COMPETITIVE ADVANTAGE

COMPETITIVE ADVANTAGE

Creating and Sustaining Superior Performance

Michael E. Porter

THE FREE PRESS
A Division of Macmillan, Inc.
NEW YORK

Collier Macmillan Publishers
LONDON

The Free Press
A Division of Macmillan, Inc.
866 Third Avenue, New York, N.Y. 10022

Collier Macmillan Canada, Inc.

Printed in the United States of America

printing number
4 5 6 7 8 9 10

Library of Congress Cataloging in Publication Data

Porter, Michael E.
Competitive advantage.

Bibliography: p.
Includes index.
1. Competition. 2. Industrial management. I. Title.
HD41.P668 1985 658 83–49518
ISBN 0–02–925090–0

To
C. Roland Christensen
and
Richard E. Caves

Contents

Preface

Competitive advantage is at the heart of a firm's performance in competitive markets. After several decades of vigorous expansion and prosperity, however, many firms lost sight of competitive advantage in their scramble for growth and pursuit of diversification. Today the importance of competitive advantage could hardly be greater. Firms throughout the world face slower growth as well as domestic and global competitors that are no longer acting as if the expanding pie were big enough for all.

This book is about how a firm can create and sustain a competitive advantage. It grows out of my research and practice in competitive strategy over the past decade. The book reflects my deepening belief that the failure of many firms' strategies stems from an inability to translate a broad competitive strategy into the specific action steps required to gain competitive advantage. The concepts in this book aim to build a bridge between strategy formulation and implementation, rather than treating the two subjects separately as has been characteristic of much of the writing in the field.

My earlier book, *Competitive Strategy,* set forth a framework for analyzing industries and competitors. It also described three generic strategies for achieving competitive advantage: cost leadership, differentiation, and focus. *Competitive Advantage* is about how a firm actually puts the generic strategies into practice. How does a firm gain a sustainable cost advantage? How can it differentiate itself from competitors? How does a firm choose a segment so that competitive advantage grows out of a focus strategy? When and how can a firm gain competitive advantage from competing with a coordinated strategy in related industries? How is uncertainty introduced into the pursuit of competitive advantage? How can a firm defend its competitive position? These are some of the questions that preoccupy this book.

Competitive advantage grows fundamentally out of the value a firm is able to create for its buyers. It may take the form of prices lower than competitors' for equivalent benefits or the provision of unique benefits that more than offset a premium price. This book uses a tool I call the value chain to disaggregate buyers, suppliers, and a firm into the discrete but interrelated activities from which value stems. The value chain will be a recurring theme throughout the book, and with it the specific sources of competitive advantage and how they relate to buyer value.

Competitive advantage is hardly a new subject. In one way or another, many books about business deal directly or indirectly with it. The control of cost has long been of concern, as has differentiation and segmentation. This book cuts across many disciplines, because marketing, production, control, finance, and many other activities in a firm have a role in competitive advantage. Similarly, a long tradition of research in business policy and in industrial economics bears on this subject. However, competitive advantage cannot be truly understood without combining all these disciplines into a holistic view of the entire firm. By examining all the sources of competitive advantage in a broad and integrated way, I hope to provide a new perspective that draws from, rather than substitutes for, previous research. It is not possible to acknowledge all the contributions in the various disciplines that have influenced in some way the ideas presented here. This book, however, would not have been possible without them.

This book is written for practitioners who are responsible for a firm's strategy and must decide how to gain competitive advantage, as well as those who seek to understand firms and their performance better. Potential sources of competitive advantage are everywhere in a firm. Every department, facility, branch office, and other organizational unit has a role that must be defined and understood. All employees, regardless of their distance from the strategy formulation process, must recognize their role in helping a firm achieve and sustain competitive advantage. Scholars working on the subject of competition outside the strategy field also need to be able to relate their research to some overall concept of competitive advantage. I hope that all these audiences will find this book valuable.

I have had a great deal of help in writing this book. The Harvard Business School has provided a uniquely fertile environment in which to explore this topic. I have drawn heavily on the multidisciplinary tradition at the School as well as the close connection between research and practice that exists there. Dean John McArthur has not only been a friend and source of encouragement to me for many years, but also extremely generous with resources and in providing the opportunity to integrate my research closely with my teaching responsibilities. Raymond Corey, Director of the Division of Research, has also been a staunch and valued ally. My heritage in the Business Policy group at Harvard has shaped my view of the subject, and I am particularly grateful to C. Roland Christensen for his support and to both he and Kenneth Andrews for sharing their wisdom with me. I have also drawn heavily on my work in industrial economics, and the constant intellectual stimulation of Richard Caves.

This book would not have been possible without the creative contributions of a number of colleagues and friends who have worked directly with me during the last several years. John R. Wells, Assistant Professor at Harvard, has not only taught with me but contributed greatly to the ideas in Chapters 3 and 9. John's own research in competitive strategy promises to make an important contribution to the field. Pankaj Ghemawat, Assistant Professor at Harvard, has also taught my strategy formulation course with me as well as provided many useful comments. He is also doing important research in the field. Mark B. Fuller, formerly Assistant Professor at Harvard and now at Monitor Company, has taught and worked with me for many years. His ideas have had a major impact on Chapter 11 and have influenced my thinking throughout the book. Catherine Hayden, also at Monitor, has been a constant source of encouragement and comments. Her ideas were of particular benefit to me in Chapter 4.

Joseph B. Fuller has worked with me in research and course development as well as in practicing in the strategy field. He has been a truly invaluable source of thoughtful comments and conceptual insights throughout the writing of manuscript. Richard Rawlinson, Associates Fellow at Harvard, has worked with me in my research as well as commented perceptively on the entire book. Others who have given generously of their time in commenting on the book and contributing ideas include Mark Albion, Robert Eccles, Douglas Anderson, Elon Kohlberg, and Richard Meyer, all Harvard colleagues. Michael Bell, Thomas Craig, Mary Kearney, and Mark Thomas have most ably worked with me in putting these ideas into practice, and contributed greatly to my thinking in the process. Jane Kenney Austin, Eric Evans, and Paul Rosetti were invaluable in commenting or in researching important topic areas. Finally, I have benefited from comments from colleagues at other schools, including Richard Schmalensee and John Stengrevics.

I could not have stood up under the demands of preparing this book without my assistant Kathleen Svensson. She has not only organized my activities but also supervised the preparation of the manuscript. I am also grateful to Robert Wallace, my editor, as well as to others at The Free Press, for their patience and support in dealing with a sometimes recalcitrant author. I must also thank my many able Harvard MBA and doctoral students who have both stimulated my thinking and been a source of joy in using these ideas. I also want to thank Deborah Zylberberg for her constant encouragement. Finally, I owe a great deal to a number of thoughtful practitioners who have shared their concerns and problems with me.

1
Competitive Strategy: The Core Concepts

Competition is at the core of the success or failure of firms. Competition determines the appropriateness of a firm's activities that can contribute to its performance, such as innovations, a cohesive culture, or good implementation. Competitive strategy is the search for a favorable competitive position in an industry, the fundamental arena in which competition occurs. Competitive strategy aims to establish a profitable and sustainable position against the forces that determine industry competition.

Two central questions underlie the choice of competitive strategy. The first is the attractiveness of industries for long-term profitability and the factors that determine it. Not all industries offer equal opportunities for sustained profitability, and the inherent profitability of its industry is one essential ingredient in determining the profitability of a firm. The second central question in competitive strategy is the determinants of relative competitive position within an industry. In most industries, some firms are much more profitable than others, regardless of what the average profitability of the industry may be.

Neither question is sufficient by itself to guide the choice of competitive strategy. A firm in a very attractive industry may still not earn attractive profits if it has chosen a poor competitive position. Conversely, a firm in an excellent competitive position may be in such a poor industry that it is not very profitable, and further efforts to enhance its position will be of little benefit.[1] Both questions are dynamic; industry attractiveness and competitive position change. Industries become more or less attractive over time, and competitive position reflects an unending battle among competitors. Even long periods of stability can be abruptly ended by competitive moves.

Both industry attractiveness and competitive position can be shaped by a firm, and this is what makes the choice of competitive strategy both challenging and exciting. While industry attractiveness is partly a reflection of factors over which a firm has little influence, competitive strategy has considerable power to make an industry more or less attractive. At the same time, a firm can clearly improve or erode its position within an industry through its choice of strategy. Competitive strategy, then, not only responds to the environment but also attempts to shape that environment in a firm's favor.

These two central questions in competitive strategy have been at the core of my research. My book *Competitive Strategy: Techniques for Analyzing Industries and Competitors* presents an analytical framework for understanding industries and competitors, and formulating an overall competitive strategy. It describes the five competitive forces that determine the attractiveness of an industry and their underlying causes, as well as how these forces change over time and can be influenced through strategy. It identifies three broad generic strategies for achieving competitive advantage. It also shows how to analyze competitors and to predict and influence their behavior, and how to map competitors into strategic groups and assess the most attractive positions in an industry. It then goes on to apply the framework to a range of important types of industry environments that I term *structural settings,* including fragmented industries, emerging industries, industries undergoing a transition to maturity, declining industries,

[1]Many strategic planning concepts have ignored industry attractiveness and stressed the pursuit of market share, often a recipe for pyrrhic victories. The winner in a fight for share in an unattractive industry may not be profitable, and the fight itself may make industry structure worse or erode the winner's profitability. Other planning concepts associate stalemates, or inability to get ahead of competitors, with unattractive profits. In fact, stalemates can be quite profitable in attractive industries.

and global industries. Finally, the book examines the important strategic decisions that occur in the context of an industry, including vertical integration, capacity expansion, and entry.

This book takes the framework in *Competitive Strategy* as a starting point. The central theme of this book is how a firm can actually create and sustain a competitive advantage in its industry—how it can implement the broad generic strategies. My aim is to build a bridge between strategy and implementation, rather than treat these two subjects independently or consider implementation scarcely at all as has been characteristic of much previous research in the field.

Competitive advantage grows fundamentally out of value a firm is able to create for its buyers that exceeds the firm's cost of creating it. Value is what buyers are willing to pay, and superior value stems from offering lower prices than competitors for equivalent benefits or providing unique benefits that more than offset a higher price. There are two basic types of competitive advantage: cost leadership and differentiation. This book describes how a firm can gain a cost advantage or how it can differentiate itself. It describes how the choice of competitive scope, or the range of a firm's activities, can play a powerful role in determining competitive advantage. Finally, it translates these concepts, combined with those in my earlier book, into overall implications for offensive and defensive competitive strategy, including the role of uncertainty in influencing strategic choices. This book considers not only competitive strategy in an individual industry but also corporate strategy for the diversified firm. Competitive advantage in one industry can be strongly enhanced by interrelationships with business units competing in related industries, if these interrelationships can actually be achieved. Interrelationships among business units are the principal means by which a diversified firm creates value, and thus provide the underpinnings for corporate strategy. I will describe how interrelationships among business units can be identified and translated into a corporate strategy, as well as how interrelationships can be achieved in practice despite the organizational impediments to doing so that are present in many diversified firms.

Though the emphases of this book and my earlier book are different, they are strongly complementary. The emphasis of *Competitive Strategy* is on industry structure and competitor analysis in a variety of industry environments, though it contains many implications for competitive advantage. This book begins by assuming an understanding of industry structure and competitor behavior, and is preoccupied with how to translate that understanding into a competitive advantage.

Actions to create competitive advantage often have important consequences for industry structure and competitive reaction, however, and thus I will return to these subjects frequently.

This book can be read independently of *Competitive Strategy,* but its power to aid practitioners in formulating strategy is diminished if the reader is not familiar with the core concepts presented in the earlier book. In this chapter, I will describe and elaborate on some of those concepts. The discussion of the core concepts will also provide a good means of introducing the concepts and techniques in this book. In the process, I will address some of the most important questions that arise in applying the core concepts in practice. Thus even readers familiar with my earlier book may find the review of interest.

The Structural Analysis of Industries

The first fundamental determinant of a firm's profitability is industry attractiveness. Competitive strategy must grow out of a sophisticated understanding of the rules of competition that determine an industry's attractiveness. The ultimate aim of competitive strategy is to cope with and, ideally, to change those rules in the firm's favor. In any industry, whether it is domestic or international or produces a product or a service,[2] the rules of competition are embodied in five competitive forces: the entry of new competitors, the threat of substitutes, the bargaining power of buyers, the bargaining power of suppliers, and the rivalry among the existing competitors (see Figure 1–1).

The collective strength of these five competitive forces determines the ability of firms in an industry to earn, on average, rates of return on investment in excess of the cost of capital. The strength of the five forces varies from industry to industry, and can change as an industry evolves. The result is that all industries are not alike from the standpoint of inherent profitability. In industries where the five forces are favorable, such as pharmaceuticals, soft drinks, and data base publishing, many competitors earn attractive returns. But in industries where pressure from one or more of the forces is intense, such as rubber, steel, and video games, few firms command attractive

[2]These concepts apply equally to products and services. I will use the term "product" in the generic sense throughout this book to refer to both product and service industries.

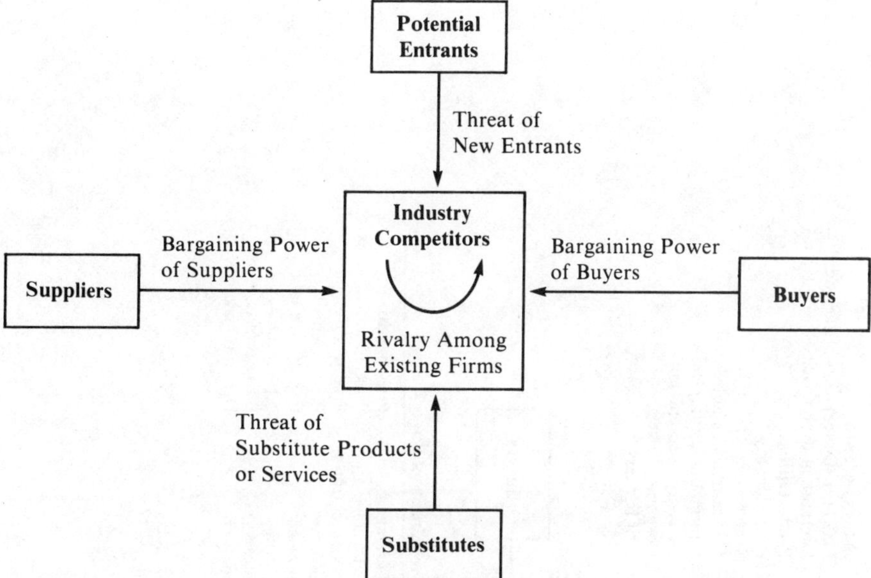

Figure 1–1. The Five Competitive Forces that Determine Industry Profitability

returns despite the best efforts of management. Industry profitability is not a function of what the product looks like or whether it embodies high or low technology, but of industry structure. Some very mundane industries such as postage meters and grain trading are extremely profitable, while some more glamorous, high-technology industries such as personal computers and cable television are not profitable for many participants.

The five forces determine industry profitability because they influence the prices, costs, and required investment of firms in an industry—the elements of return on investment. Buyer power influences the prices that firms can charge, for example, as does the threat of substitution. The power of buyers can also influence cost and investment, because powerful buyers demand costly service. The bargaining power of suppliers determines the costs of raw materials and other inputs. The intensity of rivalry influences prices as well as the costs of competing in areas such as plant, product development, advertising, and sales force. The threat of entry places a limit on prices, and shapes the investment required to deter entrants.

The strength of each of the five competitive forces is a function of *industry structure,* or the underlying economic and technical characteristics of an industry. Its important elements are shown in Figure

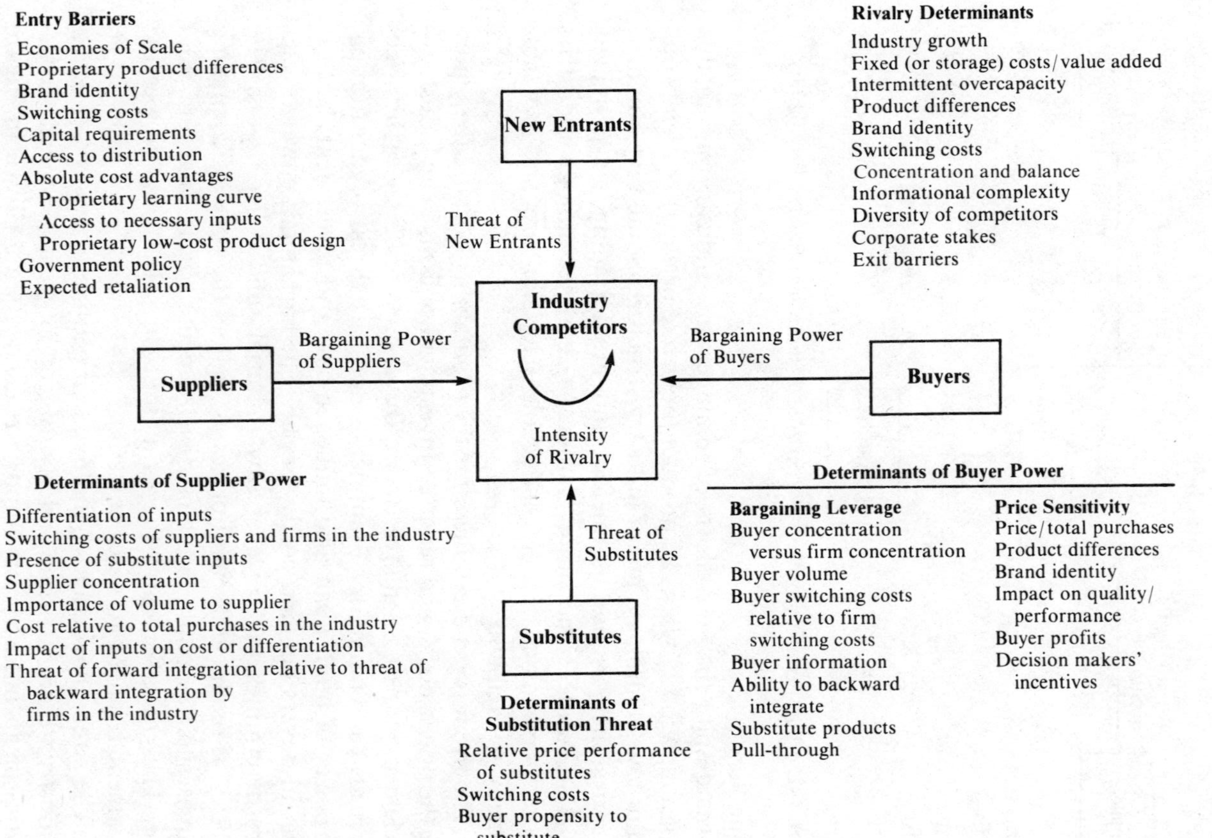

Figure 1–2. Elements of Industry Structure

1–2.[3] Industry structure is relatively stable, but can change over time as an industry evolves. Structural change shifts the overall and relative strength of the competitive forces, and can thus positively or negatively influence industry profitability. The industry trends that are the most important for strategy are those that affect industry structure.

If the five competitive forces and their structural determinants were solely a function of intrinsic industry characteristics, then competitive strategy would rest heavily on picking the right industry and understanding the five forces better than competitors. But while these are surely important tasks for any firm, and are the essence of competitive strategy in some industries, a firm is usually not a prisoner of its industry's structure. Firms, through their strategies, can influence the five forces. If a firm can shape structure, it can fundamentally change an industry's attractiveness for better or for worse. Many successful strategies have shifted the rules of competition in this way.

Figure 1–2 highlights all the elements of industry structure that may drive competition in an industry. In any particular industry, not all of the five forces will be equally important and the particular structural factors that are important will differ. Every industry is unique and has its own unique structure. The five-forces framework allows a firm to see through the complexity and pinpoint those factors that are critical to competition in its industry, as well as to identify those strategic innovations that would most improve the industry's—and its own—profitability. The five-forces framework does not eliminate the need for creativity in finding new ways of competing in an industry. Instead, it directs managers' creative energies toward those aspects of industry structure that are most important to long-run profitability. The framework aims, in the process, to raise the odds of discovering a desirable strategic innovation.

Strategies that change industry structure can be a double-edged sword, because a firm can destroy industry structure and profitability as readily as it can improve it. A new product design that undercuts entry barriers or increases the volatility of rivalry, for example, may undermine the long-run profitability of an industry, though the initiator may enjoy higher profits temporarily. Or a sustained period of price cutting can undermine differentiation. In the tobacco industry, for example, generic cigarettes are a potentially serious threat to industry structure. Generics may enhance the price sensitivity of buyers, trigger price competition, and erode the high advertising barriers that have kept out new entrants.[4] Joint ventures entered into by major aluminum

[3]Industry structure is discussed in detail in *Competitive Strategy,* Chapter 1.
[4]Generic products pose the same risks to many consumer good industries.

producers to spread risk and lower capital cost may have similarly undermined industry structure. The majors invited a number of potentially dangerous new competitors into the industry and helped them overcome the significant entry barriers to doing so. Joint ventures also can raise exit barriers because all the participants in a plant must agree before it can be closed down.

Often firms make strategic choices without considering the long-term consequences for industry structure. They see a gain in their competitive position if a move is successful, but they fail to anticipate the consequences of competitive reaction. If imitation of a move by major competitors has the effect of wrecking industry structure, then everyone is worse off. Such industry "destroyers" are usually second-tier firms that are searching for ways to overcome major competitive disadvantages, firms that have encountered serious problems and are desperately seeking solutions, or "dumb" competitors that do not know their costs or have unrealistic assumptions about the future. In the tobacco industry, for example, the Liggett Group (a distant follower) has encouraged the trend toward generics.

The ability of firms to shape industry structure places a particular burden on industry leaders. Leaders' actions can have a disproportionate impact on structure, because of their size and influence over buyers, suppliers, and other competitors. At the same time, leaders' large market shares guarantee that anything that changes overall industry structure will affect them as well. A leader, then, must constantly balance its own competitive position against the health of the industry as a whole. Often leaders are better off taking actions to improve or protect industry structure rather than seeking greater competitive advantage for themselves. Such industry leaders as Coca-Cola and Campbell's Soup appear to have followed this principle.

Industry Structure and Buyer Needs

It has often been said that satisfying buyer needs is at the core of success in business endeavor. How does this relate to the concept of industry structural analysis? Satisfying buyer needs is indeed a prerequisite to the viability of an industry and the firms within it. Buyers must be willing to pay a price for a product that exceeds its cost of production, or an industry will not survive in the long run. Chapter 4 will describe in detail how a firm can differentiate itself by satisfying buyer needs better than its competitors.

Satisfying buyer needs may be a prerequisite for industry profitability, but in itself is not sufficient. The crucial question in determining profitability is whether firms can capture the value they create for buyers, or whether this value is competed away to others. Industry structure determines who captures the value. The threat of entry determines the likelihood that new firms will enter an industry and compete away the value, either passing it on to buyers in the form of lower prices or dissipating it by raising the costs of competing. The power of buyers determines the extent to which they retain most of the value created for themselves, leaving firms in an industry only modest returns. The threat of substitutes determines the extent to which some other product can meet the same buyer needs, and thus places a ceiling on the amount a buyer is willing to pay for an industry's product. The power of suppliers determines the extent to which value created for buyers will be appropriated by suppliers rather than by firms in an industry. Finally, the intensity of rivalry acts similarly to the threat of entry. It determines the extent to which firms already in an industry will compete away the value they create for buyers among themselves, passing it on to buyers in lower prices or dissipating it in higher costs of competing.

Industry structure, then, determines who keeps what proportion of the value a product creates for buyers. If an industry's product does not create much value for its buyers, there is little value to be captured by firms regardless of the other elements of structure. If the product creates a lot of value, structure becomes crucial. In some industries such as automobiles and heavy trucks, firms create enormous value for their buyers but, on average, capture very little of it for themselves through profits. In other industries such as bond rating services, medical equipment, and oil field services and equipment, firms also create high value for their buyers but have historically captured a good proportion of it. In oil field services and equipment, for example, many products can significantly reduce the cost of drilling. Because industry structure has been favorable, many firms in the oil field service and equipment sector have been able to retain a share of these savings in the form of high returns. Recently, however, the structural attractiveness of many industries in the oil field services and equipment sector has eroded as a result of falling demand, new entrants, eroding product differentiation, and greater buyer price sensitivity. Despite the fact that products offered still create enormous value for the buyer, both firm and industry profits have fallen significantly.

Industry Structure and the Supply/Demand Balance

Another commonly held view about industry profitability is that profits are a function of the balance between supply and demand. If demand is greater than supply, this leads to high profitability. Yet, the long-term supply/demand balance is strongly influenced by industry structure, as are the consequences of a supply/demand imbalance for profitability. Hence, even though short-term fluctuations in supply and demand can affect short-term profitability, industry structure underlies long-term profitability.

Supply and demand change constantly, adjusting to each other. Industry structure determines how rapidly competitors add new supply. The height of entry barriers underpins the likelihood that new entrants will enter an industry and bid down prices. The intensity of rivalry plays a major role in determining whether existing firms will expand capacity aggressively or choose to maintain profitability. Industry structure also determines how rapidly competitors will retire excess supply. Exit barriers keep firms from leaving an industry when there is too much capacity, and prolong periods of excess capacity. In oil tanker shipping, for example, the exit barriers are very high because of the specialization of assets. This has translated into short peaks and long troughs of prices. Thus industry structure shapes the supply/demand balance and the duration of imbalances.

The consequences of an imbalance between supply and demand for industry profitability also differs widely depending on industry structure. In some industries, a small amount of excess capacity triggers price wars and low profitability. These are industries where there are structural pressures for intense rivalry or powerful buyers. In other industries, periods of excess capacity have relatively little impact on profitability because of favorable structure. In oil tools, ball valves, and many other oil field equipment products, for example, there has been intense price cutting during the recent sharp downturn. In drill bits, however, there has been relatively little discounting. Hughes Tool, Smith International, and Baker International are good competitors (see Chapter 6) operating in a favorable industry structure. Industry structure also determines the profitability of excess demand. In a boom, for example, favorable structure allows firms to reap extraordinary profits, while a poor structure restricts the ability to capitalize on it. The presence of powerful suppliers or the presence of substitutes, for example, can mean that the fruits of a boom pass to others. Thus industry structure is fundamental to both the speed of adjustment of supply to demand and the relationship between capacity utilization and profitability.

Generic Competitive Strategies

The second central question in competitive strategy is a firm's relative position within its industry. Positioning determines whether a firm's profitability is above or below the industry average. A firm that can position itself well may earn high rates of return even though industry structure is unfavorable and the average profitability of the industry is therefore modest.

The fundamental basis of above-average performance in the long run is *sustainable competitive advantage.*[5] Though a firm can have a myriad of strengths and weaknesses vis-à-vis its competitors, there are two basic types of competitive advantage a firm can possess: low cost or differentiation. The significance of any strength or weakness a firm possesses is ultimately a function of its impact on relative cost or differentiation. Cost advantage and differentiation in turn stem from industry structure. They result from a firm's ability to cope with the five forces better than its rivals.

The two basic types of competitive advantage combined with the scope of activities for which a firm seeks to achieve them lead to three *generic strategies* for achieving above-average performance in an industry: cost leadership, differentiation, and focus. The focus strategy has two variants, cost focus and differentiation focus. The generic strategies are shown in Figure 1–3.

Each of the generic strategies involves a fundamentally different route to competitive advantage, combining a choice about the type of competitive advantage sought with the scope of the strategic target in which competitive advantage is to be achieved. The cost leadership and differentiation strategies seek competitive advantage in a broad range of industry segments, while focus strategies aim at cost advantage (cost focus) or differentiation (differentiation focus) in a narrow segment. The specific actions required to implement each generic strategy vary widely from industry to industry, as do the feasible generic strategies in a particular industry. While selecting and implementing a generic strategy is far from simple, however, they are the logical routes to competitive advantage that must be probed in any industry.

[5] Without a sustainable competitive advantage, above-average performance is usually a sign of harvesting.

		COMPETITIVE ADVANTAGE	
		Lower Cost	Differentiation
COMPETITIVE SCOPE	Broad Target	**1. Cost Leadership**	**2. Differentiation**
	Narrow Target	**3A. Cost Focus**	**3B. Differentiation Focus**

Figure 1–3. Three Generic Strategies

The notion underlying the concept of generic strategies is that competitive advantage is at the heart of any strategy, and achieving competitive advantage requires a firm to make a choice—if a firm is to attain a competitive advantage, it must make a choice about the type of competitive advantage it seeks to attain and the scope within which it will attain it. Being "all things to all people" is a recipe for strategic mediocrity and below-average performance, because it often means that a firm has no competitive advantage at all.

Cost Leadership

Cost leadership is perhaps the clearest of the three generic strategies. In it, a firm sets out to become *the* low-cost producer in its industry. The firm has a broad scope and serves many industry segments, and may even operate in related industries—the firm's breadth is often important to its cost advantage. The sources of cost advantage are varied and depend on the structure of the industry. They may include the pursuit of economies of scale, proprietary technology, preferential access to raw materials, and other factors I will describe in detail in Chapter 3. In TV sets, for example, cost leadership requires efficient size picture tube facilities, a low-cost design, automated assembly, and global scale over which to amortize R&D. In security guard services, cost advantage requires extremely low overhead, a plentiful source of low-cost labor, and efficient training procedures because of high turnover. Low-cost producer status involves more than just going down the learning curve. A low-cost producer must find and exploit all sources of cost advantage. Low-cost producers typically sell a standard, or no-frills, product and place considerable emphasis on reaping scale or absolute cost advantages from all sources.

If a firm can achieve and sustain overall cost leadership, then it will be an above-average performer in its industry provided it can command prices at or near the industry average. At equivalent or lower prices than its rivals, a cost leader's low-cost position translates into higher returns. A cost leader, however, cannot ignore the bases of differentiation. If its product is not perceived as comparable or acceptable by buyers, a cost leader will be forced to discount prices well below competitors' to gain sales. This may nullify the benefits of its favorable cost position. Texas Instruments (in watches) and Northwest Airlines (in air transportation) are two low-cost firms that fell into this trap. Texas Instruments could not overcome its disadvantage in differentiation and exited the watch industry. Northwest Airlines recognized its problem in time, and has instituted efforts to improve marketing, passenger service, and service to travel agents to make its product more comparable to those of its competitors.

A cost leader must achieve *parity* or *proximity* in the bases of differentiation relative to its competitors to be an above-average performer, even though it relies on cost leadership for its competitive advantage. Parity in the bases of differentiation allows a cost leader to translate its cost advantage directly into higher profits than competitors'.[6] Proximity in differentiation means that the price discount necessary to achieve an acceptable market share does not offset a cost leader's cost advantage and hence the cost leader earns above-average returns.

The strategic logic of cost leadership usually requires that a firm be *the* cost leader, not one of several firms vying for this position.[7] Many firms have made serious strategic errors by failing to recognize this. When there is more than one aspiring cost leader, rivalry among them is usually fierce because every point of market share is viewed as crucial. Unless one firm can gain a cost lead and "persuade" others to abandon their strategies, the consequences for profitability

[6]Parity implies either an identical product offering to competitors, or a different combination of product attributes that is equally preferred by buyers.

[7]While the cost leader will be the most profitable, it is not necessary to be the cost leader to sustain above-average returns in commodity industries where there are limited opportunities to build efficient capacity. A firm that is in the lowest quartile of costs though not the cost leader will usually still be an above-average performer. Such a situation exists in the aluminum industry, where the ability to add low-cost capacity is limited by access to low-cost power, bauxite, and infrastructure.

(and long-run industry structure) can be disastrous, as has been the case in a number of petrochemical industries. Thus cost leadership is a strategy particularly dependent on preemption, unless major technological change allows a firm to radically change its cost position.

Differentiation

The second generic strategy is differentiation. In a differentiation strategy, a firm seeks to be unique in its industry along some dimensions that are widely valued by buyers. It selects one or more attributes that many buyers in an industry perceive as important, and uniquely positions itself to meet those needs. It is rewarded for its uniqueness with a premium price.

The means for differentiation are peculiar to each industry. Differentiation can be based on the product itself, the delivery system by which it is sold, the marketing approach, and a broad range of other factors. In construction equipment, for example, Caterpillar Tractor's differentiation is based on product durability, service, spare parts availability, and an excellent dealer network. In cosmetics, differentiation tends to be based more on product image and the positioning of counters in the stores. I will describe how a firm can create sustainable differentiation in Chapter 4.

A firm that can achieve and sustain differentiation will be an above-average performer in its industry if its price premium exceeds the extra costs incurred in being unique. A differentiator, therefore, must always seek ways of differentiating that lead to a price premium greater than the cost of differentiating. A differentiator cannot ignore its cost position, because its premium prices will be nullified by a markedly inferior cost position. A differentiator thus aims at cost *parity* or *proximity* relative to its competitors, by reducing cost in all areas that do not affect differentiation.

The logic of the differentiation strategy requires that a firm choose attributes in which to differentiate itself that are *different* from its rivals'. A firm must truly be unique at something or be perceived as unique if it is to expect a premium price. In contrast to cost leadership, however, there can be more than one successful differentiation strategy in an industry if there are a number of attributes that are widely valued by buyers.

Focus

The third generic strategy is focus. This strategy is quite different from the others because it rests on the choice of a narrow competitive scope within an industry. The focuser selects a segment or group of segments in the industry and tailors its strategy to serving them to the exclusion of others. By optimizing its strategy for the target segments, the focuser seeks to achieve a competitive advantage in its target segments even though it does not possess a competitive advantage overall.

The focus strategy has two variants. In *cost focus* a firm seeks a cost advantage in its target segment, while in *differentiation focus* a firm seeks differentiation in its target segment. Both variants of the focus strategy rest on *differences* between a focuser's target segments and other segments in the industry. The target segments must either have buyers with unusual needs or else the production and delivery system that best serves the target segment must differ from that of other industry segments. Cost focus exploits differences in cost behavior in some segments, while differentiation focus exploits the special needs of buyers in certain segments. Such differences imply that the segments are poorly served by broadly-targeted competitors who serve them at the same time as they serve others. The focuser can thus achieve competitive advantage by dedicating itself to the segments exclusively. Breadth of target is clearly a matter of degree, but the essence of focus is the exploitation of a narrow target's differences from the balance of the industry.[8] Narrow focus in and of itself is not sufficient for above-average performance.

A good example of a focuser who has exploited differences in the production process that best serves different segments is Hammermill Paper. Hammermill has increasingly been moving toward relatively low-volume, high-quality specialty papers, where the larger paper companies with higher volume machines face a stiff cost penalty for short production runs. Hammermill's equipment is more suited to shorter runs with frequent setups.

A focuser takes advantage of suboptimization in either direction by broadly-targeted competitors. Competitors may be *underperforming*

[8]Overall differentiation and differentiation focus are perhaps the most often confused strategies in practice. The difference is that the overall differentiator bases its strategy on widely valued attributes (e.g., IBM in computers), while the differentiation focuser looks for segments with special needs and meets them better (e.g., Cray Research in computers).

in meeting the needs of a particular segment, which opens the possibility for differentiation focus. Broadly-targeted competitors may also be *overperforming* in meeting the needs of a segment, which means that they are bearing higher than necessary cost in serving it. An opportunity for cost focus may be present in just meeting the needs of such a segment and no more.

If a focuser's target segment is not different from other segments, then the focus strategy will not succeed. In soft drinks, for example, Royal Crown has focused on cola drinks, while Coca-Cola and Pepsi have broad product lines with many flavored drinks. Royal Crown's segment, however, can be well served by Coke and Pepsi at the same time they are serving other segments. Hence Coke and Pepsi enjoy competitive advantages over Royal Crown in the cola segment due to the economies of having a broader line.[9]

If a firm can achieve sustainable cost leadership (cost focus) or differentiation (differentiation focus) in its segment and the segment is structurally attractive, then the focuser will be an above-average performer in its industry. Segment structural attractiveness is a necessary condition because some segments in an industry are much less profitable than others. There is often room for several sustainable focus strategies in an industry, provided that focusers choose different target segments. Most industries have a variety of segments, and each one that involves a different buyer need or a different optimal production or delivery system is a candidate for a focus strategy. How to define segments and choose a sustainable focus strategy is described in detail in Chapter 7.

Stuck in the Middle

A firm that engages in each generic strategy but fails to achieve any of them is "stuck in the middle." It possesses no competitive advantage. This strategic position is usually a recipe for below-average performance. A firm that is stuck in the middle will compete at a disadvantage because the cost leader, differentiators, or focusers will be better positioned to compete in any segment. If a firm that is stuck in the middle is lucky enough to discover a profitable product or buyer, competitors with a sustainable competitive advantage will quickly eliminate the spoils. In most industries, quite a few competitors are stuck in the middle.

[9]This example is discussed in more detail in Chapter 7.

A firm that is stuck in the middle will earn attractive profits only if the structure of its industry is highly favorable, or if the firm is fortunate enough to have competitors that are also stuck in the middle. Usually, however, such a firm will be much less profitable than rivals achieving one of the generic strategies. Industry maturity tends to widen the performance differences between firms with a generic strategy and those that are stuck in the middle, because it exposes ill-conceived strategies that have been carried along by rapid growth.

Becoming stuck in the middle is often a manifestation of a firm's unwillingness to make *choices* about how to compete. It tries for competitive advantage through every means and achieves none, because achieving different types of competitive advantage usually requires inconsistent actions. Becoming stuck in the middle also afflicts successful firms, who compromise their generic strategy for the sake of growth or prestige. A classic example is Laker Airways, which began with a clear cost focus strategy based on no-frills operation in the North Atlantic market, aimed at a particular segment of the traveling public that was extremely price-sensitive. Over time, however, Laker began adding frills, new services, and new routes. It blurred its image, and suboptimized its service and delivery system. The consequences were disastrous, and Laker eventually went bankrupt.

The temptation to blur a generic strategy, and therefore become stuck in the middle, is particularly great for a focuser once it has dominated its target segments. Focus involves deliberately limiting potential sales volume. Success can lead a focuser to lose sight of the reasons for its success and compromise its focus strategy for growth's sake. Rather than compromise its generic strategy, a firm is usually better off finding new industries in which to grow where it can use its generic strategy again or exploit interrelationships.

Pursuit of More Than One Generic Strategy

Each generic strategy is a fundamentally different approach to creating and sustaining a competitive advantage, combining the type of competitive advantage a firm seeks and the scope of its strategic target. Usually a firm must make a choice among them, or it will become stuck in the middle. The benefits of optimizing the firm's strategy for a particular target segment (focus) cannot be gained if a firm is simultaneously serving a broad range of segments (cost leadership or differentiation). Sometimes a firm may be able to create two largely separate business units within the same corporate entity, each with a different generic strategy. A good example is the British hotel firm Trusthouse Forte, which operates five separate hotel chains each targeted at a different segment. However, unless a firm strictly separates the units pursuing different generic strategies, it may compromise the ability of any of them to achieve its competitive advantage. A suboptimized approach to competing, made likely by the spillover among units of corporate policies and culture, will lead to becoming stuck in the middle.

Achieving cost leadership and differentiation are also usually inconsistent, because differentiation is usually costly. To be unique and command a price premium, a differentiator deliberately elevates costs, as Caterpillar has done in construction equipment. Conversely, cost leadership often requires a firm to forego some differentiation by standardizing its product, reducing marketing overhead, and the like.

Reducing cost does not always involve a sacrifice in differentiation. Many firms have discovered ways to reduce cost not only without hurting their differentiation but while actually raising it, by using practices that are both more efficient and effective or employing a different technology. Sometimes dramatic cost savings can be achieved with no impact on differentiation at all if a firm has not concentrated on cost reduction previously. However, cost reduction is not the same as achieving a cost advantage. When faced with capable competitors also striving for cost leadership, a firm will ultimately reach the point where further cost reduction requires a sacrifice in differentiation. It is at this point that the generic strategies become inconsistent and a firm must make a choice.

If a firm can achieve cost leadership and differentiation simultaneously, the rewards are great because the benefits are additive—differentiation leads to premium prices at the same time that cost leadership implies lower costs. An example of a firm that has achieved both a cost advantage and differentiation in its segments is Crown Cork and Seal in the metal container industry. Crown has targeted the so-called "hard to hold" uses of cans in the beer, soft drink, and aerosol industries. It manufactures only steel cans rather than both steel and aluminum. In its target segments, Crown has differentiated itself based on service, technological assistance, and offering a full line of steel cans, crowns, and canning machinery. Differentiation of this type would be much more difficult to achieve in other industry segments which have different needs. At the same time, Crown has dedicated its facilities to producing only the types of cans demanded by buyers in its chosen segments and has aggressively invested in modern two-piece steel canning technology. As a result, Crown has probably also achieved low-cost producer status in its segments.

There are three conditions under which a firm can simultaneously achieve both cost leadership and differentiation:

Competitors are stuck in the middle. Where competitors are stuck in the middle, none is well enough positioned to force a firm to the point where cost and differentiation become inconsistent. This was the case with Crown Cork. Its major competitors were not investing in low-cost steel can production technology, so Crown achieved cost leadership without having to sacrifice differentiation in the process. Were its competitors pursuing an aggressive cost leadership strategy, however, an attempt by Crown to be both low-cost and differentiated might have doomed it to becoming stuck in the middle. Cost reduction opportunities that did not sacrifice differentiation would have already been adopted by Crown's competitors.

While stuck-in-the-middle competitors can allow a firm to achieve both differentiation and low cost, this state of affairs is often temporary. Eventually a competitor will choose a generic strategy and begin to implement it well, exposing the tradeoffs between cost and differentiation. Thus a firm must choose the type of competitive advantage it intends to preserve in the long run. The danger in facing weak competitors is that a firm will begin to compromise its cost position or differentiation to achieve both and leave itself vulnerable to the emergence of a capable competitor.

Cost is strongly affected by share or interrelationships. Cost leadership and differentiation may also be achieved simultaneously where cost position is heavily determined by market share, rather than by product design, level of technology, service provided, or other factors. If one firm can open up a big market share advantage, the cost advantages of share in some activities allow the firm to incur added costs elsewhere and still maintain net cost leadership, or share reduces the cost of differentiating relative to competitors (see Chapter 4). In a related situation, cost leadership and differentiation can be achieved at the same time when there are important interrelationships between industries that one competitor can exploit and others cannot (see Chapter 9). Unmatched interrelationships can lower the cost of differentiation or offset the higher cost of differentiation. Nonetheless, simultaneous pursuit of cost leadership and differentiation is always vulnerable to capable competitors who make a choice and invest aggressively to implement it, matching the share or interrelationship.

A firm pioneers a major innovation. Introducing a significant technological innovation can allow a firm to lower cost and enhance differentiation at the same time, and perhaps achieve both strategies. Introducing new automated manufacturing technologies can have this effect, as can the introduction of new information system technology to manage logistics or design products on the computer. Innovative new practices unconnected to technology can also have this effect. Forging cooperative relations with suppliers can lower input costs and improve input quality, for example, as described in Chapter 3.

The ability to be both low cost and differentiated is a function of being the *only* firm with the new innovation, however. Once competitors also introduce the innovation, the firm is again in the position of having to make a tradeoff. Will its information system be designed to emphasize cost or differentiation, for example, compared to the competitor's information system? The pioneer may be at a disadvantage if, in the pursuit of both low cost and differentiation, its innovation has not recognized the possibility of imitation. It may then be neither low cost nor differentiated once the innovation is matched by competitors who pick one generic strategy.

A firm should always aggressively pursue all cost reduction opportunities that do not sacrifice differentiation. A firm should also pursue all differentiation opportunities that are not costly. Beyond this point, however, a firm should be prepared to choose what its ultimate competitive advantage will be and resolve the tradeoffs accordingly.

Sustainability

A generic strategy does not lead to above-average performance unless it is sustainable vis-à-vis competitors, though actions that improve industry structure may improve industrywide profitability even if they are imitated. The sustainability of the three generic strategies demands that a firm's competitive advantage resists erosion by competitor behavior or industry evolution. Each generic strategy involves different risks which are shown in Table 1–1.

The sustainability of a generic strategy requires that a firm possess some barriers that make imitation of the strategy difficult. Since barriers to imitation are never insurmountable, however, it is usually necessary for a firm to offer a moving target to its competitors by investing in order to continually improve its position. Each generic strategy is also a potential threat to the others—as Table 1–1 shows, for example, focusers must worry about broadly-targeted competitors and vice versa.

TABLE 1–1 Risks of the Generic Strategies

RISKS OF COST LEADERSHIP	RISKS OF DIFFERENTIATION	RISKS OF FOCUS
Cost leadership is not sustained • competitors imitate • technology changes • other bases for cost leadership erode	Differentiation is not sustained • competitors imitate • bases for differentiation become less important to buyers	The focus strategy is imitated The target segment becomes structurally unattractive • structure erodes • demand disappears
Proximity in differentiation is lost	Cost proximity is lost	Broadly-targeted competitors overwhelm the segment • the segment's differences from other segments narrow • the advantages of a broad line increase
Cost focusers achieve even lower cost in segments	Differentiation focusers achieve even greater differentiation in segments	New focusers sub-segment the industry

The factors that lead to sustainability of each of the generic strategies will be discussed extensively in Chapters 3, 4, and 7.

Table 1–1 can be used to analyze how to attack a competitor that employs any of the generic strategies. A firm pursuing overall differentiation, for example, can be attacked by firms who open up a large cost gap, narrow the extent of differentiation, shift the differentiation desired by buyers to other dimensions, or focus. Each generic strategy is vulnerable to different types of attacks, as discussed in more detail in Chapter 15.

In some industries, industry structure or the strategies of competitors eliminate the possibility of achieving one or more of the generic strategies. Occasionally no feasible way for one firm to gain a significant cost advantage exists, for example, because several firms are equally placed with respect to scale economies, access to raw materials, or other cost drivers. Similarly, an industry with few segments or only minor differences among segments, such as low-density polyethylene, may offer few opportunities for focus. Thus the mix of generic strategies will vary from industry to industry.

In many industries, however, the three generic strategies can profitably coexist as long as firms pursue different ones or select different bases for differentiation or focus. Industries in which several strong firms are pursuing differentiation strategies based on different sources of buyer value are often particulary profitable. This tends to improve industry structure and lead to stable industry competition. If two or more firms choose to pursue the same generic strategy on the same basis, however, the result can be a protracted and unprofitable battle. The worst situation is where several firms are vying for overall cost leadership. The past and present choice of generic strategies by competitors, then, has an impact on the choices available to a firm and the cost of changing its position.

The concept of generic strategies is based on the premise that there are a number of ways in which competitive advantage can be achieved, depending on industry structure. If all firms in an industry followed the principles of competitive strategy, each would pick different bases for competitive advantage. While not all would succeed, the generic strategies provide alternate routes to superior performance. Some strategic planning concepts have been narrowly based on only one route to competitive advantage, most notably cost. Such concepts not only fail to explain the success of many firms, but they can also lead all firms in an industry to pursue the same type of competitive advantage in the same way—with predictably disastrous results.

Generic Strategies and Industry Evolution

Changes in industry structure can affect the bases on which generic strategies are built and thus alter the balance among them. For example, the advent of electronic controls and new image developing systems has greatly eroded the importance of service as a basis for differentiation in copiers. Structural change creates many of the risks shown in Table 1–1.[10]

Structural change can shift the relative balance among the generic strategies in an industry, since it can alter the sustainability of a generic strategy or the size of the competitive advantage that results from it. The automobile industry provides a good example. Early in its history, leading automobile firms followed differentiation strategies in the production of expensive touring cars. Technological and market changes created the potential for Henry Ford to change the rules of competition by adopting a classic overall cost leadership strategy, based on low-cost production of a standard model sold at low prices. Ford rapidly dominated the industry worldwide. By the late 1920s, however, economic growth, growing familiarity with the automobile, and techno-

[10] *Competitive Strategy,* Chapter 8, describes the processes that drive industry structural change.

logical change had created the potential for General Motors to change the rules once more—it employed a differentiation strategy based on a wide line, features, and premium prices. Throughout this evolution, focused competitors also continued to succeed.

Another long-term battle among generic strategies has occurred in general merchandising. K Mart and other discounters entered with cost leadership strategies against Sears and conventional department stores, featuring low overhead and nationally branded merchandise. K Mart, however, now faces competition from more differentiated discounters who sell fashion-oriented merchandise, such as Wal-Mart. At the same time, focused discounters have entered and are selling such products as sporting goods (Herman's), health and beauty aids (CVS), and books (Barnes and Noble). Catalog showrooms have also focused on appliances and jewelry, employing low-cost strategies in those segments. Thus the bases for K Mart's competitive advantage have been compromised and it is having difficulty outperforming the industry average.

Another more recent example of the jockeying among generic strategies has occurred in vodka. Smirnoff has long been the differentiated producer in the industry, based on early positioning as a high-class brand and heavy supporting advertising. As growth has slowed and the industry has become more competitive, however, private label vodkas and low price brands are undermining Smirnoff's position. At the same time, PepsiCo's Stolichnaya vodka has established an even more differentiated position than Smirnoff through focus. Smirnoff is caught in a squeeze that is threatening its long-standing superior performance. In response, it has introduced several new brands, including a premium brand positioned against Stolichnaya.

Generic Strategies and Organizational Structure

Each generic strategy implies different skills and requirements for success, which commonly translate into differences in organizational structure and culture. Cost leadership usually implies tight control systems, overhead minimization, pursuit of scale economies, and dedication to the learning curve; these could be counterproductive for a firm attempting to differentiate itself through a constant stream of creative new products.[11]

[11]A more detailed review of the differing skills required by each generic strategy is given in *Competitive Strategy,* Chapter 2, pp. 40–41.

The organizational differences commonly implied by each generic strategy carry a number of implications. Just as there are often economic inconsistencies in achieving more than one generic strategy, a firm does not want its organizational structure to be suboptimal because it combines inconsistent practices. It has become fashionable to tie executive selection and motivation to the "mission" of a business unit, usually expressed in terms of building, holding, or harvesting market share. It is equally—if not more—important to match executive selection and motivation to the generic strategy being followed.

The concept of generic strategies also has implications for the role of culture in competitive success. Culture, that difficult to define set of norms and attitudes that help shape an organization, has come to be viewed as an important element of a successful firm. However, different cultures are implied by different generic strategies. Differentiation may be facilitated by a culture encouraging innovation, individuality, and risk-taking (Hewlett-Packard), while cost leadership may be facilitated by frugality, discipline, and attention to detail (Emerson Electric). Culture can powerfully reinforce the competitive advantage a generic strategy seeks to achieve, if the culture is an appropriate one. There is no such thing as a good or bad culture per se. Culture is a means of achieving competitive advantage, not an end in itself.

The link between generic strategy and organization also has implications for the diversified firm. There is a tendency for diversified firms to pursue the same generic strategy in many of their business units, because skills and confidence are developed for pursuing a particular approach to competitive advantage. Moreover, senior management often gains experience in overseeing a particular type of strategy. Emerson Electric is well known for its pursuit of cost leadership in many of its business units, for example, as is H. J. Heinz.

Competing with the same generic strategy in many business units is one way in which a diversified firm can add value to those units, a subject I will discuss in Chapter 9 when I examine interrelationships among business units. However, employing a common generic strategy entails some risks that should be highlighted. One obvious risk is that a diversified firm will impose a particular generic strategy on a business unit whose industry (or initial position) will not support it. Another, more subtle risk is that a business unit will be misunderstood because of circumstances in its industry that are *not* consistent with the prevailing generic strategy. Worse yet, such business units may have their strategies undermined by senior management. Since each generic strategy often implies a different pattern of investments and different types of executives and cultures, there is a risk that a business unit that is "odd man out" will be forced to live with inappropriate corporate policies and targets. For example, an across-the-board cost reduction goal or firmwide personnel policies can be disadvantageous to a business unit attempting to differentiate itself on quality and service, just as policies toward overhead appropriate for differentiation can undermine a business unit attempting to be the low-cost producer.

Generic Strategies and the Strategic Planning Process

Given the pivotal role of competitive advantage in superior performance, the centerpiece of a firm's strategic plan should be its generic strategy. The generic strategy specifies the fundamental approach to competitive advantage a firm is pursuing, and provides the context for the actions to be taken in each functional area. In practice, however, many strategic plans are lists of action steps without a clear articulation of what competitive advantage the firm has or seeks to achieve and how. Such plans are likely to have overlooked the fundamental purpose of competitive strategy in the process of going through the mechanics of planning. Similarly, many plans are built on projections of future prices and costs that are almost invariably wrong, rather than on a fundamental understanding of industry structure and competitive advantage that will determine profitability no matter what the actual prices and costs turn out to be.

As part of their strategic planning processes, many diversified firms categorize business units by using a system such as build, hold, or harvest. These categorizations are often used to describe or summarize the strategy of business units. While such categorizations may be useful in thinking about resource allocation in a diversified firm, it is very misleading to mistake them for strategies. A business unit's strategy is the route to competitive advantage that will determine its performance. Build, hold, and harvest are the results of a generic strategy, or recognition of the inability to achieve any generic strategy and hence of the need to harvest. Similarly, acquisition and vertical integration are not strategies but means of achieving them.

Another common practice in strategic planning is to use market share to describe a business unit's competitive position. Some firms go so far as to set the goal that all their business units should be leaders (number one or number two) in their industries. This approach to strategy is as dangerous as it is deceptively clear. While market share is certainly relevant to competitive position (due to scale economies, for example), industry leadership is *not a cause but an effect of competitive advantage.* Market share per se is not important competitively; competitive advantage is. The strategic mandate to business units should be to achieve competitive advantage. Pursuit of leadership for its own sake may guarantee that a firm never achieves a competitive advantage or that it loses the one it has. A goal of leadership per se also embroils managers in endless debates over how an industry should be defined to calculate shares, obscuring once more the search for competitive advantage that is the heart of strategy.

In some industries, market leaders do not enjoy the best performance because industry structure does not reward leadership. A recent example is Continental Illinois Bank, which adopted the explicit goal of market leadership in wholesale lending. It succeeded in achieving this goal, but leadership did not translate into competitive advantage. Instead, the drive for leadership led to making loans that other banks would not, and to escalating costs. Leadership also meant that Continental Illinois had to deal with large corporations that are extremely powerful and price-sensitive buyers of loans. Continental Illinois will be paying the price of leadership for some years. In many other firms, such as Burlington Industries in fabrics and Texas Instruments in electronics, the pursuit of leadership for its own sake seems to have sometimes diverted attention from achieving and maintaining competitive advantage.

Overview of This Book

Competitive Advantage describes the way a firm can choose and implement a generic strategy to achieve and sustain competitive advantage. It addresses the interplay between the types of competitive advantage—cost and differentiation—and the scope of a firm's activities. The basic tool for diagnosing competitive advantage and finding ways to enhance it is the *value chain,* which divides a firm into the discrete activities it performs in designing, producing, marketing, and distributing its product. The scope of a firm's activities, which I term *competitive scope,* can have a powerful role in competitive advantage through its influence on the value chain. I describe how narrow scope (focus) can create competitive advantage through tailoring the value chain, and how broader scope can enhance competitive advantage through the exploitation of interrelationships among the value chains that serve different segments, industries or geographic areas. While this book addresses competitive advantage, it also sharpens the ability of the practitioner to analyze industries and competitors and hence supplements my earlier book.

This book is organized into four parts. Part I describes the types of competitive advantage and how a firm can achieve them. Part II discusses competitive scope within an industry and its affect on competitive advantage. Part III addresses competitive scope in related industries, or how corporate strategy can contribute to the competitive advantage of business units. Part IV develops overall implications for competitive strategy, including ways of coping with uncertainty and to improve or defend position.

Chapter 2 presents the concept of the value chain, and shows how it can be used as the fundamental tool in diagnosing competitive advantage. The chapter describes how to disaggregate the firm into the activities that underlie competitive advantage, and identify the linkages among activities that are central to competitive advantage. It also shows the role of competitive scope in affecting the value chain, and how coalitions with other firms can substitute for performing activities in the chain internally. The chapter also briefly considers the use of the value chain in designing organizational structure.

Chapter 3 describes how a firm can gain a sustainable cost advantage. It shows how to use the value chain to understand the behavior of costs and the implications for strategy. Understanding cost behavior is necessary not only for improving a firm's relative cost position but also for exposing the cost of differentiation.

Chapter 4 describes how a firm can differentiate itself from its competitors. The value chain provides a way to identify a firm's sources of differentiation, and the fundamental factors that drive it. The buyer's value chain is the key to understanding the underlying basis of differentiation—creating value for the buyer through lowering the buyer's cost or improving buyer performance. Differentiation results from both actual uniqueness in creating buyer value and from the ability to signal that value so that buyers perceive it.

Chapter 5 explores the relationship between technology and competitive advantage. Technology is pervasive in the value chain and plays a powerful role in determining competitive advantage, in both cost and differentiation. The chapter shows how technological change can influence competitive advantage as well as industry structure. It also describes the variables that shape the path of technological change in an industry. The chapter then describes how a firm can choose a technology strategy to enhance its competitive advantage, encompassing the choice of whether to be a technological leader and the strategic use of technology licensing. The idea of *first-mover advantages and disadvantages* is developed to highlight the potential risks and rewards of pioneering any change in the way a firm competes.

Chapter 6 discusses competitor selection, or the role of competitors in enhancing competitive advantage and industry structure. The chapter shows why the presence of the right competitors can be beneficial to a firm's competitive position. It describes how to identify "good" competitors and how to influence the array of competitors faced. It also describes how a firm can decide what market share it should hold, an important issue since a very large share is rarely optimal.

Chapter 7 begins Part II of the book and examines how industries can be segmented. It draws on Chapters 3 and 4, since segments stem from intraindustry differences in buyer needs and cost behavior. Segmentation is clearly pivotal to the choice of focus strategies, as well as to assessing the risks borne by broadly-targeted firms. The chapter describes how profitable and defensible focus strategies can be identified.

Chapter 8 discusses the determinants of substitution, and how a firm can substitute its product for another or defend against a substitution threat. Substitution, one of the five competitive forces, is driven by the interplay of the relative value of a substitute compared to its cost, switching costs, and the way individual buyers evaluate the economic benefits of substitution. The analysis of substitution is of central importance in finding ways to widen industry boundaries, exposing industry segments that face a lower substitution risk than others, and developing strategies to promote substitution or defend against a substitution threat. Hence understanding substitution is important both to broadening and to narrowing scope. The analysis of substitution draws on Chapters 3 through 7.

Chapter 9 begins Part III of the book, and is the first of four chapters about corporate strategy for the diversified firm. The central concern of corporate strategy is the way in which interrelationships among business units can be used to create a competitive advantage. Chapter 9 explains the strategic logic of interrelationships. It describes the three types of interrelationships among industries, and why they have grown in importance over time. It then shows how the significance of interrelationships for competitive advantage can be assessed.

Chapter 10 addresses the implications of interrelationships for *horizontal strategy,* or strategy that encompasses multiple distinct business units. A firm with multiple business units in related industries must formulate strategies at the group, sector, and corporate levels that coordinate the strategies of individual units. The chapter describes the principles for doing so, as well as the implications of interrelationships for diversification into new industries.

Chapter 11 describes how interrelationships among business units can actually be achieved. Many organizational impediments stand in the way, ranging from the protection of turf to faulty incentives. The chapter identifies these impediments in detail, and shows how they can be overcome through what I call *horizontal organization.* Firms competing in related industries must have a horizontal organization that links business units together, that supplements but does not replace the hierarchical organization to manage and control them.

Chapter 12 treats a special but important case of interrelationships, where an industry's product is used or purchased with complementary products. The chapter describes the circumstances in which a firm must control complementary products rather than let other firms supply them. It also examines the strategy of *bundling,* or selling separate products together as a single package, and the circumstances in which such a strategy is appropriate. Finally, the chapter examines cross-subsidization, or pricing complementary products to reflect the relationship among them rather than setting each price separately.

Part IV of the book draws on the concepts in this book and *Competitive Strategy* to develop broad principles for offensive and defensive strategy. Chapter 13 discusses the problem of formulating competitive strategy in the face of significant uncertainty. It describes the concept of industry scenarios, and shows how scenarios can be constructed to illuminate the range of future industry structures that might occur. The chapter then outlines the alternative ways in which a firm can cope with uncertainty in its choice of strategy. Competitive strategy is more effective if there is explicit consideration of the range of industry scenarios that might occur, and recognition of the extent to which strategies for dealing with different scenarios are consistent or inconsistent.

Competitive Advantage concludes with a treatment of defensive and offensive strategy. Chapters 14 and 15 serve to pull together many of the other chapters. Chapter 14, on defensive strategy, describes the process by which a firm's position is challenged and the defensive tactics available to deter or block a competitor. The chapter then develops the implications of these ideas for a defensive strategy. Chapter 15 shows how to attack an industry leader. It lays out the conditions a firm must meet to challenge a leader, and the approaches to changing the rules of competition in order to do so successfully. The same principles involved in attacking a leader can be used in offensive strategy against any competitor.

I
Principles of Competitive Advantage

2
The Value Chain and Competitive Advantage

Competitive advantage cannot be understood by looking at a firm as a whole. It stems from the many discrete activities a firm performs in designing, producing, marketing, delivering, and supporting its product. Each of these activities can contribute to a firm's relative cost position and create a basis for differentiation. A cost advantage, for example, may stem from such disparate sources as a low-cost physical distribution system, a highly efficient assembly process, or superior sales force utilization. Differentiation can stem from similarly diverse factors, including the procurement of high quality raw materials, a responsive order entry system, or a superior product design.

A systematic way of examining all the activities a firm performs and how they interact is necessary for analyzing the sources of competitive advantage. In this chapter, I introduce the *value chain* as the basic tool for doing so. The value chain disaggregates a firm into its strategically relevant activities in order to understand the behavior of costs and the existing and potential sources of differentiation. A firm gains competitive advantage by performing these strategically important activities more cheaply or better than its competitors.

A firm's value chain is embedded in a larger stream of activities that I term the *value system,* illustrated in Figure 2–1. Suppliers have value chains (*upstream value*) that create and deliver the purchased inputs used in a firm's chain. Suppliers not only deliver a product but also can influence a firm's performance in many other ways. In addition, many products pass through the value chains of channels (*channel value*) on their way to the buyer. Channels perform additional activities that affect the buyer, as well as influence the firm's own activities. A firm's product eventually becomes part of its *buyer's value chain.* The ultimate basis for differentiation is a firm and its product's role in the buyer's value chain, which determines buyer needs. Gaining and sustaining competitive advantage depends on understanding not only a firm's value chain but how the firm fits in the overall value system.

The value chains of firms in an industry differ, reflecting their histories, strategies, and success at implementation. One important difference is that a firm's value chain may differ in *competitive scope* from that of its competitors, representing a potential source of competitive advantage. Serving only a particular industry segment may allow a firm to tailor its value chain to that segment and result in lower costs or differentiation in serving that segment compared to competitors. Widening or narrowing the geographic markets served can also affect competitive advantage. The extent of integration into activities plays a key role in competitive advantage. Finally, competing in related industries with coordinated value chains can lead to competitive advantage through interrelationships. A firm may exploit the benefits of broader scope internally or it may form coalitions with other firms to do so. Coalitions are long-term alliances with other firms that fall short of outright merger, such as joint ventures, licenses, and supply agreements. Coalitions involve coordinating or sharing value chains with coalition partners that broadens the effective scope of the firm's chain.

This chapter describes the fundamental role of the value chain in identifying sources of competitive advantage. I begin by describing the value chain and its component parts. Every firm's value chain is composed of nine generic categories of activities which are linked together in characteristic ways. The generic chain is used to demonstrate how a value chain can be constructed for a particular firm, reflecting the specific activities it performs. I also show how the activities in a firm's value chain are linked to each other and to the activities

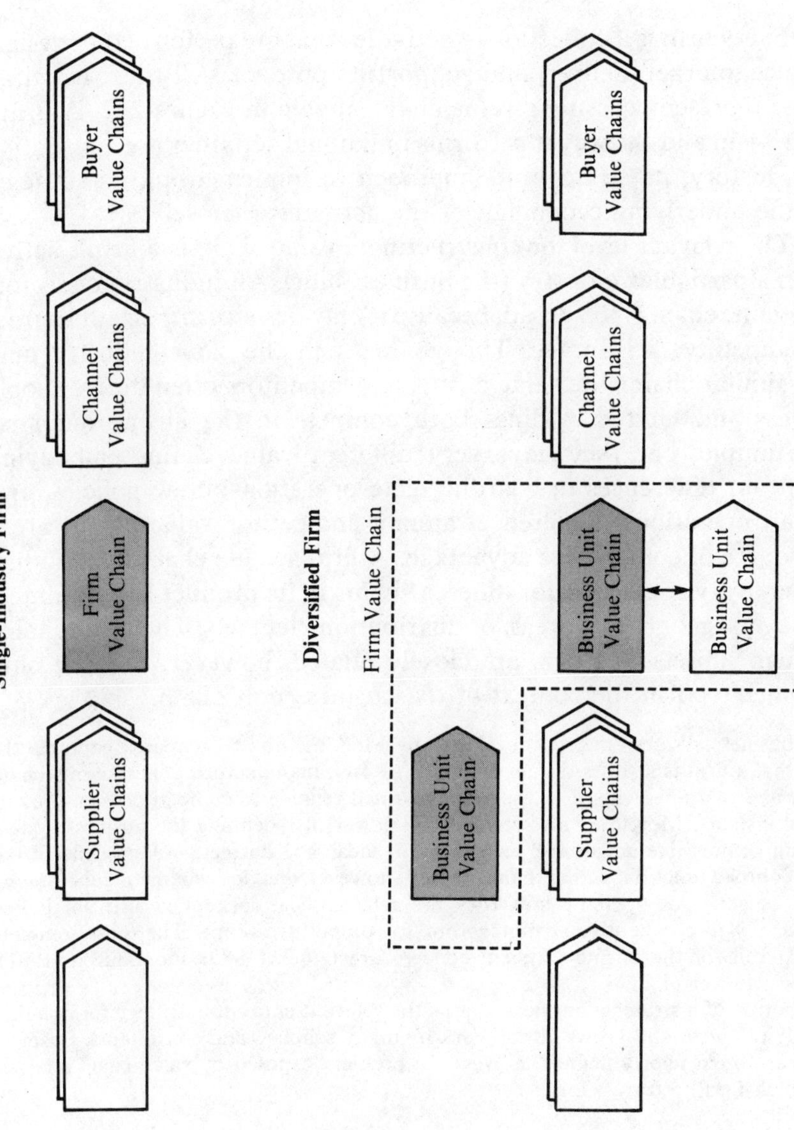

Figure 2–1. The Value System

of its suppliers, channels, and buyers, and how these linkages affect competitive advantage. I then describe how scope of a firm's activities affects competitive advantage through its impact on the value chain. Subsequent chapters will illustrate in detail how the value chain can be used as a strategic tool to analyze relative cost position, differentiation, and the role of competitive scope in achieving competitive advantage.

The Value Chain

Every firm is a collection of activities that are performed to design, produce, market, deliver, and support its product. All these activities can be represented using a value chain, shown in Figure 2–2. A firm's value chain and the way it performs individual activities are a reflection of its history, its strategy, its approach to implementing its strategy, and the underlying economics of the activities themselves.[1]

The relevant level for constructing a value chain is a firm's activities in a particular industry (the business unit). An industry- or sector-wide value chain is too broad, because it may obscure important sources of competitive advantage. Though firms in the same industry may have similar chains the value chains of competitors often differ. People Express and United Airlines both compete in the airline industry, for example, but they have very different value chains embodying significant differences in boarding gate operations, crew policies, and aircraft operations. Differences among competitor value chains are a key source of competitive advantage. A firm's value chain in an industry may vary somewhat for different items in its product line, or different buyers, geographic areas, or distribution channels. The value chains for such subsets of a firm are closely related, however, and can only be understood in the context of the business unit chain.[2]

[1]The business system concept, developed by McKinsey and Company, captures the idea that a firm is a series of functions (e.g., R&D, manufacturing, marketing, channels), and that analyzing how each is performed relative to competitors can provide useful insights. McKinsey also stresses the power of redefining the business system to gain competitive advantage, an important idea. The business system concept addresses broad functions rather than activities, however, and does not distinguish among types of activities or show how they are related. The concept is also not linked specifically to competitive advantage nor to competitive scope. The most complete descriptions of the business system concept are Gluck (1980) and Bauron (1981). See also Bower (1973).

[2]The notion of a strategic business unit as the relevant entity for strategy formulation is well accepted, and grows out of work by many scholars and consultants. Business units are often poorly defined, however, a problem exposed by value chain analysis to which I will return below.

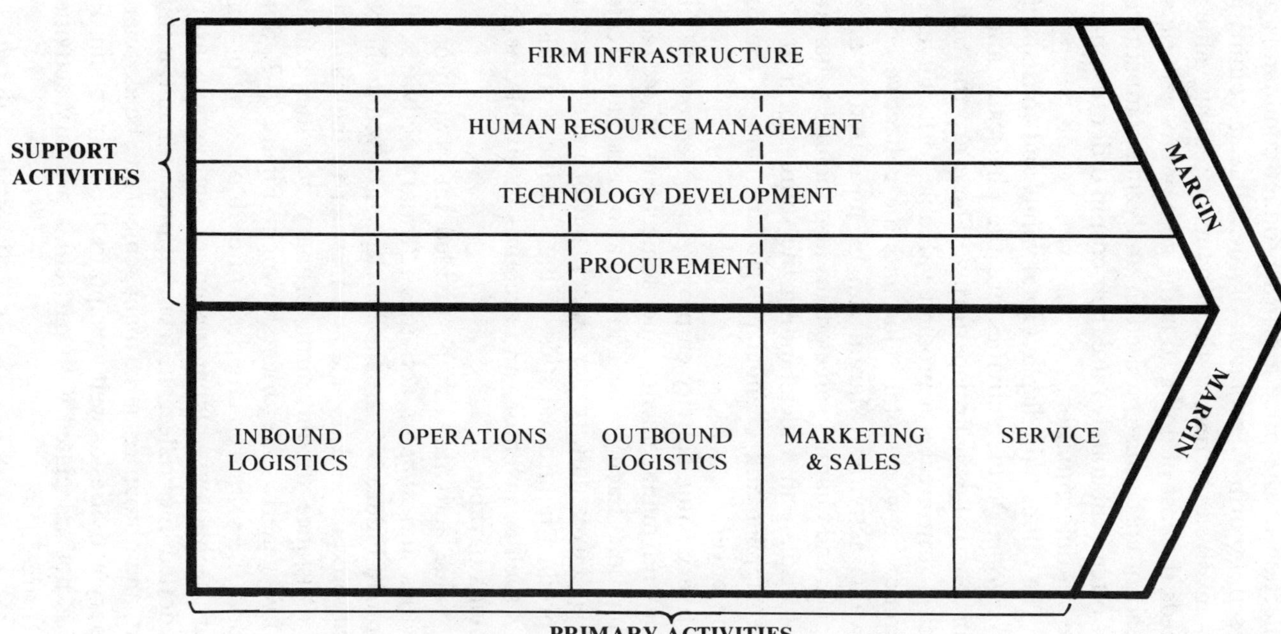

Figure 2–2. The Generic Value Chain

In competitive terms, value is the amount buyers are willing to pay for what a firm provides them. Value is measured by total revenue, a reflection of the price a firm's product commands and the units it can sell. A firm is profitable if the value it commands exceeds the costs involved in creating the product. Creating value for buyers that exceeds the cost of doing so is the goal of any generic strategy. Value, instead of cost, must be used in analyzing competitive position since firms often deliberately raise their cost in order to command a premium price via differentiation.

The value chain displays total value, and consists of *value activities* and *margin.* Value activities are the physically and technologically distinct activities a firm performs. These are the building blocks by which a firm creates a product valuable to its buyers. Margin is the difference between total value and the collective cost of performing the value activities. Margin can be measured in a variety of ways. Supplier and channel value chains also include a margin that is important to isolate in understanding the sources of a firm's cost position, since supplier and channel margin are part of the total cost borne by the buyer.

Every value activity employs *purchased inputs, human resources* (labor and management), and some form of *technology* to perform its function. Each value activity also uses and creates *information,* such as buyer data (order entry), performance parameters (testing), and product failure statistics. Value activities may also create financial assets such as inventory and accounts receivable, or liabilities such as accounts payable.

Value activities can be divided into two broad types, *primary* activities and *support* activities. Primary activities, listed along the bottom of Figure 2–2, are the activities involved in the physical creation of the product and its sale and transfer to the buyer as well as after-sale assistance. In any firm, primary activities can be divided into the five generic categories shown in Figure 2–2. Support activities support the primary activities and each other by providing purchased inputs, technology, human resources, and various firmwide functions. The dotted lines reflect the fact that procurement, technology development, and human resource management can be associated with specific primary activities as well as support the entire chain. Firm intrastructure is not associated with particular primary activities but supports the entire chain.

Value activities are therefore the discrete building blocks of competitive advantage. How each activity is performed combined with its economics will determine whether a firm is high or low cost relative to competitors. How each value activity is performed will also determine its contribution to buyer needs and hence differentiation. Comparing the value chains of competitors exposes differences that determine competitive advantage.[3]

An analysis of the value chain rather than value added is the appropriate way to examine competitive advantage. Value added (selling price less the cost of purchased raw materials) has sometimes been used as the focal point for cost analysis because it was viewed as the area in which a firm can control costs. Value added is not a sound basis for cost analysis, however, because it incorrectly distinguishes raw materials from the many other purchased inputs used in a firm's activities. Also, the cost behavior of activities cannot be understood without simultaneously examining the costs of the inputs used to perform them. Moreover, value added fails to highlight the linkages between a firm and its suppliers that can reduce cost or enhance differentiation.

Identifying Value Activities

Identifying value activities requires the isolation of activities that are technologically and strategically distinct. Value activities and accounting classifications are rarely the same. Accounting classifications (e.g., burden, overhead, direct labor) group together activities with disparate technologies, and separate costs that are all part of the same activity.

Primary Activities

There are five generic categories of primary activities involved in competing in any industry, as shown in Figure 2–2. Each category is divisible into a number of distinct activities that depend on the particular industry and firm strategy:

- *Inbound Logistics.* Activities associated with receiving, storing, and disseminating inputs to the product, such as material han-

[3]Economists have characterized the firm as having a production function that defines how inputs are converted into outputs. The value chain is a theory of the firm that views the firm as being a collection of discrete but related production functions, if production functions are defined as activities. The value chain formulation focuses on how these activities create value and what determines their cost, giving the firm considerable latitude in determining how activities are configured and combined.

dling, warehousing, inventory control, vehicle scheduling, and returns to suppliers.

- *Operations.* Actitivies associated with transforming inputs into the final product form, such as machining, packaging, assembly, equipment maintenance, testing, printing, and facility operations.
- *Outbound Logistics.* Activities associated with collecting, storing, and physically distributing the product to buyers, such as finished goods warehousing, material handling, delivery vehicle operation, order processing, and scheduling.
- *Marketing and Sales.* Activities associated with providing a means by which buyers can purchase the product and inducing them to do so, such as advertising, promotion, sales force, quoting, channel selection, channel relations, and pricing.
- *Service.* Activities associated with providing service to enhance or maintain the value of the product, such as installation, repair, training, parts supply, and product adjustment.

Each of the categories may be vital to competitive advantage depending on the industry. For a distributor, inbound and outbound logistics are the most critical. For a service firm providing the service on its premises such as a restaurant or retailer, outbound logistics may be largely nonexistant and operations the vital category. For a bank engaged in corporate lending, marketing and sales are a key to competitive advantage through the effectiveness of the calling officers and the way in which loans are packaged and priced. For a high speed copier manufacturer, service represents a key source of competitive advantage. In any firm, however, all the categories of primary activities will be present to some degree and play some role in competitive advantage.

Support Activities

Support value activities involved in competing in any industry can be divided into four generic categories, also shown in Figure 2–2. As with primary activities, each category of support activities is divisible into a number of distinct value activities that are specific to a given industry. In technology development, for example, discrete activities might include component design, feature design, field testing, process engineering, and technology selection. Similarly, procurement can be divided into activities such as qualifying new suppliers, procurement of different groups of purchased inputs, and ongoing monitoring of supplier performance.

Procurement. Procurement refers to the *function* of purchasing inputs used in the firm's value chain, not to the purchased inputs themselves. Purchased inputs include raw materials, supplies, and other consumable items as well as assets such as machinery, laboratory equipment, office equipment, and buildings. Though purchased inputs are commonly associated with primary activities, purchased inputs are present in every value activity including support activities. For example, laboratory supplies and independent testing services are common purchased inputs in technology development, while an accounting firm is a common purchased input in firm infrastructure. Like all value activities, procurement employs a "technology," such as procedures for dealing with vendors, qualification rules, and information systems.

Procurement tends to be spread throughout a firm. Some items such as raw materials are purchased by the traditional purchasing department, while other items are purchased by plant managers (e.g., machines), office managers (e.g., temporary help), salespersons (e.g., meals and lodging), and even the chief executive officer (e.g., strategic consulting). I use the term procurement rather than purchasing because the usual connotation of purchasing is too narrow among managers. The dispersion of the procurement function often obscures the magnitude of total purchases, and means that many purchases receive little scrutiny.

A given procurement activity can normally be associated with a specific value activity or activities which it supports, though often a purchasing department serves many value activities and purchasing policies apply firmwide. The cost of procurement activities themselves usually represents a small if not insignificant portion of total costs, but often has a large impact on the firm's overall cost and differentiation. Improved purchasing practices can strongly affect the cost and quality of purchased inputs, as well as of other activities associated with receiving and using the inputs, and interacting with suppliers. In chocolate manufacturing and electric utilities, for example, procurement of cocoa beans and fuel respectively is by far the most important determinant of cost position.

Technology Development. Every value activity embodies technology, be it know-how, procedures, or technology embodied in process equipment. The array of technologies employed in most firms is very broad, ranging from those technologies used in preparing documents and transporting goods to those technologies embodied in the product itself. Moreover, most value activities use a technology that combines a number of different subtechnologies involving different scientific disciplines. Machining, for example, involves metallurgy, electronics, and mechanics.

Technology development consists of a range of activities that can be broadly grouped into efforts to improve the product and the process. I term this category of activities technology development instead of research and development because R&D has too narrow a connotation to most managers. Technology development tends to be associated with the engineering department or the development group. Typically, however, it occurs in many parts of a firm, although this is not explicitly recognized. Technology development may support any of the numerous technologies embodied in value activities, including such areas as telecommunications technology for the order entry system, or office automation for the accounting department. It does not solely apply to technologies directly linked to the end product. Technology development also takes many forms, from basic research and product design to media research, process equipment design, and servicing procedures. Technology development that is related to the product and its features supports the entire chain, while other technology development is associated with particular primary or support activities.

Technology development is important to competitive advantage in all industries, holding the key in some. In steel, for example, a firm's process technology is the single greatest factor in competitive advantage. The competitive implications of the array of technologies in the value chain are treated in Chapter 5.

Human Resource Management. Human resource management consists of activities involved in the recruiting, hiring, training, development, and compensation of all types of personnel. Human resource management supports both individual primary and support activities (e.g., hiring of engineers) and the entire value chain (e.g., labor negotiations). Human resource management activities occur in different parts of a firm, as do other support activities, and the dispersion of these activities can lead to inconsistent policies. Moreover, the cumulative costs of human resource management are rarely well understood nor are the tradeoffs in different human resource management costs, such as salary compared to the cost of recruiting and training due to turnover.

Human resource management affects competitive advantage in any firm, through its role in determining the skills and motivation of employees and the cost of hiring and training. In some industries it holds the key to competitive advantage. The world's leading accounting firm Arthur Andersen, for example, draws a significant competitive advantage from its approach to recruiting and training its tens of thousands of professional staff. Arthur Andersen has bought a former college campus near Chicago, and has invested heavily in codifying its practice and regularly bringing staff from around the world to its college for training in the firmwide methodology. Having a deeply understood methodology throughout the firm not only makes all engagements more effective but also greatly facilitates the servicing of national and multinational clients.

Firm Infrastructure. Firm infrastructure consists of a number of activities including general management, planning, finance, accounting, legal, government affairs, and quality management. Infrastructure, unlike other support activities, usually supports the entire chain and not individual activities. Depending on whether a firm is diversified or not, firm infrastructure may be self-contained or divided between a business unit and the parent corporation.[4] In diversified firms, infrastructure activities are typically split between the business unit and corporate levels (e.g., financing is often done at the corporate level while quality management is done at the business unit level). Many infrastructure activities occur at both the business unit and corporate levels, however.

Firm infrastructure is sometimes viewed only as "overhead," but can be a powerful source of competitive advantage. In a telephone operating company, for example, negotiating and maintaining ongoing relations with regulatory bodies can be among the most important activities for competitive advantage. Similarly, proper management information systems can contribute significantly to cost position, while in some industries top management plays a vital role in dealing with the buyer.

Activity Types

Within each category of primary and support activities, there are three activity types that play a different role in competitive advantage:

[4]There may also be infrastructure activities at the group or sector level.

- *Direct.* Activities directly involved in creating value for the buyer, such as assembly, parts machining, sales force operation, advertising, product design, recruiting, etc.
- *Indirect.* Activities that make it possible to perform direct activities on a continuing basis, such as maintenance, scheduling, operation of facilities, sales force administration, research administration, vendor record keeping, etc.
- *Quality Assurance.* Activities that ensure the quality of other activities, such as monitoring, inspecting, testing, reviewing, checking, adjusting, and reworking. Quality assurance is *not* synonymous with quality management, because many value activities contribute to quality, as will be discussed in Chapter 4.

Every firm has direct, indirect, and quality assurance value activities. All three types are present not only among primary activities but also among support activities. In technology development, for example, actual laboratory teams are direct activities, while research administration is an indirect activity.

The role of indirect and quality assurance activities is often not well understood, making the distinction among the three activity types an important one for diagnosing competitive advantage. In many industries, indirect activities represent a large and rapidly growing proportion of cost and can play a significant role in differentiation through their effect on direct activities. Despite this, indirect activities are frequently lumped together with direct activities when managers think about their firms, though the two often have very different economics. There are often tradeoffs between direct and indirect activities—more spending on maintenance lowers machine costs. Indirect activities are also frequently grouped together into "overhead" or "burden" accounts, obscuring their cost and contribution to differentiation.

Quality assurance activities are also prevalent in nearly every part of a firm, though they are seldom recognized as such. Testing and inspection are associated with many primary activities. Quality assurance activities outside of operations are often less apparent though equally prevalent. The cumulative cost of quality assurance activities can be very large, as recent attention to the cost of quality has demonstrated. Quality assurance activities often affect the cost or effectiveness of other activities, and the way other activities are performed in turn affects the need for and types of quality assurance activities. The possibility of simplifying or eliminating the need for quality assurance activities through performing other activities better is at the root of the notion that quality can be "free."

Defining the Value Chain

To diagnose competitive advantage, it is necessary to define a firm's value chain for competing in a particular industry. Starting with the generic chain, individual value activities are identified in the particular firm. Each generic category can be divided into discrete activities, as illustrated for one generic category in Figure 2–3. An example of a complete value chain is shown in Figure 2–4, the value chain of a copier manufacturer.

Defining relevant value activities requires that activities with discrete technologies and economics be isolated. Broad functions such as manufacturing or marketing must be subdivided into activities. The product flow, order flow or paper flow can be useful in doing so. Subdividing activities can proceed to the level of increasingly narrow activities that are to some degree discrete. Every machine in a factory, for example, could be treated as a separate activity. Thus the number of potential activities is often quite large.

The appropriate degree of disaggregation depends on the economics of the activities and the purposes for which the value chain is being analyzed. Though I will return to this question in later chapters, the basic principle is that activities should be isolated and separated that (1) have different economics, (2) have a high potential impact of differentiation, or (3) represent a significant or growing proportion of cost. In using the value chain, successively finer disaggregations of some activities are made as the analysis exposes differences important to competitive advantage; other activities are combined because they prove to be unimportant to competitive advantage or are governed by similar economics.

Selecting the appropriate category in which to put an activity may require judgment and can be illuminating in its own right. Order processing, for example, could be classified as part of outbound logistics or as part of marketing. In a distributor, the role of order processing is more a marketing function. Similarly, the sales force often performs service functions. Value activities should be assigned to categories that best represent their contribution to a firm's competitive advantage. If order processing is an important way in which a firm interacts with its buyers, for example, it should be classified under marketing.

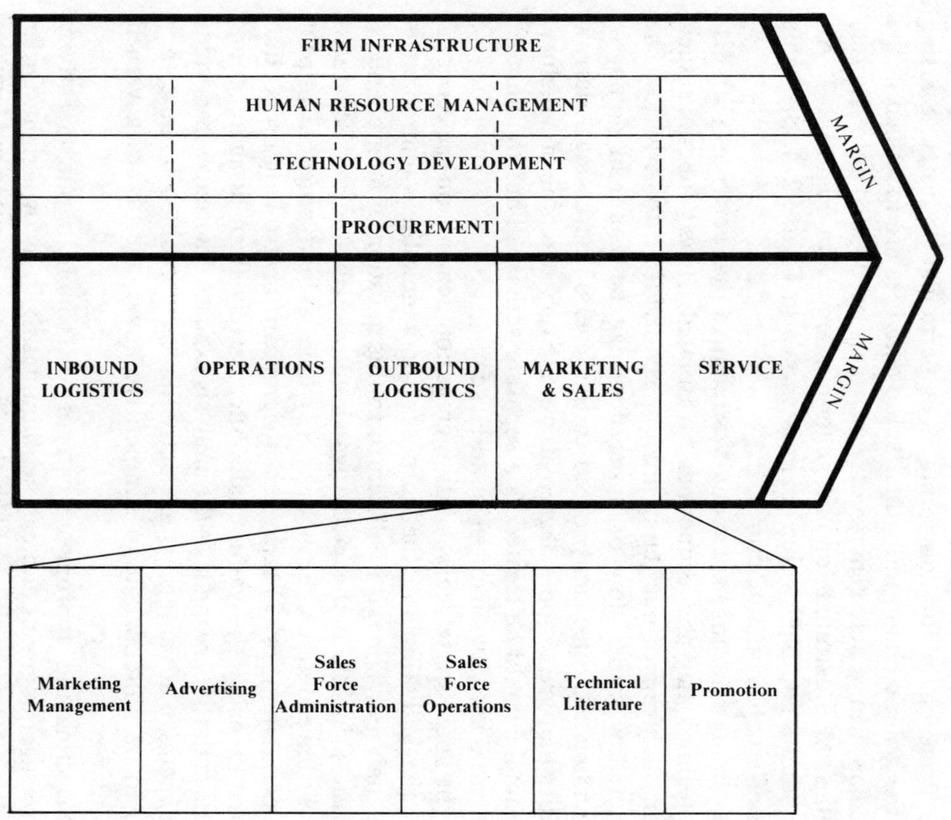

Figure 2–3. Subdividing a Generic Value Chain

	Inbound Logistics	Operations	Outbound Logistics	Marketing & Sales	Service
FIRM INFRASTRUCTURE					
HUMAN RESOURCE MANAGEMENT		Recruiting Training		Recruiting	Recruiting
TECHNOLOGY DEVELOPMENT	Design of Automated System	Component Design Machine Design Design of Assembly Line Testing Procedures Energy Management	Information System Development	Market Research Sales Aids & Technical Literature	Service Manuals and Procedures
PROCUREMENT	Transportation Services	Materials Other Parts Energy Supplies Electrical/ Electronic Parts	Computer Services Transportation Services	Media Agency Services Supplies Travel & Subsistence	Spare Parts Travel & Subsistence
	Inbound Material Handling Inbound Inspection Parts Picking & Delivery	Component Fabrication Assembly Fine Tuning & Testing Maintenance Facilities Operation	Order Processing Shipping	Advertising Promotion Sales Force	Service Reps Spare Parts Systems
	INBOUND LOGISTICS	**OPERATIONS**	**OUTBOUND LOGISTICS**	**MARKETING & SALES**	**SERVICE**

MARGIN

MARGIN

Figure 2–4. Value Chain for a Copier Manufacturer

Similarly, if inbound material handling and outbound material handling use the same facilities and personnel, then both should probably be combined into one value activity and classified wherever the function has the greatest competitive impact. Firms have often gained competitive advantage by redefining the roles of traditional activities—Vetco, an oil field equipment supplier, uses customer training as a marketing tool and a way to build switching costs, for example.

Everything a firm does should be captured in a primary or support activity. Value activity labels are arbitrary and should be chosen to provide the best insight into the business. Labeling activities in service industries often causes confusion because operations, marketing, and after-sale support are often closely tied. Ordering of activities should broadly follow the process flow, but ordering is judgmental as well. Often firms perform parallel activities, whose order should be chosen to enhance the intuitive clarity of the value chain to managers.

Linkages within the Value Chain

Although value activities are the building blocks of competitive advantage, the value chain is not a collection of independent activities but a system of interdependent activities. Value activities are related by linkages within the value chain. Linkages are relationships between the way one value activity is performed and the cost or performance of another. For example, purchasing high-quality, precut steel sheets can simplify manufacturing and reduce scrap. In a fast food chain, the timing of promotional campaigns can influence capacity utilization. Competitive advantage frequently derives from linkages among activities just as it does from the individual activities themselves.

Linkages can lead to competitive advantage in two ways: optimization and coordination. Linkages often reflect tradeoffs among activities to achieve the same overall result. For example, a more costly product design, more stringent materials specifications, or greater in-process inspection may reduce service costs. A firm must optimize such linkages reflecting its strategy in order to achieve competitive advantage.

Linkages may also reflect the need to coordinate activities. On-time delivery, for example, may require coordination of activities in operations, outbound logistics, and service (e.g., installation). The ability to coordinate linkages often reduces cost or enhances differentiation. Better coordination, for example, can reduce the need for inven-

inventory throughout the firm. Linkages imply that a firm's cost or differentiation is not merely the result of efforts to reduce cost or improve performance in each value activity individually. Much of the recent change in philosophy towards manufacturing and towards quality—strongly influenced by Japanese practice—is a recognition of the importance of linkages.

Linkages are numerous, and some are common to many firms. The most obvious linkages are those between support activities and primary activities represented by the dotted lines on the generic value chain. Product design usually affects the manufacturing cost of a product, for example, while procurement practices often affect the quality of purchased inputs and hence production costs, inspection costs, and product quality. More subtle linkages are those between primary activities. For example, enhanced inspection of incoming parts may reduce quality assurance costs later in the production process, while better maintenance often reduces the downtime of a machine. An interactive order entry system may reduce salesperson time required per buyer because salespersons can place orders faster and are freed from the need to follow up on inquiries and problems. More thorough inspection of finished goods often improves the reliability of products in the field, reducing servicing costs. Finally, frequent deliveries to buyers may reduce inventory and accounts receivable. Linkages that involve activities in different categories or of different types are often the most difficult to recognize.

Linkages among value activities arise from a number of generic causes, among them the following:

- *The same function can be performed in different ways.* For example, conformance to specifications can be achieved through high quality purchased inputs, specifying close tolerances in the manufacturing process, or 100 percent inspection of finished goods.
- *The cost or performance of direct activities is improved by greater efforts in indirect activities.* For example, better scheduling (an indirect activity) reduces sales force travel time or delivery vehicle time (direct activities); or better maintenance improves the tolerances achieved by machines.
- *Activities performed inside a firm reduce the need to demonstrate, explain, or service a product in the field.* For example, 100 percent inspection can substantially reduce service costs in the field.

- *Quality assurance functions can be performed in different ways.* For example, incoming inspection is a substitute for finished goods inspection.

Though linkages within the value chain are crucial to competitive advantage, they are often subtle and go unrecognized. The importance of procurement in affecting manufacturing cost and quality may not be obvious, for example. Nor is the link between order processing, manufacturing scheduling practices, and sales force utilization. Identifying linkages is a process of searching for ways in which each value activity affects or is affected by others. The generic causes of linkages discussed above provide a starting point. The disaggregation of procurement and technology development to relate them to specific primary activities also helps to highlight linkages between support and primary activities.

Exploiting linkages usually requires information or information flows that allow optimization or coordination to take place. Thus, information systems are often vital to gaining competitive advantages from linkages. Recent developments in information systems technology are creating new linkages and increasing the ability to achieve old ones. Exploiting linkages also frequently requires optimization or coordination that cuts across conventional organizational lines. Higher costs in the manufacturing organization, for example, may result in lower costs in the sales or service organization. Such tradeoffs may not be measured in a firm's information and control systems. Managing linkages thus is a more complex organizational task than managing value activities themselves. Given the difficulty of recognizing and managing linkages, the ability to do so often yields a *sustainable* source of competitive advantage. The specific role of linkages in cost and differentiation will be discussed in more detail in Chapters 3 and 4.

Vertical Linkages

Linkages exist not only within a firm's value chain but between a firm's chain and the value chains of suppliers and channels. These linkages, which I term vertical linkages, are similar to the linkages within the value chain—the way supplier or channel activities are performed affects the cost or performance of a firm's activities (and vice versa). Suppliers produce a product or service that a firm employs in its value chain, and suppliers' value chains also influence the firm at other contact points. A firm's procurement and inbound logistics activities interact with a supplier's order entry system, for example, while a supplier's applications engineering staff works with a firm's technology development and manufacturing activities. A supplier's product characteristics as well as its other contact points with a firm's value chain can significantly affect a firm's cost and differentiation. For example, frequent supplier shipments can reduce a firm's inventory needs, appropriate packaging of supplier products can lower handling cost, and supplier inspection can remove the need for incoming inspection by a firm.

The linkages between suppliers' value chains and a firm's value chain provide opportunities for the firm to enhance its competitive advantage. It is often possible to benefit both the firm and suppliers by influencing the configuration of suppliers' value chains to jointly optimize the performance of activities, or by improving coordination between a firm's and suppliers' chains. Supplier linkages mean that the relationship with suppliers is *not a zero sum game* in which one gains only at the expense of the other, but a relationship in which both can gain. By agreeing to deliver bulk chocolate to a confectionery producer in tank cars instead of solid bars, for example, an industrial chocolate firm saves the cost of molding and packaging while the confectionery manufacturer lowers the cost of in-bound handling and melting. The division of the benefits of coordinating or optimizing linkages between a firm and its suppliers is a function of suppliers' bargaining power and is reflected in suppliers' margins. Supplier bargaining power is partly structural and partly a function of a firm's purchasing practices.[5] Thus *both* coordination with suppliers and hard bargaining to capture the spoils are important to competitive advantage. One without the other results in missed opportunities.

Channel linkages are similar to supplier linkages. Channels have value chains through which a firm's product passes. The channel markup over a firm's selling price (which I term channel value) often represents a large proportion of the selling price to the end user—it represents as much as 50 percent or more of selling price to the end user in many consumer goods, such as wine. Channels perform such activities as sales, advertising, and display that may substitute for or complement the firm's activities. There are also multiple points of contact between a firm's and channels' value chains in activities such as the sales force, order entry, and outbound logistics. As with supplier linkages, coordinating and jointly optimizing with channels can lower cost or enhance differentiation. The same issues that existed with sup-

[5]For a discussion of some of the structural issues see *Competitive Strategy,* Chapters 1 and 6.

pliers in dividing the gains of coordination and joint optimization also exist with channels.

Vertical linkages, like linkages within a firm's value chain, are frequently overlooked. Even if they are recognized, independent ownership of suppliers or channels or a history of an adversary relationship can impede the coordination and joint optimization required to exploit vertical linkages. Sometimes vertical linkages are easier to achieve with coalition partners or sister business units than with independent firms, though even this is not assured. As with linkages within the value chain, exploiting vertical linkages requires information and modern information systems are creating many new possibilities. I will discuss the role of supplier and channel linkages in competitive advantage more fully in Chapters 3 and 4.

The Buyer's Value Chain

Buyers also have value chains, and a firm's product represents a purchased input to the buyer's chain. Understanding the value chains of industrial, commercial, and institutional buyers is intuitively easy because of their similarities to that of a firm. Understanding households' value chains is less intuitive, but nevertheless important. Households (and the individual consumers within them) engage in a wide range of activities, and products purchased by households are used in conjunction with this stream of activities. A car is used for the trip to work and for shopping and leisure, while a food product is consumed as part of the process of preparing and eating meals. Though it is quite difficult to construct a value chain that encompasses everything a household and its occupants do, it is quite possible to construct a chain for those activities that are relevant to how a particular product is used. Chains need not be constructed for every household, but chains for representative households can provide an important tool for use in differentiation analysis, to be discussed in more detail in Chapter 4.

A firm's differentiation stems from how its value chain relates to its buyer's chain. This is a function of the way a firm's physical product is used in the particular buyer activity in which it is consumed (e.g., a machine used in the assembly process) as well as *all* the other points of contact between a firm's value chain and the buyer's chain. Many of a firm's activities interact with some buyer activities. In optoelectronic parts, for example, a firm's product is assembled into the buyer's equipment—an obvious point of contact—but the firm also works closely with the buyer in designing the part, providing ongoing technical assistance, troubleshooting, order processing, and delivery. Each of these contact points is a potential source of differentiation. "Quality" is too narrow a view of what makes a firm unique, because it focuses attention on the product rather than the broader array of value activities that impact the buyer.

Differentiation, then, derives fundamentally from creating value for the buyer through a firm's impact on the buyer's value chain. Value is created when a firm creates competitive advantage for its buyer—lowers its buyer's cost or raises its buyer's performance.[6] The value created for the buyer must be perceived by the buyer if it is to be rewarded with a premium price, however, which means that firms must communicate their value to buyers through such means as advertising and the sales force. How this value is divided between the firm (a premium price) and the buyer (higher profits or more satisfaction for the money) is reflected in a firm's margin, and is a function of industry structure. The relationship between the buyer's value chain and the firm's value chain in creating and sustaining differentiation will be described in detail in Chapter 4.[7]

Competitive Scope and the Value Chain

Competitive scope can have a powerful effect on competitive advantage, because it shapes the configuration and economics of the value chain. There are four dimensions of scope that affect the value chain:[8]

- *Segment Scope.* The product varieties produced and buyers served.
- *Vertical Scope.* The extent to which activities are performed in-house instead of by independent firms.

[6]Unlike a firm, which can measure value in terms of price or profit, a consumer's measure of value is complex and relates to the satisfaction of needs. See Chapter 4.

[7]The same principles that determine a firm's differentiation also can be used to analyze the threat of substitution, as I discuss in Chapter 8.

[8]The term scope of the firm is used in economic theory to reflect the boundary between the activities a firm performs internally and those it obtains in market transactions—e.g., vertical integration (see, for example, Coase [1937, 1972]). Some recent work has begun to examine the extent of a firm's diversification as an issue in scope (see Teece [1980]). Competitive scope is used here to refer to a broader conception of the scope of a firm's activities, encompassing industry segment coverage, integration, geographic markets served, and coordinated competition in related industries.

- *Geographic Scope.* The range of regions, countries, or groups of countries in which a firm competes with a coordinated strategy.
- *Industry Scope.* The range of related industries in which the firm competes with a coordinated strategy.

Broad scope can allow a firm to exploit the benefits of performing more activities internally. It may also allow the firm to exploit interrelationships between the value chains that serve different segments, geographic areas or related industries.[9] For example, a shared sales force may sell the products of two business units, or a common brand name may be employed worldwide. Sharing and integration have costs, however, that may nullify their benefits.

Narrow scope can allow the tailoring of the chain to serve a particular target segment, geographic area or industry to achieve lower cost or to serve the target in a unique way. Narrow scope in integration may also improve competitive advantage through the firm's purchasing activities that independent firms perform better or cheaper. The competitive advantage of a narrow scope rests on *differences* among product varicties, buyers, or geographic regions within an industry in terms of the value chain best suited to serve them, or on differences in resources and skills of independent firms that allow them to perform activities better.

The breadth or narrowness of scope is clearly relative to competitors. In some industries, a broad scope involves only serving the full range of product and buyer segments within the industry. In others, it may require both vertical integration and competing in related industries. Since there are many ways to segment an industry and multiple forms of interrelationships and integration, broad and narrow scope can be combined. A firm may create competitive advantage by tuning its value chain to one product segment and exploiting geographic interrelationships by serving that segment worldwide. It may also exploit interrelationships with business units in related industries. I will discuss these possibilities in more detail in Chapter 15.

Segment Scope

Differences in the needs or value chains required to serve different product or buyer segments can lead to a competitive advantage of

[9]Interrelationships among value chains serving different segments, geographic areas and related industries are analytically the same. See Chapters 7 and 9.

focusing. For example, the value chain required to serve sophisticated minicomputer buyers with in-house servicing capabilities is different from that required to serve small business users. They need extensive sales assistance, less demanding hardware performance, user-friendly software, and service capability.

Just as differences among segments favor narrow scope, however, interrelationships between the value chains serving different segments favor broad scope. General Motors' value chain for large cars is different from that for small cars, for example, but many value activities are shared. This creates a tension between tailoring the value chain to a segment and sharing it among segments. This tension is fundamental to industry segmentation and to the choice of focus strategies, the subject of Chapter 7.

Vertical Scope

Vertical integration defines the division of activities between a firm and its suppliers, channels, and buyers. A firm may purchase components rather than fabricate them itself, for example, or contract for service rather than maintain a service organization. Similarly, channels may perform many distribution, service, and marketing functions instead of a firm. A firm and its buyers can also divide activities in differing ways. One way a firm may be able to differentiate itself is by assuming a greater number of buyer activities. In the extreme case, a firm completely enters the buyer's industry.

When one views the issue of integration from the perspective of the value chain, it becomes apparent that opportunities for integration are richer than is often recognized. Vertical integration tends to be viewed in terms of physical products and replacing whole supplier relationships rather than in terms of activities, but it can encompass both. For example, a firm may rely on a supplier's applications engineering and service capability, or it may perform these activities internally. Thus there are many options regarding what value activities a firm performs internally and what value activities it purchases. The same principles apply to channel and buyer integration.

Whether or not integration (or de-integration) lowers cost or enhances differentiation depends on the firm and the activity involved. I have discussed the factors that bear on this question in *Competitive Strategy.* The value chain allows a firm to identify more clearly the potential benefits of integration by highlighting the role of vertical linkages. The exploitation of vertical linkages does not require vertical integration, but integration may sometimes allow the benefits of vertical linkages to be achieved more easily.

Geographic Scope

Geographic scope may allow a firm to share or coordinate value activities used to serve different geographic areas. Canon develops and manufactures copiers primarily in Japan, for example, but sells and services them separately in many countries. Canon gains a cost advantage from sharing technology development and manufacturing instead of performing these activities in each country. Interrelationships are also common among partially distinct value chains serving geographic regions in a single country. For example, food service distributors such as Monarch and SISCO have many largely distinct operating units in major metropolitan areas that share firm infrastructure, procurement, and other support value activities.

Geographic interrelationships can enhance competitive advantage if sharing or coordinating value activities lowers cost or enhances differentiation. There may be costs of coordination as well as differences among regions or countries that reduce the advantage of sharing, however. The sources of competitive advantage from a global strategy and the impediments to employing one are discussed in *Competitive Strategy* and elsewhere.[10] The same principles apply to national or regional coordination of value chains.

Industry Scope

Potential interrelationships among the value chains required to compete in related industries are widespread. They can involve any value activity, including both primary (e.g., a shared service organization) and support activities (e.g., joint technology development or shared procurement of common inputs). Interrelationships among business units are similar in concept to geographic interrelationships among value chains.

Interrelationships among business units can have a powerful influence on competitive advantage, either by lowering cost or enhancing

[10]See Porter (1985).

differentiation. A shared logistical system may allow a firm to reap economies of scale, for example, while a shared sales force offering related products can improve the salesperson's effectiveness with the buyer and thereby enhance differentiation. All interrelationships do not lead to competitive advantage. Not all activities benefit from sharing. There are also always costs of sharing activities that must be offset against the benefits, because the needs of different business units may not be the same with respect to a value activity. I will describe interrelationships among business units and their implications for both corporate and business unit strategy in Chapters 9–11.

Coalitions and Scope

A firm can pursue the benefits of a broader scope internally, or enter into *coalitions* with independent firms to achieve some or all of the same benefits. Coalitions are long-term agreements among firms that go beyond normal market transactions but fall short of outright mergers. Examples of coalitions include technology licenses, supply agreements, marketing agreements, and joint ventures. Coalitions are ways of broadening scope without broadening the firm, by contracting with an independent firm to perform value activities (e.g., a supply agreement) or teaming up with an independent firm to share activities (e.g., a marketing joint venture). Thus there are two basic types of coalition—vertical coalitions and horizontal coalitions.

Coalitions can allow sharing of activities without the need to enter new industry segments, geographic areas, or related industries. Coalitions are also a means of gaining the cost or differentiation advantages of vertical linkages without actual integration, but overcoming the difficulties of coordination among purely independent firms. Because coalitions involve long-term relationships, it should be possible to coordinate more closely with a coalition partner than with an independent firm, though not without some cost. Difficulties in reaching coalition agreements and in ongoing coordination among partners may block coalitions or nullify their benefits.

Coalition partners remain independent firms and there is the question of how the benefits of a coalition are to be divided. The relative bargaining power of each coalition partner is thus central to how the gains are shared, and determines impact of the coalition on a firm's competitive advantage. A strong coalition partner may appropriate all the gains of a shared marketing organization through the terms of the agreement, for example. The role of coalitions in competitive advantage is discussed in my book on global strategy, because they are particularly prevalent in international competition.[11]

Competitive Scope and Business Definition

The relationship between competitive scope and the value chain provides the basis for defining relevant business unit boundaries. Strategically distinct business units are isolated by weighing the benefits of integration and de-integration and by comparing the strength of interrelationships in serving related segments, geographic areas, or industries to the differences in the value chains best suited for serving them separately. If differences in geographic areas or product and buyer segments require very distinct value chains, then segments define business units. Conversely, strong and widespread benefits of integration or geographic or industry interrelationships widen the relevant boundaries of business units. Strong advantages to vertical integration widen the boundaries of a business unit to encompass upstream or downstream activities, while weak advantages to integration imply that each stage is a distinct business unit. Similarly, strong advantages to worldwide coordination of the value chains imply that the relevant business unit is global, while strong country or regional differences necessitating largely distinct chains imply narrower geographic business unit boundaries. Finally, strong interrelationships between one business unit and another may imply that they should merge into one. Appropriate business units can be defined, then, by understanding the optimal value chain for competing in different arenas and how the chains are related. I will return to this issue after the principles of industry segmentation have been discussed in Chapter 7.

The Value Chain and Industry Structure

Industry structure both shapes the value chain of a firm and is a reflection of the collective value chains of competitors. Structure determines the bargaining relationships with buyers and suppliers that is reflected in both the configuration of a firm's value chain and how margins are divided with buyers, suppliers, and coalition partners. The threat of substitution to an industry influences the value activities

[11]Porter, op. cit. See also Porter, Fuller, and Rawlinson (1984).

desired by buyers. Entry barriers bear on the sustainability of various value chain configurations.

The array of competitor value chains is, in turn, the basis for many elements of industry structure. Scale economies and proprietary learning, for example, stem from the technology employed in competitors' value chains. Capital requirements for competing in an industry are the result of the collective capital required in the chain. Similarly, industry product differentiation stems from the way firms' products are used in buyers' value chains. Thus many elements of industry structure can be diagnosed by analyzing the value chains of competitors in an industry.

The Value Chain and Organizational Structure

The value chain is a basic tool for diagnosing competitive advantage and finding ways to create and sustain it, the subject that will dominate the chapters that follow. However, the value chain can also play a valuable role in designing organizational structure. Organizational structure groups certain activities together under organizational units such as marketing or production. The logic of those groupings is that activities have similarities that should be exploited by putting them together in a department; at the same time, departments are separated from other groups of activities because of their differences. This separation of like activities is what organizational theorists call "differentiation." With separation of organizational units comes the need to coordinate them, usually termed "integration." Thus integrating mechanisms must be established in a firm to ensure that the required coordination takes place. Organizational structure balances the benefits of separation and integration.[12]

The value chain provides a systematic way to divide a firm into its discrete activities, and thus can be used to examine how the activities in a firm are and could be grouped. Figure 2–5 shows a value chain with a typical organizational structure superimposed. Organizational boundaries are often not drawn around the groups of activities that are most similar in economic terms. Moreover, organizational units such as the purchasing and R&D departments frequently contain only a fraction of the similar activities being performed in a firm.

The need for integration among organizational units is a manifes-

[12]For the seminal work see Lawrence and Lorsch (1967).

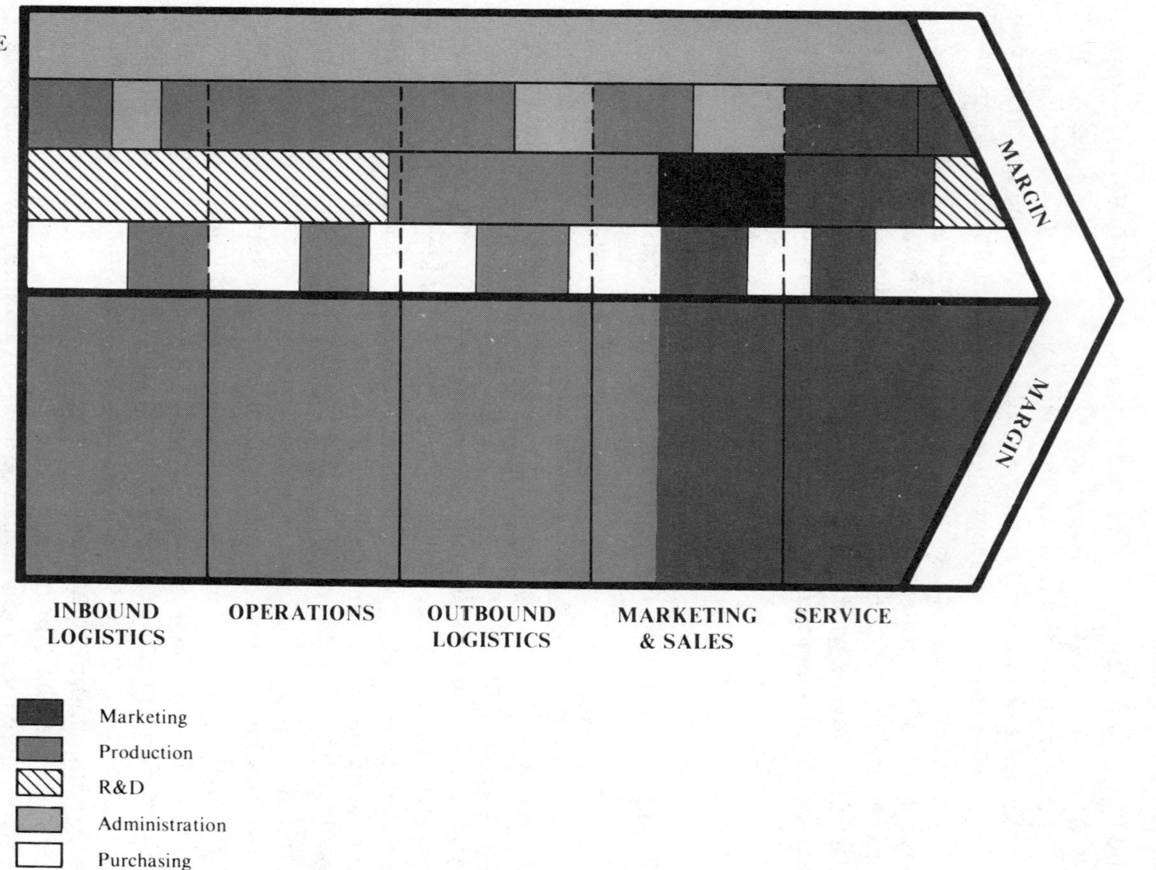

Figure 2–5. Organizational Structure and the Value Chain

tation of linkages. There are often many linkages within the value chain, and organizational structure often fails to provide mechanisms to coordinate or optimize them. The information necessary for coordinating or optimizing linkages is also rarely collected throughout the chain. Managers of support activities such as human resource management and technology development often do not have a clear view of how they relate to the firm's overall competitive position, something the value chain highlights. Finally, vertical linkages are often not well provided for in organizational structure.

A firm may be able to draw unit boundaries more in tune with its sources of competitive advantage and provide for the appropriate types of coordination by relating its organizational structure to the value chain, and the linkages within it and with suppliers or channels. An organizational structure that corresponds to the value chain will improve a firm's ability to create and sustain competitive advantage. While this subject cannot be treated in detail here, it remains an important issue in the implementation of strategy.

3
Cost Advantage

Cost advantage is one of the two types of competitive advantage a firm may possess. Cost is also of vital importance to differentiation strategies because a differentiator must maintain cost proximity to competitors. Unless the resulting price premium exceeds the cost of differentiating, a differentiator will fail to achieve superior performance. The behavior of cost also exerts a strong influence on overall industry structure.

Managers recognize the importance of cost, and many strategic plans establish "cost leadership" or "cost reduction" as goals. However, the behavior of cost is rarely well understood. Wide disagreement often exists among managers about a firm's relative cost position and the reasons underlying it. Cost studies tend to concentrate on manufacturing costs and overlook the impact of other activities such as marketing, service, and infrastructure on relative cost position. Moreover, the cost of individual activities is analyzed sequentially, without recognizing the linkages among activities that can affect cost. Finally, firms have great difficulty assessing the cost positions of competitors, an essential step in assessing their own relative positions. They often

This chapter has benefited from joint work with John R. Wells.

resort to simplistic comparisons of labor rates and raw material costs.

The absence of a systematic framework for cost analysis in most firms underlies these problems. Most cost studies address narrow issues and take a short-term viewpoint. Popular tools like the experience curve are often misused in cost analysis. The experience curve can serve as a starting point, but it ignores many of the important drivers of cost behavior and obscures important relationships among them. Cost analyses also tend to rely heavily on existing accounting systems. While accounting systems do contain useful data for cost analysis, they often get in the way of strategic cost analysis. Cost systems categorize costs in line items—such as direct labor, indirect labor, and burden—that may obscure the underlying activities a firm performs. This leads to aggregation of the costs of activities with very different economics, and to the artificial separation of labor, material, and overhead costs related to the same activity.

This chapter describes a framework for analyzing the behavior of costs, the determinants of relative cost position, and the way firms can gain a sustainable cost advantage or minimize their cost disadvantage. The framework can also reveal the cost of differentiation, and the ways a differentiated competitor can lower costs in the areas that do not undermine its differentiation. The same tools can also be used to analyze supplier and buyer cost behavior, important to both cost position and achieving differentiation.

The value chain provides the basic tool for cost analysis. I begin by showing how to define a value chain for cost analysis purposes and how to associate costs and assets with value activities. I then describe how to analyze the behavior of cost, using the concept of *cost drivers.* Cost drivers are the structural determinants of the cost of an activity, and differ in the extent to which a firm controls them. Cost drivers determine the behavior of costs within an activity, reflecting any linkages or interrelationships that affect it. A firm's cost performance in each of its major discrete activities cumulates to establish its relative cost position.

Having presented a framework for analyzing cost behavior, I turn to how a firm can assess the relative cost of competitors and achieve a sustainable cost advantage. I then describe some important pitfalls in developing an understanding of cost position. The chapter concludes with a discussion of the steps in strategic cost analysis. The techniques outlined in this chapter do not constitute a substitute for the detailed analysis of cost necessary for operations management or pricing, nor do they diminish the need for financial and cost accounting. Rather, the framework aims to help a firm understand the behavior of cost in a broad, holistic way that will guide the search for a sustainable cost advantage and contribute to the formulation of competitive strategy.

The Value Chain and Cost Analysis

The behavior of a firm's costs and its relative cost position stem from the value activities the firm performs in competing in an industry. A meaningful cost analysis, therefore, examines costs within these activities and not the costs of the firm as a whole. Each value activity has its own cost structure and the behavior of its cost may be affected by linkages and interrelationships with other activities both within and outside the firm. Cost advantage results if the firm achieves a lower cumulative cost of performing value activities than its competitors.

Defining the Value Chain for Cost Analysis

The starting point for cost analysis is to define a firm's value chain and to assign operating costs and assets to value activities. Each activity in the value chain involves both operating costs and assets in the form of fixed and working capital. Purchased inputs make up part of the cost of every value activity, and can contribute to both operating costs (purchased operating inputs) and assets (purchased assets). The need to assign assets to value activities reflects the fact that the amount of assets in an activity and the efficiency of asset utilization are frequently important to the activity's cost.

For purposes of cost analysis, the disaggregation of the generic value chain into individual value activities should reflect three principles that are not mutually exclusive:

- the size and growth of the cost represented by the activity
- the cost behavior of the activity
- competitor differences in performing the activity

Activities should be separated for cost analysis if they represent a significant or rapidly growing percentage of operating costs or assets. While most firms can easily identify the large components of their cost, they frequently overlook smaller but growing value activities that can eventually change their cost structure. Activities that represent a small and stagnant percentage of costs or assets can be grouped together into broader categories.

Activities must also be separated if they have different cost drivers, to be defined in more detail below. Activities with similar cost drivers can be safely grouped together. For example, advertising and promotion usually belong in separate value activities because advertising cost is sensitive to scale while promotional costs are largely variable. Any activity a business unit shares with others should also be treated as a separate value activity since conditions in other business units will affect its cost behavior. The same logic applies to any activity that has important linkages with other activities. In practice, one does not always know the drivers of cost behavior at the beginning of an analysis; hence the identification of value activities tends to require several iterations. The initial breakdown of the value chain into activities will inevitably represent a best guess of important differences in cost behavior. Value activities can then be aggregated or disaggregated as further analysis exposes differences or similarities in cost behavior. Usually an aggregated value chain is analyzed first, and then particular value activities that prove to be important are investigated in greater detail.

A final test for separating value activities is the behavior of competitors. Significant activities should be treated separately when a competitor performs them in a different way.[1] For example, People Express and other no-frills airlines offer very different on-board service than the established trunk carriers such as American, Eastern, TWA, and United. Differences among competitors raise the possibility that an activity is the source of a relative cost advantage or disadvantage.

Assigning Costs and Assets

After identifying its value chain, a firm must assign operating costs and assets to value activities. Operating costs should be assigned to the activities in which they are incurred. Assets should be assigned to the activities that employ, control, or most influence their use. The assignment of operating costs is straightforward in principle, although it can be time-consuming. Accounting records must often be recast to match costs with value activities rather than with accounting

[1]Including when a competitor shares the activity with related business units and the firm does not. See Chapter 9.

classifications, particularly in areas such as overhead and purchased inputs.

Since assets are expensive and their selection and use often involve tradeoffs with operating costs, assets must be assigned to value activities in some way that will permit an analysis of cost behavior. Assignment of assets to activities is more complex than assignment of operating costs. Asset accounts must usually be regrouped to correspond to activities, and assets must be valued in some consistent way. There are two broad approaches to assigning assets. They may be assigned at their book or replacement value and compared to operating costs in this form, or book or replacement value may be translated into operating costs via capital charges. Either valuation approach poses difficulties. Book value may be meaningless because it is sensitive to the timing of initial purchase and to accounting policies. Calculating replacement value is also frequently a difficult task. Similarly, depreciation schedules are often arbitrary, as are capital charges for both fixed and current assets. The particular method chosen to value assets should reflect industry characteristics, which in turn will determine the most significant biases inherent in the data and the practical considerations in collecting it. The analyst must recognize the biases inherent in whatever method is chosen.[2] It may prove illuminating for cost analysis to assign assets in several ways.

The costs and assets of shared value activities should be allocated initially to the value chain of the business unit using whatever methodology the firm currently employs, typically based on some allocation formula. The cost behavior of a shared value activity reflects the activity as a whole and not just the part that is attributable to one business unit. The cost of a scale-sensitive shared activity will depend on the volume of all involved business units, for example. In addition, the allocation formulas covering shared activities may not reflect their economics but may have been set based on convenience or political considerations. As the analysis proceeds, the costs of shared activities can be refined using more meaningful allocation methods based on the cost behavior of the activities.

The time period chosen for assigning costs and assets to value activities should be representative of a firm's performance. It should recognize seasonal or cyclical fluctuations and periods of discontinuity that would affect cost. The comparison of costs at different points in time can illuminate the effect of strategy changes, as well as help

[2]If assets are assigned by some measure of asset value, a capital charge will still be required to evaluate any tradeoffs with operating costs that are present.

diagnose cost behavior itself. Looking at the cost of an activity during successive periods can highlight learning effects, for example, while comparing costs during periods of widely differing levels of activity may give some indications about scale sensitivity and the role of capacity utilization.

It is important to remember that assigning costs and assets does not require the precision needed for financial reporting purposes. Estimates are often more than sufficient to highlight strategic cost issues, and can be employed in assigning costs and assets to value activities where generating accurate cost figures would require great expense. As the analysis proceeds and particular value activities prove to be important to cost advantage, greater efforts at precision can be made. Finally, a firm may find that competitors assign their operating costs and assets differently. The way in which competitors measure their costs is important because it will influence their behavior. Part of the task of competitor cost analysis is to attempt to diagnose competitor costing practices.

First Cut Analysis of Costs

The allocation of costs and assets will produce a value chain that illustrates graphically the distribution of a firm's costs. It can prove revealing to separate the cost of each value activity into three categories: purchased operating inputs, human resource costs, and assets by major category. The proportions of the value chain can be drawn to reflect the distribution of costs and assets among activities as shown in Figure 3–1.

Even the initial allocation of operating costs and assets to the value chain may suggest areas for cost improvement. Purchased operating inputs will often represent a larger proportion of costs than commonly perceived, for example, because all the purchased inputs in the value chain are rarely cumulated. Other insights can result from grouping value activities into direct, indirect and quality assurance activities as defined in Chapter 2, and cumulating costs in each category. Managers often fail to recognize burgeoning indirect costs and have a tendency to focus almost exclusively on direct costs. In many firms, indirect costs not only represent a large proportion of total cost but also have grown more rapidly than other cost elements. The introduction of sophisticated information systems and automated processes is reducing direct costs but boosting indirect costs by requiring

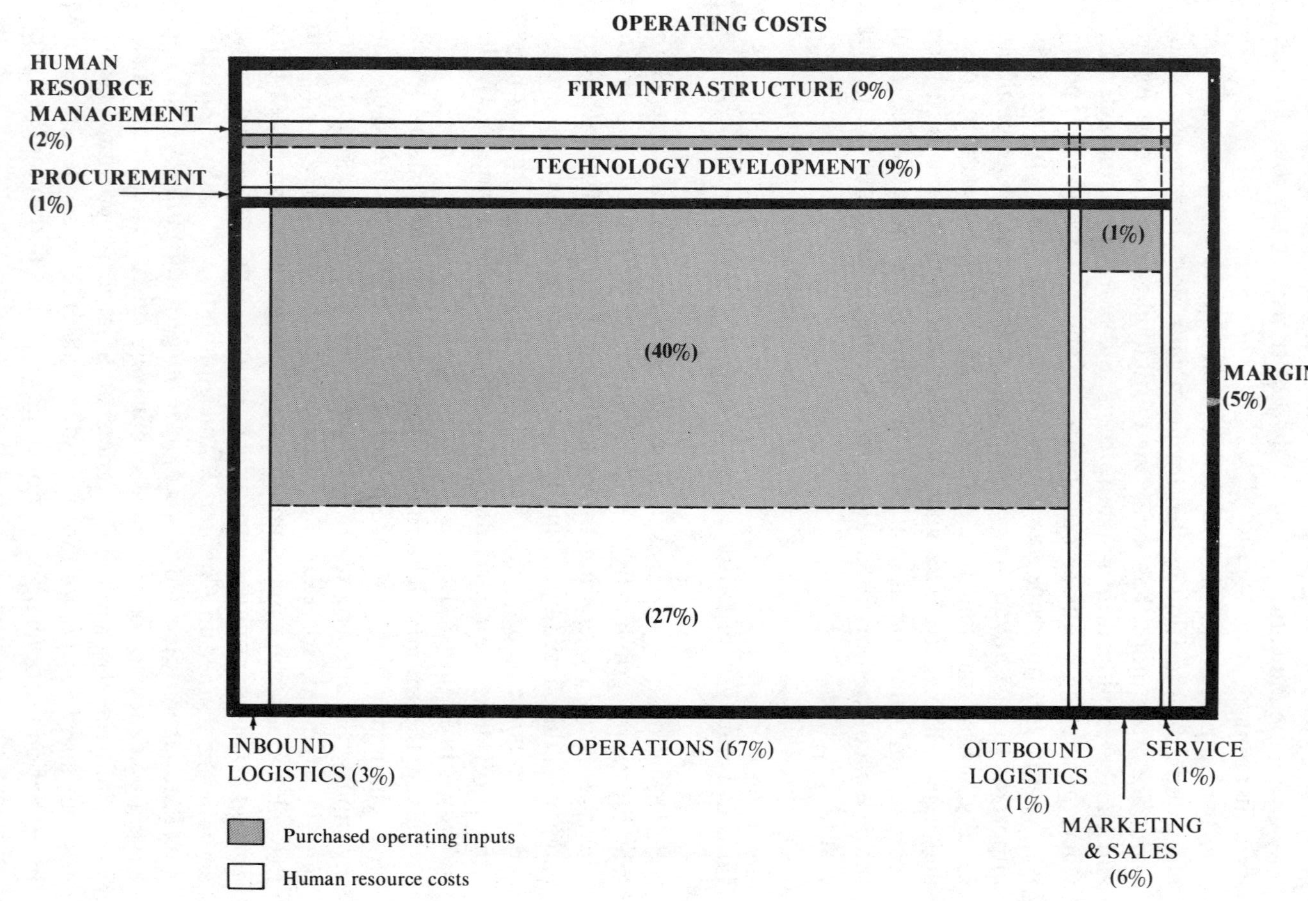
OPERATING COSTS
HUMAN RESOURCE MANAGEMENT (2%)
PROCUREMENT (1%)
FIRM INFRASTRUCTURE (9%)
TECHNOLOGY DEVELOPMENT (9%)
(40%)
(27%)
(1%)
MARGIN (5%)
INBOUND LOGISTICS (3%)
OPERATIONS (67%)
OUTBOUND LOGISTICS (1%)
MARKETING & SALES (6%)
SERVICE (1%)
Purchased operating inputs
Human resource costs

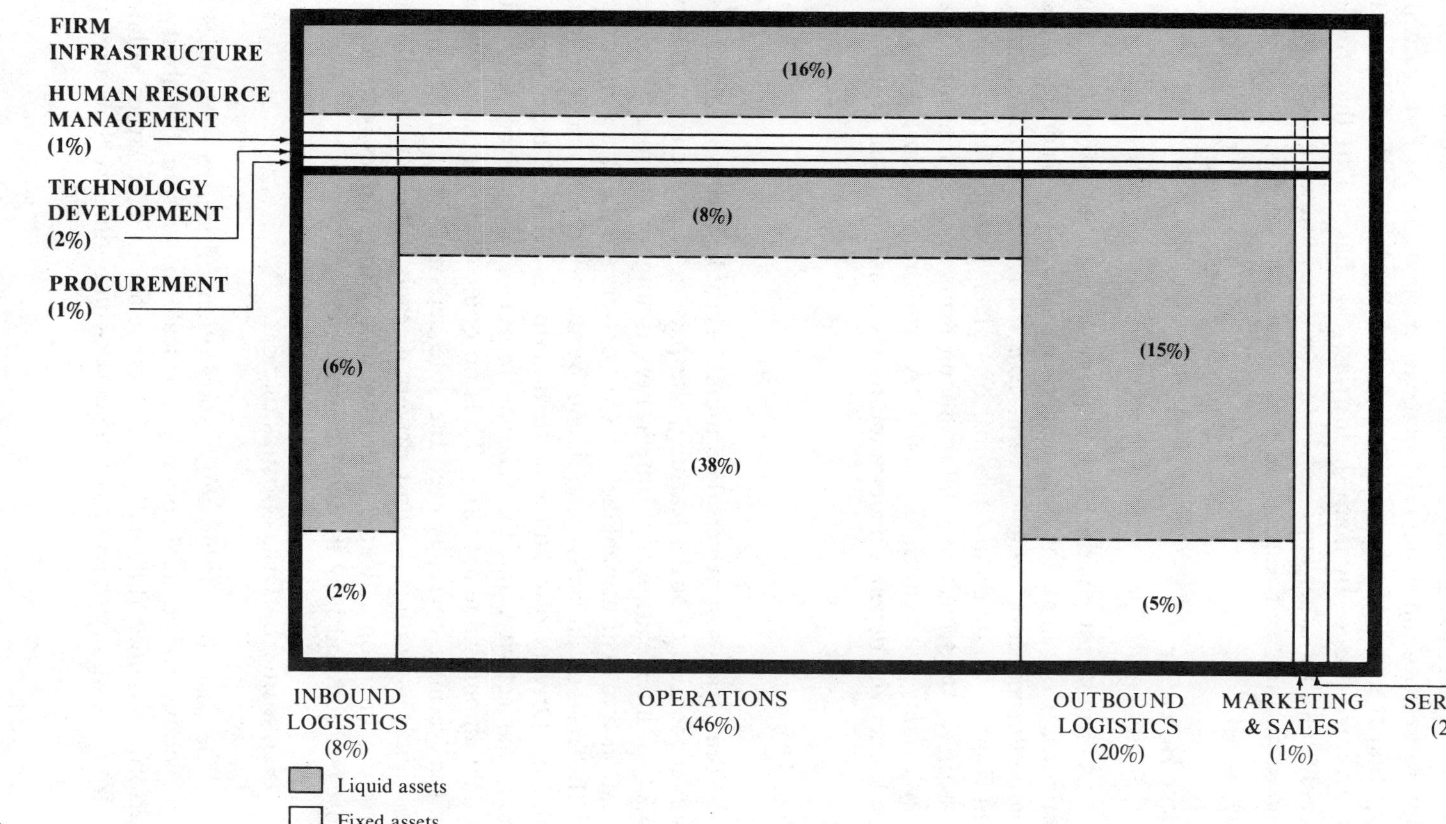

Figure 3–1. Distribution of Operating Costs and Assets in Flow Control Valves

such things as sophisticated maintenance and computer programmers to prepare machine tapes. In valve manufacturing, for example, indirect cost represents more than 10 percent of total cost. Firms can also find that the sum of all quality assurance activities in the value chain is strikingly large. In many industries, this has led to the growing conclusion that other approaches to quality assurance besides inspection, adjusting, and testing can yield large cost savings.

Cost Behavior

A firm's cost position results from the cost behavior of its value activities. Cost behavior depends on a number of structural factors that influence cost, which I term *cost drivers.* Several cost drivers can combine to determine the cost of a given activity. The important cost driver or drivers can differ among firms in the same industry if they employ different value chains. A firm's relative cost position in a value activity depends on its standing vis-à-vis important cost drivers.

Cost Drivers

Ten major cost drivers determine the cost behavior of value activities: economies of scale, learning, the pattern of capacity utilization, linkages, interrelationships, integration, timing, discretionary policies, location, and institutional factors. Cost drivers are the structural causes of the cost of an activity and can be more or less under a firm's control. Drivers often interact to determine the cost behavior of a particular activity, and the relative impact of cost drivers will differ widely among value activities. Thus no one cost driver, such as scale or the learning curve, is ever the sole determinant of a firm's cost position. Diagnosing the cost drivers of each value activity allows a firm to gain a sophisticated understanding of the sources of its relative cost position and how it might be changed.

Economies or Diseconomies of Scale

The costs of a value activity are often subject to economies or diseconomies of scale. Economies of scale arise from the ability to perform activities differently and more efficiently at larger volume, or from the ability to amortize the cost of intangibles such as advertising and R&D over a greater sales volume. Economies of scale can result from efficiencies in the actual operation of an activity at higher scale as well as from less than proportional increases in the infrastructure or overhead needed to support an activity as it grows. In a bauxite mine, for example, actual mining costs go down less with scale than do infrastructure costs.

Economies of scale must be clearly distinguished from capacity utilization. Increasing capacity utilization spreads the fixed costs of existing facilities and personnel over large volume, while economies of scale imply that an activity operating at full capacity is more efficient at larger scale. Mistaking capacity utilization for economies of scale can lead a firm to the false conclusion that its costs will continue to fall if it expands capacity once its existing capacity is full.

Increasing complexity and costs of coordination can lead to diseconomies of scale in a value activity as scale increases. When the number of lines in a metal can plant exceeds about 15, for example, the complexity of the plant becomes unwieldy. Increasing scale also sometimes dampens employee motivation and may increase wage or purchased input costs. For example, a large plant may have a greater likelihood of unionization or lead to higher expectations and greater stridency of union negotiators. Diseconomies of scale in procurement can also occur if large requirements meet an inelastic supply, forcing up input prices. Diseconomies of scale appear to be present in many fashion-sensitive industries and professional services, which rely heavily on fast response times and creative individuals who do not function well in large organizations.

The scale sensitivity of activities varies widely. Value activities such as product development, national advertising, and firm infrastructure are typically more scale-sensitive than activities such as procurement and sales force operations because their costs are heavily fixed no matter what the firm's scale is. However, economies (and diseconomies) of scale can be found to some extent in virtually every value activity of a firm.

Economies of scale reflect not only the technology in a value activity but also the manner in which a firm chooses to operate it. Scale economies in a plant can be strongly affected by the number of product varieties produced and the length of runs chosen. Similarly, the deployment of a sales force can influence economies of scale in sales force operation. In a sales force organized geographically, costs tend to fall as regional sales volume grows because a salesperson can write larger orders on each sales call and/or because travel time between accounts is reduced by greater density. If the sales force is organized by product line, however, an increase in volume in one region may create diseconomies by requiring salespersons to travel more to that region than to other regions closer to home base.

Economies of scale are not all equivalent. The relevant *measure of scale* differs among value activities and industries. Firms that overlook this often undermine their relative cost positions. For some value activities, global or worldwide scale is the relevant cost driver. For other value activities, national scale, regional scale, local scale, plant scale, project scale, scale per production line, scale per buyer, scale per order, or some other measure of scale may underlie the behavior of cost.[3]

In product R&D, for example, global or national scale are often the relevant measure of scale. Developing a new model requires a fixed investment that is amortized over all the units sold. The development cost of a standard model sold worldwide is sensitive to global scale, while the development cost of a product that must be customized for individual countries may be more sensitive to national scale. Economies of scale in transportation typically hinge on regional or local scale or on scale per buyer, depending on the mode of transportation employed. Local or regional scale is a proxy for the density of buyers and hence the distances between deliveries to different buyer's locations. Transportation suppliers also frequently offer discounts on containerload, carload, or trainload shipments to a given area that contribute to local or regional scale sensitivity. Finally, the cost of delivery to a given buyer often remains largely fixed regardless of the buyer's order size, making large buyers less costly to serve. Understanding how economies of scale affect cost, therefore, requires an identification of the specific mechanisms underpinning them and the measure of scale that best captures these mechanisms.

The appropriate measure of scale is a function of how a firm manages an activity. For example, modifying products by country instead of selling a standard product worldwide, a policy choice, changes the appropriate measure of scale. Similarly, the authorization cost of a credit card processing firm that authorizes merchant charges electronically rather than manually becomes much more sensitive to the overall volume of transactions. Thus a firm can influence not only the extent of economies of scale but also the type of scale that most

[3]Scale is not the same as market share. Depending on the relevant measure of scale, the appropriate definition of market share that will serve as a proxy for scale will differ markedly.

determines its cost in an activity. This suggests that a firm should manage its activities to maximize their sensitivity to the type of scale in which the firm has the greatest advantage over its competitors. A regional firm should accentuate the value of its regional scale, for example, while a national competitor without leadership in any region should manage its activities to maximize the value of its national scale.

Learning and Spillovers

The cost of a value activity can decline over time due to learning that increases its efficiency. The mechanisms by which learning can lower cost over time are numerous, and include such factors as layout changes, improved scheduling, labor efficiency improvement, product design modifications that facilitate manufacturing, yield improvements, procedures that increase the utilization of assets, and better tailoring of raw materials to the process. Learning can also reduce the cost of constructing plants, retail outlets, or other facilities. Thus the possibilities for learning in an activity are much broader than learning by personnel to perform their functions more efficiently.[4] The rate of learning varies widely among value activities because each offers differing possibilities for learning improvements.[5] Learning is often the cumulation of many small improvements rather than major breakthroughs. The rate of learning may increase during slack periods when attention is focused on reducing costs rather than meeting demand. Moreover, learning tends to vary with the amount of management attention devoted to capturing it.

Learning can spill over from one firm in an industry to another, through mechanisms such as suppliers, consultants, ex-employees, and reverse engineering of products. Where spillover of learning among firms is high in a value activity, the rate of learning may stem more from total industry learning than from the learning of one firm. Since a sustainable cost advantage results only from proprietary learning,

[4]The term "experience" is often used to describe cost reduction over time, reflecting the wide possibilities for learning. The "experience curve" mixes both learning and economies of scale, however, which are very different cost drivers. I use the term learning to encompass all types of cost reduction that result from improving know-how and procedures independent of scale.

[5]A 15 percent reduction in costs with a doubling of cumulative volume represents the median of a large number of academic studies. This average masks a wide variation in learning rates among activities, however. For an insightful treatment of learning, see Pankaj Ghemawat (1984).

the rate of spillover also determines whether learning serves to create a cost advantage for a firm or simply lowers cost for the industry.[6] Analysis of the rate of spillover plays a crucial role in diagnosing the relative cost differences among competitors due to differential rates of learning.

As with scale economies, the appropriate measure of the rate of learning is different for different value activities. The appropriate measure of learning reflects the specific mechanisms of learning that account for the fall in costs over time in a value activity. This will vary because mechanisms for learning are diverse and because of the influence of spillovers. In a value activity where learning affects cost behavior through improving worker efficiency, for example, the rate of learning may be tied to the cumulative volume in that activity. In this case, the rate of learning is correlated with scale because high scale makes learning accumulate rapidly. Where learning occurs through the introduction of more efficient machinery, however, its rate may reflect the rate of technological change in machinery and have little to do with the firm's volume. The rate of learning can also be a function of calendar time or the level of investment expended in modifications to an activity. Understanding the specific mechanisms for learning in each value activity and identifying the best measure of its rate are necessary if a firm is to improve its cost position.[7] The rate of learning is often subject to diminishing returns, and hence it may decline over time for some value activities as an industry matures.

Some alternative measures that may serve as a proxy for the rate of learning in an activity and typical value activities in which they apply are shown in Table 3–1.

Pattern of Capacity Utilization

Where a value activity has substantial fixed cost associated with it, the cost of an activity will be affected by capacity utilization. Fixed costs create a penalty for underutilization, and the ratio of fixed to variable cost indicates the sensitivity of a value activity to utilization. Different ways of configuring a value activity will affect its sensitivity

[6] Even if learning cannot be kept proprietary, however, there may be first-mover advantages to pioneering certain types of learning. See below and Chapter 5.

[7] The popular measure of the rate of learning, cumulative firm volume, has the benefit of simplicity. However, this measure obscures differential rates of learning in value activities and is not an appropriate proxy for the rate of learning in many activities.

TABLE 3–1 Typical Measures of Learning

Cumulative volume in the activity (typical for determining machine speed or reject rates in fabrication operations)
Time in operation (typical for work-flow layout in assembly)
Cumulative investment (typical for plant efficiency)
Cumulative industry volume (typical for product design improvements that lower cost where spillovers are high)
Exogenous technical change (typical for basic process improvements)

to capacity utilization. For example, the use of food brokers to sell to supermarkets usually reduces sensitivity to capacity utilization when compared to an in-house sales force. Brokers typically receive a commission on sales, while an in-house sales force is paid a fixed salary and expenses over and above commissions.

Capacity utilization at a given point in time is a function of seasonal, cyclical, and other demand or supply fluctuations unrelated to competitive position. Thus the pattern of utilization over the entire cycle is the correct cost driver instead of utilization at one point in time. Changes in the level of capacity utilization will involve costs of expanding or contracting, so that a firm that changes its utilization will have higher costs than one that keeps its utilization constant, though they both have the same average utilization. The pattern of utilization reflects such changes, and is thus the appropriate cost driver rather than the average level of utilization. The pattern of capacity utilization of an activity is partly determined by environmental conditions and competitor behavior (particularly competitor investment behavior) and is partly under a firm's control through its policy choices in areas such as marketing and product selection.

Linkages

The cost of a value activity is frequently affected by how *other* activities are performed. As described in Chapter 2, two broad types of linkages exist: linkages within the value chain and vertical linkages with the value chains of suppliers and channels. These linkages mean that the cost behavior of a value activity cannot be understood by examining that activity alone. Linkages create the opportunity to lower the total cost of the linked activities. They provide a potentially powerful source of cost advantage because linkages are subtle and require joint optimization or coordination of activities across organizational lines. Competitors often fail to recognize their presence or are incapable of harnessing them.

Linkages within the Value Chain

Linkages among value activities pervade the value chain. Some of the most common linkages are those between direct and indirect activities (e.g., machining and maintenance), quality assurance and other activities (e.g., inspection and after-sale service), activities that must be coordinated (e.g., inbound logistics and operations), and between activities that are alternative ways of achieving the result (e.g., advertising and direct sales, or writing airline tickets on-board the plane instead of at ticket counters or gates). Identifying linkages requires asking the question, "What are all the other activities elsewhere in a firm that have or might have an impact on the cost of performing this activity?"

When activities in the value chain are linked, changing the way one of them is performed can reduce the total cost of both. *Deliberately* raising cost in one activity may not only lower the cost of another activity but also lower total cost. As described in Chapter 2, linkages lead to opportunities for cost reduction through two mechanisms: coordination and optimization. Better coordination of linked activities such as procurement and assembly can reduce the need for inventory, for example. Inventory is typically a manifestation of a linkage between activities, and reducing inventory is possible by managing the linkage better. Jointly optimizing activities that are linked involves resolving tradeoffs among them. In copier manufacturing, for example, the quality of purchased parts is linked to the adjustment of copiers after assembly. Canon found it could virtually eliminate the need for adjustment in its personal copier line by purchasing higher precision parts.

Vertical Linkages

Vertical linkages reflect interdependencies between a firm's activities and the value chains of suppliers and channels. The firm can identify them by examining how the behavior of suppliers or channels affects the cost of each of its activities and vice versa. Vertical linkages are frequently overlooked, because identifying them requires a sophisticated understanding of supplier and channel value chains.

Linkages with suppliers tend to center on the suppliers' product design characteristics, service, quality assurance procedures, packaging, delivery procedures, and order processing. Supplier linkages also take the form of a supplier performing an activity that the firm might otherwise undertake. In these and other areas, the manner in which a supplier performs activities within its value chain can raise or lower a firm's cost. Typical examples of supplier linkages important to cost include the linkage between the frequency and timeliness of supplier deliveries and a firm's raw material inventory, the linkage between supplier application engineering and a firm's technology development cost, and the linkage between a supplier's packaging and a firm's material handling cost. As described in Chapter 2, for example, delivery of bulk chocolate in liquid form instead of ten pound molded bars can reduce a confectioner's processing costs. Often linkages with suppliers provide opportunities for cost reduction on both sides —e.g., delivery of liquid chocolate can reduce the supplier's cost as well, since it eliminates the cost of molding bars and packaging them.

Managing supplier linkages can lower total cost through coordination or joint optimization, as in all linkages. The easiest linkages to exploit are those where both a firm's and a supplier's cost fall. Sometimes exploiting a linkage requires that a supplier's cost go *up* to achieve a more than compensating fall in a firm's costs, however. A firm must be prepared to raise the price it gives suppliers in such cases to make exploiting the linkage worthwhile. The opposite case is also possible, and the firm must be prepared to elevate its own internal cost if the supplier offers a more-than-compensating price cut.

A similar analysis applies to *linkages with channels.* The typical linkages mirror those with suppliers. For example, the location of a channel's warehouses and the channel's materials handling technology can influence a firm's outbound logistical and packaging cost. Similarly, sales or promotional activities of channels may reduce a firm's sales cost. As with supplier linkages, channel linkages may allow both the firm and its channels to lower cost. However, exploiting channel linkages may require the channel to raise cost for a more than offsetting reduction in the firm's cost. It may be desirable, then, to *raise* margins paid to channels in return for changes in the way they operate that will reduce a firm's cost. In the United States, for example, Seiko paid its jewelers a generous fee for accepting Seiko watches for repair and shipping them to Seiko. This minimized Seiko's need for service locations and lowered the cost of processing repairs and of informing customers about repair procedures.

Since vertical linkages involve independent firms, reaching agreement on how to exploit them and how to divide the resulting gains can be difficult. Linkages that require a supplier or channel to raise cost to benefit the firm are quite difficult to achieve unless the firm has considerable bargaining power. Exploiting linkages may also require the creation of switching costs as a byproduct, tying one or both sides to the other. This often further complicates the task of agreeing on ways to exploit linkages, because reaching agreement involves a high level of commitment and trust. The payout to exploiting linkages may be great, however, because they are hard for competitors to match.

INTERRELATIONSHIPS

Interrelationships with other business units within a firm affect cost, as will be discussed in detail in Chapter 9. The most important form of interrelationships is when a value activity can be shared with a sister unit. American Hospital Supply has found that sharing an order processing and distribution organization across many units producing medical supplies has yielded a significant cost improvement, for example, while shared marketing and distribution are benefiting such financial services firms as Citicorp and Sears. Another form of interrelationship, that I term an intangible interrelationship, involves the sharing of know-how between separate but similar value activities. Emerson Electric, for example, uses cost reduction expertise gained in one division to help lower cost in others.

Sharing a value activity raises throughput in the activity. It reduces unit costs if cost in the activity is sensitive to economies of scale or learning, or if sharing improves the pattern of capacity utilization because different business units place demands on the value activity at different times. Sharing is potentially a way to achieve scale, go down the learning curve faster, or load capacity outside of the boundaries of a single industry. Sharing is thus a potential substitute for position in a particular industry. Sharing a value activity always involves costs, however, that must be weighed against any benefits from sharing. The other form of interrelationship, sharing know-how between separate activities, lowers cost if the activities are similar and if the know-how is significant to improving the efficiency of the activity. In effect, sharing know-how is transfering the fruits of learning from one activity to another.

Integration

The level of vertical integration in a value activity may influence its cost. The cost of an order processing system can be lower if the firm owns its own computer and software instead of contracting with a computer service bureau, for example, while the cost of an outbound logistics activity may vary depending on whether or not a firm owns its own fleet of trucks. Every value activity employs or could employ purchased inputs, and thus involves explicit or implicit integration choices.

Integration can reduce cost in a number of ways. It avoids the costs of using the market, such as procurement and transportation costs. It can allow the firm to avoid suppliers or buyers with considerable bargaining power. Integration can also lead to economies of joint operation, as where steel does not have to be reheated if it moves directly from the steelmaking to the fabrication process. However, integration can raise cost by creating inflexibility, bringing activities in-house that suppliers can perform more cheaply, undermining incentives for efficiency because the relationship with the supplying unit becomes captive, or raising exit barriers.[8] Whether integration raises, lowers, or has no effect on cost thus depends on the particular value activity and purchased input involved. Sometimes de-integration is indicated.

A firm must assess the potential benefits of integration for each important purchased input in a value activity. Conversely, it must examine those functions currently performed internally to determine whether de-integration would lower the cost of the activity without undermining the firm's strategy. Firms often ignore the de-integration option in their cost analyses. Integration and de-integration analysis must not limit itself to major inputs but should also examine ancillary services and other supporting functions. A product might be purchased without service, for example, though the two are often bundled.[9] Firms can often lower cost by integrating into some ancillary services while continuing to buy the basic product.

Timing

The cost of a value activity often reflects timing. Sometimes a firm may gain first-mover advantages from being among the first to

[8] I have described the relationship between integration and competitive advantage in detail in *Competitive Strategy,* Chapter 14.

[9] Bundling of complementary products is discussed in detail in Chapter 12.

take a particular action. The first major brand in the market may have lower costs of establishing and maintaining a brand name, for example. Gerber exploited this advantage in baby food. Learning is also inextricably linked to timing, because the timing of moves determines when learning begins. Disadvantages may also accrue to first movers. Late movers can enjoy benefits such as purchasing the latest equipment (an advantage today in computers and steel) or avoiding high product or market development costs borne by early movers. A late mover may also be able to tailor the value chain to prevailing factor costs. Another late-mover advantage may be a less senior, and therefore less costly, workforce. Newly established airlines such as People Express have much less senior workforces than established carriers such as PanAm. Furthermore, workforces assembled during difficult economic conditions may prove less interested in unionization. First-mover and late-mover advantages are discussed extensively in Chapter 5.

Timing's role in cost position may depend more on timing with respect to the business cycle or market conditions than on timing in absolute terms. For example, the timing of purchase of an offshore drilling rig in the industry's cycle strongly influences not only the interest cost but the purchase price of the rig. ODECO has purchased rigs during downturns when prices are depressed as an integral part of its cost leadership strategy. Depending on the value activity, then, timing can either raise or lower costs relative to competitors. Timing can lead to either sustainable cost advantage or a short-term cost advantage. A firm that has low cost assets because of fortuitous timing, for example, may find that the eventual need to replace those assets dramatically raises its relative cost position.

Discretionary Policies Independent of Other Drivers

The cost of a value activity is always affected by policy choices a firm makes, quite independently of other cost drivers. Discretionary policy choices reflect a firm's strategy and often involve deliberate tradeoffs between cost and differentiation. For example, an airline's cost position is determined by such policy choices as the quality of meals, which airports are used, the level of amenities in terminals, the baggage allowance offered, and whether the airline sells tickets on-board or has in-terminal ticketing and downtown ticket offices. A "no-frills" airline reduces cost by having no meals or charging for them, using secondary airports with spartan terminals, having no free baggage allowance, and ticketing on board.

Some of the policy choices that tend to have the greatest impact on cost include:

- product configuration, performance, and features
- mix and variety of products offered
- level of service provided
- spending rate on marketing and technology development activities
- delivery time
- buyers served (e.g., small versus large)
- channels employed (e.g., fewer, more efficient dealers versus many small ones)
- process technology chosen, independent or scale, timing, or other cost drivers
- the specifications of raw materials or other purchased inputs used (e.g., raw material quality affects processing yield in semiconductors)
- wages paid and amenities provided to employees, relative to prevailing norms
- other human resource policies including hiring, training, and employee motivation
- procedures for scheduling production, maintenance, the sales force and other activities

Though policy choices always play an independent role in determining the cost of value activities, they also frequently affect or are affected by other cost drivers. Process technology is often dictated partly by scale and partly by what product characteristics are desired, for example. Moreover, other cost drivers inevitably affect the *cost* of policies. For example, an automated ticketing and seat selection system may well be subject to economies of scale that make such a system very costly for a small airline to adopt.

Policies typically play a particularly essential role in differentiation strategies. Differentiation often rests on policy choices that make a firm unique in performing one or more value activities, deliberately raising cost in the process (see Chapter 4). A differentiator must understand the costs associated with its differentiation and compare them to the price premium that results. This can be done only by isolating the effects of policies on cost. Frequently, firms choose seemingly benign policies to differentiate themselves that prove enormously costly once their role in cost behavior becomes clear. In other cases, firms forego policies that can enhance differentiation with little impact on cost—or that are less expensive for them to implement than for their competitors. A market leader such as Owens-Corning Fiberglas, for example, can potentially differentiate itself at lower cost than other fiberglass competitors through a high spending rate on advertising. The resulting brand awareness is cheaper for Owens-Corning to achieve than competitors because of scale economies in advertising that are driven by national share.

Policies play a vital role in determining cost, and cost analysis must uncover their impact. Yet many firms do not recognize the extent to which the explicit and implicit policy choices they make determine cost. A firm must scrutinize each value activity to identify the explicit and implicit policy choices embodied in it. Sometimes policy choices are nearly invisible, because they are inherited or represent conventional wisdom that is unchallenged. An examination of competitors' policies in each activity often yields insight into the firm's explicit or implicit policy choices and suggests ways they might be modified or improved to lower costs. Policy choices can often be changed rapidly, yielding immediate cost reduction.

Location

The geographic location of a value activity can affect its cost, as can its location relative to other value activities. While location frequently reflects a policy choice, it can also stem from history, the location of inputs, and other factors. Hence, location should be treated as a separate cost driver.

The location of a value activity affects cost in a number of ways. Locations differ in the prevailing costs of labor, management, scientific personnel, raw materials, energy, and other factors. Prevailing wage levels and tax rates vary markedly by country, region within a country, and city, for example. Eaton Corporation has capitalized on this in automotive components, employing plants in Spain and Italy to achieve a low-cost position in Europe. Location can also affect the cost of a firm's infrastructure because of differences in available local infrastructure. Climate, cultural norms, and tastes also differ by location. These affect not only product needs but also the way in which a firm can perform value activities. The amenities required in a plant, for example, are partly a function of local norms. Finally, logistical costs often hinge on location. Location relative to suppliers is an important factor in inbound logistical cost, while location relative to buyers affects outbound logistical cost. Location of facilities relative to each other affects the costs of transshipping, inventory, transportation, and coordination. Location also shapes the transportation modes and communication systems available to a firm, which can affect cost.

Location has some influence, then, on the cost of almost every value activity. Firms do not always understand the impact of location beyond obvious differences such as wage rates and taxes, however. Opportunities often exist for reducing cost through relocating value activities or by establishing new patterns of location of facilities relative to each other. Changing location often involves tradeoffs—it lowers some costs while raising others. Locating to minimize transportation or other costs also frequently trades off against scale economies. Technological change that alters scale economies may alter historical tradeoffs, however, as may shifts in relative wages and other costs. Thus firms may be able to create a cost advantage through recognizing opportunities for changing location first.

INSTITUTIONAL FACTORS

Institutional factors, including government regulation, tax holidays and other financial incentives, unionization, tariffs and levies, and local content rules, constitute the final major cost driver. Institutional factors represent perhaps the single most important cost driver in the trucking industry in the United States in the 1980s, for example. Regulatory approval for the use of double trailers could have as much as a 10 percent impact on cost. At the same time, unionized carriers have much higher wage costs relative to nonunion carriers. These two factors outweigh all the other major cost drivers by a considerable margin in determining the relative cost position of trucking firms. Another example of the role of institutional factors as a cost driver is in power costs, the single largest determinant of cost position in aluminum smelting. Power costs depend on the rates charged by power companies, a highly political issue in areas where governments own power companies. Rapid escalation of power rates in some countries has made them uncompetitive smelting locations. Favorable institutional factors can lower costs just as unfavorable ones can raise them. While institutional factors often remain outside a firm's control, means may exist to influence them or minimize their impact.

Diagnosing Cost Drivers

The same cost drivers determine asset utilization as well as operating costs in an activity. Finished good inventory turnover, for example, is often determined by the scale of the order processing activity and policies regarding delivery time. Tradeoffs can often be made between asset utilization and operating costs. A large-scale plant may have low operating costs but less asset turnover than a small-scale one, for example. Such tradeoffs must be identified in order to optimize the combination of assets and operating cost to lower total cost. Some illustrative drivers of asset utilization are shown in Table 3–2.

The cost behavior of a value activity can be a function of more than one cost driver. While one driver may exert the strongest influence on the cost of a value activity, several drivers often interact to determine cost. For example, the cost of gate operations for an airline reflects policies regarding how much service the airline provides, local scale (which influences the efficiency with which personnel and facilities are utilized), and the pattern of capacity utilization (which is a reflection of the flight schedule). Figure 3–2 illustrates the most important cost drivers in a consumer durable manufacturing firm.

A firm must attempt to quantify the relationship between cost drivers and the cost of a value activity whenever possible. This will require estimating for each activity the slope of the scale or learning curve, the cost impact of each important policy, the cost advantage or penalty of timing, and so on for each driver. Though a high degree of precision is not required, some level of quantification is necessary in order to determine the relative significance of each cost driver. Quantification will also greatly facilitate estimates of relative cost position vis-à-vis competitors.

The technology employed in a value activity is not itself a cost driver, but rather an outcome of the interplay of cost drivers. Scale, timing, location, and other drivers shape the technology employed in combination with policy decisions a firm makes. The relationship between technology and the cost drivers is important in determining the feasibility of technology changes, one of the subjects of Chapter 5.

Interactions Among Drivers. Cost drivers often interact to determine the cost of an activity. These interactions take two forms: drivers either *reinforce* or *counteract* each other. Drivers frequently reinforce or are related to each other in affecting cost. The extent of scale economies in an activity is partly determined by policy choices

TABLE 3–2 Illustrative Drivers of Asset Utilization for Selected Value Activities

	Operations			Physical Distribution		Order Processing	
Driver	Raw Materials Inventory	Work-in-Process Inventory	Production Facilities	Logistical Facilities	Finished Goods Inventory	Computer Systems	Accounts Receivable
Scale	Purchasing scale (that determines influence over supplier delivery)	Plant scale	Scale of facilities	Scale of facilities	Regional scale	National scale	Order scale
Learning			Experience in constructing plants	Experience in construction of facilities			
Linkages	Supplier delivery schedule and packaging			Location of channel warehouses	Channel stocking levels		Channel payment policies
Pattern of capacity utilization		Seasonality/cyclicality of production	Seasonality/cyclicality of production	Seasonality/cyclicality of shipments	Fluctuations in demand		
Integration		Vertical integration	Vertical integration	Vertical integration		Vertical integration	
Timing			Date of construction Timing of asset purchases	Timing of technology choice		Timing of technology choice	
Policies	Safety stocks Payment schedule to suppliers	Safety stocks Aging or curing requirements Production technology Stability of production rate	Production technology Speed of construction of facilities	Logistics technology	Aging or curing requirements Delivery time to customers	Systems technology	Payment terms Credit policy Accounts receivable monitoring technology

	Inbound Logistics	Operations	Outbound Logistics	Marketing & Sales	Service
FIRM INFRASTRUCTURE	National Scale				
HUMAN RESOURCE MANAGEMENT			Human Resource Policies		
TECHNOLOGY DEVELOPMENT			Global Scale		
PROCUREMENT			Procurement Policies Linkages with Suppliers Global Purchasing Scale		
	Location Linkages with Suppliers	Learning Plant Scale Policy Choice of Plant Technology Timing of Asset Purchases	Order Size Interrelationships with Sister Units Regional scale	National Scale (advertising) Buyer Density (sales force utilization)	Local Scale Interrelationships with Sister Units

MARGIN

MARGIN

Figure 3–2. Cost Drivers in a Consumer Durable Manufacturing Firm

about how the activity will be performed as well as product mix, for example. The effect of location on cost is often related to institutional conditions such as unionization or regulation, while securing good locations may require early timing in such industries as retailing. Policy choices can also make linkages easier or more difficult to achieve, and the cost of policies is often affected by other drivers as noted earlier. The advantages of early timing can be reinforced by scale economies or learning effects, as will be discussed in Chapter 5. Integration also frequently increases scale economies.

Cost drivers can also counteract each other, offsetting each other's effects. This means that improving position vis-à-vis one driver may worsen a firm's position vis-à-vis another. Large scale and high levels of vertical integration frequently increase the penalty of underutilizing capacity, for example. Similarly, increased scale can increase the likelihood of unionization, while scale economies can be offset because a single location raises transportation costs.

Identifying interactions among cost drivers is a necessary part of determining the cost behavior of a value activity. Where drivers are reinforcing, a firm must coordinate its strategy in order to achieve the lowest cost. For example, policy choices should enhance the firm's ability to reap the benefits of scale economies or to achieve linkages. Early timing should be exploited by the aggressive pursuit of learning. Eliminating inconsistencies and harnessing the reinforcing effects of cost drivers can significantly improve relative cost position.

The presence of counteracting cost drivers implies the need for optimization. Location must optimize the tradeoff among scale economies, transportation costs, and wage costs, for example. The choice of plant scale must weigh the cost of underutilization. Policy choices can sometimes alter such tradeoffs—for example, the choice of a flexible manufacturing process can change the tradeoff between scale and product variety. Resolving such tradeoffs is only possible if the effect of each driver on the cost of an activity can be quantified.

Interactions among cost drivers are often subtle. They are frequently not recognized, especially if they are changing. The ability to translate insight about the interaction of cost drivers into strategy choices can thus be a sustainable source of cost advantage.

Identifying Cost Drivers. Identifying cost drivers and quantifying their effect on cost may not be easy, and a number of methods can be employed. Sometimes the cost drivers of a value activity will be intuitively clear from examining its basic economics. For example, sales force costs are often driven by local share because high local share lowers travel time. A reasonably accurate estimate of the shape of the relationship between sales force cost and share can be computed by estimating how rising share would cut average travel time. It is often illuminating for understanding and quantifying cost behavior to employ alternative measures of the efficiency of an activity besides total cost. For example, such measures as yield, scrap rates, labor hours, and others can be employed to probe the sources of cost changes in a value activity and their logic.

Another method of identifying cost drivers is for a firm to examine its own internal experience, particularly if the firm's circumstances have changed over time or it operates multiple units. Past cost data may allow a firm to plot its historical learning curve in a value activity, for example, if it adjusts for inflation and changes in policies, product design, and product mix. Cost levels at different scales of output in the past may shed some light on scale economies. If a firm sells in several geographic regions or manufactures in several plants, differences among them can illuminate cost drivers.

Cost drivers can also be determined from interviews with experts. Individuals who have extensive knowledge of a value activity can be asked "what if" questions about the effects of changing various parameters on cost. For instance, interviews with production managers might address the impact of doubling line speed on such factors as manning levels, energy consumption, and yield.

The final method for identifying cost drivers is to compare a firm's cost in a value activity to its competitors' or compare competitors' costs to each other. Since competitors will usually be situated differently vis-à-vis the cost drivers, such comparisons can expose which cost drivers are most important. Analyzing competitor cost behavior will be discussed below.

The Cost of Purchased Inputs

Procurement has strategic significance in almost every industry, but rarely has sufficient stature in firms. Every value activity employs purchased inputs of some kind, ranging from raw materials used in component fabrication to professional services, office space, and capital goods. Purchased inputs divide into purchased operating inputs and purchased assets. The total cost of purchased inputs as a percentage of firm value provides an important indicator of the strategic significance of procurement. In many industries, the total cost of purchased inputs is a very large percentage of value, yet it receives much less attention than reducing labor costs.

The cost of purchased inputs is an integral part of the cost of a value activity, and the cost drivers described above determine the behavior of input costs. However, isolating purchased inputs for separate analysis will often yield additional insights into cost behavior. The cost of purchased inputs in an activity is a function of three factors: their unit cost, their rate of utilization in an activity, and their indirect effects on other activities through linkages. While utilization of inputs in an activity and linkages with other activities are best analyzed as part of the overall cost behavior of an activity, the *unit cost* of purchased inputs often has similar drivers across activities. Firmwide procurement practices also affect the unit cost of many inputs. Thus a firm can gain insight into how to lower unit cost by analyzing the unit cost of purchased inputs as a group.

In separating the unit cost of purchased inputs for analysis, however, a firm must recognize all three factors noted above. Better quality steel may improve the yield of a forging operation, as well as simplify machining. In some instances, then, a firm may lower total cost by spending *more* on purchased inputs. Minimizing the unit cost of purchased inputs is not necessarily appropriate. However, it is still clearly desirable to seek the best possible unit cost for purchased inputs after choosing the appropriate type and quality of inputs.

Firms' analyses of purchasing typically focus on the most visible items, especially raw materials and components. However, purchased inputs other than raw materials and components, when aggregated, often constitute an even greater percentage of cost. Standard cost systems often distribute the costs of such inputs among many cost categories rather than highlighting their importance. Purchased services such as maintenance or professional services are often overlooked in purchasing analyses, while purchases from sister units seldom receive the level of examination that is applied to outside purchases. Finally, purchased assets are frequently bought outside the normal procurement system and without the associated expertise. A comprehensive analysis of the unit cost of purchased inputs can be an important tool in gaining cost advantage.

Purchasing Information

The starting point in analyzing the unit cost of purchased inputs is to develop purchasing information. A firm should begin by identifying all significant purchased inputs and determining its yearly or quarterly expenditures on them. The list should include inputs purchased from sister business units. For purchased operating inputs, usage per period represents a relatively easy means of calculating cost. This analysis, however, must account for prepayments, discounts, and inventory changes. For purchased assets, total purchase price can be used as a measure of cost, adjusted for supplier concessions such as free service, free spare parts, or low-cost financing.

All significant purchased inputs should be identified, and listed in the order of importance to total cost. They should then be divided into purchased operating inputs and purchased assets and, within these categories, into items purchased regularly such as raw materials and office space, and irregularly purchased items such as equipment and consulting. Categorizing purchased inputs in this way can direct attention to areas where opportunities for cost reduction are frequently present. Small purchased inputs often provide fruitful opportunities for cost reduction. Managers tend to focus their attention on those few purchases that represent a significant percentage of costs. As a result, suppliers frequently generate their highest margins on purchases that represent a small cost item to the buyer. Irregularly purchased inputs frequently receive inadequate attention as well, while regular purchases are monitored and most firms have procedures to govern them. A firm should also compute the change in the inflation-adjusted cost of each input over time. Such a calculation further highlights those inputs that should be scrutinized. An increase in the real unit cost of an input may indicate that a firm has either paid inadequate attention to controlling cost or that supplier bargaining power has grown.

After sorting purchased inputs by size, regularity of purchase and real cost change, a firm should then identify *where* it makes the purchasing decision. Authority for many purchases rests outside the purchasing department. Yet the purchasing department is the place where procedures, procurement expertise, systems for tracking the costs of purchases, and the mandate to manage cost reside. Although the de facto delegation of procurement authority to other parts of a firm is often a practical necessity, it tends to obscure the cost of many purchased inputs and can lead to less efficient procurement unless the firm applies the same care as it does in the purchasing department.

A final step in developing information about purchased inputs is to record the suppliers for each item and the proportion of purchases awarded to each supplier over an ordering cycle. The number and mix of suppliers will play an important role in determining the cost of purchased inputs. A firm must also systematically track *potential* suppliers that it does not currently purchase from. This will ensure that alternative suppliers are regularly considered and that a firm can gain perspective on the performance of its own suppliers. Often a simple list of suppliers for each input will lead to some interesting conclusions. For example, single-sourced items may represent a significant fraction of total purchases. Unless special circumstances are present, single sourcing is an indication that suppliers have created switching costs and that unit costs of inputs may be unnecessarily high.

Drivers of Purchased Input Costs

The same cost drivers identified above shape the cost behavior of purchased inputs, in combination with the bargaining relationship between the firm and suppliers that grows out of industry structure.[10] The structural bargaining relationship reflects the broader industry determinants of supplier margin, while the cost drivers address how a firm's specific circumstances can influence it. While a firm must expect to pay suppliers higher margins on some imputs for these structural reasons, the cost of all inputs can be reduced by controlling the drivers. Some drivers have similar effects on the cost of many purchased inputs, and Table 3–3 summarizes some of the most important ones. For each purchased input, position vis-à-vis the drivers will determine the unit cost of purchased inputs of a given quality.

As discussed in Chapter 2, a firm should seek to coordinate or jointly optimize supplier linkages to lower overall costs in addition to create bargaining power with its suppliers. Effective communication with suppliers is necessary to achieve linkages. Ideally, a firm can exploit the available linkages and capture its share of their benefits by exercising its bargaining power. Procurement policies have an important role in both harnessing supplier linkages and improving a firm's bargaining power.

Supplier Cost Behavior and the Cost of Inputs

The cost behavior of suppliers will have an important influence on both the cost of inputs and the ability of a firm to exploit supplier linkages. Suppliers of a given purchased input will often vary in relative cost position, and identifying the lowest cost source may lead to lower unit purchasing costs in the long term if the firm can exercise its

[10]For a description of the industry structural factors see Chapter 1 and *Competitive Strategy,* Chapter 6.

TABLE 3–3 Drivers of the Unit Cost of Purchased Inputs

Cost Driver	Cost Driver Applied to Procurement	Description
Economies of Scale	Purchasing scale	The volume of purchasing with a given supplier affects bargaining power
Linkages	Linkages with suppliers	Coordinating with suppliers on specifications, delivery, and other activities can lower total costs
Interrelationships	Shared purchasing with other business units	Combining purchases with sister business units can improve bargaining power with suppliers
Integration	Make versus buy	Integration may raise or lower the cost of an input
Timing	History of supplier relationships	Historical loyalty to or problems with suppliers may affect input costs, access to inputs during tight periods, and services provided by suppliers
Policies	Purchasing practices*	Purchasing practices can significantly improve bargaining power with suppliers and the willingness of suppliers to perform extra services, for example: • Selection of the number and mix of suppliers • Hedging procedures • Investment in information on supplier costs and availability • Annual contracts versus individual purchases • Utilization of by-products
Location	Supplier location	Location of suppliers can affect the cost of inputs through the cost of transportation and the ease of communication
Institutional Factors	Government and union restrictions	Government policy can restrict access to inputs or affect their cost through tariffs, taxes, and other means. Unions may affect the ability to out-source or whether nonunion suppliers can be used

* Purchasing practices that can lower input costs will be treated more completely below.

bargaining power. Supplier cost behavior will determine whether placing larger orders will lower suppliers' cost. Supplier cost behavior will also determine the impact on suppliers' cost of other practices a firm adopts or asks its suppliers to adopt. Supplier cost behavior is analyzed in the same way as a firm's cost behavior. Understanding the cost behavior of key suppliers will thus allow a firm to establish better purchasing policies as well as to recognize and exploit linkages.

Segment Cost Behavior

Thus far I have described how to analyze the cost behavior of a business unit as a whole. In practice, however, a business unit usually produces a number of different product varieties and sells them to a number of different buyers. It may also employ a number of different distribution channels. For example, a shipbuilder constructs both liquid natural gas tankers and containerships while a bank lends to sophisticated high net-worth individuals as well as to middle income customers. Any of these differences may give rise to segments in which the behavior of costs in the value chain may be different. Unless the firm recognizes differences in cost behavior among segments, there is a significant danger that incorrect or average-cost pricing will provide openings for competitors. Thus cost analysis at the segment level must often supplement analysis at the business unit level.

Chapter 7 discusses the identification and analysis of segments in more detail. Differences in cost behavior among products, buyers, channels, or geographic areas is one of the key bases for the existence of segments, and hence cost analysis is an essential input to segmentation. The value chain for segments generally parallels that of the whole business unit. However, segment value chains may differ in some respects that affect cost. For example, the large sizes of a product line may be produced on different machines than small sizes and require different handling, inspection, and shipping procedures. Similarly, they may require different purchased inputs. Identifying important differences in the value activities for different segments is a starting point in segment cost analysis.

A firm should analyze the costs of those product lines, buyer types, or other portions of its activities that

- have significantly different value chains
- appear to have different cost drivers
- employ questionable procedures for allocating costs

In practice, a firm may want to select representative product varieties or buyers to illuminate differences among segments, rather than analyze every product variety or buyer in complete detail.

The process used to analyze cost behavior for segments is the same as that used for business units. The value chain for the segment is identified and costs and assets are assigned to it. Then the cost drivers of each activity are determined and quantified if possible. While the process remains the same, however, some complications often arise in practice. The prevalence of shared value activities among segments (see Chapter 7) requires the allocation of costs among segments. Standard cost systems often employ arbitrary measures as the basis for allocating cost to segments, such as sales volume or other readily measurable variables. While these measures have the benefit of simplicity, they often have little to do with the true contribution of the segment to overall costs. For example, allocating the costs of a value activity to domestic and international buyers by volume of sales will usually seriously understate the true cost of international sales, because international sales often make disproportionate demands in terms of time and attention. The costs of support activities and the costs of indirect primary activities appear to be most susceptible to misallocation. Such misallocations result in incorrect costs and inappropriate prices for product or buyer segments.

The costs of value activities shared among segments should be allocated based on each segment's actual impact on the effort or capacity of the value activity. Such measures will capture the opportunity cost of using a shared value activity in one segment instead of another. In technology development, for example, allocation should probably be based on the estimated time spent by engineers and scientists on particular product lines rather than on the products' respective sales volumes.

It is not always feasible or necessary to allocate the costs of shared activities to segments on an ongoing basis. The required analysis for strategic purposes does not require a high degree of precision, and periodic studies can suffice. To allocate R&D costs, for example, engineers can be interviewed to determine the percentage of their time spent on various products and buyers over a period of time long enough to eliminate distortions. Some firms may also be in a position to compute time allocation by sampling engineering change orders or requests for product modifications flowing to the engineering group from the sales force. Similar methods of approximation can provide the basis for allocating effort to segments in almost any shared activity.

Cost Dynamics

In addition to analyzing cost behavior at a point in time, a firm must consider how the absolute and relative cost of value activities will change over time *independent* of its strategy. I term this *cost dynamics.* An analysis of cost dynamics enables a firm to forecast how the cost drivers of value activities may change and which value activities will increase or decrease in absolute or relative cost importance. A firm with insight into cost dynamics may be able to position itself to gain a cost advantage by anticipating these changes and moving quickly to respond to them.

Cost dynamics occur because of the interplay of cost drivers over time, as a firm grows or as industry conditions change. The most common sources of cost dynamics include:

Industry Real Growth. Growth of an industry as a whole often has a number of effects on costs. Growth can flow through to purchased inputs, affecting the scale of supplier industries and thereby the cost of inputs. In some industries, industry growth forces up the cost of purchased inputs by worsening the supply/demand balance, while in others it lowers the cost of inputs by making suppliers more efficient. Industry growth can also open up possibilities for scale economies by making the introduction of new technologies feasible in value activities.

Differential Scale Sensitivity. Real growth (or decline) in the sales of firms can dramatically change the absolute and relative costs of value activities if activities have differing scale sensitivity. For example, software cost has become increasingly high relative to hardware cost in many electronics-related industries such as computers, video games, and telecommunication equipment, as hardware cost has proven more scale- and learning-sensitive than software cost. The same process can shift the relative cost position of firms that have value chains with differing degrees of scale sensitivity. For example, Eli Lilly's DNA-based technology for manufacturing insulin is believed to be more scale-sensitive than Novo Industries' process. If this proves to be true, Lilly's relative cost position will improve as volume grows.

Different Learning Rates. The relative cost of different value activities will change if learning occurs in them at different rates. Learning reduces the relative costs of those value activities in which it proceeds most rapidly. For example, rapid learning has dramatically reduced assembly costs as a percentage of sales for many electronics firms. As a result, differences among regions and countries in labor rates for assembly workers have diminished in importance in determining relative cost position.

Differential Technological Change. Technological changes that proceed at different rates can clearly affect the relative cost of different value activities and their cost drivers. For example, the availability of low-cost computers and the development of airfreight have fundamentally shifted the economics of many distribution industries. These changes have caused dramatic reductions in order processing costs as a percentage of total costs, and have allowed the restructuring of distributors in the direction of fewer and more centralized warehouses.

Relative Inflation of Costs. The rate of inflation in key cost elements in value activities often differs and this can significantly shift their relative cost. Differential inflation rates can quickly turn an insignificant value activity into one of critical strategic importance, or can convert a modest cost item within an activity into the dominant one. For example, because of the rapid inflation in oil prices relative to salaries and equipment, fuel costs now constitute almost 50 percent of airline operating costs. As a result, the fuel efficiency of the fleet, the inherent efficiency of the route system, and operating procedures have taken on critical strategic importance.

Aging. An aging capital base or workforce can shift the relative cost of value activities. Older offshore drilling rigs require more maintenance and insurance, for example, and an older workforce typically has higher salary and benefit costs.

Market Adjustment. The operation of market forces often works to counteract high or low purchased input costs and to eliminate or reduce cost differentials based on favorable purchasing by individual firms. People Express and other new airlines have enjoyed extremely low aircraft costs by purchasing used planes during the recent glut. Imitators of their strategy will eventually eliminate the stock of used planes, and People Express will compete with other airlines on a more equal basis.

Cost dynamics can lead to significant changes in industry structure and relative cost position. In steelmaking, for example, technological change and changing material costs have shifted the stage at which the minimum efficient scale of a steelmaking complex is determined. The primary rolling mill historically set minimum scale, but now the blast furnace stage does. Continuous casting has emerged as a lower-cost process than primary rolling for producing semifinished steel slabs. It is also less scale-sensitive than primary rolling. These shifts have major implications for the relative cost positions of competitors, depending on their process configurations. They have led to the success of mini-mills such as Nucor and Lone Star that use continuous casting technology and also have lower-cost labor than established competitors. Early identification of cost dynamics can yield a significant cost advantage by directing a firm toward those value activities that will have the greatest leverage for *future* relative cost position but may not now be receiving attention.

Cost Advantage

A firm has a cost advantage if its cumulative cost of performing all value activities is lower than competitors' costs.[11] The strategic value of cost advantage hinges on its sustainability. Sustainability will be present if the sources of a firm's cost advantage are difficult for competitors to replicate or imitate. Cost advantage leads to superior performance if the firm provides an acceptable level of value to the buyer so that its cost advantage is not nullified by the need to charge a lower price than competitors.

A firm's relative cost position is a function of

- the composition of its value chain versus competitors'
- its relative position vis-à-vis the cost drivers of each activity

Competitors have value chains that may be similar to or different from the firm's. In airlines, for example, TWA and United employ similar value chains that differ from that of People Express. If competitors' value chains are different from that of the firm, the inherent efficiency of the two chains will determine relative cost position. Differ-

[11]The same principles apply to assessing the costs of *potential* competitors.

ences in value chains usually encompass only a subset of value activities and thus a firm can isolate the effect of different chains on relative cost position by comparing the cost of these differing activities.

A firm's relative cost position in value activities that are the same as competitors' depends on the firm's position vis-à-vis the cost drivers of those activities relative to competitors. If regional scale drives the cost of the sales force, for example, relative sales force cost will reflect the regional shares of competitors and the steepness of the scale curve. A firm should assess the relative cost position of common value activities one by one, and then accumulate them together with the relative cost of different activities to determine overall cost position.

Determining the Relative Cost of Competitors

The value chain is the basic tool for determining competitor costs. The first step in determining competitor costs is to identify competitor value chains and how activities are performed by them. The process is the same as that employed by a firm to analyze its own value chain. In practice it is often extremely difficult to assess competitors' costs because the firm does not have direct information. It is usually possible to estimate directly the cost of some of a competitor's value activities from commonly available public data as well as from interviews with buyers, suppliers and others. For example, a firm can often learn the number of salespersons a competitor employs as well as their approximate compensation and expense account allowances. In this way, the costs of some of the competitor's value activities can be built up to yield an accurate but partial picture of the competitor's costs.

For value activities where a competitor's costs cannot be estimated directly, the firm should employ comparisons between itself and the competitor. This requires that the relative position of the competitor with respect to the cost drivers of the value activities in question be determined. A firm then uses its knowledge of cost behavior to estimate differences in the competitor's costs. For example, if local share drives logistical costs and the competitor has a higher local share, the competitor probably possesses a cost advantage in that value activity. If the firm can estimate the scale curve for logistical costs, the share difference provides a way of estimating the extent of the firm's disadvantage.

Given the extent to which determining a competitor's costs involves estimates and deduction, it is sometimes only feasible to estimate the *direction,* and not the absolute magnitude, of the relative cost difference with a competitor in a value activity. However, this can still prove extremely useful, since the firm can combine the direction of difference with knowledge of the proportional size of each value activity to develop a general picture of a competitor's relative cost position.

A firm can typically improve the accuracy of estimates of competitors' costs by examining several competitors simultaneously. Information disclosed by one competitor can be cross-checked against the disclosures of other competitors and used to test the consistency of scale curves or other cost models for a particular value activity. In fact, analyzing a firm's cost behavior and determining the relative costs of competitors is often an iterative process.

Gaining Cost Advantage

There are two major ways that a firm can gain a cost advantage:

- *Control cost drivers.* A firm can gain an advantage with respect to the cost drivers of value activities representing a significant proportion of total costs.
- *Reconfigure the value chain.* A firm can adopt a different and more efficient way to design, produce, distribute, or market the product.

The two sources of cost advantage are not mutually exclusive. Even a firm with a very different value chain from its competitors will have some common activities, and its relative cost position in them can enhance or detract from overall cost position.

Successful cost leaders usually derive their cost advantage from *multiple* sources within the value chain. Sustainable cost advantage stems not from one activity but from many, and reconfiguring the chain frequently plays a role in creating cost advantage. Cost leadership requires an examination of every activity in a firm for opportunities to reduce cost, and the consistent pursuit of all of them. More often than not, cost leaders have a culture emanating from senior management that reinforces such behavior. It often includes symbolic practices such as spartan facilities and limited executive perquisites.

Cost reduction may or may not erode differentiation. Every firm should aggressively pursue cost reduction in activities that do not influence differentiation (see Chapter 4). In activities that contribute to differentiation, a conscious choice may still be made to sacrifice all or part of differentiation in favor of improving relative cost position.

Controlling Cost Drivers

Once a firm has identified its value chain and diagnosed the cost drivers of significant value activities, cost advantage grows out of controlling those drivers better than competitors. A firm can potentially achieve superior position vis-à-vis the cost drivers of any activity in the value chain. Activities that represent a significant or growing proportion of cost will offer the greatest potential for improving relative cost position. While the appropriate cost drivers will vary for each activity, some generalizations about how controlling each of the ten cost drivers can lead to cost advantage in an activity are as follows:

Controlling Scale

Gain the Appropriate Type of Scale. Increasing scale through acquisitions, product line extensions, market expansion, or marketing activity can lower cost. However, the type of scale that drives cost differs by activity. Boosting local or regional scale in an existing product will usually lower sales force or physical distribution costs, while raising national scale by entering a new region may actually raise these costs. By looking throughout the value chain for the types of scale that drive cost, the value of scale (and hence market share) of different types can be assessed. Pursuit of scale should be selectively tuned to the type of scale that drives the cost of important activities in the particular industry. Scale increases in different activities must be balanced, moreover, so that pursuing scale in one activity does not create diseconomies in another.

Set Policies to Reinforce Scale Economies in Scale-Sensitive Activities. Scale economies are partly a function of how activities are managed. Eaton has maximized its scale economies in engine valves, for example, by simplifying its product line.

Exploit the Types of Scale Economies Where the Firm Is Favored. A firm should manage activities in ways that bring out the types of scale economies that most favor it. A firm with high global share should manage product development to emphasize global scale, for example, by stressing world products rather than country-tailored ones.

Emphasize Value Activities Driven by Types of Scale Where the Firm Has an Advantage. Since different types of scale drive the cost of different value activities, a firm should set its strategy to emphasize as much as possible the activities in which it has superior scale of the appropriate type. For a regional producer competing with national firms, for example, this may imply that sales force assistance and service should be emphasized, rather than rapid new product introduction whose cost is driven by national or global scale.

Controlling Learning

Manage with the Learning Curve. Learning does not occur automatically but results from the effort and attention of management and employees. Attention to learning should not be confined to labor costs but also to the cost of constructing facilities, the cost of scrap, and other significant value activities. Every premise and every practice must be examined for possible revision. Management must demand learning improvements and establish targets for them, rather than simply hope that learning will occur. When setting targets, the rate of learning should be compared across facilities and regions, as well as to industry standards. A firm must also establish mechanisms to facilitate the sharing of learning across facilities and business units. The sharing of learning is often impeded by geographic distance and internal rivalry.

Keep Learning Proprietary. Learning can lower a firm's relative cost position if the firm minimizes the spillover rate to competitors. Keeping learning proprietary can become an important means of achieving cost advantage in learning-sensitive value activities. Means for accomplishing this include:

- backward integration to protect know-how, such as by building or modifying production equipment in-house
- controlling employee publications or other forms of information dissemination
- retaining key employees
- strict non-disclosure provisions in employment contracts

Learn from Competitors. Pride should not interfere with exploiting the learning of competitors. Analysis of competitor value chains allows a firm to uncover good ideas that can be applied in-house. There are many ways to acquire competitor learning, including reverse engineering of competitor products, studying published material including patent filings and articles about competitors, and maintaining relationships with competitors' suppliers to gain access to knowhow and to the latest purchased inputs.

Controlling the Effect of Capacity Utilization

Level Throughput. A firm can often increase average capacity utilization by finding ways to level the fluctuations of volume through its value chain. For example, Sun-Diamond, the agricultural cooperative that produces Sun Maid raisins, Diamond walnuts, and other products, has reduced the cost of underutilization by promoting year-round baking uses for its products. These have reduced demand differences between the Christmas season and the rest of the year. Similarly, credit card processors can level throughput by serving a mix of accounts that have peak volumes spread throughout the year, e.g., beach clubs and ski areas.

A firm can level throughput through a variety of means, including:

- peak load or contribution pricing
- marketing activity, such as increasing promotion during slack periods and finding off-season uses for the products
- line extensions into less cyclical products, or into products that can intermittently utilize excess capacity (e.g., private label)
- selecting buyers with more stable demand or demands that are counterseasonal or countercyclical
- ceding share in high demand periods and regaining it in low demand periods
- letting competitors serve fluctuating segments[12]
- sharing activities with sister business units with a different pattern of needs (see Chapter 9).

Reduce the Penalty of Throughput Fluctuations. In addition to smoothing throughput fluctuations, a firm can sometimes reduce the costs associated with fluctuations in the volume of activity. Tapered integration, for example, is a means of using suppliers to cover peak needs rather than satisfying them in-house. Canadian steel producers, for example, have avoided excess capacity despite fluctuating sales by adding capacity for trendline demand growth rather than year-to-year demand. They sell steel produced by subcontractors and foreign firms to cover shortfalls.

[12]The use of competitors to reduce volume fluctuation as well as for other strategic purposes is discussed in Chapter 6.

Controlling Linkages

Exploit Cost Linkages Within the Value Chain. A firm can improve its cost position if it recognizes linkages among value activities and exploits them. The additional cost of achieving higher precision in machining parts may, for example, be offset by a reduction in inspection costs of the finished products. Recent technological advances are making linkages stronger and more possible to achieve. Information systems are making coordination among activities easier, while computer-aided design and manufacturing is just one example of how microelectronics is linking other activities.

Work with Suppliers and Channels to Exploit Vertical Linkages. Vertical linkages imply that relations with suppliers and channels offer possibilities for all parties to gain through the coordination and joint optimization of their respective value chains. Xerox, for example, provides suppliers with its manufacturing schedule through computer terminals, enabling suppliers to ship parts precisely when needed. Seeking out and pursuing such opportunities will require careful study of supplier and channel value chains, as well as the determination to overcome suspicion, greed, and other barriers to joint action. A firm must be prepared to share the gains of linkages with suppliers and channels in order to ensure that they can be achieved.

Controlling Interrelationships

Share Appropriate Activities. A firm can often reduce its relative costs significantly by sharing value activities with sister business units, or by entering new businesses in which opportunities for sharing exist. Chapter 9 describes in detail how to identify opportunities for sharing that lower cost.

Transfer Know-how in Managing Similar Activities. A diversified firm may also be able to transfer know-how gained in managing a value activity to other business units with generically similar activities. The issues involved in doing so are also discussed in Chapter 9.

Controlling Integration

Examine Systematically Possibilities for Integration and De-integration. Both integration and de-integration offer the potential of lowering costs. As changes in management attitudes and new information system technology are making supplier linkages easier to achieve, de-integration is becoming more and more attractive in many industries.

Controlling Timing

Exploit First-mover or Late-mover Advantages. The first mover in an industry often reaps a long-lasting cost advantage by tying up the best locations, preempting the best personnel, gaining access to preferred suppliers, or securing patents. In some industries, in fact, only the first mover can gain a significant cost advantage. In other industries, late-movers may gain cost advantages because technology is changing rapidly or they can observe and cheaply imitate the actions of the pioneer. First-mover and late-mover advantages are discussed in Chapter 5.

Time Purchases in the Business Cycle. Purchasing assets during periods of soft demand can yield a major cost savings. This is the case for many capital goods such as machinery, ships, and even complete plants.

Controlling Discretionary Policies

Modify Expensive Policies That Do Not Contribute to Differentiation. Many policies that govern a firm's activities raise cost. Sometimes a firm consciously does so in the hope of creating differentiation. Often, however, firms fail to recognize the cost of a policy. Cost analysis will often highlight the need to modify such policies, and careful scrutiny may also reveal that a policy does not contribute meaningfully to differentiation because its costs outweigh the price premium it generates. Both situations offer opportunities for cost reduction. Chapter 4 will describe how to evaluate the role of value activities in differentiation.

Invest in Technology to Skew Cost Drivers in the Firm's Favor. New technology often underlies cost advantage. Technology can also allow a firm to make its competitor's advantages vis-à-vis cost drivers obsolete. The level of technology investment is a policy choice and most cost leaders invest aggressively. Iowa Beef, for example, spends

$20 million or more on plant renovations annually. Some of the important ways in which technology investment lowers costs include:[13]

- *Developing low-cost processes.* For example, Union Carbide's Unipol process for making low-density polyethylene.
- *Facilitating automation.* For example, Iowa Beef's massive beef processing plants and K Mart's automated distribution centers.
- *Low-cost product designs.* For example, Canon's NP200 copier with fewer parts.

In some cases, the ability to apply new low-cost technology depends on scale. In soft contact lenses, for example, Bausch and Lomb's dramatically lower-cost spin casting technology for manufacturing lenses is much more scale-sensitive than lathe technology. However, the choice of technology can also be related to other cost drivers such as timing, location, or integration. A firm should invest in technology development in areas that will skew cost drivers the most in its favor.

Avoid Frills. Most cost leaders control discretionary expenses throughout their value chains. National Semiconductor executives work in spartan surroundings with few private offices, and similar characteristics apply to other cost leaders including Lincoln Electric, People Express, and Crown Cork and Seal. Such policy choices not only reduce costs in their own right but also seem to have important symbolic value.

Controlling Location

Optimize Location. The location of activities in relation to each other as well as to buyers and suppliers often contributes significantly to such things as labor rates, logistical efficiency, and supplier access. The firm that locates its facilities well will often gain a significant cost advantage. The optimal location of activities changes over time, as is happening today in the steel industry with the emergence of mini-mills.

Controlling Institutional Factors

Do Not Take Institutional Factors as a Given. Firms can influence institutional factors such as government policies and unionization,

[13]Chapter 5 describes in some detail how technology can affect competition.

despite a tendency to view institutional factors as beyond their control. For example, many unionized trucking companies have established nonunion subsidiaries. Firms can also frequently influence regulation through lobbying, as Japanese firms are actively seeking to do in states that have begun taxing foreign profits. A number of states are already committed to repealing their laws to avoid scaring away foreign investors.

Procurement and Cost Advantage

Procurement practices have a potentially major impact on cost position that cuts across activities. A number of possible changes in procurement can reduce costs:

Tune Specifications of Purchased Inputs to Meet Needs More Precisely. A firm can improve its cost position by ensuring that the quality of purchased inputs meets, but does not exceed, the firm's requirements. Clark Equipment, for example, has begun to move toward automotive grade components for some lift truck models, rather than more expensive and unnecessarily high-quality truck grade components.

Enhance Bargaining Leverage Through Purchasing Policies. Firms rarely view purchasing strategically or as a bargaining problem, though purchasing practices can significantly affect cost. Firms can take a number of specific actions to enhance their bargaining power with suppliers:

- Increase bargaining power in purchasing by keeping the number of sources sufficient to ensure competition, but small enough to be an important buyer to each source.
- Select suppliers who are especially competitive with each other, and divide purchases among them.
- Vary the proportion of business awarded to suppliers over time to ensure that they do not view it as an entitlement.
- Solicit occasional proposals from new suppliers, both to test market prices and gather technological intelligence.
- Enhance the leverage of purchasing scale through contracting based on annual volume with phased deliveries, instead of making frequent smaller purchases.
- Seek out opportunities to combine purchases with sister business units.

- Appoint high-quality purchasing executives to allow more sophisticated buying practices.
- Invest in information to understand suppliers' costs and market conditions better.
- Pursue technology development to eliminate or reduce the need for expensive inputs where unit costs cannot be reduced.

Select Appropriate Suppliers and Manage Their Costs. A firm should select those suppliers which are most efficient or those that offer the least costly product to use given the firm's value chain. Purchasing practices should also include promoting supplier cost reduction, aiding suppliers where necessary with technology development, and encouraging supplier practices that lower the firm's cost through linkages. Marks and Spencer, for example, has achieved a low cost position in retailing in the United Kingdom through active efforts to help suppliers adopt the most modern technology. Managing the efficiency or effectiveness of the supplier base, using an analysis of supplier value chains essentially the same as the analysis of its own chain, can be equally as important to cost position as enhancing bargaining power over suppliers.

Reconfiguring the Value Chain

Dramatic shifts in relative cost position most often arise from a firm adopting a value chain that is significantly different from its competitors'. Reconfigured value chains stem from a number of sources, including:

- a different production process
- differences in automation
- direct sales instead of indirect sales
- a new distribution channel
- a new raw material
- major differences in forward or backward vertical integration
- shifting the location of facilities relative to suppliers and customers
- new advertising media

No-frills airlines such as People Express and Southwest Airlines provide a striking example of strategies based on reconfiguring the value chain. They have adopted chains that differ markedly from trunk carriers, as shown in Table 3–4.

TABLE 3–4 Alternative Value Chains in Airlines

	Ticket Counter Operations	Gate Operations	Aircraft Operations	On-Board Service	Baggage Handling	Ticket Offices
Trunk Airlines	Full service	Full service	Purchase new aircraft Union pilots	Full service	Free baggage checking	Ticket offices in downtown locations
No-Frills Carriers	Secondary airports and terminals No ticket counter (or check-in only) Purchase tickets on board the aircraft or from machines No interline tickets Few fare options	Secondary airports and terminals First come, first served seating No ticketing at gates	Used aircraft High-density seating Nonunion pilots Smaller crews and more flying hours per day	Nonunion flight attendants Snack only or no meals Charge for food and drink served	Provide carry-on space Charge for checked baggage No interline baggage	None

Two other examples from different industries illustrate the significant cost advantage to be gained through reconfiguration of the value chain. In beef packing, the traditional value chain involved raising cattle on isolated farms and shipping them live to labor-intensive abattoirs in major rail centers like Chicago. After the animal was slaughtered and broken, whole sides of beef were shipped to markets where they were cut into smaller pieces by retailers. Pursuing an innovative strategy, Iowa Beef Packers built large automated plants near the cattle supply and processed the meat there into smaller "boxed" cuts. This significantly reduced transportation expense, a major cost, as well as raised yield by avoiding the weight loss that occurred when live animals were shipped. Iowa Beef also reduced costs in the operations activities in the value chain by using cheaper nonunion labor, readily available in rural areas where its new plants were located.[14]

Federal Express similarly redefined the value chain for air delivery of small parcels. Traditional competitors such as Emery and Airborne collected freight of varying sizes, shipped it via the airlines, and then delivered it to the addressee. Federal Express limited itself to small packages and flew them on company-owned planes to its central hub in Memphis where the parcels were sorted. It then flew the parcels to their destinations on the same planes and delivered them in company-owned trucks. Other dramatic reconfigurations of the value chain include the early discount retailers, discount stockbrokers, and new long distance telephone companies such as MCI and Sprint.

Reconfiguring the value chain can lead to cost advantage for two reasons. First, reconfiguration frequently presents the opportunity to fundamentally restructure a firm's cost, compared to settling for incremental improvements. The new value chain may prove inherently more efficient than the old one. The success of the no-frills airlines vividly illustrates how adopting a different value chain that is inherently cheaper can allow a firm to establish a new cost standard for an industry. On some routes, no-frills airlines have achieved costs that are as much as 50 percent lower than those of trunk carriers. Not only are activities performed more cheaply in the new value chain, but linkages are exploited. By ticketing on-board, for example, People Express significantly reduces cost in other value activities such as gate operations and ticket counter operations.

The second way an alternate value chain can lead to cost advantage is by altering the basis of competition in a way that favors a

[14]For a general description of Iowa Beef, see Stuart (1981).

firm's strengths. Reconfiguration of the chain may *change the important cost drivers in a way that favors a firm.* Performing an activity differently can change its susceptibility to scale economies, interrelationships, locational effects, and virtually every other cost driver. In aluminum, for example, Japanese firms are investing in the new carbothermic reduction process that converts bauxite and related ore directly into metal, skipping the intermediate alumina stage. This would nullify the Japanese firms' serious disadvantage in power costs. In the beef processing case, Iowa Beef redefined the role of location as a cost driver and increased scale sensitivity. A firm with a large market share, like Iowa Beef, often benefits from shifting to a more scale-sensitive value chain. In the case of the no-frills airlines, the new value chain is less scale-sensitive than the old one because of the reduction in indirect activities. This has been important to the success of the newly established no-frills carriers.

Coalitions and other interfirm agreements sometimes provide firms with a way to reconfigure the value chain even if they cannot do so independently. A number of multiple system operators of cable television franchises have traded franchises to increase marketing and operating efficiency, for example. Similarly, Allied Chemical and Church & Dwight have worked out a deal to swap identical raw materials produced in different locations to save transportation costs.

To identify a new value chain, a firm must examine everything it does, as well as its competitors' value chains, in search of creative options to do things differently. A firm should ask questions such as the following for every activity:

- How can the activity be performed differently or even eliminated?
- How can a group of linked value activities be reordered or regrouped?
- How might coalitions with other firms lower or eliminate costs?

Reconfiguring Downstream

Where channel costs or other downstream costs represent a significant fraction of cost to the buyer, reconfiguration of downstream activities can reduce cost substantially. Gallo's heavy use of the supermarket channel for wine provides an example. A supermarket's costs of distribution are less than that of the liquor store channel which involves distributors. By emphasizing supermarkets, Gallo has lowered the cost of getting wine to buyers. Gallo's high sales volume and faster turnover also reduce its relative cost to the supermarket. This has made supermarkets willing to accept lower margins from Gallo than from its competitors.

The efficiency of downstream channels reflects their strategies and degree of fragmentation. Chain stores are often more efficient than single outlets, for example, and large office equipment or automobile dealers are often more efficient than smaller ones. A firm can not only choose more efficient downstream routes to the end user, but also take actions to promote consolidation or otherwise improve the efficiency of downstream entities. In extreme cases, a firm may have to integrate forward to achieve downstream efficiency.

The relative bargaining power of a firm and its downstream channels has an important influence on whether the firm will reduce its relative cost position through downstream reconfiguration. In Gallo's case, supermarkets would reap the benefits of their greater efficiency if they priced wines the same as liquor stores. However, Gallo's "pull-through" effect and intense competition among supermarkets have led to low prices and allowed Gallo to reap most of the benefits.

Cost Advantage through Focus

A focus strategy may also provide a means for achieving a cost advantage that rests on using focus to control cost drivers, reconfiguring the value chain, or both. Since the cost of value activities as well as the most efficient value chain may differ for different segments, a firm that dedicates its efforts to a well-chosen segment of an industry can often lower its costs significantly. Federal Express based its reconfiguration of the air parcel delivery value chain on small packages requiring rapid delivery. People Express has focused on price-sensitive buyers, allowing it to eliminate many costs. In the hotel/motel industry, La Quinta offers only guest rooms, and has lowered its investment and operating costs per room by eliminating costly restaurants, conference facilities, and other services not desired by its target buyer—the middle-level manager who travels frequently to the same area.

The most dramatic improvements in relative cost position through focus usually stem from employing a different and tailored value chain to serve the target segment. The Federal Express, People Express, and La Quinta examples all share this characteristic. Focus can also lower costs if the target segment *is associated with a key cost driver.* If regional market share is a key cost driver, for example, a regional focus strategy can yield a cost advantage over larger national competitors with small shares in the particular region.

Successful focus strategies frequently stem from innovative segmentation of an industry. Chapter 7 will describe how to segment industries and how to choose appropriate focus strategies. Industry segments grow, in part, out of product varieties, buyer groups, or geographic areas that require a different value chain or in which cost drivers differ.

Sustainability of Cost Advantage

Cost advantage will result in above-average performance only if the firm can sustain it. Improving relative cost position in unsustainable ways may allow a firm to maintain cost parity or proximity, but a firm attempting to achieve cost leadership strategy must also develop sustainable sources of cost advantage.

Cost advantage is sustainable if there are entry or mobility barriers that prevent competitors from imitating its sources. Sustainability varies for different cost drivers and from one industry to another. Some drivers, however, tend to be more sustainable than others:

- *Scale.* Scale is a key entry/mobility barrier, and the cost of replicating scale is often high because competitors must buy share.
- *Interrelationships.* Interrelationships with sister business units can force a competitor to diversify in order to match a cost advantage. If there are entry barriers into the related industries, sustainability can be high.
- *Linkages.* Linkages are often difficult for a firm to detect and require coordination across organizational lines or with independent suppliers and channels.
- *Proprietary learning.* Learning is difficult to achieve in practice; it can also be hard for competitors to catch up if learning can be kept proprietary.
- *Policy choices to create proprietary product or process technology.* Replicating product innovations or new production processes often poses great difficulties for competitors if innovations are protected by patents or secrecy. Process innovations are often more sustainable than product innovations because secrecy is easier to maintain.

Timing and integration can also be sources of sustainable cost advantage because they are often hard to replicate. However, their sustainability will be greatest in instances where they also translate into scale or learning advantages. Location, the pattern of capacity utilization, institutional factors, and policy choices can be sources of sustainable cost advantage in some industries, although they tend to create less sustainable cost advantage on average than other drivers. Even sources of cost advantage that are less sustainable, however, can provide formidable barriers if they interact with more sustainable drivers or with each other. Policy choices that elevate scale economies can be difficult to imitate, for example.

Sustainability stems not only from the sources of the cost advantage, but also from their *number.* Cost advantage derived from one or two value activities provides an alluring target for imitation by competitors. Cost leaders usually accumulate cost advantages gained from numerous sources in the value chain that interact and reinforce each other. This makes it difficult and expensive for competitors to replicate their cost position.

Gallo provides a good example of a sustainable cost leadership strategy based on these principles. Gallo's value chain, shown in simplified form in Figure 3–3, contains numerous sources of cost advantage in many value activities. The Gallo cost advantage draws heavily on scale and proprietary technology, two of the most sustainable cost drivers. Gallo has consistently achieved a 15 percent or greater cost advantage over its major rivals. Gallo's strength encouraged Coca-Cola's exit from the wine industry, because Gallo's cost advantage dampened Coke's profitability.

The creation of a new or reconfigured value chain is a final source of sustainability in cost advantage. Competitors almost inevitably face a high cost of matching a reconfigured chain. This is particularly true for well-established competitors, who face significant mobility barriers in moving away from the industry's traditional value chain. Iowa Beef and Federal Express, for example, have both enjoyed enduring advantages while competitors struggled to respond. Japanese aluminum producers would gain a similarly durable cost advantage in aluminum smelting if carbothermic reduction proves a success.

Implementation and Cost Advantage

This chapter has focused on how to achieve a cost advantage through changes in strategy and the way activities are performed. However, the success of cost leadership hinges on a firm's skills in

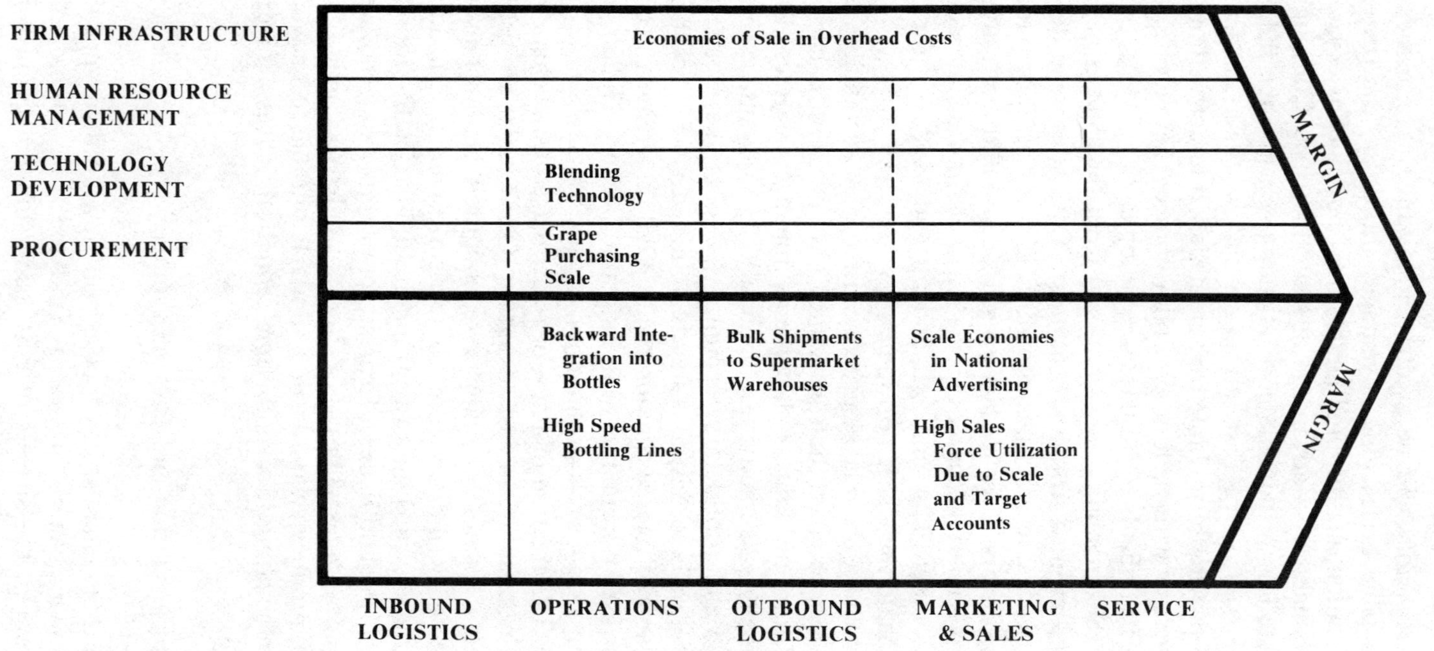

FIRM INFRASTRUCTURE
HUMAN RESOURCE MANAGEMENT
TECHNOLOGY DEVELOPMENT
PROCUREMENT

Economies of Sale in Overhead Costs

Blending Technology

Grape Purchasing Scale

Backward Integration into Bottles

High Speed Bottling Lines

Bulk Shipments to Supermarket Warehouses

Scale Economies in National Advertising

High Sales Force Utilization Due to Scale and Target Accounts

MARGIN

MARGIN

INBOUND LOGISTICS
OPERATIONS
OUTBOUND LOGISTICS
MARKETING & SALES
SERVICE

Figure 3–3. Gallo's Source of Cost Advantage in Wine

actually implementing it on a day to day basis. Costs do not go down automatically or by accident but rather as a result of hard work and constant attention. Firms differ in their abilities to lower costs, even when they have similar scale or cumulative volumes or when guided by similar policies. Improving relative cost position may not require a major shift in strategy so much as greater management attention. A firm should never assume its costs are low enough.

No cost driver works automatically. Scale economies are not achieved in an activity unless a firm's other activities are coordinated to provide the inputs necessary to operate smoothly at large scale. Policy choices must not dissipate the advantages of scale through product proliferation. Interrelationships will not lower cost unless affected business units actually coordinate their behavior. Learning curve advantages do not occur unless a firm's management strives to capture them.

A number of factors, including the training and motivation of employees, the firm's culture, the adoption of formal cost reduction programs, a constant pursuit of automation, and a strong belief in the learning curve contribute to a firm's ability to achieve cost leadership. Everyone in a firm has the potential to affect cost. Cost leaders have cost control programs in every value activity, not only in manufacturing. They compare activities against themselves over time, and among business units and competitors. The importance of symbolic factors in creating the climate for cost reduction also cannot be overstated. Successful cost leaders usually pay a great deal of attention to discretionary costs, in addition to tuning their strategy to achieve minimum operating costs.

Pitfalls in Cost Leadership Strategies

Many firms do not fully understand the behavior of their costs from a strategic perspective and fail to exploit opportunities to improve their relative cost position. Some of the most common errors made by firms in assessing and acting upon cost position include:

Exclusive Focus on the Cost of Manufacturing Activities. When one mentions "cost," most managers instinctively think of manufacturing. However, a significant, if not overwhelming, share of total cost is generated in activities such as marketing, sales, service, technology development, and infrastructure. These often receive too little attention in cost analysis. An examination of the entire value chain often results in relatively simple steps that can significantly reduce cost position. For example, recent advances in computers and computer-aided design are having dramatic impacts on the cost of performing research.

Ignoring Procurement. Many firms work diligently to reduce labor costs but pay scant attention to purchased inputs. They tend to view purchasing as a secondary staff function and devote few management resources to it. Analysis within the purchasing department too often centers solely on the purchase price of key raw materials. Firms often allow many items to be purchased by individuals with little expertise or motivation to reduce cost. Linkages between purchased inputs and the costs of other value activities go unrecognized. Modest changes in purchasing practices could yield major cost benefits for many firms.

Overlooking Indirect or Small Activities. Cost reduction programs usually concentrate on large cost activities and/or direct activities such as component fabrication and assembly. Activities that represent a small fraction of total cost seldom receive sufficient scrutiny. Indirect activities, such as maintenance and regulatory costs, often escape attention altogether.

False Perception of Cost Drivers. Firms often misdiagnose their cost drivers. For example, a firm with the largest national market share and the lowest costs may incorrectly assume that national market share drives cost. However, cost leadership may actually stem from the firm's large regional share in the regions in which it operates. Failing to understand the sources of its cost advantage may lead the firm to attempt to lower cost by raising national share. As a result it may worsen its cost position by reducing regional focus. It may also concentrate its defensive strategies on national competitors and ignore the more significant threat posed by strong regional competitors.[15]

Failure to Exploit Linkages. Firms rarely recognize all the linkages that affect cost, particularly linkages with suppliers and linkages among activities such as quality assurance, inspection, and service. The ability to exploit linkages underlies the success of many Japanese firms. Matsushita and Canon, among others, recognize and exploit

[15]See Chapter 14, which discusses defensive strategy.

linkages despite the fact that their policies contradict traditional manufacturing and purchasing practices. Failure to recognize linkages also leads to such errors as requiring each department to cut costs by the same amount, even though *raising* cost in some departments may lower total costs.

Contradictory Cost Reduction. Firms often attempt to reduce cost in ways that are contradictory. They try to gain market share to reap the benefits of scale economies while at the same time dissipating scale economies through model proliferation. They locate close to buyers to save freight costs but emphasize weight reduction in new product development. Cost drivers sometimes work in opposite directions, and a firm must recognize the tradeoffs.

Unwitting Cross Subsidy. Firms often engage in unwitting cross subsidy when they fail to recognize the existence of segments in which costs behave differently.[16] Conventional accounting systems rarely measure all the cost differences among products, buyers, channels, or geographic areas described above. Thus, a firm may charge excessive prices on some items in the line or to some buyers while subsidizing prices charged on others. For example, white wine requires less costly cooperage than red wine because of its lower aging requirements. If a winery sets equal prices for white and red wine based on average costs, then the price of lower-cost white wine will subsidize the price of red wine. Unwitting cross subsidy often provides an opening for competitors that understand costs and use them to undercut a firm's prices and improve their market position. Cross subsidy also exposes the firm to focused competitors that only compete in the overpriced segments.[17]

Thinking Incrementally. Cost reduction efforts often strive for incremental cost improvements in the existing value chain, rather than finding ways to reconfigure the chain. Incremental improvement can reach the point of diminishing returns, while reconfiguring the chain can lead to a whole new cost plateau.

Undermining Differentiation. Cost reduction can undermine differentiation if it eliminates a firm's sources of uniqueness to the buyer. Though doing so may be strategically desirable, it should be the result

[16] *Deliberate* cross subsidy can be strategically justified in some industries. See Chapter 12.

[17] Opportunities for exploiting cross subsidy to attack market leaders will be discussed in Chapter 15.

of a conscious choice. Cost reduction efforts should concentrate most on activities that do not contribute to a firm's differentiation. A cost leader will improve performance, moreover, if it differentiates in activities wherever differentiation is not costly.

Steps in Strategic Cost Analysis

The techniques described in this chapter can be summarized by outlining the steps required in strategic cost analysis:

1. Identify the appropriate value chain and assign costs and assets to it.
2. Diagnose the cost drivers of each value activity and how they interact.
3. Identify competitor value chains, and determine the relative cost of competitors and the sources of cost differences.
4. Develop a strategy to lower relative cost position through controlling cost drivers or reconfiguring the value chain and/or downstream value.
5. Ensure that cost reduction efforts do not erode differentiation, or make a conscious choice to do so.
6. Test the cost reduction strategy for sustainability.

4
Differentiation

A firm differentiates itself from its competitors if it can be unique at something that is valuable to buyers. Differentiation is one of the two types of competitive advantage a firm may possess. The extent to which competitors in an industry can differentiate themselves from each other is also an important element of industry structure. Despite the importance of differentiation, its sources are often not well understood. Firms view the potential sources of differentiation too narrowly. They see differentiation in terms of the physical product or marketing practices, rather than potentially arising anywhere in the value chain. Firms are also often different but not differentiated, because they pursue forms of uniqueness that buyers do not value. Differentiators also frequently pay insufficient attention to the cost of differentiation, or to the sustainability of differentiation once achieved.

This chapter presents a framework for analyzing differentiation and choosing a differentiation strategy. I will first describe the sources of differentiation, which can arise anywhere in a firm's value chain. Successful differentiation strategies grow out of the coordinated actions of all parts of a firm, not just the marketing department. Differentiation is usually costly, and I will show how to determine the cost of differentiation and how it varies by competitor. I will then describe how to diagnose what types of differentiation create buyer value, employing the buyer's value chain as a tool for doing so. Next I will show how to translate an analysis of buyer value into specific buyer purchase criteria. Finally, I will use all of these concepts to describe how to choose a differentiation strategy, and highlight some common pitfalls in pursuing one.

Sources of Differentiation

A firm differentiates itself from its competitors when it provides something unique that is valuable to buyers beyond simply offering a low price. Differentiation allows the firm to command a premium price, to sell more of its product at a given price, or to gain equivalent benefits such as greater buyer loyalty during cyclical or seasonal downturns.[1] Differentiation leads to superior performance if the price premium achieved exceeds any added costs of being unique. A firm's differentiation may appeal to a broad group of buyers in an industry or only to a subset of buyers with particular needs. Brooks Brothers appeals to buyers wanting traditional clothing, for example, though many buyers view Brooks Brothers clothing as too conservative. Differentiation will be treated in general terms in this chapter, and Chapter 7 will describe how differences in buyer needs within an industry can lead to opportunities for differentiation through focus.

Differentiation and the Value Chain

Differentiation cannot be understood by viewing the firm in aggregate, but stems from the specific activities a firm performs and how they affect the buyer.[2] Differentiation grows out of the firm's value chain. Virtually any value activity is a potential source of uniqueness.

[1]Hereafter I will use the term price premium to refer to all of these benefits of differentiation.

[2]The stream of research in demand theory pioneered by Lancaster sees a product as a bundle of attributes that the buyer desires. See Lancaster (1979) for a recent summary. This chapter shows how valuable attributes grow out of a buyer's value chain, how product attributes actually create buyer value, and how valuable attributes relate to the activities performed by a firm.

The procurement of raw materials and other inputs can affect the performance of the end product and hence differentiation. For example, Heineken pays particular attention to the quality and purity of the ingredients for its beer and uses a constant strain of yeast. Similarly, Steinway uses skilled technicians to choose the finest materials for its pianos, and Michelin is more selective than its competitors about the grades of rubber it uses in its tires.

Other successful differentiators create uniqueness through other primary and support activities. Technology development activities can lead to product designs that have unique product performance, as Cray Research has done in supercomputers. Operations activities can affect such forms of uniqueness as product appearance, conformance to specifications, and reliability. Perdue, for example, has bolstered its differentiation of fresh chickens by careful control of growing conditions and by feeding chickens marigolds to improve their color. The outbound logistical system can shape the speed and consistency of deliveries. For example, Federal Express has established an integrated logistical system using its Memphis hub that yields a level of delivery reliability unheard of prior to its entry into the small-parcel delivery business. Marketing and sales activities also frequently have an impact on differentiation. Timken's sales force, for example, assists its buyers to use roller bearings more effectively in their manufacturing processes.

Figure 4–1 illustrates how any activity in the value chain can potentially contribute to differentiation. Even if the physical product is a commodity, other activities can often lead to substantial differentiation. Similarly, indirect activities such as maintenance or scheduling can contribute to differentiation just as do direct activities such as assembly or order processing. For example, a dust and fume free building can dramatically improve defect rates in semiconductor manufacturing.

Value activities representing only a small percentage of total cost can nevertheless have a major impact on differentiation. For example, inspection may represent only 1 percent of cost, but shipping even one defective package of drugs to a buyer can have major negative repercussions for a pharmaceutical firm's perceived differentiation. Value chains developed for purposes of strategic cost analysis, therefore, may not isolate all activities that are important for differentiation. Differentiation analysis requires a finer division of some value activities, while others may be aggregated if they have little differentiation impact.

A firm may also differentiate itself through the *breadth* of its activities, or its competitive scope. Crown Cork and Seal offers crowns

	INBOUND LOGISTICS	OPERATIONS	OUTBOUND LOGISTICS	MARKETING & SALES	SERVICE	
FIRM INFRASTRUCTURE	Top Management Support in Selling Facilities that Enhance the Firm's Image Superior Management Information System					MARGIN
HUMAN RESOURCE MANAGEMENT	Superior Training of Personnel	Stable Workforce Policies Quality of Work Life Programs Programs to Attract the Best Scientists and Engineers		Sales Incentives to Retain Best Salespersons Recruiting Better Qualified Sales and Service Personnel	Extensive Training of Service Technicians	
TECHNOLOGY DEVELOPMENT	Superior Material Handling & Sorting Technology Proprietary Quality Assurance Equipment	Unique Product Features Rapid Model Introductions Unique Production Process or Machines Automated Inspection Procedures	Unique Vehicle Scheduling Software Special Purpose Vehicles or Containers	Applications Engineering Support Superior Media Research Most Rapid Quotations for Tailored Models	Advanced Servicing Techniques	
PROCUREMENT	Most Reliable Transportation for Inbound Deliveries	Highest Quality Raw Materials Highest Quality Components	Best Located Warehouses Transportation Suppliers that Minimize Damage	Most Desirable Media Placements Product Positioning and Image	High Quality Replacement Parts	
	Handling of Inputs that Minimizes Damage or Degradation Timeliness of Supply to the Manufacturing Process	Tight Conformance to Specifications Attractive Product Appearance Responsiveness to Specifiation Changes Low Defect Rates Short Time to Manufacture	Rapid and Timely Delivery Accurate and Responsive Order Processing Handling that Minimizes Damage	High Advertising Level and Quality High Sales Force Coverage and Quality Personal Relationships with Channels or Buyers Superior Technical Literature & Other Sales Aids Most Extensive Promotion Most Extensive Credit to Buyers or Channels	Rapid Installation High Service Quality Complete Field Stocking of Replacement Parts Wide Service Coverage Extensive Buyer Training	MARGIN

Figure 4–1. Representative Sources of Differentiation in the Value Chain

(bottle caps) and filling machinery plus cans. It thus offers a full line of packaging services to its buyers, and its expertise in packaging machinery gives it more credibility and access in selling cans. Citicorp's breadth of activities in financial services enhances its reputation as well as allowing its sales channels to offer a broader product range. A number of other differentiating factors can result from broad competitive scope:

- ability to serve buyer needs anywhere
- simplified maintenance for the buyer if spare parts and design philosophies are common for a wide line
- single point at which the buyer can purchase
- single point for customer service
- superior compatibility among products

Most of these benefits require consistency or coordination among activities if a firm is to achieve them.

Differentiation can also stem from *downstream.* A firm's channels can be a potent source of uniqueness, and may enhance its reputation, service, customer training, and many other factors. In soft drinks, for example, independent bottlers are crucial to differentiation. Coca Cola and Pepsi Cola spend a great deal of attention and money attempting to upgrade bottlers and improve their effectiveness. Coke, for example, has been arranging the sale of less effective bottlers to new, more capable owners. Similarly, observers credit Caterpillar Tractor's dealers with providing an important source of differentiation for Caterpillar. Cat's approximately 250 dealers are by far the largest in the industry on average, and their size allows them to provide extensive service and buyer financing. Selective distribution through well-chosen outlets has also proven to be an extremely important source of differentiation for such firms as Estée Lauder and Hathaway.

Firms can enhance the role of channels in differentiation through actions such as the following:

- channel selection to achieve consistency in facilities, capabilities, or image
- establishing standards and policies for how channels must operate
- provision of advertising and training materials for use by channels
- providing funding so that channels can offer credit

Firms often confuse the concept of quality with that of differentiation. While differentiation encompasses quality, it is a much broader concept. Quality is typically associated with the physical product. Differentiation strategies attempt to create value for the buyer throughout the value chain.

Drivers of Uniqueness

A firm's uniqueness in a value activity is determined by a series of basic drivers, analogous to the cost drivers described in Chapter 3. Uniqueness drivers are the underlying reasons *why* an activity is unique. Without identifying them, a firm cannot fully develop means of creating new forms of differentiation or diagnose how sustainable its existing differentiation is.

The principal uniqueness drivers are the following, ordered approximately in terms of their prominence:

Policy Choices. Firms make policy choices about what activities to perform and how to perform them. Such policy choices are perhaps the single most prevalent uniqueness driver. Johns Manville chooses to provide extensive customer training in installing its roofing products, for example, while Grey Poupon chooses to advertise mustard at a substantially higher rate of spending than historical industry practice. Much uniqueness, therefore, is discretionary.

Some typical policy choices that lead to uniqueness include:

- product features and performance offered
- services provided (e.g., credit, delivery, or repair)
- intensity of an activity adopted (e.g., rate of advertising spending)
- content of an activity (e.g., the information provided in order processing)
- technology employed in performing an activity (e.g., precision of machine tools, computerization of order processing)
- quality of inputs procured for an activity
- procedures governing the actions of personnel in an activity (e.g., service procedures, nature of sales calls, frequency of inspection or sampling)
- skill and experience level of personnel employed in an activity, and training provided
- information employed to control an activity (e.g., number of

temperature, pressure, and variables used to control a chemical reaction)

Linkages. Uniqueness often stems from linkages within the value chain or with suppliers and channels that a firm exploits. Linkages can lead to uniqueness if the way one activity is performed affects the performance of the other:

LINKAGES WITHIN THE VALUE CHAIN. Meeting buyer needs often involves coordinating linked activities. For example, delivery time is frequently determined not only by outbound logistics but also by the speed of order processing and the frequency of sales calls to take orders. Similarly, coordination between the sales force and the service organization can lead to more responsive customer service. Uniquely meeting buyer needs may also require the optimization of linked activities. In a number of industries such as copiers and semiconductors, for example, Japanese competitors have achieved dramatic reductions in defect rates by modifying every activity that influences defects instead of rclying on a single value activity such as inspection. Similarly, higher investment in indirect activities such as maintenance can improve the performance of direct activities such as finishing or printing.

SUPPLIER LINKAGES. Uniqueness in meeting buyer needs may also be the result of coordination with suppliers. Close coordination with suppliers can shorten new model development time, for example, if suppliers tool up for producing new parts at the same time as a firm is completing the design of equipment to manufacture the new model. Similarly, missionary sales efforts by suppliers to a firm's buyers can sometimes help differentiate a firm's product.

CHANNEL LINKAGES. Linkages with channels can also lead to uniqueness in a variety of ways. By coordinating with channels or jointly optimizing the division of activities between the firm and the channels, uniqueness can frequently result. Some examples of how linkages with channels can lead to uniqueness are as follows:

- training channels in selling and other business practices
- joint selling efforts with channels
- subsidizing for channel investments in personnel, facilities, and performance of additional activities.

Timing. Uniqueness may result from when a firm began performing an activity. Being the first to adopt a product image, for example, may preempt others from doing so and make the firm unique. This is one of Gerber's sources of differentiation in baby food. Early regulatory approval for its soft contact lens gave Bausch and Lomb its differentiation. In other industries, moving late may allow a firm to employ the most modern technology and thereby differentiate. Chapter 5 discusses first-mover and late-mover advantages in more detail.

Location. Uniqueness may stem from location. For example, a retail bank may have the most convenient branch and automatic teller machine locations.

Interrelationships. The uniqueness of a value activity may stem from sharing it with sister business units. Sharing a sales force for both insurance and other financial products, as some leading firms are beginning to do, may allow the salesperson to offer the buyer better service. The analysis of interrelationships is described in Chapter 9.

Learning and spillovers. The uniqueness of an activity can be the result of learning about how to perform it better. Achieving consistent quality in a manufacturing process may be learning-driven, for example. As with cost, the spillover of learning to competitors erodes its contribution to differentiation. Only proprietary learning leads to sustainable differentiation.

Integration. A firm's level of integration may make it unique. Integration into new value activities can make a firm unique because the firm is better able to control the performance of the activities or coordinate them with other activities. Integration may also provide more activities to be sources of differentiation. Providing service in-house instead of leaving it to third party suppliers, for example, may allow a firm to be the only firm to also offer service or to provide service in a unique way compared to competitors. Integration may encompass not only supplier or channel activities, but it may involve performing activities currently performed by the buyer. By connecting hospitals to its computer system and allowing on-line ordering, for example, American Hospital Supply eliminates the need for some buyer activities and differentiates itself. Integration also sometimes makes the achievement of linkages with suppliers and channels easier. Reducing integration relative to competitors may be a source of differentiation in some industries. De-integration may exploit the capabilities of suppliers or independent channels, for example.

Scale. Large scale can allow an activity to be performed in a unique way that is not possible at smaller volume. For example, Hertz's scale in car rental underlies some of its differentiation. Hertz's many locations in all areas of the United States provide more convenient pick-up and drop-off of cars, and faster field service. The relevant type of scale that leads to differentiation will vary—with Hertz it is number of rental and service locations, while in another industry it might be the scale of plant that allows precise tolerances due to high speed equipment. In some cases, however, scale can work against the uniqueness of an activity. Scale may, for example, reduce the flexibility of fashion-related firms to buyer needs.

Institutional factors. Institutional factors sometimes play a role in allowing a firm to be unique. Similarly, a good relationship with its union may allow a firm to establish unique job definitions for employees.

The drivers of uniqueness vary for each activity and may vary across industries for the same activity. The drivers interact to determine the extent to which an activity is unique. A firm must examine each of its areas of uniqueness to see what driver or drivers underlie it. This will be critical to the sustainability of differentiation because some uniqueness drivers provide more sustainability than others. Policy choices may be easier for competitors to imitate than uniqueness stemming from interrelationships or exploiting linkages, for example. Understanding what allows it to be unique will also ensure that a firm does not undermine the causes. Finally, the drivers of uniqueness may suggest new sources of differentiation.

The Cost of Differentiation

Differentiation is usually costly. A firm must often incur costs to be unique because uniqueness requires that it perform value activities better than competitors. Providing superior applications engineering support usually requires additional engineers, for example, while a highly skilled sales force typically costs more than a less skilled one. Achieving greater product durability than competitors may well require more material content or more expensive materials—Rockwell's water meters are more durable than competitors' because they employ more bronze.

Some forms of differentiation are clearly more costly than others. Differentiation that results from superior coordination of linked value activities may not add much cost, for example, nor may better product performance that results from closer parts tolerances achieved through an automated machining center. In diesel locomotives, the higher tolerances achieved through automation improve fuel efficiency at low additional cost. Similarly, differentiating through having more product features is likely to be more costly than differentiating through having different but more desired features.

The cost of differentiation reflects the *cost drivers* of the value activities on which uniqueness is based. The relationship between uniqueness and cost drivers takes two related forms:

- what makes an activity unique (uniqueness drivers) can impact cost drivers
- the cost drivers can affect the cost of being unique

In pursuing differentiation, a firm often affects the cost drivers of an activity adversely and deliberately adds cost. Moving an activity close to the buyer, for example, may raise cost because of the effect of the location cost driver. Smith International achieved differentiation in drill bits by maintaining large and more accessible inventories in the field, raising its cost.

At the same time as uniqueness often raises cost by affecting the cost drivers, the cost drivers determine how costly differentiation will be. A firm's position vis-à-vis cost drivers will determine how costly a particular differentiation strategy will be relative to competitors. The cost of providing the most sales force coverage, for example, will be affected by whether there are economies of scale in the operation of the sales force. If economies of scale exist they may reduce the cost of increased coverage and make such coverage less costly for a firm with a large local market share.

Scale, interrelationships, learning, and timing are particularly important cost drivers in affecting the cost of differentiation. Though scale can itself lead to differentiation, it most often affects the cost of differentiation. Scale can determine the cost of a firm's policy choice to advertise heavily, for example, or the cost of rapid introduction of new models. Sharing also can reduce the cost of differentiation.

IBM's highly trained, experienced sales force is made less expensive by sharing it among a variety of related office products, for example. A firm moving faster down the learning curve in a differentiating activity will gain a cost advantage in differentiating, while moving early may lower the cost of differentiating in areas such as advertising where there is an accumulating stock of goodwill or other intangible assets.

The cost drivers thus play an important role in determining the success of differentiation strategies and have important competitive implications. If competitors have different relative positions vis-à-vis important cost drivers, their cost of achieving uniqueness in the affected activity will differ. Similarly, different forms of differentiation are relatively more or less costly for a firm depending on its situation vis-à-vis the cost drivers of the affected activities. Manufacturing parts with higher precision through automation can be less costly for a firm that can share the computerized machining center via interrelationships than for a firm that cannot. Similarly, Black & Decker has a faster rate of new product introduction than competitors in power tools but this rate is proportionally less costly for Black & Decker because of its leading worldwide market share. In the extreme, a firm may have such a large cost advantage in differentiating a particular value activity that its cost in that activity is actually lower than a firm not attempting to be unique in the activity. This is one reason why a firm can sometimes be both low cost and differentiated simultaneously, as was discussed in Chapter 1.

Sometimes making an activity unique also simultaneously lowers cost. For example, integration may make an activity unique but also lower cost if integration is a cost driver. Where achieving differentiation and reducing cost can take place simultaneously, however, this suggests that (1) a firm *has not been fully exploiting all the opportunities to lower cost;* (2) being unique in an activity was formerly judged undesirable; or (3) a significant innovation has occurred which competitors have not adopted, such as a new automated process that both lowers cost and improves quality.

Firms often fail to exploit opportunities to lower cost through coordination of linked activities that also raises differentiation. Better coordination of quotations, procurement, and manufacturing scheduling may lower inventory cost at the same time as it shortens delivery lead time, for example. More extensive inspection by suppliers may lower a firm's inspection costs at the same time that the reliability of the end product is increased. Unexploited opportunities to reduce cost through linkages that also affect quality, in fact, are the reason underpinning the popular assertion that "quality is free." The possibility of simultaneously raising differentiation and reducing cost through linkages exists, however, because the firm has not been fully exploiting cost reduction opportunities and not because differentiation is not costly.

If a firm has been aggressively reducing its cost, therefore, attempts to achieve uniqueness usually raise cost. Similarly, once competitors imitate a major innovation a firm can remain differentiated only by adding cost. In assessing the cost of differentiation, then, a firm must compare the cost of being unique in an activity with the cost of being equal to competitors.

Buyer Value and Differentiation

Uniqueness does not lead to differentiation unless it is valuable to the buyer. A successful differentiator finds ways of creating value for buyers that yield a price premium in excess of the extra cost. The starting point for understanding what is valuable to the buyer is the *buyer's value chain.* Buyers have value chains consisting of the activities they perform just as a firm does, as discussed in Chapter 2.[3] A firm's product or service is a purchased input to its buyer's value chain. Steel is a raw material that is typically cut, bent, machined, or otherwise converted in its buyer's production process to become part of components and ultimately end products, for example. The buyer's value chain determines the way in which a firm's product is actually used as well as the firm's other effects on the buyer's activities. These determine the buyer's needs and are the underpinnings of buyer value and differentiation.

Although buyer value chains are easiest to visualize for industrial, commercial, or institutional buyers, individual consumers also have value chains. A consumer's value chain represents the sequence of activities performed by a household and its various members in which the product or service fits. To understand how a product fits into a household value chain it is usually necessary to identify those activities

[3]In identifying new or better products, the literature in marketing tends to focus on the physical product and assume the attributes of the product that are desired are known (for a survey see Shocker and Srinivasan [1979]). I focus here on what makes attributes valuable to buyers, and how the firm's total activities can create value.

in which a product is directly or indirectly involved, typically not all the activities a household performs. A television serves as entertainment for various members of a household during some periods of the day, and serves as a background noise during others. The set is typically switched on and off a number of times each day and the channel may be changed frequently. Traveler's checks are typically bought in quantity at a bank and then used occasionally in the course of a vacation or business trip. Redeeming any extra checks after the trip involves a visit to the bank, which means that many checks are saved for future trips instead. A commercial, institutional, or industrial buyer's value chain reflects its strategy and approach to implementation, while a household's value chain reflects its members' habits and needs. What is valuable for either type of buyer, however, grows out of how a product and the firm supplying it affect the buyer's chain.

Buyer Value

A firm creates value for a buyer that justifies a premium price (or preference at an equal price) through two mechanisms:[4]

- by lowering buyer cost[5]
- by raising buyer performance

For industrial, commercial, and institutional buyers, differentiation requires that a firm be uniquely able to *create competitive advantage for its buyer* in ways besides selling to them at a lower price. If a firm is able to lower its buyer's cost or enhance its buyer's performance, the buyer will be willing to pay a premium price. If the components supplied by a well respected bicycle parts supplier allow a bicycle assembler to improve differentiation and thereby charge a higher price, for example, the assembler will be willing to pay a premium for the components. Similarly, the fact that Kodak's Ektaprint copier lowers the cost of a finished set of collated documents with a recirculating document feeder and an in-line automatic stapler that reduces the buyer's personnel cost means that the buyer is willing to pay a premium for the copier. In both instances, the firm was able to enhance the

[4]This same analysis determines the relative value of a substitute product, discussed in Chapter 8. See Chapter 8 for further examples of how firms actually lower buyer costs or raise buyer performance.

[5]Lowering buyer risk of failure is equivalent to lowering buyer cost.

competitive advantage of its buyer even though not selling its product at a cheaper price.

The principle is the same for households and individual consumers, though the measurement of buyer cost and particularly buyer performance may be more subtle. For household buyers, the cost of a product includes not only financial costs but also time or convenience costs. The cost of time for a consumer reflects the opportunity cost of using it elsewhere, as well as the implicit cost of frustration, annoyance, or exertion. Buyer value results from lowering any of these costs for the buyer. A refrigerator that uses less electricity than other refrigerators can command a premium. A vacuum cleaner that saves vacuuming time and reduces exertion is also valuable to the household buyer. Offering direct marketing that saves the buyer shopping time may not be valuable if the buyer enjoys shopping, however.

Raising buyer performance for consumers involves raising their level of satisfaction or meeting their needs. If a TV set's better picture quality and faster warmup time lead to more satisfaction in watching it relative to competitors' sets, for example, the buyer will be willing to pay a premium. Status or prestige are important needs just as are the features of a product or its quality. Although it may be difficult to value buyer performance for consumers, their value chains will suggest the important dimensions of satisfaction.

Industrial, commercial, and institutional buyers sometimes resemble consumers in instances where their objectives are not solely profits or revenue growth. Buyers may value a supplier that provides satisfaction or prestige for executives or other employees even if it does not contribute to the profit of the company. This reflects the differences that often exist between employee and company goals. Similarly, a hospital values a diagnostic device that yields better treatment even if the hospital does not earn higher profit as a result. This reflects both the goal of providing quality patient care and the fact that a large number of hospitals are nonprofit institutions. Many organizations have other goals in addition to profitability even if they are profit making, which may enter into buyer value.

The Value Chain and Buyer Value

A firm lowers buyer cost or raises buyer performance through the impact of its value chain on the buyer's value chain. A firm may affect the buyer's chain by simply providing an input to one buyer activity. Frequently, however, a firm's product will have both direct and indirect impacts on the buyer's chain that go beyond the activity in which the product is actually used. For example, weight is important in a typewriter that is moved from place to place though it is not relevant if one views the buyer activity simply as typing. Moreover, a firm typically impacts the buyer not only through its product but also through such activities as the logistical system, order entry system, sales force, and applications engineering group. Even firm activities representing a small fraction of total cost can have a substantial impact on differentiation. Sometimes the buyer has individual contact with value activities of the firm (e.g., the sales force) while in other cases the buyer only observes the outcome of a group of activities (e.g., the ultimate on-time or late delivery). Thus, the value a firm creates for its buyer is determined by the whole array of links between the firm's value chain and its buyer's value chain, represented schematically in Figure 4–2.

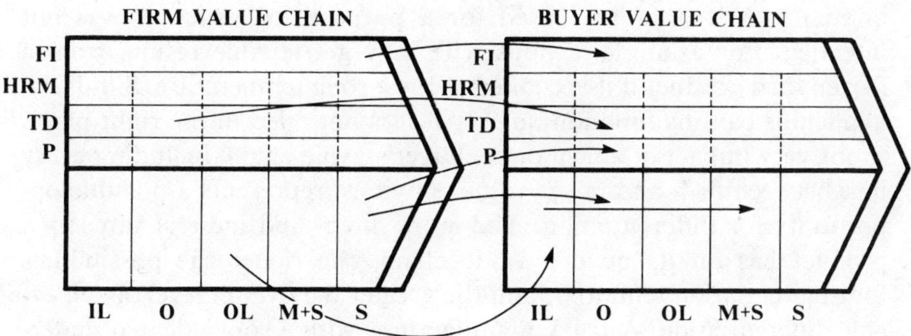

Figure 4–2. Representative Linkages Between the Firm and the Buyer's Value Chain

Heavy trucks offer a useful example of multiple links. A heavy truck directly influences its buyer's logistical costs—a function of the truck's carrying capacity, ease of loading and unloading, fuel costs, and maintenance costs. The truck will also have indirect effects on its buyer's other costs. Its capacity will influence the frequency with which the buyer makes deliveries. The truck may contribute product quality through the amount of shaking it subjects the cargo to, as well as the temperature and humidity conditions in transit. The truck may also affect the buyer's packaging costs, a function of the protection required to avoid damage. Finally, the truck may incrementally affect brand identity through its appearance and the visibility of the logo painted on the side.

Not only will the truck itself affect the buyer's value chain, but several other value activities of the truck manufacturer will probably affect the buyer as well. Spare parts availability will affect the downtime experienced by the buyer. Credit policies will affect the financing cost of the truck. The quality of the truck manufacturer's sales force may well determine their helpfulness in suggesting new maintenance procedures and truck utilization practices. All these links between a truck manufacturer's value activities and the buyer may potentially add to or subtract from buyer cost or performance. The principle also holds true for household buyers.

The links between a firm and its buyer's value chain that are relevant to buyer value depend on how the firm's product is *actually* used by the buyer, not necessarily how it was intended to be used. Even the most carefully designed product can yield unsatisfactory performance if a buyer does not understand how to install, operate, or maintain it or if it is used for a purpose for which it was not intended. For example, a housewife may get terrible results from a frozen food product if it is cooked at the wrong temperature. Similarly, a machine can malfunction quickly if it is not oiled in the right place.

Every impact of a firm on its buyer's value chain, including every link between firm and buyer value activities, represents a possible opportunity for differentiation. The more direct and indirect impacts a product has on its buyer's value chain, the richer the possibilities for differentiation tend to be and the greater the overall level of achievable differentiation. A truck manufacturer with a sophisticated understanding of how it impacts its buyer's value chain, for example, can not only design the truck to provide greater benefits to the buyer, but can perform other value activities such as service, spare parts supply, and financing to be more valuable to the buyer.

Differentiation, then, grows out of all the links between a firm and its buyer in which the firm is unique. The value of being unique in a value activity is its direct and indirect impact on the buyer's cost or performance. A firm's overall level of differentiation is the cumulative value to the buyer of the uniqueness throughout its value chain. This cumulative value can be calculated and provides the upper limit of the price premium the firm can command relative to its competitors. Since the firm must necessarily *share some of the value* it creates with its buyer in order to give the buyer an incentive to purchase, the actual price premium will be somewhat less in practice.

Lowering Buyer Cost

Anything a firm can do that lowers the buyer's total cost of using a product or other buyer costs represents a potential basis for differentiation. Actions that lower the cost of buyer value activities representing a significant fraction of the buyer's cost constitute the most significant opportunities. There are frequently many ways to lower buyer cost if a firm has a sophisticated understanding of how buyers use its product and how its various marketing, delivery, and other activities affect buyer costs.

A firm can lower its buyer's cost in a number of ways:[6]

- Lower delivery, installation, or financing cost
- Lower the required rate of usage of the product
- Lower the direct cost of using the product, such as labor, fuel, maintenance, required space
- Lower the indirect cost of using the product, or the impact of the product on other value activities. For example, a light component may reduce the transport costs of the end product
- Lower the buyer cost in other value activities unconnected with the physical product
- Lower the risk of product failure and thus the buyer's expected cost of failure.

Table 4–1 lists some of the ways in which a firm's product itself can lower the buyer's direct cost of use. In addition to lowering buyer cost through its product characteristics as illustrated by the examples in Table 4–1, a firm can lower its buyer's cost of use through many other value activities. Reliability of deliveries reduces buyer inventory, and short lead times in supplying spare parts reduce downtime. Ordering and billing procedures can reduce the buyer's accounting and procurement costs. American Hospital Supply's on-line ordering system

[6]The ways to lower the buyer's costs are discussed further in Chapter 8, in the parallel case of one product substituting for another. Forbis and Mehta (1979) also contains a useful discussion of some of the issues in lowering buyer cost.

TABLE 4–1 Illustrative Product Characteristics that Lower the Buyers' Direct Cost of Use

Differentiating Factor	Example
Reduced usage of the product to achieve an equivalent benefit (including scrap percentage)	Cut-to-size steel sheets
Faster time to process	Quick attaching fasteners
Lower labor costs of use (lower labor inputs, less training, or lower skilled labor required)	Automatic dialers
Reducing quantity of inputs or ancillary equipment required (e.g. fuel, electricity, required shielding from interference, etc.)	Fuel-efficient refrigerator
Lower required maintenance/spare parts or ease of maintenance	Reliable copiers
Less downtime or idle time	Fast-loading cargo ships
Less required adjustment or monitoring	Uniform-quality paints
Lower failure cost or risk	Blowout preventers for oil wells
Lower installation costs	Single-ply roofing material
Less incoming inspection required	Semiconductors
More rapid setup time	Programmable machine tools
Faster processing time	Tailored aluminum alloys
Reduced risk of damage of other products	Filtration equipment
Higher trade-in value	Durable cars
Compatibility with more types of ancillary equipment	Personal computers

for hospitals, for example, allows purchase orders to be placed by less skilled, lower paid clerks instead of purchasing agents. A firm can also provide buyers with advice or technical assistance that reduces their costs. Intel, for example, has a development system to help buyers design its microprocessors cheaply and rapidly into their products. A firm can also take over buyer functions, in effect forward integrating into the buyer's value chain. In wholesaling, for example, Napco stocks shelves, prices goods, and replaces slow-moving items for its buyers.[7]

A number of more extended examples will illustrate how firms have lowered their buyers' costs and achieved differentiation. Kodak's

[7]Such a strategy presupposes that the firm can perform such activities more cheaply than the buyer can.

copiers, described earlier, lower the buyer's cost of making collated and stapled copies. The industry leader Xerox was more concerned with copying speed itself, which failed to recognize the buyer's full cost of using copiers. In the moving industry, Bekins has offered guaranteed pickup and delivery dates, a fixed price for a move that is quoted in advance, a $100 late payment to the buyer if the move does not occur on time, and reimbursement for damaged goods based on their replacement costs instead of purchase price. All these lower the buyer's direct and indirect cost of a move (and increase peace of mind as well). In fasteners, Velcro uses a system involving many small plastic hooks that connect to a fibrous pad. Velcro fasteners are easier to install than other forms of fastening devices and eliminate the need for skilled labor in the fastening steps on the buyer's assembly line.

In seeking opportunities to lower buyer costs, a firm must chart in detail how its product moves through or affects the buyer's value chain, including the buyer's inventory, handling, technology development, and administrative activities. It must also be familiar with all other products or inputs its product is used with, and understand how its product interfaces with them. The firm must also identify every other value activity in its value chain that affects the buyer's chain.

Raising Buyer Performance

Raising buyer performance will depend on understanding what is desirable performance from the buyer's viewpoint. Raising the performance of industrial, commercial, and institutional buyer depends on what creates differentiation with their buyers. Thus the needs of the buyer's buyer must be understood, requiring the same analysis as the analysis of buyer value. A truck sold to a buyer who is a consumer goods company that uses it to carry goods to retail stores provides an example. If the retail stores desire frequent deliveries, the consumer goods company will be very interested in a truck with carrying capacity to make frequent deliveries at reasonable cost. Similarly, in selling to automobile manufacturers Velcro achieves differentiation because its fasteners are more flexible and allow interior design options for cars that are appreciated by consumers.

Raising performance of industrial, commercial, or institutional buyers can also be based on helping them meet their noneconomic goals such as status, image, or prestige. In heavy trucks, for example,

PACCAR has achieved a high level of differentiation for its Kenworth "K-Whopper" trucks by careful handcrafting and by tailoring them to individual owner specifications. These have little to do with the economic performance of the truck. However, many Kenworth buyers are owner-operators who derive value from the appearance and brand image of their trucks.

For products sold to consumers, raising buyer performance will be a function of better satisfying needs. American Express traveler's checks are used in a stream of consumer activities in which cash needs are irregular, travel plans change, banks are not always available, and a risk of theft or loss exists. American Express differentiates itself because its buyers value the security of redemption anywhere as well as rapid replacement of lost checks. American Express provides easy redemption anywhere via many offices throughout the world that operate long hours.

Buyer Perception of Value

Whatever the value a firm provides its buyers, buyers often have a difficult time assessing it in advance. Even careful inspection and test driving of a truck, for example, does not allow the buyer to assess completely its comfort, durability, fuel usage, and repair frequency. A detailed understanding of how the physical product affects a buyer's cost or performance often requires extensive experience in its use. A buyer faces an even more difficult challenge in knowing how all the other activities a firm performs will affect buyer value. Moreover, a buyer cannot always completely or accurately gauge the performance of a firm and its product even *after* the product has been purchased and used.

Buyers, then, frequently do not fully understand all the ways in which a supplier actually or potentially might lower their costs or improve performance—that is, buyers often do not know what they *should* be looking for in a supplier. While buyers are more likely to understand the direct impacts of a firm on their value chains, they often fail to recognize the indirect impacts or the ways in which other supplier activities besides the product affect them. Buyers can sometimes perceive too much value just as they can fail to perceive enough. For example, buyers sometimes see only the price of a product when measuring its value and do not add up other, more hidden, costs such as freight or installation. The buyer's perception of a firm and its product, therefore, can be as important as the reality of what the firm offers in determining the effective level of differentiation achieved. Moreover, buyers' incomplete knowledge of what is valuable to them can become an opportunity for differentiation strategy, since a firm may be able to adopt a new form of differentiation preemptively and educate buyers to value it.

A buyer's incomplete knowledge implies that the differentiation actually achieved may well be based in part on the factors used by the buyer to *infer* or *judge* whether a firm will lower its cost or improve its performance relative to competitors (or is doing so currently). Buyers use such indications as advertising, reputation, packaging, the professionalism, appearance, and personality of supplier employees, the attractiveness of facilities, and information provided in sales presentations to infer the value a firm will or does create. I term such factors that buyers use to infer the value a firm creates *signals of value.*

Some signals of value require ongoing expenditure by a firm (e.g., packaging, advertising) while others reflect the stock of goodwill or reputation a firm has built up over time. Similarly, some signals of value are not directly controlled by the firm at all (e.g., word of mouth). Signaling may be as necessary, in some industries, to expose hidden costs of a product on which the firm has an advantage over competitors as it is to expose unrecognized benefits. In some, if not many, industries, signals of value are as important as the actual value created in determining realized differentiation. This is particularly true where a firm's impact on buyer cost or performance is subjective, indirect, or hard to quantify, when many buyers are first-time buyers, buyers are unsophisticated, or repurchase is infrequent. Good examples would be legal services, cosmetics, and consulting. However, the need to signal value is present in virtually every industry.

Buyers will not pay for value that they do not perceive, no matter how real it may be. Thus, the price premium a firm commands will reflect both the value actually delivered to its buyer and the extent to which the buyer perceives this value. This is illustrated schematically in Figure 4–3. A firm that delivers only modest value but signals it more effectively may actually command a higher price than a firm that delivers higher value but signals it poorly.

In the long run, the upper limit of the price premium a firm can command reflects its actual impact on buyer value—impact on buyer cost and performance relative to competitors. Through effective signaling of value, a firm may be able to command a price in excess of true value for a time. Eventually, however, the failure of a firm to deliver perceived value to match its price tends to become known, partly through the efforts of competitors.[8] The converse is less true, however. By failing to signal its value effectively, a firm may never realize the price premium its actual value deserves.

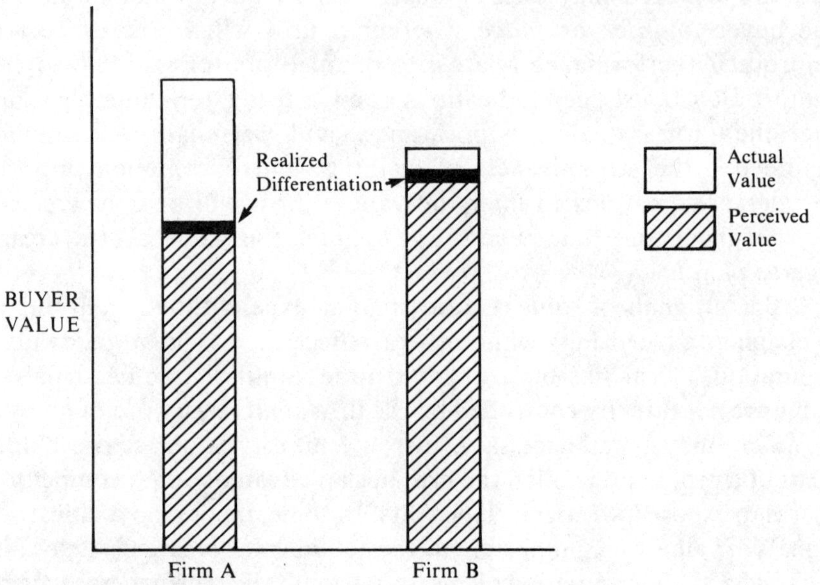

Figure 4–3. Actual Versus Perceived Buyer Value

Buyer Value and the Real Buyer

A firm or household does not purchase a product; individual decision makers do. Both actual value and signals of value are assessed and interpreted by these decision makers. The identity of the specific person or persons who make the purchase decision will influence, if not determine, the value attached to a product. The decision maker

[8]A persistent price in excess of buyer value is usually possible only when a firm and its product's effect on buyer cost or performance are very intangible and hard to measure.

may not necessarily be the person who pays for the product (e.g., the doctor, not the patient, chooses drugs) and may be different from the user (e.g., the purchasing agent chooses a product used in the plant). The channel may also make its own decision about whether to stock a firm's product and whether the firm is a desirable supplier.

Different decision makers will value different things about a supplier and use different signals to assess them. A purchasing agent may not value reliability as highly as a plant manager, for example, because the purchasing agent is more detached from the consequences of product failure. The purchasing agent may be motivated more to keep the cost of purchase to a minimum. There may also be more than one decision maker for a product. Both husband and wife typically decide on buying a house, for example, and travel agents and tour brokers all can play a role in choosing an airline or resort hotel. Similarly, the purchasing department and plant engineer often jointly choose pieces of production equipment. A number of individuals frequently influence the decision maker though they may not participate in the decision directly. Such individuals may be able to veto a supplier, despite the fact that they do not have the power to choose.

Identifying the value a firm creates for the buyer and the signals of value used by the buyer, then, rests on determining the identity of the real buyer. The process of identifying the real buyer often suggests new dimensions of performance that are not immediately apparent if the buyer is viewed as the firm or household. These can include such factors as prestige, personal relationships with supplier personnel that are valued in their own right, and the desire to avoid personal risk in the purchase decision by choosing a well-known supplier. IBM has exploited its position as a "safe" choice as a supplier, for example, as has Kodak in amateur photography. The expertise and sources of information available to the real buyer will also shape what signals of value will be convincing—an engineer might use technical publications and advertising in technical journals as signals while an accounting clerk might be more swayed by polished salespeople and glossy brochures.

Buyer Purchase Criteria

Applying these fundamentals of buyer value to a particular industry results in the identification of buyer purchase criteria—specific attributes of a firm that create actual or perceived value for the buyer. Buyer purchase criteria can be divided into two types:

- *Use criteria.* Purchase criteria that stem from the way in which a supplier affects actual buyer value through lowering buyer cost or raising buyer performance. Use criteria might include such factors as product quality, product features, delivery time, and applications engineering support.
- *Signaling criteria.* Purchase criteria that stem from signals of value, or means used by the buyer to infer or judge what a supplier's actual value is. Signaling criteria might include factors such as advertising, the attractiveness of facilities, and reputation.

Use criteria are specific measures of what creates buyer value. Signaling criteria are measures of how buyers perceive the presence of value. While use criteria tend to be more oriented to a supplier's product, outbound logistics and service activities, signaling criteria often stem from marketing activities. Nonetheless, every functional department of a firm (and most every value activity) can affect both.

The price premium a firm can command will be a function of its uniqueness in meeting both use and signaling criteria. Addressing use criteria without also meeting signaling criteria, a common error, will undermine a buyer's perception of a firm's value. Addressing signaling criteria without meeting use criteria will also usually not succeed because buyers will eventually realize that their substantive needs have gone unmet.

The distinctions among use and signaling criteria are often complex, since many of a firm's activities contribute to meeting use criteria as well as serve as signals of value. A polished sales force, for example, may both signal value and be a valuable source of applications knowledge that will lower the buyer's cost. Similarly, brand reputation may be valuable to a buyer because it removes any blame if a supplier does not perform ("How can you blame me for selecting IBM?"). Despite such situations, however, it is vital to separate use and signaling criteria and the firm's activities that contribute to both, since only use criteria represent true sources of buyer value. *Buyers do not pay for signals of value per se.* A firm must understand how well it meets use criteria and the value created in order to determine an appropriate price premium. The value of meeting signaling criteria is measured differently. The value of a signaling criterion is how much it contributes to the buyer perceiving the value created in meeting use criteria.

Use Criteria

Use criteria grow out of links between a firm's value chain and its buyer's value chain, as described earlier. Because these links are numerous, there are often many use criteria that go well beyond characteristics of the physical product. Use criteria can encompass the actual product (e.g., Dr Pepper's taste difference from Coca-Cola and Pepsi), or the system by which a firm delivers and supports its product, even if the physical product is undifferentiated. While the distinction between a product and other value activities may only be a matter of degree, it remains an important one since other value activities often provide more dimensions on which to differentiate than the physical product. Other value activities besides those associated with the product can represent an important source of differentiation because many firms tend to be preoccupied with the physical product. Use criteria can also include both the specifications achieved by a firm's product (or other value activities) as well as the consistency with which it meets those specifications (conformance). Conformance may be as important as or more important than specifications, although it too is often overlooked as a differentiating factor.

Use criteria can also include intangibles such as style, prestige, perceived status, and brand connotation (e.g., designer jeans), particularly in consumer goods. Intangible use criteria often stem from purchase motivations that are not economic in the narrow sense. Smirnoff Vodka's ability to achieve a premium price for a product that is essentially a commodity stems largely from the social context in which much drinking takes place. Buyers want to be seen consuming sophisticated vodka or to serve vodka perceived as such by their guests. While intangible use criteria are usually associated with consumers, they can be equally important with other buyers. Owning a Gulfstream III business jet can lead to considerable prestige for executives with their peers, for example. Intangible use criteria are most important in industrial, commercial, or institutional products where the real buyer is an individual with considerable discretion in purchasing.

Finally, use criteria also may encompass the characteristics of distribution channels, or downstream value. Since channels can contribute to differentiation, use criteria must reflect these in areas such as channel-provided service, and credit provided by channels. In addition, channels will have their *own* use criteria that measure sources of value in a firm's dealings with them. For example, channels will often want credit, responsiveness to inquiries, or technical support that the end buyer may not notice at all.

Since the performance of a firm in meeting use criteria may also be affected by how the buyer actually uses a product, part of a firm's challenge is to ensure that its product is actually used in a way that allows it to perform to its capabilities. This can be influenced by product design, packaging, and training. Flow control valves, for example, are often designed so they cannot be overtorqued. Factors that improve the chances that a product is used as intended often become use criteria in their own right. They may be potential bases for differentiation since firms often assume that their products are used as intended.

Signaling Criteria

Signaling criteria reflect the signals of value that influence the buyer's perception of the firm's ability to meet its use criteria. Activities a firm performs, as well as other attributes, can be signaling criteria. Signaling criteria may help a particular supplier to be considered and/or may play an important role in the buyer's final purchase decision. Typical signaling criteria include:

- reputation or image
- cumulative advertising
- weight or outward appearance of the product
- packaging and labels
- appearance and size of facilities
- time in business
- installed base
- customer list
- market share
- price (where price connotes quality)
- parent company identity (size, financial stability, etc.)
- visibility to top management of the buying firm

Often signaling criteria can be quite subtle. For example, the paint job on a medical instrument may have an important impact on the buyer's perception of its quality even though the paint job has little or no impact on the instrument's performance. Similarly, Arm & Hammer's brand extension into detergents has been perceived as differentiated in part because a box of it is heavier than competitors' products even though it yields the same number of washes.

Signaling criteria are the most important when buyers have a difficult time measuring a firm's performance, they purchase the product infrequently, or the product is produced to buyer specifications and hence past history with other buyers is an incomplete indication of the future. In professional services, for example, signaling criteria are extremely important. Services are typically customized and actually performed only after the buyer has purchased them. As a result, successful professional service firms pay very close attention to such things as office decor and the appearance of employees. Another industry where signaling criteria are important is pianos, where many buyers are not sophisticated or secure enough to judge quality very accurately. Steinway, the differentiated producer, has recognized the use of pianos by concert pianists as a powerful signaling criterion. Steinway maintains a "piano bank" of grand pianos all over the United States that approved artists can use for concerts at a nominal cost.[9] As a result, Steinway has developed excellent artist relationships, and a large percentage of concerts are performed on Steinway pianos.

Signaling criteria also grow out of the need to reinforce the buyer's perception of a firm even *after* the purchase of the product. Buyers often need continued reassurance that they made a good decision in choosing the firm and the product. They may also need education to help them evaluate the extent to which a product is meeting their use criteria. This is because buyers often remain unable to discern how well a product has met their use criteria even after purchase, and may have insufficient data or may not pay enough attention to notice product performance. Regular communication that describes a firm's contribution for its buyers can often have a major impact on differentiation.[10]

Some signaling criteria are associated with particular use criteria, while others are more generalized signals that a supplier will provide value to the buyer. Advertising may emphasize product characteristics, for example, while a firm's reputation may imply to some buyers that many of their criteria will be satisfied. It is important to attempt to draw the connections between signals of value and the particular use

[9]For a description see Steinway and Sons (1981).

[10]For an interesting discussion of this issue with further examples, see Levitt (1981).

criteria they are signaling. This will both help in identifying additional signals of value, and help the firm understand exactly those attributes its signaling should convey. If a firm recognizes that its customer list is a signal of service reliability, for example, it can present the list in a form that emphasizes this.

Identifying Purchase Criteria

Identification of purchase criteria begins by identifying the decision maker for a firm's product and the other individuals that influence the decision maker. The channels may be an intermediate buyer that must be analyzed as well. Use criteria should be identified first, because they measure the sources of buyer value and also often determine signaling criteria. A number of parallel approaches should be employed to identify use criteria. Internal knowledge of the buyer's needs constitutes an initial source of use criteria. However, conventional wisdom may color internal perception of use criteria; an internal analysis alone is insufficient. No analysis of buyer purchase criteria should ever be accepted unless it includes some direct contact with the buyer. However, even talking to buyers, as essential as it is, is insufficient because buyers often do not fully understand all the ways in which a firm can affect their cost or performance and they may also not tell the truth. In any serious effort to understand buyer purchase criteria, then, a firm must identify the buyer's value chain and perform a systematic analysis of all existing and potential linkages between a firm's value chain and its buyer's chain. This sort of analysis can not only uncover unrecognized use criteria, but also show how to assess the relative weight of well-known use criteria.

Use criteria must be identified *precisely* in order to be meaningful for developing differentiation strategy. Many firms speak of their buyers' use criteria in vague terms such as "high quality" or "delivery." At this level of generality, a firm cannot begin to calculate the value of meeting a use criterion to the buyer, nor can the firm know how to change its behavior to increase buyer value. Quality could mean higher specifications or better conformance, for example. For McDonald's, consistency of hamburger and french fry quality over time and across locations is important as is taste and portion size. Improving these two things involves very different actions by a firm. Service can also mean many things, including backing of claims, repair capability, response time to service requests, and delivery time.

Good performance in meeting each use criteria should be quantified if possible. For example, the quality of a food ingredient might be measured in terms of the particle count of extraneous material or the percentage of fat content.[11] Quantification not only forces careful thinking to determine what precisely the buyer values, but also allows the measurement and tracking of firm performance against a use criterion—this often yields major improvements in performance in and of itself. Quantification also allows a firm to assess its position against competitors in meeting important criteria. The firm can then study the practices that underlie competitors' performance.

A firm can calculate the value of meeting each use criterion by estimating how it affects the buyer's cost or performance. Such calculations inevitably involve judgments, but are an indispensable tool in choosing a sustainable differentiation strategy.[12] Determining the buyer value in meeting each use criterion will allow them to be ranked in order of importance. For some use criteria a firm must only meet a threshold value to satisfy the buyer's need, while for others more performance against them is always better. If a TV set warms up in two seconds, for example, there is little additional benefit if the time is reduced to one second. Nearly all use criteria will reach a point of diminishing returns, however, after which further improvement is not valuable or will actually *reduce* buyer value. Meeting some use criteria may also involve tradeoffs with others. Calculating the buyer value from meeting each use criterion will illuminate the relevant thresholds, tradeoffs, and buyer value that accrues to additional improvement in meeting it. A firm can only make its own assessments of the balance between the value of differentiation and its cost if it understands these things. The ranking of use criteria in terms of the buyer value of meeting them will often contradict conventional wisdom.

Signaling criteria can be identified by understanding the process the buyer uses to form judgments about a firm's potential ability to meet use criteria, as well as how well it is actually meeting them. Examining each use criteria to determine possible signals is a good place to start. If a key use criterion is reliability of delivery, for example, past delivery record and customer testimonials might be signals of value. Two other analytical steps can also provide insight into signals of value. By carefully analyzing the *process by which the buyer pur-*

[11]Even intangible use criteria such as styling can often be quantified—e.g., ratings in industry surveys.

[12]Some quantitative techniques for ranking product attributes have been developed in the marketing literature, though they are based principally on the use of competitive product sales data and customer polling and not on calculating value directly. For a survey, see Shocker and Srinivasan (1979).

chases, including the information sources consulted, the testing or inspection procedures carried out, and the steps in reaching the decision, signals of value may become apparent. This sort of analysis will yield indications about what a buyer consults or notices, including channels. A related way of identifying signaling criteria is to identify *significant points of contact* between a firm and the buyer both before and after purchase, including the channels, trade shows, accounting department, and others. Every point of contact represents an opportunity to influence the buyer's perception of a firm and thus is a possible signaling criterion.

Like use criteria, signaling criteria should be defined as precisely and operationally as possible in order to guide differentiation strategy. In a bank, for example, the appearance of facilities can signal value through its order, permanence, and security. For a designer clothing store, other dimensions of appearance would be more appropriate. Signaling criteria vary in importance, and a firm must rank them in terms of their impact on buyer perception in order to make choices about how much to spend on them. Calculating the contribution of signaling criteria to realized price is often difficult, but focus groups and interviews may be helpful. As with use criteria, meeting signaling criteria can reach the point of diminishing returns. Opulent offices, for example, may disillusion a buyer by making a firm appear wasteful or unprofessional.

The process of identifying buyer purchase criteria should result in a ranking and sorting of purchase criteria such as that in Figure 4–4, which illustrates purchase criteria for a chocolate confection product. Price should be included in the list corresponding to the ranking the buyer places on it. Use and signaling criteria that derive from

	Use Criteria	**Signaling Criteria**
End User	Taste Nutritional Value Texture Appearance *Price* Availability Package Sizes	Advertising Shelf Positioning In-Store Displays Availability
Channels	Speed of Order Processing *Channel Margin* Reliability of Service Promotional Support	Frequency of Sales Calls

Figure 4–4. Ranked Buyer Purchase Criteria for a Chocolate Confection

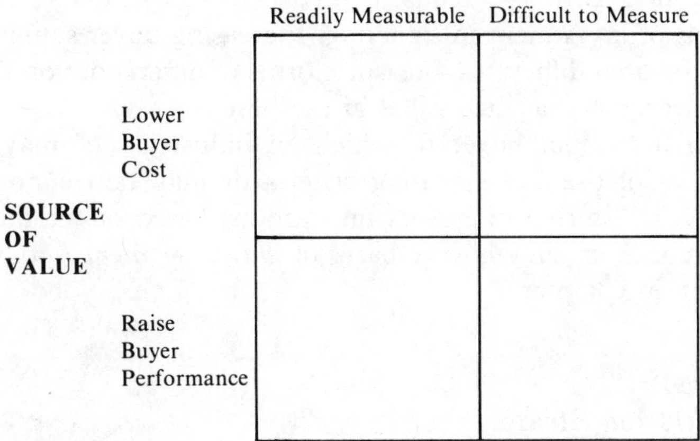

Figure 4–5. The Relationship Between Use Criteria and Buyer Value

the end user and the channel should be separated, to highlight the different entities involved and to clarify the actions required to meet each criterion. Use criteria for both end users and channels can be usefully divided into those factors that lower buyer cost and those that raise buyer performance. While meeting a use criterion can sometimes both lower cost and raise performance, often one or the other modes of value creation is predominant—in the chocolate confection example taste relates to buyer performance while availability is predominantly a measure of buyer shopping cost. Then use criteria can be further divided into those that are easy to measure and those that are difficult for the buyer to perceive and/or quantify (see Figure 4–5).

Recognizing the differences in use criteria represented in Figure 4–5 can be important for a number of reasons. Differentiation that lowers buyer cost provides a more persuasive justification for paying a sustained price premium with some buyers than differentiation that raises performance. Financial pressures on buyers (such as in a downturn) often mean that buyers are willing to pay a premium only to firms that can demonstrate persuasively that they lower buyers' cost. Differentiation with a readily measurable connection to buyer value is also frequently more translatable into a price premium than differentiation that creates value in ways that are hard to perceive or measure.

Differentiation that is difficult to measure tends to translate into a price premium primarily in situations where the buyer perceives a great deal to be at stake, such as in top level consulting or where the buyer is seeking to meet status needs. Differentiation on the right-hand side of Figure 4–5 tends to be expensive to explain, requiring high levels of investment in signaling. Increasing buyer sophistication tends to threaten difficult-to-measure forms of differentiation that may have been accepted at face value in the past.

Each individual buyer to which an industry sells may have a different set of use and signaling criteria or may rank among them differently. Clustering of buyers into groups based on similarities in their purchase criteria is one basis of *buyer segments,* to which I will return in Chapter 7.

Differentiation Strategy

Differentiation stems from uniquely creating buyer value. It can result through meeting use or signaling criteria, though in its most sustainable form it comes from both. Sustainable differentiation requires that a firm perform a range of value activities uniquely that impact those purchase criteria. Meeting some purchase criteria requires that a firm perform just one value activity well—for example, clever advertising. Other purchase criteria are affected by many of a firm's activities. Delivery time, for example, can be influenced by operations, outbound logistics, and order processing, among others.

Many value activities typically play a role in meeting some use or signaling criterion. Figure 4–6 illustrates how purchase criteria can be arrayed against value activities to help a firm identify the activities important to differentiation. The links between the firm's value chain and the buyer's value chain, highlighted earlier, underlie an analysis such as that shown in Figure 4–6.

A firm's overall level of differentiation is the cumulative value it creates for buyers in meeting all purchase criteria. The sources of differentiation in the firm's value chain are often multiple, as illustrated by Stouffer's successful differentiation strategy in frozen entrees (Figure 4–7). Stouffer's has differentiated itself in both use and signaling criteria. Heavy spending on menu development has led to Stouffer's having the highest proportion of unique dishes, as well as superior sauce technology. Care in ingredient selection and preparation has resulted

ACTIVITIES THAT INFLUENCE BUYER PURCHASE CRITERIA

		Inbound Logistics	Operations	Outbound Logistics	Marketing and Sales	Service	Procurement	Technology Development	Human Resource Management	Firm Infrastructure
USE CRITERIA	Conformance to Specifications		X	X		X	X	X	X	
	Delivery time	X	X	X	X		X			
	Product Features		X					X		
	Sales force quality				X				X	
SIGNALING CRITERIA	Sales aids				X			X		
	Attractiveness of Facilities		X							X

Figure 4–6. Relationship of Value Activities to Buyer Purchase Criteria

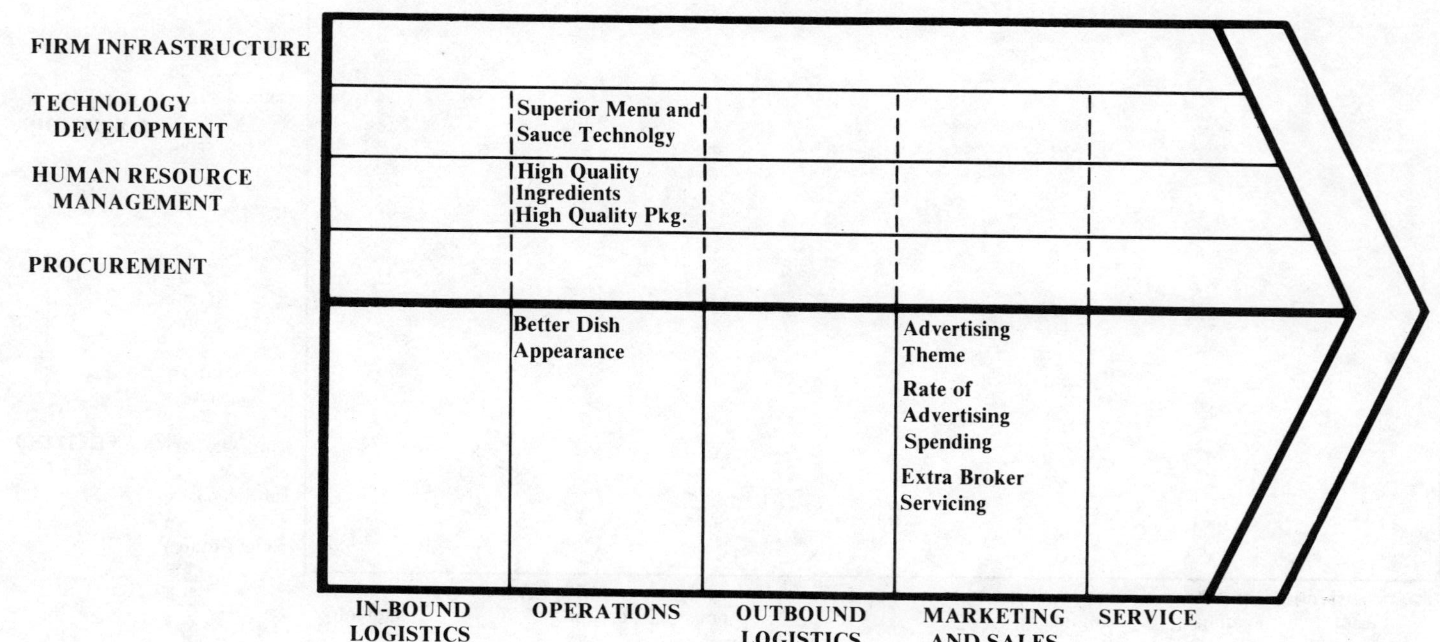

Figure 4–7. Sources of Stouffer's Differentiation in Frozen Entrees

in dishes of attractive, consistent appearance. Meals are more sophisticated in their menus and ingredients. Stouffer's attractive packaging serves as a signal of value, reinforcing its quality image. Stouffer's also pioneered high rates of spending on advertising in a product category where low spending levels had been the norm. It also innovated by advertising its frozen entrees as gourmet meals for busy people rather than as quick, filling meals for the family. Finally, Stouffer's spends a considerable amount on a direct sales force and food brokers in order to gain attractive retail shelf displays, rapid restocking, and the removal of damaged merchandise. These multiple sources of uniqueness in its value chain combine to yield Stouffer's a significant price premium over its competitors. Differentiation has also led to a substantial market share.

Differentiation will lead to superior performance if the value perceived by the buyer exceeds the cost of differentiation. Stouffer's price premium exceeds the extra costs it deliberately incurs in advertising, packaging, ingredients, brokers, and research, and estimates suggest that it has been significantly more profitable than its competitors. Differentiation strategy aims to create the largest gap between the buyer value created (and hence the resulting price premium) and the cost of uniqueness in a firm's value chain. The cost of differentiation will vary by value activity, and the firm should choose those activities where the contribution to buyer value is greatest relative to the cost. This may imply pursuing low cost sources of uniqueness as well as high cost ones that have high buyer value. The cost of differentiating in various ways will depend on the firm's position vis-à-vis cost drivers, which can influence the firm's approach to differentiation and its resulting performance. Stouffer's high share has lowered its cost of advertising, product development, and procurement to the benefit of its performance.

The final component of differentiation strategy is sustainability. Differentiation will not lead to a premium price in the long run unless its sources remain valuable to the buyer and cannot be imitated by competitors. Thus a firm must find durable sources of uniqueness that are protected by barriers to imitation.

Routes to Differentiation

A firm can enhance its differentiation in two basic ways. It may become more unique in performing its existing value activities or it may reconfigure its value chain in some way that enhances its uniqueness. Becoming more unique in its value activities requires that a firm manipulate the drivers of uniqueness described earlier. In both cases, a differentiator must simultaneously control the cost of differentiation so that it translates into superior performance. A number of approaches characterize successful differentiators:

Enhance the Sources of Uniqueness

Proliferate the sources of differentiation in the value chain. A firm can often increase its overall differentiation by exploiting sources of uniqueness in additional value activities. Stouffer's is a good example of how successful differentiation usually stems from cumulating uniqueness in many value activities. Other examples include Caterpillar Tractor, which combines uniqueness in product durability, parts availability, and its dealer network; and Heineken Beer, which combines raw material quality, consistency of taste, rapid shipping time to preserve freshness, heavy advertising, and wide distribution to differentiate in imported beer. Every value activity should be scrutinized for new ways to enhance buyer value. Some semiconductor manufacturers, for example, are offering computer-aided design facilities to their buyers who take over final design steps for their chips.

Make actual product use consistent with intended use. Since the way a buyer actually uses a product will determine its performance, differentiation can often suffer if a firm does not take steps to bring actual and intended use in line:

- Invest in understanding how the product is actually used by buyers
- Modify the product to make it easier to use correctly
- Design effective manuals and other instructions for use, rather than treating them as an afterthought
- Provide training and education to buyers to improve actual use, either directly or via channels.

Employ signals of value to reinforce differentiation on use criteria. A firm cannot gain the fruits of differentiation without adequate attention to signaling criteria. The activities chosen to influence signaling criteria must be consistent with a firm's intended bases for differentiation on use criteria. Pall Corporation, for example, showcases its extensive R&D facilities in the liquid filtration industry through advertising and buyer visits to reinforce its differentiation in product performance. Since the buyer may fail to perceive indirect or hidden costs of a product, signaling may be as necessary to show the lack of value delivered by competitors as it is to show the value delivered by the firm. In addition, a differentiator must provide reassurance about the correctness of the buyer's choice after sale. Signaling is only necessary to the extent that it helps buyers perceive the firm's value, however, and no more.

Employ information bundled with the product to facilitate both use and signaling. Information and information systems are becoming increasingly important tools in differentiation, and bundling information with a product can often enhance differentiation. Effective descriptions of how a product works, how to use it, and how to service it can align intended use with actual use, as discussed above. Giving the product the capacity to generate information as it is used (e.g., a continuous readout of gasoline mileage in a car) can improve the product's use as well as be valuable in its own right. Combining a product with information systems can raise buyer value in other ways as well. American Greetings, for example, provides retailers with an automated inventory management system to help them maintain their stock, thereby raising greeting card sales and at the same time minimizing inventory requirements. Finally, bundling information with a product about how the product was made, how unique it is, or how it performs relative to substitutes is often an effective way of signaling its value. Partagas fine cigars, for example, includes an insert with every box that explains the family history of the owners and how they have brought the Partagas brand from Cuba to the United States.

Make the Cost of Differentiation an Advantage

Exploit all sources of differentiation that are not costly. Many activities can be made more unique at little extra cost. A good case in point is the use of linkages to improve differentiation. A firm may be able to differentiate itself simply by coordinating better internally or with suppliers or channels. Similarly, changing the mix of product features may be less costly than simply adding features. Other high priority targets for enhancing differentiation are activities in which cost is also reduced in the process. Reducing product defects may also reduce service cost, for example.

Minimize the cost of differentiation by controlling cost drivers, particularly the cost of signaling. A firm can minimize the cost of differentiation by recognizing the impact of cost drivers. Firms should differentiate as efficiently as possible by paying careful attention to controlling the cost drivers of activities on which differentiation is based using the principles described in Chapter 3. General Motors, for example, is attempting to lower the cost of product variety through installing flexible manufacturing systems in a number of its auto plants. It is particularly important to find efficient ways of signaling because signaling does not itself create value. Signaling that draws on past investments or reputation (e.g., units in place, cumulative advertising) can be less costly than signaling that arises only from current expenditures.

Emphasize forms of differentiation where the firm has a sustainable cost advantage in differentiating. The cost of differentiating in various ways will differ among competitors. A firm should differentiate in those ways where it has a cost advantage. A large-share firm will have a cost advantage in differentiating in scale-sensitive activities such as advertising and R&D, for example, while a diversified firm may have an advantage in differentiating itself in ways where the cost of doing so is reduced by interrelationships with sister business units.

Reduce cost in activities that do not affect buyer value. In addition to seeking a cost advantage in differentiating, a firm must also pay attention to lowering cost in activities unrelated to the chosen differentiation strategy.

Change the Rules to Create Uniqueness

Shift the decision maker to make a firm's uniqueness more valuable. The identity of the decision maker in part defines what is valuable to the buyer, as well as the appropriate signals of that value. A firm may be able to increase its uniqueness or the perceived value of that uniqueness if it can alter the purchasing process in a way that elevates the role of decision makers who value more the firm's particular forms of uniqueness. A product with highly sophisticated features, for example, may be perceived as more unique and more valuable by an engineer than by a purchasing agent. Shifting the decision maker typically requires modifying a firm's value chain in ways such as the following:

- deploying a new type of salesperson
- involving technical people in the sale
- changing advertising media and content
- changing selling materials
- educating the buyer about new bases for the decision that requires a different decision maker.

Discover unrecognized purchase criteria. Finding important purchase criteria that buyers (and competitors) have not recognized offers a major opportunity to achieve differentiation. It can allow a firm to preempt a new basis for differentiation and gain lasting benefits in image and reputation. Purchase criteria that are unrecognized are often use criteria, particularly those based on the indirect impacts a firm or its product has on the buyer's value chain. Many great differentiation strategies were not passive responses to buyer demands, but were based on new approaches to differentiation. Stouffer's discovered an entirely new way of differentiating frozen entrees, for example, just as Procter & Gamble was the first to advertise hand and body lotion year-round to consumers instead of seasonally. It discovered that hand and body lotion was used by buyers in ways unrecognized in previous strategies.

Preemptively respond to changing buyer or channel circumstances. Buyers or channels whose purchase criteria are changing provide another important opportunity for differentiation strategies. Change creates new bases for differentiation and can lead buyers to take a new look at products that have been routinely purchased from an established supplier. Increased health consciousness by buyers, for example, has led to the rapid penetration of caffeine-free soft drinks. Increased competition in a buyer's industry can also enhance the buyer's need for applications engineering assistance, or raise the value of lowering the buyer's cost. In oil field equipment, for example, increasing financial pressure on buyers has favored suppliers who can demonstrate that they lower buyers' cost. Similarly, buyer sophistication in minicomputers may be reducing the ability to differentiate on the basis of customer service but may be enhancing possibilities for differentiation based on delivery time, cost of use, and other more subtle bases. Differentiation that lowers the buyers cost will often fare best during difficult times for the buyer industry or as buyers get more sophisticated. Similarly, differentiation based on quantifiable performance improvements for the buyer may command a more lasting price premium than that based on intangible performance advantages.

Reconfigure the Value Chain to Be Unique in Entirely New Ways

The discovery of an entirely new value chain can unlock possibilities for differentiation. For example, Federal Express differentiated itself by reconfiguring the traditional value chain for small-parcel delivery completely. It bought its own trucks and aircraft and pioneered the hub concept. It thereby improved timeliness and reliability compared to competitors using scheduled airlines and/or long-distance trucks combined with many distribution points and sorting centers. Hanes's L'eggs pantyhose, with its innovative packaging, distinctive in-store displays, and sales and delivery directly to supermarkets, serves as another example of how a new value chain can be the key to a successful differentiation strategy. Opportunities to achieve dramatic levels of differentiation often result from reconfiguring the value chain.

Conceiving of a new value chain is a creative process. Working backward from the buyer's value chain, a firm should probe for ways it might link with the buyer's chain differently or restructure its own value activities to meet purchase criteria better. Common reconfigurations involve areas such as the following:

- a new distribution channel or selling approach
- forward integration to take over buyer functions or eliminate the channels
- backward integration to control more determinants of product quality
- adoption of an entirely new process technology

The Sustainability of Differentiation

The sustainability of differentiation depends on two things, its continued perceived value to buyers and the lack of imitation by competitors. There is an ever-present risk that buyers' needs or perceptions will change, eliminating the value of a particular form of differentiation. Competitors may also imitate the firm's strategy or leapfrog the bases of differentiation a firm has chosen.

The sustainability of a firm's differentiation vis-à-vis competitors depends on its sources. To be sustainable, differentiation must be based on sources where there are mobility barriers to competitors replicating them. As discussed earlier, the drivers of uniqueness differ in their sustainability while the cost of differentiation may also vary among competitors and affect sustainability. Differentiation will be more sustainable under the following conditions:

The firm's sources of uniqueness involve barriers. Proprietary learning, linkages, interrelationships, and first-mover advantages tend to be more sustainable drivers of uniqueness than simply a policy choice to be unique in an activity as was discussed earlier. Signaling activities such as advertising can also be sustainable because they involve barriers. However, differentiation based too heavily on signaling tends to be vulnerable to increasing buyer sophistication.

The firm has a cost advantage in differentiating. A firm with a sustainable cost advantage in performing the activities that lead to differentiation will enjoy much greater sustainability.

The sources of differentiation are multiple. The overall difficulty of imitating a differentiation strategy depends in part on how many sources of uniqueness a firm has. The sustainability of a differentiation strategy is usually greatest if differentiation stems from multiple sources, rather than resting on a single factor such as product design. A single basis for differentiation provides a strong focal point for competitors. Differentiation that results from coordinated actions in many value activities will usually be more durable, since it requires wholesale changes in competitor behavior to imitate.

A firm creates switching costs at the same time it differentiates. Switching costs are fixed costs incurred by the buyer when it changes suppliers, which allow a firm to sustain a price premium even if its product is equal to that of competitors.[13] If differentiation at the same time creates switching costs, the sustainability of differentiation is increased. Switching costs, like differentiation itself, grow out of the way in which a product is used by the buyer. Activities that make a firm unique can frequently raise the cost of switching since the buyer often tailors its activities to exploit the firm's uniqueness.

The Stouffer's example described earlier provides an illustration of how the sustainability of a firm's sources of differentiation can be assessed (see Figure 4–7). Of Stouffer's sources of differentiation, the most sustainable are probably its menu and sauce technology, its product positioning and brand image, its relationships with prime food brokers, and its cost advantage in advertising because of its leading

[13]See *Competitive Strategy,* Chapters 1 and 6, for descriptions of the sources of switching costs. Switching costs are also discussed in Chapter 8.

market share. Heavy investment by competitors would likely be necessary to replicate these factors if they could be replicated at all. As a result, Stouffer's differentiation has been sustainable over a long period of time. Conversely, Hanes's new packaging of pantyhose and direct distribution to grocery stores were policy choices not protected by proprietary learning, substantial scale advantages in executing them, or other barriers to imitation. Hanes's differentiation has thus been extensively imitated by competitors and has not yielded a significant price premium.

Pitfalls in Differentiation

This chapter has suggested some common pitfalls that afflict firms pursuing differentiation strategies. Most result from an incomplete understanding of the underlying bases of differentiation or its cost.

Uniqueness That Is not Valuable

The fact that a firm is unique at something does not necessarily mean it is differentiated. Uniqueness does not lead to differentiation unless it lowers buyer cost or raises buyer performance as perceived by the buyer. The most persuasive differentiation often stems from sources of value the buyer can perceive and measure, or from difficult-to-measure sources of value that are extensively signaled. A good test of the value of uniqueness is whether a firm can command and sustain a price premium in selling to well-informed buyers.

Too Much Differentiation

If a firm does not understand the mechanisms by which its activities affect buyer value or the perception of value, it may be *too* differentiated. If product quality or service levels are higher than buyers' need, for example, a firm may be vulnerable to competitors with the correct level of quality and a lower price. Unnecessary differentiation is the result of failure to diagnose performance thresholds or diminishing returns in buyer purchase criteria. This, in turn, stems from a lack of understanding of how a firm's activities relate to the buyer's value chain.

Too Big a Price Premium

The price premium from differentiation is a function of value of differentiation and its sustainability. A differentiated competitor will be abandoned by buyers if the premium gets too high. Unless a firm shares some of the value created with the buyer in the form of a more reasonable price, moreover, it may tempt the buyer to backward integrate. The appropriate price premium is a function not only of a firm's extent of differentiation, but also of its overall relative cost position. If a firm does not keep its costs in proximity to competitors', the price premium may grow beyond sustainable levels even if a firm's differentiation is maintained.

Ignoring the Need to Signal Value

Firms sometimes ignore the need to signal value, basing their differentiation strategies on use criteria that are seen as the "real" bases for differentiation. However, signals of value exist because buyers are not willing or able to fully discern differences among suppliers. Ignoring signaling criteria can open a firm to attack from a competitor providing inferior value but having a better understanding of the buyer's purchasing process.

Not Knowing the Cost of Differentiation

Differentiation does not lead to superior performance unless its perceived value to the buyer exceeds its cost. Firms often do not isolate the cost of the activities they perform to differentiate themselves, but instead assume that differentiation makes economic sense. Thus they either spend more on differentiation than they recover in the price premium, or fail to exploit ways of reducing the cost of differentiation through understanding its cost drivers.

Focus on the Product Instead of the Whole Value Chain

Some firms see differentiation only in terms of the physical product, and fail to exploit opportunities to differentiate in other parts of the value chain. As has been discussed, the entire value chain often provides numerous and sustainable bases for differentiation, even if the product is a commodity.

Failure to Recognize Buyer Segments

Buyer purchase criteria and their ranking usually vary among buyers, creating buyer segments. If a firm does not recognize the existence of these segments, its strategy may not meet the needs of any buyer very well, making it vulnerable to focus strategies. The existence of buyer segments does not mean that a firm must choose a focus strategy, but rather that it must base its differentiation on widely valued purchase criteria. The strategic issues raised by industry segmentation will be discussed more extensively in Chapter 7.

Steps in Differentiation

The concepts in this chapter can be summarized by outlining the analytical steps necessary for determining the bases for differentiation and selecting a differentiation strategy.

1. *Determine who the real buyer is.* The first step in differentiation analysis is to identify the real buyer. The firm, institution, or household is not the real buyer, but rather one or more specific individuals within the buying entity who will interpret use criteria as well as define signaling criteria. Channels may also be buyers in addition to the end user.

2. *Identify the buyer's value chain and the firm's impact on it.* A firm's direct and indirect impact on its buyer's value chain will determine the value a firm creates for its buyer through lowering buyer cost or raising buyer performance. A firm must clearly understand all the ways it does or could affect its buyer's value chain, and how possible changes in the buyer's value chain will impact the equation. Channels may play a role in affecting the buyer's chain as well as through linkages with the firm's chain.

3. *Determine ranked buyer purchasing criteria.* Analysis of the buyer's value chain provides the foundation for determining buyer purchase criteria. Purchase criteria take two forms, use criteria and signaling criteria. Uniqueness in meeting use criteria creates buyer value, while uniqueness in meeting signaling criteria allows that value to be realized. Sometimes an analysis of the buyer's value will suggest purchase criteria that the buyer does not currently perceive. Purchase criteria must be identified in terms that are operational, and their link to buyer value calculated and ranked. The analyst must not shrink from finding ways to attach a specific value to performance and cost savings, even for household buyers. The identification of purchase criteria grows out of buyer value chain analysis, buyer interviews, and in-house expertise. The process is iterative, and the list of buyer purchase criteria is refined continuously as an analysis proceeds.

4. *Assess the existing and potential sources of uniqueness in a firm's*

value chain. Differentiation can stem from uniqueness throughout a firm's value chain. A firm must determine which value activities impact each purchase criteria (see Figure 4–6). It must then identify its existing sources of uniqueness relative to competitors, as well as potential new sources of uniqueness. A firm must also identify the drivers of uniqueness, because they bear on the question of sustainability.

Since differentiation is inherently relative, a firm's value chain must be compared to those of competitors. Careful analysis of competitors is also invaluable in understanding how value activities impact the buyer, and in seeing possibilities for creating new value chains. Another technique for uncovering possible new ways to perform value activities is to study analogies—industries producing similar products or selling to the same buyer that may do things differently.

5. *Identify the cost of existing and potential sources of differentiation.* The cost of differentiation is a function of the cost drivers of the activities that lead to it. The firm deliberately spends more in some activities to be unique. Some forms of differentiation are not very costly and pursuing them may even lower cost in ways that the firm has overlooked. Normally, however, a firm must deliberately spend more than it would have to otherwise to be unique. A firm's position vis-à-vis cost drivers will make some forms of differentiation more costly than others relative to competitors.

6. *Choose the configuration of value activities that creates the most valuable differentiation for the buyer relative to cost of differentiating.* A subtle understanding of the relationship between the firm's and the buyer's value chains will allow a firm to select a configuration of activities that creates the largest gap between buyer value and the cost of differentiation. Most successful differentiation strategies cumulate multiple forms of differentiation throughout the value chain, and address both use and signaling criteria.

7. *Test the chosen differentiation strategy for sustainability.* Differentiation will not lead to superior performance unless it is sustainable against erosion or imitation. Sustainability grows out of selecting stable sources of buyer value, and differentiating in ways that involve barriers to imitation or where the firm has a sustainable cost advantage in differentiating.

8. *Reduce cost in activities that do not affect the chosen forms of differentiation.* A successful differentiator reduces cost aggressively in activities that are unimportant to buyer value. This will not only improve profitability, but also reduce the vulnerability of differentiators to attack by cost-oriented competitors because the price premium becomes too large.

5
Technology and Competitive Advantage

Technological change is one of the principal drivers of competition. It plays a major role in industry structural change, as well as in creating new industries. It is also a great equalizer, eroding the competitive advantage of even well-entrenched firms and propelling others to the forefront. Many of today's great firms grew out of technological changes that they were able to exploit. Of all the things that can change the rules of competition, technological change is among the most prominent.

Despite its importance, however, the relationship between technological change and competition is widely misunderstood. Technological change tends to be viewed as valuable for its own sake—any technological modification a firm can pioneer is believed to be good. Competing in "high technology" industries is widely perceived as being a ticket to profitability, while other industries that are "low-technology" are viewed with disdain. The recent success of foreign competition, much of it based on technological innovation, has encouraged companies even more to invest in technology, in some cases uncritically.

Technological change is not important for its own sake, but is important if it affects competitive advantage and industry structure. Not all technological change is strategically beneficial; it may worsen a firm's competitive position and industry attractiveness. High technology does not guarantee profitability. Indeed, many high-technology industries are much less profitable than some "low-technology" industries due to their unfavorable structures.

Technology, however, pervades a firm's value chain and extends beyond those technologies associated directly with the product. There is, in fact, no such thing as a low technology industry if one takes this broader view. Viewing any industry as technologically mature often leads to strategic disaster. Moreover, many important innovations for competitive advantage are mundane and involve no scientific breakthroughs. Innovation can have important strategic implications for low tech as well as hi tech companies.

This chapter will describe some of the important links between technological change and competitive advantage as well as industry structure. It focuses not on particular technologies or on how to manage research and development, but on ways to recognize and exploit the competitive significance of technological change. I present a rather broad view of technology in this chapter because *all* the technologies embodied in a firm's value chain have potential competitive impacts.

The chapter begins by describing the linkage between technology and competition. I examine the relationship of technology to competitive advantage, growing out of technology's role in the value chain and the resulting ability of a firm to achieve low cost and/or differentiation through its value activities. I then show how technology can shape industry structure. With this framework established, the chapter examines methods for selecting a technology strategy. Technology strategy must include choices about what important technologies to invest in, whether to seek technological leadership in them, and when and how to license technology. The chapter then describes how a firm can forecast the path of technological change as an industry evolves, crucial to the selection of technology strategy. Finally, the steps in formulating technology strategy are summarized.

Technology and Competition

Any firm involves a large number of technologies. Everything a firm does involves technology of some sort, despite the fact that one or more technologies may appear to dominate the product or the production process. The significance of a technology for competition is not a function of its scientific merit or its prominence in the physical product. *Any* of the technologies involved in a firm can have a significant impact on competition. A technology is important for competition if it significantly affects a firm's competitive advantage or industry structure.

Technology and the Value Chain

The basic tool for understanding the role of technology in competitive advantage is the value chain. A firm, as a collection of activities, is a collection of technologies. Technology is embodied in every value activity in a firm, and technological change can affect competition through its impact on virtually any activity. Figure 5–1 illustrates the range of technologies typically represented in a firm's value chain.

Every value activity uses some technology to combine purchased inputs and human resources to produce some output. This technology may be as mundane as a simple set of procedures for personnel, and typically involves several scientific disciplines or *subtechnologies.* The materials handling technology used in logistics, for example, may involve such disciplines as industrial engineering, electronics, and materials technology. The technology of a value activity represents one combination of these subtechnologies. Technologies are also embodied in the purchased inputs used in each value activity, both in consumable inputs and in capital items. The technology inherent in purchased inputs interacts with the other subtechnologies to yield the level of performance of the activity.

Technology is embodied not only in primary activities but in support activities as well. Computer-aided design is an example of a technology just coming into use in product development that is replacing traditional ways of developing new products. Various types of technologies also underlie the performance of other support activities, including those not typically viewed as technologically based. Procurement embodies procedures as well as technologies for placing orders and interacting with suppliers. Recent developments in information

	Inbound Logistics	Operations	Outbound Logistics	Marketing & Sales	Service
FIRM INFRASTRUCTURE	Information System Technology Planning and Budgeting Technology Office Technology				
HUMAN RESOURCES MANAGEMENT			Training Technology Motivation Research Information Systems Technology		
TECHNOLOGY DEVELOPMENT		Product Technology Computer-aided Design Pilot Plant Technology	Software Development Tools Information Systems Technology		
PROCUREMENT		Information System Technology Communication System Technology Transportation System Technology			
	Transportation Technology Material Handling Technology Storage and Preservation Technology Communication System Technology Testing Technology Information System Technology	Basic Process Technology Materials Technology Machine Tool Technology Material Handling Technology Packaging Technology Maintenance Methods Testing Technology Building Design/ Operation Technology Information System Technology	Transportation Technology Material Handling Technology Packaging Technology Communication System Technology Information System Technology	Media Technology Audio & Video Recording Technology Communication System Technology Information System Technology	Diagnostic and Testing Technology Communication System Technology Information System Technology

MARGIN

MARGIN

INBOUND LOGISTICS | OPERATIONS | OUTBOUND LOGISTICS | MARKETING & SALES | SERVICE

Figure 5–1. Representative Technologies in a Firm's Value Chain

systems technology offer the possibility of revolutionizing procurement by changing ordering procedures and facilitating the achievement of supplier linkages. Human resource management draws on motivation research and technologies for training. Firm infrastructure involves a wide range of technologies ranging from office equipment to legal research and strategic planning.

Information systems technology is particularly pervasive in the value chain, since every value activity creates and uses information. This is evident from Figure 5–1, which shows information systems technology in every generic category of value activity in the chain. Information systems are used in scheduling, controlling, optimizing, measuring, and otherwise accomplishing activities. Inbound logistics, for example, uses some kind of information system to control material handling, schedule deliveries, and manage raw material inventory. Similarly, an information system is involved in order processing, managing suppliers, and scheduling the service force. Information systems technology also has an important role in linkages among activities of all types, because the coordination and optimization of linkages (Chapter 2) requires information flow among activities. The recent, rapid technological change in information systems is having a profound impact on competition and competitive advantages because of the pervasive role of information in the value chain.

Another pervasive technology in the value chain is office or administrative technology, because clerical and other office functions must be performed as part of many value activities. While office technology can be subsumed under information systems technology, I have separated it because of the propensity to overlook it. Change in the way office functions can be performed is one of the most important types of technological trends occurring today for many firms, though few are devoting substantial resources to it.

The technologies in different value activities can be related, and this underlies a major source of *linkages* within the value chain. Product technology is linked to the technology for servicing a product, for example, while component technologies are related to overall product technology. Thus a technology choice in one part of the value chain can have implications for other parts of the chain. In extreme cases, changing technology in one activity can require a major reconfiguration of the value chain. Moving to ceramic engine parts, for example, eliminates the need for machining and other manufacturing steps in addition to having other impacts on the value chain. Linkages with suppliers and channels also frequently involve interdependence in the technologies used to perform activities.

A good example of the interdependence of technology in value activities is American Airline's Sabre reservations system. American leases terminals to travel agents, which allows automated reservations and ticketing. The system has been a source of differentiation for American. At the same time, however, the same system is used inside American in ticketing and issuing boarding passes as well as in route scheduling. American also sells listings on the system to other airlines.

A firm's technologies are also clearly interdependent with its buyers' technologies. The points of contact between a firm's value chain and its buyer's chain, discussed in the previous chapter, define the areas of potential interdependency of technology. A firm's product technology influences the product and process technology of the buyer and vice versa, for example, while a firm's order processing technology influences and is influenced by the buyer's procurement methods.

Technology, then, is pervasive in a firm and depends in part on both the buyers' channels and suppliers' technology. As a result, the development of technology encompasses areas well outside the boundaries traditionally established for R&D, and inherently involves suppliers and buyers.[1] Some of the technologies embodied in the value chain are industry-specific, to varying degrees, but many are not. Office automation and transportation are just two areas where vital technologies, in large part, are not industry-specific. Hence technology development relevant to a firm often takes place in other industries. All these characteristics of technology have implications for the role of technology in competitive advantage.

Technology and Competitive Advantage

Technology affects competitive advantage if it has a significant role in determining relative cost position or differentiation. Since technology is embodied in every value activity and is involved in achieving linkages among activities, it can have a powerful effect on both cost and differentiation. Technology will affect cost or differentiation if it influences the cost drivers or drivers of uniqueness of value activities described in Chapters 3 and 4. The technology that can be employed in a value activity is often the result of other drivers, such as scale, timing, or interrelationships. For example, scale allows high-speed automatic assembly equipment, while early timing allowed some elec-

[1]Hence the label "technology development" in the generic value chain instead of the more limited phrase "research and development."

tric utilities to harness hydropower while sites were available. In these instances technology is not the source of competitive advantage, but rather an outcome of other advantages. However, the technology employed in a value activity is frequently itself a driver when it reflects a policy choice made independently of other drivers. A firm that can discover a better technology for performing an activity than its competitors thus gains competitive advantage.

In addition to affecting cost or differentiation in its own right, technology affects competitive advantage through *changing or influencing the other drivers* of cost or uniqueness. Technological development can raise or lower scale economies, make interrelationships possible where they were not before, create the opportunity for advantages in timing, and influence nearly any of the other drivers of cost or uniqueness. Thus a firm can use technological development to alter drivers in a way that favor it, or to be the first and perhaps only firm to exploit a particular driver.

Two good examples of the role of technology in altering relative cost position are underway in the aluminum industry and illustrate these points. The dramatic rise in energy costs has made power the largest single cost in aluminum smelting, and transformed a number of firms into high-cost producers because of the cost of their power. The great majority of Japanese aluminum smelters fall into this category, for example. To deal with the problem, Japanese firms have worked actively on carbothermic reduction, a breakthrough technology that dramatically lowers power consumption by converting bauxite and related ores directly into aluminum ingot without the intermediate alumina step. Here a new technology is itself a policy cost driver. Carbothermic reduction by reducing power consumption would also diminish the importance of location and institutional factors as cost drivers because location and government pricing policies for power strongly influence electricity costs.

The other example of the role of technology in cost is occurring in aluminum semifabrications, where a new process technology called continuous casting is emerging as a potential replacement for hot mills. The new process does not appear to result in lower cost at efficient scale, but it is less scale-sensitive. If the process proves successful, it could nullify the scale advantage of large semifabricators and allow plants to be located closer to buyers. This would reduce relatively high transport cost in regions previously served by products shipped from distant facilities. Here the new technology does not appear to be itself a cost driver, but is affecting other drivers (scale and location).

It will influence the cost position of firms asymmetrically depending on their positions vis-à-vis those drivers.

The role of technology in differentiation is illustrated by Federal Express, which reconfigured the value chain in small parcel delivery and achieved faster and more reliable delivery. The new technologies employed in Federal Express's value chain were policy choices, but also had the effect of increasing scale economies and creating a first mover advantage. Thus as Federal Express has gained a large market share, the cost of matching its differentiation has become very high for competitors. This example also demonstrates the point that a major technological development need not involve scientific breakthroughs or even technologies that were not widely available previously. Mundane changes in the way a firm performs activities or combines available technologies often underlie competitive advantage.

Since a firm's technology is often interdependent with its buyers' technology, technological change by the buyer can affect competitive advantage just as can technological change within the firm. This is particularly true in differentiation strategies. For example, a distributor that once differentiated itself by performing pricing and inventory control functions for its retail buyers may lose that differentiation if retailers switch to on-line point-of-sale systems. Similarly, changes in suppliers' technology can add to or subtract from a firm's competitive advantage if they affect the drivers of cost or uniqueness in a firm's value chain.

Tests of a Desirable Technological Change

The link between technological change and competitive advantage suggests a number of tests for a desirable direction of technological change. Technological change by a firm will lead to sustainable competitive advantage under the following circumstances:

The technological change itself lowers cost or enhances differentiation and the firm's technological lead is sustainable. A technological change enhances competitive advantage if it leads to lower cost or differentiation and can be protected from imitation. The factors that determine the sustainability of a technological lead are described below.

The technological change shifts cost or uniqueness drivers in favor of a firm. Changing the technology of a value activity, or changing the product in ways that affect a value activity, can influence the drivers of cost or uniqueness in that activity. Even if the technological change is imitated, therefore, it will lead to a competitive advantage for a firm if it skews drivers in the firm's favor. For example, a new assembly process that is more scale-sensitive than the previous process will benefit a large-share firm that pioneers it even if competitors eventually adopt the technology.

Pioneering the technological change translates into first-mover advantages besides those inherent in the technology itself. Even if an innovator is imitated, pioneering may lead to a variety of potential first-mover advantages in cost or differentiation that remain after its technological lead is gone. First-mover advantages and disadvantages are identified below.

The technological change improves overall industry structure. A technological change that improves overall industry structure is desirable even if it is easily copied.

Technological change that fails these tests will not improve a firm's competitive position, though it may represent a substantial technological accomplishment. Technological change will destroy competitive advantage if it not only fails the tests but has the opposite effect contemplated in the tests, such as skewing cost or uniqueness drivers in favor of competitors. A firm may also find itself in the situation where a technological change may meet one test but worsen a firm's position via another.

Technology and Industry Structure

Technology is also an important determinant of overall industry structure if the technology employed in a value activity becomes widespread. Technological change that is diffused can potentially affect each of the five competitive forces, and improve or erode industry attractiveness. Thus even if technology does not yield competitive advantage to any one firm, it may affect the profit potential of all firms. Conversely, technological change that improves a firm's competitive advantage may worsen structure as it is imitated. The potential effect of technological change on industry structure means that a firm cannot set technology strategy without considering the structural impacts.

Technology and Entry Barriers

Technological change is a powerful determinant of entry barriers. It can raise or lower economies of scale in nearly any value activity. For example, flexible manufacturing systems often have the effect of reducing scale economies. Technological change can also raise economies of scale in the technological development function itself, by quickening the pace of new production introduction or raising the investment required for a new model. Technological change also is the basis of the learning curve. The learning curve results from improvements in such things as layout, yields, and machine speeds—all of which are types of technological change. Technological change can lead to other absolute cost advantages such as low-cost product designs. It can also alter the amount of capital required for competing in an industry. The shift from batch to continuous process technology for producing cornstarch and corn syrup has significantly increased the capital requirements in corn wet milling, for example.

Technological change also plays an important role in shaping the pattern of product differentiation in an industry. In aerosol packaging, for example, technological change has resulted in product standardization and has made the product a near commodity, all but eliminating the ability of contract packagers to differentiate themselves based on product characteristics. Technological change can also raise or lower switching costs. Technological choices by competitors determine the need for buyers to retrain personnel or to reinvest in ancillary equipment when switching suppliers. Technological change can also influence access to distribution by allowing firms to circumvent existing channels (as telemarketing is doing) or, conversely, by increasing industry dependence on channels (if more product demonstration and after-sale service is required, for example).

Technology and Buyer Power

Technological change can shift the bargaining relationship between an industry and its buyers. The role of technological change in differentiation and switching costs is instrumental in determining buyer power. Technological change can also influence the ease of backward integration by the buyer, a key buyer bargaining lever. In the computer service industry, for example, the rapid decline in the cost of computers, driven by technological change, is having a major impact on the ability of firms such as ADP to sell timesharing, since many buyers can now afford their own machines.

Technology and Supplier Power

Technological change can shift the bargaining relationship between an industry and its suppliers. It can eliminate the need to purchase from a powerful supplier group or, conversely, can force an industry to purchase from a new, powerful supplier. In commercial roofing, for example, the introduction of rubber-based roofing membranes has introduced powerful new resin suppliers in place of less powerful asphalt suppliers. Technological change can also allow a number of substitute inputs to be used in a firm's product, creating bargaining leverage against suppliers. For example, the can industry has benefited from fierce competition between the aluminum and steel companies to supply it, brought on by technological change in aluminum cans. Technology investments by firms can also allow the use of multiple suppliers by creating in-house knowledge of supplier technologies. This can eliminate dependence on any one supplier.

Technology and Substitution

Perhaps the most commonly recognized effect of technology on industry structure is its impact on substitution. Substitution is a function of the relative value to price of competing products and the switching costs associated with changing between them, as will be discussed extensively in Chapter 8. Technological change creates entirely new products or product uses that substitute for others, such as fiberglass for plastic or wood, word processors for typewriters, and microwave ovens for conventional ovens. It influences both the relative value/price and switching costs of substitutes. The technological battle over relative value/price between industries producing close substitutes is at the heart of the substitution process.

Technology and Rivalry

Technology can alter the nature and basis of rivalry among existing competitors in several ways. It can dramatically alter the cost structure and hence affect pricing decisions. For example, the shift to continuous process technology in the corn wet milling industry mentioned above has also raised fixed cost, and contributed to greater industry rivalry. A similar increase in fixed cost as a percentage of total cost has accompanied the increasing deadweight tonnage of oil tankers, made possible by improvements in shipbuilding technology. The role of technology in product differentiation and switching costs also is important to rivalry.

Another potential impact of technology on rivalry is through its effect on exit barriers. In some distribution industries, for example, automation of materials handling has raised exit barriers because the materials handling equipment is specialized to the particular goods moving through warehouses. Hence what were once general-purpose facilities have become specialized and capital-intensive facilities.

Technological Change and Industry Boundaries

Technological change plays an important role in altering industry boundaries. The boundary of an industry is often imprecise, because distinctions between an industry's product and substitutes, incumbents and potential entrants, and incumbents and suppliers or buyers are often arbitrary. Nevertheless, it is important to recognize that regardless of where one chooses to draw industry boundaries, technological change can broaden or shrink them.

Technological change widens industry boundaries in a number of ways. It can reduce transportation or other logistical costs, thereby enlarging the geographic scope of the market. This happened in the 1960s and 1970s with the advent of large bulk cargo carriers in shipping. Technological change that reduces the cost of responding to national market differences can help globalize industries.[2] It can also enhance product performance, thereby bringing new customers (and competitors) into a market. Finally, technological changes can increase the interrelationships among industries. In industries such as financial services, computers and telecommunications, technological change is blurring industry boundaries and folding whole industries together. In publishing, automated text processing and printing technologies have made shared printing operations more feasible for several different types of publications. Interrelationships are discussed in greater detail in Chapter 9.

Technology can also narrow industry boundaries. Technological change may allow a firm to tailor the value chain to a particular segment, as will be discussed in Chapter 7. Thus segments can, in effect, become industries. Portable cassette players, for example, have

[2]See *Competitive Strategy,* Chapter 13, and Porter (1985).

become a full-fledged industry independent of larger cassette players and cassette players used in dictating due to technological advancements that improved their performance and widened their usage.

Technological Change and Industry Attractiveness

While it is sometimes believed that technological change always improves industry structure, the previous discussion should make it clear that it is just as likely to worsen industry structure. The effect of technological change on industry attractiveness depends on the nature of its impact on the five forces. If it raises entry barriers, eliminates powerful suppliers, or insulates an industry from substitutes, then technological change can improve industry profitability. However, if it leads to more buyer power or lowers entry barriers, it may destroy industry attractiveness.

The role of technological change in altering industry structure creates a potential conundrum for a firm contemplating innovation. An innovation that raises a firm's competitive advantage may eventually undermine industry structure, if and when the innovation is imitated by other competitors. Firms must recognize the dual role of technological change in shaping both competitive advantage and industry structure when selecting a technology strategy and in making technology investments.

Technology Strategy

Technology strategy is a firm's approach to the development and use of technology. Although it encompasses the role of formal R&D organizations, it must also be broader because of the pervasive impact of technology on the value chain. Because of the power of technological change to influence industry structure and competitive advantage, a firm's technology strategy becomes an essential ingredient in its overall competitive strategy. Innovation is one of the principal ways of attacking well-entrenched competitors, a subject I will return to in Chapter 15. However, technology strategy is only one element of overall competitive strategy, and must be consistent with and reinforced by choices in other value activities. A technology strategy designed to achieve differentiation in product performance will lose much of its impact, for example, if a technically trained sales force is not available to explain the performance advantages to the buyer and if the manufacturing process does not contain adequate provisions for quality control.

Technology strategy must address three broad issues:

- what technologies to develop
- whether to seek technological leadership in those technologies
- the role of technology licensing

Choices in each area must be based on how technology strategy can best enhance a firm's sustainable competitive advantage.

The Choice of Technologies to Develop

At the core of a technology strategy is the type of competitive advantage a firm is trying to achieve. The technologies that should be developed are those that would most contribute to a firm's generic strategy, balanced against the probability of success in developing them. Technology strategy is a potentially powerful vehicle with which a firm can pursue each of the three generic strategies. Depending on which generic strategy is being followed, however, the character of technology strategy will vary a great deal, as shown in Table 5–1.

In many firms, R&D programs are driven more by scientific interests than by the competitive advantage sought. It is clear from Table 5–1, however, that the primary focus of a firm's R&D programs should be consonant with the generic strategy that is being pursued. The R&D program of a cost leader, for example, should include a heavy dose of projects designed to lower cost in all value activities that represent a significant fraction of cost, as well as projects to reduce the cost of product design through value engineering. R&D by a cost leader on product performance must be aimed at maintaining parity with competitors rather than adding costly new features or the goals of R&D will be inconsistent with the firm's strategy.

Another important observation from Table 5–1 is that both product and process technological change can have a role in supporting each of the generic strategies. Firms often incorrectly assume that process technological change is exclusively cost-oriented and product technological change is intended solely to enhance differentiation. Chapter 3 has shown how product technology can be critical in achieving low cost, while Chapter 4 has shown how changes in process

TABLE 5–1 Product and Process Technology and the Generic Strategies

	Cost Leadership	Differentiation	Cost Focus	Differentiation Focus
		Illustrative Technological Policies		
Product Technological Change	Product development to reduce product cost by lowering material content, facilitating ease of manufacture, simplify logistical requirements, etc.	Product development to enhance product quality, features, deliverability, or switching costs	Product development to design in only enough performance for the target segment's needs	Product design to meet the needs of a particular segment better than broadly-targeted competitors
Process Technological Change	Learning curve process improvement to reduce material usage or lower labor input Process development to enhance economies of scale	Process development to support high tolerances, greater quality control, more reliable scheduling, faster response time to orders, and other dimensions that raise buyer value	Process development to tune the value chain to a segment's needs in order to lower the cost of serving the segment	Process development to tune the value chain to segment needs in order to raise buyer value

technology may be the key to differentiation (a favorite tactic of Japanese companies).

It is also important that a firm's technology strategy extend *beyond* product and process R&D as they are traditionally defined. Technology pervades a firm's value chain and relative cost and differentiation are a function of the entire chain. Thus a systematic examination of all a firm's technologies will reveal areas in which to reduce cost or enhance differentiation. The information system department may have more impact on technological change in some firms today than the R&D department, for example. Other important technologies such as transportation, materials handling, communications, and office automation also deserve more than ad hoc or informal attention. Finally, development in all technological areas must be coordinated to ensure consistency and exploit interdependencies among them.

Crown Cork and Seal provides a good example of the link between technology strategy and competitive advantage. Crown focuses on select customer industries and provides cans together with highly responsive service. Crown does little or no basic research and does not pioneer new products. Rather, its R&D department is organized to solve specific customer problems on a timely basis, and to imitate successful product innovations rapidly. Crown's R&D approach, then, closely supports its focus strategy. Its technological policies are quite different from those of American Can or Continental Group, which supply broad lines of packaging in addition to cans. American and Continental invest heavily on research in basic materials and new products.

The selection of specific technologies in the value chain on which to concentrate development effort is governed by the link between technological change and competitive advantage. A firm should concentrate on those technologies that have the greatest *sustainable* impact on cost or differentiation, either directly or through meeting the other tests described earlier. These tests allow a ranking of technological changes that would yield the greatest competitive benefit. The cost of improving the technology must be balanced against the benefit, as well as the likelihood that the improvement can be achieved.

Firms often confront a choice between attempting to improve an established technology for performing a value activity or investing in a new one. In aluminum smelting, for example, a firm might concentrate on improving the Hall-Heroult process now in use, or it might attempt to develop carbothermic reduction. Technologies seem to go through a life cycle in which early major improvements give way to later incremental ones. This argues that the benefit/cost tradeoff in improving mature technologies may be less (though perhaps more certain) than that in improving newer technologies.

This can be a dangerous assumption, however, that is self-fulfilling. A technology can be assumed to be mature only with great caution. Major improvements in the efficiency of the Hall-Heroult process are occurring today, for example, despite the fact that it was developed prior to 1900. Similarly, the fuel efficiency of low-speed diesel engines has risen significantly since 1974. Diesel technology is also over 80 years old and was widely viewed as mature compared to gas turbines, yet diesels have actually increased their lead over turbines. In both these examples, the rapid rise in energy prices stimulated active attention to fuel efficiency. Greater attention to improving the technologies was coupled with improvements in materials technology, instrumentation, and electronics that allowed better process control, higher temperatures, and other benefits.

As noted earlier, most products and value activities embody not one technology but several technologies or subtechnologies. It is only *a particular combination* of subtechnologies that can be assumed to be mature, not individual subtechnologies themselves. Significant changes in any one of the subtechnologies going into a product or process may create new possibilities for combining them that produce dramatic improvements, such as those achieved in smelting and low-speed diesel engines. The advent of microelectronics, a subtechnology that can be applied to many other technologies, is having a profound effect on many industries through unlocking possibilities for new technological combinations.

Thus in choosing among technologies to invest in, a firm must base its decisions on a thorough understanding of each important technology in its value chain and not on simple indicators such as age. Sometimes all that is necessary to produce technological progress is effort and investment, as both examples illustrate. In other cases, advances in subtechnologies may allow improvement in the existing technology. Efforts at improving an older technology can sometimes be futile, however. In such instances the best course of action is to attempt to leapfrog it. The decision by a firm to discard its own technology may be difficult, particularly if it was developed in-house, but such a choice may be essential to maintaining the firm's competitive position.

The choice of technologies to develop should not be limited to those few where there are opportunities for major breakthroughs. Modest improvements in several of the technologies in the value chain, including those not related to the product or the production process, can add up to a greater benefit for competitive advantage. Moreover, cumulative improvements in many activities can be more sustainable than a breakthrough that is noticeable to competitors and becomes an easy target for imitation. The success of Japanese firms in technology is rarely due to breakthroughs, but to a large number of improvements throughout the value chain.

Technological Leadership or Followership

The second broad issue a firm must address in technology strategy is whether to seek technological leadership. The notion of technological leadership is relatively clear—a firm seeks to be the first to introduce technological changes that support its generic strategy. Sometimes all firms that are not leaders are viewed as technological followers, including firms that disregard technological change altogether. Technological followership should be a conscious and active strategy in which a firm explicitly chooses not to be first on innovations, and that is the sense in which it is examined here.

While technological leadership is often thought of in terms of product or process technology, the issue is much broader. Leadership can be established in technologies employed in any value activity. The discussion here is directed at the strategic choice between pioneering innovation in any value activity and waiting for others to pioneer.

The decision to become a technological leader or follower can be a way of achieving either low cost or differentiation, as illustrated in Table 5–2:

TABLE 5–2 Technological Leadership and Competitive Advantage

	Technological Leadership	Technological Followership
Cost Advantage	Pioneer the lowest-cost product design Be the first firm down the learning curve Create low cost ways of performing value activities	Lower the cost of the product or value activities by learning from the leader's experience Avoid R&D costs through imitation
Differentiation	Pioneer a unique product that increases buyer value Innovate in other activities to increase buyer value	Adapt the product or delivery system more closely to buyer needs by learning from the leader's experience

Firms tend to view technological leadership primarily as a vehicle for achieving differentiation, while acting as a follower is considered the approach to achieving low cost. If a technological leader is the first to adopt a new lower-cost process, however, the leader can become the low-cost producer. Or if a follower can learn from the leader's mistakes and alter product technology to meet the needs of buyers better, the follower can achieve differentiation. There can also be more than one technological leader in an industry because of the many technologies involved and the different types of competitive advantage sought.

The choice of whether to be a technological leader or follower in an important technology is based on three factors:[3]

- *Sustainability of the technological lead.* The degree to which a firm can sustain its lead over competitors in a technology.
- *First-mover advantages.* The advantages a firm reaps from being the first to adopt a new technology.
- *First-mover disadvantages.* The disadvantages a firm faces by moving first rather than waiting for others.

All three factors interact to determine the best choice for a particular firm. Significant disadvantages of being a first mover may eliminate the desirability of taking the leadership role even if a firm can sustain its technological lead. Conversely, first-mover advantages may translate an initial technological lead into a sustainable competitive advantage elsewhere though the technological lead itself disappears. First-mover advantages and disadvantages occur most often in the context of technological choices, but their significance for competitive strategy formulation extends beyond technological strategy. They address the wider question of how timing translates into competitive advantage or disadvantage and into entry and mobility barriers.

Sustainability of the Technological Lead

Technological leadership is favored if the technological lead can be sustained because (1) competitors cannot duplicate the technology, or (2) the firm innovates as fast or faster than competitors can catch

[3]The same ideas can be generalized to evaluate pioneering of any kind, such as pioneering in marketing or in the approach to procurement.

up. The second condition is important because technology often diffuses, requiring a technological leader to remain a moving target. Kodak, for example, has maintained leadership in amateur photography in large part through a succession of camera systems and film chemistries, most recently including the disc camera, rather than possessing a single technology competitors could not match. If a technology lead cannot be sustained, technological leadership can only be justified if the initial lead translates into first-mover advantages, because of the greater cost of leadership compared to followership.

The sustainability of a technological lead is a function of four factors:

The Source of Technological Change. The sustainability of a technological lead depends heavily on whether technology is being developed inside the industry or is coming from outside it. An important proportion of technological change comes from external sources such as suppliers, buyers, or completely unrelated industries. In many process industries, for example, the key source of technology is construction engineering firms that design production processes and build plants.

Where important sources of technology are external to an industry, sustaining a technological lead is generally more difficult. External technology sources decouple a firm's access to technology from its technological skills and R&D spending rate, because many companies can get access to external developments. Hence external technological changes act as an equalizer among competitors. Technological leaders in industries with key external sources of technology must capture the best of those sources through coalitions or exclusive arrangements in order to sustain their lead, or have a superior ability to adapt externally developed technology to the industry.

The Presence or Absence of a Sustainable Cost or Differentiation Advantage in Technology Development Activity. A technological lead is more likely to be sustainable if a firm has a cost or differentiation advantage in performing technology development. The tools in Chapters 3 and 4 can be used to analyze a firm's relative cost and differentiation in the development of technology. For example, scale economies or learning effects in technological development give large-share or experienced firms an R&D cost advantage. Where the costs of developing a model are largely fixed, a firm with a large share has proportionally lower R&D costs than a smaller-share firm. It may thus be able to spend more money on R&D in order to maintain its technological lead without a cost penalty. This seems to have occurred in large turbine generators, where General Electric has outspent Westinghouse in absolute terms and maintained a significant technological lead although its R&D as a percentage of sales is still lower than Westinghouse's. Rising costs of product development in an industry also work in favor of large-share firms. As the cost of bringing out a new herbicide has risen to over $30 million, for example, the advantages of the industry leaders in agricultural chemicals are widening.

A firm's relative cost or effectiveness in performing technology development can also be strongly influenced by interrelationships among related business units within the parent company. Interrelationships can allow the transference of skills or sharing of costs of R&D activity. The types of interrelationships involving R&D are described in Chapter 9. Technological leaders often aggressively pursue technological interrelationships, entering new businesses with related technologies. They also create mechanisms for R&D transfer among business units, and tend to invest at the corporate level in core technologies with a potential impact on many business units.

Different parts of the innovation cycle—basic research, applied research, development—tend to offer differing opportunities for sustainable cost advantages in R&D spending. Basic product innovation is often less scale-sensitive than the subsequent rapid introduction of new product types and the incorporation of new features. This is one of the reasons Japanese firms often overtake innovative U.S. firms that fail to maintain their lead in subsequent product improvements. Many successful technological leaders do not reap all of the benefits of scale, learning, or interrelationships in R&D in the form of higher profits, but reinvest to maintain their technological lead. They also exploit any scale or learning advantages in R&D by rapid new model introduction. Honda, for example, has reinforced its competitive advantage in motorcycles through a continual stream of new models.

Relative Technological Skills. A firm with unique technological skills vis-à-vis competitors is more likely to sustain its technological lead than a firm with comparable R&D personnel, facilities, and management to competitors. Technological skills will influence the output from a given rate of spending on technology, regardless of scale, learning, or interrelationship effects. Technological skills are a function of many factors—management, company culture, organizational structure and systems, company reputation with scientific personnel, and others. NEC Corporation, for example, is the company most highly ranked by engineering graduates in Japan. This contributes to its ability to attract the best graduates, reinforcing its strong R&D capability.

Successful technological leaders pay close attention to their stock of R&D skills. They avoid cutting back R&D staff in industry downturns or profit squeezes. They also seek out relationships with the leading scientific centers in appropriate fields, and attempt to develop an image as the best place to work for the types of research personnel that support their technology strategy.

Rate of Technology Diffusion. A final important factor in determining the sustainability of a technological lead is the rate of diffusion of the leader's technology. Superior technological skills or cost advantages in performing R&D are nullified if competitors can easily copy what a firm develops. Diffusion of technology occurs continually, though at different rates depending on the industry. Some of the mechanisms for diffusion of a leader's technology are as follows:

- direct observation by competitors of a leader's products (reverse engineering) and methods of operating
- technology transfer through equipment suppliers or other vendors
- technology transfer through industry observers such as consultants and the trade press
- technology transfer through buyers who desire another qualified source
- personnel losses to competitors or spinoff firms
- public statements or papers delivered by a leader's scientific personnel

The diffusion of technology is often greater for the basic product and process innovations than it is for later improvements. Product and process refinements are more likely to be kept proprietary, particularly when based on process improvements. Since Japanese firms have emphasized constant process innovations, they often develop more sustainable advantages than U.S. or European firms that pioneered the process.

The rate of technological diffusion is partly intrinsic to an industry and partly under a firm's control. Most of the technology of a mobile home producer, for example, is readily observable by examining the product. Disposable diaper technology diffuses more slowly because much of it hinges on the way the product is manufactured on customized machines. Some factors that slow down the rate of diffusion are as follows:

- patenting of the firm's technology and related technologies
- secrecy
- in-house development of prototypes and production equipment
- vertical integration into key parts that embody or give clues to the technology
- personnel policies that retain employees

Successful technological leaders are aggressive in trying to slow down diffusion. They patent extensively where patents can be obtained, and enforce them by *always* challenging infringers. They view all contact with outsiders, even buyers, as a threat to proprietary know-how. Plant tours are a rarity, and even buyers are not told about key innovations. Technological leaders are also often vertically integrated, building or modifying equipment in-house to protect technology, and are discrete in public disclosures. It is striking how many of the firms known to be secretive are also technological leaders. These include DuPont, Kodak, Procter & Gamble, and Michelin.

First-Mover Advantages

Technological leadership is strategically desirable when first-mover advantages exist. These allow a leader to translate a technology gap into *other* competitive advantages that persist even if the technology gap closes. First-mover advantages rest on the role of timing in improving a firm's position vis-à-vis sustainable sources of cost advantage or differentiation. In general terms, a first mover gets the opportunity to *define the competitive rules* in a variety of areas.

The most important types of potential first-mover advantages include the following, and can also accrue to moving first into a geographic area or to pioneering that does not involve technology per se:[4]

Reputation. A firm that moves first may establish a reputation as the pioneer or leader, a reputation that emulators will have difficulty overcoming. Leadership places a firm, at least temporarily, in the posi-

[4]Some of these advantages also accrue to other early movers besides the first.

tion of being unique which can produce long-term image benefits not available to others. A first mover also may be first to serve buyers and thus to establish relationships where there may be loyalty. The significance of any reputation advantage from leadership will depend on the credibility of a firm and its capacity to invest in marketing. A small company may not succeed in enhancing its reputation by moving first because it lacks the resources to publicize its lead.

Preempting a Positioning. A first mover may preempt an attractive product or market positioning, forcing competitors to adopt less desirable ones. Stouffer's preempted the gourmet concept in frozen entrees, for example. A first mover gets the opportunity to shape the way a product is defined or marketed in a way that favors it. A first mover can also put capacity in place to preempt the ability of competitors to profitably expand.

Switching Costs. A first mover can lock in later sales if switching costs are present. In hospital management contracts, for example, the pioneer that signed up hospitals first gained a significant edge in contract renewals because of the substantial costs to the hospital of changing management firms. Switching would result in disruption caused by a new administrator, a new computer system, and other changes.

Channel Selection. A first mover may gain unique channel access for a new product or product generation. It can pick the best brokers, distributors, or retailers, while followers must either accept the second best, establish new channels, or persuade the first mover's channels to shift or divide their loyalties.

Proprietary Learning Curve. A first mover gains a cost or differentiation advantage if there is a proprietary learning curve in value activities that are affected by the early move. The first mover begins down the learning curve first in the affected activities, and may establish a durable cost or differentiation advantage if it can keep its learning proprietary.

Favorable Access to Facilities, Inputs, or Other Scarce Resources. A first mover can often enjoy at least a temporary advantage in access to purchased inputs or other resources, because it contracts for them before market forces reflect the full impact of the change it is pioneering. A firm may get its pick of sites for facilities, for example, or favorable deals with raw material suppliers eager for new business. A good case in point is the airline industry, where the early no-frills carriers have acquired cheap surplus aircraft and/or low-cost terminal space, and hired out-of-work pilots. Market forces will eventually bid up the prices of these inputs as the no-frills strategy is imitated.

Other examples come from several extractive industries. New mines and processing plants are being constructed in increasingly remote locations, raising infrastructure costs. They are also being forced to bear higher environmental costs. Early movers, then, have lower costs.

Definition of Standards. A first mover can define the standards for technology or for other activities, forcing later movers to adopt them. These standards, in turn, make the firm's position more sustainable. For example, RCA defined the standards in color TV which meant that competitors had to go down the learning curve RCA had already started down rather than create a new one.

Institutional Barriers. A first mover may enjoy institutional barriers against imitation. The first mover may secure patents, or being first into a country may give it special status with government. Institutional factors often facilitate a first mover's ability to define standards as well.

Early Profits. In some industries, a first mover may be in a position to enjoy temporarily high profits from its position. It may be able to contract with buyers at high prices during early scarcity of a new item, for example, or sell to buyers who value the new technology very highly.

Successful technological leaders actively pursue first-mover advantages rather than rely solely on their technological edge. They take every opportunity to use their technological leadership to define the competitive rules in ways that benefit them. They invest in marketing to reinforce the reputation benefits of being the leader, and price aggressively to make early sales to buyers with the highest switching costs. It is striking how many firms that were first movers have remained leaders for decades. In consumer goods, for example, such leading brands as Crisco, Ivory, Life Savers, Coca-Cola, Campbell's, Wrigley, Kodak, Lipton, and Goodyear were leaders by the 1920s.

First-mover advantages can be dissipated through aggressive spending by later entrants unless the first mover invests to capitalize on them. As happened to Bowmar in electric calculators, small pioneers are often overwhelmed by later entrants. Their lead is overcome not because first-mover advantages were not present, but because the resources were not present to exploit them. IBM in personal computers is providing a more recent example of a late mover succeeding against early movers based on resources and interrelationships with other business units.

Where the first mover does not have adequate resources, the first early mover with resources can often be the firm to gain the benefits of first-mover advantages. In minicomputers, for example, Digital Equipment did not introduce the first machine but gained many first-mover advantages because it was the first to develop the product aggressively. Digital invested heavily to exploit its advantages through expanding its product line, going down the learning curve, and increasing the size of its sales force. A similar situation occurred in video cassette recorders, where Ampex pioneered the product but Japanese firms invested heavily to improve the technology, produce units cheaply, and translate their lead into first-mover advantages.

FIRST-MOVER DISADVANTAGES

First movers often face disadvantages as well as advantages. First-mover disadvantages stem from two broad sources, the costs of pioneering and the risk that conditions will change.

Pioneering Costs. A first mover often bears substantial pioneering costs, including the following:[5]

- gaining regulatory approvals
- achieving code compliance
- educating buyers
- developing infrastructure in areas such as service facilities and training
- developing needed inputs such as raw material sources and new types of machinery
- investing in the development of complementary products (see Chapter 12)
- high costs of early inputs because of scarcity of supply or small scale of needs

[5]The costs of pioneering are discussed in the context of an emerging industry in *Competitive Strategy,* Chapter 10.

Pioneering costs vary widely depending on the type of technological innovation and can be reduced by sharing them with good competitors (see Chapter 6). However, they are often unavoidable for the first mover.

Demand Uncertainty. A first mover bears the risk of uncertainty over future demand. It must put capacity in place first, while later movers can base their decisions on more current information. Though committing before competitors has some advantages, it also has some significant risks. RCA was the first mover into color TV, for example, betting on an early takeoff of the new technology. Later movers learned from RCA's experience that demand for color sets was some years away and avoided a period of losses.

Changes in Buyer Needs. A first mover is vulnerable if buyer needs change and its technology is no longer valued. A first mover's reputation advantage may also be eliminated if buyers' needs change and the first mover is identified with the old generation of technology. Unless buyer needs shift radically, substantially changing the technology required to serve them, however, a first mover can maintain its lead by modifying technology over time.

Specificity of Investments to Early Generations or Factor Costs. A first mover may be at a disadvantage if early investments are specific to the current technology and cannot be easily modified for later generations. In semiconductors, for example, Philco moved early for leadership with a large automated plant. It enjoyed a period of success, but the later development of a different manufacturing process for semiconductor chips made its earlier investment obsolete. Similarly, the early movers will be disadvantaged if its product or process reflected factor costs or factor quality that have changed.

Technological Discontinuities. Technological discontinuities work against the first mover by making obsolete its investments in the established technology. Technological discontinuities are major shifts in technology that a first mover may be ill prepared to respond to given its investment in the old technology. Discontinuity favors the fast follower who does not bear the high cost of pioneering. Where technology evolves along a relatively continuous path, however, a first mover's head start is an advantage. It can transfer learning from the old technology to the new and stay ahead on the learning curve.

Low-cost Imitation. A first mover exposes itself to followers who may be able to imitate the innovation at lower cost than the cost of innovating. Followers often have to bear some costs of imitation and adaptation, however, which work to the benefit of the first mover.

Licensing of Technology

The third broad issue in technology strategy is technology licensing, a form of coalition with other firms.[6] Firms with a unique technology are often asked for licenses, or are forced to license by government regulations. Licensing is also a way to gain access to technology. Where technology is an important source of competitive advantage, decisions on licensing are vital. Yet many firms have squandered technology-based competitive advantages through inappropriate licensing decisions.

When Should a Firm License?

If technology is a source of competitive advantage, a firm must treat licensing other firms as a risky step that should be taken only under special conditions. Licensing fees are rarely large enough to offset a loss of competitive advantage. However, awarding licenses may be strategically desirable under a number of circumstances.

Inability to Exploit the Technology. Awarding licenses is appropriate if a firm cannot exploit the technology itself. This may be because a firm lacks resources or skills to establish a sustainable position, is harvesting the business unit involved, or competitors are too entrenched to yield market position. The first motivation for licensing is at work today in biotechnology and electronics, where creative startup firms lack the capability to commercialize innovations. Even where the firm has substantial resources, it may be unable to gain a substantial share on the basis of its new technology because competitors are too committed or because of government demands for local ownership. The former seems to be one reason why Standard Brands widely licensed its technology for high fructose corn syrup, a sugar substitute.

Where the firm cannot exploit the market itself, failure to license will create the motivation for competitors to invent around its technol-

[6]Another possible form of coalition is joint technology development with another firm. Joint development involves many of the same issues as licensing.

ogy. Eventually one or more competitors may succeed, and the firm will be left with a small market position. By licensing, however, competitors gain a cheaper and less risky alternative to investing in their own technology. Thus, instead of being imitated, the firm licensing its technology may be able to set the standard and collect licensing royalties in addition to profits from its own market position.

Tapping Unavailable Markets. Licensing may allow a firm to gain some revenue from markets otherwise unavailable to it. This includes other industries where the technology is valuable but where the firm has little possibility of entering, or other geographic markets a firm cannot or does not want to enter.

Rapidly Standardizing the Technology. Licensing may accelerate the process by which the industry standardizes on a firm's technology. If several firms are pushing the technology, licensing not only will legitimize it but also may accelerate its development. The pioneers of the VHS and Beta formats in video cassette recorders licensed them widely to promote standardization, for example, because standardization was so critical to increasing the availability of software.

Poor Industry Structure. Licensing can be desirable where industry structure is unattractive. In such instances, a firm may be better off collecting royalties than investing in a market position that will not yield high returns. The more bargaining power a firm has in extracting high licensing fees, the more attractive it is to license and retain only a modest position in the industry for itself.

Creating Good Competitors. Licensing may be a vehicle for creating good competitors, which in turn can play a variety of important roles such as stimulating demand, blocking entry, and sharing the costs of pioneering. Magnavox widely licensed its video game patents, for example, reasoning correctly that it could expand the market faster through encouraging competitors to introduce a wide range of products. Entry barriers were also low enough that Magnavox was unlikely to be able to develop a sustainable position. Chapter 6 describes the potential benefits of good competitors in detail, along with how a good competitor can be identified.

Quid Pro Quo. A firm may award a license in return for a license of another firm's technology, as ATT and IBM are prone to do. A firm must ensure that the trade is a fair one, however.

Choosing a Licensee

Firms should award licenses only to noncompetitors or to good competitors. Since noncompetitors can rapidly become competitors, a firm must minimize the risk of this through the terms of the license or convince itself that a noncompetitor will remain so. To ensure that a potential licensee is a noncompetitor, a firm must consider not only the existing markets or segments it serves, but also markets it might want to enter in the future. Licensing buyers to make some of their needs internally can sometimes be desirable to shrink the available market for competitors or potential competitors.

Where a firm licenses a competitor, it should be a good competitor and not just anyone. The same is true when a firm is compelled to license by governments. When licensing noncompetitors, a firm ideally should license noncompetitors that would be good competitors if they later decided to enter the industry. Similarly, licenses should contain renewal clauses, when possible, in order to avoid a perpetual commitment to turn over technology in the event that a licensee becomes a competitor.

Pitfalls in Licensing

Firms often hurt rather than help their competitive position by awarding licenses. The two most common pitfalls in licensing are to create competitors unnecessarily in the process, and to give away a firm's competitive advantage for a small royalty fee. Licensing often is an easy way of increasing short-term profits, but it can result in a long-term erosion in profits as a firm's competitive advantage dissipates.

Firms often fail to perceive who their potential competitors are, and thus award licenses that come back to haunt them. They may license foreign firms that later enter their home markets. Similarly, many firms have licensed firms in other industries only to have the licensees ultimately enter their own industry. Often the process by which a license agreement sours can be quite subtle. A firm licenses another amid talk of a long-term alliance that will strengthen both. Over time, though, the licensee learns everything possible, not only about the licensor's technology but about its other value activities. The licensee then decides it can attack the licensor successfully and becomes a serious competitor. Asian firms, which have licensed widely, have sometimes used licenses in this way.

Technological Evolution

Since technological change has such a powerful role in competition, forecasting the path of technological evolution is extremely important to allow a firm to anticipate technological changes and thereby improve its position. Most research on how technology evolves in an industry has grown out of the product life cycle concept. According to the life cycle model, technological change early in the life cycle is focused on product innovations, while the manufacturing process remains flexible. As an industry matures, product designs begin to change more slowly and mass production techniques are introduced. Process innovation takes over from product innovation as the primary form of technological activity, with the aim of reducing the cost of an increasingly standardized product. Finally, all innovation slows down in later maturity and declines as investments in the various technologies in the industry reach the point of diminishing returns.

The product life cycle model has been refined by the work of Abernathy and Utterback.[7] Initially, in their framework, product design is fluid and substantial product variety is present. Product innovation is the dominant mode of innovation, and aims primarily at improving product performance instead of lowering cost. Successive product innovations ultimately yield a "dominant design" where the optimal product configuration is reached. As product design stabilizes, however, increasingly automated production methods are employed, and process innovation takes over as the dominant innovative mode to lower costs. Ultimately, innovation of both types begins to slow down. Recently, the concept of "dematurity" has been added to the Abernathy[8] framework to recognize the possibility that major technological changes can throw an industry back into a fluid state.

While these hypotheses about the evolution of technology in an industry are an accurate portrayal of the process in some industries, the pattern does not apply in every industry. In industries with undifferentiated products (e.g., minerals, many chemicals), the sequence of product innovations culminating in a dominant design does not take place at all or takes place very quickly. In other industries (e.g., military and commercial aircraft, large turbine generators), automated mass production is never achieved and most innovation is product-oriented. Technology evolves differently in every industry, just as other industry

[7]See Abernathy and Utterback (1978).
[8]Abernathy, Clark, and Kantrow (1983).

characteristics do.[9] The pattern of technological evolution is the result of a number of characteristics of an industry, and must be understood in the context of overall industry structural evolution. Innovation is both a response to incentives created by the overall industry structure and a shaper of that structure.

Technological evolution in an industry results from the interaction of a number of forces:

- *Scale change.* As firm and industry scale increase, new product and process technologies may become feasible.
- *Learning.* Firms learn about product design and how to perform various value activities over time with resulting changes in the technology employed.
- *Uncertainty reduction and imitation.* There are natural pressures for standardization as firms learn more about what buyers want and imitate each other.
- *Technology diffusion.* Technology is diffused through a variety of mechanisms described earlier.
- *Diminishing returns to technological innovation in value activities.* Technologies may reach limits beyond which further improvement is difficult.

The product life cycle pattern of technological evolution would result if these forces interacted in the following way. Through successive product innovation and imitation, the uncertainty about appropriate product characteristics is reduced and a dominant design emerges. Growing scale makes mass production feasible, reinforced by the growing product standardization. Technological diffusion eliminates product differences and compels process innovation by firms in order to remain cost competitive. Ultimately, diminishing returns to process innovation set in, reducing innovative activity altogether.

Whether the life cycle pattern of technological innovation or some other pattern will occur in a particular industry will depend on some particular industry characteristics:

Intrinsic Ability to Physically Differentiate. A product that can be physically differentiated, such as an automobile or machine tool, allows many possible designs and features. A less differentiable product will standardize quickly and other forms of technological activity will be dominant.

[9]See *Competitive Strategy,* Chapter 8, for a broader discussion of industry evolution and its causes.

Segmentation of Buyer Needs. Where buyer needs differ substantially, competitors may introduce more and more specialized designs over time to serve different segments.

Scale and Learning Sensitivity. The extent to which the industry technologies are scale- or learning-sensitive relative to industry size will influence the pressure for standardization. High scale economies will create pressure over time for standardization despite segmented buyer needs, while low scale economies will promote the flowering of product varieties.

Technological Linkage Among Value Activities. The technologies in the product and in value activities are often linked. Changing one subtechnology in the product often requires changing others, for example, while changing the production process alters the needs in inbound and outbound logistics. Technological linkages among value activities will imply that changes in one activity will beget or be affected by technology changes in others, affecting the pattern of technological change.

Substitution Logic. The pressure from substitutes (Chapter 8) is an important determinant of the pattern of technological evolution. Whether substitutes are threatening based on cost or differentiation will lead to a corresponding emphasis in technological change. For example, the initial challenge for disposable diapers was to bring their cost into proximity with those of cloth diapers and diaper services. A great deal of early innovation was in manufacturing methods.

Technological Limits. Some technologies offer much richer possibilities for cost or performance improvement than others. In products like commercial aircraft and semiconductors, for example, diminishing returns from efforts at product innovation come relatively slowly. The technological limits in the various technologies and subtechnologies in the value chain will thus affect the path of technological change.

Sources of Technology. A final industry characteristic that shapes the pattern of technological change is the source of the technologies employed in the industry. The path of technological change is usually more predictable when industry-specific technologies are dominant, and the impact of technologies emanating from outside the industry is small.

Continuous Versus Discontinuous Technological Evolution

The pattern of technological evolution differs widely among industries based on whether technological change is incremental or subject to discontinuity. Where there is incremental technological change, the process is more likely to be determined by actions of industry participants or spinoffs from these participants. External sources of technology are likely to be existing suppliers to an industry.

Where there is technological discontinuity, the sources of technology are much more likely to be outside the industry. Entirely new competitors or new suppliers to the industry are more likely to have an important role. Technological discontinuity also tends to decouple the pattern of technological innovation from the state of industry maturity, because outside sources of technology are less responsive to industry circumstances than the R&D departments of industry participants.

Technological discontinuity creates the maximum opportunity for shifts in relative competitive position. It tends to nullify many first-mover advantages and mobility barriers built on the old technology. Discontinuity also may require wholesale changes in the value chain rather than changes in one activity. Hence a period of technological discontinuity makes market positions more fluid, and is a time during which market shares can fluctuate greatly.

Forecasting Technological Evolution

A firm can use this framework to forecast the likely path of technological evolution in its industry. In commercial aircraft, for example, the product is highly differentiable. However, there are large scale economies in product design which limit the number of product varieties that are developed. The flexibility of production means that the production process is no barrier to continuous and long-lasting efforts at product innovation. Thus the aircraft industry is one where we would expect continuous product R&D. The flexibility of the production process would also allow us to expect a continuous search for new materials and components that would be much less likely in an industry with heavy automation.

With some insight into the likely pattern of technological evolution, a firm may be able to anticipate changes and move early to reap competitive advantage. However, there will always be uncertainty wherever technology is involved. Uncertainty over future technological evolution is a major reason why a firm may want to employ industry scenarios in considering its choice of strategies. Industry scenarios are discussed in detail in Chapter 13.

Formulating Technological Strategy

The concepts in this chapter suggest a number of analytical steps in formulating technological strategy in order to turn technology into a competitive weapon rather than a scientific curiosity.

1. *Identify all the distinct technologies and subtechnologies in the value chain.* Every value activity involves one or more technologies. The starting point in formulating technological strategy is to identify all the technologies and subtechnologies, no matter how mundane, that are employed either by the firm or its competitors. In addition, a firm must gain a similar if not as deep understanding of the technologies in its suppliers' and buyers' value chains, which often are interdependent with its own. Firms often focus on product technology or on technology in the basic manufacturing operation. They ignore technologies in other value activities, and pay little attention to the technology for developing technology.

2. *Identify potentially relevant technologies in other industries or under scientific development.* Often technologies come from outside an industry and such technologies can be a source of discontinuous change and competitive disruption in an industry. Each value activity must be examined to see if outside technologies are present that might be applicable. Information systems, new materials, and electronics should always be investigated thoroughly. All three are having a revolutionary impact in creating new technologies or allowing new technological combinations of old technologies.

3. *Determine the likely path of change of key technologies.* A firm must assess the likely direction of technological change in each value activity and in buyer and supplier value chains, including technologies whose sources are unrelated to the industry. No technology should be assumed to be mature. Subtechnologies of it may be changing or maturity may be only a sign of little effort at technological innovation.

4. *Determine which technologies and potential technological changes are most significant for competitive advantage and industry structure.* Not all the technologies in the value chain will have signifi-

cance for competition. The significant technological changes are those that meet the four tests described in this chapter:

- Create a sustainable competitive advantage themselves
- Shift cost or uniqueness drivers in favor of a firm
- Lead to first-mover advantages
- Improve overall industry structure

A firm must isolate these technologies, and understand how they will affect cost, differentiation, or industry structure. Supplier and buyer technologies are often among the most important in this respect. Critical technologies will be those with a major effect on cost or differentiation, and where a technological lead is sustainable.

5. *Assess a firm's relative capabilities in important technologies and the cost of making improvements.* A firm must know its relative strengths in key technologies, as well as make a realistic assessment of its ability to keep up with technological change. Considerations of pride should not obscure such an assessment or a firm will squander resources is an area in which it has little hope of contributing to its competitive advantage.

6. *Select a technology strategy, encompassing all important technologies, that reinforces the firm's overall competitive strategy.* Technology strategy must reinforce the competitive advantage a firm is seeking to achieve and sustain. The most important technologies for competitive advantage are those where a firm can sustain its lead, where drivers of cost or differentiation are skewed in its favor, or where the technology will translate into first-mover advantages. As described earlier, firms can do a lot to reinforce advantages gained through technology through investments in other areas.

Included in a firm's technological strategy should be the following:

- A ranking of R&D projects that reflects their significance for competitive advantage. No project should be approved without a rationale describing its effect on cost and/or differentiation.
- Choices about technological leadership or followership in important technologies.
- Policies toward licensing that enhance overall competitive position rather than reflect short-term profit pressures.
- Means of obtaining needed technology externally, if necessary, through licenses or otherwise.

7. *Reinforce business unit technology strategies at the corporate level.* While technology is ultimately linked to individual business units, a diversified firm can play two key roles to strengthen its overall technological position. The first is to assist in monitoring technologies for possible business unit impacts. A corporate group can usefully invest in identifying and analyzing all streams of technology that might have wide impact, and then feed that information to business units. A corporate role in monitoring such technologies as information systems, office automation, factory automation, materials, and biotechnology is often highly desirable.

The second key corporate role in technological strategy is in finding, exploiting, and creating technological interrelationships among business units. A business unit can gain competitive advantage if it can exploit technological interrelationships with others, as Chapter 9 describes in some detail.

The following specific actions at the corporate, sector, or group level can strengthen a firm's overall technological position:

- Identify core technologies for the corporation that impact many units.
- Ensure that active and coordinated research efforts are underway, and that technology migrates among business units.
- Fund corporate research in important technologies to create a critical mass of knowledge and people.
- Use acquisitions or joint ventures to introduce new technological skills to the corporation, or to invigorate existing skills.

6
Competitor Selection

Competitors are viewed by most firms as a threat. Attention is centered on how a firm can gain share against them and how their entry can be prevented in the first place. Competitors, goes this line of thought, are the enemy and must be eliminated. More market share is also usually seen as being better than less, a viewpoint given reinforcement by adherents of the experience curve.

While competitors can surely be threats, the right competitors can *strengthen* rather than weaken a firm's competitive position in many industries. "Good" competitors can serve a variety of strategic purposes that increase a firm's sustainable competitive advantage and improve the structure of its industry. Accordingly, it is often desirable for a firm to have one or more "good" competitors, and even to deliberately forgo market share rather than to attempt to increase it. More market share can frequently be *worse* than less. At the same time, a firm should concentrate its efforts on attacking "bad" competitors while maintaining relative position vis-à-vis good ones. These principles apply to market leaders and followers alike.

This chapter will describe how a firm can understand and influence its array of competitors to increase its competitive advantage and improve industry structure. It will help a firm identify which are the right competitors to attack, and avoid battling competitors who are benefiting its own position and industry structure. I begin by identifying the potential benefits of having competitors. Next I describe how a firm can recognize a "good" competitor and distinguish it from a bad one. Having laid this groundwork, I show how a firm can influence whom it competes with, and how it can avoid the risk of eroding industry structure in the process of competing. I then identify the considerations that bear on the choice of an optimal configuration of competitors in an industry from a firm's viewpoint, and how it can take actions that preserve industry stability. Finally, the chapter highlights some pitfalls in dealing with competitors that follow from the principles of competitor selection.

Competitors are not only beneficial to competition, but can be more beneficial to a firm than is usually recognized. A firm can never be complacent towards its competitors or stop seeking ways to gain competitive advantage. Sustainable competitive advantage is the only reliable way to achieve superior performance. At the same time, however, a firm must know which competitors to attack, and how the array of competitors it faces will influence industry structure. Each competitor will carry with it different implications for competitive strategy.

The Strategic Benefits of Competitors

The presence of the right competitors can yield a variety of strategic benefits that fall into four general categories: increasing competitive advantage, improving current industry structure, aiding market development, and deterring entry. The particular benefits achieved will differ by industry and the strategy a firm is pursuing.

Increasing Competitive Advantage

The existence of competitors can allow a firm to increase its competitive advantage. The mechanisms are described below, along with the industry characteristics that make them particularly valuable.

Absorb Demand Fluctuations. Competitors can absorb fluctuations in demand brought on by cyclicality, seasonality, or other causes, allowing a firm to utilize its capacity more fully over time. Having competitors is thus a way to control the capacity utilization cost driver described in Chapter 3. Market shares of industry leaders commonly rise during downturns and fall during upturns, for example, a manifestation of this phenomenon. Competitors gain share when the leader's capacity is short during an upturn because the leader cannot or chooses not to meet all the demand. In a downturn, the leader gains share because it is the preferred source and now has capacity available. Letting competitors absorb the fluctuations is often preferable to maintaining the necessary capacity to meet demand over the cycle. However, a firm must ensure enough overall capacity in the industry to serve key buyers and not attract entrants, and that it has enough excess capacity to control industry prices if the product is a commodity.

Enhance the Ability to Differentiate. Competitors can enhance a firm's ability to differentiate itself by serving as a standard of comparison. Without a competitor, buyers may have more difficulty perceiving the value created by a firm, and may, therefore, be more price- or service-sensitive. As a result, buyers may bargain harder on price, service, or product quality. A competitor's product becomes a benchmark for measuring relative performance, however, which allows a firm to demonstrate its superiority more persuasively or lower the cost of differentiation. Competitors, then, can be signals of value for a firm's product (Chapter 4). In consumer industries, for example, the existence of generic brands may actually allow a branded product to sustain higher margins in some circumstances. The benefit of a competitor as a benchmark, however, presupposes that the buyer can perceive product and other differences, and that a firm is really differentiated so that the presence of a benchmark does not expose an unsustainable price premium.

A related situation in which having a competitor enhances differentiation is where a firm is too superior to most of its rivals. It may be difficult to command a large premium over standard-quality producers without a competitor somewhere in between, even if the value created by the firm fully justifies the premium. For example, IBM reportedly had difficulty securing high prices in its management information system software development business until the Big Eight accounting firms entered the industry and charged high prices. The Big Eight had credibility, and their prices made it easier for buyers to accept the premiums IBM was asking over independent software houses.

The benefits of a standard of comparison are most important in industries where accepted standards for product quality and service are not apparent, where a wide range of cost/quality tradeoffs are possible, and where buyers would be prone to price sensitivity in the absence of perceived differentiation. In such industries, pressure from buyers to continually improve products and services in the absence of a benchmark is likely to place downward pressure on a firm's profitability.

Serve Unattractive Segments. A firm's competitors can be happy to serve industry segments that it finds unattractive, but that it would otherwise be forced to serve in order to get access to desirable segments or for defensive reasons. Unattractive segments are those which are costly for the firm to serve, where buyers have bargaining power and price sensitivity, where the firm's position is not sustainable, or where participation undermines a firm's position in more attractive segments. The concepts in Chapter 7 can be used to identify strategically-relevant industry segments and their attractiveness.

A common example of the value of competitors is where particular items in the product line are difficult for a firm to differentiate and do not earn acceptable returns. If buyers must have them, they will seek a supplier for the items that may gain an edge in selling the whole line. A good competitor supplying these items is less threatening than the buyer finding an entirely new source. The essential factor that makes a good competitor valuable in this situation is that demand for items in the line is linked.

In a related situation, a particular buyer group may be price-sensitive and possess bargaining power. Without a good competitor, however, the firm may have to serve the unattractive buyers for defensive reasons to cut off a logical entry avenue for a bad competitor (see Chapter 14). Major mass merchandisers such as Sears, for example, are more powerful and price-sensitive than smaller chains because they are larger and compete with cost rather than differentiation strategies. If a firm serves the large mass merchandisers, it will earn a lower return than it does in serving the smaller chains and its overall profitability will be lower unless the incremental volume from the unattractive buyers is sufficient to improve its overall cost position. However, the large chains provide an inviting target for threatening new entrants unless served effectively by a good competitor.

A typical situation in industries where there is government procurement will illustrate how serving one segment can undermine performance in others. The sealed bids required in selling to government agencies are frequently open to public inspection. Thus the bid prices become known to less price-sensitive industrial buyers, potentially compromising a firm's ability to charge them premium prices. A firm may be better off with a good competitor serving such a segment. Allowing a competitor to serve a segment can also be beneficial in situations where a firm has a weak product offering in the segment that would undermine its credibility in other segments.

A competitor can also be beneficial to a firm if it competes in segments with a buyer group that is particularly costly for a firm to service. If a firm is unable for legal reasons to price-discriminate[1] sufficiently among buyers to reflect differences in servicing cost (e.g., because of the Robinson-Patman Act), or if possibilities for reselling among buyers prevent differential pricing, then a firm's profits are increased if a competitor who can serve them more cheaply or has lower profit standards serves the high-cost customers.

A segment must truly be unattractive structurally to justify the benefits of a competitor, however. Sometimes seemingly unattractive segments are not really unattractive, but rather are being priced or served incorrectly. Rather than have competitors, then, a firm can profit from serving the segments itself. The risks of incorrect pricing are discussed in Chapter 3.

Provide a Cost Umbrella. A high-cost competitor can sometimes provide a cost umbrella that boosts the profitability of a low-cost firm. It is a common view that industry leaders provide a price umbrella for industry followers, and this is indeed the case in some industries.[2] What is less often recognized, however, is that market price is often set by the cost position of the high-cost competitor in stable and particularly in growing industries. If a high-cost competitor prices at or near its costs, the low-cost competitor can earn a substantial margin if it matches that price. Without the high-cost competitor, however, the price sensitivity of buyers may be greater because there is a larger price premium that attracts buyers' attention to price. The cost umbrella from a high-cost competitor is particularly valuable where buyers

[1]Price discrimination is the sale of identical products to different buyers at different prices.

[2]I will have more to say about this below. The vulnerabilities of leaders resulting from this and other practices are discussed in Chapter 14.

(including retailers) desire a second or third source and will therefore give the high-cost competitor a portion of their business.

The risk of letting a high-cost competitor set the price is that this price will attract entry. In order for the strategy to succeed, then, there must be some entry barriers. It is also important that the high-cost competitor gain enough business to remain viable or its demise may attract the entry of a bad competitor.

Improve Bargaining Position with Labor or Regulators. Having competitors can greatly facilitate bargaining with labor and government regulators, where negotiations are partly or wholly industrywide. A leader is vulnerable to being pressured for concessions in union negotiations, or into meeting stringent standards for product quality, pollution control, and so on.[3] The presence of a competitor can have a moderating effect on such demands if the competitor is less profitable, less well capitalized, or more precariously positioned.

Lower Antitrust Risk. The presence of viable competitors may be necessary to reduce the risk of antitrust scrutiny and prosecution, in both government and private suits. Eastman-Kodak and IBM are notable examples of companies that have faced repeated antitrust prosecution that has consumed a great deal of management time and perhaps distracted attention from running the business.[4] Even if the chances of government antitrust prosecution are low, having too large a market share can expose a firm to private litigation every time it takes a significant action such as a new product introduction, technology license, or price change. The risk of litigation often leads high-share firms to be consciously or unconsciously cautious in making moves, to the detriment of their competitive advantage. The presence of a viable competitor would improve the situation.

Increase Motivation. A role of competitors that is hard to overestimate is that of motivator. A viable competitor can be an important motivating force for reducing cost, improving products, and keeping up with technological change. The competitor becomes a common adversary that brings people together to achieve a common goal. Hav-

[3]In the particular case of rate-of-return regulation, allowable rates are often determined by average costs of competitors. Hence having competitors may allow an efficient producer to be more profitable.

[4]For further examples of the effect of antitrust considerations on leader behavior, see Bloom and Kotler (1975).

ing a viable competitor has important psychological benefits inside an organization. Xerox, for example, is showing signs of benefiting from the emergence of serious competitors in copiers. Its manufacturing cost position appears to be improving after years where cost was unimportant to success, and its pace of new product development has quickened. The histories of firms with monopoly or near-monopoly positions, on the other hand, frequently provide examples of situations where a dominant firm was complacent and ultimately blinded to changes to which it failed to respond.

Improving Current Industry Structure

Having competitors can also benefit overall industry structure in a variety of ways:

Increase Industry Demand. The presence of competitors can increase overall industry demand and, in the process, a firm's sales. If primary demand for a product is a function of total industry advertising, for example, a firm's sales can benefit from competitors' advertising. Followers often spend disproportionately on advertising because they are too small to reap economies of scale. A regular stream of product introductions by a firm and competitors may also broaden industry appeal and raise awareness of the industry, boosting demand. Finally, the entrance of competitors can sometimes lend credibility to a product, as the entrance of IBM did with personal computers.

Competitors can also boost industry demand where an industry's product line includes complementary products, as with cameras and film, razors and blades, and laboratory instruments and consumable supplies. A firm with a proprietary position in one product can benefit if one or more competitors sell the complementary product. For example, Kodak has licensed camera technology to allow numerous competitors to sell cameras, thereby stimulating the sales of proprietary Kodak film. This strategy is based on the ability of competitors to enhance primary demand for a complementary good through their collective marketing efforts. The strategy is also a good one where it is difficult to earn an adequate return on the complementary product and thus the firm wants to meet only a portion of the demand itself.[5]

[5]Strategies such as this that link complementary products are described more fully in Chapter 12.

Provide a Second or Third Source. In many industries, particularly those involving important raw materials or other important inputs, buyers want a second or third source in order to mitigate the risk of supply disruptions and/or to hedge against the bargaining power of suppliers. This sort of buyer behavior occurs in turbine generators, metal cans, sugar, and chemicals, for example. The presence of a good competitor as the second or third source takes the pressure off a firm. It can prevent buyers from inviting more threatening competitors into such industries as well as delay or reduce the risk that buyers will backward integrate themselves.

Kyocera, the U.S. subsidiary of Kyoto Ceramics, has experienced the problem of not having credible competitors in supplying the semiconductor industry. Its share of ceramic housings for semiconductor chips is so dominant that U.S. semiconductor companies have been actively searching for new sources, and have actually invested resources to help new suppliers get into the business. With a more credible competitor, Kyocera would have been less vulnerable to such destabilizing behavior by its buyers and perhaps under less scrutiny from them on pricing.

While the examples cited above have been drawn from industrial products, the same issues apply in consumer goods. Retailers often desire more than one brand to provide a counterweight to any one manufacturer's power. Having a good competitor can lower the chances that retailers will actively help other competitors enter the industry through favorable shelf positioning, heavy promotion, and other support.

Reinforce Desirable Elements of Industry Structure. A good competitor can reinfore desirable aspects of industry structure or promote structural change that improves the attractiveness of the industry. For example, a competitor that stresses product quality, durability, and service can help reduce buyer price sensitivity and mitigate price rivalry in the industry. Or a competitor that heavily advertises may hasten the evolution of the industry into one with a few strong brands and high entry barriers. Conversely, a bad competitor can undermine the structure of an industry in the pursuit of its own competitive advantage. In baby foods, for example, Beech-Nut historically reinforced positive aspects of the industry through its high levels of advertising, frequent product introductions, and stable prices before its acquisition by Squibb in the mid-1970s. Heinz, on the other hand, has undermined industry structure with a low cost/low price strategy in a futile effort to overtake Gerber. Squibb's acquisition of Beech-Nut turned Beech-Nut into a bad competitor as well by altering its goals and strategy.

Aiding Market Development

Competitors can help develop the market in emerging industries or in industries where product or process technology is evolving:

Share the Costs of Market Development. Competitors can share the costs of market development for new products or technologies. Market development often involves costs of inducing buyer trial, battling substitutes (see Chapter 8), legal compliance, and promoting the development of infrastructure such as independent repair facilities.[6] In addition, R&D spending is often necessary to refine the basic technology, to overcome switching costs faced by any prospective buyer, and to develop procedures for installation and service that are widely useful. Competitors can lower a firm's cost of market development, particularly if competitors spend disproportionately on it relative to their sales and if their market development efforts are in areas that represent industrywide problems.

Reduce Buyers' Risk. Competitors may be necessary in a new market (or a new technology) in order to provide an alternate source for buyers, even if buyers would not normally require another source later on. Buyers are often reluctant to purchase a new product if only one or two firms produce it, particularly where the cost of switching is high or the buyer would be hurt if a supplier failed to provide adequate service or went out of business.

Help to Standardize or Legitimize a Technology. Having competitors that employ the same technology as a firm can accelerate the process by which the technology is legitimized or becomes the standard. Buyers are often reluctant to accept a technology as the standard when only one firm is backing it, and may hold back from initial purchases to wait for technological change to progress further. When a credible competitor is also pushing the technology (and sharing in the cost of marketing it), buyers' reluctance to adopt it can be much reduced. The move of the pioneers of VHS and Beta format video cassette recorders to license other leading firms to use their

[6]The problems of launching an emerging industry are discussed in *Competitive Strategy,* Chapter 10.

technology is a good example. A competitor with the same technology may also facilitate the process of gaining approvals by government or other standard-setting organizations for the technology.

Promote the Image of the Industry. The right competitors can enhance the image of an industry. Established companies with reputations in other businesses can lend credibility to an industry by signaling that the industry is legitimate and that promises by firms will be met.

The benefits of having competitors during market development are often transient ones, applying most strongly to the emerging or growth phases of an industry's development. Having several competitors may thus be most strategically beneficial early in an industry's development, with the ideal number of competitors declining thereafter.

Deterring Entry

Competitors play a crucial role in deterring other entrants, or enhancing the sustainability of a firm's competitive advantage. The right competitors can contribute to defensive strategy (Chapter 14) in a variety of ways:

Increase the Likelihood and Intensity of Retaliation. Competitors can increase the likelihood and severity of retaliation perceived by potential entrants. Competitors can also act as a first line of defense against new entrants, battling them with tactics such as price cutting that would be prohibitively expensive for a firm with a large market share because its revenues across the board would be reduced. Further, an entrant may be less prone to enter if it faces a number of credible competitors than if it sees a dominant firm that is potentially vulnerable to focus strategies. Dominant firms often have mixed motives in serving particular segments that expose them to focused entrants.[7]

A competitor does not deter other entrants, however, if it is perceived as too weak. Instead, a weak competitor provides a new entrant with an inviting beachhead in the industry though the entrant would not dare to attack the leader directly.

[7]Chapter 15 describes how market leaders can be successfully attacked with focus strategies.

Symbolize the Difficulty of Successful Entry. A competitor can bear witness to the difficulty of successfully competing against a firm, and demonstrate the unspectacular profitability of a follower position. The limited increase in market share and poor profitability of Procter & Gamble's Folgers, for example, is a good lesson in the costs of gaining share in the coffee industry against General Foods' Maxwell House. Without a competitor, a potential entrant may underestimate the height of entry barriers and the competitive strength of the leader.

Block Logical Entry Avenues. Competitors can occupy positions that represent logical entry paths into an industry, blocking them from potential entrants. In the lift truck industry, for example, small lift trucks sold to smaller buyers are a logical entry path. Small lift trucks require less service, and smaller buyers face fewer switching costs in changing suppliers because they often have only one lift truck and face no issues of fleet commonality. Thus the barriers to entry into this segment are lower than into other segments. In this example, however, the moderate profitability of the segment caused leading U.S. manufacturers to neglect it. Unfortunately for U.S. lift truck manufacturers, there was no credible U.S. competitor to block entry into the segment, and Japanese manufacturers successfully used the segment as a way to enter the U.S. market. Even though an industry leader might serve such a segment itself, it may be more profitable for the leader to cede the segment to a good competitor if the segment is structurally less attractive than the core business (see Chapter 7).

Competitors can also fill product niches that would themselves be too small for the leader, or in relation to which the leader faces mixed motives. Having competitors filling these niches increases the difficulty of entry because a potential entrant is forced to enter with a "me too" product, instead of having a protected niche in which to create a base for expansion.[8] The desire of buyers for a second or third source also opens up logical entry avenues for competitors. Having a good competitor to fulfill this role can deter more threatening entrants.

Crowd Distribution Channels. Having a competitor gives distributors and/or retailers multiple brands, and may make it more difficult for a new entrant to gain access to distribution. Where there are only one or two firms in an industry, on the other hand, the channels

[8]The effect of product proliferation in breakfast cereals on entry is analyzed by Schmalensee (1978).

may welcome new competitors to mitigate the bargaining power of the leaders or to supply private label merchandise. The presence of competitors can thus force a new entrant to bear much higher costs of gaining channel access because the channels already have a full complement of brands.

It may also be desirable for a leader to supply private label goods as a defensive move if no good competitor is present to serve the private label market. Despite this, many leaders tend to avoid private label business because they see it as undercutting the position of their branded goods, as RCA and Zenith reasoned in TV sets. This can be too narrow a viewpoint when the risks of future entry are considered; in TV sets, Sears actively encouraged Japanese entry into the U.S. color set market because of its inability to source a quality private label set from RCA, Zenith, or other capable U.S. manufacturers.

What Makes a "Good" Competitor?

Competitors are not all equally attractive or unattractive. A good competitor is one that can perform the beneficial functions described above without representing too severe a long-term threat. A good competitor is one that challenges the firm not to be complacent but is a competitor with which the firm can achieve a stable and profitable industry equilibrium without protracted warfare. Bad competitors, by and large, have the opposite characteristics.

No competitor ever meets all of the tests of a good competitor. Competitors usually have some characteristics of a good competitor and some characteristics of a bad competitor. Some managers, as a result, will assert that there is no such thing as a good competitor. This view ignores the essential point that some competitors are a lot better than others, and can have very different effects on a firm's competitive position. In practice, a firm must understand where each of its competitors falls on the spectrum from good to bad and behave accordingly.

Tests of a Good Competitor

A good competitor has a number of characteristics. Since its goals, strategy, and capabilities are not static, however, the assessment of whether a competitor is good or bad can change.

Credible and Viable. A good competitor has sufficient resources and capabilities to be a motivator to the firm to lower cost or improve differentiation, as well as to be credible with and acceptable to buyers. The competitor cannot serve as a standard of comparison or aid in market development unless it has the required resources to be viable in the long term and unless buyers view it as at least a minimally acceptable alternative. The credibility and viability of a good competitor are particularly important to its ability to deter new entry. A competitor must have resources sufficient to make its retaliation a credible threat to new entrants and it must represent an acceptable alternative to buyers if they are to forgo looking for new sources. Finally, a competitor must be strong enough to keep the firm from becoming complacent.

Clear, Self-Perceived Weaknesses. Though credible and viable, a good competitor has clear weaknesses relative to a firm which are *recognized.* Ideally, the good competitor believes that its weaknesses will be difficult to change. The competitor need not be weaker everywhere, but has some clear weaknesses that will lead it to conclude that it is futile to attempt to gain relative position against a firm in the segments the firm is interested in.

Understands the Rules. A good competitor understands and plays by the rules of competition in an industry, and can recognize and read market signals. It aids in market development and promotes the existing technology rather than attempting strategies that involve technological or competitive discontinuities in order to gain position.

Realistic Assumptions. A good competitor has realistic assumptions about the industry and its own relative position. It does not overestimate industry growth potential and therefore overbuild capacity, or underinvest in capacity and in so doing provide an opening for newcomers. A good competitor also does not overrate its capabilities to the point of triggering a battle by attempting to gain share, or shy from retaliating against entrants because it underestimates its strengths.

Knowledge of Costs. A good competitor knows what its costs are, and sets prices accordingly. It does not unwittingly cross-subsidize product lines or underestimate overhead. As in the areas described above, a "dumb" competitor is not a good competitor in the long run.

A Strategy that Improves Industry Structure. A good competitor has a strategy that preserves and reinforces the desirable elements of industry structure. For example, its strategy might elevate entry barriers into the industry, emphasize quality and differentiation instead of price cutting, or mitigate buyer price sensitivity through the nature of its selling approach.

An Inherently Limiting Strategic Concept. A good competitor's strategic concept inherently limits it to a portion or segment of the industry that is not of interest to the firm, but that *makes strategic sense* for the competitor. For example, a competitor following a focus strategy based on premium quality might be a good competitor if it does not want to expand its share.

Moderate Exit Barriers. A good competitor has exit barriers that are significant enough to make its presence in the industry a viable deterrent to entrants, but yet not so high as to completely lock it into the industry. High exit barriers create the risk that the competitor will disrupt the industry rather than exit if it encounters strategic difficulty.

Reconcilable Goals. A good competitor has goals that can be *reconciled* with the firm's goals. The good competitor is satisfied with a market position for itself which allows the firm to simultaneously earn high returns. This often reflects one or more of the following characteristics of a good competitor:

HAS MODERATE STRATEGIC STAKES IN THE INDUSTRY. A good competitor does not attach high stakes to achieving dominance or unusually high growth in the industry. It views the industry as one where continued participation is desirable and where acceptable profits can be earned, but not one where improving relative position has great strategic or emotional importance. A bad competitor, on the other hand, views an industry as pivotal to its broader corporate goals. For example, a foreign competitor entering what it perceives to be a strategic market is usually a bad competitor. Its stakes are too high, and it may also not understand the rules of the game.

HAS A COMPARABLE RETURN-ON-INVESTMENT TARGET. A good competitor seeks to earn an attractive return on investment and does not place greater priority on gaining tax benefits, employing family members, providing jobs, earning foreign exchange (e.g., some government-owned competitors), providing an outlet for upstream products, or other goals that translate into unacceptable profits in the industry. A competitor with compatible profit objectives is less likely to undercut prices or make heavy investments to attack a firm's position. Differences in goals make McDonnell-Douglas a much better competitor to Boeing in aircraft than the state-owned Airbus Industries, for example.

ACCEPTS ITS CURRENT PROFITABILITY. A good competitor, while seeking to earn attractive profits, is typically satisfied with its current returns and knows that improving them is not feasible. Ideally the competitor is satisfied with profitability that is somewhat lower than the firm's in segments that they jointly serve. In such a situation the competitor is not prone to upset the industry equilibrium in order to improve its relative profitability, and its modest returns may serve to discourage entry by new competitors.

DESIRES CASH GENERATION. A good competitor is interested enough in generating cash for its stockholders or corporate parent that it will not upset industry equilibrium with major new capacity or a major product line overhaul. However, a good competitor does not harvest its position in the industry because this will threaten its credibility and viability.

HAS A SHORT TIME HORIZON. A good competitor does not have so long a time horizon that it will fight a protracted battle to attack a firm's position.

IS RISK-AVERSE. A good competitor is concerned about risk and will be satisfied with its position rather than take large risks to change it.

Smaller divisions of diversified firms can often be good competitors if they are not viewed as essential to long-term corporate strategy. They are often given tough profitability targets and expected to generate cash flow. Divisions that are slotted for growth may be bad competitors, however. Squibb's acquisition of Beech-Nut's baby food business was predicated on the perception that Beech-Nut had significant growth potential. This led Beech-Nut to take some actions that proved unsuccessful but that undermined the industry.

Even a competitor with considerable strengths can be a good competitor if it has the right goals and strategy. Its goals and strategy create a situation where a firm and the competitor can coexist. A clear and self-perceived weakness is thus not a prerequisite for a good competitor. Conversely, however, a competitor with a very long time horizon, little short-run need for cash flow, or a willingness to take substantial risks is usually a bad competitor from the point of view of achieving a stable industry equilibrium, whether or not it has any real strengths.

Sometimes a competitor can be a good competitor to a firm but the firm is not a good competitor to it. One competitor plays by the rules, but the other attacks it anyway. Industries are most stable when firms are mutually good competitors—the segment one competitor focuses on is profitable for it but not of interest to the other, for example. Mutually good competitors play to their respective strengths and succeed at doing so given their respective internal standards.

"Good" Market Leaders

These tests of a good competitor also shed light on what makes a good market leader from the perspective of followers. If a firm is not in a position to be among the leaders in the industries it serves, its success may well be highly dependent on picking industries with good leaders. The single most important quality of a good leader from a follower's perspective is that the leader has goals and a strategy that provide an umbrella under which the follower can live profitably. For example, a leader with high return-on-investment goals, concern for the "health of the industry," a strategy built upon differentiation, and a disinclination to serve certain industry segments due to mixed motives will offer opportunities for followers to earn attractive returns in a relatively stable industry environment. Conversely, a leader that fails to understand the benefits of viable followers, that is satisfied with low returns, or whose strategy works in other ways to erode industry structure is unlikely to provide an attractive environment for followers. For example, a leader pursuing a strategy based on going down the learning curve rapidly through low prices in an industry where buyers are powerful and price-sensitive will often destroy the industry for followers (and perhaps for itself).

Diagnosing Good Competitors

Diagnosing whether a rival is a good competitor requires a complete competitor analysis. A competitor's goals, assumptions, strategy, and capabilities all play a part in determining whether it is a good or bad competitor for a particular firm.[9] Since no competitor ever meets all the tests of a good competitor completely, it is necessary to decide whether a competitor's desirable characteristics outweigh those that undermine the industry or a firm's position.

A number of examples may serve to illustrate the process of weighing and balancing a competitor's characteristics to reach a net assessment of whether it is good, bad, or somewhere in between. In the computer industry, Cray Research seems to be a good competitor for IBM, while Fujitsu is a bad competitor. Cray is a viable rival that plays by accepted rules in a focused segment of the industry, and does not appear to misjudge its ability to take on IBM. Fujitsu, on the other hand, has high stakes in succeeding against IBM, low standards for profitability in markets it is attempting to penetrate, and a strategy that may worsen industry structure by undermining differentiation.

In the copier industry, Kodak is a relatively good competitor for Xerox. Kodak is concentrating on the high-volume end of the market and emphasizing quality and service. Though it has taken some profitable market share away from Xerox, Kodak has high rate-of-return standards and is playing by the same rules as Xerox. Thus it has pushed Xerox to improve its quality. Moreover, Kodak does not appear to view copiers as a linchpin of an office automation strategy that would justify accepting low profits, but as a profitable business area in its own right.

In fertilizer and chemicals, conversely, oil companies have proven to be bad competitors. They have had excess cash to invest, and have looked for big markets in which they could gain large market shares so as to have a noticeable impact on their financial statements. Instead of emphasizing R&D and customer service, most oil companies have competed on price and accelerated the commoditization of the industries they entered. They have also had poor forecasting ability, and tended to build huge new plants during the peaks of the business cycle rather than acquiring facilities during troughs. This has meant that they have created or exacerbated problems of excess capacity.

The competitive situation in CT scanners illustrates a case where a follower seems to understand the benefits of a good market leader. The Israeli company Elscint has gained a number two or three market position. GE is the leader in the industry, and Elscint has publicly

[9] Competitor analysis is described in detail in *Competitive Strategy,* Chapters 3 through 5.

disclaimed a desire to overtake GE. Elscint views GE as a good market leader because it maintains high prices, differentiates based on service and reputation, and has invested heavily to educate and develop the market. Another historically good market leader is Coca-Cola. Coke avoided price competition and vigorous retaliation against followers' moves, opting for a statesman's role instead. Pepsi Cola, Dr Pepper, and Seven-Up enjoyed many years of stable profits as followers. Perhaps as a result of Pepsi's misjudgment in attempting to take too much share from Coke combined with the ascendance of new top management, however, Coke is showing signs of becoming much more aggressive. Pepsi's apparent triggering of Coke's change of behavior illustrates a pitfall in dealing with good competitors that I will discuss further below.

If competitors are bad enough, even a firm with a significant competitive advantage may find it unattractive to compete in an industry. In mushrooms, for example, Ralston-Purina had some potential advantages but faced many family firms with low return-on-investment standards as well as imports from Taiwan and the People's Republic of China. Ralston finally exited the industry.

Influencing the Pattern of Competitors

The benefits of good competitors suggest that it may be desirable for a firm to attack some current competitors and not others, and to encourage the entry of new competitors provided they meet the tests of a good competitor. Since it is usually desirable to have more competitors early in an industry's development than during maturity, it may also make sense to encourage the early entry of competitors that will not be able to succeed in the long run. Nothing in these statements implies that a firm should be complacent toward competitors, or that a firm should not aggressively seek to increase competitive advantage. Rather, the principles of competitor selection imply that a firm must adopt a more sophisticated perspective towards its competitors than is commonly done.

Who a firm competes with is determined by a wide range of factors, many of which are largely outside a firm's control. Which competitors choose to enter an industry is, to a considerable extent, a matter of the luck of the draw, as will be discussed in Chapter 14 in more detail. Whether or not a particular firm perceives an industry to be attractive at a particular time and has the resources available to enter is partly a matter of chance. Once a few competitors have entered, however, others may no longer perceive the industry as an opportunity, particularly if the early entrants were credible firms. If a firm can somehow influence who enters early, then, the entire pattern of entry into the industry may be changed.

Competitor selection seeks not only to influence the pattern of entry, but to influence which competitors gain the market share necessary to be viable and which segments they compete in.[10] The following tactics to select competitors are available in many industries:

Technology Licensing. A firm can license its technology early to good competitors under favorable terms (see Chapter 5). If it picks the right competitors, further entry may be effectively deterred. Given the desire of buyers for a second or third source in semiconductors, for example, licensing is relatively common in that industry and careful choice of licenses can have a beneficial effect. In an interesting recent move, Intel has licensed IBM and Commodore to make the 8088 microprocessor. Here the licenses are having the effect of making *buyers* competitors in a sense, but blocking other more threatening competitors in the process.

Selective Retaliation. A firm can retaliate vigorously against bad competitors, leaving good competitors to enter or gain share unopposed. The firm's choice of products to introduce or geographic markets to enter will often impact one competitor more than another, for example.

Selective Entry Deterrence. A firm can refrain from investing in creating entry barriers to those segments where the presence of a good competitor can improve the firm's position. The risk is that the wrong competitor chooses to occupy the undefended segments, as part of a more ambitious sequenced entry strategy.[11]

Coalitions to Draw in New Entrants. A firm can contract with a good potential competitor to become a source of supply for some item in the product line, to be sold through a firm's distribution channels. This competitor may then logically expand to serve other seg-

[10]See Chapter 14 for a fuller discussion of defensive strategy.
[11]See Chapter 14.

ments undesirable to the firm. Other forms of coalitions that can encourage good competitors include sourcing agreements for components, and private label arrangements where a competitor supplies goods sold under a firm's name. Both can have the effect of lowering barriers to entry for a good competitor.

Damaging Good Competitors in Battling Bad Ones

It is often difficult to battle bad competitors without the battle spilling over to harm good competitors. An increase in advertising, new product introduction, or change in warranty policy designed to thwart a bad competitor, for example, can reduce a good competitor's market share or even threaten its viability. Weakening the good competitor in turn may erode the attractiveness of the industry or invite new entry.

It is important, therefore, to tailor offensive or defensive moves against bad competitors to minimize their impact on good competitors. Sometimes this is impossible, because of the segments a bad competitor is threatening or the seriousness of the threat. However, the challenge is to maintain the delicate balance between improving a firm's position and vigorously responding to threats, on the one hand, and preserving good competitors, on the other. It is important that good competitors not perceive that they are the target of attacks or they may change their goals in desperation. Also, a firm must inhibit good competitors from becoming bad ones by continued rivalry to keep them from revising their objectives.

Changing Bad Competitors into Good Ones

Sometimes bad competitors can be transformed into good ones. Ideally, market signaling to correct a competitor's faulty assumptions is all that is necessary. Alcoa has been attempting to influence overly optimistic demand forecasts of its competitors in the aluminum industry, for example. In other cases, time will convert a bad competitor into a good one. The futility of the competitor's strategy will become apparent to it, and it will alter its goals or strategy in ways that make it a better competitor.

A firm must often be prepared to fight battles in order to convert bad competitors to good ones, however. A battle may be necessary to demonstrate its relative weakness to a competitor, or to convince it that the firm will not tolerate erosion of position. While battles can be expensive, they are often cheaper than the cost of a protracted siege. With bad competitors, a protracted siege is often a fact of life in an industry.

Some bad competitors will never become good competitors. With them, a firm must accept the fact that continued challenges to its position will be forthcoming. The full range of offensive and defensive tactics described throughout this book will be necessary to sustain competitive advantage and avoid undermining industry structure.

The Optimal Market Configuration

The principles of competitor selection imply that holding a 100 percent market share is rarely, if ever, optimal.[12] It is sometimes more sensible for firms to yield position and allow good competitors to occupy it than to maintain or increase share. While this is contrary to managers' beliefs in some firms and almost heretical in others, it may be the best way to improve competitive advantage and industry structure in the long run. The right question a firm should ask is: What configuration of market shares and competitors is optimal? Having described the way in which a firm can identify and influence good competitors, I will now consider the configuration of competitors that is likely to best serve a firm's long-run strategic position.

The determinants of the ideal market share for a firm in general terms are numerous and complex. It is possible, however, to lay down some general principles for assessing the share a firm should hold and the ideal pattern of competitors. I first describe the factors that determine the ideal configuration, and then consider how a firm should move toward the ideal configuration given the existing competitor configuration.

The Optimal Competitor Configuration

A firm's optimal share of the part of the industry it is targeting should be high enough not to tempt a competitor to attack it. A firm must also have sufficient market share superiority (combined with its other competitive advantages not related to share) to maintain

[12]The undesirability of a 100 percent share is also recognized by Bloom and Kotler (1975), based on valid reasons. Bloom and Kotler cite the antitrust problems of high share, the possible effect of high share in attracting entry, and risks faced by high-share companies of the attack by consumerist or public interest organizations.

an equilibrium in the industry. The gap between leader and follower shares required to preserve stability will vary from industry to industry as I will describe below.

A number of structural characteristics influence a leader's optimal share:

Factors Implying a High Optimal Market Share for Leaders[13]

- Significant economies of scale[14]
- A steep learning curve that is proprietary
- Few industry segments
- Buyers willing to purchase from a single source
- No distribution channels stocking multiple brands
- Competitors who can *share* value activities with related business units, implying that small competitor share positions are an effective bases from which to attack a leader (see Chapter 10)
- Other high entry barriers

Factors Suggesting a Lower Optimal Share for Leaders

- Few economies of scale
- A modest learning curve
- There are unattractive segments
- Buyers demand a second or third source
- Channels have bargaining power and desire multiple suppliers
- Competitors are single-business firms who cannot share activities
- Followers are necessary as credible entry deterrents against more threatening firms
- A follower needs a meaningful share to be viable
- The industry has a history of antitrust problems or vulnerability to them.[15]

The distribution of market shares among firms in an industry that leads to the greatest industry stability is critically dependent on industry structure and whether competitors are good or bad competitors. The most important industry structural variables determining the ideal pattern of shares are the degree of differentiation or switching costs present in the industry and whether or not the industry is seg-

[13]For an empirical study supporting some of these factors, see Caves, Fortunato, and Ghemawat (1981).

[14]Industry growth interacts with scale economies to determine the optimal share. In a rapid-growth industry, scale economies yield less of an entry barrier and cost advantage than in a slow-growth industry.

[15]See Bloom and Kotler (1975).

mented. Where there are few segments and little differentiation or low switching costs, significant market share differences are usually necessary for a stable industry. With segmentation or high levels of differentiation, conversely, firms can coexist profitably despite similar shares because they are less prone to see the need or opportunity to attack each other.

The nature of competitors is equally important. Where competitors are bad competitors, large share differences among firms are necessary to preserve stability because bad competitors tend to take destabilizing actions if they perceive any opportunity to succeed. Where competitors are good competitors, conversely, little share differential may be necessary to discourage attacks.

These considerations combine to yield the implications shown in Figure 6–1.[16]

The pattern of generic strategies in an industry is also vital. Firms with different generic strategies can coexist much more easily than firms that all converge on the same generic strategy. Thus a firm must look beyond market shares alone in assessing the configuration of competitors in its industry.

COMPETITORS	EXTENT OF DIFFERENTIATION/ SEGMENTATION: Low	EXTENT OF DIFFERENTIATION/ SEGMENTATION: High
Good Competitors		Modest share difference needed for stability
Bad Competitors	Large share difference needed for stability	

Figure 6–1. Competitor Configuration and Industry Stability

[16]Evidence from examining a cross section of industries suggests that a significant difference in share among competitors is associated with greater stability. Buzzell's (1981) statistical test suggested that stable market share patterns often follow a semilogarithmic distribution, where each competitor's share is a constant proportion of the next higher-ranking firm's. Boston Consulting Group (1976) has also hypothesized that a stable market share distribution will have only three significant competitors with market shares in the proportion 4:2:1. This is a special case of the semilogarithmic distribution. Such generalizations can be misleading, however, because they do not reflect other industry and competitor characteristics besides share. BCG's hypothesis, for example, will not hold in all industries, but is most likely to hold in commodity industries where there are bad competitors.

It may be beneficial for the share not controlled by leaders to be split among followers rather than held by one. This means that followers will be pitted against each other instead of eyeing the position of the leader. Followers who are pursuing different focus strategies are even better than followers who are competing head on. It is also essential that followers be truly viable and offer a credible deterrent to new entrants, or fragmentation of the follower group can backfire and invite new entry.

Maintaining Competitor Viability

A firm must pay close attention to the health of its good competitors. Good competitors cannot play their role unless they are viable, and even a good competitor may undermine a firm's competitive advantage or industry structure if driven to desperation. Desperate competitors have a tendency to violate beneficial industry conventions or engage in other practices that undermine industry structure and damage industry image. They also have a tendency to look for salvation through being acquired, and may in the process introduce a threatening new player into the industry. Finally, the managements of desperate competitors are frequently changed. A new management can convert a good competitor into bad one.

The market position necessary for a competitor to be viable varies from industry to industry depending on entry/mobility barriers; it is less than 5 percent in soft drinks, but probably more than 10 percent in frozen entrees. A firm must know the market position necessary to keep its good competitors viable, and how this may be changing as a result of structural evolution. It must also allow good competitors enough successes to lead them to perpetuate their strategies, rather than change them in the face of repeated problems.

Moving Toward the Ideal Competitor Configuration

The considerations described above suggest how competitors should ideally be distributed. To decide whether to move toward the ideal, however, a firm must calculate the cost of gaining position or, conversely, the risk of incrementally yielding it. Yielding share can be destabilizing by tempting competitors to take even more, or by sending unfortunate signals to potential entrants.

A firm may need to gain share not only to increase its own sales but also, as we have seen, to improve industry structure through a more stable competitor configuration. The cost of gaining share will be a function of who will lose share in the process. The losing competitors' goals, capabilities, and barriers to shrinkage will be especially critical. A competitor's goals, commitment to the business, and the importance it attaches to share are important to assess. Its capabilities will determine the cost of wooing away buyers from the competitor. *Barriers to shrinkage* are barriers to reducing position in (though not completely exiting) an industry. These are closely analogous to exit barriers, and will be high where fixed costs are high because of the high penalty for reducing volume in existing facilities. Where competitors have high stakes in an industry, goals stressing market share, or high barriers to shrinkage, it may well be more costly to gain share than it is worth. In such industries, upward movement toward the ideal share should be slow and take advantage of opportunities posed by unfolding industry events.

The risk of yielding share to improve competitive advantage or industry structure will be a function of the difference in relative strength between the firm and competitors. If the gap is large, then a loss of share is unlikely to tempt competitors (or potential entrants) to upset the industry equilibrium by attempting to take even more share. The risk of yielding share is also a function of the inherent credibility of the firm in retaliating—a firm with a tough image faces less risk than one with a statesman's image. Finally, the risk of yielding share also depends on the ability of a firm to yield share in a way that will appear logical to other firms (including potential entrants) rather than be taken as a sign of weakness.

Maintaining Industry Stability

Maintaining the stability of an industry requires continual attention and effort by a firm, even if its competitors are good competitors. This is because competitors' goals or circumstances may change. Having enjoyed for some years a relatively profitable number two position, for example, a competitor may decide that more would be better. Or a change in its corporate parent or a shift in top management may lead a competitor to change its goals or assumptions. For example, the acquisition of Beaird-Poulan by Emerson Electric dramatically raised the ambitions of this regional chain saw manufacturer. Changes in industry structure may also create pressures on a competitor to gain share in the short or long run in order to remain viable. Driven to the wall, even a good competitor can touch off a process that destroys an industry.

These considerations suggest that a firm must continually work to manage its competitors' expectations and assumptions. This may require periodic competitive moves, aggressive market signaling, and investing in mobility barriers. The aim is to make sure competitors do not make faulty estimates of their strengths or a firm's commitment to the industry. Procter & Gamble is a good example of a firm that manages expectations through regular product changes and marketing investment. A firm that rests on its laurels vis-à-vis its competitors is starting a time bomb ticking that may transform a stable and profitable industry into one in which there is a costly battle for market share.

Pitfalls in Competitor Selection

The principles of competitor selection are not always followed. The following pitfalls seem to be among the most common:

Failure to Distinguish Good and Bad Competitors. Many companies do not recognize which of their competitors are good competitors and which are not. This leads them to pursue across-the-board moves, or worse yet, to attack good competitors while leaving the bad ones alone. In the process, industry structure is often severely damaged. Typical is the case of a specialty rubber manufacturer that viewed another major specialty rubber manufacturer as its mortal enemy and behaved accordingly. The view was not surprising, because this competitor's market share was similar to the firm's and made it a natural focal point for attention. In fact, this competitor was a nearly ideal competitor that was desperately trying to avoid a battle. The real enemies of the specialty rubber firm were the specialty divisions of the tire companies, who were using specialty markets as a dumping ground for excess capacity. By damaging its good competitor, the specialty rubber firm was helping the tire companies get established in the industry and eroding industry attractiveness.

It is very common for firms to view the competitor that is closest to them in market share or has the most similar strategy as the greatest enemy. This is the competitor that is repeatedly attacked, while other competitors are ignored. In fact, such a competitor is often a good competitor who offers very little threat.

Driving Competitors to Desperation. Companies often fail to think through the consequences of *too much success* against competitors. Driving competitors to desperation runs the risk of serious consequences that I have described earlier. In soft contact lenses, for example, Bausch and Lomb may have sown the seeds of some of its own problems. It moved very aggressively against other soft lens manufacturers in the late 1970s, slashing prices and behaving like a true believer in the experience curve. What happened was that Bausch and Lomb indeed gained share, but one by one its desperate competitors sold out. Their acquirors included Revlon, Johnson & Johnson, and Schering-Plough, all much larger than Bausch and Lomb and viewing contact lenses as an avenue for growth. With infusions of capital to its competitors, Bausch and Lomb now has a serious fight to contend with. It may have converted good competitors into bad ones.

Having Too Big a Share. Beyond a point, growing invites problems that are best avoided by ceding share to good competitors. Moreover, a large market share may actually lead to lower rates of return. Often the best course of action for a high share firm is to look for growth elsewhere rather than to push for more share in an industry. Similarly, high share firms may be better off finding ways to increase overall industry size or profitability, rather than try to gain share. They will enjoy the biggest piece of an expanding pie, and avoid the risks of destabilizing the industry. It is all too tempting, however, for a firm to push for incremental gains in relative position in an industry where it feels strongest.

Attacking a Good Leader. Followers sometimes commit the fatal error of attacking a good leader. The leader is then forced to retaliate, and what has been a profitable position for the follower turns into a marginal one. Western Company launched a market share attack on Halliburton in oil well completion and stimulation services, for example, despite the fact that Halliburton competed on differentiation and Western had been very profitable. Halliburton's reaction, no doubt a grudging one, has severely reduced Western's profits. Halliburton, if anything, has gotten stronger.

Entering an Industry with Too Many Bad Competitors. Entering an industry with too many bad competitors can doom a firm to a protracted siege, even if the firm has a competitive advantage. The cost of converting many bad competitors into good ones may be very great, and nullify the fruits of entry. Faced with an industry with many bad competitors, a firm may be better off finding another industry.

Competitors are both a blessing and a curse. Seeing them only as a curse runs the risk of eroding not only a firm's competitive advantage but also the structure of the industry as a whole. A firm must compete aggressively but not indiscriminately.

II
Competitive Scope Within an Industry

7
Industry Segmentation and Competitive Advantage

Industries are not homogeneous. Segments of industry have a structure just as industries do, and the strength of the five competitive forces often differs from one part of an industry to another. Segments also frequently involve differing buyer value chains and/or the value chain a firm requires to serve them well. Segments of an industry thus frequently differ widely in their structural attractiveness and in the requirements for competitive advantage in them. Crucial strategic questions facing a firm become (1) where in an industry to compete and (2) in what segments will focus strategies be sustainable because barriers can be built between segments.

Industry segmentation is the division of an industry into subunits for purposes of developing competitive strategy. Industry segmentation for competitive strategy must be broader than the familiar notion of market segmentation, though encompassing it. Market segmentation is concerned with identifying differences in buyer needs and purchasing behavior, allowing a firm to serve segments that match its capabilities with distinct marketing programs. Market segmentation tends to focus on the marketing activities in the value chain. Industry segmentation combines buyer purchasing behavior with the behavior of costs, both production costs and the costs of serving different buyers. Industry segmentation encompasses the entire value chain. It also exposes the differences in structural attractiveness among segments, and the conflicts in serving segments simultaneously. This broader approach to segmentation can provide insights into new segmentation approaches and can be the basis of creating and sustaining competitive advantage.

Industry segmentation is necessary to address the central question of competitive scope within an industry, or what segments of an industry a firm should serve and how it should serve them. It is also the basis for the choice of focus strategies,[1] since it exposes segments that are poorly served by broadly-targeted competitors in which focus can be both sustainable and profitable. Broadly-targeted competitors must also understand industry segmentation, because it reveals areas where they are vulnerable to focusers and may suggest unattractive segments that are best left to competitors. Attention to segmentation from a strategic perspective is increasingly important because new developments in technology are altering some of the old rules of segmentation, with implications for both focusers and broadly-targeted firms.

This chapter describes the way an industry can be segmented for strategic purposes, as well as some of the implications for creating and sustaining competitive advantage. I begin by describing the underlying factors that create industry segments and the observable indicators that can be used to define them in practice. These principles provide the basis for constructing and interpreting an industry segmentation matrix and for evaluating alternative ways of segmenting an industry. Having defined how to segment an industry, I develop some important strategic implications that arise from segmentation. The conditions that make a segment structurally attractive are identified, as are the factors that lead to strategic interrelationships between segments. I then describe how a firm can choose the segments on which to base a focus strategy, and test its sustainability against competitors. The chapter concludes by showing how industry segmentation relates to industry definition.

[1]Focus strategies are described in Chapter 1.

Bases for Industry Segmentation

An industry is a market in which similar or closely related products are sold to buyers, as shown schematically in Figure 7–1.[2] In some industries a single product variety is sold to all buyers. More typically, however, there are many existing or potential items in an industry's product line, distinguished by such characteristics as size, performance, and functions. Ancillary services (repair, installation, applications engineering) are also in fact distinct products that can be and often are provided separately from physical products.[3]

In some industries there is a single buyer (e.g., in some defense and space industries). More typically, though, there are many existing or potential buyers. These buyers are usually not all alike, but vary according to demographics, the characteristics of the industry in which they compete, location, and in other ways. Firms provide the link between products and buyers. Firms produce, sell, and deliver products through value chains (Chapters 2–4) in competition with each other. In some industries, there are independent distribution channels between firms and buyers involved in all or part of industry sales.

The boundaries of an industry are frequently in flux. Product lines are rarely static. Firms can create new product varieties that perform new functions, combine functions in new ways, or split off particular functions into separate products. Similarly, new buyers can

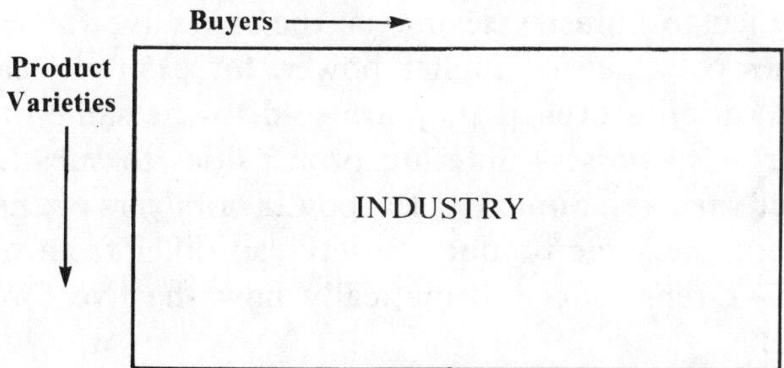

Figure 7–1. An Industry as an Array of Products and Buyers

[2]Throughout this book the term "product" has been used to describe both products and services. In most industries producing products there are some services that are part of the offering, and these are important to segmentation. The principles of analyzing both products and services for segmentation purposes are the same.

[3]Chapter 12 describes the strategic issues in bundling together physically distinct products and selling them as a package, something that many companies do without knowing it.

become part of an industry, existing buyers can drop out, or buyers may alter their purchasing behavior. The current array of products and buyers reflects the products that firms have chosen to introduce and the buyers that have chosen to buy them, and not the products and buyers that an industry could potentially encompass.

Structural Bases for Segmentation

The reason that industries must be segmented for competitive strategy formulation is that the products, buyers, or both within an industry are dissimilar in ways that affect their *intrinsic attractiveness* or the way in which a firm gains *competitive advantage* in supplying them. Differences in structural attractiveness and in requirements for competitive advantage among an industry's products and buyers create industry segments.[4] Segments grow out of both differences in buyer behavior as well as differences in the economics of supplying different products or buyers. Product and buyer differences that do not affect structure or competitive advantage (e.g., differences in the color of an otherwise identical product variety) may be important for production or marketing, but responding to them is not essential to competitive strategy.

Structural Differences and Segmentation. Differences in products or buyers create industry segments if they alter one or more of the five competitive forces. Chapter 1 showed how the five competitive forces determine overall industry attractiveness. Structural analysis can also be applied to industry segments; the same five forces are at work. Economies of scale or supplier power, for example, can vary among product varieties even if they are sold to the same buyer. A given buyer may also possess differing propensities to substitute for different product varieties. Similarly, the power of buyers or the threat of substitution for the same product variety can differ from buyer to buyer. Figure 7–2 represents schematically how the five forces can vary by segment.[5]

[4]As we will see, industry segmentation flows from the intrinsic characteristics of an industry's products and buyers, irrespective of firms' existing strategies. Strategic groups (*Competitive Strategy,* Chapter 7) are the result of differences in firms' strategies, one dimension of which may be the different segments they serve. Thus industry segmentation is a building block for analyzing strategic groups.

[5]The threat of substitution and the threat of entry tend to be greater for segments than for an industry as a whole, because other product varieties are often substitutes for a product variety and competitors operating in other segments are often well-placed potential entrants to a segment.

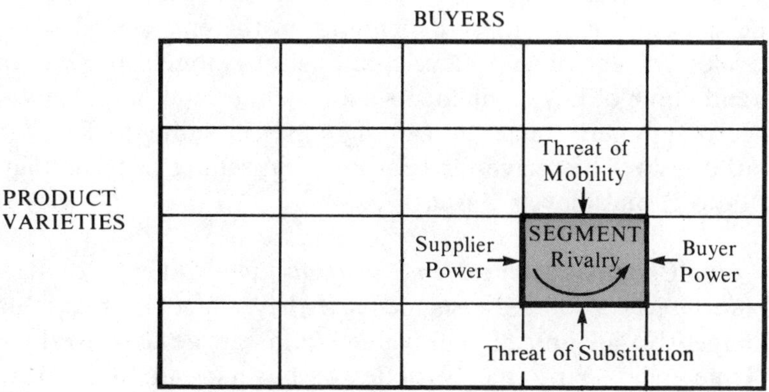

Figure 7–2. Differences in the Five Forces Among Segments

The television set industry provides an example of how the five forces can differ by product variety independently of who the buyer is. TV sets can be segmented by configuration (portables, table models, consoles and combination units). Small screen portables have become largely a commodity, while console TVs offer more opportunities for differentiation through styling, furniture, finish, and features. Moreover, console set production employs a different production process and different suppliers than the production of portables, and is less sensitive to economies of scale. These differences affect mobility barriers, supplier power, buyer power, and rivalry pressures. Similar differences which affect the five forces exist for other TV product varieties.

Large turbine generators illustrate how differences among buyers may also often have structural implications, *independent* of the product variety they purchase. Investor-owned electric utilities can be distinguished from municipally-owned utilities from a structural viewpoint. Investor-owned utilities tend to be more technologically sophisticated and purchase through a negotiation process, while municipal utilities are less sophisticated and purchase through public bidding. This creates differences in price sensitivity and in the ability of a firm to create mobility barriers in selling to the two types of utilities such as brand identity, switching costs, and proprietary product differences.

Both product varieties and buyers in an industry can potentially differ in all five of the competitive forces. In TV sets, for example, the distinction between console and portable sets has implications for mobility barriers, supplier power, and rivalry. In the turbine generator industry, investor-owned utilities and municipal utilities differ in their bargaining power, the rivalry among firms in serving them, and the opportunity to erect mobility barriers. Even supplier power can vary for the same product variety depending on the end buyer's identity. In bicycles, for example, a bicycle enthusiast is much more aware of the brand name of key components such as hubs and derailleurs. This gives parts suppliers greater bargaining power in selling to firms targeting enthusiasts. They have far less power in selling to firms that sell bicycles to casual bicycle purchasers.

Value Chain Differences and Segmentation. Differences in products and buyers also create segments if they affect the requirements for competitive advantage. The value chain can be used to diagnose this. Differences in product varieties or buyers lead to segments if:

- they affect the drivers of cost or uniqueness in the firm's value chain
- they change the required configuration of the firm's value chain
- they imply differences in the buyer's value chain

An example of a product difference that affects the value chain is the difference between standard and premium bicycles. Standard bikes are built with an automated manufacturing process, while premium bikes are frequently handcrafted. Many other value activities differ for the two as well, and the drivers of cost and uniqueness of value activities differ accordingly. Thus the sources of competitive advantage for standard and premium bikes are quite different, making them different segments. Another good example of how different product varieties can affect the value chain is draft beer compared to canned beer. While the beer is the same, many other value activities are not.

An example of how differences in buyers can affect the firm's value chain is building insulation. Since many costs in the insulation industry are driven by regional scale and by the location of buyers in relation to plants, buyers located in different geographic regions constitute important segments. This example shows not only how buyers can differ in purchasing behavior, but also how the behavior of cost in serving buyers can be quite different, even with the identical product.

Value chains also differ among buyers. The way a hotel chain uses a TV set is different from how a household uses it, with strong implications for use criteria and signals of value (Chapter 4). Differences in use criteria and signals of value among buyers define segments, because they affect the requirement for competitive advantage. It is also important to recognize that the way different product varieties fit into the *same* buyer's value chain can differ—for example, a new part versus a replacement part. Product differences that affect the buyer's use and signaling criteria define segments.

The Array of Industry Segments. In theory, every individual buyer or product variety in an industry could be a segment, because the five forces or the value chain were somehow different for each. In TV sets, for example, every screen size or feature might potentially constitute a different segment. Similarly, in turbine generators, every utility has a somewhat different value chain. In practice, however, product varieties and buyers should be grouped into categories that reflect their important differences. Deciding how to group products and buyers to capture the most important differences is a key to good segmentation and a subject to which I will return later.

An industry segment is always a *combination* of a product variety (or varieties) and some group of buyers who purchase it. In some cases, buyers do not have important structural differences and segments are defined by product varieties, and vice versa. Usually, however, structural differences in both product varieties and buyers are present in industries, leading to segments consisting of a subset of products sold to a subset of buyers. Note that product varieties are often associated with particular types of buyers that purchase them, as was true in both the TV set and turbine generator industries.

Industry segments must also be defined *independently* of the scope of activities chosen by existing competitors. Segments stem from structural differences within an industry that competitors may or may not have perceived. A segment may be important even though no competitor is yet focusing on it. Industry segmentation should include *potential* product varieties and buyer groups as well as those that already exist. The tendency in segmentation is to focus on observed differences in product varieties and buyers. Yet there are typically product varieties that are feasible but not yet produced, and potential buyer groups that are not currently being served. Unobserved or potential segments can be the most important to identify because they offer opportunities for preemptive moves that create competitive advantage.

Segmentation Variables

To segment an industry, each discrete product variety (and potential variety) in an industry should be identified and examined for structural or value chain differences from others. Product varieties can be used directly as segmentation variables. Buyer segments can be identified in a similar fashion, by examining all the buyers in the industry and probing for structural or value chain differences among them. Since buyers vary in a multiplicity of ways, experience has shown that a good starting point in identifying buyer segments is to look for buyer differences along three broad and observable dimensions: buyer type, buyer geographic location, and distribution channel employed. Buyer type encompasses such things as the buyer's size, industry, strategy, or demographics.

While these three dimensions of buyers are often related, each has an independent effect. Location can significantly affect purchasing behavior and the value chain required to serve a buyer even if all other buyer characteristics are equal. Similarly, in many industries the same buyer is reached through different channels, though the channel employed is often related to buyer type (and also to product variety). For example, buyers of electronic components purchase small, rush orders of chips from distributors and purchase larger orders directly from manufacturers.

To segment an industry, then, four observable classes of segmentation variables are used either individually or in combination to capture differences among producers and buyers. In any given industry, any or all of these variables can define strategically relevant segments:

- *Product variety.* The discrete product varieties that are, or could be, produced.
- *Buyer type.* The types of end buyers that purchase, or could purchase, the industry's products.
- *Channel (immediate buyer).* The alternative distribution channels employed or potentially employed to reach end buyers.
- *Geographic buyer location.* The geographic location of buyers, defined by locality, region, country, or group of countries.[6]

Identifying segmentation variables is perhaps the most creative part of segmenting an industry, because it involves conceiving of dimensions along which products and buyers differ that carry important structural or value chain implications. This requires a clear understanding of industry structure as well as the firm's and the buyer's value chain.

[6]Geographic buyer location reflects the importance of geographic scope, defined in Chapter 2. For practical reasons, scope within the industry and geographic scope are best treated together in segmentation.

Product Segments

To identify product segments, all the physically distinct product types produced or potentially produced by an industry should be isolated, including ancillary services that could feasibly be offered separately from the product. Replacement parts are also a distinct product variety. Groups or bundles of products that can be sold together as a single package should also be identified as a product variety, in addition to the items currently sold separately.[7] In the hospital management industry, for example, some firms sell a complete management package at a single price, while others sell individual services such as physician recruiting. The package should be viewed as a separate product variety for purposes of segmentation. Similarly, in industries where the product requires service, there are often three product varieties—the product sold separately, service sold separately, and the product and service sold together. In many industries, the list of product varieties that results from going through such a process is quite long.

Product varieties in an industry can differ in many ways that translate into structural or value chain differences and hence segments. Some of the most typical product differences that are good proxies for structural or value chain differences that define segments are as follows, along with some illustrative examples of why they reflect segments:

Physical size. Size is often a proxy for technological complexity or how a product is used, both of which affect the possibilities for differentiation. For example, different sized forklifts are typically used for different applications. Size may also imply differences in the value chain required to produce different varieties. Different sized varieties must often be manufactured on different machines, and require different components. For example, a miniature camera requires a different manufacturing process and higher precision components than a standard camera.

Price level. The price level of product varieties is often associated with buyer price sensitivity. Price also serves as a good proxy in some industries for the design and nature of manufacturing or selling value activities.

[7]Chapter 12 describes the strategic issues involved in bundling in some detail.

Features. Product varieties with different features may be associated with different levels of technological sophistication, different production processes, and different suppliers.

Technology or design. Differences in technology (e.g., analog versus digital watches) or design (front opening versus side opening valves) among product varieties can involve different levels of technological complexity, different production processes, and other factors.

Inputs employed. Sometimes product varieties differ significantly in their use of raw materials or other inputs (e.g., plastic versus metal parts). Such differences often have implications for the manufacturing process or supplier bargaining power.

Packaging. Varieties may differ in the way they are packaged and subsequently delivered, such as in bulk versus bagged sugar or draft versus canned beer. This translates into value chain differences in both the firm and buyers.

Performance. Performance differences such as pressure rating, fuel economy, and accuracy are related to the technology and design of product varieties, and often reflect differences in R&D, manufacturing sophistication, and testing.

New versus aftermarket or replacement. Replacement products often go through entirely different downstream value chains than identical new products, and may be different in other ways such as buyer price sensitivity, switching costs, and required delivery time.

Product versus ancillary services or equipment. The distinction between a product and ancillary products or services is often a key indicator of price sensitivity, differentiability, switching costs, and the value chain required to provide them.

Bundled versus unbundled. Selling various products as a package (bundle) versus selling individual items (unbundle) can have implications for mobility barriers, the ability to differentiate, and the value chain required (see Chapter 12).

The product differences that are most meaningful for industry segmentation are those that reflect the most important structural differences. There are often a number of different product descriptors that are related. Price level, technology, and performance may all be correlated, for example, and reflect the same basic differences among products. If each descriptor is measuring the same difference, the measure that most closely measures or proxies the structural or value chain differences should be chosen.

More than one product dimension may define relevant segments, and all product differences that affect structure should be identified. The best method for segmenting an industry in which there are multiple segmentation variables will be discussed below. It is also important in product segmentation to include product varieties that are feasible though not currently being produced, such as service sold independently of the product or a product variety with a new mix of features. Good examples are cordless telephones and the "no name" food items now sold in grocery stores.

BUYER SEGMENTS

To identify buyer segments, all the different types of end buyers to which an industry sells must be examined for important structural or value chain differences. In most industries, there are several ways in which buyers can be classified. In consumer goods, for example, some key factors include age, income, household size, and decision maker. In industrial, commercial, or institutional products, buyer size, technological sophistication, and nature of use for the product are among the factors that distinguish buyers.

There is an active debate among marketers about the best means of segmenting buyers.[8] In fact, no one variable can ever capture all the buyer differences that might determine segments, particularly since differences that affect the cost of serving buyers (and the value chain for doing so) are often just as important for segmentation as differences in their purchasing behavior. Buyer segmentation should reflect the underlying structural and value chain differences among buyers rather than any single classification scheme, because the goal of segmentation is to expose all these differences.

Industrial and Commercial Buyers

Common factors which serve as proxies for structural or value chain differences that distinguish buyer segments among industrial

[8]For a good survey, see Moriarty (1983). Bonoma and Shapiro (1984) present a very useful analysis of industrial market segmentation and its implications for marketing strategy.

and commercial buyers are as follows, along with some illustrative examples of how they reflect segments:

BUYER INDUSTRY. The buyer's industry is often a proxy for how a product is used in the buyer's value chain and what fraction of total purchases it represents. For example, candy bar manufacturers buy and use chocolate much differently than dairy product firms, who use less chocolate and have less need for product quality. Differences such as these can affect factors such as buyer price sensitivity, susceptibility to substitution, and the cost of supplying the buyer.

BUYER'S STRATEGY (E.G., DIFFERENTIATION VERSUS COST LEADERSHIP). A buyer's competitive strategy is often an important indicator of how a product is used and of price sensitivity, among other things. Strategy shapes the buyer's value chain and the role a product plays in it. For example, a differentiated high-margin food processor is more concerned with ingredient quality and consistency than a private label food manufacturer that competes on cost.

TECHNOLOGICAL SOPHISTICATION. A buyer's technological sophistication can be an important indicator of its susceptibility to differentiation and resulting price sensitivity. Major oil companies tend to be more sophisticated buyers of oil field services and equipment than independents, for example.

OEM VERSUS USER. Original equipment manufacturers (OEMs) that incorporate a product into their product and sell it to other firms often have differing levels of price sensitivity and sophistication than firms that use the product themselves.

VERTICAL INTEGRATION. Whether a buyer is partially integrated into the product or into ancillary or related products (e.g., in-house service) can greatly affect the buyer's bargaining power and a firm's ability to differentiate itself.

DECISION-MAKING UNIT OR PURCHASING PROCESS. The particular individuals involved in the decision-making process can have a major impact on the sophistication of the purchase decision, the desired product attributes, and price sensitivity. Many industrial products are purchased in complex processes involving many individuals (see Chapter 4), and the procedures often vary markedly even among buyers in the same industry. Some users of electronic components purchase through trained and dedicated purchasing agents, for example, and are much more price-sensitive than other component buyers that employ engineers in purchasing or use purchasing agents also responsible for purchasing other items.

SIZE. A buyer's size can indicate its bargaining power, how it uses a product, the purchasing procedures employed, and the value chain with which it is best supplied. Sometimes *order size* is the relevant measure of size, while in other industries it may be *total annual purchases.* In still other cases *company size* may be the best determinant of bargaining power and purchasing procedures.

OWNERSHIP. The ownership structure of a buyer firm may have a major impact on its motivations. Private companies may value different product characteristics than public companies, for example, while a division of a diversified firm may be guided by purchasing practices determined by the parent.

FINANCIAL STRENGTH. A buyer's profitability and financial resources can determine such things as its price sensitivity, need for credit, and frequency of purchase.

ORDER PATTERN. Buyers can differ in their ordering pattern in ways that affect buyer bargaining power or the value chain required to supply them. Buyers that place regular and predictable orders, for example, may be much less costly to serve than those whose orders come at erratic intervals. Some buyers also typically have more seasonal or cyclical purchasing patterns than others, affecting a firm's pattern of capacity utilization.

Consumer Goods Buyers

Typical proxies of buyer differences that define segments among consumer goods buyers are as follows, along with illustrative examples of how they reflect segments:

DEMOGRAPHICS. Buyer demographics can be a proxy for the desired product attributes, price sensitivity, and other use and signaling criteria. For example, single persons have different needs and purchasing patterns for frozen entrees than families with children. Many aspects of demographics can be important, including family size, income, health, religion, sex, nationality, occupation, age, presence of working females, social class, etc. In banking, for example, wealth, annual income, and the education level of household members all determine what banking services are purchased and how price sensitive the buyer is.

PSYCHOGRAPHICS OR LIFESTYLE. Hard-to-measure factors such as lifestyle or self-image can be important discriminators of purchasing behavior among consumers. Jetsetters may value a product differently than equally wealthy conservatives, for example.[9]

LANGUAGE. Language also may define segments. In the record industry, for example, the Spanish speaking market worldwide is a relevant segment.

DECISION-MAKING UNIT OR PURCHASING PROCESS. The decision-making process within the household can be important to desired product attributes and price sensitivity. One spouse may be more interested in performance features of a car, for example, while the other opts for comfort and reliability.

PURCHASE OCCASION. Purchase occasion refers to such things as whether a product is purchased as a gift or for the buyer's own use, and whether the product is to be part of a special event or used routinely. A buyer's use and signaling criteria are often very different depending on the occasion, even if the buyer is the same person and the product is similar. Purchasers of pens for gifts, for example, will favor recognized brands names such as Cross that may carry less weight in purchasing for personal use.

Several buyer dimensions may be important in defining buyer segments. In oil field equipment, for example, buyer size, technological sophistication, and ownership are all relevant variables. In frozen entrees, household size, age of family members, whether both parents are working, and income are all relevant variables. *Potential* buyers of a product not currently purchasing may also constitute segments. Buyer segmentation variables may also be related and the task is to select the variables that best reflect structural and value chain differences.

[9]Marketers have proposed a number of other related ways of segmenting consumers, such as personality and loyalty. For a survey, see Kotler (1980).

Channel Segments

To identify segments based on channels, all existing and feasible channels through which a product can or does reach buyers should be identified. The channel employed usually has implications for how a firm configures its value chain and the vertical linkages (Chapter 2) that are present. The channel can also reflect factors which are important cost drivers such as order size, shipment size, and lead time. Large orders of electronic components are sold direct, for example, while small orders are sold through distributors (often to the same buyers). Channels can also differ greatly in bargaining power. Mass merchandisers such as Sears and K-Mart have a great deal more power than independent department stores.

Typical differences in channels that define segments include:

Direct versus distributors. Selling direct removes the need to gain access to channels and may imply a very different value chain than selling through distributors.

Direct mail versus retail (or wholesale). Direct mail eliminates the potential bargaining power of the intermediate channel. It also usually carries implications for value activities such as the logistical system.

Distributors versus brokers. Brokers typically do not hold inventory and may handle a different product line than distributors.

Types of distributors or retailers. Products may be sold through retailers or distributors of very different types, which carry different assortments and have different strategies and purchasing processes.

Exclusive versus nonexclusive outlets. Exclusivity may affect a channel's bargaining power and also the activities performed by the channel versus those performed by the firm.

There are often several types of channels in an industry. In copiers, for example, machines are sold direct as well as through copier distributors, office products distributors, and retailers. Channel segmentation must also include any *potential* channel that might be feasible. For example, L'eggs resegmented the hosiery market by discovering a new channel, the direct sale of hosiery to supermarkets.

Geographic Segments

Geographic location can affect both buyer needs and the costs of serving buyers. Geographic location may be important directly as a cost driver and may also affect the value chain required to reach the buyer. Geographic location also frequently serves as a proxy for desired product attributes due to differences in weather, customs, government regulation, and the like. For example, commercial roofs in the southern United States require less insulation than in the North, while the roofing membrane is more likely to be ballasted with gravel in the North than in the South because a roof designed to take a snow load can handle the extra weight.

Typical geographic segments are based on variables such as the following:

Localities, regions or countries. Geographic areas may have differences in such areas as transportation systems and regulations. Geographic buyer location also plays a key role in defining scale economies. Depending on the geographic scope of scale economies (Chapter 3), different sized geographic areas may be the relevant segments. In the residential roofing shingle industry, regions are the appropriate segments because high logistical costs limit the effective radius of a plant. In food distribution, metropolitan areas are the appropriate segments because of dense customer location and use of trucks for local delivery.

Weather zones. Climatic conditions often have a strong impact on product needs or on the value chain required to serve an area.

Country stage of development or other country groupings. Buyers located in developing countries may have very different needs than those in developed countries. In addition, packaging, logistical systems, marketing systems, and many other aspects of the value chain may differ significantly. Similarly, other groupings of countries may expose similarities that define segments.

The relevant measure of geographic location for segmentation purposes will differ from industry to industry. In most cases, the relevant location to use in segmentation is the location where a product is actually *consumed* or used. However, sometimes the location to which a product is *shipped* (e.g., the warehouse) is more relevant. In other cases, the location of the buyer's *headquarters or primary dwelling* emerges as the most important geographic segmentation variable, even though the buyer uses the product somewhere else.

There can also be more than one meaningful geographic segmentation. For example, regions may be meaningful segments for determining cost position in industries where the costs of key value activities are driven by regional scale, whereas countries may be meaningful segments for determining desired product attributes and the ability to differentiate.

Finding New Segments

Some segmentation variables are readily apparent as a result of industry convention or competitor behavior. There are often established norms for dividing buyers or grouping geographic areas, based on historical data collected by trade associations or government agencies. In the oil industry, for example, the distinction between majors and independents is an accepted segmentation. Traditional categorization schemes for product varieties in an industry are also typical. Competitors may also define apparent segments through their choice of focus strategies.

However, segmentation must go beyond conventional wisdom and accepted classification schemes. Correct industry segmentation should reflect important differences for structure or the value chain among products, buyers, channels, or geography, whether or not they are recognized and used currently. The greatest opportunity for creating competitive advantage often comes from *new* ways of segmenting, because a firm can meet true buyer needs better than competitors or improve its relative cost position.

In searching for potential new product segments, the following questions can be usefully considered:

- Are there *other technologies or designs* to perform the required functions in the buyer's value chain?
- Could *additional* functions be performed by an enhanced product?
- By *reducing* the number of functions the product performs (and possibly lowering the price), could the needs of some buyers be better served?
- Are there *different bundles* (either narrower or broader) of products and services that could be feasibly sold as a package?

Off-price retailers are an example of a new segmentation based on reducing the number of functions the product performs. Firms such as Loehmann's eliminate costly services such as credit and returns while selling through spartan outlets without extensive dressing rooms or sales help. This stripped down value chain, without many traditional value activities, has created an entirely new segment. A similar process is occurring in the hotel/motel industry, where budget chains such as La Quinta are selling rooms without other services such as restaurants and bars, and other chains are combining services in new ways.

The possibility of employing new channels also frequently exists. Firms can sell direct where the norm has been to use agents or distributors or employ new types of distributors or retailers. Timex did this in watches, and Avon did it in cosmetics. Any feasible channel is a potential segment.

In identifying new geographic and buyer segments, creativity is often required in two areas. The first is finding important new ways that geography or buyers can be divided to reflect structural or value chain differences. As discussed earlier, Stouffer's discovered important differences in purchase criteria for frozen entrees by isolating single households and households with two working parents. The second area for creativity in geographic or buyer segmentation is in identifying potential *new* buyer types or geographic areas not presently being served by the industry. Sometimes reaching a new buyer type or geographic area will require product modifications, while in other cases it just requires that a firm gain a better understanding of its buyers' needs and potential new applications for its product. For example, Arm & Hammer baking soda found a large market in deodorizing refrigerators, and Johnson & Johnson Baby Shampoo proved popular with adults. No product change was required for reaching either new buyer group.

The Industry Segmentation Matrix

Having identified the relevant segmentation variables with structural or value chain implications, the next task is to combine them into an overall segmentation of the industry. The task is usually difficult because there are many relevant segmentation variables—in some industries there can be dozens. The challenge is to distill these variables into the most meaningful segments for developing competitive strategy.

The first step in the distillation process is to apply a significance test to each segmentation variable. Only those variables with a truly *significant* impact on the sources of competitive advantage or industry structure should be isolated for strategic analysis. Other less important, though still meaningful, segmentation variables that are identified can be used for fine tuning in marketing or operations management.

The basic tool for translating the remaining variables into a segmentation is the *industry segmentation matrix.* A simple segmentation matrix based on two segmentation variables is shown in Figure 7–3, illustrating the oil field equipment industry in which the size of the buyer oil company and the stage of development of the country in which the buyer is headquartered have been identified as the two segmentation variables.

The first practical problem in constructing a segmentation matrix is choosing the number of categories of each segmentation variable to select. In Figure 7–3 I have chosen three discrete categories of buyer size and two categories of a country's stage of development. In reality, buyer size is a continuous variable and country development goes through many stages. The way in which each segmentation variable is broken into discrete categories should reflect the categories that capture the most significant structural or value chain differences, balanced against the practical need to limit the number of segments to a manageable number. Deciding on the best discrete categories for strategic purposes almost always requires judgment and is an iterative process.

The cells in Figure 7–3 are the individual segments in the industry. It may well be that some of the cells are presently unoccupied. In

		BUYER TYPE		
		Major Oil Companies	Large Independents	Small Independents
GEOGRAPHIC LOCATION	Developed Countries			
	Developing Countries		Null	Null

Figure 7–3. A Simple Industry Segmentation Matrix for an Oil Field Equipment Industry

addition, if there were no small independent oil companies based in developing countries and not likely ever to be any, this segment would be a null cell. For purposes of illustration, Figure 7–3 shows null cells involving both large and small independents. Segments can often be eliminated from consideration if they are null cells. However, it is important to remember that null cells should be *infeasible* combinations of the segmentation variables and not merely cells in which no firm is currently operating. Feasible cells where no firm is operating represent a potential opportunity and it is important that such segments be highlighted, not eliminated, in segmentation.

Figure 7–3 portrays a case where there are two relevant segmentation variables. In practice, there may be many variables grouped under the four broad categories of product, buyer type, channel, and geography. Looked at closely, most industries are quite heterogeneous. With many significant segmentation variables, the number of segmentation matrices that could be plotted multiplies rapidly. The problem, then, is to convert the segmentation variables into a small number of segmentation matrices that will be most illuminating for the strategy formulation process.

Relationships Among Segmentation Variables

To move from a number of segmentation variables to the most meaningful segmentation matrices, the first step is to probe the relationships among the segmentation variables. The number of important segmentation variables can be reduced by collapsing segmentation variables together that are correlated, or which effectively measure the same thing. For example, geographic location may be associated with a particular buyer type (e.g., automobile companies are located in the Midwest), or buyer type may be closely related to channel (small roofing contractors are all served through distributors). Constructing a segmentation matrix with correlated segmentation variables will produce a matrix in which many cells are null.

Segmentation variables that are highly correlated can be combined, because one variable is a surrogate for the effect of the other. In less extreme cases, the correlation among segmentation variables is partial, but allows a significant reduction in the number of possible segments because many cells in the matrix are null. It is important to identify all the relationships among the segmentation variables and use this to combine variables together and identify null cells.

It is also important to understand *why* variables are related, because this will often have important ramifications. If one variable is not a good surrogate for another but rather a reflection of current firm behavior or happenstance, combining variables is a mistake. It will obscure unoccupied segments that may represent an unexploited opportunity. For example, if small roofing contractors were served through distributors not for economic reasons but for historical reasons, then eliminating direct sale to small contractors as a segment would be a mistake. Telemarketing or remote order entry by salespersons with portable computer terminals might make the segment feasible though it had not been previously.

Combining Segmentation Matrices

The significant and independent segmentation variables that remain after the process described above represent the potential axes for industry segmentation matrices. Where there are more than two segmentation variables, the industry segmentation matrix will no longer fit on a two-dimensional page. One way of proceeding is to construct a number of different segmentation matrices for each pair of variables. Each of these matrices can then be analyzed for its strategic implications. This approach is not fully satisfactory, however, because meaningful segments may be the result of combining more than two segmentation variables and may be overlooked.

To deal with more than two segmentation variables, it is usually useful to create *combined* segmentation matrices. The process is illustrated in Figure 7–4. In oil field equipment there are at least two other relevant buyer segmentation variables besides buyer type and geographic buyer location: the technological sophistication of the oil company and its ownership. In Figure 7–4, I have plotted the four variables in pairs and then combined the two segmentations together after eliminating null cells.

The process of combining matrices not only reduces the number of segments by eliminating some null cells, but also exposes correlations among variables that may have been missed. In Figure 7–4, I have noted the null cells representing infeasible combinations. Combining matrices is usually best done by combining all segmentation variables within a category first. In Figure 7–4, for example, I have combined all the buyer segmentation variables together.

After combining segmentation variables of the same broad cate-

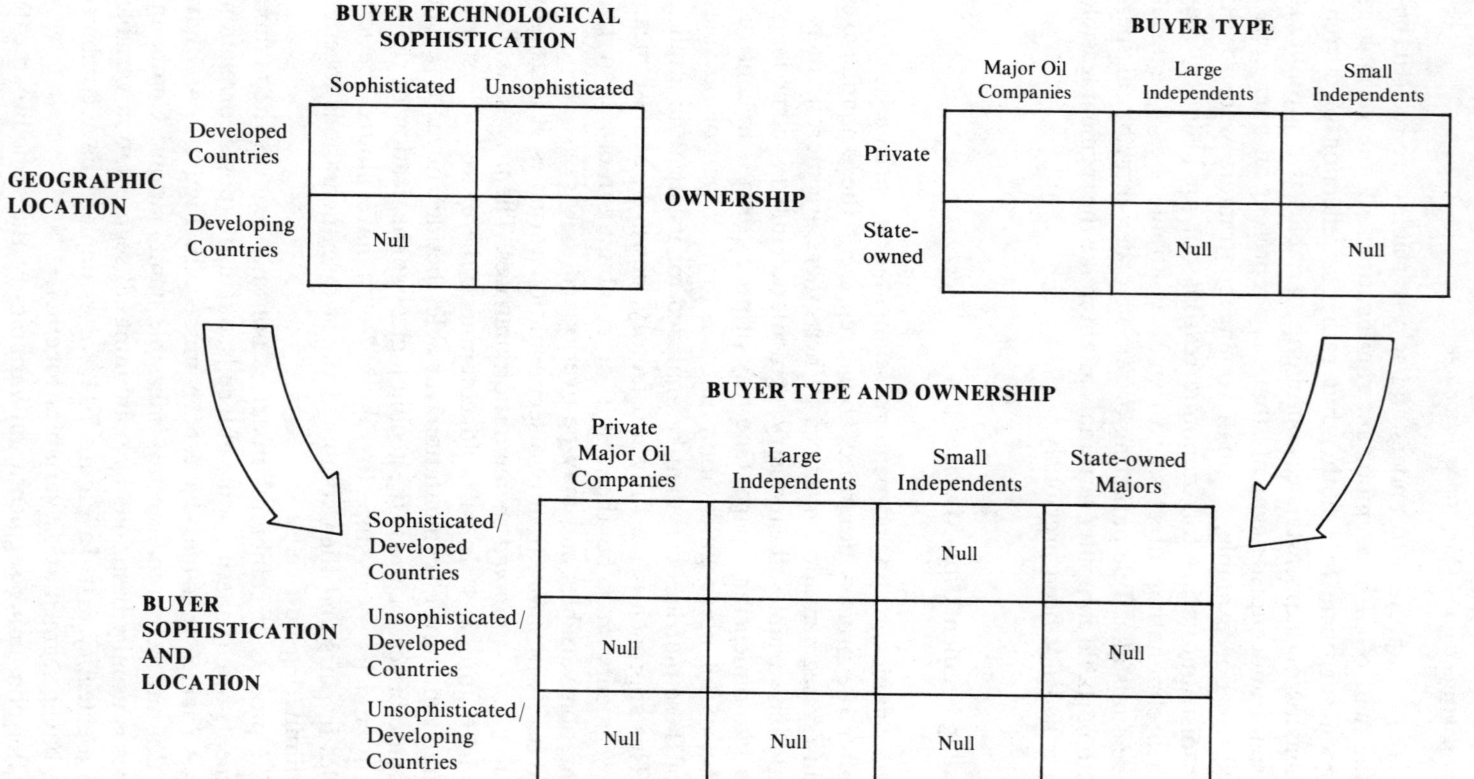

Figure 7–4. Combined Segmentation Matrix for an Oil Field Equipment Industry

		BUYERS					
		SOPHISTICATED			UNSOPHISTICATED		
		Private Majors	State-owned Majors in Developed Countries	Large Independents	Large Independents	Small Independents	State-owned Majors in Developing Countries
PRODUCT VARIETY	Premium/ Deep Drilling						
	Standard/ Deep Drilling						
	Standard/ Shallow Drilling						

Figure 7–5. Illustrative Industry Segmentation Matrix for an Oil Field Equipment Industry

gory, one proceeds to combine variables in different categories. In doing so, it is usually best to create a segmentation matrix in which one axis reflects the combined *product* segmentation variables and the other axis combines all the *buyer-related* variables (buyer type, channel, geography). Where the number of segmentation variables is manageable, it is possible using this procedure to construct one two-dimensional industry segmentation matrix. This matrix may be quite large, but has the advantage of displaying the entire industry in a way that facilitates strategic analysis. Figure 7–5 shows such a matrix for oil field equipment, after adding to the segmentation two product segmentation variables—premium versus standard quality products, and products with ratings for deep versus shallow drilling.

Sometimes the number of relevant segmentation variables and resulting segments is so great as to make a single matrix unwieldy. The presence of a very large overall segmentation matrix should prompt the reexamination of the segmentation variables and the discrete categories of each to ensure that the differences are truly significant. Where this is the case, it may be desirable to use two or three segmentation matrices in subsequent analysis to avoid missing important strategic implications.

The industry segmentation matrix should contain potential segments and not just segments that are currently occupied. Potential segments may imply entirely new segmentation variables (e.g., channel is added because there is the possibility that some direct sales may be possible in the future instead of handling all sales through distributors) or new discrete categories of existing variables (e.g., a new performance rating for an alloy).

A segmentation matrix is an analytical tool, not an end in itself. The analyst should start with the longest list of segmentation variables to avoid overlooking possibilities. Only over the course of the analysis are variables combined or eliminated and the working segmentation matrix refined. The whole process usually involves trying a number of different segmentation schemes in which the product and buyer differences that are most important for industry structure are gradually exposed.

A segmentation matrix should be tested by examining the strategies of competitors. If the scope of competitors' activities is plotted on the matrix, new segments or segmentation variables may be exposed. Conversely, competitors' activities may draw attention to segments that must inevitably be served together. I will have more to say about this below when interrelationships among segments are discussed. Figure 7–6 summarizes the steps required in industry segmentation.

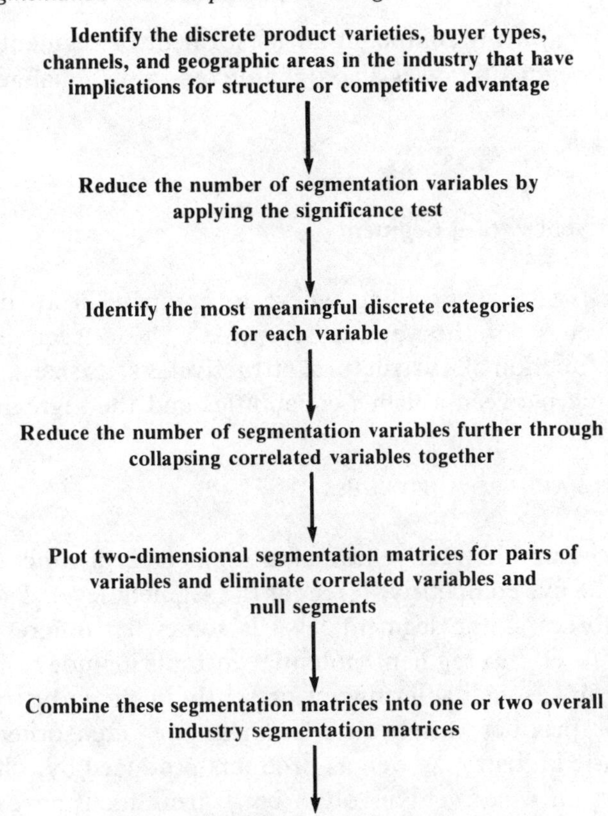
Identify the discrete product varieties, buyer types, channels, and geographic areas in the industry that have implications for structure or competitive advantage
Reduce the number of segmentation variables by applying the significance test
Identify the most meaningful discrete categories for each variable
Reduce the number of segmentation variables further through collapsing correlated variables together
Plot two-dimensional segmentation matrices for pairs of variables and eliminate correlated variables and null segments
Combine these segmentation matrices into one or two overall industry segmentation matrices
Test the matrices by locating competitors on them

Figure 7–6. The Industry Segmentation Process

Industry Segmentation and Competitive Strategy

Industry segments differ in their attractiveness and the sources of competitive advantage for competing in them. The key strategic questions that arise out of segmentation are:

- where in the industry a firm should compete (*segment scope*)
- how its strategy should reflect this segmentation

A firm can adopt a broadly-targeted strategy that addresses many segments, or exclusively address a small number of segments in a focus strategy. A broadly-targeted firm must also be aware of the vulnerabilities it faces because segments have structural differences, just as a focused firm must recognize and deal with the threat of broadly-targeted firms competing in its segment or segments together with others. Segmentation is also dynamic and must change to reflect structural changes.

The Attractiveness of a Segment

The first issue in deciding where to compete in an industry is the attractiveness of the various segments. The attractiveness of a segment is a function of its structural attractiveness, its size and growth, and the match between a firm's capabilities and the segment's needs.

Structural Attractiveness

The structural attractiveness of a segment is a function of the strength of the five competitive forces at the segment level. The analysis of the five forces at the segment level is somewhat different than at the industry level. In a segment, potential entrants include firms serving other segments, as well as firms not presently in the industry. Substitutes for the product variety in a segment are often other product varieties in the industry, as well as products produced by other industries. Rivalry in a segment involves both firms focusing exclusively on the segment and firms that serve other segments well. Buyer and supplier power tend to be more segment-specific, but may well be influenced by buyer purchases in other segments or supplier sales to other segments. Thus the structural analysis of a segment is usually influenced heavily by conditions in other segments, more so than the structural analysis of an industry is affected by other industries.

The segments in an industry will often differ widely in structural attractiveness. In large turbine generators, for example, the segment consisting of large-capacity generators sold to large, privately-owned utilities is structurally attractive. Large-capacity generators are very sophisticated technologically and the scale and learning curve barriers to developing and producing them are high. Large units also offer many more opportunities for differentiation than smaller units. Greater thermal efficiency of large units creates lower costs of use for buyers, reducing buyer price sensitivity. Large utilities also tend to be more technologically sophisticated buyers and appreciate more features, enhancing competitors' ability to differentiate themselves. Large utilities also command the financial resources to be less price sensitive. Finally, the selling process to private utilities involves secret negotiations rather than public bidding in which the lowest qualified bid must be selected.

Analyzing the attractiveness of each segment is an important first step in deciding where to compete. As a test of the analysis, it is often quite illuminating to compute a firm's profitability in the various segments in which it competes and to compare this to both the structural analysis and any industry profitability data by segment that are available. Focused competitors may provide data on the profitability of the segments they occupy, for example. Differences in profitability by segment can be truly striking. Existing segment profitability is not necessarily an indication of potential profitability, however, because a firm may not be optimizing its strategy for each segment or, for that matter, for any segment.

Segment Size and Growth

Segments will frequently differ in their absolute size and growth rate. Size and growth will be important in their own right to the choice of where to compete. Size and growth also have an impact on structural attractiveness. The expected growth rate of each segment is important to rivalry and to the threat of entry, while size may affect the attractiveness of a segment to large competitors. Sometimes firms can sustain a position in smaller segments because large firms are not interested in them.

Determining the size and expected growth of segments is typically not easy. Data are hardly ever collected in ways that exactly match meaningful segment boundaries, especially segments determined by demand and cost considerations rather than industry convention. Hence a firm may need to invest in special data collection or market research to produce estimates of size and growth by segment.

Firm Position vis-à-vis a Segment

A firm's resources and skills, reflected in its value chain, will usually be better suited to some segments than others, influencing the attractiveness of a segment for a particular firm. Each segment will have somewhat different requirements for competitive advantage that are highlighted in constructing the segmentation matrix. The tools described in Chapters 3 and 4 can be used to determine a firm's relative position for competing in various segments and the possibilities for changing it.

Segment Interrelationships

Segments are often related in ways that have an important effect on the segments in which a firm wants to compete. Segments are related where activities in the value chain can be shared in competing in them—I call such opportunities *segment interrelationships.* There are often many opportunities to share value activities among segments. For example, the same sales force can sell to different buyer types, or the same manufacturing facilities can produce different product varieties.

Figures 7–7 and 7–8 illustrate a typical situation where interrelated value chains serve two segments. Strongly related segments are those where the shared value activities represent a significant fraction of total cost or have an important impact on differentiation. Segment interrelationships are analogous to interrelationships among business units competing in related industries. Segment interrelationships are within an industry, however, while interrelationships among business units are between industries.[10] Similarly, segment interrelationships are analogous to interrelationships involved in competing in different geographic areas.

The analysis of interrelationships is treated in detail in Chapter 9, where I focus on interrelationships among business units. The same concepts apply here, and I will summarize them briefly. Interrelationships among segments are strategically important where the benefits of sharing value activities exceed the cost of sharing. Sharing value activities leads to the greatest benefit if the cost of a value activity is subject to significant economies of scale or learning, or sharing allows a firm to improve the pattern of capacity utilization of the value activity. Economies of scale or learning in a value activity imply that sharing across segments may yield a cost advantage relative to single-segment competitors. Sharing activities among segments is also beneficial where it increases differentiation in the value activity or lowers the cost of differentiation. Sharing a value activity is most important to differentiation where the value activity has a significant impact on differentiation and sharing allows a significant improvement in uniqueness or a significant reduction in the cost of providing it. The firm with a shared service organization across segments, for example, will gain an advantage over the single segment competitor if service is vital to differentiation and sharing lowers the cost of hiring better service

[10]The strength of interrelationships within an industry and between industries determine the boundaries of strategically distinct industries.

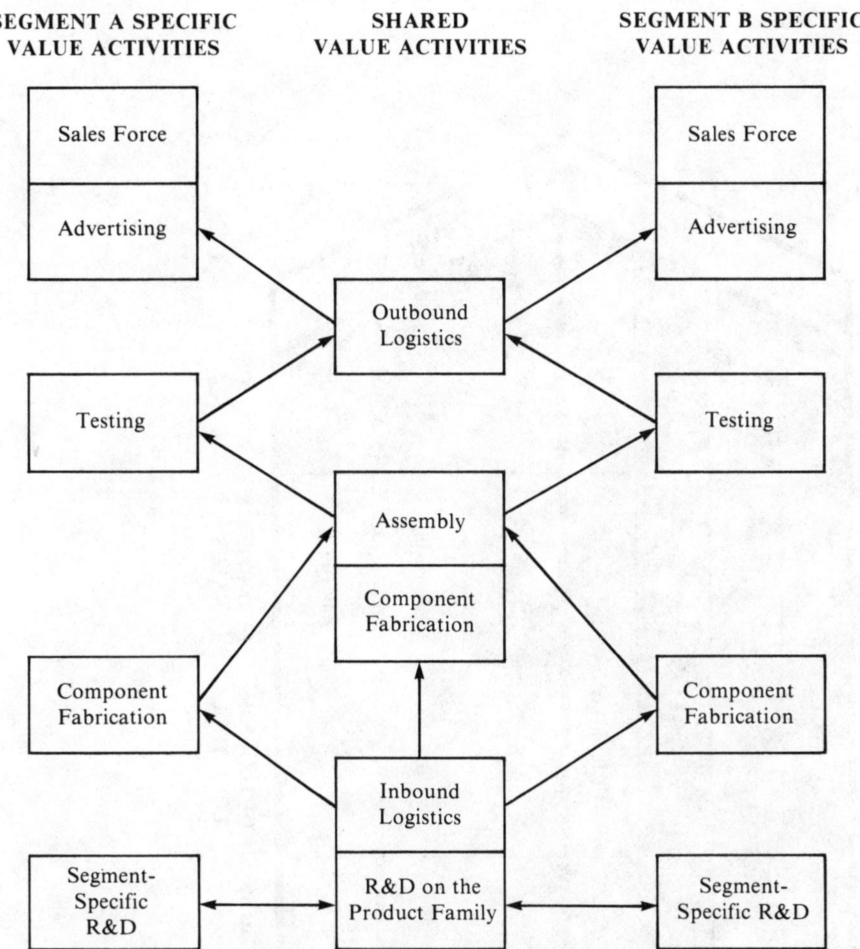

Figure 7–7. Interrelated Value Chains for Different Segments

personnel. Sharing a brand name across segments is also often a source of differentiation.

The benefits of interrelationships among segments are offset by costs of *coordination, compromise,* and *inflexibility* in jointly serving segments with shared activities. Coordination costs simply reflect the greater complexity of operating in multiple segments with shared value activities. Compromise costs occur when the value chain designed to serve one segment is not optimal in serving another segment, and serving both undermines a firm's ability to serve either. For example, the brand name, advertising, and image appropriate to a premium product may be inconsistent with the needs of a low-end product variety or vice versa. Here a firm has to create and advertise two

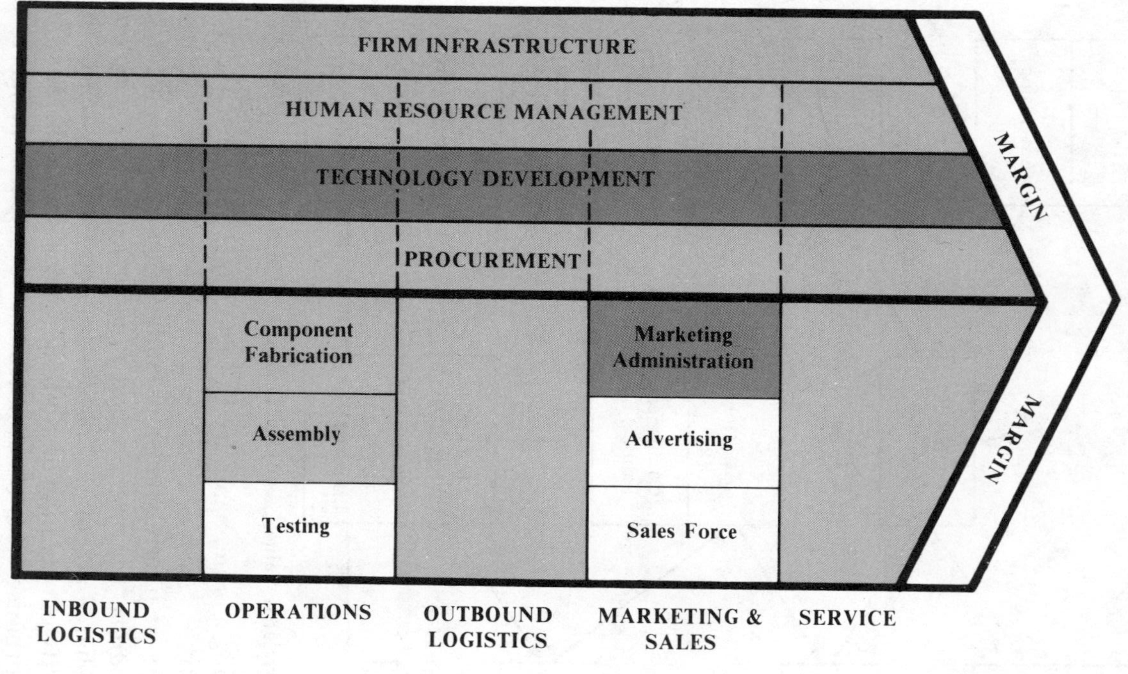

Figure 7–8. Segment Interrelationships Displayed on the Value Chain

separate brand names if it wants to operate in both segments. K. Hattori, for example, uses the Seiko name for higher-priced watches, and the Pulsar name for medium-priced watches. Even then, retailers often tell customers that a Pulsar is really a Seiko.

A less extreme form of compromise cost is where the optimal value chain for serving one segment is somewhat different from the optimal value chain for serving another, but the same chain will serve both at some penalty in cost or differentiation. For example, a sales force selling to two buyer segments may not be as effective as a sales force specializing in one, or a manufacturing process with the flexibility to produce two product varieties may not be as efficient as one that is designed to produce one.

Segment spillover is a form of compromise that occurs when a firm tries to serve multiple segments. Buyers in one segment may demand the same terms as buyers in another. For example, the prices charged in one buyer segment may spill over to other segments because buyers demand equal treatment, a problem a single segment competitor does not have. Because the bases for segmentation include differences in the optimal value chain, the need to compromise in jointly serving segments is quite prevalent.

The need to compromise in jointly serving segments can partially or completely nullify the ability of a firm to gain competitive advantage from sharing value activities among segments. The firm is thus forced to trade the cost of creating parallel value activities to serve different segments (e.g., a separate production process or a different brand name) against the cost of compromise. In extreme cases, the compromise required to serve multiple segments goes beyond nullifying the advantages of sharing value activities and creates disadvantages. Because of major inconsistencies in such areas as brand image or production process, for example, competing in one segment can make it very difficult to operate in another segment even with a completely separate value chain.

The final cost of sharing activities among segments is the cost of inflexibility. Sharing value activities limits the flexibility of modifying strategies in the different segments, and may create exit barriers in leaving a segment. The cost of inflexibility, as well as the other costs of sharing, are discussed extensively in Chapter 9.

The net competitive advantage of competing in multiple segments versus focusing on one or a few is a function of the balance between the advantages of sharing value activities and the costs. In most industries the pattern of segment interrelationships is not symmetric. Some pairs of segments have stronger interrelationships than others. A firm may also be able to share some value activities across one group of segments and another group of value activities across another, perhaps overlapping, group of segments.

As a result of the pattern of segment interrelationships, firms often cluster in the group of segments they serve. In copiers, for example, Xerox, Kodak, and IBM have traditionally competed in high-volume copiers, while Ricoh, Savin, Canon, Minolta, and several others have served the low-volume convenience copiers. High-volume copiers are characterized by low unit manufacturing volumes, direct sales forces, and different technological issues than low-volume machines, which are mass-produced and sold through distributors. Only through having what amounts to a separate company (Fuji Xerox) has Xerox spanned the whole product range, while Canon has had to broaden its line upward painstakingly through major investments in the new value activities needed to compete in the high end. This example illustrates the point that the greater the cost of sharing activities among segments, the more the broadly-targeted firm is required to create essentially separate value chains if it is to be successful. Yet separate value chains negate the benefits of broad targeting.

A good way to test a firm's understanding of interrelationships among segments is to plot competitors on the segmentation matrix (see Figure 7–9). If all competitors in one segment also compete in another, chances are good that strong interrelationships are present. By looking at the pattern of competitors, one can often gain insight into the pattern of interrelationships.[11] However, competitors may

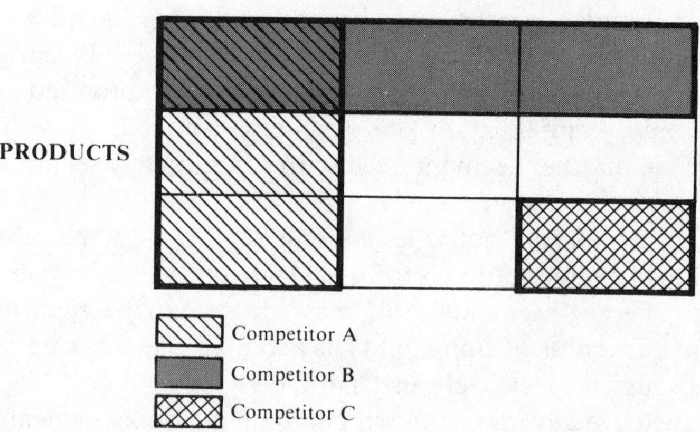

Figure 7–9. Competitor Positions on the Segmentation Matrix

[11]It may also be illuminating to distinguish among strong and weak positions in each segment.

well have failed to recognize or exploit all segment interrelationships.

Interrelationships among segments may suggest further collapsing of the industry segmentation matrix. Segments with very strong interrelationships can be combined if a firm cannot logically serve one without serving the other. Once a firm has entered one such segment the barriers to entering the adjacent segment are low. By examining interrelationships, therefore, an industry segmentation matrix may be simplified for strategic purposes.

Segment Interrelationships and Broadly-Targeted Strategies

Interrelationships among segments provide the strategic logic for broadly-targeted strategies that encompass multiple segments if they lead to a net competitive advantage. Strong interrelationships among segments define the cluster of segments a firm should serve. Strong interrelationships will also define the logical paths of mobility of firms in the industry from one segment to another. A firm competing in one segment will be most likely to enter other segments where there are strong interrelationships.

The broadly-targeted competitor bets that the gains from interrelationships among segments outweigh the costs of sharing, and designs its strategy to strengthen the interrelationships and minimize the coordination and compromise costs. Developments in manufacturing technology are working today to lower the cost of compromise in serving different product segments because of enhanced flexibility to produce different varieties in the same facility. These or other developments that increase the flexibility of value activities without a cost or differentiation penalty will work toward the benefit of broadly-targeted competitors.

A broadly-targeted competitor should usually not serve *all* industry segments, however, because the benefits of sharing value activities are nearly always outweighed in some segments by the cost of compromise. Serving all segments is also often not desirable because all segments are not structurally attractive. A broadly-targeted firm may have to serve some unattractive segments, however, because they contribute to the overall cost or differentiation of shared value activities, or to defending its position in structurally attractive segments. As will be discussed further in Chapter 14, occupying some unattractive segments may prevent a competitor from establishing beachheads in those segments from which it can build on interrelationships into the firm's segments. The gap left by U.S. automobile firms in less profitable small cars, for example, seems to have provided the Japanese automakers with the opportunity to enter the U.S. market.

The Choice of Focus

Focus strategies rest on *differences* among segments, either differences in the firm's optimal value chain or differences in the buyer value chain that lead to differing purchase criteria. The existence of costs of coordination, compromise, or inflexibility in serving multiple segments is the strategic underpinning of sustainable focus strategies. By optimizing its value chain for only one or a few segments, the focuser achieves cost leadership or differentiation in its segment or segments compared to more broadly-targeted firms that must compromise. Focus strategies involve the entire value chain and not just marketing activities, as in market segmentation.

Focus strategies can encompass more than one segment and encompass several segments with strong interrelationships. However, the ability of a firm to optimize for any segment is generally diminished by broadening the target. Note that a firm can focus within an industry *at the same time* as it achieves interrelationships with business units competing in other industries that do not force it to compromise in serving the target segments. The choice of competitive scope involves simultaneously understanding interrelationships at both levels (see Chapter 15).

Firms can choose different groups of segments on which to focus, which may or may not overlap. Figure 7–10 illustrates a case where a number of firms are supplying information products to financial services firms. Company A has adopted a product-based focus strategy of supplying one product variety (data bases) to all buyers. Company B, on the other hand, has adopted a buyer-based focus strategy in which it sells the full array of products to insurance companies. Company C has yet another focus strategy which concentrates exclusively on providing consulting advice to finance companies. Its buyers either acquire the data elsewhere or generate it themselves. Company C's focus strategy does not overlap with the segments served by companies A and B.[12]

As noted above, focus strategies involving several segments rest on the presence of strong interrelationships among the segments that outweigh the suboptimization of serving more than one. For example,

[12]There is no need for strategies that combine segments to be horizontal or vertical on the segmentation matrix. However, focus strategies are often horizontal or vertical because product, buyer, channel, or geographic focus strategies are common.

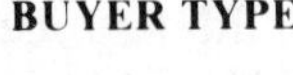

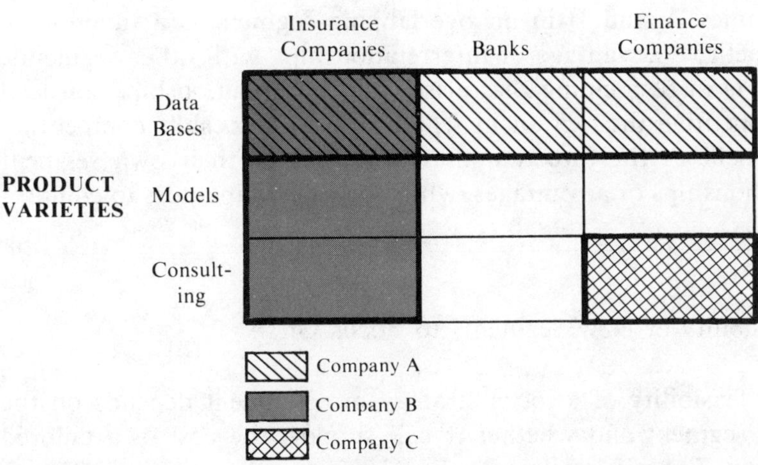

Figure 7–10. Alternative Focus Strategies in a Financial Information Industry

company A has maximized interrelationships based on shared R&D and production of only data bases, which offset the fact that each buyer type would ideally prefer a somewhat different type of data base and perhaps a different delivery system. Company B, on the other hand, has chosen a buyer-based focus strategy that gains competitive advantage through optimizing its delivery and selling system for insurance companies. Company C has opted for the potential differentiation benefits of offering only consulting to finance companies and the internal benefits of product specialization, while forgoing potential scale economies of a broader focus. Thus each company has built a focus strategy based on different interrelationships and different competitive advantages, and each bears different costs of compromise.

Interesting competitive issues arise in segments where focus strategies with different segment interrelationships overlap. In Figure 7–10 this occurs in the upper left-hand segment in the matrix. In that segment, the different focus strategies create competitive advantages and disadvantages of different types for the two firms competing in the segment. Company A brings extensive low-cost data bases and an acute understanding of data base design, while Company B brings an in-depth understanding of insurance companies and cost advantages from offering a full line. Just as interrelationships can lead to competitive advantages, they can also make a firm inflexible in competing in a segment. For example, company A could not easily modify its data base management system to better respond to the needs of insurance company buyers because of the effect this would have on its activities with banking and finance companies. The relative position of companies A and B in an overlapping segment is a function of net competitive advantage of interrelationships with other segments. Constraints in responding that arise from interrelationships can lead to a competitive interaction in which firms try to shift competition in a segment in the direction that best exploits their own segment interrelationships or advantages, while forcing competitors to compromise theirs.

The Feasibility of New Segments to Focus On

The feasibility of a focus strategy in a segment depends on the size of a segment and whether it will support the cost of a tailored value chain. Even if a tailored value chain would be more responsive to the needs of a particular new segment, the costs of the tailored chain may not be recoupable. Thus many potential segments should not be served with focus strategies.

There are four ways that new segments emerge as viable for focus strategies. The first is that tailoring gets less costly. Falling economies of scale may allow a focus strategy, for example. The second reason focus on a new segment becomes viable is that the segment grows enough to overcome the fixed cost of serving it. A third reason is that firms exploit interrelationships with other industries to overcome scale thresholds in serving the segment. Finally, a segment may become viable if a firm pursues it globally, using volume in many countries to overcome scale economies. Here the firm is pursuing geographic interrelationships.

Firms can preempt new focus strategies by perceiving new segmentation schemes or by identifying opportunities to make new segments viable. Recent reductions in scale economies have occurred in some technologies, including computerized manufacturing and design. These, coupled with enhanced ability to exploit interrelationships among business units (Chapter 9) and compete globally, will be continually creating opportunities for new focus strategies in the 1980s.

The Sustainability of a Focus Strategy

I have discussed how a firm can choose a segment or small group of segments on which to focus, based on the attractiveness of those segments and the interrelationships among them. A final issue in choosing a focus strategy is the sustainability of the focus strategy against competitors. The sustainability of a focus strategy is determined by three factors:

- *Sustainability against broadly-targeted competitors.* The size and sustainability of the competitive advantage created through focus vis-à-vis more broadly-targeted competitors.
- *Sustainability against imitators.* The mobility barriers to imitating the focus strategy or being outfocused by a competitor with an even narrower target.
- *Sustainability against segment substitution.* The risk that buyers will be drawn away to other segments the focuser does not serve.

Sustainability Against Broadly-Targeted Competitors

Broadly-targeted competitors may either already compete in a focuser's segment or be potential entrants to the segment as an extension of their existing base in other segments. The focuser's competitive advantage over a more broadly-targeted competitor is a function of:

- the degree of compromise a broadly-targeted competitor faces in serving the focuser's segments and other segments at the same time
- the competitive advantage of sharing value activities with other segments in which the broadly-targeted competitor operates

The more *different* the focuser's value chain is from the value chain required to serve other segments, the more sustainable is the focus strategy. In the airconditioning industry in the United States and Europe, for example, the distribution channels that serve the residential and commercial market are separate from those that serve the industrial market. In Latin America, Asia, and the Middle East, however, the same channels tend to stock the whole line. A focus strategy has been much more successful and sustainable in the United States and Europe than in other parts of the world, because focusers can tailor the value chain to the channel that specializes in their target segment. The focus strategy is more sustainable as buyer needs in the target segment are more *different* and *unusual* vis-à-vis other segments.

The problems of Royal Crown in the soft drink industry illustrate these principles. Royal Crown focuses on colas, unlike Coke and Pepsi, which supply a broader line of soft drink flavors. Supplying only colas does not involve a significantly different value chain than supplying a broad line. Buyer needs and purchasing behavior are not much different for colas than for other flavors except for the flavor preference. Conversely, supplying a broad line allows significant benefits of sharing activities in production, distribution, and marketing. Hence Royal Crown's focus strategy leads to no competitive advantage against its broadly-targeted competitors, only disadvantages. On the other hand, Mercedes gains strong advantages through focus in automobiles by using a tailored value chain compared to its broad-line competitors.

Mead's strategic evolution in the paper container industry illustrates how the factors underlying the sustainability of a focus strategy can change. In response to intense cost competition in high volume containers in the late 1970's, Mead chose a focus strategy targeted at low volume, high value-added segments. In the early 1980's, however, new continuous-run paper corrugators were developed that operated faster but at the same time required much less setup time. This made it increasingly possible for broad line competitors to service small orders economically. Mead was forced to modify its focus strategy and serve a broader range of segments while investing in the new equipment. In this case, the value chain required to serve Mead's target segments became less different from that required to efficiently serve the high volume segments.

The sustainability of a focus strategy will erode if a segment's differences from others fall over time, if technological change reduces the cost of compromise in serving multiple segments or increases the ability to reap interrelationships (see Chapter 9), or if a tailored value chain for the segment becomes too expensive relative to a more standardized chain. Hence there is an important dynamic element in choosing the segments on which to focus, reflecting an ongoing tradeoff between the advantages of focus on a particular segment and the gains of sharing through competing in multiple segments.

Sustainability Against Imitators

The second type of risk facing a focuser is that another firm will choose to replicate the focus strategy, either a firm new to the industry or one dissatisfied with its existing strategy. The sustainability of a focus strategy against imitators is based on the sustainability of the competitive advantage a focuser possesses, analyzed using the concepts in Chapters 3 and 4. The mobility barriers to imitating a focus strategy are the scale economies, differentiation, channel loyalty, and/or other barriers unique to the focus strategy. The height of the barriers against imitation of a focus strategy thus depends on the structure of the particular segment. Imitating Kodak's high-end focus in copiers, for example, requires that a firm overcome barriers due to proprietary technology as well as economies of scale in establishing an in-house sales and service network.

The size of a segment can affect the threat of imitation of a focus strategy. In a small segment, even modest scale economies may be significant relative to segment size if they cannot be offset by interrelationships, and competitors may not be interested in entering. Conversely, in a growing industry there is the continual possibility not only that a focus strategy will be imitated but also that a focuser will be "outfocused" as ever-narrower segments become viable. In the rapidly growing information industry, for example, outfocusing is pervasive as firms develop ever more specialized data bases for narrower target buyer groups.

Sustainability Against Segment Substitution

The final determinant of the sustainability of a focus strategy is the risk of segment substitution. A focus strategy concentrating on a segment is vulnerable to the disappearance of that segment. This may be the result of changes in the environment, technology, or competitor behavior. The risk of segment substitution is analyzed in the same way as substitution in general (see Chapter 8). Segment substitution can be influenced by competitors just as industry-level substitution can—if anything, even more so. Competitors often attempt to shift demand away from a focuser's segments through techniques such as marketing, technological innovation, or even lobbying for government standards that worsen conditions in the segment. Where a focuser faces competitors serving much larger segments, there is a risk that their advertising spending and other marketing may shape buyer attitudes and lead buyers away from the focuser's segment.

Pitfalls and Opportunities for Focusers and Broadly-Targeted Competitors

Several important lessons emerge from this analysis both for focusers and for broadly-targeted competitors:

Successful focus strategies must involve compromise costs for competitors. Focusing on a segment or group of segments is not sufficient to achieve competitive advantage in and of itself. The chosen segments must involve buyers with different needs, or require a value chain that differs from that which serves other segments. It is differences between the focuser's segment and other segments that lead to suboptimization by broadly-targeted competitors, and provide the source of a sustainable competitive advantage for the focuser.

Identifying a new way of segmenting an industry can be a major opportunity. A properly constructed industry segmentation matrix will often expose segments that are not reflected in the behavior of existing competitors. By identifying a new way of segmenting the industry, a firm can often design a focus strategy around a product variety, buyer group, channel, or geographic subdivision that has not previously been recognized as a segment but that has structural or value chain differences. New segments can be narrower or broader than segments currently recognized. Its differences imply that the new segment needs a distinctive strategy and value chain, and that competitors serving it together with other segments will be suboptimizing.

The firm that recognizes a meaningful new segmentation first can often gain a sustainable competitive advantage preemptively. Federal Express, for example, saw the small parcel requiring overnight delivery as a segment that no firm had focused on before. Federal Express designed a strategy around this segment involving a reconfigured value chain, and gained enormous advantages over competitors who were serving it as part of broader strategies. Similarly, Century 21 was first to recognize a broader nationwide segment in real estate brokerage.

Broad targeting does not necessarily lead to competitive advantage where there are industry segments. A broadly-targeted competitor must gain sustainable competitive advantage from competing in multiple segments if it is to enjoy above-average returns. These competitive advantages usually come from the interrelationships among segments. A cost leadership strategy rests on achieving a low-cost position through the scale and other advantages of competing in many segments. A differentiation strategy is based on achieving uniqueness in meeting use or signaling criteria that are widely valued by many segments. Without some tangible competitive advantage from breadth, the structural differences among segments will usually guarantee that a broadly-targeted competitor will be "stuck in the middle."

Broadly-targeted firms often serve too many segments. A firm aiming at an overly broad strategic target runs the risk of suboptimization, increasing its vulnerability to focusers. Reducing the number of segments served may decrease vulnerability, as well as increase profitability through eliminating unattractive segments. A broadly-targeted firm should consider dropping out of segments where:

- it gains little advantages from interrelationships with other segments
- it is forced to modify its entire strategy in order to serve the segment
- the segment is structurally unattractive
- sales and growth potential in the segment is limited
- defensive considerations do not require presence in the segment to block competitors

The relevant segments and breadth of target must be continually examined. The strategically meaningful segments in an industry will evolve over time due to shifts in buyer behavior, the emergence of new buyer groups, and technology that alters segment interrelationships. Thus the choice competitive scope within an industry must be continually reexamined. A firm cannot automatically accept a historically important segmentation as meaningful, despite the fact that old segmentations have a tendency to fade slowly from managers' minds. Viewing the choice of segments served as a permanent decision will inevitably bring strategic disaster.

New technology is changing old assumptions about segmentation. New technology, particularly microelectronics and information systems, is creating opportunities for both new focus and new broadly-targeted strategies. Flexibility in manufacturing, logistics, and other value activities is making it possible for broadly-targeted firms to tailor activities to segments while maintaining a single value chain. This is reducing opportunities for sustainable focus in some industries. At the same time, the same technological revolution is making strategies tailored to new segments viable. Computer-aided design, for example, is lowering the design cost of new product varieties. Firms must pay particular attention to how the new technologies might shake up the traditional logic of focus or broad targeting in their industries.

Industry Segmentation and Industry Definition

Drawing industry boundaries is always a matter of degree. Structural and value chain differences among product varieties and buyers work towards a narrower industry definition. Industry segmentation is thus a tool to probe for narrower industry definitions by exposing structural heterogeneity within an industry. Interrelationships among segments and business units (Chapter 9) create possibilities for broader industry definitions.

A useful working industry definition should encompass all segments for which segment interrelationships are very strong. Segments where interrelationships with other segments are weak may sometimes be separate industries from a strategic viewpoint. Related industries linked by strong interrelationships may in strategic terms be a single industry.

Where one actually chooses to draw industry boundaries is not so essential as long as both segmentation and strategic interrelationships are examined as part of structural analysis. Such an analysis will expose all the key determinants of competitive advantage that derive from competitive scope.

8
Substitution

All industries face the threat of substitution. Substitution is the process by which one product or service supplants another in performing a particular function or functions for a buyer. The analysis of substitution applies equally to products and processes, because the same principles govern a buyer's choice to do something in a new way anywhere in its value chain. Substitution is one of the five competitive forces determining the profitability of an industry, because the threat of substitution places a ceiling on industry prices. At the same time, substitution plays a prominent role in determining industry and a firm's demand. Penetration against substitutes is a major reason why industries and firms grow, and the emergence of substitutes is a major reason why they decline. Substitution is also inextricably tied to a firm's competitive scope within an industry, because it widens or narrows the range of segments in an industry.

How can a firm best defend against a substitute? What is the best strategy for promoting substitution if the firm is on the offensive? These are important questions in competitive strategy in many industries. This chapter will present a framework for analyzing substitution and answering those questions. I will first consider how to identify substitutes, an essential but often subtle step in substitution analysis. Next I will describe the economics of substitution, which define the threat of a substitute and provide the underpinnings of any strategic moves intended to influence it. I will then outline how the threat of substitution changes over time. With this as a background, the factors that influence the path of substitution will be identified. Substitution proceeds in some characteristic ways over time, which are important to recognize both in assessing the extent of the threat and in forecasting the penetration of a substitute. Finally, I will describe the strategic implications of the framework for both offensive and defensive strategy towards substitutes. The discussion is framed in terms of substitution at the industry level (e.g., carbon fiber substituting for titanium and aluminum), but the same basic principles apply to the substitution of one product form for another.

Identifying Substitutes

The first step in substitution analysis is to identify the substitutes an industry faces. This seemingly straightforward task is often not easy in practice. Identifying substitutes requires searching for products or services that perform the same generic function or functions as an industry's product, rather than products that have the same form. A truck differs greatly from a train, but they both perform the same generic function for the buyer—point-to-point freight transportation.[1]

The function a product performs depends on its role in the buyer's value chain. A product is used by the buyer in performing some activity or activities—a truck or a train is used in inbound or outbound logistics, for example, while skis are used as part of a buyer's recreation in winter. As discussed in Chapter 4, a product often affects not only the buyer value activity in which it is used but also many other activities. A component used in a product passes through inbound logistics, is held in inventory before it is used, and must be serviced in the field after sale, for example. Similarly, baby diapers are not only worn by the baby but also must be put on by the parent, laundered if they are reuseable, and purchased and stored. All the impacts of a product on the buyer are relevant in defining substitutes and their relative

[1]See Levitt (1960) for the classic statement of the need to think functionally.

performance. Finally, the value activity in which a product is used may be connected to other activities through linkages. The precision of a part can influence the need for product adjustment and for after-sale servicing, for example. Linkages affecting a product can also influence substitution, because they often create possibilities for discovering new ways to combine activities.

In the simplest form of substitution, one product substitutes for another in performing the same function in the same buyer value activity. This is the case of a ceramic engine part substituting for a metal engine part. Though the substitution is direct, linkages can still exist. A ceramic part may require different handling, for example. Even in simple substitutions, it is also important to define the function of a product in the activity generically rather than literally—what the product does rather than how it does it. The generic function of a product is often very broad, particularly in consumer goods. A manufacturer of metal downhill skis faces substitution not only from epoxy or fiberglass skis but also from cross-country skis, other winter sports equipment, other leisure products that can be used in winter, and from the buyer taking more leisure time in the summer rather than winter. The generic function of metal skis, most broadly defined, is recreation. The more generically the function of an industry's product is expressed, the greater the number of potential substitutes there usually are.

In the more complex forms of substitution, a substitute performs a different range of functions than an industry's product and/or affects buyer activities in a different way. In the case of a truck substituting for a train, for example, loading, unloading, packaging, and shipment size may all be different though both perform the same transportation function. A substitute may also perform a *wider or narrower range of functions* than an industry's product. For example, a word processor is not only a substitute for the functions of a typewriter but also for other functions such as calculating and small-quantity copying; a heat pump performs both heating and cooling, while a conventional boiler system can be used only for heating; a disposable diaper removes the need for laundering. Conversely, a waffle maker performs fewer functions than a toaster oven, and a specialty retailer sells only one line of goods that are a subset of the product assortment of a department store. In identifying substitutes, then, it is necessary to include products that can perform functions in addition to those of an industry's product, as well as products that can perform any significant function among those the industry's product can perform.

Because a substitute can perform a wider or narrower range of functions, chains of substitution for a product can go in very different directions. For example, the functions of a racetrack include both gambling and entertainment. Substitutes for the gambling function include casinos, off-track betting, and bookies, while substitutes for the entertainment function are even more numerous and include movies, books, sporting events, and so on. The more functions a product performs in the buyer's value chain, the greater the number of chains of substitutes.

While one usually thinks of substitutes only in terms of different products, in many industries there are at least four other options that must be considered as substitutes in a broad sense. One option is that the buyer *does not purchase anything at all* to perform the function, the most extreme form of a substitute with a narrower range of functions. In water meters, for example, the primary substitute is not to meter water usage at all. Similarly, the leading U.S. salt producer, Morton-Norwich, is being threatened by concern over the health effects of sodium that has reduced consumption.

A second potential substitute is to *lower the usage rate of the product required* to perform the function. In aluminum, for example, new beverage cans require thinner walls and hence less aluminum. Similarly, in offshore drilling rigs, new directional drilling techniques and down-hole measurement of the drilling process promise to reduce the amount of rig time required to drill.

A third substitute that is often overlooked is *used, recycled, or reconditioned products.* In aluminum, for example, perhaps the most threatening substitute facing primary aluminum producers is secondary (recycled) aluminum. Secondary consumption has grown rapidly in both the United States and Japan. Used products are important substitutes for new products in many industries producing durable goods, such as automobiles and recreational vehicles. Reconditioned products are an important substitute in aircraft engine components, where remachined and recoated engine parts are a threat to new spare parts.

A final potential substitute is for the buyer to perform the function internally, or *backward integration.* For example, the key substitute for many distribution industries is for the buyer to purchase directly from the manufacturer and perform the distribution function internally. Or in property and casualty insurance, a buyer can self-insure or establish a captive insurance subsidiary.

The relevant substitutes will differ by industry segment (Chapter 7). Different buyers use a product in different ways and hence value its functions differently. At a racetrack, for example, some buyers will come to enjoy the spectacle and an evening with friends, while others will spend most of their time at the betting windows or consulting tip sheets. Thus the relevant substitutes will differ by buyer or buyer segment. Similarly, different product varieties are used differently and hence may face different substitutes. Thus the pattern of substitutes changes by industry segment, and a firm's most threatening substitutes will be a function of what segments it actually serves.

Several substitutions can occur simultaneously. In the video game industry, for example, programmable video games with replaceable software cartridges are substituting for dedicated games that cannot be changed, at the same time that personal computers (on which game programs can be run) are substituting for programmable games. Multiple substitutions often involve the broadening or narrowing of product functions, as this example illustrates.

Multiple substitutions interact in shaping the overall substitution rate in an industry and may lead to counterintuitive consequences. Aspartame is a new artificial low calorie sweetener, for example, that is substituting for saccharin. Both aspartame and saccharin are substituting for sugar. The success of aspartame is expected by some observers to *increase* rather than decrease the demand for saccharin for a time, by expanding the overall market for artificial sweeteners faster than it substitutes for saccharin. Here the later substitute benefits an earlier substitute. The process can also work in reverse. The success or failure of the first substitute can make it harder (or easier) for the next one.

Even if an industry faces no direct substitutes, it may still be affected by substitution if there is the threat of substitution *downstream* if the buyer's product faces substitutes. For example, diesel engines and gasoline engines are contending substitutes for use in medium-sized trucks, diesel engines having long replaced gasoline engines in heavy trucks. If diesel engines win out, the demand for gasoline engine *parts* will fall, even though the parts themselves face no substitutes directly. Downstream substitution can also occur when the buyer's product depends on the sale of a complementary product that is threatened. If microwave ovens replace conventional ovens, for example, not only will the manufacturers of parts for conventional ovens be adversely affected but so will the manufacturers of cookware used in conventional ovens. In downstream substitution, the buyer no longer needs to perform the function of the firm's product.

Downstream substitution can both lower industry demand, and

can alter buyer behavior. A threat of downstream substitution will often be transmitted to suppliers in the form of greater price sensitivity. It may also lead buyers to look for help from their suppliers in meeting the threat through innovations in suppliers' products or other actions that raise the buyer's differentiation or lower the buyer's cost.

The number of substitutes for an industry's product will vary widely from industry to industry. Potential substitutes will differ in how they replace a product and in the level of threat they represent. It is important in substitution analysis to begin with the longest list of potential substitutes, because firms are much more prone to be blindsided by a substitute than to take a particular substitute too seriously.

The Economics of Substitution

One product substitutes for another if it offers buyers an inducement to switch that exceeds the cost or overcomes the resistance to doing so. A substitute offers an inducement to switch if the substitute provides the buyer with more value relative to its price than the product currently being used. There is always some cost of switching to a substitute because of the disruption and potential reconfiguration of buyer activities that must result, however. The threat of a substitute will vary depending on the size of the inducement relative to the required switching costs.

In addition to relative value to price and switching cost, the pattern of substitution is influenced by what I term the *buyer's propensity to switch.* Faced with equivalent economic inducements for substitution, different buyers will often evaluate substitution differently.

The threat of substitution, then, is a function of three factors:

- the relative value/price of a substitute compared to an industry's product
- the cost of switching to the substitute
- the buyer's propensity to switch

This simple statement of the economics of substitution masks the often subtle analysis required to understand it. The inducement a substitute offers to switch is properly measured over the *entire period the buyer will use it,* and discounted to the present. The cost of switching to a substitute is typically incurred immediately or even before the substitute provides any benefits at all. Both relative value/price (RVP) and the costs of switching are functions of a wide variety of factors, and are subject to change over time. Both can also involve considerable uncertainty. Understanding both requires a clear understanding of how a product affects the buyer's value chain, as well as the structure of the industry producing the substitute. Understanding the buyer's propensity to switch requires a further knowledge of the buyer's competitive circumstances, resources, and other characteristics that play a part in predicting its behavior towards a substitute.

Relative Value/Price

The value/price of a substitute is the value it provides to the buyer compared to the price the buyer pays for it. Relative value/price is the value/price of a substitute relative to the value/price of the product it seeks to replace (which I term the *product*). When there are no switching costs and the product is consumed quickly, the relevant RVP is solely a function of current conditions. Future circumstances are not important because the buyer can rapidly and without cost shift back and forth between the substitute and the product depending on the RVP at the time. When there are costs of switching or the product is durable, however, the relevant measure of the attractiveness of a substitute is the *expected* RVP of the substitute over the planning horizon.

The current prices of a substitute and a product are relatively easy to determine. The *expected* relative prices over the planning horizon are what should enter the RVP calculation, and must reflect the price changes forecasted over time. The purchase prices of both a substitute and a product must be adjusted for any discounts, rebates, or free ancillary products or services involved in their purchase. In office equipment, for example, free service is often part of the deal with a buyer, and must be included in comparing the prices of substitutes such as copiers and offset duplicators. Prices must be also adjusted for any tax credits the buyer gains in purchase.

The relative value of a substitute is based on exactly the same factors that determine differentiation, discussed in Chapter 4. A substitute is valuable if it lowers buyer cost or improves buyer performance relative to the product. This value must be *perceived* by the buyer, however, and hence a substitute's ability to signal value relative to the product is part of the value comparison. As with relative price, it is the expected relative value of the substitute over its period of use that enters into RVP, not just its current value.

The role of signaling in substitution is often as or more important than its role in differentiation. Substitution frequently involves a new product replacing a well established one. The substitute is typically unproven and its value may be quite uncertain, while the established product is proven and its qualities are well known. The ability of the substitute to signal value may, as a result, take on a significance that exceeds the role of signaling in differentiation.

The relative value of a substitute depends on its cumulative impact on the buyer's value chain compared to the product's, including both direct and indirect impacts. The principles of the analysis are the same as described in Chapter 4, though in practice there tend to be greater complexities in the analysis in substitution not usually present when comparing one brand of a product to another. A substitute and a product are often not directly comparable, and a substitute is more likely to involve a *different* pattern of impacts on the buyer's value chain than a competing brand. Two brands of cloth diapers have essentially the same impact on the household, for example, while disposable diapers are used very differently than cloth diapers. The differing patterns of use of a substitute and a product typically necessitate adjustments in order to determine the relative value of a substitute.

The following adjustments in measuring impact on buyer cost or buyer performance are commonly necessary when comparing the value of a substitute with the value of a product:

Usage Rate. The effect of a substitute on a buyer's cost depends on the amount of the substitute necessary to perform the same function. A substitute can lower buyer cost if less usage of it is required for a given result. For example, aspartame is much sweeter than saccharin, which means that less is necessary to achieve a comparable sweetening effect. Aspartame's much higher price per pound must thus be adjusted accordingly. The usage of a substitute required for a given outcome will be affected by such factors as its purity, concentration, reject rate, or operating speed.

Delivered and Installed Cost. The effect of a substitute on buyer cost depends on the delivered and installed cost of the substitute relative to the product. Delivered and installed cost may include such factors as the cost of transportation, installation, calibration, expanding or modifying space to house the substitute, and many other costs that frequently differ for a substitute and the product.

Financing Cost. The effect of a substitute on buyer cost depends on the cost of financing the purchase of the substitute relative to the product. In comparing mobile homes and conventional houses, for example, it is important to recognize that mobile homes are financed as vehicles while conventional houses are financed as real estate. Interest rates and/or terms differ for these different types of financing, generally in the form of easier credit availability but higher rates for financing mobile homes. Financing costs can be a large fraction of total cost in some industries.

Relative Variability of Price or Availability. The cost of a substitute to the buyer is a function of expected fluctuations in its price or availability (of both the product and ancillary items such as parts or service). Price fluctuations are often costly for a buyer to deal with, as are periods of tight supply. One of the potential benefits of ceramics, for example, is that it uses a plentiful and cheap raw material while metal parts are subject to greater price fluctuations because of changing metal prices. Both price fluctuations and the risk of nonavailability are partly a function of how many credible sources there are for a substitute relative to the product.

The cost of a substitute to the buyer is also affected by whether adequate capacity is present to serve key buyers' needs, particularly in the case of important inputs. Buyers are often unwilling to switch until enough capacity and suppliers are available to place the buyer in a tenable bargaining position. This creates the need in many substitutions to add capacity *ahead* of demand.

Direct Costs of Use. The effect of a substitute on buyer cost depends not only on its initial cost, but also on the present value of the *cost of using the substitute over its entire life* compared to that product. Direct costs of use involve such things as:

- cost of labor (reflecting the quality of labor necessary)
- consumables such as materials, fuel, or filters
- insurance
- time before replacement
- frequency and cost of maintenance

- cost of spare parts
- breakdown time (valued at its opportunity cost or the cost of reserve capacity)
- costs of maintaining the space required
- salvage value
- dismantling cost

In consumer goods, the cost of labor to use the substitute is the implicit cost of the buyer's time. In frozen entrees, for example, a major benefit to the buyer is time savings in preparation compared to most other meal types. Valuing a consumer's time is often difficult because it does not involve a money cost, though the techniques described in Chapter 4 provide a place to start.

In many industries, such as elevators and aircraft engines, the costs of using a substitute over its life are equal or are greater than the initial purchase price, and can be decisive in determining its attractiveness. For example, radial truck tires get approximately 25 percent more mileage than bias ply tires. Radials also have lower downtime from punctures, and can be retreaded twice compared to once for bias ply tires. Radials also improve the fuel efficiency of a truck on the order of 2 to 6 percent. These improvements in cost of use more than offset the 40 to 50 percent price premium for radial truck tires.

Indirect Costs of Use. The relative cost of use of a substitute must reflect costs throughout the buyer's value chain, and not just costs in the value activity in which a substitute is directly employed. Such indirect or system impacts are often overlooked by both firms and buyers. An automated material handling conveyor, for example, can reduce the number and required skill levels of workers on the assembly line, the number of lift trucks needed in the factory, and the required strength of shipping containers compared to conventional materials handling methods. Similarly, disposable diapers eliminate the need for storage and laundering of soiled diapers in addition to making diapering the baby easier because of attached fastening tapes and a form-fitting shape. Another example is the electronic cash register, which can help a retailer to lower required inventory and to control operating costs better than a mechanical cash register that cannot generate extensive on-line transactions data.

A substitute may affect the cost of other activities in the buyer's value chain if it:

- affects productivity in other value activities
- influences the need for other raw materials or their required quality
- requires different ancillary equipment
- affects the need for inventory
- affects the frequency and complexity of required quality control checks
- affects the amount and type of packaging materials needed in shipping
- affects product weight and hence transport costs

Buyer Performance. The value of a substitute must reflect any differences in its impact on the buyer's performance relative to the product. An electronic switching system for telecommunications can be more easily adapted to new requirements than an electromechanical switch, for example. A color TV provides more realistic pictures than a black and white set and therefore greater entertainment. Another example of a substitution based heavily on improving buyer performance is disposable diapers. Disposable diapers offer greater cleanliness than cloth diapers and are softer and less likely to cause diaper rash. As is often true in differentiation, the performance of a substitute from the buyer's perspective may involve intangibles such as perceived status and the quality of personal relationships. The effect of a substitute on buyer performance is not always easy to measure, though it always can be estimated.

The substitution of robotics for a conventional manned machine tool provides an example of a complex substitution that involves direct cost of use effects, indirect cost of use effects, and effects on buyer performance. A robot reduces labor cost by increasing capital cost, and may increase the output rate of the production step in which it is employed. Robots can also save raw material cost and do not take sick leave, though they must be maintained. Indirectly, robots can alter the material preparation needed in previous production steps as well as material handling needs. Potential performance effects of robots include higher reliability, greater flexibility, and higher workplace safety.

Number of Functions. The effect of a substitute on buyer cost and performance must be adjusted for the range of functions it can perform relative to the product. Wider functionality usually improves the relative value of a substitute if buyers value the additional functions.

This is not always the case, however, since wider functionality may come at the expense of the quality of performance of particular key functions. For example, personal computers that play video games have many more functions than video game machines, but video game machines are still easier to use and the games playable on them have better quality graphics. Lower functionality usually reduces the value of the substitute but this can be offset by the corresponding reduction in price or superior performance of the narrower range of functions. Changing functionality can not only affect buyer performance but also alter the buyer's cost of use, as the electronic cash register example demonstrated.

Attaching a value to additional functions (or missing functions) that affect performance in RVP calculations is often difficult, just as it is in differentiation analysis. The problem is particularly severe in consumer goods, because buyer performance often involves satisfying intangible needs. The principle of valuing different functionality is to examine how the functions involved impact the buyer's value chain, and calculate the effect on buyer cost or performance. One approach to valuing particular functions is to look for stand-alone products that perform the functions, and see what buyers are willing to pay for them. Valuing differences in functions that affect buyer cost is typically easier than valuing those that affect buyer performance.

Cost and Performance of Complementary Products. The effect of a substitute on buyer cost and performance may be a function of the cost and performance of complementary products used with it relative to those used with the product.[2] For example, movie theaters face the threat of substitution by home TV and videotape recorders, among other products. The cost to the buyer of going to a movie in a theater includes the time and cost of transportation to the theater and parking, and the cost of buying popcorn. The cost of these complementary purchases that are not necessary with home entertainment is one of the reasons movies fell from 8.2 percent of U.S. recreational expenditures in 1936 to under 3 percent by the mid-1970s.[3] Similarly, substitution of recreational vehicles such as motor homes depends on such complements as gasoline, roads, and campgrounds.

Uncertainty. There is usually some uncertainty involved in how a substitute will affect the buyer's cost or performance, and this must

[2]Chapter 12 describes the strategic issues raised by complementary products in more detail. Differential cost and quality of complementary products are rarely issues in differentiation among brands.

[3]"General Cinema Corporation," 1976.

be reflected in the RVP calculation. One major source of uncertainty is the possibility that the substitute will be improved in subsequent generations of the product. This can substantially delay switching by buyers. Uncertainty can be introduced into RVP by lowering the assumed value of a substitute by some discount factor.

Perception of Value. It is the buyer's perception of the RVP of a substitute that will determine the threat of a substitute, not necessarily the reality of RVP. Buyer awareness of a substitute is often not as great as that of the established product, and knowledge about the benefits and features of a substitute is often incomplete. Relative inability to signal value will thus effectively reduce the perceived RVP of a substitute. Buyers are least likely to perceive the benefits of a substitute when:

- the advantage of the substitute is in lowering the costs of use over time rather than immediately
- the advantages of the substitute are indirect and involve a number of value activities rather than direct advantages in the value activity in which the substitute is employed
- the advantages of the substitute are in raising performance over time rather than immediately
- gaining the advantages of the substitute requires a significant change in behavior or use patterns by the buyer
- the credibility of the substitute's benefit is hard to assess

In all these cases, a buyer may not fully understand the impact of a substitute on its value chain; hence the need for signaling value through a variety of means is great. The substitution of robotics for conventional production equipment, described earlier, is a good example of a substitution where accurate perception of value has been a barrier to substitution, particularly in the United States relative to Japan.

While it is more common that buyers have difficulty recognizing the value of a substitute, sometimes the opposite occurs. Sometimes substitution occurs for glamour or to appear progressive, with little understanding of the actual value of the substitute. In power supplies, for example, some buyers are changing to the new switch mode technology whose needs are probably better met by the older linear technology. In such cases, time may lower the perception of a substitute's actual value.

A substitute signals value in the same ways a firm does generally (see Chapter 4), using tools such as advertising, the sales force, demonstrations, and placement of units with opinion leaders. The stock of knowledge about a substitute as well as the expenditures by the substitute industry on signaling will determine how accurately the value of a substitute is perceived. Word of mouth and other sources of information not directly controlled by a firm are also vital.

Switching Costs

Substitution always involves some costs of switching to the substitute for the buyer, which are weighed against RVP. The higher the switching cost relatively, the more difficult substitution will be. Switching costs in substitution are analogous to those of changing from one supplier to another in an industry.[4] Switching costs are usually higher in substitution than in switching suppliers, however, because substitution may require switching to a new supplier *plus* switching to a new way of performing a function.

Switching costs potentially arise from all the impacts a substitute has on the buyer's value chain. Both the value activity in which the substitute is employed as well as other value activities it indirectly affects may require one-time costs of changeover. Switching costs most common in substitution are the following:

Identification and Qualification Sources. Finding sources for the substitute and gathering information about them are switching costs. So is the need to test a substitute to see if it meets performance standards. The cost of qualifying a 64K memory chip to replace a 16K chip has been estimated at $50,000, for example, and the process can take as long as a year.

Cost of Redesign of Reformulation. A buyer's product or value activities must often be redesigned to accept a substitute. Reformulating a consumer food product to accept high-fructose corn syrup instead of sugar, for example, requires out-of-pocket costs as well as the time and opportunity cost involved in testing the reformulated product.

[4]The costs of switching suppliers are described in *Competitive Strategy,* Chapters 1 and 6.

Redesign costs can affect many value activities. The layout of an entire plant must be changed to get the benefits of a new materials handling system, for example. Similarly, purchasing synthetically produced gas made from coal gasification instead of natural gas requires a user to modify gas burning equipment because of synthetic gas's slightly different qualities. The cost of redesign or reformulation will be lower if the buyer is changing product generations or building a new facility anyway.

Retraining or Relearning Costs. Switching to a substitute often requires learning how to use the substitute or changing use patterns. A typist who has been using a manual typewriter must get used to the much lighter touch of an electric one, for example, while a cook must learn a new set of cooking procedures to use a microwave. Similarly, plant engineers and maintenance personnel must go down the learning curve with a new type of machine tool.

The cost of retraining includes the cost of downtime and higher reject rates during the shakedown period and other such costs besides the out-of-pocket costs of learning or training themselves. Retraining costs will be highest where a substitute is used very differently from the product. Shifting from black and white to color TV is easy, for example, while shifting from conventional ovens to microwave ovens requires learning about oven operation, procedures, cooking times, and how to get the best results with different foods.

Changing Role of the User. Quite apart from the need to learn new behavior, substitution frequently involves a change in role for the user that can be a positive or negative influence on the cost of switching. Automating a manufacturing process can relegate equipment operators or engineers to passive or noncritical roles, for example, which can be reflected in subtle or open resistance to a substitute. A husband or wife who cooks for the family may resist a food product that removes all the opportunity for a personal touch that demonstrates caring.

Risk of Failure. The risk that a substitute will fail to perform is a cost of switching. The cost of failure will vary widely from product to product. In fiber optics, the severe consequences of failure because of the role of fiber optics as the communications link in larger systems have made buyers conservative in switching from copper wire and cable.

New Ancillary Products. Changing to a substitute may require investments in new related equipment or material such as testing gear, spare parts, and software. While the cost of use of such ancillary products is included in the RVP of a substitute, the one-time cost of reequipping is a cost of switching. The need to invest in new ancillary products depends primarily on the compatibility of the equipment or parts used with the substitute with those used with the product, and the extent to which the substitute involves different types of interfaces with related products. Like redesign costs, the cost of investing in new ancillary products is lowest when the ancillary products would have been replaced anyway.

Switching Costs Versus Switching Back Costs. Both the cost of failure of a substitute and the risk that its RVP will shift adversely are a function of the cost of *switching back* to the original product. If it is easy and inexpensive to switch back, the risk of switching is lower. The cost of switching back to the original product is usually less than the cost of switching to the substitute, because prior use of the product implies that the buyer already knows how to use it and has the required ancillary products. However, some switching costs, such as changeover costs and layout changes, cannot be avoided in switching back. There may also be some unique cost of switching back, such as confusing the buyer.

The cost of switching back usually rises as a function of the time since substitution, though some switching back costs are typically present no matter how short the experience with the substitute is. The relationship between switching cost and switching back costs has implications for substitution strategy that I will discuss below.

Buyer Propensity to Substitute

Buyers with different circumstances and in different industries do not all have equal propensities to substitute when faced with a comparable economic motivation. Differences in their circumstances lead buyers to respond to a given RVP and switching cost differently. While such differences might be treated as factors that modify RVP or switching costs, it is more helpful in practice to isolate them.

Resources. Substitution often involves up-front investments of capital and other resources. Access to such resources will differ from one buyer to another.

Risk Profile. Buyers often have very different risk profiles, the result of such things as their past history, age and income, ownership structure, background and orientation of management, and nature of competition in their industry. Buyers prone to risk taking are more likely to substitute than buyers that are risk-averse.

Technological Orientation. Buyers experienced with technological change may be less concerned with some kinds of substitution risks, while extremely aware of others that a less technologically sophisticated buyer would be oblivious to.

Previous Substitutions. The second substitution may be easier for a buyer than the first, unless the first substitution has been a failure. The buyer's uncertainties over undertaking a substitution may have diminished if a past substitution has been successful, or risen if a past substitution has led to difficulties. In the soft drink industry, this seems to have worked to the benefit of aspartame.

Intensity of Rivalry. Buyers under intense competitive pressure and searching for competitive advantage will tend to substitute more quickly to gain a given advantage than those that are not.

Generic Strategy. The RVP of a substitute will have different significance depending on the competitive advantage that industrial, commercial, or institutional buyers are seeking or the value of time and particular performance needs of the household buyer. A substitute that offers a cost saving will tend to be of more interest to a cost leader than a differentiator, for example.

Many of these factors that shape the buyer's propensity to substitute will be a function of the particular decision maker who is involved in the purchase decision.

Segmentation and Substitution

Both the identity of substitutes and the threat of substitution often differ by industry segment. This is because the economics of substitution are different for different product varieties and buyers, reflecting their structural and value chain differences. Thus a merging of the analysis in Chapter 7 and that in this chapter will not only expose differences in the substitution threat among segments but also assist in the construction of the industry segmentation matrix itself.

The threat of substitution will vary by buyer group if RVP, switching costs, or the propensity to substitute vary. The RVP of a substitute often varies among buyers in an industry because of differences in how they use a product, the value they attach to various product attributes, and the other impacts of the product on their value chain. In the racetrack case discussed earlier, for example, buyers attending primarily for entertainment will have different substitutes than buyers attending primarily for gambling. Similarly, the advantages of radial truck tires in mileage and retreading ability will have more value to a long-haul fleet operator than to a local pickup and delivery service. In the same vein, the value of the convenience of disposable diapers is probably higher to families with two working spouses than to families in which one spouse stays home.

Switching costs also differ from buyer to buyer within an industry. Retraining costs are a function of existing procedures. The need for redesign or new ancillary products will relate to the specifics of how a product is used. Buyer propensity to substitute can also vary dramatically among buyers, a function of buyer resources, orientation, and so on. In many consumer goods, for example, substitution occurs first with high-income buyers who have the resources to purchase new items while they are expensive.

A good example of how substitution threat varies by buyer segment is in the adoption of personal computers by small businesses. Personal computers are a substitute for manual methods (e.g., standard office machines) and computer service bureaus. As Figure 8–1 indicates, the degree of penetration of personal computers in small businesses is correlated to the size of the business. Personal computers have penetrated much further within larger companies because those firms have more complex paperwork needs and thus a greater need for automation, and also greater resources to invest in capital purchases.

The substitution threat can vary not only for buyer segments but also for different product varieties, geographic areas, and channels. In each case the substitute may perform different functions or be used in different ways and hence its RVP or switching costs may differ. Full-size office typewriters are more vulnerable to substitution from word processors than are portable electric typewriters, for example, because the special features and correcting capabilities of word processors are more valuable in office uses than for intermittent personal typing.

The penetration of a substitute often follows such segment differ-

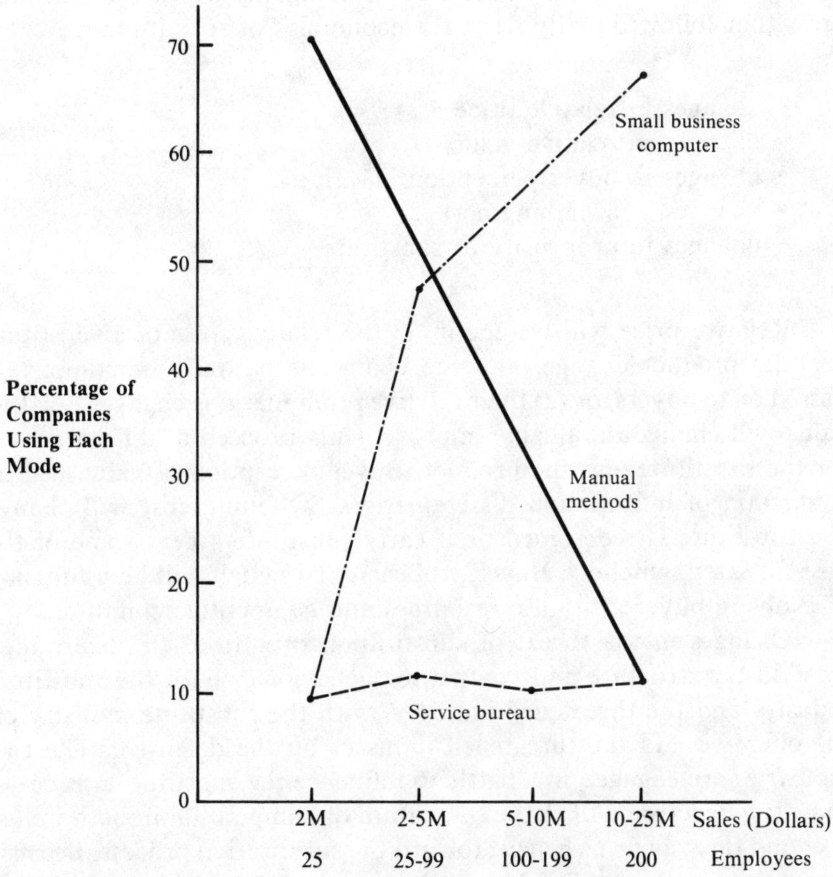

Figure 8–1. Use of Personal Computers in Small Business, 1981

ences. A substitute penetrates by expanding the number of segments it serves, penetrating new segments in order of the size of RVP of the substitute and the cost of switching in them. Thus the interaction of segmentation and substitution is often vital to understanding the path of substitution, a subject that I will treat below.

Changes in the Substitution Threat

The threat of a substitute often changes over time, with a corresponding impact on the pattern of substitution. Many of the sources of change in the substitution threat are predictable and can often be influenced through a firm's offensive or defensive substitution strategy.

Changes in the threat of substitution occur in five broadly defined areas that follow directly from the economics of substitution:

- changes in relative price
- changes in relative value
- changes in buyer perception of value
- changes in switching cost
- changes in propensity to substitute

Relative price will change if (1) the relative costs of a substitute and the product change, and the change is partially or completely passed on to buyers, or (2) their relative profit margins change. Relative value will change if valuable improvements proceed at different rates for the substitute and the product. Buyer perception of value will be a function of information dissemination. Switching cost will change if a substitute is redesigned or if early substituters bear some of the cost for later switchers. Buyer propensity to switch will be a function of evolving buyer attitudes, resources and competitive conditions.

Changes in the threat of substitution over time are determined by industry structure and competitor behavior in both the substitute industry and the threatened industry, with the substitute industry on the offensive and the threatened industry on the defensive. The two industries are engaged in a battle to influence the substitution process. Industry structure will shape the nature of competition in both industries and the way firms behave toward the substitution process. Because competitors' moves will influence the course of the substitution process in one direction or another, *where* competitors place bets is vital. If competitors in the substitute industry are better capitalized, for example, they can tip the balance in its favor because they will make greater investments to reduce costs, signal value, or set low initial prices. Similarly, other competitor strategic moves can impact the substitution process, such as RCA's decision to widely license its color TV patents. Determining future changes in the threat of substitution is thus an exercise in forecasting the effects of industry structure and competitor behavior on each of the components of the substitution calculation.

Some important determinants of changes in each of the five areas that determine substitution are as follows:[5]

[5]The discussion of industry evolution in *Competitive Strategy,* Chapter 8, provides tools for forecasting structural changes in the substitute and threatened industries;

Changing Relative Price

Changes in Relative Cost. A substitute and a product are in a competition to improve relative cost. A substitute often improves its relative cost as substitution proceeds through the operation of economies of scale or the learning curve. For example, the price of carbon fibers fell from $100 per pound in the early 1970s to $20 to $25 in 1982 for these reasons, promoting the substitution of carbon fibers for steel and aluminum in automotive and aircraft applications. Another factor that often lowers the relative cost of a substitute over time is that technological change reduces the amount necessary to perform the required function, as illustrated in the aluminum and offshore drilling examples earlier in this chapter. Such improvements, of course, come at the expense of the volume of the substitute sold. A substitute's cost can just as easily escalate, however, if its success forces up the cost of its key raw materials.

There may be fewer opportunities to reduce cost in the industry being threatened by a substitute because of its age and maturity. Moreover, penetration of the substitute may reduce the scale and capacity utilization of firms in the threatened industry, raising their costs. However, industries that have been sleepy have achieved remarkable cost reductions under the threat of a substitute, so one cannot generalize about how relative costs will change.

The relative cost behavior of a substitute over time is analyzed using the framework in Chapter 3. The important cost drivers for both the substitute and the product should be identified. Cost behavior over time will be a function of the interplay of these cost drivers coupled with the likely behavior of competitors. Sometimes the projection of past cost trends for the substitute and the product will clearly indicate future relative cost. It is dangerous to count on the continuation of past trends, however, because the threatened industry may respond and the early pace of cost reduction by the substitute may be unsustainable. Predicting relative cost changes thus often requires that the impact of increasing scale, learning, and other factors on cost is estimated for a substitute and compared to the ability of the product to reduce cost through redesign, relocation, or introduction of new process technologies. The sources of cost dynamics described in Chapter 3 will suggest other important relative cost changes that might occur, such as differential inflation.

---

the analysis of emerging industries in *Competitive Strategy,* Chapter 10, is also often applicable to substitute industries because they are frequently new industries.

Changes in Profit Margins. The prices of a substitute and a product contain profit margins.[6] The relative profit margins of a substitute and a product are a key factor that can shift over time. A common reason for the change in relative margins is that the threatened industry lowers its margins to fight the substitute. Video game margins are falling rapidly to fight personal computers, for example. The extent to which a threatened industry's margins can be reduced before firms begin to exit is a function of how high margins were initially, and whether exit barriers keep firms in the industry despite low returns.

The margins of a substitute can also change as substitution proceeds, depending on industry structure in the substitute industry. If early entrants into the substitute industry were skimming and entry barriers are not high, the substitute's margins can fall dramatically as new companies enter. Initial success in penetration may also lead firms selling the substitute to set low penetration prices. Rivalry in selling a substitute often increases over time as it becomes more standardized and explosive growth slackens, as is happening in personal computers. Increasing penetration of the substitute may also raise the threat of backward integration by buyers. All these factors can squeeze a substitute's margins. Margins of a substitute and a product, then, will be a function of the influence of their changing industry structures over time, partly in response to each other.

Changing Relative Value

The relative value to the buyer of a substitute will often change because of changing technology, better service, and a myriad of other causes. Producers of a substitute may gain expertise in tailoring their value chains to meet buyer needs, though producers of the threatened product will look for ways to enhance value as well. While any of the factors that determine buyer value described in Chapter 4 may be changing, three important sources of change are the *relative pace of technological change* in the substitute and the product, the *development of infrastructure,* and *institutional factors.*

A substitute and the threatened product are engaged in a technological race to see which can improve value faster. The likely pace and extent of technological change can be analyzed using the concepts in Chapter 5. A substitute may have the edge in technological change if it is a new industry, but several examples in Chapter 5 have shown

[6]Margins can be negative, and sometimes are for a substitute that is beginning its penetration.

how a threatened product or process can often achieve significant technological improvements. The relative pace of technological change is also strongly influenced by the resources and skills of competitors. In the substitution of plastics and aluminum for steel, for example, the greater technological orientation of plastics and aluminum firms was one of the factors leading to a faster pace of change in those industries.

RVP often changes in favor of the substitute over time as better infrastructure develops to support it. As a substitute becomes established, for example, it frequently spawns independent repair shops and is added to the product lines of established wholesalers. Availability improves and the perceived risk of shortages falls.

RVP of a substitute can also change as a result of a wide variety of other exogenous influences and institutional factors. The rapid substitution of polyvinyl chloride (PVC) for materials such as aluminum in residential siding was set back by the revelation that vinyl chloride was a possible carcinogen. Similarly, the penetration of solar heating has been buffeted by shifts in government policy and a fluctuating energy price outlook, while the relative value of food products has been altered by rising concerns about cholesterol and sodium. Such exogenous influences are often as hard to predict as they are powerful.

Changing Buyer Perception of Value

The perception of value by buyers frequently changes over time in substitution because time and marketing activity are working to alter the way buyers view a substitute compared to a product. A substitute may gain in perceived value position over time as buyers become more and more familiar with how to use it. One of the inhibiting factors in the use of carbon fibers in aircraft wings and other applications (as a substitute for steel, titanium, or aluminum), for example, has been that most engineers had no idea how to design with fibers. Yet the properties of carbon fibers are sufficiently unique that their benefits can be fully reaped only if the designer understands the material. As this has begun to happen, the perceived value of fibers is increasing. While time often benefits a substitute, it can also hurt it. Many substitutes emerge amid overinflated buyer perceptions of their value, and time and trial are moderating influences.

The perception of a substitute and a product can also be affected by the relative intensity and creativity of signaling activities. Campaigns to increase the awareness of a substitute are pitted against efforts by the threatened industry to improve its perceived value. The U.S. record industry, for example, has responded to flattening sales at the expense of video entertainment products with its "Gift of Music" campaign. Record manufacturers contribute one-half cent per record for advertising, stressing the value of records as a gift. The appropriate signaling activities will depend on signaling criteria for the product.

Changing Switching Costs

The costs of switching to a substitute often change over time, frequently in a downward direction. One reason is that early switchers can bear some of the costs for later switchers, by developing procedures, designs, or standards. An early switcher from steel to aluminum beverage cans, for example, might develop product standards and methods of lithographing labels on the cans that can easily be copied. Switching costs can also fall over time because the substitute is redesigned to be more compatible with ancillary equipment, or suppliers develop procedures to minimize the buyer's switching costs. In addition, third parties may spring up to lower the cost of switching, such as consultants, installers and training firms. In office equipment, for example, consultants and training firms are proliferating to ease the changeover to office automation.

Switching costs are partly determined by a buyer's technological choices, and thus change over time as buyers alter their products and processes. In the substitution of aluminum for steel and cast iron, for example, new buyer technology has reduced switching costs. Automakers have built more flexible plants that can machine either aluminum or cast iron, while can makers' new lines can accept both aluminum and tinplate can stock.

Changing Propensity to Switch

The propensity to switch to a *successful* substitute frequently grows over time. Early success with a substitute allays buyer risk aversion, at the same time as competitive considerations lead buyers to switch so as not to have a disadvantage relative to early switchers.

Substitution and Overall Industry Demand

In addition to taking share from existing products, a substitute can raise or lower overall industry demand. A substitute with a longer useful life than the product it is replacing will lower overall demand after the initial period when the substitute stimulates faster replacement. This pattern seems to have occurred in the substitution of longer-lasting radial tires for bias ply tires.

The penetration of a substitute can also increase overall industry demand if the substitute expands the industry or increases the usage or replacement rate. Portable cassette players such as Sony's Walkman, for example, have surely expanded the total market for cassette players at the same time as they have taken share from conventional cassette players. Similarly, the introduction of disposable ballpoint pens, championed by BIC Corporation, led to substitution for conventional pens but also stimulated the purchase of more ballpoint pens per buyer. Any impact of a substitute on overall demand for a product must be combined with a forecast of the path of substitution in order to predict the absolute volume of sales of a substitute over time.

Substitution and Industry Structure

Penetration of a substitute may have second order effects on the resulting industry structure. A substitute may shift the buyer's cost structure, for example, in ways that increase or decrease price sensitivity. A substitute may also require new suppliers, and entry barriers may differ from those of the product it replaces. Thus the substitute must be analyzed as a new industry, not merely as a change in product. The substitute industry can be more or less attractive structurally than the industry it replaces, a fact that has important implications for strategy towards a substitute.

The Path of Substitution

The path of substitution in an industry is a function of how RVP, the perception of RVP, switching costs, and the propensity of buyers to switch evolve over time. The rate of penetration of substitutes differs widely from industry to industry. Some substitutes gain quick acceptance, while others penetrate slowly or not at all and are discontinued. In many industries, however, the path of substitution for successful substitutes looks like an S-curve, when substitution as a percent of total demand is plotted against time (see Figure 8–2).

The S-shaped substitution curve is closely related to the familiar product life cycle curve, because products early in their life cycles are frequently substituting for some other products. An S-shaped substitution path is *not* characteristic of every successful substitution. However, it is important to understand why an S-curve might occur so that the economic factors that underlie it are recognized.[7] Where the underlying economics of a particular substitution suggest an S-curve path, a number of techniques are available to help forecast the rate of substitution.

In an S-curve path such as that shown in Figure 8–2, substitution is initially modest and often continues at low levels for a considerable period of time in what can be called the "informing and testing phase." Unless a product flaw emerges with the substitute or the threatened industry responds to nullify the substitute's advantages, the penetration of the substitute then often climbs rapidly in a "takeoff phase" toward an upper bound that represents maximum penetration. This upper

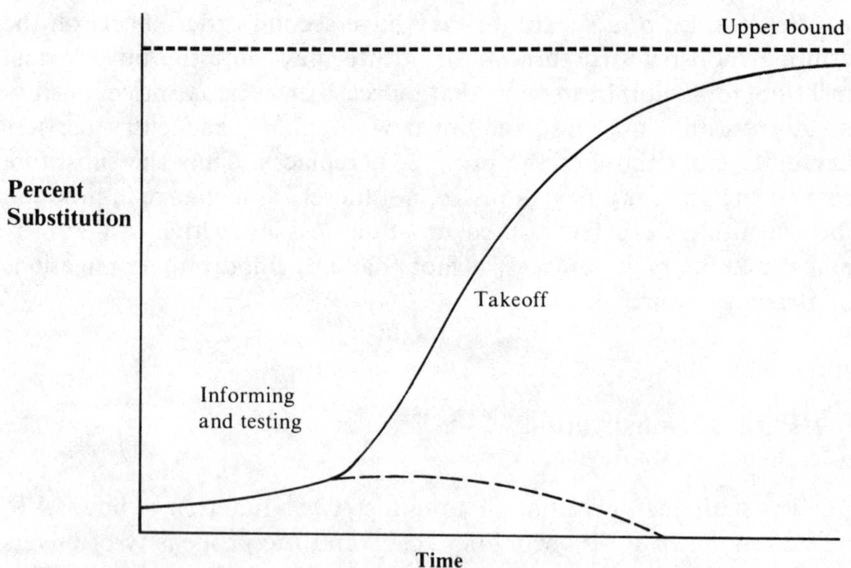

Figure 8–2. A Typical S-Shaped Substitution Path

[7]Chapter 8 in *Competitive Strategy* describes how the product life cycle is a poor generalization about industry structural change. The S-shaped path of sales growth, though by no means universal, is among the most commonly occurring predictions that grow out of life cycle theory.

bound is determined by the number of buyers for whom the substitute is potentially valuable. The upper bound of substitution can itself change over time as changes in technology or buyer needs bring buyers in or out of the pool.

The reasons that an S-shaped substitution curve occurs reflect a set of assumptions about the interplay of actual and perceived RVP, switching costs, and the buyer's propensity to switch over time. Initially, the performance of a substitute is likely to be uncertain, and there may be few capable firms to supply it. Many buyers are not even aware of the substitute or what its characteristics are. The price of the substitute is likely to be high because of its low volume or because suppliers are skim-pricing. Though the value of the substitute is often uncertain, however, the cost of switching is usually very clear and made particularly high by the unfamiliarity of both buyers and suppliers with how the substitute should be used. Moreover, the cost of switching must be borne up front, before the benefits of the substitute are realized.

During the informing and testing period, some adventurous buyers or buyers who attach a particularly high value to the substitute's qualities will switch to the substitute to experiment with it or will switch permanently because the RVP of the substitute to them appears particularly high. During this period, either the substitute begins to prove its value or product flaws become apparent. The product flaws prove uncorrectable (and penetration never increases), or the substitute is improved (sometimes the substitute is completely withdrawn from the market and then reintroduced). At the same time, marketing activity and word of mouth tend to widen the group of buyers that are aware of the substitute and thus the perception of value improves.[8]

Assuming that the substitute eventually achieves acceptable performance with early buyers, the rate of penetration of the substitute can start to increase rapidly along the S-pattern for a number of reasons. First, the uncertainty of perceived value and the risk of failure of the substitute both fall as early buyers have successful experiences. Second, once a few buyers successfully switch, competitive pressures force other buyers to switch to maintain their cost position or differentiation (or self-image for consumers). Third, the cost of switching may decline for reasons discussed earlier. Fourth, rising adoption leads to increasing awareness of the substitute and raises its credibility. Fifth,

[8]The path of substitution is analogous to the diffusion of an innovation. Diffusion research has emphasized the information and attitudinal factors that affect the diffusion process. See Robertson (1971) for a survey.

rising penetration of the substitute often reduces its cost through economies of scale and learning.[9] Sixth, introduction of new varieties of the substitute opens up new industry segments. Finally, increasing penetration of the substitute prompts its suppliers to become more aggressive in pricing, marketing, and R&D, often as a result of entry by new competitors into the substitute industry. All of these factors tend to be self-reinforcing, and can lead to the extremely rapid penetration of the substitute.

Eventually, the penetration of a substitute begins to approach 100 percent of the buyers to which the substitute is attractive. As this happens, penetration tends to level off as the penetration of new buyers becomes more and more difficult. However, improvements in RVP or new varieties of a substitute may *widen* the pool of potential buyers beyond those initially foreseen, fueling new opportunities for growth of the substitute. The upper bound in Figure 8–2 can thus expand to contain a larger and larger number of buyers.

At the same time, the buyers' usage of the substitute may change in ways that increase or decrease demand. In TV sets, for example, sales of black and white sets were very robust even after color sets began to penetrate because buyers bought second, third, and even fourth TV sets. Similarly, in the substitution of electric shavers for conventional razors, the recent introduction of small, portable electric razors may well be shifting the upper bound of penetration of electric shavers by making them more versatile and less expensive. Thus the upper bound in Figure 8–2 can include a growing volume of units.

The length of the informing and testing phase is a function of a number of factors. Clearly important is the size of the RVP improvement offered by the substitute—the bigger the inducement, the shorter the period will be. The length of time necessary to prove the performance of a substitute also differs by product, and can greatly influence the length of the testing period. The performance of an automatic drip coffee maker can be proven in weeks or months, for example, while a new piece of capital equipment may require years of production line testing to assess its true performance. The period required for the industry producing the substitute to make necessary improvements in performance or cost, and to build adequate capacity to serve major buyers, also influences the length of the testing phase. Finally, the intensity of competition of the buyer's industry and the significance of the specific RVP of the substitute to that competition influence

[9]Falling cost of the substitute, like most of these reasons for increasing penetration, should not be treated as inevitable as noted earlier.

the length of the testing phase, by determining the pressures for imitation if one buyer switches to a substitute.

The steepness of the takeoff phase is a function of how compelling in an industry are the reasons for rising penetration described above. In selling a substitute to an intensely competitive buyer industry, for example, takeoff can be very rapid. The steepness of takeoff is also a function of the time required to change over to a substitute and the adequacy of capacity. The purchasing cycle in the buyer industry is also important, because buyers are more likely to switch to a substitute when they would normally reorder or replace the product anyway. This reduces the switching costs associated with scrapping a product which has years of useful life remaining or where the buyer has substantial inventory on hand. For similar reasons, switching to a substitute in durable goods tends to occur faster when the buyer industry is growing and therefore investing in new facilities and equipment.

The response of the threatened industry is also clearly important to the path of substitution. An aggressive response by the threatened industry can sometimes stop the penetration of a substitute altogether or delay it considerably. Conversely, entry into the substitute industry by credible competitors can accelerate penetration, as IBM's entry into personal computers and Kodak's entry into instant cameras seem to have done. Smooth substitution curves such as the one portrayed in Figure 8–2 are most characteristic of industries where there are many buyers of a substitute. Where there are few buyers, a decision by a major buyer can dramatically shift the curve overnight. In such cases, substitution analysis is best conducted on a buyer-by-buyer basis.

Segmentation and the Substitution Path

The substitution path in an industry is often very closely related to industry segmentation. Early penetration occurs in industry segments where a substitute offers the highest RVP, requires the lowest switching costs, and/or encounters the most adventurous or highest value buyers. Early segments support the cost reduction or performance improvement necessary to penetrate later segments. The high value of the substitute to early segments either offsets the high initial cost of the substitute, or allows its producers to earn extremely high profits. Margins often will fall over time in the substitute industry as additional segments are penetrated where the substitute has lower value.

The substitution of minicomputers provides a good example of how the substitution path relates to industry segmentation. The early segments penetrated by minicomputers were scientific and computer center applications where computational power was needed but where users could do their own programming, adapt machines to their needs, and perform some maintenance in-house. Later penetration was in applications such as industrial controls, where the buyer was still sophisticated and support requirements were moderate. Only after some time did minicomputers develop the service and support capabilities to penetrate small business applications.

The same factors that lead to early penetration in some segments also mean that the rate of penetration *within* segments will vary. Since segments vary in RVP and switching costs, penetration will proceed much faster in some segments than others. Hence the industry substitution curve is actually a collection of segment substitution curves.

Substitution Forecasting Models

The observation that successful substitution often follows an S-shaped penetration curve can be used in forecasting. A variety of models that are based on the assumption of S-shaped penetration have grown out of research on diffusion processes. Data from the early years of a substitution can be used to forecast the entire substitution curve using such models, under the assumption that an S-shaped process will occur. The forecasted substitution curve may then become a base case from which an analysis of the underlying economics of a substitution can begin. Adjusting the standard S-shaped curve to reflect the economics of a particular substitution allows a prediction of the extent of substitution in future years. The premise underlying such a procedure is that the tendency toward an S-shaped penetration curve is strong enough so that the plotting of such a curve—derived from the early penetration data—is a useful beginning point for analysis.

The most commonly used diffusion model is the so-called "logistic function," a form of exponential function.[10] The functional form of the relationship as applied to substitution is as follows:

[10]Diffusion models have been widely used in forecasting the growth of new brands and in forecasting the rate of diffusion of technology. Important diffusion models are those of Mansfield (1961), Bass (1969), and Fisher and Pry (1971). The logistic model described here is similar to Fisher and Pry's.

$$\frac{F}{1-F} = \text{exponential K (time)}$$

where F = fraction of the total potential market that has switched to a substitute

K = a constant set equal to the early growth rate of a substitute

The logistic function makes two important assumptions: (1) if substitution has progressed as far as a few percent, it will proceed to completion; and (2) the fractional rate of fractional substitution of a substitute for the product is proportional to the remaining amount of the product left to be substituted for. It is the latter assumption that produces the S-curve shape. If F/(1 − F) is plotted as a function of time on semilogarithmic paper, the logistic function results in a substitution curve that is a straight line with the slope K as shown in Figure 8–3.[11]

If the logic underlying an S-shaped substitution curve is believed to hold in a particular substitution process, as well as the assumption

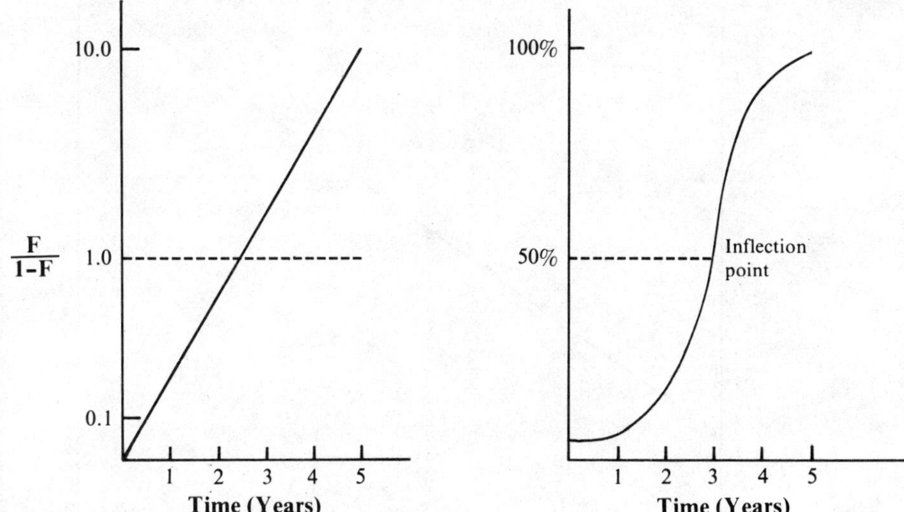

Figure 8–3. A Typical Logistic Curve

[11]The logistic function produces an inflection point of the S-curve at 50 percent substitution. A related function, known as the Gompertz function, has its inflection point at 37 percent penetration. While both functions have received empirical support, the logistic function is easier to use in practice. For a survey of diffusion models, see Mahajan and Muller (1979).

about a constant fractional rate of fractional substitution, the logistic function can be used to forecast the path of substitution that will occur. To do this, data on substitution history are used to determine F/(1 − F) for each year. Then F/(1 − F) is plotted on semilogarithmic paper against time, and a straight line is fitted through the early history. Extending this line projects the future substitution path under the assumption that it will follow the logistic curve.[12]

The procedure is shown in Figure 8–4, which plots the early

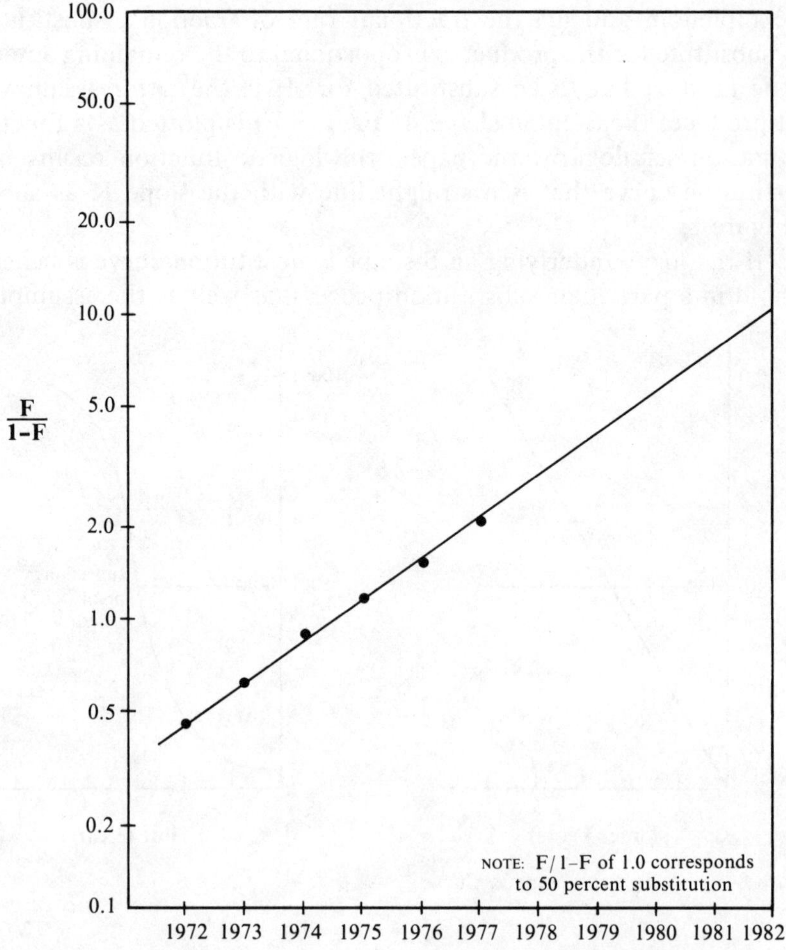

Figure 8–4. Early Substitution of Steel for Aluminum in Beer Cans

[12]Penetration rates must be adjusted if there were capacity constraints in supplying the substitute.

substitution history of aluminum for steel in beer cans. The early history fits the logistic curve quite closely. Based on this history, we could expect the extent of substitution by 1982 to be approximately 91 percent if the assumptions of the logistic curve hold. The accuracy of this forecast, however, depends on how well the logistic curve reflects the economics of substitution in the particular industry. One important issue is the size of the potential market, and hence the upper bound. In the beverage can case the upper bound is fairly clear. Where the upper bound is increasing, the logistic curve will have a tendency to overestimate the rate of penetration. Another important issue later in the substitution process is whether the intensity of use of the substitute required to perform its function will change over time.

Perhaps the most important issue in whether substitution will follow the logistic curve growing out of the early substitution history is the extent to which the RVP that is driving the substitution will change over time. The logistic curve assumes a stable motivation for substitution. If RVP falls, the penetration of a substitute may actually *decrease,* something that never happens with the logistic curve. If the RVP of a substitute improves, on the other hand, the rate of penetration will increase from early history—the substitution path may jump to a new curve. Figure 8–5 illustrates how this has actually happened in beer cans.

After 1976, the introduction of two-piece steel can technology helped slow the penetration of aluminum cans. Working with steel companies, Crown Cork and Seal introduced a cheaper way of making steel cans that reduced the RVP of aluminum cans. In 1978, however, Miller Beer (number two in the beer industry) announced a major test of aluminum cans against steel. The rate of substitution slowed further pending the outcome. Miller's decision in 1979 was to switch to aluminum. Once Miller's switch occurred, substitution accelerated to a faster pace than before 1976, in part because Miller legitimized the substitute. An additional factor in the faster penetration of aluminum after 1979 was the growing recycling of aluminum cans, which are more recyclable than steel cans. As infrastructure allowed for more widespread recycling, the RVP of aluminum became even better than before because recycling reduced the cost of metal. By 1982, penetration of aluminum was actually about 98 percent instead of the 91 percent that would have been forecasted using the early history.

As the beverage can example illustrates, the *logistic curve is not a substitute for substitution analysis.* It is a simple tool that can serve as a starting point for more careful analysis of the economics of

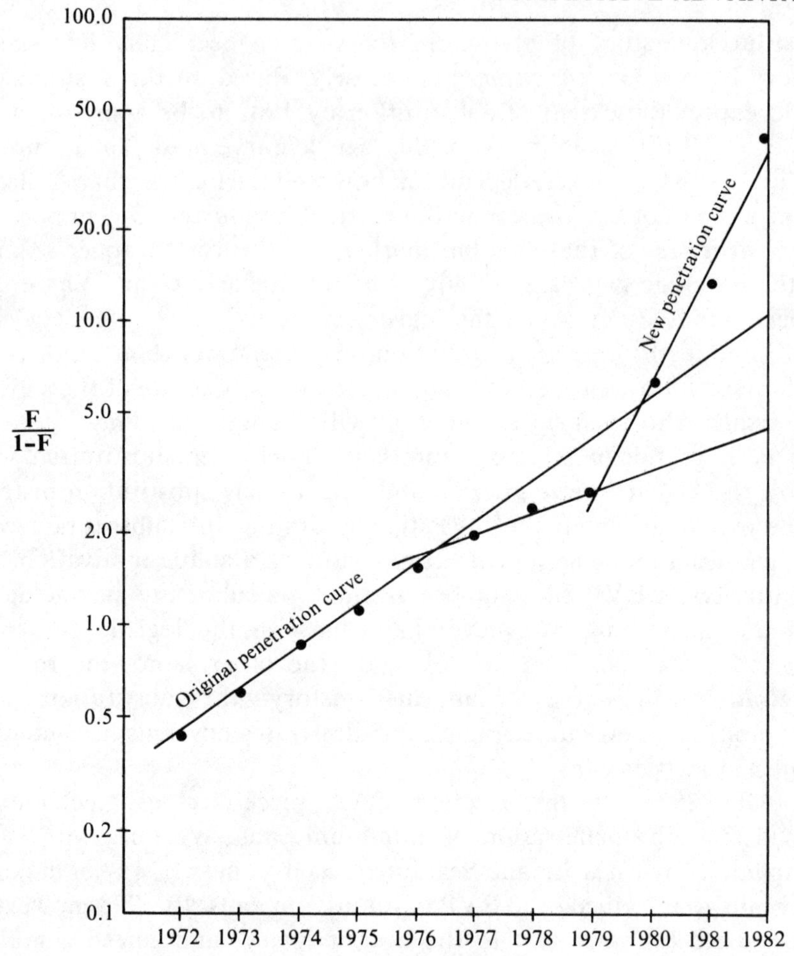

Figure 8–5. Substitution of Steel for Aluminum in Beer Cans

substitution.[13] The substitution path will vary from industry to industry, and will be affected by technological changes and competitive moves. In order for the logistic curve to be meaningfully used, the factors that determine RVP, switching costs, and propensity to substitute in a particular industry must be understood and expected changes in them forecasted. Since the economics of a substitute often differ by industry segment, logistic curves should usually be plotted at the segment level and not the industry level. Beer producers, for example, have different needs in cans than other can users. A logistic curve for aluminum's substitution against steel in cans overall would not be as meaningful as one for beer cans alone.

[13]Logistic curves have often been misused by both managers and their advisors. Decisions have been made with too little diagnosis of the underlying economics of substitution.

Substitution and Competitive Strategy

The economics of substitution carry a variety of strategic implications for firms attempting to promote substitution, as well as for firms attempting to defend against it. Defenses against substitution are, by and large, the reverse of offensive strategies that promote substitution. I will first describe some principles of promoting substitution and then turn to defense.

Promoting Substitution

A firm can trigger or accelerate substitution through strategic moves that enhance RVP, lower switching costs, or raise the propensity of buyers to switch. While none of these moves are without costs and risks, the following concepts for promoting substitution can be considered:

1. *Target early switchers.* As the section "Segmentation and Substitution" emphasized, some buyers and buyer segments in an industry will be much more likely to adopt a substitute than others because of greater RVP from the substitute, lower switching costs, or greater propensity to switch. The order of segments that are targeted for penetration is one of the most important components of a substitution strategy. A firm attempting substitution should focus its efforts on the most likely early switchers first, and use the track record it gains with these buyers and their support to trigger the self-reinforcing take-off phase. Early switchers may be buyers who are redesigning their products, are replacing equipment, face a pressing need for the value the substitute provides, or are adventurous purchasers. To reach these buyers, a firm may have to subsidize trial. For example, Mauna Loa macadamia nuts are sold on very favorable terms to some airlines to gain trial of target buyers.

2. *Improve the firm's offering in areas with the highest RVP impacts.* The impact of improvements in the product and elsewhere in the value chain on substitution will be greater the more RVP is affected. With a sophisticated understanding of the bases of RVP, drawn from the framework presented earlier, a firm can determine its R&D and marketing priorities accordingly. In color TV, for example, picture quality was much more important to RVP initially than features or

styling, given the preferences of buyers substituting from black and white sets with high picture quality. Similarly, in many industries the problem is not actual product performance but the buyer's uncertainty about it. Here, guarantees can be an effective tool to promote substitution.

3. *Reduce or subsidize switching costs.* Investments to reduce switching costs can have a major role in stimulating substitution, presuming a substitute has superior RVP. A firm should direct part of its technical development to improvements that lower switching costs, and create mechanisms for information dissemination among buyers that have the same effect. This may be as simple as manuals or newsletters.

A firm may also find it advantageous to subsidize switching costs for some buyers. A firm need not subsidize the switching costs of all buyers, but only a core group of buyers whose adoption of a substitute is likely to trigger the takeoff phase. These buyers should be opinion leaders who will serve as credible signals of value to other buyers. Subsidizing switching costs can involve such things as free training, paying for product reformulation or testing, supplying or assisting in the design of ancillary equipment, providing free assistance in modifying production procedures, giving high trade-in allowances, offering money-back guarantees, and giving free in-home demonstrations.

4. *Invest in signaling.* A major barrier faced by a substitute may be the lack of awareness and knowledge by potential buyers. A firm must identify the most important signaling criteria used by buyers to judge the value of a substitute, and invest to influence them. Buyers often misperceive the RVP of a substitute, particularly where RVP is not obvious but has the characteristics described earlier in this chapter. Hence the importance of signaling can frequently be great to successful substitution.

5. *Use tapered forward integration or induce backward integration to create pull-through.* A strategy practiced successfully by the aluminum industry, among others, is to forward integrate selectively into downstream products to create pull-through demand for a substitute. A related strategy is to induce end users to backward integrate into the intermediate industry to get around intermediate producers who are unwilling to substitute. By integrating forward and creating demand with end users, a firm can sometimes force recalcitrant intermedi-

ate buyers to bear the switching costs of substitution. Forward integration can also demonstrate the performance of the substitute, and be a means for developing procedures for its use or for lowering switching cost.

Tapered forward integration is most effective where the end user faces few, if any, costs of switching to a substitute, while intermediate buyers face significant switching costs. This was the case in metal cans, where beverage companies could switch to aluminum cans relatively easily but can companies faced heavy investment costs in new equipment.

6. *Ensure multiple sources and/or adequate capacity.* Often major buyers will not incur the costs and risk of substitution when there is only one source for a substitute or if there is insufficient capacity for it on stream to meet expected future demand. Substitution can be accelerated by remedying these concerns, through encouraging entry into the substitute industry or by building capacity ahead of demand. This is an example of how good competitors can benefit a firm (Chapter 6).

7. *Promote improvements in complementary products or infrastructure.* A firm can often improve RVP or switching costs if it can stimulate improvements in the cost or quality of necessary complementary goods or infrastructure. This may justify investing in technology for complementary products and sharing the results freely with other firms. It may also suggest the formation of joint ventures or other relationships with producers of complementary goods, or creating needed infrastructure such as service facilities.[14] RCA originally trained many of the repair personnel who serviced all color TV sets, for example.

8. *Price to balance capturing RVP against creating barriers.* The price of a substitute must share some of the value created with the buyer in order to give the buyer an inducement to switch. How close the price of a substitute approaches RVP should depend on industry structure. Where there are high entry barriers, a firm may be better off substituting slowly by penetrating high-value segments first at high prices and moving prices down gradually to capture lower-value segments. Where there are first-mover advantages (Chapter 5), the firm instead should sacrifice short-term profits to penetrate quickly and

[14]The strategic role of complementary goods is discussed in more detail in Chapter 12.

build barriers that protect long-term profits. With low barriers, a firm must attempt to reap profits quickly before entry erodes its position.

9. *Conceive of new functions to widen a substitute's market.* Conceiving of new functions a substitute can perform may greatly expand the potential market. This not only is important in product design and selecting features, but also in pricing strategy. In fresh flowers, for example, European retailers recognized that low prices could open up a whole new function for flowers—everyday use in decorating—in addition to the traditional use of fresh flowers in weddings and for other special occasions. As a result, the European market for flowers is much bigger than the U.S. market, where pricing has tended to be higher. Many industries have accepted maturity of demand rather than looked for new substitution possibilities.

10. *Harvest if competitive position in the substitute is not sustainable.* Investments to build share in a substitute are indicated if a firm can sustain its competitive advantage in the substitute industry and if the industry structure is attractive. Otherwise, a firm may be better off skimming profits early in the substitution process rather than pricing to deter entry or widen the market. A successful substitute is not necessarily a good business.

Defense Against Substitutes

The first step in defense against substitutes is to identify all of them. This is often a difficult task, because it requires a look at the basic functions a product performs. Strategies to combat substitutes are the reverse of many of the steps described above:

- improve RVP relative to the substitute by reducing costs, improving the product, improving complementary goods, etc.
- modify the product image
- raise switching costs
- block pull-through attempts by aggressive selling efforts directed at the buyers' buyers

Where switching back costs are high, a firm must invest aggressively in a short-term holding action to deter switching while it seeks more fundamental long-term improvements in RVP. With high switching back costs, buyers lost to a substitute will be hard to regain.

In addition to these actions, a number of other possibilities in defending against substitutes warrant consideration:

1. *Find new uses unaffected by the substitute.* Sometimes a product facing substitution can be repositioned into entirely new uses. A good example is Arm & Hammer baking soda. As a result of a ten-year marketing campaign, Arm & Hammer is used in over 50 percent of American refrigerators for odor control, a use that has far surpassed the original use of baking soda.

2. *Redefine competition away from the strengths of the substitute.* A substitute's RVP advantage generally stems from either low price or certain dimensions of value. A good defensive strategy may be to attempt to influence industry competition away from these advantages. Repelling a low price substitute might involve such actions as longer warranties, more engineering support, or new product features.

3. *Enlist suppliers to help in defense.* Suppliers of important purchased inputs often have a big stake in fighting substitution too, and can bring important resources and technological skills to the defense. Suppliers of inputs that are large cost items or that have an important influence on value are the best candidates for alliances.

4. *Redirect strategy toward segments least vulnerable to substitution.* Some product or buyer segments will be less vulnerable to substitution than others. A firm under attack from substitutes may be better off focusing its defensive investments on such segments. A firm may also exit from or harvest its position in the segments most vulnerable to substitution. Early withdrawal from these segments can allow the firm to generate the most cash from harvesting or from liquidating assets, while exiting later will generate little or no cash.[15]

5. *Harvest instead of defend.* Depending on the likely future RVP of a substitute and the feasibility of defensive strategies, the best strategy for a firm facing substitution may be to harvest its position instead of investing in defense at all. Such strategy involves such actions as concentrating attention on the segments where substitution will be the slowest, and raising prices.

[15]These concepts are important in declining industries. See *Competitive Strategy,* Chapter 12, which also discusses harvest strategies.

6. *Enter the substitute industry.* Rather than viewing a substitute as a threat, it may be better to view it as an opportunity. Entering the substitute industry may allow a firm to reap competitive advantages from interrelationships between a substitute and the product, such as common channels and buyers.[16]

Industry Versus Firm Substitution Strategy

A substitution process is partly under the control of a firm and partly a function of the industry as a whole. No matter what it does, the individual firm is affected by such things as the industry's image and the consistency of industrywide product offerings, which influence buyer attitude and confusion about the benefits of a substitute. This implies that industrywide actions can usefully supplement individual firm efforts to promote or defend against substitution. For example, New Zealand producers of kiwi fruit have greatly stimulated its substitution for other fruits through an industry-sponsored R&D program to breed one uniform variety of fruit (down from twenty) and adoption of this single variety by all the growers.[17] This campaign has been reinforced by advertising of the fruit.

Some industrywide activities that can promote (or prevent) substitution include:

- Image advertising of the product. Total industry advertising can affect overall industry demand.
- Collective R&D expenditures to develop uses for the product, or techniques for integrating the product into buyers' value chains.
- Establishment and enforcement of product standards to allay buyers' fears of poor quality or inadequate performance.
- Gaining the necessary regulatory approvals for the product to lower buyers' switching costs and perceived risks.
- Joint actions to improve the quality, availability, and cost of complementary products, thereby improving RVP.

Expenditures made by a firm to promote or discourage substitution also may benefit competitors, who get a free ride. In order to deal with this problem, collective industry action through trade associa-

[16]See Chapter 9.
[17]For a discussion, see *World Business Weekly* (1981).

tions or other industry groups is a common approach to promoting or defending against substitution. For example, the coal industry has recently embarked on a television and print advertising campaign in the United States to improve the image of coal as an abundant, easy-to-obtain, and "American" fuel. Without some collective action, fragmented industries often have difficulty promoting or fighting substitution because of the free-rider problem.

Pitfalls in Strategy Against Substitutes

Substitution is a positive or negative force, to some degree, in every industry. Yet firms often make some common errors in dealing with substitutes. A discussion of these will provide a summary of some of the important concepts in this chapter:

Failing to Perceive a Substitute. Firms often fail to recognize substitutes at all until the substitution process is well under way, because they view their product's function too narrowly, do not recognize the different substitutes faced by different segments, or overlook downstream substitution.

Not Understanding RVP. The determinants of RVP are complex, and firms often have a simplistic view of why a substitute is succeeding or failing. For example, they may believe that superior product performance is the cause of substitution when the real reason is lower cost of use for the buyer because of easier installation. Not knowing why a substitute is succeeding or failing can be a ticket to the wrong offensive or defensive strategy, or to an unpleasant surprise when a substitute takes off.

Misreading of Slow Early Penetration. The slow early penetration of a substitute can be misread as a sign that it is not a serious threat, rather than as a manifestation of the S-shaped nature of the substitution process. While many substitutes do indeed fail, slow early penetration is not a reliable sign that this will happen. What is necessary is a careful analysis of RVP, and early buyer experience with the substitute.

A Static View of RVP. Both offensive and defensive strategy towards substitution should be driven by the *future* as well as present

RVP of a substitute. A firm can mistakenly direct its product and marketing improvements toward the wrong areas, or fail to plan for improvements in RVP or reduction in margins by the substitute over time.

Fighting Versus Joining. Many firms invest heavily to defend against substitutes when long-term RVP is compellingly against them. Similarly, their defense against a substitute is across the board, instead of reflecting differences in vulnerability to the substitute in different segments. Early moves to focus on certain segments, harvest, or enter the substitute industry are sometimes called for.

Accepting Maturity. Perhaps the most unfortunate pitfall of all is accepting the maturity of one's product, and not considering substitution as a possibility. Firms often look inward, and become preoccupied with battling rivals. It may be better to expand the size of the pie through substitution. The age of an industry is not a reliable indicator of the substitution possibilities. Industry maturity may be just an illusion.

III
Corporate Strategy and Competitive Advantage

9
Interrelationships among Business Units

As strategic planning theory and practice have developed, most firms have come to recognize two types of strategy: business unit strategy and corporate strategy. Business strategy charts the course for a firm's activities in individual industries, while corporate strategy addresses the composition of a firm's portfolio of business units. Reflecting this distinction, most major firms have divided their businesses into some type of strategic business units (SBUs), and instituted formal planning processes in which SBUs submit plans for review by top management on an annual or biannual basis. At the same time, corporate strategy has become increasingly viewed as portfolio management, typically using some variation of the portfolio planning techniques that were widely adopted in the 1970s.[1]

As these developments in formal planning have been occurring, the concept of synergy has become widely regarded as passé. The

[1]In a recent article, Haspeslagh (1982) found evidence that portfolio planning techniques were in use in someway by over 300 of the Fortune 1000.

idea that combining different but related businesses could create value through synergy was widely accepted and used as a justification for the extensive diversification that took place in the United States in the 1960s and early 1970s. Statements describing hoped-for areas for synergy accompanied many merger announcements, and were common in annual reports. By the late 1970s, however, the enthusiasm for synergy had waned. Synergy, it seemed, was a nice idea *but rarely occurred in practice.* Instead of in synergy, the answer seemed to lie in decentralization where business unit managers would be given authority and responsibility and rewarded based on results. Recent popular business writing has identified decentralization as a foundation of many successful firms, and many major corporations now practice decentralization with near-religious reverence. Decentralization, coupled with disenchantment with synergy, has reinforced the view that portfolio management is the essential task of corporate strategy.

The failure of synergy stemmed from the inability of companies to understand and implement it, not because of some basic flaw in the concept. Firms often used it to justify actions taken for other reasons. Ill-defined notions of what constituted synergy underlay many companies' acquisition strategies. Even in instances where companies possessed a genuine opportunity to harness synergy, they often failed because the tools for analyzing it were lacking or they could not overcome the substantial organization problems of implementation.

Compelling forces are at work today, however, that mean that firms must reexamine their attitude toward synergy. Economic, technological, and competitive developments are increasing the competitive advantage to be gained by those firms that can identify and exploit interrelationships among distinct but related businesses. These interrelationships are not the fuzzy notions of "fit" which underlay most discussions of synergy, but tangible opportunities to reduce costs or enhance differentiation in virtually any activity in the value chain. Moreover, the pursuit of interrelationships by some competitors is compelling others to follow suit or risk losing their competitive position.

These developments have made *horizontal* strategy, which cuts across divisional boundaries, perhaps the most critical item on the strategic agenda facing a diversified firm. Horizontal strategy is a coordinated set of goals and policies across distinct but interrelated business units. It is required at the group, sector, and corporate levels of a diversified firm. It does not replace or eliminate the need for separate business units and/or business unit strategies. Rather, horizontal strategy provides for explicit coordination among business units that makes corporate or group strategy *more* than the sum of the individual business unit strategies. It is the mechanism by which a diversified firm enhances the competitive advantage of its business units.

Horizontal strategy is a concept of group, sector, and corporate strategy based on competitive advantage, not on financial considerations or stock market perceptions. Corporate strategies built on purely financial grounds provide an elusive justification for the diversified firm. Moreover, the benefits of even successful financial strategies are often temporary. Without a horizontal strategy there is no convincing rationale for the existence of a diversified firm because it is little more than a mutual fund.[2] Horizontal strategy—not portfolio management—is thus the essence of corporate strategy.

Strategically important interrelationships have long been present in many diversified firms. Little attention has been given to identifying and exploiting them systematically, however, and many interrelationships have remained untapped. Achieving interrelationships involves far more than simply recognizing their presence. There are a number of organizational barriers to achieving interrelationships in practice, which are difficult to surmount even if the strategic benefits are clear. Without organizational mechanisms to facilitate interrelationships that work in tandem with a decentralized corporate organizational structure, horizontal strategy will fail.

This chapter will provide a framework for analyzing interrelationships among business units and how they relate to competitive advantage. First, I will describe the reasons for the growing importance of interrelationships, and show how they affect many firms. I will next describe the three broad types of interrelationships among business units: tangible interrelationships, intangible interrelationships, and competitor interrelationships. Then I will discuss how each form of interrelationship leads to competitive advantage, and how interrelationships can be identified.

Chapter 10 will draw together the principles of interrelationships to describe how a firm can formulate a horizontal strategy for its existing business units, and a diversification strategy for entry into new industries. Chapter 11 goes on to treat the organizational issues involved in achieving interrelationships. In achieving interrelationships, strategy and organization are inextricably linked. There are strong parallels between interrelationships among business units, seg-

[2]Recent work on stock market valuation has identified a conglomerate discount, where unrelated business units in a firm are worth less than if they were stand-alone units. Without a horizontal strategy that actually exploits interrelationships, a conglomerate discount is often justified.

ment interrelationships (see Chapter 7), and geographic interrelationships, or interrelationships among activities located in different regions or countries. My focus in this chapter is on interrelationships among business units in different industries, but many of the principles of strategy can be readily applied to these other forms of interrelationships.[3]

The Growing Importance of Horizontal Strategy

Horizontal strategy is something that few firms today can afford to ignore. Interrelationships among business units and the ability to exploit them have been increasing in the last decade, and powerful and interconnected forces are likely to accelerate the trend in the 1980s and 1990s.[4]

Diversification philosophy is changing. The philosophy guiding many firm's diversification strategies has shifted markedly since the early 1970s. Most now emphasize related diversification. This has led to more attention being paid to "fit," and widespread pruning of corporate portfolios. Unrelated or marginally related business units added during earlier phases of diversification have been sold off, and many firms have boosted their stock price through this process, including Borden, Scoville, Trans World Corporation, and IU International. A significant fraction of today's merger activity involves firms selling divisions to other firms where the fit is closer.

Emphasis is shifting from growth to performance. The environment in most of the developed world is one of relatively slow growth coupled with growing global competition, a dramatic change from the previous decades. The emphasis has thus shifted from growth to improving competitive advantage. While largely independent business units may have been an appropriate vehicle for pursuing growth, a more difficult environment has made it increasingly important to coordinate business unit strategies to exploit interrelationships. Buyers, themselves under pressure, are often a force for coordination. Increasingly sophisticated purchasing by hospitals, for example, is compelling firms such as Johnson & Johnson and American Hospital Supply to integrate the sales forces and distribution systems of business units

[3]For a treatment of geographic interrelationships, see Porter (1985).
[4]Some of the same forces are leading to the globalization of industries.

serving hospitals in order to maintain competitive advantage. Both of these firms have been among the strongest advocates of decentralization.

Technological change is proliferating interrelationships and making them more achievable. Technology is breaking down barriers between industries and driving them together, particularly those based on electronics/information technology. Microelectronics, low-cost computers, and communications technology are permeating many businesses and causing technologies to converge. As these technologies are assimilated into many products and production processes, the opportunities for shared technology development, procurement, and component fabrication are increasing. The rush of many large diversified firms such as Gould and United Technologies to acquire electronics firms is a manifestation of this trend.

These same technologies are changing the functions of products and making them parts of larger systems, sometimes controlled centrally with a common computer. Integrated aircraft cockpits, office automation, telecommunications, and lighting, heating, airconditioning, security, and elevator systems in buildings are just a few examples where historically distinct businesses are now becoming strongly related.

New technology is also making it possible to share activities across business unit lines where it was not feasible previously. So-called "flexible automation" is one important example, in which a computer-controlled machine can produce a variety of similar products with minimal setup time. While flexible automation is penetrating slowly and its limits have yet to be defined, it is enhancing the possibilities for sharing component fabrication and assembly facilities among business units with related products. Flexibility that allows sharing also holds promise in other areas such as automated testing and computer-aided design.

The growing sophistication of information systems is also a powerful force in opening up possibilities for interrelationships. With the increasing capacity to handle complex on-line data, information technology is allowing the development of automated order processing systems, automated materials handling systems, automated warehouses, and systems to automate other value activities outside of manufacturing. These systems can often be shared among related businesses.[5] Information technology is also restructuring distribution channels and

[5]While the availability of cheap computing power may be reducing the need to share computers in some applications, a stronger trend seems to be for the technology to spawn new opportunities for sharing.

the selling process in industries such as banking and insurance, in ways that can facilitate sharing.

At the same time that technology is creating interrelationships, it is also reducing costs of exploiting them. The ease of communication has increased just as dramatically as its costs have fallen, reducing the costs of coordinating the activities of business units. Information processing technology has allowed management information systems to be established in areas such as logistics, inventory management, production scheduling, and sales force scheduling. Flexibility in activities has become increasingly possible. While sharing activities may have involved unmanageable complexity and unacceptable costs in the past, this is less often the case today.

Multipoint competition is increasing. A final compelling motivation for horizontal strategy is a logical outgrowth of the other three. As more and more firms seek out or are forced to pursue interrelationships among business units, there is an increasing presence of what I term *multipoint competitors.* Multipoint competitors are firms that compete with each other not only in one business unit but in a number of related business units. For example, Procter & Gamble, Kimberly-Clark, Scott Paper, and Johnson & Johnson compete with each other in varying combinations of consumer paper products industries including disposable diapers, paper towels, feminine napkins, toilet tissue, and facial tissue. General Electric, Westinghouse, Square D, and Emerson Electric similarly meet each other in a number of electrical products industries. Where a firm has multipoint competitors, it must view its competitors more broadly than at the business unit level because competitive advantage will be more broadly determined.

Many important industry sectors are being affected by these forces. Financial services are being revolutionized by interrelationships created by information technology and unleashed by regulatory changes. Such firms as American Express, Citicorp, Sears, Prudential-Bache, and Merrill Lynch are aggressively linking previously separate financial services industries together. In health care, I have already noted how producers of medical equipment and supplies are beginning to pursue interrelationships more aggressively. A few health care providers are also just beginning to see the possible interrelationships in operating facilities such as hospitals, nursing homes, retirement communities, and home care services, though these interrelationships are not yet being exploited. Entertainment firms have begun to recognize the possibilities for coordinated strategies in different media. Information companies such as McGraw-Hill and Dun and Bradstreet are moving to combine many data base products. Computers and telecommunications firms are combining together and/or invading each other's turf, as evidenced by such recent moves as IBM's link with Rolm and AT&T's entry into computers. Automation of the factory and the office is connecting many industries and spawning broadly-based strategies by such firms as GE, Westinghouse, and Xerox. This list of industries being connected by interrelationships is by no means exhaustive.

The forces leading to increasing interrelationships are also illustrated in a study I conducted of business units in 75 diversified Fortune 500 firms in 1971 and 1981. These 75 firms had organized their thousands of business units into 300 groups in 1971 and 315 groups in 1981. The nature and strength of the interrelationships among business units in each group were examined for both time periods. The number and strength of *potential* interrelationships within the groups increased over the ten-year period, as portfolios were reconfigured. However, the firms' success at exploiting the potential interrelationships was less clear. From examining how firms changed their organizational structure over the period, it does appear that firms became more prone to group related businesses together.

Many factors point to the growing importance of horizontal strategy, and imply that past experience with synergy is a poor guide for the future. At the same time, though, many firms have not converted potential interrelationships into sources of competitive advantage. The same firms that are assembling groups of related business units continue to manage them like a portfolio. Thus diversified firms must learn how to manage interrelationships at the same time as they will increasingly have to identify and build upon them.

Interrelationships among Business Units

There are three broad types of possible interrelationships among business units: tangible interrelationships, intangible interrelationships, and competitor interrelationships. All three types can have important, but different, impacts on competitive advantage and are not mutually exclusive:

Tangible Interrelationships. Tangible interrelationships arise from opportunities to share activities in the value chain among related business units, due to the presence of common buyers, channels, technologies, and other factors. Tangible interrelationships lead to competitive advantage if sharing lowers cost or enhances differentiation enough to exceed the costs of sharing. Business units that can share a sales force, for example, may be able to lower selling cost or provide the salesperson with a unique package to offer the buyer. Achieving tangible interrelationships often involves jointly performing one value activity while in other cases it involves multiple activities. When sister business units cross-sell each other's product, for example, they are sharing both of their sales forces.

Intangible Interrelationships. Intangible interrelationships involve the transference of management know-how among separate value chains. Businesses that cannot share activities may nevertheless be similar in generic terms, such as in the *type* of buyer, *type* of purchase by the buyer, *type* of manufacturing process employed and *type* of relationship with government. For example, beer and cigarettes are both frequently purchased recreational products sold on the basis of image as well as taste, while trucking and waste treatment both involve the management of multiple sites.

Intangible interrelationships lead to competitive advantage through transference of *generic skills* or know-how about how to manage a particular type of activity from one business unit to another. This may lower the cost of the activity or make it more unique and outweigh any cost of transferring the know-how. For example, Philip Morris applied product management, brand positioning, and advertising concepts learned in cigarettes to the beer business, substantially changing the nature of competition and dramatically enhancing the competitive position of the Miller brand. It performed marketing activities for cigarettes and beer separately, but used expertise gained in managing activities in one industry to manage them more effectively in another.

Often intangible interrelationships are manifested in a firm's use of the same generic strategy in a number of business units, reflecting management's skills in executing a particular strategy. For example, Emerson Electric and H. J. Heinz compete by using cost leadership strategies in many of their business units. Emerson and Heinz have learned how to manage many activities to achieve low cost, and transfer this know-how to similar but separate value activities in many business units.

Competitor Interrelationships. The third form of interrelationship, competitor interrelationships, stems from the existence of rivals that actually or potentially compete with a firm in more than one industry. These *multipoint competitors* necessarily link industries together because actions toward them in one industry may have implications in another. While competitor interrelationships occur without tangible or intangible interrelationships being present and vice versa, the two often coexist because tangible and intangible interrelationships can provide the basis for diversification. Competitors in one industry, therefore, often expand in the same directions.

Competitor interrelationships make tangible and intangible interrelationships all the more important to recognize and exploit. A multipoint competitor may compel a firm to match an interrelationship or face a competitive disadvantage. Multipoint competitors can also have an overlapping but different set of business units linked by *different* interrelationships than the firm's, making the matching of such interrelationships difficult.

The three types of interrelationships can occur together, as has already been suggested. Tangible interrelationships involving some value activities can be supplemented by intangible interrelationships in others. Activities shared between two business units can be improved by know-how gained from similar activities in other business units. Both tangible and intangible interrelationships are often present when multipoint competitors are present. Each type of interrelationship, however, leads to competitive advantage in a different way.

Synergy is not one idea, then, but three fundamentally different ideas. Thus it is no surprise that what is meant by synergy has been vague. Synergy has most often been described in terms that suggest that what was meant was intangible interrelationships—transference of skills or expertise in management from one business unit to another. This form of interrelationship is perhaps the most ephemeral, however, and its role in creating competitive advantage often is uncertain though potentially significant. Hence it is not surprising that many firms have had great difficulty realizing the fruits of synergy in practice.

I will discuss all three forms of interrelationships in this chapter. Tangible and competitive interrelationships have the most compelling link to competitive advantage, and are easier to implement. Intangible interrelationships are fraught with pitfalls and are often difficult to implement, but can still be a powerful source of competitive advantage in some industries. All three types play a role in horizontal strategy, as will be discussed in Chapter 10.[6]

Tangible Interrelationships

The value chain provides the starting point for the analysis of tangible interrelationships. A business unit can potentially share any value activity with another business unit in the firm, including both primary and supporting activities. For example, Procter & Gamble enjoys interrelationships between its disposable diaper and paper towel businesses. Certain raw materials can be procured and handled jointly, the development of technology on products and processes is shared, a joint sales force sells both products to supermarket buyers, and both products are shipped to buyers via the same physical distribution system. The interrelationships are shown schematically in Figure 9–1. As this example illustrates, tangible interrelationships between two business units can involve one or many value activities. If most value activities are shared between two business units, however, they are not strategically distinct business units but in fact one business unit.

Sharing an activity can lead to a sustainable competitive advantage if the advantage of sharing outweighs the cost, provided the sharing is difficult for competitors to match. Sharing leads to a competitive advantage if it reduces cost or enhances differentiation. Sharing always involves some cost, however, that ranges from the cost of coordinating among the business units involved to the need to modify business unit strategies to facilitate sharing.

Sharing and Competitive Advantage

Sharing a value activity will lead to a significant cost advantage if it involves an activity that represents a significant fraction of operating costs or assets (I term this a *large* value activity), and sharing lowers the cost of performing the activity. Sharing will significantly enhance differentiation if it involves an activity important to differentiation in which sharing either increases the uniqueness of the activity or reduces the cost of being unique. Thus sharing leads to a competitive advantage if it affects the drivers of cost position or differentiation described in Chapters 3 and 4.

[6]John R. Wells (1984) has done an important study on interrelationships that provides evidence of how portfolio membership has affected business units in a sample of diversified firms.

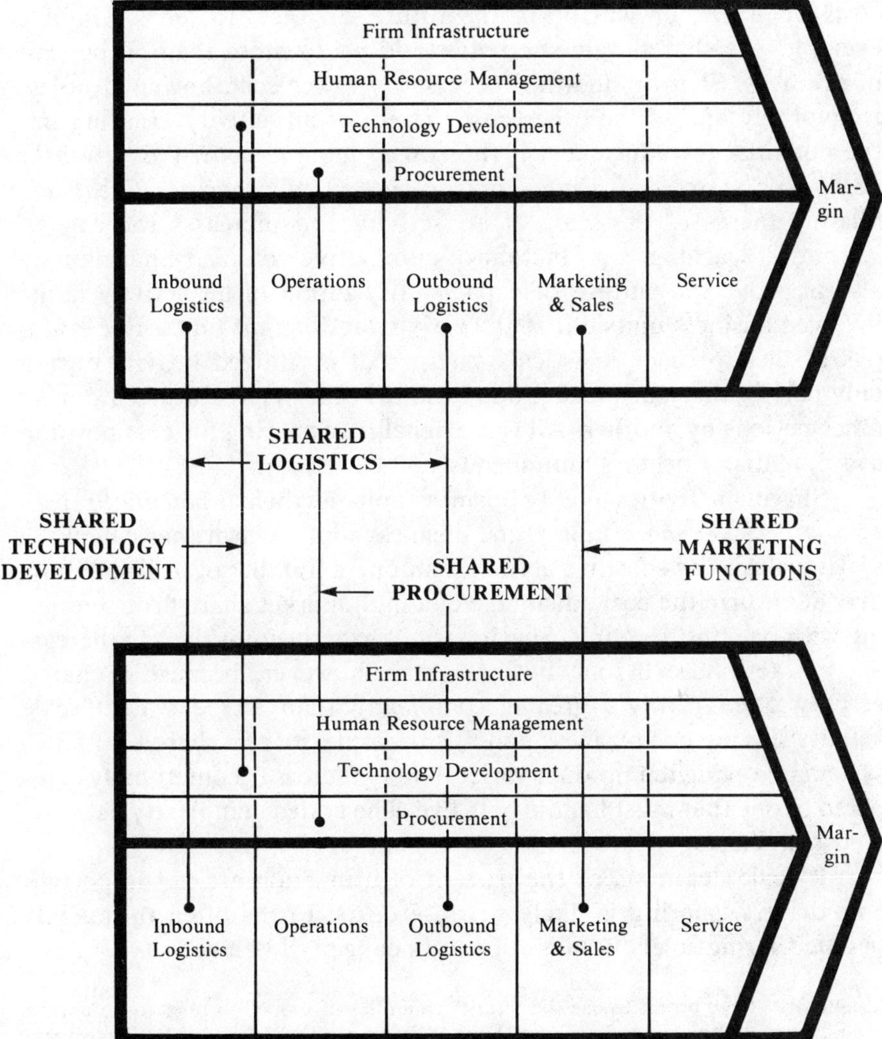

Figure 9–1. Illustrative Interrelationships Between Value Chains in Paper Products

SHARING AND COST

Sharing will have a material impact on overall cost position only if the value activities involved are a significant proportion of operating costs or assets, or will be in the future. In the Procter & Gamble example, the shared value activities add up to more than 50 percent of revenues. Sharing does not necessarily lower cost, however, unless it favorably affects the other cost drivers of an activity. Sharing has the potential to reduce cost if the *cost of a value activity is driven by economies of scale, learning, or the pattern of capacity utilization.*[7] Sharing increases the scale of an activity and increases the rate of learning if learning is a function of cumulative volume.[8] Sharing may also improve the pattern of capacity utilization of an activity if the involved business units utilize the activity at different times. For example, a sales force or logistical system that is utilized heavily during only part of the year serving one business unit may be utilized during other periods by another. All three benefits of sharing for cost position can potentially occur simultaneously.[9]

Sharing activities among business units is, then, a *potential substitute for market share* in any one business unit. A firm that can share scale- or learning-sensitive activities among a number of business units may neutralize the cost advantage of a high market share firm competing with one business unit. Sharing is not exactly equivalent to increasing market share in one business unit, however, because a shared activity often involves greater *complexity* than an equivalent scale activity serving one business unit. The complexity of a shared logistical system involving ten product varieties may increase geometrically compared to one that must handle only five. The added complexity becomes a cost of sharing.

If scale, learning, or the pattern of utilization are not important cost drivers, sharing is likely to raise costs. Firms often mistakenly pursue sharing solely because of excess capacity in an activity. If shar-

[7]Economists have begun to use the term "economies of scope" to refer to economies available to multiproduct firms (see Baumol, Panzar, and Willig, 1982). The sources of economies of scope have not been operationalized, nor have the conditions that nullify them.

[8]Sharing can increase the rate of learning in an activity by increasing its throughput. Intangible interrelationships are also a form of learning, but one in which knowledge gained in one business unit is transferred to another though each business unit has separate activities.

[9]Terms such as shared experience or shared resources are sometimes used to reflect the possibility that activities can be shared. Such terms are not well defined, however; nor do they grow out of a framework that specifies the potential competitive advantages of sharing and its costs.

ing does not lead to scale or learning advantages or improve the long-term pattern of utilization, however, the costs of sharing will usually mean that sharing creates a disadvantage. The correct solution would have been to reduce capacity in the activity rather than share it.

Figure 9–2 illustrates how these principles can be used to highlight activities where sharing is potentially important to cost position. Interrelationships involving value activities in the upper right-hand quadrant of the diagram are of potentially greatest significance due to their large costs and sensitivity to scale, learning, or utilization. Interrelationships involving value activities in the upper left-hand quadrant are not currently important because sharing will not reduce cost, though the value activities represent a large fraction of costs or assets. However, changes in the technology for performing such activities can quickly make interrelationships crucial if their cost becomes more sensitive to scale, learning, or utilization. The change in order processing technology from manual systems to on-line computers in many distribution industries, for example, has begun to create important advantages from sharing order processing across related product lines. Interrelationships involving value activities in the lower right-hand quadrant can become important for cost position if changes in the cost structure raise the percentage of operating costs or assets they represent. The increasing capital cost of a plant and supporting infra-

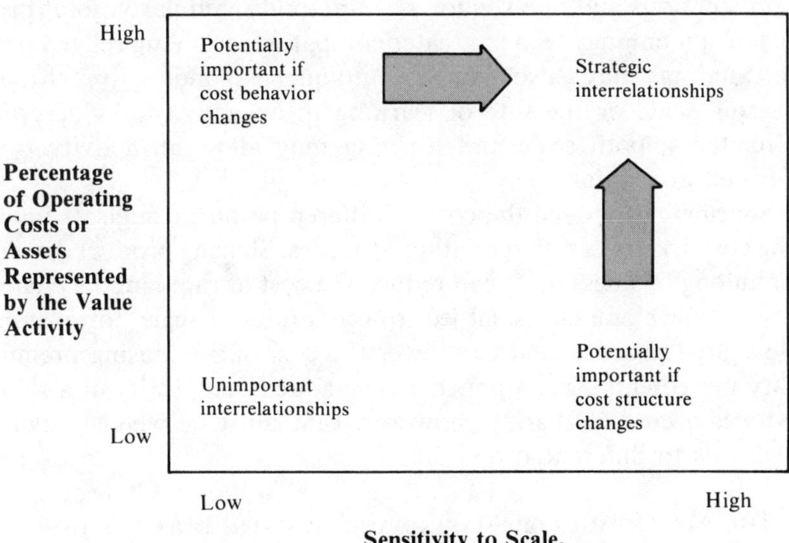

Figure 9–2. Shared Value Activities and Cost Position

structure, for example, will raise the potential advantage of sharing facilities.

Sharing and Differentiation

Sharing affects differentiation in two ways. It can enhance differentiation by increasing the uniqueness of an activity, or it can lower the cost of differentiation. Chapter 4 described how many activities can affect buyer value and, thus, differentiation. Sharing will be most important to differentiation if it affects value activities that are important to actual value or to signaling value. In consumer electronics, for example, sharing product development is important to differentiation because differentiation is heavily affected by product design. Sharing will also be important to differentiation where it reduces the cost of expensive forms of differentiation, such as an extensive sales and service network (e.g., IBM in office products).

Sharing can make an activity more unique both directly and through its impact on other drivers of uniqueness. Sharing enhances uniqueness directly if the shared activity is more valuable to buyers because it involves more than one business unit. Selling several products through the same sales force may increase convenience for the buyer, for example, or allow for the differentiation advantages of bundling (see Chapter 12). In telecommunications, for example, buyers want system solutions and one-vendor accountability. Similarly, joint product development may lead to greater compatibility among related products. Sharing may also increase uniqueness indirectly, through increasing scale or the rate of learning in an activity. As described in Chapter 4, both scale and learning may allow an activity to be performed in a unique way.

Sharing can reduce the cost of differentiation through its impact on the cost drivers of differentiating activities. Sharing product development among business units can reduce the cost of rapid model changes if product development is subject to economies of scale, for example, while shared procurement can lower the cost of purchasing premium quality ingredients or components. The added complexity of a shared activity is a cost of sharing, however, that must be weighed against the benefits to differentiation.

The Advantages of Sharing and Business Unit Position

Sharing an activity will usually not lead to an equal improvement in cost or differentiation for each of the business units involved. Differences in the scales of the business units are one important reason. A business unit that uses a large volume of a component may not gain much of a cost advantage from sharing fabrication of the component with a business unit that uses a small volume of it. However, the unit that is the smaller user may enjoy a tremendous improvement in cost position through gaining the benefits of the larger unit's scale. The advantages to the unit that is the smaller user may allow it to substantially improve its market position. Given such asymmetries, it should come as no surprise that larger business units are rarely enthusiastic about interrelationships with smaller units.[10]

Differences in the structure of the industries in which business units compete may also lead to differential benefits from sharing. A small improvement in cost position may be very important in a commodity industry, for example, but less significant in an industry where product differentiation is high and firms compete on quality and service. The significance of an interrelationship also depends on the strategies of the business units involved. An interrelationship may lead to uniqueness that is valuable for one business unit but much less valuable to another. It is rare, then, that all the business units involved in an interrelationship will perceive it as equally advantageous. This point has important implications for horizontal strategy and for the ability of senior managers to persuade business units to pursue interrelationships.

The Costs of Sharing

Interrelationships always involve a cost, because they require business units to modify their behavior in some way. The costs of sharing a value activity can be divided into three types:

- cost of coordination
- cost of compromise
- cost of inflexibility

The *cost of coordination* is relatively easy to understand. Business units must coordinate in such areas as scheduling, setting priorities, and resolving problems in order to share an activity. Coordination involves costs in terms of time, personnel, and perhaps money. The

[10]The important scale differences among business units are those *in the value activity being shared,* which is not necessarily the same as the overall scale of the business unit. A small business unit may utilize logistics very intensively, for example.

cost of coordination will differ widely for different types of sharing. A shared sales force requires continual coordination, for example, while joint procurement may require nothing more than periodic communication to determine the quantity of a purchased input required per period by each business unit. Different business units may also see the cost of coordination differently. The costs of coordination are often viewed as higher by smaller business units, who see a continual battle over priorities and the risk of being dictated to by larger units. Business units that do not manage a shared activity or are located at a distance from it also tend to fear that their best interests will not be protected.[11]

The cost of coordination will be influenced by the potentially greater complexity of a shared activity noted earlier. The added complexity involved in sharing will vary, depending on the specific activity. Sharing a computerized order entry system among business units will usually add little complexity, for example, in contrast to sharing a logistical system between two business units with large product lines. The added complexity of a shared activity can sometimes offset economies of scale or reduce the rate of learning compared to an activity serving one business unit. Thus sharing can both increase scale and/or learning at the same time as it alters the relationship between scale or learning and cost. This is important because changing the scale- or learning-sensitivity of an activity may benefit or hurt the firm's cost position depending on its circumstances. Computerization generally has reduced the cost of handling the complexity of sharing. That is one of the reasons why interrelationships are getting more important.

A second, often more important, cost of sharing is the *cost of compromise.* Sharing an activity requires that an activity be performed in a consistent way that may not be optimal for either of the business units involved. Sharing a sales force, for example, may mean that the salesperson gives less attention to both business units' product and is less knowledgeable about either product than a dedicated sales force would be. Similarly, sharing component fabrication may mean that the component's design cannot exactly match one business unit's needs because it must also meet another's. The cost of compromise may include costs not only in the shared value activity but also in other linked value activities. Sharing a sales force, for example, may reduce the availability of salespeople to perform minor service functions, thereby increasing the number of service technicians required. Policy choices required to facilitate sharing, then, can adversely affect

[11]The cost of coordination is clearly dependent on a firm's organizational practices. See Chapter 11.

the cost or differentiation of one or more of the business units involved.

That business units must in some way compromise their needs to share an activity is almost a given. The cost of compromise may be minor, or may be great enough to nullify the value of sharing. For example, attempting to share a logistical system among business units producing products of widely differing sizes, weights, delivery frequencies, and sensitivities to delivery time may well lead to a logistical system that is so inappropriate to any of the business unit's needs that the cost savings of sharing are overwhelmed. However, sharing a brand name or sharing procurement of commodities may involve little or no compromise.

The cost of compromise to share an activity will often differ for each of the affected business units. A business unit with a product that is difficult to sell may have to compromise the most in employing a shared sales force, for example. The cost of compromise may also differ because the particular value activity plays a differing role in one business unit compared to another because of its strategy. The compromise involved in joint procurement of a common grade of milk or butter may be more serious for a business unit of a food manufacturer pursuing a premium quality strategy than it is for one attempting to be the low-cost producer if the common grade is not top quality.

The cost of compromise required to achieve an interrelationship is much less if the strategies of the business units involved are consistent with respect to the role of the shared value activity. Achieving such consistency often involves little or no sacrifice to the affected business units *if their strategic directions are coordinated over time.* A particular component can be highly effective in the products of two business units if both units design their products with the component in mind, for example. If the design groups of the two business units are allowed to proceed independently, however, the chances are high that the common component will not meet either business unit's needs. Consistency among business units' strategies that facilitates sharing will rarely happen naturally. An example of both the opportunities to shape the cost of compromise and the indirect costs of compromise that must be weighed comes from General Foods' successful new Pudding Pops. Pudding Pops were designed to melt at a higher temperature than ice cream so that distribution then could be shared with General Foods' Birds Eye frozen vegetables. While frozen foods are transported at zero degrees Fahrenheit, ice cream must be transported at 20 degrees below zero or it will build up ice crystals. While the benefits in shared logistics were clear, however, sharing had some unforseen consequences elsewhere in the value chain. Because Pudding Pops had to be ordered by supermarket frozen food managers along with vegetables, instead of with other freezer case novelty items, Pudding Pops were often forgotten. As this example illustrates, the benefits and costs of an interrelationship must be examined *throughout the value chain* and not just in the activity shared.

The cost of compromise is frequently reduced if an activity is *designed for sharing* rather than if previously separate activities are simply combined or if an activity designed to serve one business unit simply takes on another with no change in procedures or technology. Recent events in financial services have highlighted this point. Merging computer systems initially designed for separate financial products has proven difficult, though a system designed to process many products would be effective. Similarly, attempting to sell insurance and other financial products through a distribution system designed for selling stocks and bonds has not served any of the products very well and has created organizational problems. However, a new conception of a brokerage office is emerging that combines brokers, customer service personnel to handle simple problems and screen clients, and specialists to sell other financial products together with a new shared information system. The cost of compromise in sharing distribution is likely to be much less as a result.

The third cost of sharing is the *cost of inflexibility.* Inflexibility takes two forms: (1) potential difficulty in responding to competitive moves, and (2) exit barriers. Sharing can make it more difficult to respond quickly to competitors because attempting to counter a threat in one business unit may undermine or reduce the value of the interrelationship for sister business units. Sharing also can raise exit barriers. Exiting from a business unit with no competitive advantage may harm other business units sharing an activity with it.[12] Unlike other costs of sharing, the cost of inflexibility is not an ongoing cost but a potential cost should the need for flexibility arise. The cost of inflexibility will depend on the likelihood of the need to respond or exit.

Some costs of coordination, compromise, or inflexibility are involved in achieving any interrelationship. These costs, particularly any required compromise to achieve an interrelationship, will be very real concerns raised by business units when sharing is discussed. They may appear far more obvious than the advantages of the interrelationship, which may appear theoretical and speculative. Business units will also tend to view a potential interrelationship in the light of their

[12]See *Competitive Strategy,* Chapter 1, for a discussion of exit barriers.

existing strategy, rather than weigh its cost if their strategies are modified to minimize the costs of sharing. Finally, the value of interrelationships is often clouded by organizational issues involved in sharing, including those of turf and autonomy which are addressed in Chapter 11. Thus business units can sometimes oppose interrelationships that may result in a clear competitive advantage to them.

The advantages of sharing an activity must be weighed against the costs of coordination, compromise, and inflexibility to determine the *net* competitive advantage of sharing. The assessment of the competitive advantage from an interrelationship must be performed separately for each of the involved business units, and the value of an interrelationship to the firm as a whole is the sum of the net advantages to the involved business units. The net competitive advantage from sharing an activity will almost inevitably vary for each business unit involved. In some cases, the net value of an interrelationship may even be *negative* from the viewpoint of one business unit because of the required compromise, but will be more than offset by a positive net value for other affected business units. For this reason and because of the natural biases in approaching interrelationships noted above, then, business units will often not readily agree on pursuing interrelationships that will benefit a firm as a whole. Interrelationships will *only* happen under such circumstances if there is an explicit horizontal strategy.

While there are always costs of sharing, forces are at work to reduce them in many industries. The new technologies described earlier in this chapter are having the effect of reducing the cost of coordination, compromise, and, to a lesser extent, the cost of inflexibility. Easier communication and better information systems make coordination easier. Low-cost computers and information systems also introduce flexibility into value activities, or the technical capability to minimize the cost of compromise. Programmable machines and robots can adapt to the different needs of business units sharing them. Many firms are only beginning to perceive these possibilities for lowering the cost of sharing, but continue to base their assessment of interrelationships on outdated methods.

Difficulty of Matching

The sustainability of the net competitive advantage of an interrelationship will depend on the difficulty competitors have in matching it. Competitors have two basic options in matching the competitive advantage of an interrelationship: (1) duplicating the interrelationship, or (2) offsetting it through other means such as gaining share in the affected business unit or exploiting a different interrelationship. The ease of duplicating an interrelationship will vary depending on whether competitors are in the same group of related industries involved. The most valuable interrelationships from a strategic point of view are those involving industries that competitors are not in and that have high barriers to entry. For example, Procter & Gamble's advantage from the interrelationships between its disposable diaper and paper towel business units is quite sustainable because its paper towel competitors are blocked from entering the diaper business by enormous entry barriers. A competitor may also face higher or lower costs of coordination and compromise than the firm in achieving an interrelationship depending on the strategies and circumstances of its business units. Other things being equal, then, a firm should pursue most aggressively those interrelationships that its competitors will find the most difficult to match because of the costs of coordination or compromise.

The ability of competitors to offset an interrelationship is a function of whether they can find some other way of improving position in the affected business unit through changes in its strategy or by pursuit of *different* interrelationships.[13] Since nearly any value activity can potentially be shared, a competitor may be able to forge an interrelationship among a different group of business units or share different value activities among the same group of businesses. If a firm, through pursuing an interrelationship, causes a competitor to respond by pursuing different interrelationships, it faces the danger that the ultimate outcome will be an erosion in its relative position.

A final consideration in assessing the difficulty of matching an interrelationship is whether the same benefits can be achieved by a competitor through a coalition or long-term contract. Sometimes a firm can gain the benefits of sharing through a joint venture or other form of coalition with another firm, without actually entering another industry. While such coalitions may be difficult to forge, they should always be considered in assessing the value of an interrelationship and how to achieve it.

Identifying Tangible Interrelationships

To aid in identifying the tangible interrelationships present in a firm, a useful starting point is to catalog all the forms of sharing

[13]For a summary discussion of the ways of gaining competitive position in an industry see Chapter 15.

that occur in practice as well as the alternative ways they can create competitive advantage. Figure 9–3 divides forms of sharing into five categories: production, market, procurement, technology, and infrastructure. I have included shared human resource management as part of shared infrastructure. It is useful to separate these categories of interrelationships because they raise different issues in sharing. Interrelationships ultimately stem from *commonalities* of various types among industries, such as common buyers, channels, or production processes. These commonalities define potential interrelationships; whether the interrelationships lead to a competitive advantage is a function of the benefits and costs described earlier. The sources of each category of interrelationship and the possible forms of sharing to capture it are shown in Table 9–1.

Market Interrelationships

Market interrelationships involve the sharing of primary value activities involved in reaching and interacting with the buyer, from outbound logistics to service. When business units have only the geographic location of their buyers in common, sharing is usually restricted to physical distribution systems, order processing, and to servicing and sales if the products have similar sales and servicing needs. Richer opportunities for sharing are present when business units also have common buyers, common channels, or both. If buyers or channels are the same, sharing of physical distribution or order processing systems among business units usually involves less complexity and lower costs of sharing. In addition, common buyers or channels open up a wide variety of other possible forms of sharing shown in Table 9–1.

The subtleties in identifying potential market interrelationships stem from the tendency to view the buyer or channel too broadly. A wide variety of products and services are sold to oil companies, for example, including drilling equipment, refinery equipment, and transportation equipment such as oil tankers and tanker trucks. Thus oil companies might be identified as a common buyer by business units in many industries. The various products are sold to different parts of the oil company, however, which often have little contact with each other. Even within a product category such as drilling equipment, equipment used in exploration is frequently sold to a different organizational unit than production equipment. Even in instances when the same unit of the oil company makes the purchase, the particular individuals making the purchase decision or influencing the decision

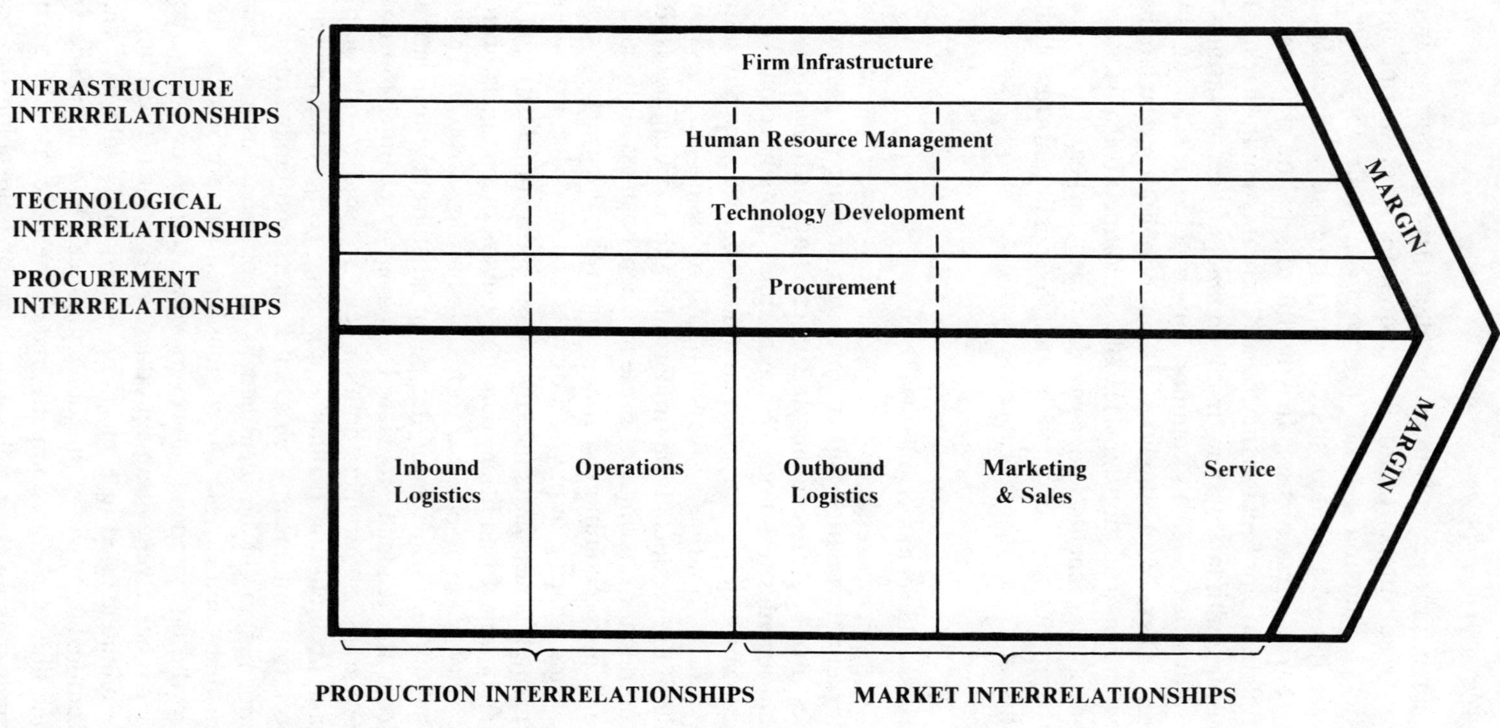

Figure 9–3. Categories of Tangible Interrelationships

TABLE 9–1 Possible Sources of Interrelationships

Procurement Interrelationships		Technological Interrelationships		Infrastructure Interrelationships	
Source of Interrelationship	Possible Forms of Sharing	Source of Interrelationship	Possible Forms of Sharing	Source of Interrelationship	Possible Forms of Sharing
Common purchased inputs	Joint procurement	Common product technology	Joint technology development	Common firm infrastructure needs	Shared raising of capital (financing)
		Common process technology	Joint interface design	Common capital	Shared cash utilization
		Common technology in other value activities			Shared accounting
		One product incorporated into another			Shared legal department
		Interface among products			Shared government relations
					Shared hiring and training
					Other shared infrastructure activities

(continues)

TABLE 9–1 *Continued*

Production Interrelationships		Market Interrelationships	
Source of Interrelationship	Possible Forms of Sharing	Source of Interrelationship	Possible Forms of Sharing
Common location of raw materials	Shared inbound logistics	Common buyer	Shared brand name
Identical or similar fabrication process	Shared component fabrication	Common channel	Cross selling of products
Identical or similar assembly process	Shared assembly facilities	Common geographic market	Bundled or packaged selling
Identical or similar testing/quality control procedures	Shared testing/quality control facilities		Cross subsidization of complementary products
Common factory support needs	Shared factory indirect activities		Shared marketing department
	Shared site infrastructure		Shared sales force
			Shared service/repair network
			Shared order processing system
			Shared physical distribution system
			Shared buyer or distributor financing organization

maker will often differ for different pieces of equipment. Engineers may be responsible for choosing some high-technology equipment such as blowout preventers, for example, while purchasing agents often choose more standard items such as pipe.

Another example of viewing the buyer too broadly is becoming apparent from recent experience in financial services. The traditional buyer of stocks and bonds is a different individual than the average life insurance buyer. Both are different individuals than the typical buyer of futures. These differences are nullifying simplistic efforts to achieve market interrelationships in financial services. Meaningful opportunities for exploring market interrelationships among business units are usually present only where the decision makers for the products are the same or have some contact with each other.

The same issues arise in identifying common channels. Though two products might both be sold through department stores, few actual channel interrelationships are likely to be present if one is sold through discount department stores and the other through exclusive department stores such as Lord & Taylor and Neiman-Marcus. There are also often different buying executives responsible for different classes of products in the same channel. In most supermarket chains, for example, frozen foods are typically bought by a different buyer than meats, even though some frozen foods are meat products. Even if the decision makers are different, however, opportunities for sharing logistical and order processing systems may exist with both common buyers and common channels.

Whether products sold to a common buyer are substitutes or complements can also affect the advantage of sharing market-related activities. Shared marketing can yield less of a cost advantage when products are substitutes because the buyer will purchase either one product or the other but not both. However, offering substitute products to buyers can reduce the risk of substitution because losses in one product can be compensated in the other (see Chapter 8). Joint marketing of substitutes can also enhance a firm's differentiation.

When business units sell complementary products to common buyers, the advantage of sharing is often greater than if the products are unrelated or substitutes. Complementary products usually have correlated demand that facilitates the efficient utilization of shared value activities, and other practices such as common branding, joint advertising and bundling. The strategic issues raised by complementary products, a subset of market interrelationships, are treated separately in Chapter 12.

The potential competitive advantages of the important forms of market interrelationships and the most likely sources of compromise cost are shown in Table 9–2. Indirect activities such as market research, sales force administration and advertising production (e.g., artwork, layout) can often be shared more easily than direct activities because they require lower compromise costs.[14] The benefits of market interrelationships can often be enhanced by changes in the strategies of the involved business units that reduce the cost of compromise. Standardizing sales force practices, repositioning brands to make their images more compatible, or standardizing delivery standards or payment terms may make sharing easier, for example.

Production Interrelationships

Interrelationships in production involve the sharing of upstream value activities such as inbound logistics, component fabrication, assembly, testing, and indirect functions such as maintenance and site infrastructure. All these forms of sharing require that activities be located together. Doing so can lead to a compromise cost if the suppliers or buyers of the business units sharing the activities have greatly different geographic locations since inbound or outbound freight costs may be increased. Shared procurement is different from production interrelationships because merging facilities is not implied. Purchased inputs can be procured centrally but shipped from suppliers to dispersed facilities.

Production interrelationships can be illusory when apparently similar value activities are examined closely. For example, though the machines themselves are generically the same, a job-shop manufacturing process for one product may involve different machine tolerances than another, or lot sizes or run lengths can be quite different. As with market interrelationships, indirect value activities offer particularly attractive opportunities for sharing because the compromise costs are often low. For example, such activities as building operations, maintenance, site infrastructure, and testing laboratories can be shared despite the fact that the actual manufacturing processes are different.

Table 9–3 shows the potential competitive advantages of important forms of production interrelationships, and the likely sources of compromise cost. The balance will depend on the strategies of the

[14]See Wells (1984).

TABLE 9–2 Determinants of Net Competitive Advantage from Market Interrelationships

Form of Sharing	Potential Competitive Advantages	Most Likely Sources of Compromise Cost
Shared brand name	Lower advertising costs Reinforcing product images/reputations	Product images are inconsistent or conflicting Buyer is reluctant to purchase too much from one firm Diluted reputation if one product is inferior
Shared advertising	Lower advertising costs Greater leverage in purchasing advertising space	Appropriate media or messages are different Advertising effectiveness reduced by multiple products
Shared promotion	Lower promotion costs through shared couponing and cross couponing	Appropriate forms and timing of promotion differ
Cross selling of products to each others' buyers	Lower cost of finding new buyers Lower cost of selling	Product images are inconsistent or conflicting Buyer is reluctant to purchase too much from one firm
Interrelated pricing of complementary products	See Chapter 12	See Chapter 12
Bundled selling	See Chapter 12	See Chapter 12
Shared marketing department	Lower cost of market research Lower marketing overhead	Product positionings are different or inconsistent Buyer's purchasing behavior is not the same
Shared channels	Enhanced bargaining power with the channels leading to improvements in service, shelf positioning, maintenance/repair/support, or channel margins One-stop shopping for the buyer improves differentiation Lower cost of channel support infrastructure	Channel gains too much bargaining power vis-à-vis the firm Channel unwilling to allow a single firm to account for a major portion of its sales Use of shared channel will erode support from other channels

TABLE 9–2 ***Continued***

Form of Sharing	Potential Competitive Advantages	Most Likely Sources of Compromise Cost
Shared sales force or sales offices	Lower selling costs or sales force infrastructure costs	Different buyer purchasing behavior
	Better quality salespersons	Buyer reluctance to purchase large amounts from a single salesperson
	More products to sell improves access to the buyer or enhances buyer convenience	Salesperson is not allowed adequate time with the buyer to present a number of products effectively
	Better sales force utilization if the pattern of utilization is not the same	Different type of salesperson is most effective Certain products get more attention than others
Shared service network	Lower servicing costs	Differences in equipment or knowledge necessary to make typical repairs
	More sophisticated or responsive servicing, due to improved technology or denser service locations	Differences in the need for timeliness in service calls
	Better capacity utilization if demand for service is inversely correlated	Differing degrees to which the buyer performs service in-house
Shared order processing	Lower order processing costs	Differences in the form and composition of typical orders
	Lower cost of employing improved technology that improves responsiveness or billing information	Differences in ordering cycles that lead to inconsistent order processing needs
	Better capacity utilization if order flows are inversely correlated	
	One-stop shopping for the buyer improves differentiation	

TABLE 9–3 Determinants of Net Competitive Advantage from Production Interrelationships

Form of Sharing	Potential Competitive Advantages	Most Likely Sources of Compromise Cost
Shared inbound logistical system	Lower freight and material handling costs Better technology enhances delivery reliability, reduces damage, etc. Sharing allows more frequent, smaller deliveries that reduce inventory or improve plant productivity	Input sources are located in different geographic areas Plants are located in differing geographic areas Varying physical characteristics of inputs imply that a logistical system which can handle all of them is suboptimal Needs for frequency and reliability of inbound delivery differ among business units
Shared components (identical components used in different end products)	Lower cost of component fabrication Better technology for component manufacturing improves quality	Needs for component design and quality differ among business units
Shared component fabrication facilities (similar or related components are produced using the *same* equipment and facilities)	Lower component costs Better fabrication technology improves quality Capacity utilization is improved because demand for similar components is not perfectly correlated	High setup costs for different component varieties Needs for component quality or tolerances differ among business units Flexible manufacturing equipment has higher cost than specialized equipment Larger workforce in one location leads to potential hiring, unionization or productivity problems
Shared assembly facilities (similar or related end products are assembled using the same equipment/lines)	Lower assembly costs Better assembly technology improves quality Utilization is improved because demand is not perfectly correlated A shared materials handling system can feed different assembly lines	High setup costs for different products Needs for quality or tolerances differ Flexible assembly equipment is higher cost Larger workforce in one location leads to potential hiring, unionization or productivity problems

TABLE 9–3 ***Continued***

Form of Sharing	Potential Competitive Advantages	Most Likely Sources of Compromise Cost
Shared testing/quality control	Lower testing cost	Testing procedures and quality standards differ
	Better technology increases the extensiveness of testing and improves quality control	Flexible testing facilities and equipment are higher cost
Shared indirect activities (including maintenance, plant overhead, personnel department, cafeteria, etc.)	Lower indirect activity costs	Differing needs for indirect activities among business units
	Improved quality of indirect activities	Larger workforce in one location leads to potential hiring, unionization, or productivity problems

involved business units. For example, two business units with differentiation strategies are more likely to have similar needs in terms of component specifications, manufacturing tolerances, and testing standards than if one business unit pursues cost leadership while another offers a premium product.

Procurement Interrelationships

Procurement interrelationships involve the shared procurement of common purchased inputs. Common inputs are frequently present in diversified firms, particularly if one looks beyond major raw materials and pieces of capital equipment. Suppliers are increasingly willing to make deals based on supplying the needs of plants located around the world, and negotiate prices reflecting total corporate needs. Some firms go overboard in shared procurements, however, because they fail to recognize the potential costs of compromise or they establish a rigid procurement process that does not allow for opportunism in negotiating attractive opportunities.

The potential competitive advantage of shared procurement and the likely sources of compromise cost are shown in Table 9–4:

TABLE 9–4 Determinants of Net Competitive Advantage from Procurement Interrelationships

Form of Sharing	Potential Competitive Advantage	Most Likely Sources of Compromise Cost
Joint procurement of common inputs	Lower costs of inputs	Input needs are different in terms of quality or specifications, leading to higher costs than necessary in business units requiring less quality
	Improved input quality	Technical assistance and delivery needs from suppliers vary among business units
	Improved service from vendors in terms of responsiveness, holding of inventory, etc.	Centralization can reduce the information flow from factory to purchasing, and make purchasing less responsive

Technological Interrelationships

Technological interrelationships involve the sharing of technology development activities throughout the value chain. They are distinguished from production interrelationships because their impact is on the cost or uniqueness of technology development, while production interrelationships involve sharing activities involved in the actual production of the product on an ongoing basis. It is important to recognize, however, that interrelationships in process development often occur together with production or market interrelationships. Interrelationships in process technology typically grow out of interrelationships in the primary activities.

As with other forms of interrelationships, apparently promising technological interrelationships can be illusory. Scientific disciplines that overlap for two business units may be of minor importance to success compared to scientific disciplines that do not overlap. Harris Corporation, for example, thought it could reduce the development expense involved in entering word processing through adapting software from its text editing system sold to newspapers. Harris discovered that the text editing system had so many features that were specific to the needs of newspapers that development of a word processing system had to start from scratch.

Truly significant technological interrelationships are ones involving technologies important to the cost or differentiation of the products or processes involved, as microelectronics technology is to both telecommunications and data processing. Many products have superficial technological similarities, making the identification of true technological interrelationships difficult. As with other types of interrelationships, the net competitive advantage of a technological interrelationship will differ depending on the industry and strategies of the business units involved. For example, the benefits of sharing microelectronics technology will tend to be greater for two consumer products business units than for a defense business unit and a consumer business unit. Rockwell International learned this lesson when it put a team of engineers from its defense business into its Admiral TV set division. The sensitivity to cost was so much greater in TV sets than in defense equipment that sharing did not succeed. The same thing occurred in business aircraft, where a design developed originally for military use (the Sabreliner) proved too expensive for the commercial market.

Table 9–5 shows the potential competitive advantages that can stem from sharing technology development as well as the most likely sources of compromise costs.

Infrastructure Interrelationships

The final category of interrelationships involve firm infrastructure, including such activities as financing, legal, accounting, and human resource management. Some infrastructure activities are almost always shared in diversified firms, as described in Chapter 2. In most cases, the effect of sharing on competitive advantage is not great because infrastructure is not a large proportion of cost and sharing has little impact on differentiation. It is ironic, therefore, that the vast majority of literature on sharing has been on sharing infrastructure—principally finance and the utilization of capital. Interrelationships in finance, particularly, have been seen as a significant benefit the diversified firm contributes to its business units.

There are two basic sources of financial interrelationships: joint raising of capital and shared utilization of capital (primarily working capital). Economies of scale in raising capital may indeed exist, especially up to a certain quantity of capital needed. Efficient utilization of working capital is made possible by countercyclical or counterseasonal needs for funds among business units, which allows cash freed up by one business unit to be deployed in another. Financial interrelationships typically involve relatively few compromise costs that must

TABLE 9–5 Determinants of Net Competitive Advantage from Technological Interrelationships

Form of Sharing	Potential Competitive Advantages	Most Likely Sources of Compromise Cost
Shared technology development (for separate products or where one product is incorporated into another)	Lower product or process design costs (including shorter design time)	Technologies are the same, but the tradeoffs in applying the technology are different among business units
	Larger critical mass in R&D, or the ability to attract better people improves the innovativeness of product or process designs	
	Transference of developments among product areas enhances differentiation or allows early entry into new technologies	
Shared interface design for products with a technological interface	Lower interface design costs	A nonstandard interface reduces the available market
	Differentiation through superior and proprietary interface performance	Risks of bundling (Chapter 12)
	Bundling opportunities created through a nonstandard interface (see Chapter 12)	

be offset against any savings. Moreover, financial interrelationships are among the easiest to achieve if they are present, perhaps a reason why they are so frequently discussed.

The major limitation to the competitive advantage of shared financing is the *efficiency of capital markets.* Scale economies in financing appear to be moderate for most firms and lead to a relatively small difference in financing costs. Firms can also borrow to cover short-term cash needs and lend excess cash in the highly efficient markets for commercial paper and other instruments, mitigating the value of sharing working capital. Hence financial interrelationships are rarely the basis for creating a significant competitive advantage, unless the size and credit rating of competitors differ greatly. Other forms of infrastructure interrelationships can be important in particular industries. Shared infrastructure for hiring and training is important in some service industries, while shared government relations can be significant in natural resource firms.

Intangible Interrelationships

Intangible interrelationships lead to competitive advantage through the transfer of skills among separate value chains. Through operating one business unit, a firm gains know-how that allows it to improve the way another generically similar business unit competes. The transference of skills can go in either direction—e.g., from existing business units to a new business unit or from a new business unit back to existing business units. The transference of generic know-how can occur anywhere in the value chain. Philip Morris transferred generic know-how in the marketing of consumer packaged goods from its cigarette business to Miller Beer, while Emerson Electric transferred plant design and cost reduction skills when it acquired the chain saw firm Beaird-Poulan. In both cases, the transference of skills *changed* the way that the receiving business unit competed and enhanced its competitive advantage.

Intangible interrelationships lead to a competitive advantage if the improvement in cost or differentiation in the business unit receiving the know-how exceeds the costs of transferring it. Know-how residing in one business unit has already been paid for, and hence transferring it may involve little cost compared to its cost of development. The actual transference of know-how always involves some cost, however, whether it be the cost of time of skilled personnel or perhaps the greater risk that proprietary information will leak out. Using the know-how that is transferred will also typically involve some cost in adapting it to the circumstances of the receiving business unit. These costs of transferring know-how must be weighed against the potential benefits to determine whether an intangible interrelationship will create competitive advantage.

Intangible interrelationships are important to competitive advantage when the transference of know-how or skills allows the receiving business unit to lower costs or enhance differentiation. This occurs if the transference of skills leads to policy changes that lower cost or enhance differentiation, or because the transference of skills gives the receiving business unit better insight into its other drivers of cost or uniqueness. The transference of skills from Philip Morris to Miller Beer, for example, resulted in policy changes in the way beer was positioned and marketed, as well as an escalation of advertising spending that increased scale economies in the industry and worked to the advantage of large brands like Miller.

Identifying Intangible Interrelationships. Intangible interrelationships arise from a variety of generic similarities among business units:[15]

- same generic strategy
- same *type* of buyer (though not the same buyer)
- similar configuration of the value chain (e.g., many dispersed sites of mineral extraction and processing)
- similar important value activities (e.g., relations with government)

Although value activities cannot be shared, these similarities among business units mean that know-how gained in one business unit is valuable and transferable to another.[16]

Because of the myriad possible generic similarities among business units, it is not possible to be as complete in identifying the important types as it was with tangible interrelationships. However, the value chain provides a systematic way of searching for intangible interrelationships. A firm can examine the major value activities in its business units to unearth similarities in activities or the way the chain is configured that might provide the basis for transference of know-how or highlight generic skills that might be applied to new industries.

Intangible Interrelationships and Competitive Advantage. Intangible interrelationships of one type or another are very widespread. It is always possible to point to some generic similarity in some value activity between almost any two business units. An airline is widely dispersed, has multiple sites, and relies heavily on scheduling, charac-

[15]John R. Wells's (1984) study contains important work on intangible interrelationships that provides further insight into when and how they arise.

[16]There may be a fine line in some cases between transferring know-how and sharing technology development. The basis for separating tangible and intangible interrelationships is whether an activity is shared in some way on an ongoing basis, or whether know-how is transferred between essentially separate activities.

teristics shared by trucking companies, international trading companies and industrial gas producers. Widespread similarities of some kind make the analysis of intangible interrelationships quite subtle.

The key tests in identifying intangible interrelationships that are important to competitive advantage are the following:

- *How similar* are the value activities in the business units?
- *How important* are the value activities involved to competition?
- *How significant* is the know-how that would be transferred to competitive advantage in the relevant activities?

These questions must be answered together. The similarity of two business units is a function of how much know-how can be usefully transferred. The importance of the transferred know-how is a function of its contribution to improving competitive advantage in the receiving business unit. The transference of just one insight can sometimes make an enormous difference to competitive advantage, so even business units that are not very similar can have important intangible interrelationships. However, truly important intangible interrelationships are much less common than an initial search for them might imply. It is frequently difficult, moreover, to predict whether the transference of know-how will prove to be valuable.

The most common pitfall in assessing intangible interrelationships is to identify generic similarities among business units that are not important to competition. Either the know-how that can be transferred does not affect value activities that are important to cost or differentiation in the receiving business unit, or it does not provide insights that competitors do not already have. Philip Morris's acquisition of the Seven Up soft drink company provides a possible example of the latter. While the beer industry had historically been populated by family firms with little marketing flair, the soft drink industry has long been characterized by sophisticated marketing by the likes of Coke, Pepsi, and Dr Pepper. Philip Morris's marketing expertise appears to have offerred much less of an advantage for Seven Up than it did for Miller.

Many firms have fallen into the trap of identifying intangible interrelationships that are illusory or do not matter for competitive advantage. Often, it seems, intangible interrelationships are forced, and represent more of an ex poste rationalization of diversification moves undertaken for other reasons. Intangible interrelationships were prominent in discussions of synergy. The difficulty of finding and implementing significant intangible interrelationships is one of the reasons synergy proved such a disappointment to many firms.

The effective exploitation of intangible interrelationships thus requires an acute understanding of the business units involved as well as the industries they compete in. The importance of an intangible interrelationship for competition can only be truly understood by identifying *specific* ways in which know-how can be transferred so as to make a difference. The mere hope that one business unit might learn something useful from another is frequently a hope not realized.

Even intangible interrelationships where the benefits of transferring know-how far exceed the cost of transferring it do not lead to competitive advantage unless the transference of know-how actually takes place. Know-how is transferred through interchange between managers or other personnel in the affected business units. This process does not occur without active efforts on the part of senior management. Personnel in the receiving business unit may be wary or unsure of the value of know-how from a "different" industry. They may even openly resist it. Business units with know-how may be hesitant to commit the time of important personnel and may view the know-how as highly proprietary. Finally, transference of know-how is subjective and the benefits of doing so often are hard for managers to understand when compared to tangible interrelationships. All these factors imply that even important intangible interrelationships can be very difficult to achieve. Doing so requires a sustained commitment and the existence of formal mechanisms through which the required transference of skills will take place. A conducive organizational setting can greatly reduce the cost of transferring know-how.

Competitor Interrelationships

Competitor interrelationships are present when a firm actually or potentially competes with diversified rivals in more than one business unit. Any action taken against multipoint competitors must consider the entire range of jointly contested businesses. In addition, a firm's competitive advantage vis-à-vis a multipoint competitor depends in part on the interrelationships that both have achieved. The competitive position of a multipoint competitor is often more a function of its *overall* position in a group of related industries than its market share in any one industry because of interrelationships. While multipoint

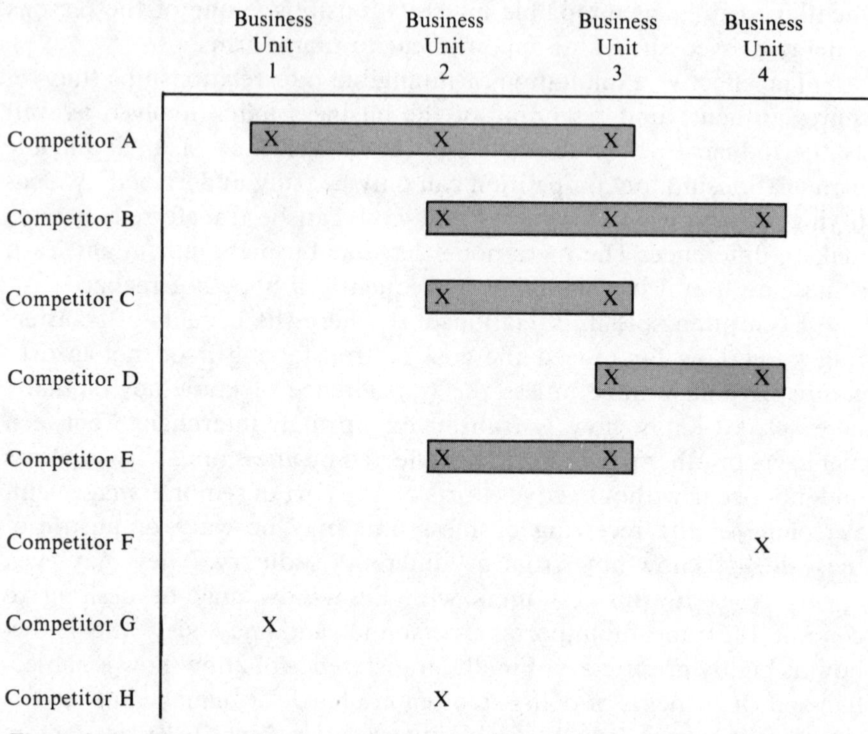

Figure 9–4. Corporate Competitor Matrix

competitors and interrelationships do not necessarily occur together, they often do because both tangible and intangible interrelationships lead firms to follow parallel diversification paths.[17]

Identifying existing multipoint competitors is relatively easy with a diagram such as that shown in Figure 9–4. For the firm shown in Figure 9–4, competitors A, B, C, D, and E are multipoint competitors. The other competitors are single point, but represent *potential* multipoints. Analysis of the figure suggests that business units 2 and 3 are in strongly related industries, because four competitors compete in both industries. The presence of many competitors in two industries is a relatively strong, though not perfect, indication that they are related. The relatedness of industries is also a clue to predicting which

[17]The analysis of multipoint competitors in both related and unrelated industries has strong parallels to the analysis of competitors in local or regional industries, as well as to competitive analysis in global competition. In a regional industry such as airlines, for example, firms compete with each other in a number of overlapping routes. Internationally, firms often compete in a number of country markets. The principles described here can be applied in all of these settings (see Porter 1985).

firms are the most likely potential multipoint competitors. Given the apparent relationship of the industries in which business units 2 and 3 compete, competitor H may be the most likely potential multipoint competitor.

Table 9–6 shows the multipoint competitor matrix for the consumer paper products sector in 1983, along with each firm's year of entry. It is clear that competitor interrelationships are numerous and that they have increased significantly over time, particularly during the 1960s and 1970s. We would observe a similar pattern in many other groups of industries. The pattern of competitor interrelationships in the table will be discussed further below.

Closely analagous to the analysis of multipoint competitors is the analysis of single-point competitors with *different patterns of interrelationships* from the firm's. For example, Xerox, Canon, and Matsushita all compete in convenience copiers. However, Xerox draws on interrelationships with its high-volume copiers and office automation equipment. Canon's interrelationships have historically been strongest with its calculator and camera businesses, while Matsushita draws on interrelationships involving its broad range of consumer electronic and other electronic products. Interestingly, both Canon and Matsushita are diversifying into office automation to match Xerox's interrelationships there.

Single-point competitors with different patterns of interrelationships are important because they bring differing sources of competitive advantage to an industry. These may be difficult for a firm to match and may shift the basis of competition. Moreover, as the copier example illustrates, single-point competitors with different patterns of interrelationships are sometimes prime candidates to become multipoint competitors.

Multipoint Competitors in Unrelated Industries

Where a firm faces a multipoint competitor in industries that are not related, the strategic issues revolve around how actions in one business unit can lead to reactions in another and how equilibrium with the competitor can be reached in several contested industries. Because a firm and a multipoint competitor meet each other in a number of industries rather than one, a greater number of variables enter into determining their relative position. This implies that firms need more information about each other to avoid mistaken interpretations of moves. It also often means that destabilizing events in one

TABLE 9–6 Competitor Interrelationships in Consumer Paper Products, 1983

	Disposable Diapers	Bathroom Tissue	Paper Towels	Facial Tissue	Paper Napkins	Feminine Napkins	Tampons	Towel Wipes
Scott Paper	In and out (1966)	X (1904)	X (1931)	X (1943)	X (1958)			X (1976)
Kimberly-Clark	X (1968)	X (1924)	X (1976)	X (1924)	X (1951)	X (1924)	X (1960)	X (1975)
Procter & Gamble	X (1966)	X (1957)	X (1965)	X (1960)		X (1983)	Entered and exited (1974)	
Georgia-Pacific		X (1909)	X (1909)	X (1909)	X (1909)			
Johnson & Johnson	X (1972)					X (1927)	X (1978)	X* (1980)
Weyerhaeuser	X							
Tampax						X (1981)	X (1936)	

* Towel wipes of this competitor are designed primarily for use with babies.

industry can spread to others. This added complexity of the game makes peaceful coexistence potentially difficult.

On the other hand, competing in a number of industries also opens up greater possibilities for signaling, making threats, establishing blocking positions, and taking reciprocal actions. For example, a firm threatened in one industry might retaliate in a different industry, sending a signal of displeasure but creating less risk of escalation than if the response were direct. The threat that a firm can retaliate in several industries (and inflict a higher cost on the competitor) may also tend to deter a competitor from making a threatening move in the first place.

Another stabilizing factor in multipoint competition is the fact that focal points, or natural equilibrium points for competition, may be more prevalent.[18] Where only one industry is contested, the number of focal points consistent with each competitor's perception of its relative strength is likely to be small. With equally balanced competitors, for example, an equal division of market shares may be the only focal point. It may well be an unstable one because any temporary shift in market shares is likely to trigger a strong response to preserve the balance. With two jointly contested industries, there may be a number of additional focal points that are more stable, and one of them will tend to be found sooner.

Table 9–7 illustrates this. Here focal points 2 and 3 will tend to be more stable than focal point 1. In each industry, the high-share competitor will tend to have a clear competitive advantage, and hence a small disturbance will be less likely to cause either firm to precipitate a war. Similarly, the asymmetry of positions reduces the chances that the high-share competitor in one industry will seek an even greater share, since it remains vulnerable to retaliation in the industry in which it is weak.

Multipoint competitors must be viewed in their totality for purposes of offensive and defensive strategy. Most competitor analysis is done at the business unit level, however, and looks exclusively at competitors' positions in a single industry. Some corporate or group-level analysis of multipoint competitors is essential. Minimally, a broader perspective on multipoint competitors needs to be applied to test that business unit actions against them will not have adverse consequences in other business units. Ideally a more comprehensive

[18]For a definition and discussion of focal points, see Thomas Schelling (1960) and *Competitive Strategy*, Chapter 5.

TABLE 9–7 Focal Points and Multipoint Competitors

	Focal Point 1		Focal Point 2		Focal Point 3	
	Share of Market 1	Share of Market 2	Share of Market 1	Share of Market 2	Share of Market 1	Share of Market 2
Competitor A	50	50	60	40	70	30
Competitor B	50	50	40	60	30	70

analysis of existing and potential multipoint competitors should be done to uncover opportunities for a coordinated offensive or defensive strategy across business units.

Some additional considerations in developing strategy vis-à-vis multipoint competitors in unrelated businesses are as follows:

Forecast possible retaliation in all jointly contested industries. A multipoint competitor may retaliate against a move in any or all jointly contested industries. It may well choose to respond in the industry where its response will be the most cost-effective (see Chapter 14). For example, it may respond in an industry in which it has a small share because it can inflict a large penalty on the firm at low cost. Each industry is not a separate battlefield.

Beware of a small position by a multipoint in a key industry. A small position held by a multipoint in an industry in which the firm has a large share (or high cash flow) can give the multipoint a lever against the firm. Such a position may be an effective blocking position (see Chapter 14).

Look for opportunities to exploit overall corporate position vis-à-vis a multipoint. The overall corporate position vis-à-vis a multipoint may provide less costly and less risky means of responding to threats. Similarly, coordinated actions in a number of industries may make it difficult and very costly for a competitor to respond.

Establish blocking positions for defensive purposes. A small presence in one of a multipoint competitor's key industries can provide a way to inflict serious penalties on it at relatively low cost.

Strategy toward a multipoint competitor is affected by whether or not the competitor *perceives* the connections among industries. Perceiving the connection among jointly contested industries cannot be assumed where a multipoint competitor is managed via highly autonomous business units. In some cases, a competitor's ignorance of multi-industry linkages may allow the firm to gain in relative position. For example, an attack on one business unit may divert competitor attention and resources from defending its position in a more important business unit.

Multipoint Competition in Related Industries

When a firm faces multipoint competitors in related industries, the strategic problem increases in complexity. The issues discussed in the previous section still apply and are often even more important because relatedness increases the likelihood that a competitor will perceive the linkages among businesses. The presence of tangible interrelationships among industries, however, complicates the assessment of relative position.

A firm's competitive advantage or disadvantage in any business unit that faces a multipoint competitor is a function of *overall position* in value activities involving interrelationships. If a firm and the competitor employ a shared sales force or logistical system, for example, the relative cost or differentiation of the sales force or logistical system as a whole is what matters. The extent to which interrelationships are *actually achieved* is what determines their effect on competitive advantage, not the potential to share. In addition, the net competitive advantage from an interrelationship for both a firm and a competitor will be influenced by their respective strategies. A competitor may potentially face higher or lower costs of coordination or compromise than the firm does, making an interrelationship more or less valuable to it.

A competitor's group of interrelated business units may not exactly overlap with the firm's. For example, Procter & Gamble competes in disposable diapers, paper towels, feminine hygiene products, and bathroom tissue, but not in paper napkins and towel wipes. Kimberly Clark, on the other hand, is in all these businesses. When the related industries that are jointly contested do not overlap exactly, the comparison between a firm and a competitor must center on the firm's whole array of interrelationships relative to the competitor's. Each shared activity must be analyzed for the competitor as a whole, and compared to the firm's cost or differentiation in that activity. The volume provided by all five of Procter & Gamble's paper-related business units compared to that of Kimberly's eight business units will affect their relative position in shared value activities such as the logistical system, for example. Relative position in any business unit is built up by comparing all shared activities as well as value activities that are not shared.

A weak relative position in one related business unit can be partially or completely offset by superior positions in other related business units. Procter & Gamble is in fewer paper products industries than Kimberly-Clark, for example, but it is the market leader in diapers, toilet tissue, and paper towels. Diapers, particularly, is a very large industry relative to the others. Procter & Gamble's total consumer paper products volume is undoubtedly higher than Kimberly's. Analyzing a firm's relative position vis-à-vis multipoint competitors thus requires an examination of the complete portfolios of the two firms.

The most basic strategic implication of multipoint competition in related industries is the same as in unrelated industries—competitor analysis must encompass the competitor's entire portfolio of business units instead of examining each business unit in isolation. Competitive advantage in one business unit can be strongly affected by the extent of potential interrelationships with other business units in the competitor's portfolio and by whether they are achieved.

Balance or superiority in shared value activities relative to a multipoint competitor can potentially be achieved in many ways. Investing to gain a stronger position in industries where a firm is already strong can offset the advantages a competitor has from being in a broader array of related industries. If the competitive advantage from shared activities is significant and no compensating advantages can be found, a firm may be forced to match a competitor's portfolio of related business units. Matching can be important for defensive reasons as well as offensive ones. It may be necessary to match a competitor's diversification even if the firm has a competitive advantage in its existing business units, to prevent the competitor from gaining the advantages of interrelationships without opposition. Conversely, if a firm can discover new related industries that competitors are not in, it may be able to strengthen position in important shared value activities.

In consumer paper products, for example, there has been a great deal of offensive and defensive diversification. Table 9–6 shows the dates of entry of each competitor into the respective industries. Competitors' portfolios of businesses have broadened since the late 1950s. Procter & Gamble's actions triggered this sequence of moves. P&G began in toilet tissue and then moved into facial tissue, disposable diapers, and paper towels defensively.

Competitors with Different Patterns of Interrelationships

Single-point and multipoint competitors may well pursue different types of interrelationships, involving different shared activities or activities shared in a different way. A good example of this situation is again the consumer paper products field (Table 9–6). Competitors have pursued interrelationships in paper products in different ways, reflecting their overall portfolios of business units and the strategies employed in them. In disposable diapers, for example, Procter & Gamble enjoys joint procurement of common raw materials, shared technology development, a shared sales force, and a shared logistical system among its paper product lines. However, Procter & Gamble has separate brand names for each paper product line. In contrast, Johnson & Johnson (J&J) competes in disposable diapers as well as a wide line of other baby care products, all sold under the Johnson & Johnson brand name. Its interrelationships include that shared brand name, plus a shared sales force and shared market research in the baby care field. J&J enjoys little sharing in production, logistics, and product or process technology development. Each competitor in Table 9–6 has a somewhat different pattern of interrelationships.

A competitor with a different pattern of interrelationships represents both an opportunity and a threat. It is a threat because the competitive advantage gained through interrelationships cannot be readily replicated, since a firm may not be in the appropriate group of industries, or have the right strategy to allow matching the interrelationships. To match J&J's shared brand name, for example, Procter & Gamble would have to change its strategy of using a different brand for each product. This would probably fail, however, because of the inappropriateness of using the diaper brand name on other paper products unrelated to babies. Thus to match this particular advantage of J&J's, Procter & Gamble would probably have to diversify further into baby care, where J&J is dominant.

A smart competitor with different interrelationships will attempt to shift the nature of competition in each industry in the direction that makes its interrelationships more strategically valuable than the firm's. An escalation in advertising spending in diapers would work to the advantage of J&J because of its shared brand, for example, holding other things constant. A competitor with different interrelationships might also attempt to reduce the ability of a firm to achieve its interrelationships. For example, a move by J&J to make diapers from textile-based materials would, if feasible, reduce P&G's ability to share value activities because of its broad presence in paper products. Similarly, a competitor might shift its strategy in a way that raised the cost of compromise for the firm to achieve its type of interrelationships, thereby forcing the firm to damage one business unit in responding to a threat to another.

Thus the essence of the competitive game between firms pursuing different forms of interrelatedness is a tug of war to see which firm can shift the basis of competition to compromise the other's interrelationships, or to enhance the value of its own. The disposable diaper industry offers a good illustration of how this game can play itself out. Procter & Gamble has retained leadership in the diaper industry, while J&J was forced to exit from the U.S. market after costly losses. Though J&J's market interrelationships were strong, advertising is a relatively small proportion of total costs in disposable diapers. Sales force and logistical costs, where Procter & Gamble enjoyed comparable if not superior interrelationships to J&J, are each as high or higher than advertising. J&J could not match Procter & Gamble's production, procurement, and technological interrelationships, and this proved fatal since total manufacturing costs for diapers are a very large percentage of total cost and the pace of technological change in both product and process is rapid. Without a markedly superior product, therefore, J&J was unable to match the combination of Procter & Gamble's large market share and its interrelationships.

Forecasting Potential Competitors

Tangible interrelationships, intangible interrelationships, and competitor interrelationships can be used to forecast likely potential competitors. Likely potential entrants into an industry will be firms for which that industry is:

- a logical way to create or extend an important interrelationship
- a necessary extension to match the interrelationships of competitors

To forecast potential competitors, all possible interrelationships involving an industry are identified, including competitor interrelationships. Each potential interrelationship will typically lead to a number of other industries. The industries in which existing competitors compete besides the industry may suggest possible interrelationships of other types. By identifying related industries, a firm can locate potential competitors for whom entry into the firm's industries would be logical. Analysis must assess the probability that these potential competitors will actually choose to enter the industry rather than pursue their other investment opportunities.

10 Horizontal Strategy

There are two fundamental issues in corporate strategy for the diversified firm. The first is the selection of industries in which the diversified firm should compete. The second issue is how the strategies of the firm's business units should be coordinated. How both issues are addressed should be driven by competitive advantage—how the corporation can contribute to the competitive advantage of business units. Business units inevitably incur costs as part of a diversified firm, both in overhead and potentially through constraints imposed by corporate policies. Unless the corporation can make a more than offsetting contribution to the competitive advantage of business units, diversification becomes a liability.

Of the two fundamental issues in corporate strategy, diversified firms have devoted much more attention to the first issue than to the second. While much attention is placed on selecting new industries, however, this selection has too often been based on tenuous forms of relatedness. Many diversified firms have devoted little or no attention to coordinating business unit strategies. As the previous chapter demonstrated, however, there is a growing need to do so as well as to enter new industries in which contributions to competitive advantage within the corporation are clear. The presence of multipoint competitors and competitors with different patterns of interrelationships also dictates that a firm must exploit the available interrelationships to maintain relative position.

Horizontal strategy coordinates the goals and strategies of related business units. It encompasses both existing business units and the selection of new industries to enter based on interrelationships with existing units. Horizontal strategy can and should exist at the group, sector, and corporate level. Few firms, however, have anything but the most informal horizontal strategy, regardless of how thoroughly they formulate strategies for individual business units. Yet tangible interrelationships constitute a major potential source of competitive advantage. An *explicit* horizontal strategy should be at the core of group, sector, and corporate strategy.

A new pattern of competition is emerging in many industries, driven by the strong trends described earlier. Competition will be among clusters of related business units rather than among individual business units. Coordinated business unit strategies and related diversification into new industries will deepen and extend interrelationships. Strategic choices will increasingly involve a partnership of the business unit and the firm as a whole. Business unit managers will seek new ways to gain competitive advantage from being part of the diversified firm other than capital availability.

Horizontal strategy cannot be left implicit or allowed to emerge on a bottom-up basis from business units. Firms without an explicit horizontal strategy will have difficulty resisting the strong pressures that always exist to undermine corporate performance by optimizing that of individual business units, particularly those firms with a tradition of decentralized decision-making. Moreover, it is a widely held fallacy that business units should propose and all agree on the desirability of an interrelationship for it to be strategically sound. This attitude is based on theories of business unit autonomy that developed in the 1970s. It promotes a hands-off posture by corporate and group executives and places the burden of identifying and exploiting interrelationships on business unit managers who lack the resources and influence to do so. Bottom-up horizontal strategy rarely ever happens.

The Need for Explicit Horizontal Strategy

Organizational structure in most firms works against achieving interrelationships. However, organizational impediments alone do not explain why related business units, proceeding independently, will rarely optimize the competitive position of the firm as a whole. Without a horizontal strategy, business units may well act in ways that reduce rather than enhance their ability to exploit interrelationships:

Business units will value interrelationships differently and not agree to pursue them. Business units will rarely reap equal benefits from an interrelationship because of differences in size, strategy, or industry. The costs of compromise required to pursue an interrelationship can differ among business units, as can the impact of sharing on their cost positions or differentiation. Some business units may rightly conclude that the costs of coordination and compromise outweigh the value of the interrelationship to them, and interrelationships of value to the firm as a whole will never be achieved. Large and currently successful business units often prove the most resistant to pursuing interrelationships, as do business units which are asked to transfer their know-how to others to gain intangible interrelationships.

Business unit strategies will evolve in ways that weaken interrelationships. Left to formulate strategies independently, business units may well proceed in *inconsistent* directions that can make interrelationships more difficult to achieve. For example, when two business units share a common buyer or channel, one may pursue a differentiation strategy while another evolves toward striving for a low-cost position. Though these strategies may well be appropriate for the business units in isolation, the potential interrelationships between the two units imply that the inconsistent strategies will confuse buyers or channels, blur the overall brand image of the firm in the related industries involved, and diminish opportunities to share a brand name and sales force. Another example is the case where two business units specify slightly different components even though they could use a common one. Independent business unit strategies will always undervalue benefits that accrue not to them, but to the firm as a whole.

Pricing and investment decisions taken independently may erode firm position. Interrelationships imply that profits should be taken in some business units and not other related ones. For example, lowering prices in one business unit to boost volume can lead to lower costs in another business unit through increasing the overall firm purchasing power in shared components or raw material.[1] Yet this sort

[1]Other examples of coordinated pricing are discussed in Chapter 12.

of action would never be contemplated by business units that develop strategies independently and are evaluated solely by their own results. This problem cannot be solved through transfer pricing, because it arises even though business units do not buy or sell from each other.

There is also a risk of suboptimal investment decisions if related business units proceed independently. For example, one business unit sharing a component may have buyers which are extremely price-sensitive while the buyers served by other business unit are not. The second business unit will attach little value to investments that reduce the cost of the common component and will allocate its resources elsewhere. The business unit benefiting greatly from cost reduction may not be able to justify the investment on its own.

Business units will have a tendency to go outside to form alliances to achieve interrelationships available internally. Business units acting independently may not fully appreciate the benefits of internal projects in areas such as shared marketing, production, technology development, and sourcing compared to alliances with outside firms. Achieving interrelationships internally implies that all the benefits accrue to the firm. Interrelationships achieved through coalitions with outside firms must share some of the benefits with coalition partners. Outside alliances can also strengthen coalition partners that eventually emerge as competitors, and can lead to the diffusion of the firm's proprietary technology. These arguments imply that in many instances business units should accept *greater* costs of compromise to work with sister units on an interrelationship. However, managers rarely see it this way. In fact, they often take the opposite view; they undervalue the benefits to the firm as a whole and prefer to deal with independent firms where they have full control over the relationship. Some of the organizational problems that reinforce these tendencies are described in Chapter 11.

Business units may ignore key potential competitors or the true significance of existing competitors. As described earlier, competitor analyses by business units will often fail to uncover potential competitors or the interrelationships that are vital to their existing competitors' relative positions. This narrow perspective of competitors also obscures the way in which competitors view an industry within their broader strategies, an important determinant of competitor behavior. Business units proceeding independently will rarely consider the ways in which their actions might trigger competitive response that affects sister business units.

Transfer of know-how among generically similar business units will not occur. The transfer of know-how that underpins intangible interrelationships does not occur naturally. Business units will want to develop their own strategies, and believe that they know their industries the best. They can rarely be expected to seek out know-how elsewhere in the firm. Business units with the know-how will have little incentive to transfer it, particularly if it involves the time of some of their best people or involves proprietary technology that might leak out.

Without an explicit horizontal strategy, there will be no systematic mechanism to identify, reinforce, and extend interrelationships. Business units acting independently simply do not have the same incentives to propose and advocate strategies based on interrelationship as do higher level managers with a broader perspective.

Formulating Horizontal Strategy

Formulating horizontal strategy involves a number of analytical steps that flow from the framework described in Chapter 9:

1. *Identify all tangible interrelationships.* The starting point in formulating horizontal strategy is to identify systematically all the tangible interrelationships that are actually or potentially present among a firm's business units. The first step in doing so is to examine value chains of each business unit for actual and possible opportunities for sharing. Initially, all interrelationships that seem to be present should be identified; illusory or insignificant interrelationships can be eliminated through further analysis. In searching for interrelationships, the specific characteristics of value activities that would provide a basis for sharing must be identified. For example, meaningful production interrelationships must be based on similarities in specific production equipment or process steps rather than a generalized view that there are similar processes. Similarly, specific technologies and subtechnologies are the basis of technology interrelationships, and common decision makers in buyers or channels are the basis of key market interrelationships.

Diagrams like Figure 10–1 provide a simple mechanism to use in identifying interrelationships within a firm.

A. Interrelationship Matrix

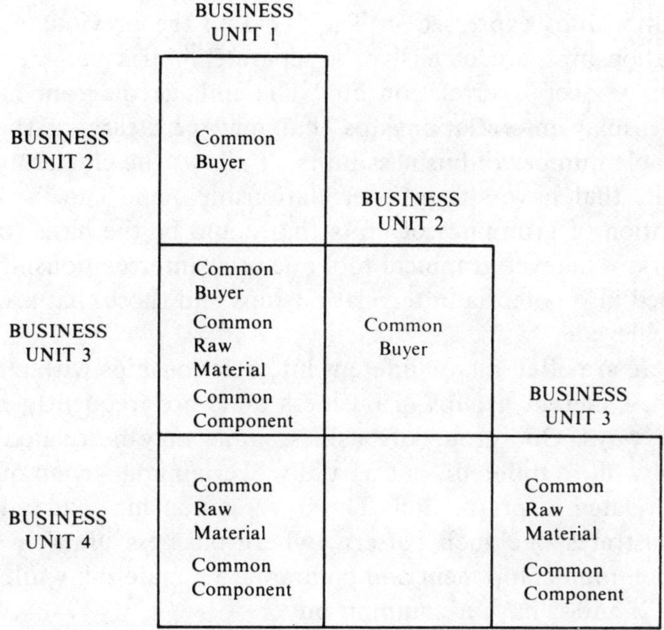

B. Linkage Diagram

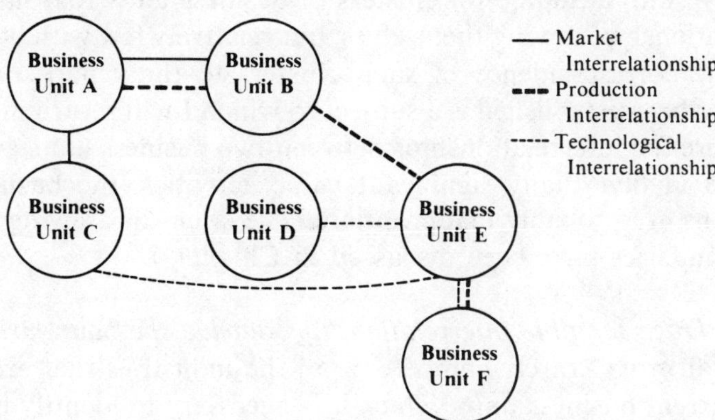

Figure 10–1. Tangible Interrelationships in a Diversified Firm

Each cell of the interrelationship matrix displays the interrelationships between a pair of business units, drawing from the types of interrelationships expressed in Table 9–1 in the previous chapter. If interrelationships are extensive, a separate matrix can be prepared for each type of interrelationship. The linkage diagram is another way to display interrelationships that may be clearer if there are a manageable number of business units. It allows the clustering of business units that have strong interrelationships, and can facilitate the visualization of groupings of units that could be the basis for groups or sectors. Whatever graphical tool one uses, interrelationships should be divided into potential interrelationships and those that are actually being achieved.

There are often many different interrelationships within a diversified firm. Different groups of business units are frequently related in different ways. One group of business units may be related by their markets, while a different, but partially overlapping, group of business units is related in production. The interrelationship matrix in Figure 10–1 illustrates one such pattern, where business units 1, 3, and 4 have a common component and common raw material, while business units 1, 2, and 3 have a common buyer.

In a diversified firm with many business units, a complex pattern of interrelationships often emerges. To simplify the analytical task of identifying interrelationships, it may be possible to break up a diversified firm into a number of clusters of business units that have many interrelationships among themselves, but relatively few with other clusters. The correspondence of such clusters to the groups or sectors that have been established is a subject to which I will return in Chapter 11. Where the interrelationships between two business units are pervasive and involve many significant value activities, the business unit definitions are probably inappropriate. The issues in drawing business unit boundaries have been discussed in Chapter 7.

2. *Trace tangible interrelationships outside the boundaries of the firm.* A firm will rarely compete in all the industries that are related to its current business units. Thus, it is necessary to identify interrelationships between a firm's existing business units and other industries not currently in its portfolio. This requires that a firm examine important value activities to look for related industries where sharing or further sharing might be feasible. A firm with an effective sales force serving a particular buyer group, for example, should identify other products purchased by the same buyer group or products that fit the

sales force's expertise that might be sold to other buyer groups. Similarly, each brand name, distribution channel, logistical system, technological development activity, and other important value activity should be probed for potential opportunities for sharing with other industries.

Identifying paths of interrelationship outside a firm is a creative task, but one that will yield considerable benefits in diversification planning and in the development of defensive strategies to anticipate and block potential entrants. The portfolios of diversified competitors can often provide important clues to industries with important interrelationships to the firm's. However, detecting *new* interrelationships not exploited by any competitor can be even more valuable.

3. *Identify possible intangible interrelationships.* After identifying tangible interrelationships, the next step is to seek out intangible interrelationships. This involves the isolation of value activities in which a firm has valuable know-how that might be useable in other business units or in new industries. It also requires identifying new industries in which a presence would lead to know-how that is valuable in the firm's existing business units. Signals of potential intangible interrelationships include similarities in generic strategy, buyer type, or value chain configuration. While identifying intangible interrelationships is subtle, it can be important. Many potential intangible interrelationships are usually present, which makes screening them to access their importance to competitive advantage an essential task.

4. *Identify competitor interrelationships.* A firm must identify all its multipoint competitors, potential multipoint competitors, and competitors pursuing different patterns of interrelationships. A diagram such as that in Figure 9–4 above can provide a structure for doing so. The existence of multipoint competitors often provides clues about the presence of interrelationships, and can aid in their identification. Conversely, interrelationships often are useful predictors of potential new competitors, as described above. After the array of multipoint competitors has been identified from a firmwide perspective, the interrelationships within each important competitor's portfolio must be charted. Often competitors have different interrelationships that involve different sets of businesses.

5. *Assess the importance of interrelationships to competitive advantage.* The net competitive advantage from a tangible interrelationship is a function of the advantage from sharing, the costs of sharing,

and the difficulty of matching the interrelationship. Shared activities must be measured against the corresponding activities of competitors on all three dimensions. The tangible interrelationships present in a diversified firm are often numerous. However, experience has shown that the number with strategic importance is likely to be relatively small. The challenge is to isolate the important ones, including those that involve industries in which a firm has no presence currently. The fact that an interrelationship is not being achieved is not a reliable sign that it is not important. The interrelationship may have been overlooked, or the costs of compromise associated with it may be reduced by making business unit strategies more consistent.

Intangible interrelationships lead to competitive advantage if the benefits of transferring know-how exceed the cost of transferring it. Transferring know-how is beneficial if the similarities among value activities are significant, the activities are important to competitive advantage in the industries involved, and the firm has know-how that can materially enhance competitive advantage if it is transferred. Experience suggests that skepticism is warranted in assessing intangible interrelationships to avoid pursuing intellectually plausible but practically useless similarities among businesses.

6. *Develop a coordinated horizontal strategy to achieve and enhance the most important interrelationships.* Important interrelationships can be achieved or enhanced in a variety of ways.

Share Appropriate Value Activities. Value activities of related business units should be shared if the benefits exceed the costs. This may involve measures such as combining sales forces, rationalizing manufacturing facilities, coordinating procurement, and rebranding product lines. Sharing will always require some adjustments to current practices. Business unit strategies may need to be modified to gain maximum advantage from sharing. Similarly, activities may have to be redesigned to reduce the cost of compromise.

Coordinate Strategic Postures of Related Business Units. The strategies of related business units should be coordinated to increase the competitive advantage of interrelationships and reduce the costs of compromise. This can involve everything from minor adjustments of business unit strategies to major repositionings, including acquisitions and divestitures. The coordination of strategies requires that marketing programs and investment spending plans are consistent, and that business units are aware of each other's plans in product development and other important areas. Coordination also implies that actions toward competitors are part of an integrated group, sector, or corporate battle plan. Market interrelationships often create the greatest need for consistent business unit strategies, in order to gain the maximum impact with common customers or channels. However, a degree of consistency is required for achieving and exploiting any form of interrelationship. Coordinating business units can involve difficult tradeoffs between enhancing interrelationships and the position of individual business units. These tradeoffs are often difficult. However without a horizontal strategy they will rarely even be considered regardless of the benefits to the firm.

Distinguish the Goals of Business Units. The goals of business units should be set to reflect the role of business units in interrelationships. Some business units, for example, might be given more ambitious sales targets but lower profit goals because of the contribution of their volume to the position of other business units. Asking all business units to meet the same goals may seem to be the "fairest" solution, but it also threatens to undermine some important sources of competitive advantage.

Business unit goals that reflect interrelationships are broader than those prescribed in portfolio planning techniques, commonly involving mandates such as build, hold, or harvest. Portfolio models typically ignore interrelationships, and set different goals for business units only in the sense that some business units are expected to generate cash while other are expected to use it. Interrelationships provide a broader perspective of corporate strategy based on competitive advantage, within which cash flow considerations are subsumed.

Coordinate Offensive and Defensive Strategies Against Multipoint Competitors and Competitors with Different Interrelationships. There must be an overall firm game plan for dealing with each significant multipoint competitor and each competitor with a different pattern of interrelationships that could be threatening. Ideally, a firm should seek to promote industry evolution in directions that increase the value of its interrelationships and compromise the value of competitors. More specific options for offensive and defensive strategy are discussed in Chapters 14 and 15.

Exploit Important Intangible Interrelationships through Formal Programs for Exchanging Know-How. A firm must actively encourage the transfer of know-how among business units with potentially important generic similarities. Receiving business units may not be receptive because of "not invented here" problems, and business units asked to transfer expertise may resent the commitment of time and people involved. Achieving intangible interrelationships will require a shared understanding of their value, and organizational mechanisms to facilitate the transference of know-how.

Diversify to Strengthen Important Interrelationships or Create New Ones. Diversification strategy should focus on finding and entering new businesses that reinforce the most important interrelationships or creating new interrelationships of high strategic importance. Diversification strategy will be treated in the next section.

Sell Business Units That Do Not Have Significant Interrelationships with Others or That Make the Achievement of Important Interrelationships More Difficult. Business units that have no important interrelationships to others in a firm or are not likely bases of further diversification are candidates for sale in the long term. Even if they are attractive and profitable, such business units will be worth as much or even more to other owners, since being part of the firm does not enhance their competitive advantage and being part of another firm might. A firm can thus be in a position to recover the full value to it or more of such business units by selling them. The proceeds can then be invested in business units where interrelationships can enhance competitive advantage. Practical considerations mean that such a strategy may have to be implemented over the long-term, however. Buyers that recognize the value of a business unit may not be easy to find, and it may be hard to replace a highly profitable, albeit unrelated business unit with an equally attractive one, no matter how great the potential interrelationships might be.

The presence of some marginally related business units may make it more difficult to achieve other, more important interrelationships. They, too, are candidates for sale. A firm may be less able to build a shared distribution channel, for example, if it has another business unit that uses a different and competing channel to reach the same buyer group. Similarly, a firm may be less able to exploit opportunities for sharing a sales force and marketing to reach a particular buyer group if it has a business unit in the buyer group's industry that competes with it. Interrelationships may create conflicts with buyers, suppliers, or channels. American Express has experienced this as it increasingly competes with banks which are also a key outlet for its travelers checks. Unlocking some interrelationships, then, may require a firm to get out of some industries.

When there are several patterns of interrelationships within a firm involving different groups of business units, taking some of the steps noted above may involve tradeoffs. Coordinating strategic postures to facilitate one type of interrelationship can reduce the ability to achieve another. Distinguishing business unit goals can lead to the same sort of tradeoff. Where such tradeoffs exist, the principle must be to reinforce those interrelationships that have the greatest impact on competitive advantage, even at the expense of others. However, organizational mechanisms described in the next chapter can often allow interrelationships among different groups of business units to be achieved simultaneously.

7. *Create horizontal organizational mechanisms to assure implementation.* Firms cannot successfully exploit interrelationships without a horizontal organizational structure that encourages coordination and transfers skills across business unit lines. Such tasks as defining the right business units, clustering them into the proper groups and sectors, and establishing incentives for business unit managers to work together are vital to success. The principles of horizontal organization are the subject of Chapter 11.

Interrelationships and Diversification Strategy

Diversification based on interrelationships is the form of diversification with the greatest likelihood of increasing competitive advantage in existing industries or leading to sustainable competitive advantage in new industries. Both tangible and intangible interrelationships have an important role in diversification strategy. Tangible interrelationships should be the starting point for formulating diversification strategy. Intangible interrelationships have a less certain effect on competitive advantage and are more difficult to achieve in practice than tangible interrelationships.

Interrelationships can allow a firm diversifying through internal development to overcome entry barriers into a new industry more cheaply than other potential entrants that lack them.[2] The presence of interrelationships also facilitates entry through acquisition because an acquisition candidate will have greater value to the firm than it does to its present owners or to other bidders without similar interrelationships. Hence profits associated with the acquisition are less likely to be bid away in setting the purchase price. The presence of interrelationships also means that diversification through either an acquisition or internal development will benefit *existing* business units that have interrelationships with the new business unit.

Any diversification move must also pass the test of structural attractiveness (Chapter 1). Industries that are related to a firm's existing business units are not more structurally attractive simply because of their relatedness. A new business unit must be in an industry that is actually or potentially structurally attractive. The presence of interrelationships per se is not sufficient justification for entering an industry unless they allow a firm to transform an unattractive industry into an attractive one. Thus seeking industries with *both* an attractive structure and interrelationships that will yield the firm a competitive advantage in competing in those industries are the dual guides to diversification strategy.

Diversification Based on Tangible Interrelationships

Diversification strategy can seek to extend any of the types of tangible interrelationships described in Table 9–1. The most desirable directions for diversification are those that lead to interrelationships offering the greatest impact on competitive advantage, using the criteria described earlier. In some cases, diversification will strengthen a firm's position against key competitors, while in others it will be dictated by the need to match competitors' diversification defensively. A firm may also enter industries where it can use interrelationships to overwhelm single-business competitors or competitors with poorly conceived arrays of business units. The benefits of tangible interrelationships can flow in two directions. It is just as valuable to pursue interrelationships that enhance the position of existing units as it is to use existing unit positions to improve new business units.

Three of the broad types of tangible interrelationships shown in Table 9–1—market, production, and technological—represent three

[2]See *Competitive Strategy,* Chapter 16, for the basic strategic logic of entry into a new business.

broad diversification avenues. A market-oriented diversification strategy aims to sell new products to common buyers, channels, or geographic markets in order to reap the benefits of market interrelationships. A production-oriented diversification strategy aims to produce similar products with shared production value activities. Procurement interrelationships often stem from production interrelationships. A technology-oriented diversification strategy aims to develop or enter new industries based on similar core technologies, that involve products sold to either existing or new markets. The successful Japanese typewriter firm Brother, for example, uses its "technology tree" in driving diversification. Brother has built on technologies developed in one business to enter another. Small motor technology from the original sewing machine business led to entering small appliances and electric typewriters, while electronics expertise gained in typewriters has led to entering electronic printers.

These three broad diversification paths often lead a firm in different directions. Broadening the range of products sold to common buyers, channels or geographic areas often involves different technologies and production processes, while broadening the range of products with similar technologies or production processes implies getting into new markets. This is not always true, however. In consumer electronics, for example, firms such as Sony and Matsushita have diversified into new products with technology shared with their existing products. Opportunities also existed at the same time for market and production interrelationships. Sony and Matsushita (Panasonic) have each developed shared value activities such as brand names, service organizations, plants, and procurement across wide product lines. Interrelationships, in fact, are one of their primary sources of competitive advantage. Another example is Black and Decker's entry into small appliances, which exploits technological interrelationships and production interrelationships involving small electric motors used in its core business, power tools.

Diversification will offer the greatest potential for enhancing overall firm position when several important value activities can be shared. The most successful diversifiers do not view market-, production-, and technology-oriented diversification as mutually exclusive, but seek ways to combine them. In my study of interrelationships in 75 Fortune 500 companies in 1971 and 1981 described in Chapter 9, high-technology companies showed the greatest ability to increase interrelationships in markets, production, and technology simultaneously. This finding is consistent with the role of electronics/information processing technology in linking industries together. As technology develops, firms should be able to find more avenues for diversification where multiple forms of interrelationships can be exploited.

Diversification Through Beachheads

Firms will differ in their ability to achieve important interrelationships through diversification. The opportunities a firm has may be limited by a number of factors:

- The existing mix of business units in the firm may enjoy few meaningful interrelationships with other industries.
- The significant interrelationships may have already been exploited.
- The industries that are related to a firm's existing industries may be structurally unattractive.
- No feasible strategy may exist for entering related industries because competitors have preempted.
- Antitrust considerations preclude entry into some related industries.

When opportunities to diversify along tangible interrelationships are few or exhausted, a firm should consider diversification based on intangible interrelationships. Since intangible interrelationships involve the transference of generic skills and not actual sharing of activities, there will usually be more industries with potential intangible interrelationships to existing business units than industries with tangible interrelationships. Finding opportunities in which intangible interrelationships will lead to competitive advantage is a subtle process, though, because it requires that a firm understand a new industry well enough to see how transference of skills will really make a difference.

Generic similarity of a new industry to an existing industry does not itself imply that transference of skills will create competitive advantage. Competitors in the new industry can have equal or superior skills themselves. The relevance of a firm's skills in a new industry must also be questioned, and superficial analyses of generic similarities can be very misleading. Basing diversification on imagined or irrelevant generic similarities among industries led to the failure of diversification strategies in the 1960s and 1970s. All these caveats aside, however, careful industry analyses can uncover new industries in which intangible interrelationships are a sound basis for diversification.

Diversification based on intangible interrelationships should be viewed not only as a stand-alone opportunity, however, but also as a potential *beachhead.* Once a firm enters a new industry based on intangible interrelationships, it can then use this beachhead to spawn new opportunities for diversification based on tangible interrelationships. A good example is Procter & Gamble's initial acquisition of Charmin Paper Company, a beachhead which allowed Procter & Gamble to build the highly interrelated cluster of paper products business units described earlier. Figure 10–2 illustrates schematically the process of diversifying through beachheads. An intangible interrelationship with the original cluster of tangibly related business units becomes

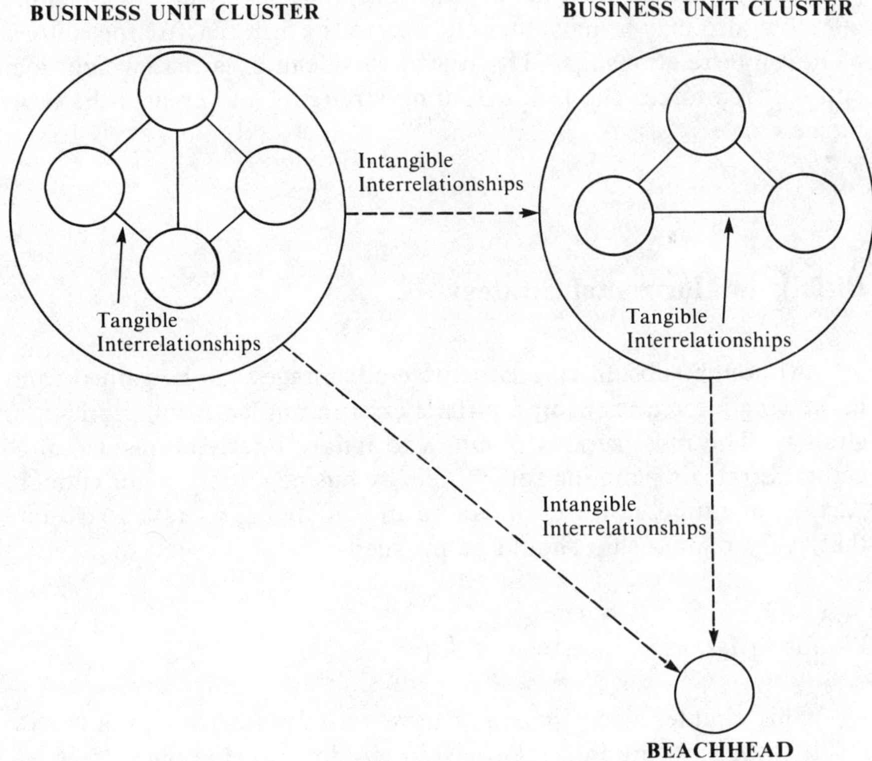

Figure 10–2. Interrelationships and the Pattern of Diversification

the foundation for a new cluster. The diversified firm emerges as a number of clusters of business units related by tangible interrelationships, with the clusters related by intangible interrelationships. A key test of diversification opportunities based on intangible interrelationships, therefore, is their potential as a beachhead.

Diversification and Corporate Resources

The unique corporate assets of a diversified firm are the existing and potential interrelationships that reside in the value chains of its business units. These interrelationships represent the major contribution of a diversified firm to its business units, and to the new industries it might enter. The central role of the diversified firm is to nurture and expand these interrelationships.

Diversification is a means to widen a firm's stock of assets and skills by expanding the perimeter of the value activities in which it participates. Each new industry not only may be related to existing ones, but also may bring value activities to the firm that are the sources of *new* interrelationships. The best diversification is that which does both—it reinforces the firm's existing strengths and creates the basis for new ones.

Pitfalls in Horizontal Strategy

Although substantial competitive advantages can be gained from harnessing interrelationships, pitfalls exist in implementing horizontal strategy. The most serious pitfall is to ignore interrelationships altogether. Strategic planning solely done by business units is not enough. At the same time, however, it can be an equally big mistake to assume that every relationship should be pursued.

Pitfalls in Ignoring Interrelationships

This chapter and Chapter 9 have raised numerous pitfalls that result from ignoring interrelationships. A few notable ones are mentioned here:

Misreading the Strategic Contributions of Business Units. A firm that fails to understand interrelationships will measure business unit performance on a stand-alone basis. It may, in the process, encourage units to take actions that will undermine interrelationships and erode overall firm position.

Misreading Position Vis-à-vis Key Competitors. A firm that plans only at the business unit level will fail to diagnose its position vis-à-vis key diversified competitors. It will also fail to formulate moves against them that enhance overall firm position.

Portfolio Management. The presence of interrelationships, particularly tangible interrelationships, limits the usefulness of portfolio planning models as they are usually applied. Portfolio planning models are narrowly conceived tools designed to aid a diversified corporation in achieving a financially balanced portfolio. In doing so, they may obscure the most essential strategic issue in constructing a firm's portfolio of businesses—the creation and enhancement of interrelationships. When interrelationships exist, decisions to build or harvest business units cannot be made independently. The use of portfolio tools is particularly dangerous at the group or sector level, because business units within a group or sector tend to have tangible interrelationships and need to be managed accordingly.

Corporate, sector, and group executives must not mistake portfolio planning for horizontal strategy. Horizontal strategy is more difficult to formulate than portfolio strategy, but is the way a diversified firm creates true economic benefits for its business units.

Pitfalls in Pursuing Interrelationships

It can be equally risky to pursue interrelationships indiscriminately:

Negative Leverage from Sharing or Transfering Know-how. Tangible interrelationships usually involve some compromise in the strategies of the business units involved. Because of this, pursuing ill-chosen interrelationships can harm all the involved business units for little net strategic gain. Transferring know-how also involves costs, and transferring know-how that is in fact inappropriate to competition in another business unit in the name of supposed intangible interrelationships can also do great harm. There must be clear potential net benefits of sharing or transfer of know-how for the related business units in order for an interrelationship to be strategically desirable.

Pursuing Interrelationships Involving Value Activities That Are Small, Have Few Scale or Learning Economies, or Have Little Effect on Differentiation. In their zeal to build a related diversification strategy, firms can fall into the trap of making too much of an interrelationship that, while indeed present, has little competitive significance. The presence of an interrelationship does *not* imply that a horizontal strategy should be built around it, even if it is the only one available.

Illusory Interrelatedness. Often superficial similarities in technologies, logistical systems, fabrication processes, and buyer groups are not, in fact, a basis for shared activities. A technology that appears similar in two business units may, upon closer scrutiny, be sold to buyers with very different needs that compromise the ability to employ a shared R&D organization. Despite the apparent similarity to outsiders between offshore drilling for oil and onshore drilling, for example, few activities in fact can be shared by drilling contractors. Intangible interrelationships can also be illusory. There are many generic similarities among business units that are not important for competition. Potential interrelationships should be scrutinized carefully *before* being translated into shared activities or altered strategies, to prevent discovering the lack of compatibility through a failure.

11
Achieving Interrelationships

Achieving interrelationships in practice has proven to be extraordinarily difficult for many firms. Part of the reason is that the costs of sharing mean that some interrelationships do not enhance competitive advantage and should not be implemented. Even for interrelationships that clearly create competitive advantage, however, a formidable array of organizational impediments work against achieving them in practice, ranging from organizational structure to cultural and managerial factors. In fact, achieving interrelationships among business units contradicts the philosophy prevailing in many diversified firms.[1]

Most major diversified firms have decentralized into business units with profit responsibility, embracing the principle of autonomy. Some firms practice decentralization with near-religious devotion. Uncon-

[1]The literature on organizational behavior contains some useful insights into the problems of achieving interrelationships among business units, but little research that treats the subject directly. Most literature in organizational behavior examines the organizational problems of coordination *within* business units, or how to divisionalize. Lorsch and Allen (1973) and Galbraith (1973) contain the most useful ideas for cross-business unit coordination, but have not treated interrelationships as a major theme.

trolled decentralization, however, undermines the pursuit of interrelationships by encouraging business unit managers to pursue strategies that maximize unit performance and not the corporations. Moreover, portfolio planning techniques have reinforced the view of business units as unconnected cash generators or users. Many other organizational practices typical of large diversified firms also work against interrelationships, such as incentive plans and transfer pricing policies. The organizational difficulties of achieving even clearly beneficial interrelationships is perhaps the single biggest reason many managers have rejected the concept of synergy.

Any treatment of strategic interrelationships among business units must confront the difficulties of actually achieving them or horizontal strategies will fail.[2] Throughout this chapter, I will make the assumption that a firm has identified interrelationships that meet the tests of strategic significance described in Chapter 9. The focus here is on mechanisms for exploiting them.

I will first identify the organizational impediments to achieving interrelationships that are present in many firms and their causes. Having done so, I will describe the ways in which firms can overcome these impediments through what I term *horizontal organization.* The predominant form of corporate organization in diversified firms is a vertical organization, through which top management directs the activities of the various business units. Information, decisions, and resources flow vertically, from business units to top management and vice versa. Organizational subunits in between, often referred to as groups and sectors, are designed primarily to oversee this vertical process and reduce the span of control of top management. Firmwide strategic planning and incentive systems further reinforce the vertical nature of decision making and control.

In contrast, horizontal organization in a diversified firm overlays the business unit structure and facilitates collaboration among business units. Horizontal organizational mechanisms include the grouping of business units, standing committees, management systems, human resources policies, and a variety of other formal and informal devices designed to coordinate business unit activities. Any firm with significant interrelationships needs a horizontal corporate organization to supplement its vertical organization. The pervasiveness of interrelationships suggests that a new organizational form for managing the diversified firm will become increasingly necessary—one that involves a much

[2]Thus this book on strategy must contain an unexpected chapter on organization.

closer balance between the horizontal and vertical dimensions of organization.

Horizontal organization does *not* seek to eliminate or replace decentralization. The logic of decentralization is sound and some diversified firms, in fact, have failed to decentralize enough. Horizontal organization overlays a set of mechanisms on the vertical organization to ensure that interrelationships yielding a competitive advantage are exploited.[3] The result is not a matrix organization, but independent business units that are connected by organizational devices and a set of shared values. While business unit autonomy may be reduced in the process, the real purpose of horizontal organization is to *redefine* business unit autonomy in terms more conducive to the firm's overall success.

Impediments to Achieving Interrelationships

Achieving tangible interrelationships requires a business unit to share activities in its value chain with other units while remaining a separate entity that acts independently in other value activities and maintains profit responsibility. Similarly, achieving intangible interrelationships requires the transfer of know-how among business units. The pursuit of interrelationships may well lead to joint activity with more than one sister unit in different parts of the value chain. A business unit may share a sales force with one division, for example, and a plant with another.

Implementing any interrelationship inevitably requires costs of coordination no matter how a firm is organized. However, a variety of organizational impediments can raise these costs unnecessarily for many firms. These impediments bear some relationship to the factors that make functional coordination difficult *within* a single business unit. However, the organizational impediments to interrelationships are usually much stronger than impediments to functional coordination. Nothing compels coordination among business units, while the functions within a business unit must coordinate in order to do business. In fact, business units often view each other as rivals competing

[3]If a diversified firm does not have a well functioning decentralized organization, in fact, it may need to decentralize further before it begins to overlay a horizontal organization across its business units.

for limited resources and senior management attention on the basis of performance.

Sources of Impediments

Impediments to business unit coordination grow out of the differences between the perspective of business unit and corporate managers. Some of the most important impediments are as follows:

Asymmetric Benefits

Interrelationships are often resisted by some business units because the benefits are or appear to be asymmetric. As I discussed in previous chapters, differences in the size and strategy of business units often mean that the competitive advantage arising from an interrelationship accrues more to one business unit than another. In some cases, an interrelationship can have a net negative impact on one business unit while being clearly beneficial to the firm as a whole. Unless the motivation system reflects these differences, it will be extremely difficult to get business units to agree to pursue an interrelationship and to work together to implement it successfully. Instead, they become embroiled in fruitless negotiations over the allocation of shared costs or over procedures for sharing revenue. The result is that interrelationships that clearly benefit *all* the involved business units are quickly adopted when recognized, but those with asymmetric benefits frequently remain untapped.

Loss of Autonomy and Control

In addition to resistance on economic grounds, managers often vigorously resist interrelationships to avoid a perceived or actual loss of autonomy. Some of the common sources of resistance include:

Protection of Turf. Business unit managers may jealously guard their "turf." They exercise full control over their operations and draw personal satisfaction from it as well as perceived influence within the corporation. Autonomy has become associated in many firms with full control over all functions, which makes managers loath to give up any of them.

Perceived Dilution of Buyer Relationships. Business units often resist market interrelationships because of fears that they will lose control of their buyers, or that relations with buyers will be damaged. Business units are concerned that sister units will steal "their" buyers, damage their image, or create confusion in buyers' minds over the appropriate point of contact with the firm. Stockbrokers, for example, have been reluctant to share client lists with sister units in their parent companies despite the existence of interrelationships in financial services.

Inability to "Fire" a Sister Division. Business units often feel in more control when dealing with an outside company, rather than being saddled with a sister unit's service, delivery, or product problems. Working with a sister unit is perceived as locking the business unit into an adverse bargaining situation, because corporate management will be prone to intervene in disputes and not allow an interrelationship to be severed in the event of poor sister unit performance. Managers perceive fewer constraints in dealing with an outside firm, because an outside firm can be "fired" if the interrelationship fails.[4]

Conflicts Over Priorities in Shared Activities. Business units are often quick to recognize the risk of conflicting priorities in shared value activities such as a shared sales force, shared logistical network, or shared development center. In a shared development center, for example, engineering time may be allocated in favor of the business unit with the most pressing need; a shared sales force will inevitably concentrate more on some products than others. While setting such priorities is rational from a corporate viewpoint, business unit managers do not welcome the prospect of compromising their plans. Thus business units resist sharing in the first place, or press to create their own autonomous unit once the shared activity has been established.

Unfair Blame for Poor Performance. Business unit managers often fear that they will be unfairly blamed for the failure of an interrelationship. Managers see the possibility that they will be evaluated for results over which they lack full control. This can encourage them to forgo the benefit of an interrelationship to ensure control over their own destiny.

[4]In economists' terms, the perceived transaction costs of dealing externally are lower than those of dealing internally.

A firm's history and organizational configuration have an important influence on the strength of managers' desire for complete autonomy. In many diversified firms, business unit autonomy is a longstanding policy that has been carefully nurtured and emphasized. In companies such as Consolidated Foods, Beatrice Foods, Johnson & Johnson, Emerson Electric, and Hewlett-Packard, for example, the belief in business unit autonomy is strongly held and has been emphasized as a key to the firm's success. While autonomy does indeed play an important positive role, there is a strong tendency to carry it too far and ignore changing competitive circumstances. Business units in firms with a long history of autonomy may resist even the most worthwhile joint projects. Emerson Electric, for example, has had to struggle to get divisions to cooperate on such relatively nonthreatening interrelationships as joint R&D centers on selected technologies.

Firms with a long commitment to business unit autonomy have trained and promoted those managers who have performed well in an environment stressing independence. Self selection has also attracted managers who value independence to join the firm. Moreover, acquisitions are also often consummated by a promise of autonomy. With such a legacy, managers are likely to resist any intrusion on their autonomy or any corporate move toward centralization on principle.

Firms that have pushed the principle of decentralization down to the smallest viable business units often face the most difficulty in achieving interrelationships, despite the fact that they frequently have the greatest need to achieve the scale economies that result from them. Autonomy can be most jealously guarded when business units are small. For example, American Hospital Supply has many small divisions selling various kinds of medical products to the same buyers, via many separate yet overlapping sales forces. It seems to have experienced difficulties in achieving coordination among its many units, due to the fierce independence of many of its managers.

Biased Incentive Systems

Corporate incentive plans often exacerbate the difficulties of implementing interrelationships by indirectly penalizing managers for pursuing them. Business units often lack any positive incentive to participate in interrelationships. They see little gain in changing the way they perform activities to facilitate sharing or transferring know-how, both essential to a successful interrelationship. Worse yet, some incentive systems actually encourage the formation of outside coalitions in preference to interrelationships with sister units.

Some of the ways in which incentive systems work against interrelationships include:

Lack of Credit for Contributions to Other Units. Incentive systems typically measure only a business unit's performance and fail to value its contribution to sister units. A business unit's contribution to an interrelationship, and hence to overall corporate performance, is often difficult to measure. Uniform financial objectives across business units and mechanical transfer pricing and allocation formulas are easy to administer and convey the impression of precision. However, they can fail to measure a business unit's total contribution to firm performance.

Managers are reluctant to spend time and resources on interrelationship projects if they are uncertain to receive credit for them. They see no point in participating in interrelationships in which they must bear compromise costs or, worse yet, get less benefit from the interrelationship than a sister unit. In Matsushita, for example, cross-divisional product development teams have encountered some problems of this type. Participants do not know if the new products will contribute to their division's profits and therefore are reluctant to contribute to their development.

Measurement Biases. In some firms, there are biases in the way revenues, costs, or assets are measured and allocated that prompt business units to ignore or resist interrelationships. For example, investing in assets or making acquisitions is capitalized, while the cost of pursuing an interrelationship must be expensed. Business units that are measured on return on sales will tend to invest in assets rather than diminish their profitability, while business units with narrowly conceived revenue growth objectives will be loath to split revenues with other units on an interrelationship project. They will prefer instead to incur the cost of contracting with an outside firm.

Differing Business Unit Circumstances

Interrelationships are difficult to achieve where business units have different organizational circumstances. Such differences raise problems of communication, and cause business units to perceive sister units as "other companies." Some of the most common organizational differences among business units that impede interrelationships include:

Strong Business Unit Identities. Pursuing interrelationships is difficult where business units have distinct histories and identities apart from the parent firm's. For example, business units may have originally been separate companies that were acquired, or have long been free-standing units with their own names. In such cases, managers and staff often identify more with the business unit than with the parent. The problem is exacerbated by past success. If business units have been industry leaders or pioneers, for example, they often resist any move toward joint efforts with sister units.

Differing Cultures. Cooperation can prove very difficult to achieve if business units have differing cultures. Relevant cultural differences include such things as norms of interpersonal behavior, terminology and basic business philosophy. Such differences can inhibit communication and make working relationships hard to negotiate and maintain. American Express's banking subsidiary has struggled to integrate with the Swiss based Trade Development Bank it acquired, for example, because of different styles and language barriers, among other reasons.

Corporate and business unit managers are also sometimes uneasy about interrelationships between culturally distinct units on the grounds that they will blur the differences among them. They see interrelationships as threats to the distinct cultures that made the business units successful in the first place. This issue is particularly likely to arise in business units that were acquired, or in a diversified firm with a strong tradition of autonomy. For example, the senior management of Brunswick has expressed such fears.[5] Brunswick operates in a variety of leisure-oriented industries and has acquired a number of well-known companies. It is hesitant to integrate them for fear of disrupting their cultures.

Management Differences. If the profile, skills and style of managers differ among business units, forging interrelationships may prove difficult. Contacts may be uncomfortable or strained, making agreements harder to reach. Management differences that may inhibit interrelationships include differences in age, titles, educational background, technical skills, and tenure in office.

[5]For a discussion of the Brunswick example see Stengrevics (1981).

Differing Procedures. Business units may have different operating procedures that make interrelationships difficult to achieve, including different accounting and information systems, approval limits, and union agreements. Procedural differences create friction and confusion when units attempt to work together, and add extra costs of coordination.

Geographic Separation. Business units separated geographically can have difficulty achieving the ongoing coordination required to make interrelationships a success. Distance reduces the ongoing interchange so necessary to work out problems.

Fear of Tampering with Decentralization

The impediments to achieving interrelationships discussed so far stem largely from the orientation and motivation of business unit managers. Corporate management may be equally hesitant to tamper with decentralization. A number of common reasons for this include:

Dampening Entrepreneurship. Corporate management may fear that anything that tampers with decentralization will undermine the entrepreneurial spirit in business units.[6] No fundamental contradiction exists between entrepreneurship and interrelationships, however, unless one equates entrepreneurship narrowly with independence. While there is some justification for extreme decentralization in startup ventures, business unit managers can often create the greatest competitive advantage through entrepreneurship that identifies and exploits interrelationships. Nevertheless, the view that pure decentralization provides the greatest entrepreneurial incentives remains deeply ingrained in many firms. Business unit managers often raise reduced incentives as an argument for resisting interrelationships as well.

Desire for a Consistent Organization. Many diversified firms have tended to organize all business units identically. This may simplify management's task in some ways, but it is inconsistent with interrelationships. Interrelationships imply that different business units (and groups of business units) should have varying degrees of autonomy and control over different activities, as well as different measures of performance and objectives.

[6]Entrepreneurship is viewed as so important in some firms that business units are even encouraged to compete among themselves.

Difficulty of Measuring Performance. Many firms base incentives solely on objective, quantifiable criteria such as growth and profitability. Interrelationships almost inevitably introduce some subjectivity into performance measurement, however, because business unit contributions to the firm as a whole are often hard to quantify precisely. In some firms, however, subjectivity is considered undesirable.

Fear of Providing "Excuses." Interrelationships almost inevitably cloud the clean lines of authority and responsibility in business units. Hence top management may fear that business unit managers will use interrelationships as excuses to justify poor performance.

Interrelationships and Equity

Many of these organizational impediments to achieving interrelationships are based on the perceived conflict between interrelationships and equity. Equity, or fairness, is a principle embraced by virtually all firms. It is part of the fabric of an organization that allows conflicts to be reconciled and underpins the motivation of managers. Yet interrelationships can conflict with equity in the minds of some managers. Interrelationships can yield differing benefits to the business units involved. Interrelationships also imply that managers should have different degrees of autonomy, differing objectives, and differing bases for incentives. Managers may complain that they are "carrying" other business units, and that rewards are given to other managers whose performance is not as good.

Many diversified firms have explicitly or implicitly adopted a narrow view of equity that stems from their decentralized organizational structures. Equity is defined to mean treating every business unit the same and avoiding any subjectivity in decision making—particularly in such sensitive areas as incentives or transfer prices. Equity is further defined as meaning that all business units must agree on interrelationships.

A narrow view of equity is not only logically incorrect but makes interrelationships achievable only in those rare cases where all business units benefit equally or the interrelationship can be achieved through arm's-length dealings with little loss of autonomy. A more constructive view of equity, which emphasizes fairness rather than sameness in the ways in which top management treat business units, is a prerequisite to successfully achieving interrelationships. Creating such a view of equity, as well as building allegiance to a higher corporate purpose, is an essential task of horizontal organization.

Differences in Impediments among Firms

The extent of impediments to achieving interrelationships differs widely among firms, as a result of their histories, mix of businesses, organizational structures, and policies. The greatest difficulties in achieving interrelationships tend to occur under the following conditions:

- Highly decentralized firms with many small business units
- Firms with a strong tradition of autonomy
- Firms built through the acquisition of independent companies
- Firms that have made little or no effort to create a corporate identity
- Firms with little or no history of interrelationships, or who have had a bad experience in attempting to pursue an interrelationship

Organizational Mechanisms for Achieving Interrelationships

A purely vertical corporate organizational structure is insufficient to assure that beneficial interrelationships will be recognized and achieved. The impediments to achieving interrelationships not only get in the way of interrelationships at the working level, but also provide business unit managers with a set of arguments with which to counter efforts by group or corporate management to champion important interrelationships. Business unit managers will also clearly see the compromises required to achieve interrelationships, and may be suspicious of the benefits. Senior management may be ill equipped to counter the resistance without an in-depth knowledge of the industries involved.

Companies tend to react in one of two broad ways to these organizational impediments to achieving interrelationships. Some companies conclude that, despite their strategic logic, interrelationships can never work. After encountering such problems, business unit managers give up on working with sister units and resolve instead to proceed independently. Corporate management becomes frustrated with resolving disputes and dealing with unclear accountability, and opts for extreme decentralization. In other companies, however, there is recognition that the benefits of interrelationships are so important that the traditional ways of managing diversity must change to accomodate them.

Interrelationships will not occur by accident or by fiat. Positive organizational mechanisms must be put in place to encourage business unit managers to pursue interrelationships and to ease the inherent coordination and communication difficulties in making them work. I term organizational practices that facilitate interrelationships *horizontal organization.* Horizontal corporate organization links business units together within a vertical structure. A balance must be struck between the vertical and horizontal elements in a diversified firm if the potential of interrelationships is to be unleashed.

Horizontal organization can be divided into four broad categories:

- *Horizontal structure.* Organizational devices that cut across business unit lines, such as grouping of business units, partial centralization, interdivisional task forces, and market or channel focus committees.
- *Horizontal systems.* Management systems with a cross business unit dimension, in areas such as planning, control, incentives and capital budgeting.
- *Horizontal human resource practices.* Human resource practices that facilitate business unit cooperation, such as cross-business unit job rotation, management forums and training.
- *Horizontal conflict resolution processes.* Management processes that resolve conflicts among business units. Such processes can be usefully distinguished from horizontal structure and systems, and relate more to the style of managing a firm.

Organizational structure and systems frequently have both a horizontal and vertical dimension. Grouping business units, for example, can be a purely vertical device to reduce the span of control of top management or can play a major role in horizontal strategy, depending on how groups are managed. Similarly, corporate incentives systems can be entirely vertical or contain provisions that encourage cross-business unit cooperation. I will concentrate on the horizontal aspects of organizational practices, recognizing that the horizontal and vertical aspects will interact. The issues raised by vertical aspects of organizational structure and systems in diversified firms have been the subject of considerable study.[7]

No single device for encouraging and facilitating cooperation among business units is sufficient to ensure that all strategically beneficial interrelationships are achieved. Instead, a variety of practices that reinforce each other are required. Firms with successful horizontal strategies tend to employ an array of practices simultaneously to gain the maximum benefits from interrelationships. The array of appropriate practices can differ for each business unit, because each will have its own pattern of interrelationships with other units with a different balance of benefits and costs.

Corporate management also has a powerful role in reinforcing horizontal organization through its behavior, the way in which it articulates corporate purpose, and its choice of modes of entry into new businesses. After describing the use of horizontal organization in achieving interrelationships, I will return to the role of top management.

Horizontal Structure

Horizontal structure refers to temporary or permanent organizational entities that cut across business unit boundaries, supplementing the business unit structure. A variety of such entities, which are not mutually exclusive, may be employed to facilitate interrelationships.

Grouping Business Units

Perhaps the most common form of horizontal structure is the group or sector, in which a number of business units report to a single executive. Most group and sector structures were originally created to reduce the CEO's span of control, or to train and evaluate managers in managing diversity as a stepping stone to corporate management. Groups and sectors have long played an important role in the vertical organization.

Group and sector executives have tended to play a relatively passive role in strategy formulation, however. They review and approve business unit strategies and coach business unit managers, rather than initiate strategy. Yet the group or sector executive should have a vital role in identifying, pursuing, and managing interrelationships, provided

[7]Leading works include Lorsch and Allen (1973), Galbraith (1973), Lawrence and Lorsch (1967), and Kotter (1982).

the boundaries of the group or sector are properly drawn and the role of the group or sector executive is properly constituted.

The grouping of business units into groups and sectors should reflect strategically important interrelationships. The boundaries of groups and sectors are often difficult to draw, however, because there are multiple patterns of interrelationships among business units. In General Foods, for example, some business units have common buyers and channels while different but overlapping groups of business units are related by product form and production technology (e.g., frozen food). Where there are several possible bases for grouping business units reflecting different types of interrelationships, a firm must choose one. Interrelationships are frequently not equally significant for all the business units involved, making the selection of a basis for grouping all the more difficult.

While grouping business units is never an exact science, the principle is clear. Groups (and sectors) should be constructed around the interrelationships that are most significant for competitive advantage, growing out of a systematic look at all the interrelationships within the firm. For example, if a large percentage of cost or the most significant sources of differentiation reside in product positioning, advertising, and distribution, groups should be formed around market interrelationships. In a consumer package goods company, for example, it may be more appropriate to group businesses by buyer or channel than to organize around manufacturing technology. In a high-technology company with a differentiation strategy, conversely, it may make more sense to group business units around technologies, since exploiting technological interrelationships will be a key to competitive advantage. Tangible interrelationships should generally be the primary basis for grouping, with intangible interrelationships serving as the basis if tangible interrelationships are minor or are exhausted. For example, groups may link business units with strong tangible interrelationships, while sectors may be based on weaker tangible interrelationships and/or intangible interrelationships.

Business units should be grouped around the most strategically important interrelationships because grouping is perhaps the single most powerful device for focusing attention on and reinforcing interrelationships, if groups are managed accordingly. Where all business units report to a single group (or sector) executive, coordination, the management of shared activities, conflict resolution, transfer or know-how, and setting of the appropriate objectives and incentives are all facilitated.

The principle that business units should be grouped around the most important interrelationship does *not* imply that all groups in a diversified firm should be based on the same type of interrelationship. All groups need not and should not be market-based, production-based, or technology-based, though firms sometimes have a tendency to use the same basis for grouping all their business units. Unless one form of interrelationship is dominant throughout an entire firm, different groups should be based on different types of interrelationships.

The strength of interrelationships among the business units in a group may well vary from group to group, depending on a firm's particular mix of businesses. Some groups may have strongly interrelated business units, while others may be characterized by few if any interrelationships and exist largely to reduce span-of-control. The way groups are managed should reflect these differences. Within a group, moreover, the interrelationship present will vary in strategic importance for the different business units. Business units that perceive few benefits of being in the group will have to be managed differently from others since they will have the greatest tendency to choose strategies that are inconsistent with strengthening interrelationships in the group. The way their performance is measured and their incentives may well have to be modified. It is important, however, that such business units are not forced to compromise their strategies so greatly as to undermine their relative competitive position. Managing any interrelationship is always a process of balancing the overall competitive advantage gained against the cost, using the tools described in Chapter 9.

Role of the Group Executive[8]

Historically, the role of many group executives has sometimes been ambiguous and uncomfortable.[9] Business unit managers frequently are the strategists in diversified firms, while group executives act as reviewers. Many group executives feel, as a result, that they receive much blame but little credit for the group's performance.

Identifying and achieving interrelationships both within and out-

[8]The sector executive's role is analogous to the role of the group executive and equally important to horizontal strategy.

[9]There has been little research on the role of the group executive, surprising given the prevalence of group structures. Stengrevics' (1981) work is the only known comprehensive study, and provides many useful insights into the group executive's role and job satisfaction.

side the group may well be the single most important task of a group executive. In a group with significant interrelationships, the group executive must become the chief strategic officer of the group. What a "group strategy" is is ambiguous in many diversified firms. Group executives have had the tendency to behave as if they were mini-portfolio managers, balancing the capital needs of different business units in the group. Where there are interrelationships, this conception of the group executive's role is fundamentally flawed. Group strategy must be more than the summation of independently proposed business unit strategies. It must include a horizontal strategy that encompasses all the business units. A group strategy does not replace the need for business unit strategies, but integrates them.

In order to achieve interrelationships, the group executive must have ultimate authority to modify business units' strategies. Furthermore, the group executive must be willing to *initiate* horizontal strategy as well as respond to business unit proposals. For all the reasons described earlier, business units acting independently will rarely propose the strategies necessary to reap the benefits of interrelationships, or risk compromising their objectives for the benefit of the group. To play the role of chief strategist, a group executive will typically require the capacity to identify and analyze interrelationships within and outside the group and to analyze multipoint competitors. An in-depth knowledge of the businesses in the group will be necessary. The role of the group executive as a horizontal strategist must also be reinforced by other horizontal devices that orient business unit managers toward the goal of achieving interrelationships. Partial centralization of key value activities, control over part of incentives, and a role in recruiting will all reinforce the ability of the group executive to build a true horizontal strategy.[10]

Partial Centralization

Another type of horizontal structure is partial centralization. It may be appropriate to centralize value activities because of important interrelationships, while still maintaining the profit responsibility of business units. Centralized value activities may also sometimes serve more than one group.

Partial centralization is relatively common in activities such as procurement, sales, and logistical systems. In General Foods, for example, manufacturing, procurement, and logistics are quite centralized

[10]For a supporting view, see Stengrevics (forthcoming).

across a range of divisions that span groups, while product development and marketing functions all report directly to division managers. McGraw-Hill has a shared order fulfillment system that serves many book, magazine, and other business units, while Castle and Cooke has a shared marketing and distribution system for many types of fresh foods.

Shared activities can have a variety of reporting relationships. One business unit can have formal control while others have a dotted-line relationship. Alternatively, shared activities can report to several business units, or shared activities can report directly to a group or corporate executive. It is desirable that centralized activities report to a line executive in order to maintain a marketplace orientation. The responsible executive must take an active role in managing the coordination between the centralized value activity and the business units, mindful of the issues raised in this and the previous chapter. Such a management provides a contrast to the passive, arm's-length approach sometimes employed in guiding relations between business units and shared activities.

Success in partial centralization requires creating the proper structure and incentives for business units to manage an activity themselves, or assigning the activity to a line executive with authority over the involved business units. Success also requires an awareness on the part of all concerned that the interrelationship is valuable to the firm, as well as the creation of formal and informal coordinating mechanisms between centralized activities and involved business units. Joint planning for centralized activities that involve the affected business units is beneficial, as is regular formal contact between activity managers and business units.

Other Cross-Business Unit Organizational Mechanisms

Grouping of business units and partial centralization of value activities are the strongest forms of organizational impetus to achieve interrelationships. Group structure should be designed to capture the most important interrelationship. It may not encompass all interrelationships, however, because secondary interrelationships may be present that go outside the group but that also enhance competitive advantage. Thus temporary and permanent cross-business unit mechanisms that provide a means of achieving interrelationships not captured in the primary organizational structure are an important part of horizontal structure. Such mechanisms can serve not only as ways of initiating and implementing interrelationship projects, but also as mechanisms for educating managers about the importance of interrelationships.[11] They should not be misconstrued as a "matrix" organization, but rather as devices to facilitate cross business unit cooperation.

Some of the most important organizational devices to serve this purpose are as follows:

1. *Market focus committees.* Where a firm is organized around products or technologies, there are often important though secondary interrelationships around markets. McGraw-Hill, for example, has established its primary organization around product forms such as books, magazines, and data bases. However, there are a number of markets, such as construction and financial services, into which many of the business units sell. McGraw-Hill can harness these interrelationships if it can attack the markets in a coordinated way, while exploiting the interrelationships around products through the primary organizational structure.

A firm can gain market interrelationships through what might be termed market focus committees. To form such committees, a firm identifies the critical markets where potential interrelationships exist and designates an executive to be responsible for overseeing the firm's efforts in each such market. A standing committee is constituted consisting of senior managers of business units serving or potentially serving the market, which meets regularly to supervise market research, identify and plan for the achievement of interrelationships in existing product areas, and identify gaps that need to be filled to strengthen the firm's overall position in the market. Staff resources are drawn in to perform the necessary analysis. Specific interrelationship projects are then assigned to line executives within the affected business units. While such committees can be time consuming, competitive advantage will be lost without them to competitors who can organize to achieve interrelationships.

Market focus committees can also serve as an interim step in shifting from a product- or technology-based organization to a market-based organization in a diversified firm, if market interrelationships become the most strategically important. If a firm shifts to a market-based primary organization, however, it should probably establish some organizational mechanisms to reinforce the production or technological interrelationships present.

[11]Galbraith (1973) provides a useful description of a number of such "lateral" organizations and conditions their success. His and other discussions are primarily oriented to within business unit rather than cross-business unit efforts, however.

2. *Technology, channel and other interrelationship committees.* Standing committees or working groups involving a number of business units can also be created around other important interrelationships, in products (e.g. office automation), production, procurement, technologies, shared distribution channels, logistical systems, or order processing systems. Their function is analogous to market focus committees, and the principles for organizing them are similar. A senior line executive must accept overall responsibility for the effort, and regular progress reviews are required so that the effort will be taken seriously.

3. *Temporary Task Forces.* While important interrelationships that cut across the primary organization structure may well require standing committees to manage their ongoing implementation, some interrelationships may be best exploited through temporary cross-business unit task forces. Temporary task forces are a very common mechanism to achieve the transfer of know-how involved in intangible interrelationships and some tangible interrelationships can be implemented this way. In addition, temporary task forces can be a device for studying interrelationships and recommending permanent ways to achieve them, whether through partial centralization, a standing committee, or a one-time change in the way business units operate.

Temporary cross-business unit task forces may address numerous types of interrelationships. General Motors, for example, forms project centers to manage critical projects that cut across business unit lines. Staff members are completely detached from existing organizational units to participate for periods of up to several years. An example of a less formal temporary organization is McGraw-Hill's Information Resources Task Force, which studied the management of computing capacity across the corporation. This temporary organization used part-time staff drawn from divisions, supported by staff from the corporate planning department. Another example is Sears, that is now using study groups to search for interrelationships among its businesses and to pursue interrelationships in financial services.

Group or Corporate Interrelationship Champions

A final structural device to facilitate interrelationships is the appointment of executives at the group, sector, or corporate level to act as champions for interrelationship. While staff roles such as this have fallen out of favor in some firms, they can contribute significantly to managing interrelationships. Staff executives can take responsibility for identifying key interrelationships in their areas, and then work with the affected business units to assist in achieving them. For example, a marketing staff executive can coordinate the procurement of advertising space to maximize bargaining leverage, or coordinate plans vis-à-vis a shared distribution channel. Staff executives can also assist in the management of other mechanisms to harness interrelationships such as committees and task forces of business unit managers.

Managing Cross-Business Unit Organizations

Cross-business unit organizations are difficult to manage, particularly in U.S. firms. Because the principle of autonomy is so ingrained and because committees are often viewed as a "waste of time" rather than an integral part of the management function, careful design of cross-business unit organizations is necessary if they are to be accepted.

A cross-business unit organization must report to a senior line executive, in order to provide it with the necessary influence within the firm and to ensure that its efforts remain focused on important issues. The cross-business unit organization must also be headed by a credible executive who is not too closely identified with a particular point of view, and who is held responsible for results. The organization must result in tangible action, or it will not be taken seriously. Top management should assign line executives from each affected business unit to the cross-business unit organization to help ensure that plans for achieving interrelationships will be implemented once developed. The representatives assigned should be senior enough to be able to influence their units to action. Some staff capability must be made available to cross-business unit organizations, or members may be called on to contribute personnel to allow meaningful analysis and thoughtful recommendations. Finally, cross-business unit organizations must be supplemented by other types of horizontal organization to help overcome the other impediments to interrelationships. In a firm with significant interrelationships, simply overcoming the cynicism toward cross-business committees will yield a major competitive advantage.

Horizontal Systems

A second aspect of horizontal organization is horizontal systems—management systems that reinforce coordination and linkages among business units. While most management systems have a strong vertical element, they can also be designed to support the achievement of interrelationships. A number of systems have particular significance for achieving interrelationships.

Horizontal Strategic Planning. Most diversified firms employ vertical strategic planning systems. Business units prepare strategic plans and submit them to senior management for approval. When there are important interrelationships, however, a horizontal component must be overlaid on the vertical strategic planning process to make planning truly meaningful.

There are a number of possible approaches for introducing a horizontal dimension into strategic planning. First, the corporate planning department can accept responsibility for identifying interrelationships and initiating steps to exploit them. Second, group and sector executives can be given responsibility for horizontal strategy and the content of the group plan should concentrate on interrelationships. A third approach is to add an interrelationships section to business unit plans. Each business unit is asked to identify important interrelationships it has with other units inside and outside its group, and to develop action plans to exploit important ones. A final approach is to require separate, joint strategic plans from business units involved in important interrelationships.

NEC Corporation has opted for the final approach, and has adopted two planning systems. In addition to a normal business unit planning system, it has established the CBP (Corporate Business Plan) system in which separate strategic plans are prepared for critical investments or programs that cut across business unit lines. The system forces business unit managers involved in an interrelationship to meet and agree on a strategic plan for dealing with it over the long term. In effect, this system requires a special plan for important horizontal issues.

The various approaches to adding a horizontal component to planning are not mutually exclusive. Usually, several should be pursued simultaneously. At the very least, mechanisms for horizontal planning must exist at both the group and corporate levels, since the horizontal strategy issues at these levels differ. No business unit will have the perspective to identify all interrelationships or develop plans to achieve them.

Horizontal Procedures. Interrelationships are facilitated by the presence of procedures governing cross-business unit activities. Many firms have transfer pricing policies, and some firms have policies governing in-house versus external purchasing. Relatively few firms, however, have guidelines for issues such as revenue or cost sharing on joint projects, or capital budgeting procedures for joint projects. Without such guidelines, pursuing interrelationship will involve a great deal of administrative turmoil and protracted negotiations. General guidelines can greatly facilitate interrelationships, limiting incentives for business units to seek outside coalitions or avoid internal interrelationships.

Transfer pricing and purchasing rules often reflect a misunderstanding of interrelationships. Simple transfer pricing rules, based on market prices, treat business units as stand-alone entities in arm's-length relationships with each other. This negates the logic underlying interrelationships, no matter how administratively appealing it may be. Interrelationships imply that transfer pricing and other decisions should be designed to improve the firm's overall position and not the financial results of individual business units.[12] For example, Perkin-Elmer has a system in which the selling division sells at market price, while the buying division buys at cost. Both have the incentive to do business, while the buying division sets prices based on the true cost to the corporation.[13] Business unit goals also may need to be adjusted in order to make them consistent with transfer pricing rules. Business units that transfer at cost, for example, should not be held to firmwide profitability targets.

Purchasing rules are another area where administrative simplicity often outweighs strategic logic. Firms defeat the purpose if they adopt the hands-off view that units can buy from the "best" source, external or internal. Most firms that are successful at achieving interrelationships treat in-house purchasing as the assumption, and business units that supply sister units view them as their most important buyers. Senior management should clearly communicate this expectation throughout the firm, and ensure that business units who treat their sister units as unimportant buyers or suppliers are not rewarded.

Horizontal Incentives. The incentive system must recognize that the firm can gain from interrelationships, and should reward business unit and group managers for achieving them instead of encouraging

[12]Eccles (1985) provides an excellent discussion of transfer pricing that reflects many of these issues.

[13]See Stengrevics (1981). No transfer pricing scheme is ever perfect, but arms-length schemes are almost always flawed where there are significant interrelationships.

them to concentrate on their individual results. It is also necessary to remove any biases in measurement that favor external or go-it-alone investments instead of joint efforts with other business units. In firms with important interrelationships, the incentive system should reward business units and their managers to some extent on *group and corporate results* as well as on business unit results. In nearly every firm I have observed that is successful at achieving interrelationships, compensation plans emphasize group or corporate performance. These firms have proven that business unit managers do not need to have all their compensation based on business unit results in order to be highly motivated. Tying compensation solely to business unit results reflects a simplistic view of motivation. Instead, business unit managements can and should be made part of the firm's general management team through a broader basis of compensation.[14] Performance measurement should differ for each unit. Performance targets should reflect the differing balance between individual business units' results and their broader contribution to the firm through interrelationships. Senior management must accept the responsibility to convince all its business unit managers that this is fair and reflects a higher corporate purpose.

Incentives should contain a *subjective* component in firms with important interrelationships. A business unit's contribution to the firm cannot usually be measured quantitatively. Any one quantitative standard will not be able to weigh all factors and may indirectly bias behavior against a firm's interests. Instead, group and corporate management must be prepared to judge a business unit's contribution to group or corporate strategy. While firms have traditionally avoided subjective incentives, top management must communicate to groups and business units a need for them and a sense of fairness in rewarding contributions to the firm as a whole.[15]

Horizontal Human Resource Practices

A third aspect of horizontal organization is human resource policies. These are policies for hiring, training, and managing human resources that facilitate cross-business unit collaboration, as well as

[14]Lorsch and Allen (1973) provide an illustration of this role of incentives in a vertically integrated firm.

[15]For a study supporting the need for subjective incentives when interrelationships are high, see Gupta and Govindarajan (1983).

successful relationships between business units and centralized functions. As with horizontal systems, horizontal human resource policies should apply to an entire firm or to those parts with significant interrelationships.

Personnel Rotation among Business Units. The rotation of personnel among business units facilitates the achievement of interrelationships in a number of ways. It helps to reduce cultural and procedural differences among business units, creates personal relationships that facilitate joint projects, educates managers about areas of opportunity for interrelationships with other units, and promotes a corporate (or group) identity in addition to the business unit identity.[16] Though there may be some cost in terms of training time and continuity when rotating personnel, the long-term benefits can be significant not only for interrelationships but also in retarding the onset of conventional wisdom in business units. Firms such as DuPont, General Electric, and Citicorp have active rotation programs that seem to have facilitated interrelationships.

Some Firmwide Role in Hiring and Training. A firmwide (or group) role in hiring and training can help build a corporate identity and an awareness of the overall interests of the firm. Corporate orientation and training programs can educate managers about other business units, and encourage personal relationships among incoming managers who will eventually be dispersed to different units. Ongoing management development programs can also facilitate interrelationships. Programs that bring managers from different units together not only can have an educational function, but also develop understanding and encourage personal relationships. Such a corporate role in orientation and training need not reduce the ability of business units to hire personnel that fit their needs.

Promotion from Within. Promotion from within tends to reinforce a corporate perspective, and can lead to managers adopting a longer time horizon. Both of these effects can facilitate interrelationships. Home-grown managers not only tend to identify more strongly with a firm, but are also more likely to develop a network of personal relationships within the firm that facilitates horizontal collaboration. While there are risks of reinforcing conventional wisdom, a general

[16]It may be valuable, for example, to switch business managers or other executives in two business units involved in an interrelationship.

preference to promote from within (though not necessarily from within the same business unit) can be important to firms with strong interrelationships.

Cross-business Unit Forums and Meetings. Carefully designed meetings that bring managers from different business units together can facilitate the discovery and achievement of interrelationships. It is particularly effective in such meetings to ask managers to brief their peers about their respective businesses, and to encourage group discussions of issues that cut across unit lines.

Education on Interrelationship Concepts. It is vital that key managers understand the strategic logic of interrelationships and have a language system for discussing and an analytical framework for identifying them in their own businesses. This education can be part of management development programs, companywide meetings, and other forums. While top management often understand the concept of interrelationships, middle managers frequently do not and changes in their behavior will make or break the achievement of interrelationships in practice.

Horizontal Conflict Resolution Processes

The fourth aspect of horizontal organization is management processes for resolving conflict among business units. Any successful organizational structure combines formal structures and systems with ongoing processes through which managers interact. While less tangible than structure and systems, these processes can be just as important to success, particularly where responsibilities are not clear and frequent interaction among organizational units is necessary.

Achieving interrelationships nearly always involves the sharing of authority, the need for frequent coordination, and subjective performance evaluation. Hence processes for resolving conflict among business units are vitally important to achieving interrelationships. The processes themselves vary greatly from firm to firm, though senior management always plays an important role by setting the tone for how business units should interact and by acting as final arbiters of any disputes. What is important is not the exact form of the process in a firm, but the existence of some process that is managed by group, sector, and corporate management which is perceived as fair.

The Corporate Role in Facilitating Interrelationships

A purely bottom-up approach to interrelationships rarely succeeds. Chief executive officers can have a major impact on the achievement of interrelationships through their behavior, as can other line executives above the business unit level. There are many opportunities available to senior management to define a larger corporate purpose, to stress the importance of interrelationships, and to discourage parochial behavior by business unit, group, and sector managers. A strong set of firmwide values and a strong corporate identity are vital links in reducing cynicism toward committees, resolving conflicts, and so on.

One important way to reinforce interrelationships is through articulating a unifying theme. A unifying theme at the corporate, sector, and group levels that stresses interrelationships can be a powerful tool for motivating managers to find and implement them. It should be prominently and repeatedly stressed by senior management both externally and internally, and at all levels of the company. NEC Corporation, for example, has the theme of "C&C" (computers and communications), which symbolizes the converging of electronics and communications technology into integrated C&C systems. Going hand in hand with the theme is a diagram that vividly displays the merging of the technologies. This theme is a constant one in top management speeches, annual report copy, and internal discussions. NEC's managers at all levels understand the theme, and it has reinforced the search for interrelationships by business units.

Interrelationships are also facilitated if the corporate identity is displayed prominently in each business unit on logos, signs, and stationery. This does not imply the abandonment of valuable business unit trade names. Instead, it suggests that a firm should develop both its corporate identity as well as those of business units, within the firm and outside. This not only affects management's view of themselves, but can directly facilitate the achievement of market interrelationships by making buyers more aware of the connection among business units.

Interrelationships and the Mode of Diversification

The achievement of interrelationships is facilitated by developing new businesses internally rather than acquiring them. Internal development is typically based on interrelationships, and organically grown units are likely to have strategies consistent with other parts of the firm. Shared value activities are more likely to be designed for sharing. Acquisitions, on the other hand, require that interrelationships be forged with a heretofore separate organization, with all the associated impediments. Acquisitions also raise the odds that compromises in strategy will be necessary to pursue interrelationship opportunities.[17] Firms such as IBM, Kodak, GE, DuPont and Procter & Gamble, which have successfully exploited interrelationships, have traditions of creating many businesses internally.

The difficulties posed by acquisitions for achieving interrelationships do not imply that firms should never make acquisitions. Rather, they suggest that firms apply a rigorous test in choosing between acquisitions and internal entry, and that horizontal strategy issues be prominent in the search for acquisitions. The choice of acquisition should reflect the added difficulty of achieving interrelationships with acquired firms. Many firms have chosen to acquire to minimize start-up losses and to have a quicker impact on revenues, sacrificing interrelationships in the process that were important to the firm's long term strategy.

If acquisition emerges as the best way to enter a new business, horizontal strategy issues should not be ignored. Unless an acquisition is in an unrelated field, the ability to integrate the acquired firm in a way that achieves interrelationships must be weighed. Many acquirers almost guarantee that interrelationships will not occur by promising complete autonomy to the management of prospective acquisitions. For example, in Transamerica's purchase of Fred S. James Company, an insurance broker, Transamerica pledged that the James Company would be independent and report directly to the CEO instead of through Transamerica's insurance group. Despite the fact that the James acquisition offered great possibilities for achieving interrelationships, achieving them has been made substantially more difficult, at least for a time.

Managing Horizontal Organization

Achieving interrelationships is a function of instituting an array of horizontal practices. As many companies have discovered, organizational structure alone is not sufficient. Merely grouping related busi-

[17]Acquiring a toehold in an industry through a smaller acquisition, and then building it, resembles internal development more than acquisition in this respect.

nesses together will not guarantee the exploitation of interrelationships. Structure must be reinforced by group and sector executives who understand their roles as horizontal strategists, as well as appropriate management systems and human resource policies. The array of horizontal practices must not be uniform across the firm, but tailored to reflect the patterns of interrelationships that are present. Some business units are more connected than others, and hence the balance between vertical and horizontal organization should vary. Top management must also reinforce interrelationships by sending clear signals about their importance, and promoting a culture where the corporation has an identity that transcends and reinforces that of business units.

Achieving interrelationships usually requires the creation of some shared values within a firm. Managers must perceive that collaboration with other business units is important and will be rewarded, and that senior management will act fairly in measuring the performance of the individual units involved. While interrelationships can sometimes be imposed, interrelationships that are imposed on business units will rarely be so strong or durable as those based on common understanding and consensus. Instituting horizontal organizational mechanisms throughout the firm is usually necessary for this attitude to occur. The process takes time, and cannot be expected to occur just because the potential for interrelationships is discovered.

Promising Examples

American Express provides an example of a firm with a corporate strategy built on interrelationships. It has set out to be a broadly based financial services company for upwardly mobile affluent consumers, as well as providing specialized services for financial institutions and corporations. The acquisition of Shearson Loeb Rhoades was a major step in this strategy, as was the earlier acquisition of Fireman's Fund. There are many interrelationships among the businesses of American Express, Shearson, and Fireman's Fund, as well as many potential new businesses that could add to American Express's overall competitive position in financial services via interrelationships. American Express and Shearson had different cultures, however, exacerbating the problems inherent in achieving interrelationships. Moreover, American Express had traditionally been run with quite autonomous units.

To achieve interrelationships, American Express has employed a wide range of horizontal devices. A coordinated financial services strategy has become the overall theme for American Express, and top management has frequently stated and reinforced this theme. A quotation from American Express's Annual Report is illustrative:

> Key to the Company's future is our ability to work as "one enterprise," with staff offices at each of our major business segments interacting with one another to blend products, services, distribution and expertise to meet the demands of sophisticated customers and add to their convenience and satisfaction. Last year's Annual Report cover graphically depicts the one enterprise concept: our American Express logo at the center of four distinct but interrelated business lines.[18] (See Figure 11–1.)

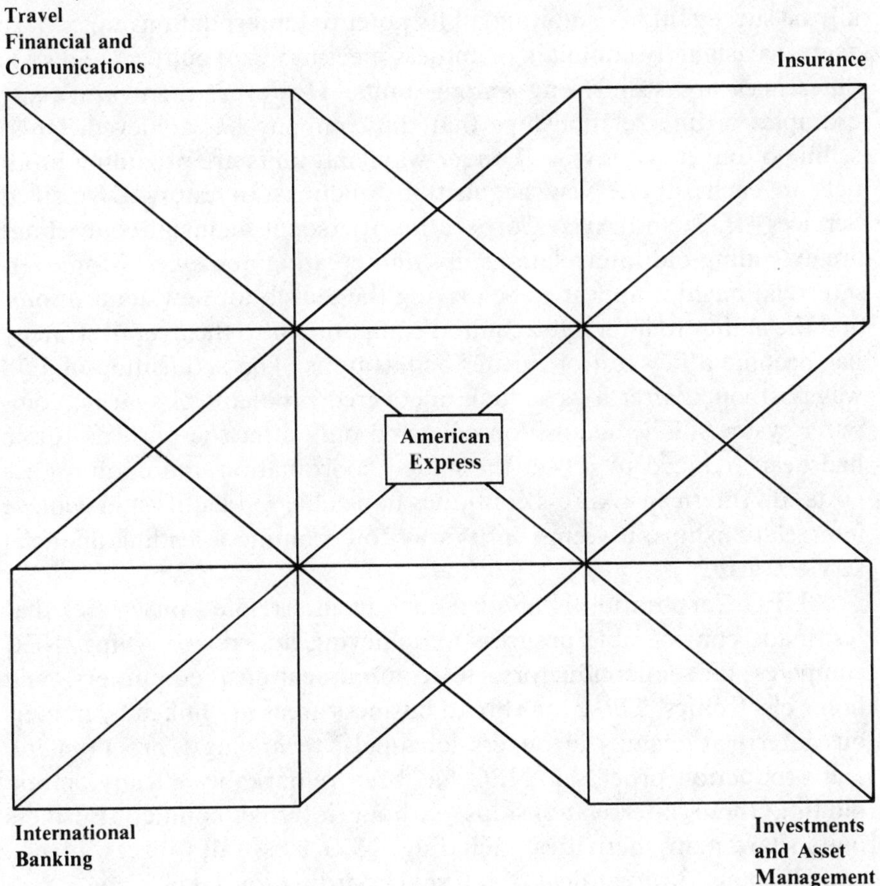

Figure 11–1. The American Express Logo

[18]American Express Company, Annual Report, 1982.

A financial services committee composed of executives from American Express and Shearson was constituted, with responsibility for developing an overall scheme for approaching the financial marketplace. Shearson's name was changed to Shearson/American Express, reinforcing a firmwide identity. Executives, including many at senior levels, have been cross-posted. A coordinating group has been established to manage the financing of the various units. Unity across the company is stressed at management meetings. American Express has also recognized that although cultures are different in acquired units and homogenization of cultures should not be the goal, some parts of each business unit's culture can usefully be transplanted.

It remains to be seen to what extent American Express will actually be successful in exploiting all its potential interrelationships. Managers occasionally complain of endless meetings, and cultural and style differences are still strong among units. However, there are many examples of interrelationships that the company has achieved. Cross selling of buyers is now well under way, and units are providing products to each other. New acquisitions such as Investors Diversified Services (IDS) and Ayco Corporation (personal financial counseling) are extending old interrelationships and creating new ones. Moreover, interrelationships appear to be driving the search for new acquisitions, and the ability to integrate acquired companies into the overall strategy has become a key test of further acquisitions. The acquisition of IDS was postponed after a close look uncovered problems of sharing computer systems. The acquisition occurred only after the purchase price had been reduced to reflect the added coordination and compromise costs. If American Express continues to be able to identify and achieve interrelationships, it seems on its way to becoming a leading financial services firm.

NEC Corporation is another firm in interrelated businesses that has made considerable progress in achieving interrelationships. NEC competes in semiconductors, telecommunications, computers, and home electronics. These four broad business areas are linked by numerous interrelationships in buyers, channels, technology, procurement, and production processes. NEC has been remarkably effective in exploiting these interrelationships without internal conflict. Business units share many activities, including R&D labs, sales forces, plants, and channels. A great deal of internal coordination takes place across divisions in joint selling, transfers of technology, buyer/supplier relationships, and many other areas. Given NEC's moderate size relative to its competitors in each of its four main business areas, an important reason for its success is its ability to exploit interrelationships while its larger competitors were largely focusing on only one or two business areas.

How has NEC been able to achieve these interrelationships? The answer lies in the extensive horizontal organization NEC has put in place to facilitate interrelationships. This overlays an equally well-developed vertical organization, in which decentralized business units are managed through planning, control, resource allocation, and incentive systems. Structurally, NEC has organized itself into four broad groups—electron devices, telecommunications, computers, and home electronics—that each reflect strong interrelationships in products, markets, and technology. Note that the computer, telecommunications, and electron devices groups are organized around technology while home electronics is a market-oriented grouping. Within these broad groups, related products such as switching equipment and transmission equipment have been grouped together, reflecting even stronger interrelationships.

To promote interrelationships across groups there are forty-four ongoing corporatewide committees, many involving important interrelationships. Perhaps the most powerful of these is the "C&C Committee," charged with identifying and exploiting the potential interrelationships created by the convergence of computers and communications. Partial centralization of activities is also prevalent at NEC in sales, distribution, manufacturing, and technology development. Corporate units in areas such as production technology and software development share the development of widely used technologies. Finally, many temporary committees are employed to get managers in different business units together.

NEC's C&C theme has constantly reinforced the need to exploit interrelationships. Every division also identifies itself with the NEC brand. The vast majority of businesses have been developed internally. Managers rotate among divisions and undergo extensive training upon joining the corporation (all personnel are hired centrally) and throughout their careers. Frequent forums allow managers to meet with counterparts in related business units.

The strategic planning process at NEC includes the CBP system described earlier, which allows unified planning for businesses with interrelationships. Incentives are not solely linked to financial results, but reflect the business unit's overall contribution to the company. Internal customers are viewed as the most important, and external sourcing is practiced only if superior quality and price are available from outside. The net result is a clear culture at NEC which reinforces finding and exploiting interrelationships.

Japanese Firms and Interrelationships

While there are many non-Japanese firms that have achieved interrelationships, a number of characteristics of many, though not all, Japanese firms make them well positioned for exploiting interrelationships:

- strong belief in overarching corporate themes
- internal development of new businesses
- a less rigid tradition of autonomy
- more flexible incentives, less based on business unit results
- willingness to centralize activities
- greater tradition of committees and frequent personal contact among executives
- intensive and continuing in-house training
- corporatewide hiring and training

Given their history, Japanese firms may be in a position to strike a better balance between horizontal and vertical organization in the diversified firm than U.S. and European firms, which tend to have either a strong tradition of autonomy or a high degree of centralized control. In many ways, the ability of Japanese firms to achieve interrelationships can be viewed as a major future challenge in competing with Western firms as interrelationships grow in importance. The first Japanese challenge, low labor costs, has been replaced by the second Japanese challenge of quality and productivity. Perhaps interrelationships will emerge as the next Japanese source of competitive advantage, coupled with an increasing ability to innovate.

It is also intriguing to note that the U.S. companies that have achieved interrelationships, such as GE, DuPont, IBM, and Procter & Gamble, have many of the same characteristics. As interrelationships become increasingly critical to competitive advantage, these firms may serve as role models for firms steeped in the tradition of extreme autonomy and diversification through acquisition so characteristic of U.S. industry.

A New Organizational Form

The principles underlying horizontal organization imply a new organizational form for diversified firms. The concept of decentralization has revolutionized the way diversified firms are managed, bringing with it a wide range of practices and management expectations. Many leading companies have successfully made the transition to decentralization.

Diversified firms must undergo further organizational evolution if they are to respond to today's competition. Because of the importance of interrelationships, there is a growing need for a new corporate organizational form that recognizes both vertical and horizontal dimensions. Decentralization in diversified firms is still a necessity, but must be overlaid with mechanisms to achieve the important interrelationships. The balance between the vertical (decentralization) and horizontal dimensions in the organization of the diversified firm is an ever changing one, and the ideal is perhaps a constant shifting of the balance as the need to emphasize different activities changes. However, a balance that combines significant elements of both vertical and horizontal will be increasingly necessary.[19] The balance must also reflect differing interrelationships from business unit to business unit.

Increasingly, *diversity does not imply the absence of interrelationships.* Business units can be distinct and benefit from decentralization, while being linked by interrelationships. Hewlett-Packard, a firm noted for its strong tradition of decentralization, is just one example of the growing need to balance vertical with horizontal. Recently, HP has recombined a number of divisions involved in the design and manufacture of personal computers and related products. These divisions were proceeding independently, but lacked the scale economies and cross-product coordination to mount a concerted attack on IBM and Apple.

This new organizational form requires a modification of rigid or narrow views of autonomy, as well as changing attitudes toward incentives systems and toward the role of group and sector executives. Instead of seeking autonomy and viewing committees and other joint efforts as a waste of time, business unit managers will have to modify their conception of what "managing their own business" means. The new requirements of the diversified firm will involve a price in terms of less simplicity, greater ambiguity, more subjectivity, and potentially more conflict. However, diversified firms that can successfully negotiate this transition will reap rewards in terms of competitive advantage. If they can make this new transition, there will be little debate over whether diversified firms add value.

[19]This new organizational form is more complex than Williamson's (1973) M-form, which is distinguished by a pattern of top management control of divisions in which top management is not involved in operating affairs. The importance of interrelationships suggests that divisionalization in its traditional sense is no longer appropriate in many firms.

12
Complementary Products and Competitive Advantage

Most industries are affected in some way by complementary products—that is, products that are used jointly with their product by the buyer. Computer software and computer hardware, for example, are complements. Complements are the opposite of substitutes, because the sale of one promotes the sale of another. Sometimes a number of complements are part of a firm's product line, while in other cases complements are supplied by other industries.

Complementary products represent one type of interrelatedness among industries, and raise important issues for a firm's competitive scope. Though interrelationships among industries in general terms have been the subject of the previous chapters, complementary products are singled out for attention here because they involve not only questions of the breadth of a firm's competitive scope but also of how it should compete within particular industries.

This chapter examines the three important strategic practices in industries that have important complementary products:

- *Control over complementary products.* Offering a full range of complementary products rather than leaving some of them to be supplied by others ("we sell both").
- *Bundling.* Selling a group of distinct but complementary products together only as a bundle, at a single price ("we only sell both together").
- *Cross subsidization.* Selling one product at terms that deliberately promote the sale of complementary products ("we sell one to sell another").

The first strategic choice a firm must make is whether it should supply complementary products itself or allow outside suppliers to provide some of them. This is an issue in competitive scope. Having resolved this question, a firm must then decide how to compete in the complementary products. One option is to bundle, or sell the complements together as a package. Bundling in some form is present in almost every industry, though it is frequently not recognized as such. Cross subsidization is a different approach to selling complementary products, in which products are not sold together at one price but sold separately with prices that reflect their complementarity. A firm whose products have important complements must make choices in all three areas.

These three practices are pervasive and affect competitive advantage and industry structure in some form or another in many industries. Yet all three issues are frequently overlooked, and the pitfalls in dealing with them are numerous. Many firms do not even recognize that they are bundling, for example. Or firms maintain cross subsidization after the conditions supporting it have changed, thereby creating an opening for competitors to attack them by focusing on the products being used to subsidize.

In this chapter I will describe in detail the conditions under which control over complements, bundling, and cross subsidization can lead to competitive advantage, as well as the risks of each practice. I will also describe how a firm's strategy toward complements should change as its industry evolves. Finally, some of the strategic pitfalls that firms have encountered in pursuing each of the three practices will be identified.

Control Over Complementary Products

In nearly every industry, products are used by the buyer in conjunction with other complementary products. Computers are used with software packages and programmers, for example, and mobile homes are often used in mobile home parks—plots of land specially designed as permanent sites for mobile homes, complete with streets, electricity, and sewer hookups. Tennis equipment is used with tennis courts, and jet engines are used with spare parts.

The sales of complementary products are necessarily linked, so that their fortunes tend to rise and fall together. However, complementary products can have a strategic relationship to each other that goes far beyond related growth rates. One complementary product often affects another's market image and perceived quality, as well as the cost of using the other from the buyer's viewpoint. Both of these effects are important to differentiation (Chapter 4). The relationship among complements can also affect the cost of supplying them (Chapter 3).

Where an industry's product is used with complements, an important strategic issue arises: the extent to which a firm should offer the full range of complements or leave some to be provided by independent suppliers. Offering the range of complements provides an important competitive advantage in some industries, but represents an unnecessary and even risky distraction in others. Control over complements is a distinct issue from bundling, though the two issues are related. A firm that supplies complements may or may not choose to bundle, because the benefits of controlling complements can often be gained even if they are sold separately.

Competitive Advantages from Controlling Complements

A firm can potentially gain competitive advantage from controlling complements in one of several ways, depending on the firm's strategy and industry structure. Broadly, the advantages stem from coordinating the value chains of a firm's product and complements in order to gain interrelationships that are similar in character to those discussed in Chapter 9:

Improve Buyer Performance and Thus Differentiate. Complements often affect the performance of a product or the firm's overall value to the buyer. Well-designed software can improve the performance of a personal computer, just as toner affects the copy quality of plain paper copiers. Similarly, a food concessionaire can significantly affect the buyer's satisfaction with a racetrack. Gaining the performance benefit of controlling complements often requires bundling. A firm that controls a complement may thus be able to enhance differentiation.

A firm gains a competitive advantage in differentiation from controlling complements if competitors do not. Even if control over a complement is widespread in an industry, however, it can still be beneficial if it improves overall industry structure though no firm gains a competitive advantage.

Improve the Perception of Value. Complements frequently affect each other's image or perceived quality. If mobile home parks look shoddy or are poorly designed, for example, this can adversely affect how buyers perceive mobile homes. Because of their association in the buyer's mind, complements are frequently signaling criteria for each other.[1] Controlling a complement can yield a competitive advantage in signaling even if a firm does not bundle. For example, Kodak's strong position in film improves its perceived differentiation vis-à-vis other camera manufacturers that do not sell film, even though Kodak sells cameras and film separately.

Controlling complements to signal value may be beneficial to industry structure even if no one firm gains a competitive advantage from doing so. In the mobile home industry, for example, the overall image of mobile homes could be improved if all mobile home producers also developed high-quality mobile home parks. This would increase the demand for mobile home versus other forms of housing and benefit the entire industry. Control over complements by one firm may, in fact, have little impact on buyer perceptions unless a sufficient number of competitors also control the complement. In these cases a firm should actually work to encourage its competitors to enter the complementary industry along with it.

Optimal Pricing. The buyer's purchase decision is frequently based on the total cost of a product and complements, rather than on the cost of the product alone. For example, buyers usually measure the cost of a condominium or automobile by the total monthly payment

[1]Signaling criteria are described in Chapter 4.

required (including principal and financing cost), rather than looking solely at the price of the condominium or automobile itself. Similarly, buyers may evaluate the cost of going to a movie in terms of the cost of the movie plus the cost of parking.[2]

Under these circumstances, prices must be set jointly to maximize profits, and this is difficult to do without controlling the complement. When setting the price of parking at a movie theater, one must recognize that lowering the cost of parking may increase the number of movie tickets sold, for example. I will discuss when such deliberate cross subsidization is the best strategy in the final section of this chapter.

As with differentiation, the benefits of controlling a complement for pricing do *not* require that the firm sell the product and complements as a bundle, or even that the firm have a market share in the complement that is comparable to its share of the base product. Even with a relatively small position in the complement, a firm can influence pricing in the complementary industry by initiating pricing moves that competitors are forced (or inclined) to follow. By lowering its own parking prices, for example, a movie theater firm may be able to force down prices at other parking garages in the area to some extent. Thus a position in the complement gives the firm a leverage point with which to influence the development of the complement's industry, and its position in the complement need only be big enough to allow exercising such leverage.

Reduce Marketing and Selling Cost. Control over complements can lead to economies in marketing, because the demands for a product and for complements are related. Advertising and other marketing investments for one complement often boost demand for the other, and complements may be susceptible to shared marketing or selling. Similarly, an installed base in one product can lower the cost of marketing complements. In video games, for example, an installed base of machines helps the firm sell game cartridges. The economies are sometimes large enough so that a firm not controlling complements is unable to reach the threshold spending on marketing needed to be effective.

A firm gains a cost advantage in marketing if it is one of relatively few firms that controls a complement. Widespread control over complements can benefit the industry as a whole, however, if it raises marketing expenditures and boosts overall industry demand relative to

[2]The cost of complements is hence part of the comparison between a product and substitutes. See Chapter 8.

substitute products. Widespread control over complements may also help overcome the "free rider" problem, where firms selling one complement piggyback on the marketing investments of firms selling others. Even if a firm's decision to control a complement is quickly imitated by competitors, such a move will still be beneficial to the industry as a whole.

Sharing Other Activities. Controlling a complement may allow a firm to share other activities in the value chain besides marketing and sales. The same logistical system may be employed to deliver a product and complements, for example, or the same order entry system. Opportunities for sharing will often be present because of the fact that complements are sold to the same buyers. The circumstances under which sharing value activities leads to a competitive advantage are discussed in Chapter 9.

Raise Mobility Barriers. Where controlling a complement leads to one or more of the competitive advantages described above, it may also increase overall entry/mobility barriers into the industry *if* entry barriers into the complementary product are significant. For example, a real estate developer that could own a bank (and get preferential access to financing) would significantly increase the sustainability of its competitive advantage because the barriers to entry into banking are significant for most real estate developers. Today real estate developers are legally prohibited from owning banks, though deregulation may change this in the future.

The benefits of controlling a complement are not mutually exclusive, and any or all can be present in an industry. For example, the food concession can not only affect the buyer's satisfaction with the racetrack, but prices should be set jointly on concessions and admission. Depending on the characteristics of buyers, low admission prices may well raise the number of patrons who will buy high priced hot dogs. Control over both the racetrack and the food concession can lead at the same time to economies in marketing. The sustainability of the competitive advantage from controlling a complement depends on the presence of some barriers to entering the complementary good. Without them, competitors can readily replicate the advantage through entering the complementary industry themselves.

The benefits of controlling a complement can sometimes be achieved through coalitions with other firms without the need for actual ownership. For example, a firm and the supplier of a complement can agree to coordinate prices, or agree to pool their marketing budgets. The problem with such arrangements is the difficulty of reaching a stable agreement. As long as firms supplying complements are independent, each will be tempted to free-ride on the other, and to set prices and strategies to maximize its profits rather than the joint profits of both. Nevertheless, the possibilities of using coalitions to achieve the benefits of controlling complements must always be explored. If the possibility exists it may be the most cost-effective option for a firm (or for the firm's competitors). Sometimes equity investments or other forms of quasi-integration between a firm and the supplier of a complementary product can overcome the difficulties of coordinating behavior.[3]

Problems of Controlling Complements

Against the benefits of controlling complements must be weighed some potential problems. The first is that the structural attractiveness of a complementary industry may be low, and its profitability significantly lower than in the base industry. Though control of the complement may improve profitability in the base industry, this must be weighed against the profitability of the complement relative to alternative uses for the funds. The tradeoff does not always favor control of the complement.

A second problem with controlling complements is that the complementary industry may involve very different managerial requirements for which a firm is ill-equipped and a firm may have little competitive advantage in the complementary industry. Thus any benefits from controlling a complement must be weighed against the risk that the firm will fail or only achieve a weak competitive position. The lack of skills in the complementary industry cannot be completely overcome by acquiring a complementary product supplier and managing it as a free-standing entity, because close coordination between complements is required to achieve most of the benefits.

Control over Complements and Industry Evolution

The value of controlling complements may well shift as an industry evolves. The need to control complements to improve their quality

[3]For a discussion of quasi-integration, see *Competitive Strategy,* Chapter 14.

or image may be greatest early in the evolution of the complementary industry, because of uneven quality or the presence of fly-by-night firms.[4] In the early years of color TV, for example, RCA's need to have an in-house service organization was much greater than later when independent service shops had mastered color set repair techniques. As a complementary industry matures, it may become desirable to exit or harvest a firm's position in the complementary industry. Independent suppliers may be able to do an adequate job, and the firm may no longer be able to offer anything unique in the complementary industry to bolster its overall differentiation. Staying in a complement too long when there are capable outside suppliers can actually erode differentiation rather than enhance it.

The pricing advantages of controlling a complement also may erode as the complementary industry matures. In the emerging phase, prices of complements are more likely to be higher than would be desirable because suppliers are skimming or inefficient. Early fragmentation of the complementary industry may also lead to inefficiency of complementary products suppliers, and to under-investment in marketing.

While there is a tendency for the need to control complements to decline with industry maturity, this is by no means a universal pattern. The advantages of controlling complements for marketing costs and other shared activities often persist, for example. A resort that owns not only a hotel but also the golf course, other sports facilities, and transportation may have a compelling advantage over one who only operates the hotel. What is necessary is for a firm to ask itself periodically whether there are benefits to controlling each complement. For some complements the benefits will persist or even increase, while for others a timely exit may be justified.

Identifying Strategically Important Complements

In view of the potential importance of complements both to a firm's competitive position and to industry structure, a firm must be aware of what products are complements to its product. The identification of complements is sometimes subtle, and often complements can be uncovered that are not generally perceived as such. Most industries will have a rather long list of products that are complementary to some degree. Table 12–1 gives an illustrative (and partial) list of prod-

[4]For a discussion of the problems of emerging industries, including the role of complementary products, see *Competitive Strategy,* Chapter 10.

TABLE 12–1 Partial List of Complements to Houses

Financing	Lawn mowers
Homeowner's insurance	Grass seed
Real estate brokerage	Swimming pools
Furniture	Barbecue grills
Appliances	Light bulbs
Carpets	Pets
Nurseries	Garden hose

ucts that are at least somewhat complementary to residential home building.

Given the potentially numerous complements in many industries such as home building, it is necessary to distinguish those complements that are strategically important from those that are not. It is clear that a house builder such as U.S. Home will gain little competitive advantage from competing in all the industries listed in Table 12–1, though it may well gain an advantage from competing in some of them.

Strategically important complements have two characteristics: (1) they are or could be associated with each other by the buyer, and (2) they have a significant impact on each other's competitive position. Some association of a complement and a firm's product by the buyer is implied in most of the potential competitive advantages of controlling a complement. The association among complements leads the buyer to connect their images, measure their performance collectively rather than individually, or measure their cost as a group. This association is also what underlies joint marketing or sales.

The strategic relationship among complements is thus in large part a function of buyer perceptions. A firm can rank complements based on how strong the association with its product is or could be. Houses and financing are commonly associated by buyers, for example, while houses and grass seed are rarely associated though their demand is undeniably related. Similarly, movies and parking costs are commonly associated, while the cost of driving to the movie is rarely associated with the cost of the movie. If products are in fact connected but not presently associated by buyers, a firm may be able to gain competitive advantage by educating buyers to make the association. A sophisticated knowledge of buyer purchasing behavior is necessary to uncover actual or potential buyer associations among complements.

The second test of the strategic significance of a complement is the effect of controlling it on competitive advantage or industry structure. A complement will not be important for a firm to control unless it has a material effect on overall cost or differentiation of the group of related products. Light bulbs are complements to lamps, for example, but light bulbs do not have a meaningful impact on the differentiation of a lamp or on the cost of marketing it. Since widespread control over complements can be a significant benefit for industry structure, however, some complements are important to control even if they cannot be turned into a competitive advantage.

Bundling

Bundling is selling separable products or services to buyers *only* as a package, or "bundle." For example, IBM bundled computer hardware, software, and service support for many years, while the manufacturers of antiknock additives for gasoline have traditionally provided various technical services along with their product all at a single price. Bundling in some form is pervasive, though not always recognized. Identifying when bundling is occurring often requires a rather fundamental look at an industry akin to that in segmentation (Chapter 7). All the potentially separable products and services that are offered must be isolated, even though they may not be seen as separate by industry participants. For example, delivery and after-sale service are often included as part of the product although they are potentially separable and could be sold separately. Similarly, retailers often provide free parking, while airlines provide free meals and baggage handling. Because some forms of bundling are age-old industry practices, firms may not even perceive that they are bundling.

Bundling means that all buyers are provided with the same package of products and services, regardless of differences in their needs. Some buyers of antiknock compounds, for example, would prefer to sacrifice the service provided by manufacturers in return for a lower price, but they do not have that option. Buyers often differ in their receptiveness to bundling because they want different collections of products or services, or because they differ in the intensity of their need for the various products or services. In either case, bundling is suboptimal for some buyers.

Bundling will not be desirable unless it has some countervailing benefits that overcome the fact that it is suboptimal for some buyers. Bundling can create competitive advantage in a number of ways, however, that vary in importance from industry to industry and even by industry segment. In some industries bundling also has significant risks that must be identified.

Competitive Advantages of Bundling

The potential competitive advantages grow broadly out of the ability to share activities in the value chains for providing parts of the bundle if the entire bundle is supplied together. The advantages of bundling can be grouped into a number of categories:

Economies of Providing the Bundle. A firm may lower its costs by providing only a single package instead of whatever mix of products or services a particular buyer desires. These economies arise from interrelationships in a firm's value chain that can be exploited by supplying only the package. Bundling can allow a firm to better share activities in the value chain in supplying the parts of the bundle. If the same bundle of products is sold to each buyer by the same salesperson, shipped on the same truck, or serviced by the same technician, for example, there may be cost savings in providing the bundle together. The price of the bundle could thus be lower than the collective price of the individual parts. For example, in providing services for offshore drilling for oil, a firm that provides two related services together may need only one person on the rig while competitors require a person for each service. Economies from bundling can also result from shared cost of gathering information about buyers. A consulting firm may learn about a client through providing one service, and apply this knowledge at low cost in providing other services in the bundle. The unbundled competitor must make the full investment in information even though it provides only one service.

Bundling may also reduce costs by promoting manufacturing economies of scale or learning. Providing the same package to all buyers guarantees an equivalent volume of all items in the bundle, perhaps lowering cost. For example, manufacturing a fire engine with standard features would allow a manufacturer to achieve greater economies of scale and learning than if each engine gets a different collection of bells and whistles, the current U.S. industry practice. Providing a common package may also increase the productivity of the sales force, by eliminating the need to inform the buyer about what parts of the bundle to select. Finally, bundling can significantly reduce administrative and selling costs. Providing the same package to all buyers usually simplifies transaction costs, including paperwork, logistical arrangements, and the like. Economies of standardization, scale, or learning can in some cases allow a firm to sell the bundle at a lower price than it would have to to charge customers who only wanted part of it.

Economies from bundling will yield a substantial competitive advantage to a bundled firm only if unbundled competitors cannot duplicate them through coalitions or contractual arrangements among themselves. However, the difficulties of reaching agreement on such coordination with independent firms often preclude a contractual solution.

Increased Differentiation. Bundling may allow a firm to differentiate itself vis-à-vis competitors selling only parts of the bundle. The role of bundling in differentiation arises from linkages among parts of the bundle in the buyer's value chain because they are used or purchased together. Without bundling, a firm may not only forgo differentiation but be forced to compete with each specialist competitor in its area of greatest strength. Bundling can increase differentiation in the following ways:

MORE BASES FOR DIFFERENTIATION. A firm that can bundle has more dimensions on which to differentiate itself than a competitor with a more limited offering. For example, a bundled firm may be able to guarantee reliability of the entire bundle or offer a single point for after-sale service. Similarly, it may differentiate itself or its service even though its product is not unique.

HIGH-PERFORMING INTERFACE. Bundling may be necessary when the interface among complementary products is not standardized. Compatibility among items in the bundle is facilitated if the same firm provides the whole package of items needed jointly to meet the buyer's needs. This presumes that interface technology is relatively difficult, and that compatibility cannot be achieved.

OPTIMIZED PACKAGE PERFORMANCE. Even if the interface among products in the bundle is standard, the bundled firm may be able to optimize the performance of the whole package (system) by controlling the design, manufacture, and service of all the parts. It may have better information about the capabilities of each part of the bundle than a specialist competitor who must gather information externally about parts of the bundle and cannot control their design directly. This advantage of bundling presumes that the parts of the bundle are interdependent in determining its overall performance.

ONE-STOP SHOPPING. Bundling simplifies the buyer's shopping task. Offering the bundle may also reassure the buyer that all the items in the bundle will work, and reduce the buyer's perceived risk of purchase. A single point of responsibility, a single place where complaints can be lodged, and a single service organization may also be valued by buyers. Buyer frustration over divided responsibility in the newly deregulated Bell System is a good example of how unbundling can lower differentiation through this mechanism.

Enhanced Opportunity for Price Discrimination. Bundling may allow a firm to increase total profits where different buyers have different price sensitivities for the individual parts of the bundle. Particularly in a "mixed" bundling strategy—where a firm offers both the full bundle at one price and the individual parts of the bundle at prices which sum to greater than the bundle price—bundling may increase total revenue compared to selling the parts separately.[5]

The mechanism by which this occurs is a function of the cost of the bundle versus the cost of the parts of the bundle a buyer would want if they could be purchased separately. Bundling can cause some buyers to buy the whole bundle even though they would not buy all the parts individually, provided the incremental cost of the whole bundle over the cost of the parts they desire is low. In addition, a mixed bundling strategy can allow the firm to extract high prices from buyers who strongly desire only one part of the bundle, while at the same time selling the whole bundle to other buyers.

The value of bundling in pricing depends on the distribution of buyer needs in the industry. Bundling is most likely to raise profits if buyers have widely differing price sensitivities for parts of the bundle. Bundling is a way of capturing differing price sensitivities without charging different prices to different buyers for the same product.

Increased Entry/Mobility Barriers. Bundling may lead to higher entry/mobility barriers, *presuming* there are one or more of the other

[5]For a demonstration of this in the case of a monopolist, see Adams and Yellen (1976).

competitive advantages of bundling. Bundling raises barriers because a competitor must develop capabilities in all parts of the bundle rather than being able to specialize.

Mitigated Rivalry. Rivalry among a group of bundled competitors may be more stable than rivalry in an industry containing both bundled and unbundled competitors. If all competitors offer the same bundle and the only industry price is the bundle price, the ability to recognize mutual dependence among firms is likely to be higher and the incentives for price cutting may be less than if competitors offer any part of the bundle separately.

Risks of Bundling

A bundled strategy involves a number of risks, which vary in importance depending on a firm's strategy and industry structure. The risks of bundling are determined by the potential vulnerability of a bundled firm to attack by an unbundled competitor employing a more focused strategy.[6] Sometimes a firm with a substantial competitive advantage can preserve bundling despite significant risks, as IBM did for many years in computers.

Diversity of Buyer Needs. Bundling presumes that a significant proportion of buyers desire and are willing to pay for the whole bundle. If buyer needs vary widely in an industry, a bundled strategy may be suboptimal for a segment of buyers and thereby vulnerable to a focused competitor who tailors the particular bundle it offers to the needs of the segment. For example, if the need for after-sale service varies widely among buyers in an industry, a focused competitor may be able to enter by selling only the product with no service included, and achieve enough market share to be viable. People Express, for example, unbundled the airline product by eliminating free meals, free baggage handling, and other parts of the traditional airline bundle. This appealed to price-sensitive buyers who had little need for the parts of the bundle that were eliminated. Similarly, off-price retailers have successfully attacked traditional retailers with strategies involving little service, no credit, no alterations, and no advertising to appeal to a particular buyer segment.

[6]Unbundling is one important variant of the focus strategy which involves performing fewer functions for the buyer. See Chapter 7.

Buyer Ability to Assemble the Bundle. In a bundled strategy, the firm assembles the bundle and sells it as a package to the buyer. This strategy is vulnerable if buyers have the technological, financial, and administrative capabilities to assemble the bundle themselves. The buyer may purchase the parts of the bundle individually from suppliers and put them together, or purchase some parts from suppliers and produce others (e.g., service) in-house.

Specialist Ability to Provide Parts of the Bundle on More Favorable Terms. A bundling strategy is vulnerable if specialists that focus on one or a few parts of the bundle can achieve low cost or differentiation in producing them. A specialist may gain a competitive advantage for the reasons described in Chapter 7. It can tailor its value chain to produce and sell just one item in the bundle that it views as its primary business. A specialist may also avoid costs of coordination or compromise with shared activities supplying other parts of the bundle that are borne by a bundled competitor.

A specialist that focuses on one part of the bundle can also potentially reap advantages from interrelationships with other industries. A specialist electronics company may have a cost advantage in producing an electronic part for an electromechanical system vis-à-vis a bundled competitor who provides the entire system, for example, because the electronics company can share value activities (e.g., R&D, test equipment) with other related electronics businesses.[7]

Bundling Through Coalitions. A bundled competitor is vulnerable if the advantages of bundling can be duplicated by focused competitors who form coalitions among themselves. Coalitions can take many forms, such as technology sharing and joint sales or service organizations.

Bundled Versus Unbundled Strategies

The balance between the competitive advantages of bundling and its risks determines the appropriateness of the bundled strategy for a firm. The risks of bundling provide the strategic levers with which focused competitors attack bundled competitors. Bundling will be the predominant strategy in an industry if the competitive advantages of

[7]See Chapter 9.

the bundled firm are significant and the risks of bundling low. Bundled and unbundled strategies are natural adversaries, however, and the balance between them can shift quickly in an industry in either direction.

In many industries, it may be difficult for the bundled and unbundled strategies to coexist. If a successful unbundled competitor becomes established, this creates pressure on the bundled competitor to unbundle. The presence of an unbundled competitor makes buyers more aware that their needs are not being exactly met by the bundled firm, and provides an alternative to purchasing the whole bundle.

In entering an industry against bundled firms, an unbundled competitor is likely to attack those parts of the bundle that by themselves would fully satisfy the needs of a significant group of buyers, such as a basic product without the ancillary services. Another likely avenue of attack is to supply a peripheral item such as spare parts or service, where the bundled competitor is inefficient or overcharging. Attacking a bundled firm through unbundling is one of the characteristic ways of gaining market position that are discussed in detail in Chapter 15.

After the first entry by an unbundler, the incentive is created for other unbundled competitors to enter and offer other parts of the bundle. Over time, then, more buyers are able to construct the particular bundle they desire. Once a number of unbundled competitors achieve significant market penetration, some of the motivations for bundling, such as scale economies, rivalry reduction, or building barriers, are often eliminated. Thus the remaining bundled competitors may be forced to unbundle.

The bundled and unbundled strategies can coexist in an industry, however, if there are wide differences in buyer needs and compelling advantages to bundling for some buyer segments that are *not* a function of volume (or of bundling being the dominant strategy). For example, optimization of system performance through bundling may be particularly critical for some buyers, and thus a bundled strategy will remain sustainable for this buyer segment despite the fact that specialist competitors supply parts of the bundle to other segments. Bundling may also be particularly valued by less sophisticated buyers, even though sophisticated buyers want to assemble the bundle themselves. In business aircraft, for example, Cessna is offering a bundle including a plane, maintenance, pilots, a hangar, office space, and landing fees all for a single monthly price. This appeals to buyers that want the convenience of one firm's taking responsibility for everything. A strategy of mixed bundling may also be appropriate depending on the particular competitive advantages sought from bundling. While offering the buyer an option to purchase either the whole bundle or parts of it from the same firm tends to undermine the firm's ability to sell the bundle, mixed bundling may be appropriate if the key advantage to bundling is differentiation or price discrimination.

Bundling and Industry Evolution

The appropriateness of bundling often changes as an industry evolves, because industry structural change alters advantages of bundling or the risks. There is no valid generalization possible about whether bundling becomes more or less attractive as an industry evolves, because many patterns are observed in practice. In the majority of industries, however, there seems to be a *tendency towards unbundling as an industry evolves.* In commercial insurance, for example, standardized insurance packages have been replaced by the separate sale of services such as loss prevention counseling. Buyers are able today to purchase broad coverage or specialized services depending on their needs. Another industry where unbundling may well occur is video systems. Just as audio systems were once bundled but are now often unbundled, video systems are likely to unbundle into displays, speakers, controllers, game units, and so on. Unbundling trends have also been evident in such other industries as building control systems, gasoline retailing, computers, and hospital management services.

The tendency for unbundling to occur over time is due to some characteristic changes in the competitive advantages and risks of bundling that accompany industry evolution:[8]

Buyer Ability to Assemble the Bundle Increases. Buyer learning over time, coupled with diffusion of technology, implies that buyers may become more able to assemble the bundle themselves. Buyers can gain the expertise to ensure compatibility, and need less reassurance from a single source of responsibility. This is reinforced by the tendency of buyers to backward integrate as industry volume grows. Buyers become more able to make some parts of the bundle themselves, and therefore do not desire the whole package.

[8]Chapter 5 discusses how the pattern of technological change in an industry evolves over time, important to these changes.

Product/Technological Standardization Occurs. Standardization of the product as an industry matures often reduces the need to control the entire package in order to optimize system performance. It also lowers entry barriers into parts of the bundle, and simplifies the buyer's task of assembling the bundle in-house. The problems of interface compatibility also tend to be reduced over time as an industry matures and standards are established. Qualified suppliers thus appear for parts of the bundle where there were none previously, and trigger the unbundling process described above.

Needs for Various Parts of the Bundle Are Reduced/Changed. Industry maturity tends to reduce the need of many buyers for service, applications engineering, and other parts of the bundle. Early in industry development, product quality is often erratic, products are unproven, and the perceived risk of purchase is often high (see Chapter 8). All of these characteristics lead buyers to seek the security of a bundled competitor, and bundling may be necessary to get an industry off the ground (the case in fiber optics and in electronic fuel injection systems for cars). As the industry matures, however, service and support either move in-house or are less needed by buyers. In addition, new buyers are often attracted to the industry and/or competitors segment the industry more finely, increasing the diversity of buyer needs. Different bundles thus become appropriate for different buyers, and the stage is set for an unbundled competitor to enter.

Industry Size Offsets Bundling Scale Economies. As an industry passes from emerging to maturing, the increase in industry size may make it possible for specialists to viably provide only parts of the bundle. Growth in demand for the parts of the bundle overcomes manufacturing scale thresholds as well as fixed selling costs. This is a special case of the emergence of a new segment as viable for a focus strategy, discussed in Chapter 7.

Increasing Buyer Price Sensitivity Leads to Pressures for Cost Reduction through Unbundling. Increasing buyer price sensitivity leads buyers to press for cost savings. One avenue is often for a buyer to purchase parts of the bundle and assemble it in-house, or to purchase just those parts of the bundle that it needs. Buyers often provide the impetus for unbundling even if no specialist competitors emerge.

Specialist Competitors Are Attracted. The success and growth of bundled firms may attract competitors looking for a way to get into the industry. Since entering with a bundled strategy usually involves overcoming higher entry barriers, new entrants naturally gravitate toward unbundled strategies (see Chapter 15). All the other forces described above provide the opening for them to succeed.

The tendency for unbundling to occur over time tends to be accentuated where an industry has powerful, capable buyers. Such buyers often have the technological strength to quickly develop in-house capability to assemble the bundle themselves, the bargaining leverage to force suppliers to unbundle, and the resources to lower the barriers facing specialist competitors. For example, the leading automobile firms purchase entire systems such as brake systems or fuel injection systems only very early in their development. Later, when the technology becomes developed, these firms break the systems into parts to be sourced from separate suppliers. They in the process often help put unbundled suppliers in business.

Unbundling is also triggered or accelerated during periods of intense industry rivalry, such as an economic downturn. Desperate competitors turn to unbundling for incremental revenue, setting in motion an often irreversible process. This pattern seems to have been at work in commercial insurance, where a disastrous downcycle has made firms anxious to gain incremental sales.

Industry followers or new entrants are often the first to break down the bundle. Followers tend to lead unbundling because of their desire to neutralize their competitive disadvantages in competing with bundled competitors. Often the best hope is to change the competitive rules in order to lower mobility barriers. New entrants also often break down the bundle by identifying latent or emerging segments or situations where there is no clear economic motivation for bundling, where bundling creates mixed motives in retaliation for bundled firms, or where buyer needs are changing. A prime source of new entrants that unbundle is spinoffs from bundled competitors, who recognize that some buyers' needs are not being served.

Despite a tendency for unbundling to occur over time, bundling is sustainable if the competitive advantages from bundling remain significant and unattainable any other way. Performance or cost benefits of bundling can persist, for example, even after the buyer's need for reassurance or assistance in assembling the bundle disappears. Bundling is also sustainable if an industry leader controls a proprietary part of the bundle and buyers are forced to purchase the entire bundle to gain access to it. Moreover, a leader can sometimes protect the bundle by protecting proprietary interfaces among parts of it. By making the problem of interfacing with its products difficult, the leader can deter the entry of specialist competitors.[9] IBM has been accused of such behavior, for example.

While the more common direction of change is from bundled to unbundled competition, it is important to recognize the opposite possibility. Technological changes may lead to product performance or interface motivations for bundling. Economies of scale in providing the bundle may also sometimes increase over time if the manufacturing process changes. Regulatory barriers that prevented economically rational bundling may fall. Unbundled strategies may also have developed over time in an industry where in fact there are economic motivations for bundling. If many specialists initially entered the industry and no firm had the resources or orientation to develop total capability in the whole bundle, buyers may have been forced to take the role of assembling the bundle themselves. A strategic innovation by one firm in bundling may transform the industry structure.

Two cases where bundling appears to be supplanting unbundled strategies are financial services and health care. Services such as Merrill Lynch's Cash Management Account (CMA), which combine stock brokerage, a checking account, a credit card, and other financial services, are bundles of previously separate services. They are a manifestation of deregulation as well as developments in information system technology that made such accounts feasible. Similarly, health maintenance organizations are combining separate services. In the same health care sector, however, home care services and specialized emergency room or firms performing minor surgery are a form of unbundling of the product line offered by hospitals. This example illustrates how the competitive advantages of bundling must be viewed on a segment-by-segment basis.

Strategic Implications of Bundling

The analysis of bundling carries important strategic implications for both bundled and unbundled competitors. There is usually a constant tension between bundled and unbundled strategies that requires that both be continually reexamined:

Bundle Where the Advantages Outweigh the Risks. Bundling can be a powerful source of competitive advantage where the benefits de-

[9]Protecting the bundle is sometimes part of defensive strategy. See Chapter 14.

scribed above outweigh the risks. Where producers of products have lost sight of the buyer's ultimate need to integrate them into a system, a bundled competitor can sometimes transform the industry in its favor. Sophisticated analysis of the buyers value chain and how it varies by segment is a prerequisite to effective choices to bundle and unbundle.

Avoid Unconscious Bundling. Many companies have de facto bundled strategies though they do not recognize them as such. Unconscious bundling is dangerous because a bundled firm may be vulnerable to attack by a focused competitor but may not perceive the threat. A bundled strategy should be the result of a conscious decision in which the advantages of bundling are judged to outweigh the risks, and not the result of a failure to distinguish among the potentially separable products or services that the firm offers.

Be Prepared to Unbundle Over Time if Conditions Change. Given the tendency for unbundling to occur over time, a bundled competitor must be constantly aware of the potential need to unbundle if the balance of advantages and risks shifts. A firm must distinguish between hard economic reasons for bundling and reasons based on lack of buyer sophistication that may be transient. Many bundled competitors have surrendered market share unnecessarily because they have stubbornly clung to bundled strategies.

Bundled Competitors May Represent Opportunities for Industry Restructuring. Bundling can create vulnerabilities that an unbundled competitor can exploit, particularly if bundling is unconscious or if the industry is evolving structurally. Industries in which bundling is being practiced, ideally as a long-standing industry convention, are potential entry targets for a firm.

Cross Subsidization

When a firm offers products that either are complementary in the strict sense of being used together or are purchased at the same time, pricing can potentially exploit the relatedness among them. The idea is to *deliberately* sell one product (which I term the base good) at a low profit or even a loss in order to sell more profitable items (which I term profitable goods).

The term "loss leadership" is commonly used to describe the application of this concept in retailing. Some products are priced at or below cost in order to attract bargain-conscious buyers to the store. The hope is that these buyers will purchase other more profitable merchandise during their visit. Loss leader pricing is also a way of establishing a low price image for the store.

The same pricing principle is at work in the so-called "razor and blade" strategy, which involves complementary products. The razor is sold at or near cost in order to promote future sales of profitable replacement blades. This same strategy is also common in amateur cameras, aircraft engines, and elevators. The complementary good is either a consumable item used with the product (e.g., film), a nonconsumable product used with the item (e.g., software cartridges with video games), replacement parts (e.g., aircraft engine parts), or service (e.g., elevator maintenance and repair).

Another variation of cross-subsidization is a trade-up strategy. Here product varieties that are typically first purchases are sold at low prices, in the hopes that the buyer will later purchase other more profitable items in the line as trade-up occurs. This strategy is sometimes employed, for example, in light aircraft, motorcycles, copiers, and computers.

Conditions Favoring Cross Subsidization

The motivation for cross subsidization is clear—increase total profit by selling larger quantities of profitable goods as a result of discounting the base good. The logic of this strategy depends on the existence of a number of conditions:

Sufficient Price Sensitivity in the Base Good. Demand for the base good must be sufficiently sensitive to price that discounting increases volume (or foot traffic) enough to result in a more than compensating increase in profit through the induced sales of the profitable good. If demand for the base good is not sensitive to price, however, the firm is better off making normal profits on both the base good and profitable good.

Sufficient Price Insensitivity in the Profitable Good. The profitable good must have demand that is not very sensitive to price, so that raising price does not greatly lower volume. Unless this is the case, profits lost in discounting the base good will not be recouped through profits on profitable goods. Insensitivity of demand to price in the profitable good is a function of the value it creates for the buyer and the threat of substitution for it.

Strong Connection between the Profitable and Base Good. The sale of profitable goods must also somehow be tied to the sale of the base good, so that buyers do not cherry-pick by purchasing only the low-priced base good. The connection between the products does not necessarily have to be binding, but it should be strong enough so that the proportion of buyers that purchase both from a firm is sufficient to justify discounting the base good.

The source of the connection between the base good and profitable good will vary from industry to industry. In retailing, the connection is created by shopping costs, which lead buyers to purchase other goods during the same visit to the store. In trade-up, brand loyalty and switching costs are the connection between one product and another. In a razor and blade strategy, brand loyalty and switching costs also may cause the buyer to purchase the blade from the firm that supplies the razor. In addition, perceived or actual compatibility may connect the goods (e.g., in film, spare parts), as does the belief of the buyer that the manufacturer of the product is best qualified to provide parts, maintenance, or repair (e.g., in elevators). The connection between the base and profitable goods also depends on the possibility of substituting for the profitable good. If spare parts can be refurbished, for example, then there is no longer the same relationship between equipment sales and parts sales.

Barriers to Entry into the Profitable Good. It must be difficult to enter the profitable good in order for cross subsidization to succeed, unless the base good and profitable good are strongly tied. Barriers to copying spare parts or consumables are essential, for example, to the logic of the razor and blade approach.

Risks of Cross Subsidization

The risks of cross subsidization tend to arise from failure to meet the third condition above. If the connection between the base good and profitable good is not sufficiently strong, a firm practicing cross subsidization may find itself selling only the low-priced base good and not the profitable good, which is purchased by the buyer from competitors. This can happen in a number of ways:

Buyer Cherry-picking. The buyer only purchases the base good, and either does without the profitable good or purchases it from another supplier that is not cross subsidizing.

Substitutes for the Profitable Good. If the need for the profitable good can be eliminated or reduced, cross subsidization is compromised because the buyer will not purchase the profitable good. For example, refurbishing spare parts instead of buying new ones or increasing the life of consumable items would have this effect.

Buyer Vertical Integration. The buyer purchases the base good but integrates to produce the profitable good internally. For example, service is performed in-house, or the buyer fabricates or refurbishes its own spare parts.

Specialist (Focused) Competitors. A specialist competitor sells the profitable good at lower prices. For example, independent service companies are common in a number of industries which specialize in servicing a particular brand of equipment, or in copying spare parts. They target an industry leader, and perform relatively simple types of service or copy the most frequently replaced parts. The equipment manufacturer's margins on parts and service are thus undermined, and it may increasingly be left with only exotic repairs or low-volume parts. Sulzer Brothers, for example, is the prime target of unlicensed parts suppliers in marine diesel engines. The risk of entry by a specialist competitor is a function of the tightness of the connection between the base good and profitable good, and the barriers to entry into the profitable good.

Cross Subsidization and Industry Evolution

The appropriateness of cross subsidization often changes as an industry matures. As in bundling, the tendency is for it to become less appropriate over time, though this not always the case. Cross subsidization can become less attractive for the following reasons:

The Strength of the Connection between the Base Good and Profitable Goods Falls. As the buyer becomes knowledgeable and more price-sensitive, the perceived need to purchase the profitable good from the same firm that sells the base good often diminishes. The tie between the goods may also weaken as diffusion of technology reduces switching costs, or compatible imitations for the profitable good become available.

Barriers to Entry into the Profitable Good Fall. More available technology and falling differentiation tend to reduce barriers to entry into the profitable good. One outcome may be buyer integration into the profitable good.

Substitution Possibilities for the Profitable Good Increase. Substitutes are sometimes discovered for the profitable good as the industry matures. For example, new technology for parts refurbishing appears (e.g., aircraft engine parts), or methods of conserving consumables are discovered (e.g., reuse of dialysers in artificial kidney machines).

Strategic Implications of Cross Subsidization

Cross subsidization can be a way to significantly improve performance if the necessary conditions hold. Such well-known firms as Gillette, Kodak, and Xerox have practiced the strategy successfully. However, the conditions supporting cross subsidization can be fleeting, and require active efforts to sustain. Moreover, a firm must be sure that cross subsidization is intended rather than unintended.

Some important strategic implications flowing from cross subsidization are as follows:

Create Barriers to Entry into the Profitable Good. Sustaining a cross subsidization strategy requires that a firm create or enhance barriers to entry into profitable goods. This implies, for example, that a firm must protect its proprietary servicing procedures, parts fabrication technologies, and designs for consumable supplies against imitators. Doing so may require aggressive patenting, deliberately creating different consumables for use in different models, and active marketing of the need to purchase profitable goods from the supplier of the base good. Many firms have squandered the advantages of cross subsidization by not paying attention to such factors.

An example of a firm that has worked hard to protect its profitable goods is Xerox. Consumables are a major contributor to profitability in copiers, and Xerox has maintained specialized toners for different models and actively marketed the benefits of purchasing consumables from the manufacturer to ensure highest quality.

Strengthen the Connection between the Base Good and Profitable Goods. Anything that tightens the connection between the base good and profitable goods will help defend a firm's ability to cross-subsidize. Designs that increase the competitor's difficulty in achieving a compatible interface are one such tactic. Another is Kodak's tactic of advertising to consumers about the desirability of finishing pictures on Kodak paper, attempting to more closely tie the sales of machines and paper to photofinishers.

Be Prepared to Modify Cross Subsidization as the Industry Evolves. A firm must be prepared to modify cross subsidization if the supporting conditions change. The relative margins on the base good and profitable goods should often be gradually equalized over time. A firm may also benefit from devising more complex pricing schemes over time that lower the price of the profitable good to those buyers most susceptible to defection. A firm must avoid the tendency to provide an umbrella that encourages entry by competitors into the profitable good.

Encourage Entry into the Base Good to Boost Sales of the Profitable Good. If the profitable good is proprietary, it may be desirable to encourage entry into the base good to boost sales of the profitable good with such tactics as licensing.[10] Kodak has encouraged entry into cameras that use its film formats, for example.

Avoid Unintended Cross Subsidization. A firm should cross-subsidize only as a deliberate strategy and not because it fails to understand its true costs. Failure to understand how costs differ by segment will almost guarantee that cross subsidization is occurring. A good system for strategic cost analysis, described in Chapter 3, is essential to effective cross subsidization. Unintended cross subsidy is an invitation to cherry-picking by competitors, as well as a way of attracting new entrants.

[10]This is one of a series of reasons why having competitors can be beneficial (see Chapter 6).

Complements and Competitive Strategy

Complements are pervasive in industries. A firm must know what complementary products it depends on, and how they affect its competitive advantage and the structure of the industry as a whole. A firm must decide which complements it should produce itself, and how to package and price them. Bundling and unbundling of complements is one of the ways in which fundamental industry restructuring takes place. The challenge is to make strategy towards complements an opportunity rather than a source of competitive advantage for competitors.

IV
Implications for Offensive and Defensive Competitive Strategy

13 Industry Scenarios and Competitive Strategy under Uncertainty

How does a firm choose a competitive strategy when it faces major uncertainties about the future? Oil field suppliers currently are agonizing, for example, over how long the drop in drilling activity will last; the estimates range from less than a year to the rest of the decade. Industry structure is not static, and firms in many industries face considerable uncertainty about how structure will change in the future. The sources of uncertainty are numerous and originate both within the industry and in the industry's broader environment. Most observers would agree that uncertainty has increased dramatically in the last decade, due to such things as fluctuating raw material prices, swings in financial and currency markets, deregulation, the electronics revolution, and the growth of international competition.

This chapter has benefitted from comments by participants in the Colloquium on Scenario Planning and Competitive Strategy held at the Harvard Business School, June 1983, especially Pierre Wack, Richard Rumelt, and Ruth Robitschek.

Every firm deals with uncertainty in one way or another. Uncertainty is not often addressed very well in competitive strategy formulation, however. Strategies are frequently based either on the assumption that the past will repeat itself, or on managers' own implicit forecasts about the most probable future of an industry. Explicit and implicit forecasts of the future structure are often biased by conventional wisdom, and by their very design may average out all the potential uncertainties facing the industry. Managers often fail to consider—or underestimate the probability of—radical or discontinuous changes that might be unlikely but would significantly alter industry structure or a firm's competitive advantage.

A few firms construct contingency plans as part of the strategic planning process, in an attempt to test strategies against major sources of uncertainty. Contingency planning is rare in practice, however, and usually tests strategies incrementally against only one or two key uncertainties such as the inflation rate or the price of oil. Contingency plans seldom examine alternative future industry structures, or compel managers to consider their implications. When facing considerable uncertainty, firms tend to select strategies that preserve flexibility, despite the costs in terms of required resources or diminished competitive position.

Scenarios as a Planning Tool

As the perceived need to address uncertainty explicitly in planning has grown, a few firms have begun to use scenarios as tools to understand the strategic implications of uncertainty more fully. A scenario is *an internally consistent view of what the future might turn out to be.* By constructing multiple scenarios, a firm can systematically explore the possible consequences of uncertainty for its choice of strategies. The use of scenarios started to become significant after the 1973 oil crisis magnified certain forms of uncertainty.

The scenarios traditionally used in strategic planning have emphasized macroeconomic and macropolitical factors—I refer to these types of scenarios as *macroscenarios.* Scenario building has concentrated on creating alternative views of the national or global economic and political environment, including such things as the rate of economic growth, inflation, protectionism, regulation, energy prices and interest rates. The use of macroscenarios reflects the fact that oil, natural resources, and aerospace companies were the early leaders in employing scenarios for planning, with Royal Dutch/Shell widely recognized as a pioneer.[1,2] Global macroeconomic and political events can have a profound effect on the success of an international oil or natural resource company. Moreover, scenarios have usually been developed at the corporate level in diversified firms, hence the attention to variables that broadly impact many business units.

Macroscenarios, despite their relevance, are too general to be sufficient for developing strategy in a particular industry. The implications of macroscenarios for individual industries are often poorly understood. Constructing macroscenarios requires the analysis of a broad and highly subjective set of factors. Few aspects of the macroeconomic and political environment have important strategic ramifications for all but the most basic industries. Other uncertainties that macroscenarios leave out such as technological change and competitor behavior can emerge as dominant factors driving industry structural change in particular industries. As a result, macroscenarios have encountered skepticism from many operating managers, and have not become integral to strategic planning in a widespread way.

Industry Scenarios

Scenarios are a powerful device for taking acount of uncertainty in making strategic choices. They allow a firm to move away from dangerous, single-point forecasts of the future in instances when the future cannot be predicted. Scenarios can help encourage managers to make their implicit assumptions about the future explicit, and to think beyond the confines of existing conventional wisdom. A firm can then make well-informed choices about how to take the competitive uncertainties it faces into account.

In competitive strategy, the appropriate unit for analysis of scenarios is the industry—I term such scenarios *industry scenarios.* Industry scenarios allow a firm to translate uncertainty into its strategic implica-

[1]A survey in 1979 estimated that between 8 and 22 percent of the Fortune 1000 had made some use of scenarios. The users were concentrated in process industries and aerospace firms (Klein and Linneman [1979]). A more recent survey of European companies by Malaska et al. (1983) showed a higher percentage of users. However, in interpreting data such as these, it is important to recognize that the definition of scenarios varies widely and that the way scenarios are used can and does vary widely.

[2]The approach to scenario planning pioneered by Shell is described in "Shell's Multiple Scenario Planning" (1980), Mandell (1982), and Wack (1984).

tions for a particular industry. By focusing on the industry, macroeconomic, political, technological, and other uncertainties are not analyzed for their own sake but probed for their implications for competition. Industry scenarios also explicitly include competitor behavior, a key source of uncertainty in the choice of strategies.

This chapter describes how to construct industry scenarios, and how to use them to guide the choice of competitive strategy. I begin by describing how to identify the sources of uncertainty facing an industry and how to translate them into the most meaningful industry scenarios. Next, I discuss how to analyze scenarios, and how to identify those with the greatest implications for industry structure and competitive advantage. I then show how a firm can select the best strategy in light of the uncertainties confronting it. The chapter concludes with a discussion of how industry scenarios should fit into a firm's ongoing strategic planning process.

Constructing Industry Scenarios

An industry scenario is an internally consistent view of an industry's future structure. It is based on a set of plausible assumptions about the important uncertainties that might influence industry structure, carried through to the implications for creating and sustaining competitive advantage. An industry scenario is *not a forecast* but one possible future structure. A set of industry scenarios is carefully chosen to reflect the range of possible (and credible) future industry structures with important implications for competition. The entire set of scenarios, rather than the most likely one, is then used to design a competitive strategy. The time period used in industry scenarios should reflect the time horizon of the most important investment decisions.

An industry typically faces many uncertainties about the future. The important uncertainties are those that will influence industry structure, such as technological breakthroughs, entry of new competitors, and interest rate fluctuations. External factors such as macroeconomic conditions and government policy affect competition through, and not independently of, industry structure. Structural change almost always requires adjustments in strategy and creates the greatest opportunities for competitors to shift their relative positions.

The five competitive forces described in Chapter 1 constitute the conceptual foundation for constructing industry scenarios. Uncertainties that affect any of the five competitive forces will have implications for competition, and therefore must be considered in constructing scenarios. Constructing industry scenarios begins by analyzing current industry structure and identifying all the uncertainties that may affect it. These uncertainties are then translated into a set of different future industry structures. An overview of the process is shown in Figure 13–1.

The process shown in Figure 13–1 is deceptively simple. Constructing industry scenarios requires several iterations and is a judgmental process. It can be difficult to determine fully what uncertainties are the most important for strategy until a number of preliminary scenarios have been analyzed, hence the feedback loops on Figure 13–1.

The process shown in Figure 13–1 postpones the introduction of competitor behavior into each scenario until the industry structure and requirements for competitive advantage have been developed, despite the fact that competitor behavior can influence structure and

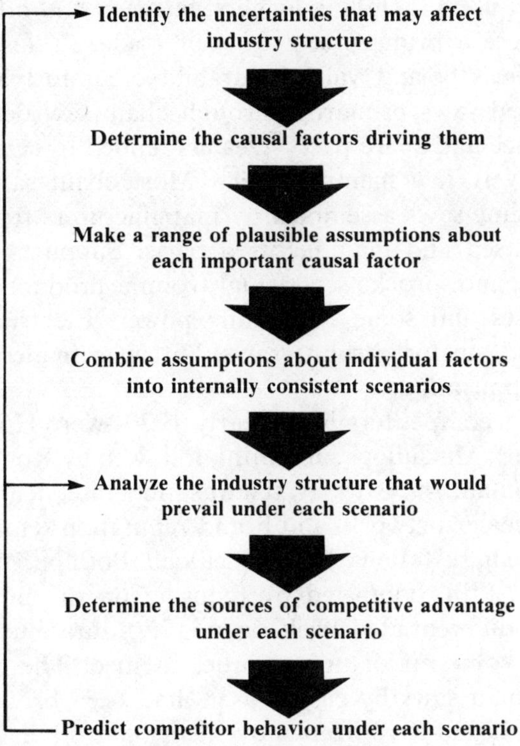

Figure 13–1. The Process of Constructing Industry Scenarios

is often a source of uncertainty in its own right. However, predicting competitor behavior in a scenario poses a nearly impossible task without some understanding of the structural environment in which competitors will operate. Expected behavior of competitors under a scenario may serve to modify industry structure; uncertainty about competitor behavior may lead to additional scenarios.

I will use an extended example drawn from the U.S. chain saw industry in describing how to construct industry scenarios. It is necessary to provide some background on the U.S. chain saw industry so that the scenarios can be better understood. The chain saw industry had enjoyed a stable and profitable structure for decades prior to the 1970s. In the early 1970s, however, there were indications that the industry might be on the threshold of a major structural change. It was believed that sales of small chain saws to homeowners and other "casual users" might enter a period of explosive growth. If this happened, a major structural change in the industry would be triggered which could proceed in several directions.

In the early 1970s, the great majority of chain saws were sold to professional users including loggers, farmers, and others for whom chain saws were a primary tool of their trade. Professionals tended to use saws heavily and valued durability, comfort and reliability. They purchased saws primarily through chain saw dealers that also provided service and spare parts. Dealers tended to carry the product lines of relatively few manufacturers. Most chain saws were large, powerful gasoline saws assembled by manufacturers from a combination of purchased and manufactured parts. Suppliers of parts such as chains, bars, and sprockets were high-volume producers that enjoyed scale economies and some bargaining power. Electric saws were a potential substitute for gasoline saws, but were inadequate for most professional applications.

The major competitors in the early 1970s were Homelite (a division of Textron), McCulloch, and Stihl, followed by Roper, Remington and Beaird-Poulan. Industry rivalry was moderate, centering on quality, features, dealer network, and brand reputation. Homelite had the largest market share, followed by McCulloch. Both pursued differentiation strategies. Stihl competed by focusing on the premium-quality segment, and differentiated itself on quality, durability, and service.

By 1973, some major uncertainties loomed. The initial spurt in demand for chain saws by casual users had been brought on by the energy crisis, the do-it-yourself movement, and other causes. Casual users were much less sophisticated than professionals and used their saws less intensively for less demanding applications. Casual users also did not necessarily purchase saws from servicing dealers, and distribution channels for chain saws were broadening to include hardware chains, catalog showrooms and department stores, among others. This encouraged new entrants into the market. Black & Decker acquired McCulloch, and Beaird-Poulan was acquired by Emerson Electric. These acquisitions had created the potential for an injection of resources into competitors that had previously been financially constrained. In the remainder of this chapter, I will construct a set of industry scenarios for the chain saw industry while describing the principles that underlie scenario building.

Identifying Industry Uncertainties

Identifying uncertainties with the most important ramifications for competition lies at the heart of the industry scenario technique. Yet the sources of uncertainty can be hard to recognize and managers may find it difficult to detect discontinuous changes or shed their conventional wisdom. To identify uncertainties each element of industry structure must be examined and placed into one of three categories: *constant, predetermined,* and *uncertain.* Constant elements of industry structure are those aspects of structure that are very unlikely to change. Predetermined elements of structure are areas where structure will change, but the change is largely predictable. Predetermined trends may well proceed faster or slower depending on the scenario. Often a variety of structural changes are predetermined if a thoughtful industry analysis is done. Uncertain elements of structure are those aspects of future structure which depend on unresolvable uncertainties. Constant and predetermined structural variables are part of each scenario, while uncertain structural variables actually determine the different scenarios.

A way to begin determining which elements of industry structure fall into each category is to list all apparent industry trends and any possible major industry changes that have been discussed internally or mentioned by industry observers. While only those uncertainties that might affect structure will be important to scenario-building, it is important initially to identify all the uncertainties to avoid omitting important variables. Uncertainties with a low probability of occurrance but with a potentially large impact on structure must also not be overlooked. Each trend or possible change is then analyzed to determine whether it could have a significant impact on industry structure, and how uncertain or predictable its impact is. Such a procedure will tend to produce a list of uncertainties that mixes causes and effects.

By considering only apparent trends, however, important discontinuities may be overlooked. Scenarios built only on apparent trends may reflect conventional wisdom and may not provide insights into future structure not available to competitors. One way to guard against overlooking discontinuities is to uncover observers of the industry who might foresee new possibilities. Soliciting opinions from outsiders new to the industry, who can view it objectively, provides another mechanism for overcoming conventional wisdom.

A wide range of environmental factors can lead to both predetermined and unpredictable industry changes, including technological trends, government policy shifts, social changes, and unstable economic conditions. Environmental changes are not important for their own sake, but because of their possible effect on industry structure. A number of underlying evolutionary processes, at work in every industry, are shown in Table 13–1.[3] These provide a census of the forces that drive industry structural change. Each should be examined to see if and how it might affect the industry. Sometimes the evolutionary processes will proceed in predictable ways, while in other cases their

TABLE 13–1 Evolutionary Forces Driving Industry Structural Change

Long-run changes in growth
Changes in buyer segments served
Buyer learning
Reduction of uncertainty
Diffusion of proprietary knowledge
Accumulation of experience
Expansion (or contraction) in scale
Changes in input and currency costs
Product innovation
Marketing innovation
Process innovation
Structural change in adjacent industries
Government policy changes
Entries and exits

[3]The evolutionary forces are discussed in detail in *Competitive Strategy*, Chapter 8.

speed and direction will be uncertain and lead to uncertainty about some elements of structure.

The possible industry changes that are most difficult to anticipate are frequently those that originate *outside* an industry. For example, many firms in industries that had little or no previous contact with electronics were taken by surprise by the development of microcomputers. New entrants also have less predictable and often more profound impacts on industry structure than do start-up competitors.

In some industries, therefore, scenarios are best constructed by starting inside the industry and looking outward for additional sources of uncertainty. In other industries, it is more appropriate to begin with macroscenarios and then narrow the focus to the industry. Macroscenarios can provide important insights into possible industry changes. They can expose possible shifts in macroeconomic, political, or social variables that are not foreseen in a more industry-centered view of the external environment. Another way of identifying uncertainties is broadly based technological forecasting. A systematic look at how any of the technologies in the firm's value chain (Chapter 5) might be affected by outside developments can sometimes help to reveal changes unforeseen by technical personnel inside a firm.

In constructing scenarios, it is important to try to identify one or more major discontinuities that would have a significant impact on structure, such as a revolutionary technological change. If major discontinuities have a material probability of occurring, they should be treated as one of the important uncertainties in developing scenarios. If a major discontinuity will have a fundamental impact on structure but is very remote, it is usually best treated separately from the normal scenarios.

To illustrate the application of these ideas, Table 13–2 lists the uncertain elements of structure in the chain saw industry in 1973. Significant uncertainties existed in all of the five forces except for suppliers. Since each uncertain element of structure can serve as the basis for several scenarios and the list of uncertainties can be quite long, as it is in the chain saw industry, these sources of uncertainty must be distilled into the few scenarios that will be truly important to strategy.

Independent Versus Dependent Uncertainties

Converting the list of uncertain structural elements into scenarios begins by dividing them into independent and dependent uncertainties:

- *Independent uncertainties.* Those elements of structure whose uncertainty is independent of other elements of structure. The sources of the uncertainty may be inside the industry (e.g., competitor behavior) or outside the industry (e.g., oil prices).
- *Dependent uncertainties.* Those elements of structure that will be largely or completely determined by the independent uncertainties. In chain saws, for example, the future level of advertising on television is quite uncertain but will be primarily a function of the size of casual user demand. Casual users are receptive to television advertising while professional and farm buyers are best reached through specialized magazines.

TABLE 13–2 Uncertain Elements of Structure in the U.S. Chain Saw Industry

Entry Barriers

Will there be new proprietary product designs?

How high will future scale economies in manufacturing be?

How high will future scale economies in marketing (media mix and spending rates) be?

How difficult will gaining access to each channel be?

What safety regulations will be enacted?

Buyers

What will casual user demand be?

What will professional/farm demand be?

What will be the mix of dealer versus nondealer sales?

How significant will private labeling be outside of the servicing dealer channel?

Will distribution be direct or through distributors?

How price sensitive will buyers be?

Rivalry

What will be the shape of the casual user penetration curve?

How will traditional competitors behave?

How will newly acquired competitors behave?

Will additional foreign firms be attracted to the U.S. industry?

How high will fixed costs be?

How committed is each competitor to chain saws?

Substitutes

How much will electric saws penetrate versus gas saws?

Suppliers

Relatively constant.

Independent uncertainties are the *scenario variables* on which scenarios are based. *Only independent uncertainties are an appropriate basis for constructing scenarios* because they are true sources of uncertainty. Dependent uncertainties are resolved once assumptions about the independent uncertainties have been made, and thus become part of each scenario.

Independent and dependent uncertainties often differ only in degree, because many industry structural characteristics will be determined in part by independent uncertainties and partly influenced by other industry characteristics. Industry concentration, for example, is largely based on the height of entry barriers and hence dependent, but is also a function of independent factors such as an unexpected acquisition or entry by a strong competitor. Thus, as in all phases of scenario construction, one must attempt to assess the most significant factors influencing each uncertain variable and use them to classify it as either dependent or as a true scenario variable. It is often not apparent in the beginning of an analysis which uncertainties are dependent. Once scenarios are analyzed, it may be necessary to modify the way a particular element of structure is classified.

Separating uncertain elements of industry structure into those that are scenario variables and those that are dependent requires that the *causal factors* of uncertain elements of structure be identified. Causal factors determine the future state of each uncertain structural element. For example, the level of casual user demand in chain saws will be a function of such causal factors as energy prices, the rate of household formation, how many new houses are built with fireplaces, and so on.

Practical considerations may dictate not going all the way back to the most fundamental causal factors determining an uncertain variable since they may be numerous and hard to measure. However, causality must be traced back far enough to separate scenario variables from dependent variables. Causal factors also are important in determining the appropriate range of assumptions that should be made about each scenario variable. If the level of casual user demand is strongly influenced by energy prices, for example, then forecasting the range of possible energy prices is necessary to understand the range of feasible levels of demand.

Table 13–3 identifies the scenario variables in the chain saw industry from the full list of uncertainties that were shown in Table 13–2 and ranks them in terms of their importance to industry structure. The scenario variables in the chain saw industry are relatively few,

TABLE 13–3 Scenario Variables in Chain Saws

Most Important Scenario Variables
Level of casual user demand
Shape of casual user penetration curve
Mix of dealer versus non-dealer sales
Extent of private label versus branded sales through nondealers
Less Important Scenario Variables
Professional and farm demand
Penetration of electric saws

because many of the uncertainties in the industry will be resolved once the demand for casual user saws and the channels through which they are sold become clear. Future safety regulations by government, for example, will probably be introduced if casual user demand grows and the number of accidents increases with the number of less sophisticated users. Marketing activity will also increase sharply and shift toward television advertising if casual user sales grow.

Table 13–4 shows the causal factors for the four important scenario variables in the chain saw industry. Several causal factors underlie each variable, as is typically the case. Causal factors reflect forces both within and external to the industry. It is also apparent from Table 13–4 that some of the causal factors reflect other aspects of industry structure or competitor behavior. Casual user demand, for example, is partly determined by the intensity of marketing activity and pricing behavior of competitors. The future mix of channels will in turn be influenced by the level of casual user demand, because casual users prefer different channels than professionals. It is not uncommon for scenario variables to have some internal causes along with external ones, and the analysis of scenarios must reflect such interdependencies.

The uncertainty that surrounds the causal factors of each scenario variable leads to scenarios. Assumptions about the scenario variables will determine the outcome of dependent uncertainties. Predetermined and constant elements of structure are then added to the scenario to complete the profile of the future structure of the industry, recognizing that the rate of change of predetermined trends may be different under each scenario. Figure 13–2 illustrates the process schematically.

Constructing a useful scenario involves developing a logic for how the various elements of industry structure interrelate, separating

TABLE 13–4 Causal Factors Determining the Uncertainties in Chain Saws

SCENARIO VARIABLE	CAUSAL FACTORS
Level of casual user demand	*External* Social trends Energy costs Woodburning stove and fireplace installations Number of households formed Channels selling casual saws *Internal* Marketing activity of competitors Product changes by competitors
*Shape of the casual user penetration curve**	*External* Economic conditions Pattern of energy price changes Pattern of social trends Replacement rate for saws Channel strategies regarding chain saws *Internal* Marketing activity by competitors
Mix of dealer versus nondealer sales	*External* Channel product line policies Consumer shopping habits for chain saws Ability of channels to provide service Usage patterns of casual saws (which determine replacement behavior, spare parts usage and service needs) *Internal* Channel policies of competitors
Extent of private label versus branded sales through nondealers	*External* Channel branding policies Channel product policies *Internal* Channel policies of competitors Branding policies of competitors

* The penetration curve is the growth in the number of households who own chain saws.

true scenario variables from dependent and predetermined industry changes. A scenario must seek to expose second-order effects of structural changes that result from one industry change affecting others. Such a logic for how various aspects of industry structure interrelate is at the heart of the usefulness of the scenario technique because it is usually important to understanding the implications of scenarios for strategy.

Identifying a Set of Scenarios

An industry scenario is based on a set of plausible assumptions about each of the scenario variables, derived from the causal factors. The consequences of this set of assumptions for industry structure flows from the process diagrammed in Figure 13–2. A scenario emerges as an *internally consistent* view of the future industry structure under one set of assumptions. The range of plausible assumptions about the potential outcomes of scenario variables determines the appropriate set of scenarios for analytical purposes.

Constructing a set of industry scenarios would be relatively simple once the scenario variables had been determined if there was only one scenario variable. If the only scenario variable in the chain saw

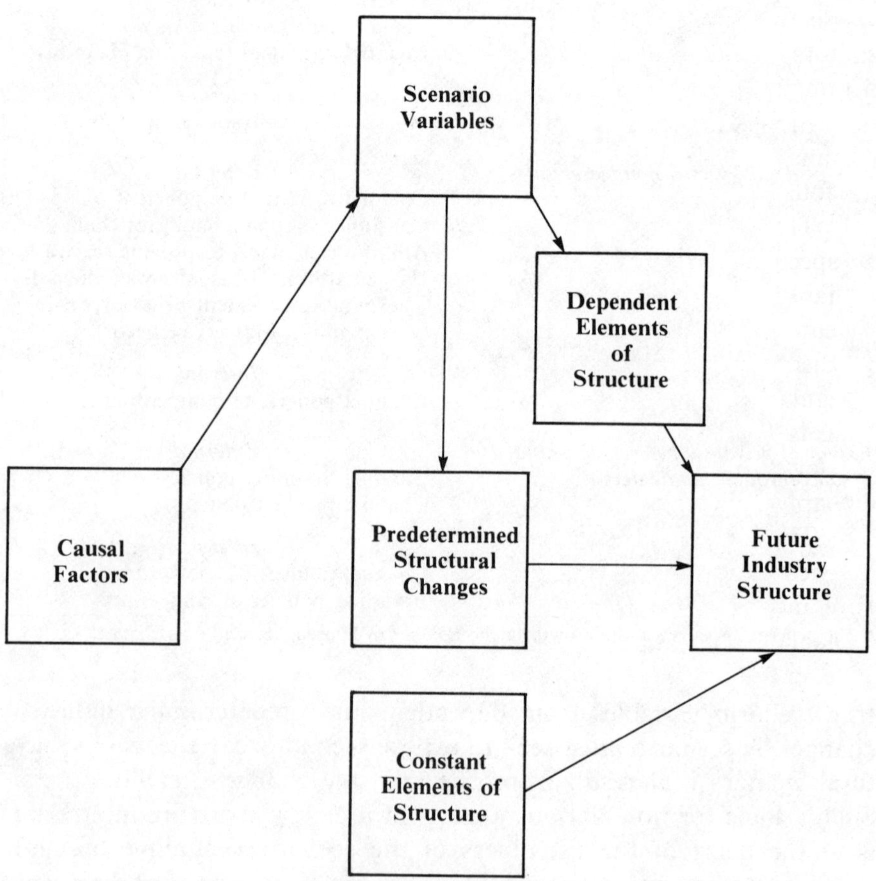

Figure 13–2. Determinants of Future Industry Structure

industry was the level of casual user demand, for example, then a manageable number of scenarios could be constructed by making several plausible assumptions about demand. However, the number of relevant scenario variables is greater than one in most industries. The number of combinations generated by differing assumptions about each scenario variable can multiply rapidly, and with it the number of scenarios that might be analyzed. With four scenario variables in chain saws, for example, dozens of scenarios could easily be constructed.

There are two ways to limit the proliferation of scenarios—reducing the number of scenario variables and reducing the number of assumptions made about each one. The first step is to ensure that the scenario variables are all truly uncertain and independent. This test may lead to the elimination of some variables. Another way to reduce the number of scenario variables is to concentrate on only those with a significant potential impact on structure. While many factors will have some impact on future structure, fewer will have an impact significant enough to influence competitive strategy. Sometimes the impact of a variable on structure only becomes clear once the analysis of scenarios has begun. In the chain saw industry, however, all four scenario variables are important.

The next step in determining the set of scenarios to analyze is to specify the different assumptions to be made about each scenario variable. The appropriate range of assumptions will depend on the extent to which its causal factors could differ. Scenario variables can be discrete or continuous. When a scenario variable is discrete (e.g., a regulation is either signed into law or it is not), the choice of assumptions is relatively clear. When the scenario variable is continuous (e.g., the level of casual user demand), a question arises as to how to make the appropriate assumptions about its value.

The choice of assumptions should be governed by four factors: the need to bound the uncertainty, regularity of the impact on structure, managers' beliefs, and practicality. Assumptions about a scenario variable should bound the feasible range of values that variable could take, exposing the important differences in possible industry structure. Since scenarios are not meant to be forecasts, it is important that those with a low probability of occurrence not be ignored. The use of extreme values can increase the understanding of the directions in which industry structure could evolve. Wide differences in the level of casual user demand, for example, will strongly influence the path of evolution in the chain saw industry. However, this does not mean that very unlikely values for a variable should be used in constructing scenarios unless these very unlikely outcomes would lead to industry structures that differ substantially from more likely outcomes. The credibility of scenarios can be damaged if they are based on highly implausible assumptions.

Having bounded the feasible range of uncertainty, the number of assumptions in between about each variable must be selected. If changes in the value of a scenario variable affect structure in a predictable way between its extremes, the number of assumptions can be small. If this is not the case, however, the range of assumptions must reflect major discontinuities. In chain saws, for example, a medium level of casual user demand is likely to have an impact on structure that is not simply between that of very low and very high demand. A medium level of demand provides room for only one or two new efficient-scale manufacturing facilities, and thus raises the possibility that several competitors will expand simultaneously, leading to overcapacity. An even more striking case of irregularity of impact is in the extent of sales through servicing dealers. It is possible that the percentage of saws sold through dealers will fall rapidly as casual user demand grows, but recover once first-time chain saw buyers trade up to larger saws and require service. This has quite different structural implications from scenarios featuring low or high dealer share.

A third consideration in choosing what assumptions to make about each scenario variable is the beliefs held by senior management. It is important to build at least one scenario around assumptions that reflect their commonly held beliefs. This lends credibility to the scenario building process. Scenarios reflecting managers' assumptions can also be useful in exposing the differences in the assumptions of various senior managers, as well as in testing the overall consistency of assumptions that managers have made independently about each scenario variable. If the scenario that results from combining these assumptions is implausible, managers' thinking about the future may be changed. All this is also important in demonstrating the validity of employing multiple scenarios rather than a single scenario.

A final consideration in choosing the number of assumptions about each scenario variable is the practical limit on the number of scenarios that can be meaningfully analyzed. A proliferation of scenarios beyond three or four may make analysis so onerous that the strategic issues are obscured. Thus compromises may well be necessary to reduce the number of assumptions examined. Since scenarios can be added, eliminated, or combined later in the analysis, it is important not to impose this constraint too strongly.

TABLE 13–5 Range of Assumptions in Chain Saw Industry Scenarios

SCENARIO VARIABLES	ASSUMPTIONS		
Level of casual unit demand	Low	Medium	High
Shape of casual user penetration curve	Steady increase	Peaked	
Mix of dealer versus nondealer sales	Dealers dominate	High nondealer share	Short-term shift to nondealers, with return to dealers in the long term
Extent of private label versus branded sales through nondealers	High percent branded	High percent private label	

Table 13–5 shows the range of assumptions chosen for the scenario variables in the chain saw industry. Except for the level of casual user demand and mix of dealer versus nondealer sales, two assumptions about each variable are sufficient to expose the implications for industry structure. The key distinction in the shape of the penetration curve is whether it rises smoothly, or rises rapidly and then levels off (peaking). Peaking raises the risk of excessive capital investment by competitors. The extent of private label sales is important in determining the bargaining power of buyers and the relative position of well-known brands such as McCulloch and Homelite (manufacturers' brands are clearly not as important in private label sales). Each assumption shown in Table 13–5 can be quantified.

Consistency of Assumptions

A scenario should be an internally consistent view of what future industry structure could be. Internal consistency is partly ensured by separating the scenario variables from the dependent ones. Another critical requirement, however, is the consistency of the assumptions made about each scenario variable with each other.

Often scenario variables affect one another, and thus some combinations of assumptions about them are not internally consistent. This can lead to the elimination of some scenarios. Figure 13–3 and 13–4 illustrate the process in the chain saw industry. Figure 13–3 compares the level of casual user demand and the shape of the casual user penetration curve. It is unlikely that the penetration curve will be peaked unless casual user demand is high. Hence, two combinations

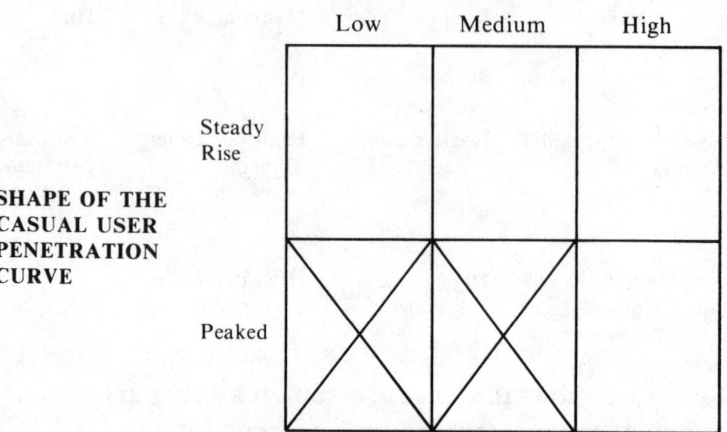

Figure 13–3. Consistency of Casual User Demand and the Penetration Curve in Chain Saws

of assumptions (cells in Figure 13–3) are inconsistent. Figure 13–4 compares the four consistent combinations of assumptions about demand and the shape of the penetration curve against the mix of channels. Once again, some combinations of assumptions are not mutually consistent and can be eliminated. Servicing dealers will dominate only if casual user demand is not high. Nondealers will not gain a high share of sales unless casual demand is medium or high. A short-term shift to nondealers is likely only if demand for casual users is high and peaked, leading to an increase in nondealer share followed by a

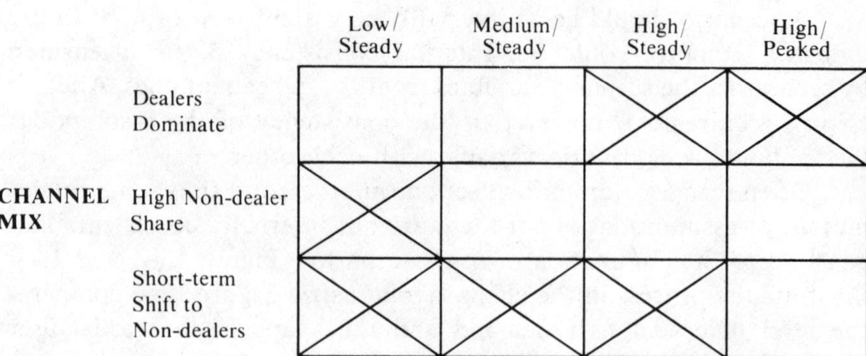

Figure 13–4. Consistency of Demand and Mix of Channels in Chain Saws

CHANNELS			CASUAL USER DEMAND: Low/ Steady	Medium/ Steady	High/ Steady	High Peaked
	Dealers Dominate		1	2	X	X
	High Percent Through Non-dealers	High Percent Branded	X	3	4	5
		High Percent Private Label	X	6	7	8
	Short-term Shift to Non-dealers	High Percent Branded	X	X	X	9
		High Percent Private Label	X	X	X	10

Figure 13–5. Consistent Scenarios for the Chain Saw Industry

fall-off in casual demand and the migration of the more serious casual users to dealers. The fourth scenario variable, the percentage of saws sold under private label versus sold branded through nondealers, is not shown on Figure 13–4. However, high private label penetration is clearly inconsistent with domination by the dealer channel.

Thus we can reduce the number of consistent scenarios in the chain saw industry to the ten shown in Figure 13–5. These ten combinations of assumptions about the scenario variables are internally consistent and, therefore, are candidates for further analysis. The process of determining internally consistent assumptions is vitally important to constructing industry scenarios, because consistency in viewing the future is one of the principal benefits of the scenario technique.

Analyzing Scenarios

The next step in scenario planning is to analyze the implications of each scenario for competition. The analysis of a scenario involves the following:

- determining future industry structure under the scenario
- developing the implications of the scenario for industry structural attractiveness
- identifying the implications of the scenario for the sources of competitive advantage

To determine the implications of a scenario for future industry structure, the process diagrammed in Figure 13–2 is carried out. Assumptions about scenario variables determine the dependent elements of structure. These are combined with the predetermined and constant elements of structure to complete the scenario. Predetermined changes in structure may be speeded up or slowed down for different scenarios. Each scenario will provide a picture of the five forces representing the industry's structure in the event that the assumptions about the scenario variables come true.

This future structure will be more or less attractive in terms of profitability. The industry structure under each scenario will determine, and possibly shift, the sources of competitive advantage. For example, a scenario characterized by low casual user demand will imply very different requirements for competitive advantage than a scenario where casual user demand is high and the mix of channels shifts away from servicing dealers. In the latter scenario, differentiation will be based more on advertising and having light, compact saw designs rather than on traditional sources of uniqueness such as excellent dealers and durable saws. The analysis of each industry scenario must specify the resulting implications for competitive advantage in the value chain.

Scenarios may differ in:

- the relative importance of value activities
- the appropriate configuration of the value chain
- the drivers of cost or uniqueness
- the importance of interrelationships
- the sustainability of different sources of competitive advantage
- the choice of generic strategies

Table 13–6 illustrates the analysis of two of the chain saw industry scenarios. Scenario 1 results in a structure quite similar to the current industry structure, while Scenario 7 results in a very different structure with quite different requirements for competitive advantage.

An important part of analyzing a scenario is determining *when* it will become clear that the particular scenario has come to pass.

TABLE 13–6 Analysis of Chain Saw Scenarios

	SCENARIO 1 "Casual user market never materializes"	SCENARIO 7 "Private label dominates"
Future Industry Structure	Same as currently	Entry barriers shift toward scale economies and absolute cost advantages Channels increase in power and price sensitivity Rivalry pressures increase Electric saws become a major product line
Structural Attractiveness	High	Mediocre on average, though a leader can be profitable
Sources of Competitive Advantage	Basically unchanged	Market share of causal units Low-cost product designs Scale economies in advertising Automated plants in low labor-cost areas *or* Extreme strength in professional/farm segment to insulate a firm from the battle in the casual user segment

Sometimes a scenario emerges quickly. In chain saws, however, a year passed before the uncertainty over the level of casual user demand was reduced. Several more years went by before the peaking of casual user demand was known. Competitors must choose between committing to a strategy early or waiting until better information becomes available. Therefore, a firm must estimate when uncertainties will be resolved in order to predict competitor behavior and to set the firm's own strategy.

Introducing Competitor Behavior into Scenarios

If the firm has a dominant position in its industry or if competitor behavior has little potential effect on structure, the analysis of each scenario can stop at the industry level. In most industries, however, competitors can affect industry structure and their strategies will influence a firm's options and likely success. Thus the analysis of scenarios must include competitors. In industries where a few powerful competitors exist, competitor analysis can be the most important part of analyzing each scenario.

The future industry structure under each scenario will usually have different consequences for different competitors. Increased casual user demand, for example, will greatly benefit firms with existing casual user models and representation in mass distribution channels compared to firms that exclusively serve professionals. Competitors will respond to structural change in ways that reflect their goals, assumptions, strategies, and capabilities. For example, Beaird-Poulan's response to growing casual user demand is likely to be aggressive, conditioned by its parent company's (Emerson Electric) aggressive growth goals. The behavior of competitors may, in turn, affect the speed and direction of structural changes in the scenario through a feedback loop. In chain saw Scenario 7, for example, aggressive investment in new capacity by Beaird-Poulan and McCulloch would enhance rivalry compared to the situation where one or both chose a conservative stance.

The full arsenal of competitor analysis tools should be brought to bear in predicting how competitors will behave under different scenarios. Strategic mapping is often a useful tool for integrating predictions of likely competitor's responses under a scenario.[4] The axes of the map are chosen to reflect the critical sources of sustainable competitive advantage implied by the scenario. Since each scenario implies a different future industry structure, the variables that will most influence the relative position of competitors may vary. For example, since industry structure under chain saw Scenario 7 will shift toward more price rivalry, manufacturing scale will become an important source of competitive advantage though it is not as important under Scenario 1.

Strategic mapping allows the simultaneous display of all competitors' expected behavior under a scenario. It also facilitates the analysis of interactions among competitors and their responses to each others' moves. If all competitors are forecast to move in one direction under a scenario, for example, some may modify their strategies as the scenario unfolds to avoid a head-on confrontation.

Often competitor behavior is difficult to predict. If the behavior

[4]See *Competitive Strategy,* Chapters 3–5 for a description of competitor analysis techniques. *Competitive Strategy,* Chapter 7, describes strategic mapping.

of one or more important competitors under a scenario is both uncertain and likely to have an important impact on competition, this introduces an *additional scenario variable* into the scenario. Scenarios under which there are key uncertainties about competitors must then be split into two or more additional scenarios based on assumptions about how competitors' behavior will differ. This same approach may be necessary to deal with uncertainty about the likelihood of potential new entrants with differing resources and skills from existing competitors.

Figure 13–6 illustrates the most important competitor uncertainties in the chain saw industry scenarios analyzed in Table 13–6. Under Scenario 1, the major uncertainty is whether McCulloch and Beaird-Poulan will aggressively invest in new capacity and advertising even though the casual user market never fully materializes. Both have strong proclivities to be aggressive given their new parent companies. Moreover, it will not be immediately clear to either firm which scenario is coming to pass. Under Scenario 7, Homelite's strategy poses the key uncertainty because McCulloch and Poulan's actions are quite predictable. Homelite may choose to pursue the entire casual user market despite the shift in strategy implied, or remain in its traditional segments and earn high profits at the expense of share. While Homelite's parent company may be prone to demand high profits, the opportunity for rapid growth could also influence Homelite's choice.

The Number of Scenarios To Analyze

Since the analysis of a scenario is often complex and time consuming, scenarios should be analyzed in a sequence that yields the necessary

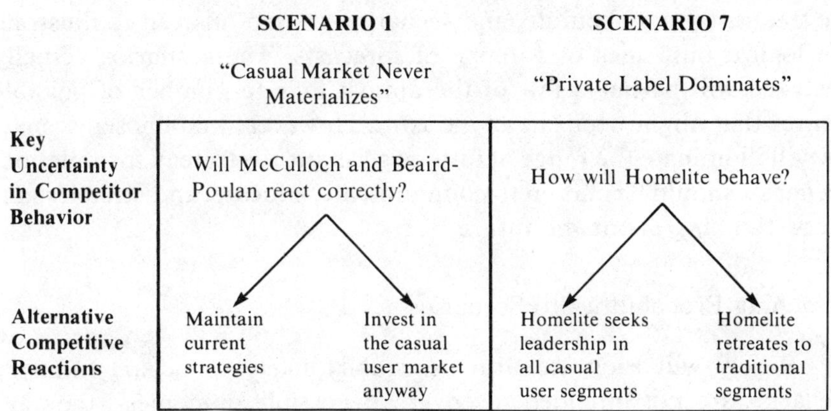

Figure 13–6. Competitor Behavior under Chain Saw Scenarios

insight for the selection of a strategy without requiring full blown analysis of every possible scenario. A good starting point is to analyze the *polar,* or most widely separated, scenarios first. The polar scenarios typically lead to the most different industry structures and thus will help bound the range of strategic options. The stark contrast between polar scenarios is often very stimulating to strategic thinking. In the chain saw industry, Scenarios 1 and 7 were the polar scenarios on Figure 13–5.

The next scenario analyzed after the polar scenarios should be one where the structural outcome is expected to differ significantly from the polar scenarios. The scenario deemed most likely to occur should also be analyzed. This process should continue until the way in which the scenario variables determine future structure is understood. In addition, major discontinuities with a low probability of occurring should be included as special scenarios which are analyzed less extensively but factored into strategic choices.

Figure 13–7 shows the analysis of an intermediate chain saw scenario, Scenario 9. This is very different scenario from Scenarios 1 and 7, because it assumes that casual user saws are a fad and private label sales will never catch on. Thus Scenario 9 creates a dilemma for firms about how to capitalize on the short-lived casual user boom without alienating dealers or sacrificing key competitive strengths. It is clear from Figure 13–7 that the determinants of competitive advantage and likely competitor behavior will be quite different under Scenario 9 than under the other two scenarios. Briefer consideration of other chain saw scenarios suggests that these three industry scenarios are representative of the impact of uncertainty on competition.

The purpose of scenarios is to understand the different ways in which industry and competitive conditions might change. Forecasts are frequently not accurate, and scenarios attempt instead to illustrate the logical outcomes of a range of forecasts. The scenarios actually analyzed will be but a few of the almost infinite number of possible futures that might occur in an industry. However, well-chosen scenarios will illuminate the range of futures germane to strategy formulation. Scenarios should be chosen to communicate, educate, and stretch managers' thinking about the future.

Attaching Probabilities to Scenarios

Rarely will each scenario be equally likely to occur. Industry scenarios are not intended to cover all possible outcomes—they are

SCENARIO 9

"Casual User Saws Are a Fad"

Future Industry Structure	Entry barriers shift but not to the extent of Scenario 7 Buyer power varies over time as the mix of channels shifts Rivalry becomes vicious after the growth spurt is over
Structural Attractiveness	Moderate in the long term
Sources of Competitive Advantage	Capacity to reap short-term profits on casual saws Brand awareness with professional users Low cost position to cope with rivalry Maintaining dealer loyalty Avoiding excess capacity Maintaining traditional strengths
Competitor Behavior	How aggressively will McCulloch and Beaird-Poulan invest? Aggressive / Cautious

Figure 13–7. Analysis of an Intermediate Chain Saw Industry Scenario

devices for exploring the strategic implications of possible future industry structures. However, the strategic implications of scenarios are partly a function of their likelihood of occurring. It is important to determine the relative probabilities of outcomes that are broadly similar to each scenario. If the scenarios analyzed are well chosen, they will represent the range of industry outcomes that might occur. In chain saws, outcomes close to Scenario 1 are the least likely to occur, while outcomes close to Scenarios 7 and 9 are about equally likely.

Attaching probabilities to scenarios is beset with problems of bias and conventional wisdom. It is important to find unbiased ways to assess the probabilities of scenarios, based on the underlying causal factors of each scenario variable. Managers' own implicit probabilities should be identified and confronted if they vary widely or contradict those indicated by industry analysis.

Summary Characteristics of Industry Scenarios

A number of characteristics distinguish industry scenarios. Each scenario is, in effect, a full analysis of industry structure, competitor behavior, and the sources of competitive advantage under a particular set of assumptions about the future. The whole range of techniques available for analyzing industries and competitive advantage must be brought to bear; the scenario tool is merely a framework for identifying the key uncertainties and analyzing them, not an end in itself. The *process* of understanding how uncertainty affects future industry structure is as important as the scenarios that are actually constructed.

The successful analysis of industry scenarios hinges on judgment and compromise. Constructing scenarios is a process of abstracting those elements of uncertainty that will drive strategic choices. Selecting and analyzing a few scenarios from the range of future industry structures requires picking the most important cases and simplifying them. The process is nearly always iterative, because the analyst will better understand the relationship between the key uncertainties and industry structure as the analysis proceeds.

Finally, it should be clear that a major purpose of industry scenarios is to ensure internal consistency of a firm's view of the future. A scenario aims to create a view of future industry structure that recognizes the interactions among variables and the need for consistency among assumptions about different industry characteristics. Scenarios provide a way of linking uncertain trends together into a number of alternate but consistent views of the future. Thus scenarios emphasize the ways in which industry trends and competitor behavior will interact or reinforce each other. Scenarios aim to reduce the chances that actions taken to deal with one element of uncertainty in an industry will unintentionally worsen a firm's position vis-à-vis other uncertainties.

Industry Scenarios and Competitive Strategy

Having developed and analyzed a set of industry scenarios, the next task is to use them to formulate competitive strategy. Scenarios are not an end in themselves. Many companies falter in translating scenarios into strategy. The bulk of attention is often placed on developing scenarios and not on determining their implications. There is also little guidance in the literature on scenarios about how to use them to formulate strategy.

A firm's optimal strategy would usually—though not always—be different under each scenario *if the firm knew the scenario would occur.* Each scenario involves a different industry structure, behaviors of key competitors, and requirements for competitive advantage. Figure 13–8 illustrates this in the chain saw industry, where the strategy for a leading firm is quite different under each scenario.

A firm does not know which scenario will occur, so it must choose the best way to cope with uncertainty in selecting its strategy, given its resources and initial position. The typical prescription for coping with uncertainty is to choose a strategy that is "robust," or viable regardless of which scenario occurs.[5] However, this is by no means the only option. A firm might decide instead to prepare for one scenario despite the risk that it will not occur. Conversely, a firm with massive resources may sometimes be able to pursue the strategies necessary to cope with all scenarios simultaneously and wait for events to unfold before focusing its efforts. If there is uncertainty over the mix of channels, for example, a strong chain saw competitor might develop its position in all likely channels.

A strategy built around one scenario is risky, while a strategy designed to ensure success under all scenarios is expensive. Moreover, the strategies implied by the different scenarios are often contradictory. For example, developing nondealer channels for chain saws will run a high risk of alienating dealers, and it is hard to pursue nondealers and dealers at the same time. In such circumstances, positioning for several scenarios may leave the firm "stuck in the middle" with no competitive advantage, a blurred brand image, and a suboptimal organizational structure (see Chapter 1). The inconsistency of implied strategies under different scenarios often raises a serious strategic dilemma. In chain saws, preparing for all three scenarios would clearly lead to suboptimization, and thus chain saw competitors will have to resolve some difficult tradeoffs before selecting their strategies. One of the important functions of scenarios is to reveal elements of strategy for which a firm must make such choices.

Strategic Approaches Under Scenarios

There are five basic approaches to dealing with uncertainty in strategy selection when a firm faces plausible scenarios with differing

[5]For example, see Hamilton (1981).

	SCENARIO 1 "Casual User Market Never Materializes"		SCENARIO 7 "Private Label Dominates"		SCENARIO 9 "Casual User Saws Are a Fad"
OPTIMAL STRATEGY	Stay the course Signal to avoid mistaken moves by competitors	←→ **Strategies totally inconsistent for leaders**	Aggressively seek cost leadership Early entry into new channels Emphasize direct sales Followers must choose focus strategies or disinvest First mover advantages make timing important	←→ **Strategies largely inconsistent**	Do not overreact to the casual segment Avoid alienating dealers or eroding reputation/franchise with professional users Pick up dealers alienated by competitors Reduce costs to defend against price competition by firms who invested in the casual segment

Figure 13–8. Competitive Strategy Under Alternative Chain Saw Scenarios

strategic implications. The approaches can sometimes, though not always, be employed sequentially or in combination.

1. *Bet on the most probable scenario.* In this approach, the firm designs its strategy around the scenario (or range of scenarios) that is seen to be most probable, accepting the risk that it may not occur. In chain saws, a firm would bet on whichever of the three scenarios it believed to be the most likely.

In practice, betting on the most probable scenario is a common approach to strategy formulation under uncertainty though it is done implicitly. Managers often base their strategies on implicit assumptions about the future. Without becoming explicit, however, a scenario may be based on ignorance and may fail the test of internal consistency so critical to good planning under uncertainty.

The desirability of consciously designing strategy for the most probable scenario depends on how likely it is that the most probable scenario will occur, how adverse the consequences are if other scenarios in fact occur, and how close the fit is between the resources and initial position of the firm and the strategy for dealing with the most probable scenario. The risk of designing strategy around the most probable scenario is that other scenarios will occur which make the strategy inappropriate, and it is difficult to modify the strategy mid-course.

2. *Bet on the "best" scenario.* In this approach, a firm designs its strategy for the scenario in which the firm can establish the most sustainable long-run competitive advantage given its initial position and resources. This approach seeks the highest upside potential by tuning the strategy to the possible future industry structure that yields the best outcome for the firm. The risk, of course, is that the best scenario does not occur and the chosen strategy is thereby inappropriate.

3. *Hedge.* In this approach, a firm chooses a strategy that produces satisfactory results under all scenarios, or at least under all scenarios that are deemed to have an appreciable probability of occurring. This is one approach to designing a robust strategy. The idea is similar to the "minimax" strategy in game theory, where a player makes the move that minimizes his maximum loss. In chain saws, hedging might entail developing a very wide model line, or entering nondealer channels with slightly different models sold under a different brand name at the same time as the firm continued to serve dealers.

Usually hedging will yield a strategy that is not optimal for *any* scenario. The resulting sacrifice in strategic position is traded off in favor of a reduction in risk. Moreover, hedging usually implies higher costs (or lower revenues) than a betting strategy because it must prepare a firm for several different possible competitive circumstances rather than one.

4. *Preserve flexibility.* Another approach to dealing with uncertain scenarios is to choose a strategy that preserves flexibility until it becomes more apparent which scenario will actually occur. This is another way of creating a robust strategy and illustrates that robustness must be carefully defined. The firm postpones resource commitments that lock it into a particular strategy. Once the uncertainties begin to resolve themselves, a strategy that fits the scenario that appears to be occurring is chosen, taking into account the firm's resources and skills. In chain saws, flexibility might be preserved by maintaining the firm's strategy in the professional segment and sourcing casual user saws initially from another firm.

A firm preserving flexibility often pays a price in strategic position because of first-mover advantages gained by firms that commit early. First-mover advantages—e.g., reputation, a proprietary learning curve, and ability to tie up the best retail channels—were discussed in detail in Chapter 5. In chain saws, the firm that moves into new channels first may well get its pick of the best ones. Preserving flexibility sacrifices first-mover advantages in return for a reduction in risk. It is different from hedging because it involves delaying commitment, rather than embarking on a strategy that works reasonably well under all feasible scenarios. If a firm can recognize early which scenario is going to occur, it can minimize the cost of preserving flexibility.

5. *Influence.* In the final approach to addressing uncertainty, a firm attempts to use its resources to bring about a scenario that it considers desirable. A firm seeks to raise the odds that a scenario will occur for which it has a competitive advantage. Doing so requires that a firm try to influence the causal factors behind the scenario variables. Since a causal factor in casual user demand for chain saws is woodburning stove installations, for example, a firm might try to influence stove demand. This might involve coalitions with woodburning stove manufacturers, or advertising that stressed the value of woodburning stoves at the same time that it advertised chain saws. Technological changes, channel policies, government regulation, and

many other sources of uncertainty can sometimes be influenced. The possibility for influence and its cost must be weighed against the competitive advantage to be gained if a firm can raise the odds that its preferred scenario will occur.

Combined and Sequenced Strategies

It is often possible and desirable to employ combined and sequential strategies. Betting on the most probable or best scenario can be combined with attempting to influence which scenario occurs. Similarly, the approach of preserving flexibility is logically part of a sequential strategy that ultimately involves a bet on the most probable scenario. A firm can also choose to hedge initially and then bet on a future industry structure as the actual scenario becomes clearer, though this is usually more costly than preserving flexibility and then betting.

A firm may also be able to *set policies in some activities in the value chain to bet on a scenario, while hedging or preserving flexibility in others.* In chain saws, for example, a firm might bet on high casual demand in its manufacturing and technology development activities through building new low-cost facilities and designing several inexpensive, lightweight models. At the same time, though, it could hedge its bet by minimizing the level of vertical integration in manufacturing to reduce capital investment and thereby transfer some of the risk to suppliers. It could also hedge its bets by spending heavily on marketing and sales activities to maintain dealer relations and preserve market position in the professional and farm segment.

A firm may also choose to contain risk in another way, by committing early to reversible actions (advertising) while postponing commitments on irreversible investments (e.g., plants). Any form of avoiding commitments or hedging will usually involve some sacrifice in competitive advantage, though, and may also be confusing to both employees and outside observers such as security analysts.

The Choice of Strategy Under Industry Scenarios

Each of the ways of coping with uncertain industry structural change has its potential benefits, costs, and risks in terms of competitive advantage. The following factors are most important in choosing a firm's approach:

First-mover Advantages. The size of first-mover advantages (Chapter 5) has a major influence on the attractiveness of betting versus postponing commitments. Where the first mover gains a significant competitive advantage, for example, the option of flexibility may be ruled out. In chain saws, gaining access to new channels may well involve significant first-mover advantages, because many mass merchandisers are unlikely to carry multiple lines of saws.

Initial Competitive Position. Scenarios will differ in their potential for a firm given its initial competitive position. Designing a strategy for the scenario that fits a firm's initial position may produce a significantly better outcome than designing a strategy around the most probable scenario. This difference in performance may compensate for the risk of betting on a less probable scenario. Influencing which scenario occurs is an attempt to shift probabilities in the direction of the scenario where a firm has the most advantages.

Cost or Resources Required. Hedging and influence tend to require greater resources or imply higher costs than does betting on one scenario. Preserving flexibility is usually somewhere in between.

Risk. The risk of each approach is a function of a number of factors:

TIMING OF RESOURCE COMMITMENT. Early commitment is usually riskier than later commitment. Preserving flexibility minimizes risk by postponing commitment, while hedging seeks to reduce risk in a different way. How long the firm can delay its commitment depends on first-mover advantages and the lead time in making moves.

THE DEGREE OF INCONSISTENCY OF STRATEGIES FOR ALTERNATE SCENARIOS. Risk is a function of how poorly a strategy will perform if the "wrong" scenario occurs. Hedging minimizes this risk at the price of higher costs or poorer position. The degree of inconsistency among strategies for alternate scenarios is a function of how different industry structure and the sources of competitive advantage are under each scenario.

RELATIVE PROBABILITY OF THE SCENARIOS. The choice of approaches depends on the relative probability of the scenarios. Hedging is a way to deal with risk by reducing the exposure of a firm to any scenario, while influence seeks to reduce risk by shifting probabilities toward the desired scenario. Betting on the most probable scenario is more risky than hedging, while betting on the best scenario can be the most risky approach.

THE COST OF CHANGING STRATEGIES ONCE UNCERTAINTY IS RESOLVED. Risk depends on the degree to which a firm is locked in once it commits to a strategy by setting its product line, channels, advertising policies, facilities, and so on. This will depend on the degree of irreversibility of the required investments, which will differ from industry to industry and strategy to strategy. Preserving flexibility seeks to minimize the cost of changing strategies.

Competitors' Expected Choices. A firm's choice of how to deal with uncertainty must reflect the choices its competitors have made or are expected to make. Competitor bets may preempt a firm from certain strategies and open up others. Hedging or preserving flexibility by competitors usually raises the payoff to the firm that makes a bet that proves correct.

The best way to deal with uncertainty is to make a *conscious* choice to follow one or more approaches, rather than a choice based on inertia or an implicit scenario. Weighing the factors involved in choosing an approach described above requires a logic for each scenario that portrays the interdependencies between various aspects of industry structure. The most challenging part of dealing with uncertainty is to find creative ways to minimize the cost of preserving flexibility or hedging, and to maximize the advantages of betting correctly. Understanding the way in which each activity in the value chain can contribute to competitive advantage under the various scenarios may allow the firm to do so.

Scenario Variables and Market Intelligence

Which scenarios will occur is determined by the scenario variables. Scenario variables are thus key indicators of the path of industry structural change—they can become clear quickly or the uncertainty may persist for long periods. Scenario variables and their causal factors should be the focal point for gathering market intelligence. Changes affecting scenario variables are warning signals of industry structural change. A firm preserving flexibility, for example, will want to closely monitor the state of scenario variables to decide when to commit.

Early information about the future state of scenario variables has a high strategic value. The earlier a firm can confidently predict the occurrence of a particular scenario, the sooner it can commit to a strategy with the accompanying gains in position described above. Thus investments in information gathering should concentrate on scenario variables rather than on indiscriminate tracking of the myriad other changes that accompany industry evolution.

Good information on scenario variables is also extremely valuable at the time when industry scenarios are constructed. Since the scenario variables are essential to structural change, understanding them may improve the set of scenarios investigated or even turn what initially appear to be scenario variables into predetermined elements of structure. In chain saws, for example, good data about household formation, the number of dwellings with fireplaces and other causal factors could reduce the range of assumptions that had to be made about casual user demand.

Scenarios and the Planning Process

Every plan is based on an industry scenario in one form or another, though the process is frequently an implicit one. The use of explicit industry scenarios brings the uncertainty in planning out into the open, and bases strategy on a conscious and complete understanding of the likely significance of uncertainty for competition. The resistance to employing scenarios will be greatly mitigated if they are seen in this light—as nothing fundamentally new or arcane. Industry scenarios are a useful device for getting a management team involved in thinking about the future systematically, and modifying unrealistic assumptions in a nonthreatening way because scenarios are not intended as forecasts.[6]

Industry scenarios are best developed by business unit managers, with guidance and input from others in the firm as well as outsiders. This places the task of understanding the effects of uncertainty in

[6]For a fascinating discussion of the process of changing management thinking at Royal Dutch Shell through scenarios see Wack (1984).

the hands of those who must actually set competitive strategy, and ensures that scenarios are truly relevant to the business unit. Industry scenarios should be constructed well into the planning process, once basic industry, competitor, and value chain analysis has been done. Industry scenarios will be ineffective without a good base of knowledge, and probably should not be introduced into the planning systems of firms without good basic planning skills. Scenarios are best used to guide the choice of a strategy, rather than as a means of confirming one.

Scenarios are not needed every year for every business unit. They are necessary only when significant uncertainties are present in an industry. However, constructing industry scenarios irregularly runs the risk that managers will overlook key uncertainties in their industries. Scenarios force a creative search for possible structural changes. How often scenarios are constructed must depend in part on the confidence of top management in the objectivity and vision of business unit managers.

An important organizational issue in using industry scenarios is the relationship between recognizing uncertainty and the level commitment of management to a direction. Scenarios emphasize the uncertainty present in an industry, while successful implementation of strategies is usually more effective if there is widespread commitment to the chosen strategy within an organization. This suggests that scenarios should be constructed by the management team of a business unit, but only the chosen strategy should be widely communicated in the organization. Organizations can only cope with so much uncertainty and ambiguity.

Corporate Role in Constructing Industry Scenarios

A corporate planning group or other corporate level managers can play a role in industry scenarios, even though industry scenarios should be constructed at the business unit level.

Macroscenarios as an Input. A corporate group can provide macroscenarios to business units, as a part of the environmental analysis needed to construct industry scenarios. Macroscenarios can stretch traditional modes of thinking by business unit managers in a way that is difficult if scenarios are purely business unit driven.

Technology Forecasting. A corporate group can conduct or sponsor technological forecasting in core technologies areas or in technologies with a potentially broad impact on many industries, a suggestion I made in Chapter 5. Such research may help expand the horizons of business unit managers about possible technological impacts on their industries, a key source of uncertainty.

Training and Challenging. A corporate planning group can play an important role in providing training and guidance in the use of the industry scenario technique itself. Constructing scenarios is a complicated task that gets much easier with experience, and experience can be shared within a firm.

In addition to training, an outside perspective can often be useful in identifying scenario variables, determining the most important ones, assigning objective probabilities, probing ways of hedging or preserving flexibility at low cost, and devising ways to influence which scenario will occur. Corporate, sector, or group managers can play a useful role through participating in these ways in business unit scenario building efforts.

Corporate Risk Analysis. By analyzing each business unit's industry scenarios, higher-level managers can identify scenario variables that have widespread importance for a diversified firm. The overall consequences to the firm should a particular scenario variable turn out one way or another can thus be assessed. In cases where corporate exposure to a particular scenario variable is great, some business unit strategies may have to be modified. At the same time, large investments may be justified in attempting to influence a scenario variable if it affects a number of business units. This approach to corporate risk analysis is based on well-informed assessments of uncertainties by business units. Top-down approaches to corporate risk analysis in many firms tend to be based on aggregate and oversimplified assessments of risks in each business unit by outsiders.

Industry Scenarios and Creativity

Most strategic plans are based on single-point estimates about the future, usually the best guess of the managers involved. Rarely are managers able to perceive fundamental shifts in their competitive environment ahead of time, and find imaginative ways of dealing with them. Industry scenarios are a systematic tool for examining the impact of uncertainty on competition by explicitly identifying the key uncertainties—the scenario variables. Scenarios aim to stretch thinking about the future and widen the range of alternatives considered. Scenarios provide a mechanism for improving the chances that views of the future are consistent. Having identified industry scenarios, a firm can then either mitigate uncertainty through its choice of strategy (influence, hedging, preserve flexibility) or make a bet on the future mindful of the risk involved. Industry scenarios also illuminate the consequences of mistaken forecasts about the future, and the key information to be acquired in forecasting efforts. Thus industry scenarios are fundamentally a tool to improve the creativity of strategic planning. They cannot insure creativity, but they can significantly raise the odds.

The industry scenario tool is *not* sufficient for strategy formulation in and of itself. Rather, scenarios provide a framework for formulating strategy under conditions of uncertainty. When combined with substantive conceptual tools for understanding industry structure, competitor behavior, and competitive advantage, the scenario tool can be an important part of the strategist's arsenal.

14
Defensive Strategy

Every firm is vulnerable to attack by competitors. Attacks come from two types of competitors—new entrants into the industry and established competitors seeking to reposition themselves. I will use the term "challenger" to describe either type. A well implemented offensive strategy constitutes the single best defense against attack by a challenger. A firm that continuously invests to gain competitive advantage by improving its relative cost position and differentiation will be difficult to challenge successfully. Even with a vigorous offensive strategy, however, an important role remains for defensive strategy. A firm can make it harder for challengers to attack it through the way it chooses to compete.

Defensive strategy aims to lower the probability of attack, divert attacks to less threatening avenues, or lessen their intensity. Instead of increasing competitive advantage per se, defensive strategy makes a firm's competitive advantage more sustainable. Almost all effective defensive strategies require investment—a firm foregoes some short term profitability to enhance sustainability. The most successful competitive strategies combine offensive and defensive components.

This chapter describes the principles of defensive strategy. Defensive strategy rests on influencing competitors' decision-making processes in order to make an attack on a firm's position less desirable from the challenger's perspective. This is done by reducing the inducement for a competitor to challenge the firm, or raising barriers to entry and mobility to make a challenge more difficult. Since an attack by any challenger changes character over time, appropriate defensive steps will change at different stages of the process. I will describe how defensive strategy should evolve, and the range of defensive tactics a firm can employ as well as some of their important characteristics. I will then show how a firm can identify the most effective defensive tactics in a particular industry. These considerations are drawn together to show how firms can formulate an overall defensive strategy. Finally, I describe the circumstances in which a firm should consider disinvesting in an industry rather than investing heavily in defense.

The Process of Entry or Repositioning

Defensive strategy rests on an acute understanding of how a challenger views the firm and on the perceived profitability of the challenger's various options for improving position. The formulation of defensive strategy must begin by recognizing that an attack by either a new or an established competitor is a time-phased sequence of decisions and actions. Appropriate defensive strategy must be formulated in the context of the entire assault, and not just one move. The appropriate modes of defense will change at different stages because of the challenger's differing levels of commitment and investment as the process proceeds.

The process of entry or repositioning consists of four periods. I will discuss them first for the case of a new entrant, and later show how the same process applies to an established competitor seeking to reposition itself.

Preentry. This is the period before an entrant has commenced its entry, during which it examines the industry as an entry target. Investments by an entrant during this period typically are limited to market studies, product and process technology development, contacts with investment bankers regarding acquisitions, and the like. This is the hardest stage to detect, because the entrant's intentions regarding entry are frequently not known with certainty. At the conclusion of the preentry period many potential entrants decide not to enter.

Entering. During this period an entrant invests in establishing a base position in the industry. This period involves such activities as continued product and process technology development, test markets, national rollout, assembling a sales force, and plant construction. The entrant hopes to have gained a viable position in the industry at the end of this period. The entering period can last a few months or several years, depending on the lead times involved in the activities necessary for establishing an initial position. In a service business, such as a restaurant, the period might only be a few months; in a natural resources industry it could be five years or more.

Sequencing. This is the period during which an entrant's strategy evolves from its entry strategy to its long-run target strategy. This period does not occur in every entry, but reflects the benefits of a sequenced entry strategy in many industries.[1] Procter & Gamble's entry into the consumer paper products industry provides an example. P&G acquired Charmin Paper, a regional firm with little brand identity, and then repositioned its strategy by going national, investing heavily in advertising, and improving products. During the sequencing period, an entrant may take such actions as broadening its product line, vertically integrating, or widening its geographic coverage. These activities involve continued investment in the industry beyond the investment necessary to gain a foothold position.

Postentry. This is the period after entry has fully occurred. At this stage in the entry process, investment by the entrant has shifted to that needed to maintain or defend its position within the industry.

The process of repositioning by an existing competitor involves the same stages. A competitor first contemplates repositioning, then actually begins to invest in repositioning, and ultimately reaches or fails to reach its sought-after position. An established competitor may also reposition itself through a sequence of steps. Therefore, the initial

[1]A firm may enter an industry without a sequenced entry strategy in mind, but initial success may lead to sequencing nonetheless. See *Competitive Strategy,* Chapter 16, for a discussion of the motivations for a sequenced entry strategy.

moves a challenger makes in repositioning often do not reliably indicate its ultimate target strategy.

The stages in the entry or repositioning process are important to defensive strategy for a number of reasons. First, a challenger's level of *commitment* to its strategy may well differ in the various stages. Generally, a challenger's commitment increases as it progresses in the process if some success is achieved. The initial level of commitment to an entry or repositioning strategy will vary, reflecting the unanimity of management opinion about the appropriateness of the decision in the first place and the attractiveness of other opportunities available to the challenger. However, commitment will tend to rise as decisions are made, resources are committed, time passes, and the strategy progresses. The level of commitment of a challenger is crucial to defensive strategy, since it mirrors the difficulty of forestalling or limiting a challenger's objectives.

Exit and shrinkage barriers will also tend to rise as the process proceeds.[2] The presence of high exit or shrinkage barriers make it difficult to dislodge a challenger or force it to limit or scale down its objectives. Exit and shrinkage barriers increase as the challenger commits to specialized assets, long-term contracts, horizontal strategies with sister business units, and investments in product or process development. In some industries, establishing even a foothold position implies the creation of significant exit barriers. In other industries, a challenger may be able to postpone the risk of increasing exit barriers until late in the entry process.[3] Developing an understanding of the height of a challenger's exit and shrinkage barriers and how they will change over time is essential to defensive strategy.

Defense becomes more difficult the greater are a challenger's commitment and exit barriers. Since commitment and exit barriers usually rise, often in discrete steps as investment commitments are made, the timing of defensive moves is critical. Defensive actions taken just before a challenger must decide whether to take steps that will raise exit or shrinkage barriers may cast a shadow over the challenger's internal decision-making process.[4] Critical junctures for a challenger

[2]Shrinkage barriers, discussed in Chapter 6, are barriers to reducing sales volume. They are closely related to exit barriers.

[3]Postponing of risk is one of the important motivations for a sequenced entry strategy.

[4]Much research by economists on entry does not recognize that entry is an extended investment process, and hence concludes that many entry-deterring investments are irrational once an initial entry investment has been made. For example, see A. Dixit (1980). An example would be a firm that attempts to deter entry by building excess capacity as a threat to potential entrants that a price war will be triggered if they

can be predicted by identifying costly or risky investments necessary in configuring the value chain. An important principle of defensive strategy, then, is to take defensive action *before* exit barriers have risen.

A challenger learns continuously as its entry or repositioning process proceeds. Assumptions were made in its initial decision that experience will verify or contradict. Its experience will also shape its future assumptions, and a challenger may modify its strategy based on events early in the process. This presents the defender with an important opportunity to *shape a challenger's information and assumptions.* Often a firm will know more about the industry than the challenger, and may be able to predict better than the challenger where the challenger's strategy will lead. This may allow a firm to influence the direction of a challenger's strategy in such a way as to minimize its negative impact.

A defender must also try to prevent a challenger's commitment from building. When considering risky and uncertain moves into new territory, a challenger's management may be particularly sensitive to setbacks or signs of early success or failure. A skillful defender seeks to prevent a challenger from meeting its initial targets and attempts to change industry competition in such a way as to cause the challenger to question its original assumptions about the attractiveness of the industry or a particular position.

As the entry or repositioning proceeds, uncertainty about the intentions of the challenger diminishes. This also has important implications for defensive strategy. Before entry or repositioning begins, a firm can only speculate about the identity of potential entrants or of competitors intending to launch an attack. Once entry or repositioning begins, however, the identity of the challenger becomes known. The challenger's strategy and long-term intentions may still not be clear

---

enter. Once the entrant has come into the industry, however, it has been argued that it is no longer rational to carry out the threat. This, of course, makes excess capacity less effective as a threat in the first place.

The flaw in the argument is that the commencing of entry does not mean that resources have been fully committed to the industry, or that the entrant should be viewed as an incumbent. Thus a price war during the entering or sequencing phases may well be effective if it causes the entrant to conclude that its ultimate target strategy cannot be achieved at acceptable cost. Entry may thus be terminated or a less ambitious target set, an outcome that has occurred in many industries such as video games and semiconductors. Entry deterrence also rests heavily on shaping potential competitor assumptions, and thus on the lack of complete information by potential competitors.

at first. However, they will emerge more clearly as the process proceeds. A challenger's ultimate strategy will not be known until well into the sequencing stage when significant investments have been made.

A firm cannot defend against attacks of any conceivable type, mounted by every conceivable competitor or potential competitor. Therefore, defense before a challenger appears must be more generalized, and effective defense of this type can be very costly. Once a challenge is under way, defensive strategy can be tailored to meet the threat posed by a specific challenger. A principle that emerges is that there is a high payout to *anticipating* which firms represent the most likely challengers and what their logical avenues of attack might be. This will allow defense to be more cost-effective, by focusing defensive investments where they are most needed.

Defensive Tactics

Defensive strategy aims to influence a challenger's calculation of the expected return from entry or repositioning, causing the challenger to conclude that the move is unattractive or to opt for a strategy that is less threatening. To do this, a defender invests in defensive tactics. Most defensive tactics are costly and reduce short-term profitability in order to raise the longer-term sustainability of a firm's position. However, most firms cannot eliminate the threat of attack completely, except at prohibitive costs. Hence a defender should invest to reduce the threat of attack to an acceptable level, balancing the risk of attack against the cost of defense.

Three types of defensive tactics underlie any defensive strategy:

- raising structural barriers
- increasing expected retaliation
- lowering the inducement for attack

Structural barriers to entry/mobility are sources of disadvantage for a challenger relative to the firm (see Chapter 1). The presence of structural barriers worsens the challenger's expected profit from a move. For example, General Foods' Maxwell House Coffee brand enjoys scale economies in marketing that will force a challenger to bear higher than proportional marketing costs relative to General Foods until it reaches proximity in market share. These higher costs will reduce the challenger's projected profit from entry below that of General Foods, and therefore reduce the likelihood of a challenge.

The second type of defensive tactic is those that increase the threat of retaliation perceived by challengers. Expected retaliation by the firm will lower a challenger's revenues or raise its costs, and thus erode the challenger's expected profitability. Raising structural barriers and increasing expected retaliation both seek to worsen a challenger's position vis-a-vis cost drivers or drivers of uniqueness, thereby eroding its relative position.

A third type of defensive tactic involves lowering the inducement for challengers to attack. While raising barriers and expected retaliation is aimed at reducing a challenger's expected profit, lowering the inducement requires that a firm accept lower profits. If a firm reduces prices or takes profits in an interrelated business unit instead of in the industry, for example, a challenger will see less to gain if an attack is successful.

All three types of tactics can be employed both before a challenge has occurred and once it has begun. Once a challenge has begun, however, a firm must consider not only its position toward the challenger but also how its behavior toward the challenger might discourage or encourage others. Investments in defensive tactics cannot and should not be measured against conventional short-term profitability targets. This ignores their purpose. Actions that deter challengers deliberately reduce short-term profitability to ensure long-term profitability.

Raising Structural Barriers

Chapter 1 summarized the types of structural barriers to entry/mobility that may be present in an industry. Every type of barrier can be influenced by a defender. In some industries, the levels of spending on advertising, sales force, plant capacity, and other activities that is necessary for doing business (ignoring defensive considerations) creates high barriers as a by-product. If the barriers naturally created by ongoing activities are very high, a firm is in the happy position of not having to make further defensive investments in barriers. However, in the long run it may be profitable to invest in building barriers even higher than natural barriers.

While offensive moves to enhance competitive advantage in the value chain can raise structural barriers, I concentrate here on defensive moves to raise barriers. Defensive tactics that raise structural barriers are actions that block logical avenues of attack for challengers. Some of the most important are the following:

Fill Product or Positioning Gaps. Barriers are increased when a firm fills gaps in its product line or preempts alternative marketing themes that a challenger might logically employ. Such moves force a challenger to take the defender head-on instead of being able to gain an unopposed beachhead, or command premium prices that can be used to offset higher costs. Filling gaps can take a number of forms:

- Broadening the product line to close off possible product niches. Seiko acquired the Pulsar watch brand to block attacks at the low end by Citizen and Timex.
- Introducing brands that match the product characteristics or brand positionings the challenger has or could use. These blocking or fighting brands raise barriers without undermining the position of the principal brand.
- Foreclosing alternative marketing themes by using such themes on secondary product lines or in secondary marketing campaigns.
- Defensive low pricing of product varieties adjacent to competitors' lines in order to discourage competitor line extensions (Chapter 7).
- Encouraging good competitors (Chapter 6) that fill gaps without threatening the firm.

Defensive product varieties and marketing activities should *not* be expected to be as profitable as a firm's core business, and prices must reflect their defensive value.[5] However, the defensive value of such products or marketing activities does not necessarily require that a firm spend heavily on them. Even if gap-filling products are not pushed aggressively, their mere presence acts as a deterrent because of the threat that they will be activated if a challenger threatens. Raising barriers may thus at the same time lead a challenger to expect greater retaliation.

Block Channel Access. When a firm makes it more difficult for a challenger to gain access to distribution channels it raises a major

[5]New brands and new positionings can be offensive opportunities. I focus here on situations where they are not attractive enough to be offensive opportunities, but yet have high defensive value because they block a likely avenue of attack.

structural barrier. Defensive strategy should be directed not only toward a firm's own channels but also toward blocking access to other channels that may be a substitute channel or a springboard for the challenger's entry in the firm's channels. For example, challengers often gain incremental volume and experience by using private label channels.

Channel-blocking tactics include the following:

- Exclusive agreements with channels.
- Filling product line gaps in order to offer the channel a full line. Competitors then have a harder time getting established.
- Expanding the product line to include all possible sizes and forms of a product, in order to clog the channels' shelf or warehouse space.
- Bundling or unbundling as appropriate to reduce vulnerability to challengers (Chapter 12).
- Aggressive volume discounts or discounts based on the channels total purchases to discourage experimentation with new suppliers.
- Attractive after-sales service support of a firm's products that prompts channels to forgo their own investment in after-sales support personnel and facilities.
- Willingness to supply private label sellers in order to preempt a challenger's access to volume.
- Encouraging good competitors, who fill up channels without threatening the firm.

Raise Buyer Switching Costs. The firm can raise barriers by raising the switching cost of buyers. I have described the ways to increase switching costs in Chapters 4 and 8. Some common approaches in defensive strategy include:

- Free or low-cost training of buyer personnel in the use or maintenance of a firm's product, or in specialized procedures such as record keeping that are only compatible with purchasing from the firm. Johns Manville has employed buyer training effectively to raise the switching costs of roofing contractors in buying roofing products.
- Participating in joint product development with buyers, or providing applications engineering assistance to them to help integrate a firm's product into the buyer's product or process.

- Establishing ties to the buyer through the use of dedicated computer terminals to allow direct ordering or inquiries, or through maintaining buyer data bases on the firm's computer.
- Ownership of on-premise storage facilities or equipment that is used at the buyer's location. In motor oil, for example, leading suppliers own tanks for bulk storage located on the garage or repair shop's premises.

Raise the Cost of Gaining Trial. If a challenger faces high costs of getting buyers to try its product, it faces a considerable barrier. Raising this barrier requires that a firm understand those product varieties that are purchased first, as well as the types of buyers that are most likely to be early experimenters and purchasers of a challenger's product. Steps to close off these avenues of trial for competitors include:

- Selective price reduction on items in the line most likely to be purchased first.
- High levels of couponing or sampling of buyers most prone to experiment.
- Discounting or deals that increase the inventory held by the buyer, lengthen the time between orders, or lengthen the period of contracts. All these impede a challenger's access to orders.
- Announcing or leaking information about impending new products or price changes that cause buyers to postpone purchases.

Defensively Increase Scale Economies. Barriers increase if economies of scale grow. It is often possible to increase scale economies in areas such as advertising and technology development, where scale thresholds are competitively determined. By boosting its spending rate on technology development and hence increasing the rate of new product development, for example, a firm can increase the challenger's required technology development investment, which is amortized over a smaller base of sales. A firm can increase scale economies most effectively in value activities where minimum scale is determined by competitive spending levels rather than determined by technology (see Chapter 3). Often this implies differentiating in ways where the firm has a cost advantage in differentiation (Chapter 4).

Scale thresholds are often increased defensively in a number of ways:

- Increased advertising spending.
- Increased spending to boost the rate of technological change.
- Shorter model life cycles, where models require fixed or quasi-fixed development costs.
- Increased sales force or service coverage.

Defensively Increase Capital Requirements. If a firm can raise the amount of capital needed to compete with it, a challenger may be discouraged. While many defensive tactics in effect raise a challenger's capital requirements by increasing start-up costs, a number of defensive moves have a particular impact on capital requirements:

- Raising the amount of financing provided to dealers or buyers.
- Increasing warranty coverage or liberalizing policy toward returns.
- Reducing delivery time for products or spare parts, implying an increase in the amount of inventory required or the need for excess manufacturing capacity.

Foreclose Alternative Technologies. If a firm can foreclose alternative technologies a challenger might employ, it blocks this avenue of attack. Some tactics for foreclosing technologies are:

- Patenting the feasible alternative technologies in the product or process, as Xerox did effectively in the early phases of the copier industry.
- Maintaining a participation in alternative technologies, through purchasing licenses, maintaining pilot plants employing alternative technologies, forming coalitions with other firms with expertise in alternative technologies, or actually producing products using an alternate technology. All these tactics let a challenger know that the firm has access to the alternative technologies if it needs them.
- Licensing or encouraging good competitors to employ alternative technologies (see Chapter 6).
- Discrediting alternative technologies through signaling.

Invest in Protecting Proprietary Know-how. If a firm can protect its proprietary know-how in products, processes, or other activities in the value chain, it raises barriers. Firms often have no systematic program in place to limit the diffusion of their know-how. Building on the discussion in Chapter 5, some elements of such a program include:

- Strictly limiting access to facilities and personnel.
- Fabricating or modifying production equipment in-house.
- Vertical integration into key components to avoid passing know-how to suppliers. Michelin practices this aggressively in tires.
- Human resource policies to minimize personnel turnover and prevent disclosures.
- Aggressive patenting of inventions.
- Litigation against all infringers. Litigation may delay investments by challengers until the uncertainties are resolved, even if the possibility of success in the litigation is low.

Tie Up Suppliers. Barriers increase if a firm can foreclose or limit a challenger's access to the best sources of raw materials, labor, or other inputs. Some representative tactics are as follows:

- Exclusive contracts with the best suppliers.
- Backward integration or partial or complete ownership of suppliers to foreclose sources of supply.
- Purchasing key locations (mines, forest lands, etc.) in excess of needs to preempt them from competitors.
- Encouraging suppliers to customize their value chains to meet a firm's needs, raising supplier switching costs to serving new competitors.
- Signing long-term purchasing contracts to tie up supplier capacity. Coca-Cola reportedly pursued this strategy in sourcing high-fructose corn syrup, a low cost substitute for sugar.

Raise Competitors' Input Costs. If a firm can raise a challenger's relative input costs, it raises barriers. Most opportunities to do so rest on differences in competitors' (or potential competitors') cost structures, so that a given input price change has a greater impact on them than on the firm. Some common tactics are as follows:

- Avoiding suppliers that also serve competitors or potential competitors, raising these suppliers' costs and avoiding the transfer of some of the firm's scale economies to competitors through the suppliers.
- Bidding up the price of labor or raw materials if they represent

a higher percentage of costs for competitors. This tactic may well have been used by large beer companies against smaller firms with less automated plants.

Defensively Pursue Interrelationships. A firm can often reduce its costs or enhance differentiation by harnessing interrelationships that competitors cannot match (Chapter 9). At the same time, pursuit of interrelationships by competitors that a firm cannot match are threats that must be defended against. Defensive considerations may suggest that a firm pursue particular interrelationships, including entering some new businesses, to enhance its defensive posture.

Encourage Government Policies That Raise Barriers. Government policies can become major structural barriers in areas such as product or plant safety, product testing and pollution control. Policies such as these can increase economies of scale, capital requirements, and other potential barriers. A firm can often shape the character of government policies in ways that are favorable to defending its position. It can:

- Encourage stringent safety and pollution standards.
- Challenge competitors' products or practices in regulatory proceedings.
- Support requirements for extensive product testing.
- Lobby for trade financing or other favorable trade policies to deal with foreign competitors.

Form Coalitions To Raise Barriers or Coopt Challengers. Coalitions with other firms can raise barriers in many of the ways described above, such as foreclosing alternative technologies or filling product gaps. At the same time, coalitions with likely challengers may be a way to convert a threat into an opportunity.

Increasing Expected Retaliation

A second type of defensive tactic is an action that increases the threat of retaliation perceived by challengers. The threat of retaliation hinges on both the perceived probability of retaliation and its expected severity. A range of tactics are available to a defender to signal its intentions to retaliate against potential challengers. For example, Dow

Chemical has built capacity in advance of demand in magnesium for many years, indicating its commitment to defending its share. Had Dow been continually constrained for capacity, challengers might have been more tempted to enter.

Expected retaliation can be increased by tactics that indicate that a firm intends to vigorously defend its position, that create conditions making it inevitable that the firm must retaliate, or that indicate it has the resources to do so. The threat of retaliation perceived by potential challengers is continually being influenced by a firm's behavior. A firm's reputation for retaliation is strongly influenced by its history, particularly its response to past challengers. The firm must carefully manage the image it projects to actual and potential competitors. Some of the most important ways of increasing a firm's perceived threat of retaliation include:[6]

Signal Commitment To Defend. A firm increases expected retaliation if it consistently signals its intention to defend its position:

- Announced intentions by management to defend market share in the industry.
- Corporate pronouncements of the importance of a business unit to the firm.
- Announced intention to build adequate capacity ahead of demand.

Such signaling can and should be carried out consistently via all the available channels, such as public statements, trade press, distributors, and buyers, in order to have the greatest defensive impact.

Signal Incipient Barriers. Most tactics that raise effective structural barriers require the firm to make a significant investment. However, a firm may sometimes be able to achieve the same effect through market signaling or partial investment. Market signaling of planned moves or partial investment has the purpose of increasing expected retaliation by the firm in the future. For example, a firm might announce or leak information about a new product generation, a fighting brand or new process technology, raising the risk perceived by a challenger that the actual move will be forthcoming. Such market signaling

[6]Some conditions for achieving credible commitment to retaliate are described in *Competitive Strategy,* Chapter 5.

can cause challengers to postpone future commitments until more information can be gained to learn if the signals are credible. IBM frequently announces new product generations well in advance, for example.

Establish Blocking Positions. A firm can provide a lever for retaliation by maintaining blocking or defensive positions in other countries or industries occupied by competitors or potential competitors (see Chapter 9). Blocking positions in business units where competitors generate a disproportionate share of their cash flow or profitability become the basis for particularly effective retaliation.

Their value rests on the principle that price cutting and other retaliatory tactics may be less costly in industries or countries where a firm has a small position than in a firm's key industries. Blocking positions may also be a less risky form of retaliation than direct retaliation, which has a greater propensity to trigger escalation and to spill over to damage good competitors.

Match Guarantees. A firm raises the expectation of retaliation if it commits itself to match or better prices or other terms offered by competitors ("We will not be undersold"). A public stance that it will do so often deters challengers from attempting to gain position through discounting, particularly if a firm backs its claim once or twice in a publicized way. Of course the firm must be capable of supporting such a claim in the eyes of challengers.

Raise the Penalty of Exit or Lost Share. Anything that increases the economic need for a firm to maintain its market share (raises its shrinkage barriers) is often a convincing way to demonstrate seriousness about retaliation:

- Constructing capacity well ahead of demand.
- Entering into long-term supply contracts for fixed quantities of inputs.
- Increasing vertical integration.
- Investing in specialized facilities.
- Publicized contractual relationships that raise the fixed cost of exit.
- Interrelationships with other business units in the firm that demonstrate an overall corporate commitment to succeeding in the industry.

Raising the penalty of lost share or exit surely introduces the risk that a firm will actually have to pay that penalty. However, this and most other effective defensive tactics raise cost or risk in order to enhance the sustainability of position.

Accumulate Retaliatory Resources. The threat of retaliation is increased if a firm has the resources in place needed to retaliate effectively. Some ways of demonstrating the capacity to retaliate include:

- Maintaining excess cash reserves or liquidity (a "war chest").
- Holding new models or product generations in reserve, though leaking their existence.

Encourage Good Competitors. Good competitors increase the threat of retaliation in many industries by serving as a first line of defense against challengers (see Chapter 6). The presence of the right competitors may also divert attacks in their direction.

Set Examples. A firm affects its image for retaliation through its behavior toward competitors that may not be real threats as well as through its behavior in response to threatening challengers. Defensive value is often reaped from using moves against nonthreatening challengers to demonstrate how tough the firm is in responding to real challengers. A very vigorous response to one challenger sends a message to others.

Establish Defensive Coalitions. Coalitions with other firms may increase the threat of retaliation by affecting many of the factors described above. A coalition, for example, may provide blocking positions or retaliatory resources a firm itself does not have.

Many of the ways to increase the perceived threat of retaliation force the firm to increase its level of risk. Indeed, by raising the firm's risk the tactics become significant to competitors. Thus a firm must be prepared to invest if it wants to improve the sustainability of its position in this way.

Retaliation During Attack

So far I have discussed the steps a firm can take to increase the perceived threat of retaliation and prevent an attack. The period immediately after a move has begun is a particularly delicate one for a challenger, however, during which it is hungry for information on its progress and is sensitive to early successes or setbacks. Challengers have a tendency to read a great deal into early results, often using them as a basis for longer-term projections. Hence, even if a defender's retaliation is unsustainable for long, it may serve to shape a challenger's expectations. As a general rule, quick and vigorous retaliation is necessary to limit an attack.

A number of additional tactics become possible once an attack has been mounted, because a firm then knows the identity of the challenger and something about its strategy.

Disruption of Test Markets or Introductory Markets. A wide range of actions can disrupt market introductions and cloud the interpretation of early results. Procter & Gamble is a tenacious rival in competitor test markets, for example. Such actions can raise a challenger's level of uncertainty about its position or cause it to adopt a more pessimistic view of future prospects. Typical disruptive tactics include:

- High but erratic levels of advertising, couponing, or sampling.
- Low-cost service, warranties, or trade-ins.

Leapfrogging. If a firm can introduce a new product or process during a challenger's attack, this can be very discouraging to the challenger. This is particularly true if such a move forces the challenger to make further investments to stay in the game just after it has expended considerable resources.

Litigation. Litigation can raise the risks or costs of further investment by a challenger, thereby delaying its progress. Forms of litigation that can be used in retaliation are as follows:

- Patent suits that raise uncertainty about the future of a challenger's product or process.
- Antitrust suits that contest any aggressive tactics used by the challenger.
- Suits that dispute product performance claims by challengers.

Lowering the Inducement for Attack

A third type of defensive tactic is actions that lower the inducement for attack instead of raise its cost. Broadly, profit serves as the inducement for a challenger to attack a firm. The profits expected by a challenger if it succeeds are a function of a firm's own profit targets as well as the assumptions held by potential challengers about future market conditions.

Reducing Profit Targets. The profits earned by a firm are a highly visible indication of the attractiveness of its position. An essential part of any defensive strategy, then, is to decide what current price and profit levels are sustainable. Many firms have invited attack by being too greedy. A firm can deliberately choose to forgo current profits to reduce the inducement for attack. This may imply lowering prices, raising discounts, and so on.

There must be a balance between structural entry/mobility barriers and threat of retaliation on the one hand, and a firm's profitability on the other.[7] If a firm's profitability is very high, challengers will attempt to cross even high barriers or combat strong retaliation. The high historical profitability in oil field services and pharmaceuticals industries, for example, attracted many firms to invest heavily in entry despite the presence of high entry barriers and entrenched competitors. For example, TRW has moved into oil field services while Procter & Gamble has entered pharmaceuticals. Many entrants attracted by high profitability fail to consider carefully the costs of entry, and often underestimate them. Similarly, high temporary profits in a cyclical industry are frequently misread as a long-term opportunity. The effect of being too greedy is thus to begin an implicit or explicit harvesting strategy as challengers erode the firm's position.

Managing Competitor Assumptions. A challenger's assumptions about future industry prospects may lead it to attack a firm. If challengers believe that an industry possesses explosive growth potential, for example, they may attack a firm despite high barriers. Managing competitor assumptions was discussed in general terms in Chapter 6. While a firm cannot credibly cause potential competitors to dismiss realistic assumptions about the industry, defensive strategy should attempt to make potential challengers' assumptions more realistic. Some options include:

- Making realistic internal growth forecasts public.
- Discussing realistic interpretations of industry events in public forums.

[7]At the industry level, this balance is reflected in the concept of the entry-deterring price discussed in *Competitive Strategy,* Chapter 1.

- Sponsoring independent studies that will question unrealistic assumptions held by competitors.

Defensive strategy can be viewed in a broad sense as influencing competitor assumptions, including their assumptions about retaliation and the height of barriers. Influencing competitor assumptions about future industry conditions is an important part of the task.

Evaluating Defensive Tactics

The defensive tactics described above differ greatly in their characteristics and in their appropriateness for a firm. A firm must decide which tactics will be most effective in its industry in view of the potential challengers it faces. A number of important tests can be used to assess defensive tactics:

Value to Buyers. A firm should select those defensive tactics which are valuable to buyers (Chapter 4). Many defensive tactics involve investments in such things as advertising, fighting brands, and price reductions on certain product varieties. A tactic directed toward buyers will not be effective for defensive purposes *unless the buyer values it.* If increased advertising leads to no increase in buyer awareness or loyalty, for example, then higher advertising spending will have no defensive value because a challenger need not match it. If buyers are highly sensitive to credit, on the other hand, then offering more credit will force a challenger to provide comparable credit or face a disadvantage.

A defensive tactic that enhances differentiation at the same time as it increases the sustainability of the firm's competitive position partly pays for itself. The buyer response to a defensive tactic need not pay for its entire cost, however, but only enough to place a challenger that fails to match the defensive tactic at a disadvantage. The defensive value of an advertising increase should not be measured only by whether the ads pay for themselves in increased sales, for example, but also whether they also force any challenger to spend at higher levels to attack the firm's position.

Cost Asymmetry. A firm should choose defensive tactics that place potential challengers at the greatest relative cost disadvantage. The effectiveness of a defensive tactic is a function of the asymmetry between the *cost of the tactic to the firm* and the *cost imposed on the challenger*. For example, an increase in national network TV advertising by a large share firm usually imposes proportionally greater spending requirements on a challenger with smaller share, because national network TV advertising is subject to economies of scale driven by national market share. Introducing a new product generation may also raise a challenger's cost proportionally more than the firm's, since new-product development costs are largely fixed and the challenger must amortize them over a much smaller initial volume. Conversely, a price cut may cost a firm the same or even more than it costs a challenger. Any fool can cut the price, goes the old maxim, and a firm often hurts itself more than the challenger in defending in this way.

Cost asymmetry stems from differences in the firm's and challenger's position vis-à-vis cost drivers such as scale, learning, location, or interrelationships. The firm should select defensive tactics which elevate its cost position less than they elevate challengers'—frequently these are differentiating factors where the firm has a cost advantage in differentiating (Chapter 4). In some industries boosting advertising will put challengers at the greatest disadvantage, while in other industries it may be increasing the size of a sales force. The analysis of cost behavior described in Chapter 3 provides the starting point for identifying such asymmetries.

Cost asymmetry in a defensive tactic is strongly influenced by whether the tactic can be *targeted* at likely avenues of attack or threatening challengers, or whether it is more generalized. Tactics that must apply across the board (e.g., a cut in list price) are generally more expensive than those that can be targeted. For example, the ability to cut price only on products that are likely initial purchases by new buyers is clearly much less costly than a price reduction on the entire line. Good defensive strategy requires that defensive investment be targeted as much as possible towards the most serious threats.

The cost asymmetry of defensive tactics is also clearly a function of the specific challenger involved. For example, an increase in national advertising is one thing if challengers are start-up firms, but quite another thing if the challenger is a large and successful consumer goods firm. Cost asymmetry in defensive tactics, then, is *relative* and not absolute.

Sustainability of Effect. A firm should select defensive tactics that have a lasting effect. The cost effectiveness of any defensive tactic is a function of the need to reinvest to maintain its defensive value. An increase in advertising has some effect beyond the current period, for example, but a firm must continually reinvest in advertising in order to maintain the barrier. An investment in a new production process, however, may not decay as a barrier as rapidly. Similarly, investing in foreclosing access to suppliers may yield a long-lasting barrier requiring little reinvestment. If a firm is unable to create lasting barriers or a credible long-term threat of retaliation, then little or no defensive investment in them is justified. A firm should invest instead in lowering the inducement to enter or it should harvest its position.

Clarity of the Message. A firm should select defensive tactics it is confident that potential challengers will detect as well as understand their implications. Competitors often differ in their understanding of industry economics and in their ability to perceive signals. Signals can be missed and the significance of some tactics misunderstood. Generally, tactics involving price, credit, advertising, sales force, and new products are particularly visible, while those involving indirect signals (e.g., announced capacity expansion), process changes, or raising exit and shrinkage barriers are often less visible.

The likelihood of a defensive tactic's being noticed and understood is a function not only of the tactic but also of the likely challengers. Competitors without a good cost system may not understand the impact of a defensive tactic on their cost positions. In addition, challengers' assumptions about the industry and about the firm will influence their interpretation of the firm's behavior.

Credibility. A firm should select defensive tactics that will be credible. Defensive tactics differ greatly in the degree to which a challenger will take them seriously. A defensive tactic that raises barriers will not be credible unless challengers view it as a permanent or long-lasting feature of competition. The credibility of a threat of retaliation rests on having resources to carry it out and a communicated resolve to do so.

Impact on Competitors' Goals. A firm should pick defensive tactics that have a measurable impact on the particular goals of its potential challengers. Since challengers' goals may vary, not all tactics may be equally effective. Defensive tactics that are effective against a competitor with a similar ownership structure to the firm, for example, may not be at all effective against a state-owned competitor. Similarly, challengers will differ in their sensitivity to start-up losses and short-term profits. Managers sometimes complain that they are attacked even though it is not "rational" to do so. Seemingly irrational attacks are often the result of a challenger having different goals. Defensive tactics should reflect challengers' goals, and not the firm's.

Other Structural Effects. A firm should select defensive tactics that have a positive or neutral influence on other elements of industry structure, and avoid those tactics that permanently erode industry structure. A new product generation that raises switching costs and encourages substitution, for example, is a better defensive tactic than a price cut that has the effect of increasing long-term buyer price sensitivity. Tactics that increase the perceived threat of retaliation sometimes have the undesirable side effect of creating rivalry pressures in an industry. Raising exit barriers, for example, can increase the risk of warfare among incumbents if they choose to follow. Leaders are particularly likely to influence industry structure through their defensive moves.

Defensive tactics may also hurt good competitors. Increases in advertising spending or price cuts can worsen the relative position of good competitors and compromise their ability to play the beneficial roles described in Chapter 6. Good competitors must perceive that defensive moves are not directed at them but at other challengers. Defensive strategy must not be set in a vacuum, then, but recognize its other structural effects.

Matching by Other Incumbents. Defensive tactics will usually have their greatest impact in defending against new entrants if they are imitated by other incumbents. Matching by other incumbents implies that a potential entrant cannot avoid the barriers created in defensive investments by attacking others in the industry. Smaller competitors may underinvest in defense and accept a free ride from the leaders, however. Efforts to prod other incumbents into matching a defensive move may well have a strategic advantage in industries where new entrants pose a greater threat than attacks by incumbents.

Defensive Strategy

Combined with an offensive strategy to increase a firm's competitive advantage, an explicit defensive strategy can raise the sustainability of whatever competitive advantages a firm possesses. The ideal of defensive strategy is usually *deterrence*—preventing a challenger from initiating a move in the first place or deflecting it to become less threatening. The other type of defensive strategy, *response,* is one in which the firm reacts to challenges as they occur. Response seeks to lower the challenger's objectives for a move once begun, or lead the challenger to rescind it altogether. In both deterrence and response, the principle is to alter a challenger's assessment of the attractiveness of a move.

Deterrence

The cost of deterrence is often less than the cost of fighting battles once a challenge has begun. A firm cannot deter challengers, however, unless it understands the nature of the threat. A maxim of defense in military strategy is that it is extremely costly to defend an entire perimeter against attack from any direction where the challenger may employ any weapon. The same principle applies in competitive strategy. A firm must determine which competitors and potential competitors are most dangerous, and the ways in which they might choose to behave. Only then can the appropriate defensive tactics be marshaled. Scenarios (Chapter 13) can be a useful device for examining the possibilities.

The important steps in deterrence can be summarized as follows:

1. *Thoroughly understand existing barriers.* A firm must have a clear understanding of what entry and mobility barriers it currently possesses, their specific sources, and how they might change. Is the firm protected by economies of scale? Where do these stem from in the value chain? Is access to channels difficult? What underlies this difficulty? What are the value activities that lead to differentiation? How sustainable are the sources of the firm's cost position and differentiation (Chapters 3 and 4)?

The height of existing barriers shapes the extent of the threat to a firm's position. If barriers are falling, for example, they must be rebuilt or replaced if the firm is to preserve profitability. The specific barriers present will also determine the types of strategies that challengers will employ, and the areas in which defensive tactics might prove most effective. A firm protected by high barriers to channel access, for example, is more likely to face competitors' attempts to create new channels than invasions of the existing ones. Conversely, a firm without scale or other sustainable cost barriers may be vulnerable to small, low-overhead competitors that are satisfied with what for the firm would be a poor return on investment. Challengers will usually try to find ways to sidestep existing barriers or somehow nullify them (see Chapter 15).

A firm must have precise knowledge of the specific sources of each barrier if it is to exploit them effectively. In residential roofing products, for example, a firm must recognize that economies of scale are driven primarily by regional scale due to high transport costs, the economics of production and sales force utilization, and regional differences in product mix. If a roofing products firm is satisfied in attributing its barriers only to scale but does not understand the specific sources of its scale barriers, it may mount the wrong defensive strategy.

2. *Anticipate the likely challengers.* A firm must anticipate the most likely challengers, whether they be potential entrants or competitors attempting to reposition themselves. Knowing who the likely challengers are is essential to focus and target defensive investments. The height of barriers and the impact of retaliation are also relative to who the likely challengers are, and not absolute. In motor oil, for example, the likely potential entrants facing Castrol, Quaker State, and other competitors are the oil majors. Given the resources of the majors, barriers such as capital and scale become less important than they would be if likely entrants were independents.

There are three questions to answer in anticipating likely challengers:

Which existing competitors are not satisfied? The most likely challengers will be existing competitors that are not satisfied with their current position. Competitors that consistently fail to meet their goals will be prone to attempt to reposition themselves. An assessment of competitors' assumptions, strategies, and capabilities should illuminate whether they are likely to reposition themselves in a way that threatens the firm. Good competitors (Chapter 6) pose a less serious threat of repositioning than bad competitors. Often the acquisition of a competitor by another firm will alter the competitor's goals, and may create a would-be challenger. In beer, for example, Miller's acquisition by Philip Morris was a precursor of an aggressive challenge of Anheuser-Busch.

Who are the most likely potential entrants? Determining the existing competitors that are most likely to reposition themselves is not easy, but anticipating likely potential entrants is often even more difficult. A way to identify potential entrants is to isolate those firms for which entry into the industry would represent a logical extension of their existing activities. The most common potential entrants tend to fall into the following categories:

- Regional competitors in other regions.
- Foreign firms not now operating in a country.
- Firms for which the industry would be backward or forward integration.
- Firms that can achieve tangible interrelationships, intangible interrelationships, or create blocking positions by entering the industry (see Chapter 9).

Regional firms often enter other regions or go national. This has been a popular strategy recently in the food industry. A number of major food companies such as Consolidated Foods and H. J. Heinz have acquired regional companies in order to take them national. Foreign entry into a country is also common as industries globalize—a contemporary example is the attack on Upjohn in the U.S. antiarthritic drug market by Boots Company, headquartered in Britain.

There are many forms of tangible interrelationships among businesses that represent a path for diversification into an industry, described in Chapter 9. The potential interrelationships leading to an industry should be traced to identify logical entrants. For example, entry into copiers was a logical extension of Kodak's chemical and optical expertise, and of Matsushita's office automation strategy.

The major challenge in identifying potential entrants is to avoid being trapped by conventional wisdom. Many companies overlook serious potential competitors such as foreign firms or related diversifiers by focusing too closely on traditional sources of new competitors such as regional firms or spinoffs. The list of most likely potential entrants may also shift as an industry evolves.[8]

Are there substitute competitors? In some industries, substitutes may be the most dangerous competitors, and thus should be the appropriate focal point for defensive strategy. Chapter 8 describes how to identify substitutes, and how threatening substitutes can be deterred.

[8]See *Competitive Strategy* Chapters 8 and 16, for further discussion of potential entrants and how they can change.

3. *Forecast likely avenues of attack.* The third step in formulating a strategy for deterrence is forecasting the likely avenues of attack. A firm must determine the best ways in which its position might be attacked so that it can focus its defensive investments on the most vulnerable areas. Every management team should ask itself the question, "Given what I know, how would I attack this firm if I were a competitor?"

The likely avenues of attack will be a function of the barriers to entry or mobility that are present, and how they might be changing. In the mustard industry, for example, Grey Poupon has increased advertising spending dramatically and attacked French's with a differentiation strategy. This was much more logical than a head-on price battle given French's scale-related advantages. The same sort of logic would suggest that SCM's portable typewriters were vulnerable to private labeling by Brother combined with new electronics technology, given SCM's channel and brand loyalty. U.S. farm equipment firms were more vulnerable in small tractors than in large tractors, where their U.S. base gave them volume advantages over Japanese firms.

The likely avenue of attack will also reflect the assumptions, strategies, and capabilities of likely challengers. Miller Beer stressed heavy advertising and market segmentation in the beer industry. This was not surprising given the intangible interrelationships present involving its parent, Philip Morris. Texas Instruments' ill-fated price cutting in personal computers was similarly predictable, given its traditional posture in semiconductors. Acquisition of second-tier competitors is a common way for potential entrants to challenge a firm, and this possibility must always be considered. In the truck business, for example, Daimler Benz acquired Freightliner (number six in the industry), Volvo acquired the truck operations of White Motor (number seven), and Renault formed a coalition with Mack.

4. *Choose defensive tactics to block the likely avenues of attack.* Effective deterrence requires that a firm block the challenger's likely avenues of attack. This requires choosing defensive tactics that raise structural barriers or increase expected retaliation that will be most cost-effective from those described. The appropriate mix of defensive tactics will vary from firm to firm, and must meet the tests outlined above. If a firm is most vulnerable to private labeling, for example, it may have to invest in a special private label model and signal its willingness to price-compete. In addition, the defensive tactics chosen must be targeted against the most likely challengers. It is particularly

important that defensive tactics reflect the actual goals of likely challengers and that they be noticed.

5. *Manage the firm's image as a tough defender.* In addition to investing in defense, a firm must clearly communicate its intentions to defend. A firm is continuously sending signals about its commitment to defend and must carefully manage the image it projects. Every public statement and every action in the marketplace must be weighed to determine the signals that will be sent. Ideally, a firm can achieve the image that Procter & Gamble (P&G) has. A poll of almost any group of managers, in and out of consumer goods, will show overwhelmingly that P&G is viewed as totally committed to defending share in its business. The fact that P&G has this image is not an accident, but the result of statements and actions over a long period of time.

6. *Set realistic profit expectations.* No defensive strategy can be effective unless a firm has realistic profit expectations. A firm's profit expectations must reflect the barriers it possesses and those that can be created through defensive investments. Often reducing profitability today will allow the firm to earn superior profits in the future.

Response

If deterrence fails, a firm must decide how to react to a challenger once an attack is under way. Deterrence cannot and should not try to reduce the chance of attack to zero. Doing so is usually too expensive and every possible challenge can rarely be anticipated. Hence responding to attacks effectively and in a timely way is an important part of defensive strategy.

Effective response is based on shifting a challenger's expectations. The whole arsenal of defensive tactics I have described can be employed to accomplish this, matched to the goals, assumptions, and capabilities of the particular challenger. For example, General Foods' Maxwell House has mounted a tough and effective defense against P&G, and no doubt caused P&G to reconsider its targets in the coffee industry. Aggressive pricing, advertising, and fighting brands have been employed to hold position and demonstrate General Foods' commitment. The vigor of the defense has meant that P&G is believed to be earning little return on its investment in the coffee business.

A number of important principles should guide response:

Respond in Some Way as Early as Possible. A firm must respond in some way to an attack as early as possible, because a challenger's exit barriers and commitment will grow as it meets its early targets and makes incremental investments. While a firm is often not in a position right away to completely counter an attack, making some immediate response is still important to holding the challenger's expectations in check. Even an inadequate holding action, such as increased advertising, may be necessary to keep a competitor from meeting its initial targets and thereby gaining the confidence necessary to increase its capital investment and raise its goals.

Invest in Early Discovery of Actual Moves. Given the advantages of responding early in the entry or repositioning process, the firm can gain substantial advantages in detecting actual moves of challengers very early. This can be facilitated through activities such as:

- Regular contact with raw material suppliers, equipment suppliers, and engineering firms to learn of orders or interest.
- Close contact with advertising media to detect purchases of advertising space.
- Monitoring of attendance at trade shows.
- Regular contact with the most adventurous buyers in the industry, who might be approached first by a new competitor or most prone to be seeking alternative sources.
- Monitoring of technical conferences, schools, and other places when technical people might be recruited.

Base the Response on the Reasons for the Attack. A firm must attempt to understand *why* a challenger is attacking, what its goals are, and what long-term strategy it has adopted. An attack based on desperation should be responded to differently than one emanating from parent company pressure on a business unit for growth. A challenger's goals and timetable must also be assessed, because good response requires that they be disrupted and ultimately modified. A good response also recognizes how one move by a challenger might fit into a longer term strategy.

Deflect Challengers in Addition to Trying to Stop Them. Part of the purpose of response is to make a move less threatening even if it cannot be stopped. It is often easier to get a challenger to focus or redirect its strategy than to withdraw it. A firm must identify ways in which a challenger's goals could be partially or completely met in less threatening ways and respond accordingly.

Take Every Challenger Seriously Enough. There is no such thing as a challenge that can be ignored. Every challenger must be analyzed for its motivations and capabilities. Even weak challengers have the potential of disrupting industry structure or damaging good competitors. Moreover, the response to less threatening competitors sends signals to more threatening ones. At the same time, however, a firm must avoid the tendency to overreact to a challenger. Response is costly, and must be directed at real and not imagined threats.

View Response as a Way to Gain Position. Response can often be used to gain position rather than just to stop a competitor. A battle between strong competitors often hurts weaker competitors more than the strong competitors hurt each other, as has been the case in soft drinks and beer. Moreover, an attack by a competitor in one segment may open that competitor to vulnerabilities in another segment that can be exploited.

Response to Price Cutting

Price cutting is among the most difficult forms of attack to counter, due to its rapid effect on profitability and the risk of an irreversible downward price spiral. Thus a firm must be particularly careful in how it responds to price cutting. Some additional issues may be useful to consider in responding to a price cut in addition to those discussed above:

Reasons for Competitor Price Cutting. A competitor may be price-cutting out of necessity to raise cash in the short term, or as part of a long-term campaign to increase share. It might also be price-cutting because it does not understand its costs and thinks it is pricing to achieve a fair return. Worse yet, the competitor may be price-cutting because it enjoys significantly lower costs. The correct response to price cutting will be very different depending on the reason underlying it. Therefore, the reason must be diagnosed as rapidly and accurately as possible.

Willingness To Do Battle. Price cutting by a competitor often rests on the assumption that a firm will not react aggressively, but will maintain a price umbrella in the hope of preserving profits. Early and vigorous response is thus often necessary if price cutting is to be contained. The response need not always be a corresponding price cut, but it must be something besides hoping the price cutter will go away. A firm must convince a price cutter that mixed motives will not paralyze it.

Localized Response. Often the response to price cutting can and should be localized to particularly vulnerable buyers, or to product varieties where differentiation is lowest, and not involve across-the-board actions. Localizing the response reduces its cost.

Cross Parry. Price cutting may be contained or eliminated if the firm immediately attacks (with price and other moves) the price cutter's key buyers or product lines. Similarly, price cutting can sometimes be stopped if blocking positions in other industries are employed to respond. The principle is to demonstrate that the price cutter has more to lose from initiating a price war than it is likely to gain.

Cut Price in Other Ways. Sometimes prices can be effectively reduced to respond to a price cutter through providing free service, discounting ancillary equipment, or other means that are easier to reverse than a price cut itself. Also, indirect price cuts may be more susceptible to localization, and less easy for competitors to match. Failing indirect price cuts, rebates or other special discounts may be less difficult to reverse later than reductions in list prices.

Create or Employ "Special" Products. Price cutting can sometimes be met more effectively with fighting brands or stripped-down products (e.g. no free service), than by lowering the price of the primary product line. The buyer can be offered a low price on special products, but reminded that they are inferior to the firm's normal offering.

Defense or Disinvest

In many industries, defensive investments yield a high return. However, a firm should *optimize* rather than maximize its investment in defense. In some industries, defensive investment is not appropriate at all, or is only appropriate as a temporary delaying action. This is true where a firm's position is not ultimately sustainable. In such industries, the best defensive strategy is to "take the money and run." This means that the firm generates as much cash as possible, knowing that entry or repositioning will ultimately erode its position. Part of such a strategy may sometimes be to *encourage* the entry of competitors to boost the growth rate of the market while harvesting takes place.

The conditions that suggest that disinvestment is preferable to investing in defense are as follows:

- low barriers, or falling barriers as the industry evolves
- little opportunity to create barriers
- potential entrants and existing competitors with superior resources
- competitors with low return-on-investment targets or other characteristics of a bad competitor

Pitfalls in Defense

There are many pitfalls in defending position. Even strongly positioned leaders are regularly attacked successfully because they make errors in defensive strategy. The single biggest pitfall in defense is a narrow concern with short-term profitability, which conflicts with the reality that defense requires investment. Internal decision-making processes in many firms are biased against defensive investments. They reward short-term profitability, and fail to reward the reduction of risk that defensive strategy seeks. The benefits of a successful defensive strategy are often hard to measure, since a successful defense means that nothing happens.

The second largest pitfall in defensive strategy is complacency. Firms often do not examine their environment for potential challengers, or seriously consider the possibility that challenge will occur. As a result, it is striking how often firms fail to make simple and inexpensive defensive moves. Moreover, firms often actually invite competitors into their industry by earning unsustainable margins or by ignoring buyer needs. A number of the other pitfalls in defensive strategy will become apparent when I discuss the principles of gaining competitive position in the next chapter.

15

Attacking an Industry Leader

When is a leader vulnerable? The market share and profitability of leaders can be inviting to a firm contemplating entry or repositioning in an industry. Yet industry leaders usually enjoy some advantages in defending themselves, such as reputation, economies of scale, cumulative learning, and preferred access to suppliers or channels. Moreover, most leaders are committed to their industry and possess the resources for protracted and damaging retaliation against challengers. A firm thus confronts a formidable and risky task in seeking to gain market position against a leader.

However, leaders are often vulnerable. NIKE deposed ADIDAS in athletic shoes. Stouffer's overcame Banquet and Swanson in frozen dinners. While successful strategies differ widely from industry to industry, a common thread runs through them. They all seek to nullify the competitive advantages of the leader, while avoiding full-scale retaliation. Though industry structural change sometimes is what makes a leader vulnerable, a follower or potential entrant that can understand the existing structure better may be able to overtake a leader as well.

This chapter draws on the entire book to present a framework for identifying vulnerable industry leaders, and for developing strategies to attack leaders successfully. I take the point of view of a challenger—a follower in the leader's industry or a firm contemplating entry. The chapter identifies the stringent conditions that must be satisfied in order for a challenger to attack a leader successfully. Next, I describe the types of strategies that challengers can employ against leaders, ranging from those that attempt to shift the basis of competition to those that exploit a leader's inflexibility. I also describe the characteristics of industries and leaders that signal a leader's vulnerability. The chapter concludes with a discussion of some common pitfalls in attacking leaders.

While every chapter in this book has provided suggestions for offensive strategy, the difficult task of attacking a leader successfully is a way of drawing them together. Though the chapter is framed in terms of attacking leaders, the same principles apply in choosing an offensive strategy against any competitor. Moreover, industry leaders can employ these same concepts to understand their own vulnerabilities and to develop defensive strategies more effectively.

Conditions for Attacking a Leader

The cardinal rule in offensive strategy is not to attack head-on with an imitative strategy, regardless of the challenger's resources or staying power. The built-in advantages inherent in a leader's position will usually overcome such a challenge and the leader will in all likelihood retaliate vigorously. The ensuing battle will almost inevitably exhaust the challenger's resources before those of the leader.

Procter & Gamble (P&G) has violated this rule in the coffee industry in challenging General Foods' Maxwell House brand. In coffee, unlike many of its other products, P&G's Folger's has little or no product superiority over Maxwell House. P&G also produces and markets Folger's using the same value chain as General Foods. Maxwell House has retaliated vigorously with a broad array of defensive tactics, benefitting from its large market share and favorable cost position. Folger's has gained some share, primarily at the expense of smaller competitors, but has yet to achieve acceptable profitability. Maxwell House, conversely, has maintained its profitability and continues to resist Folger's attempt to gain share successfully.

Coca-Cola's sale of its wine operations, called the Wine Spectrum, to Seagrams is still another manifestation of violating the rules for attacking leaders. While Coke gained market share against second-tier competitors in the wine industry, it faced a substantial cost disadvantage to Gallo (see Chapter 3) and had no innovative approach in product or marketing to counteract it, only heavy spending. Gallo's strong resistance to Coke meant that Coke never earned acceptable profits in wine. IBM has faced similar difficulties in copiers. It has achieved little differentiation or cost advantage and faces stiff resistance from Xerox and Kodak in medium- and high-volume copiers.

Successfully attacking a leader requires that a challenger meet three basic conditions:

1. *A sustainable competitive advantage.* A challenger must possess a clear and sustainable competitive advantage over the leader, in either cost or differentiation. If the advantage is low cost, the firm can cut price to gain position against a leader, or earn higher margins at industry average prices to allow reinvestment in marketing or technology development. Both will allow a challenger to gain share. Alternatively, if the firm achieves differentiation, it will allow premium prices and/or minimize the cost of marketing or gaining trial against the leader. Either source of competitive advantage the challenger possesses must be sustainable, using the criteria for sustainability in Chapters 3 and 4. Sustainability ensures that the challenger will have a sufficiently long period to close the market share gap before the leader can imitate.

2. *Proximity in other activities.* A challenger must have some way of partly or wholly neutralizing the leader's other inherent advantages. If the challenger employs a differentiation strategy, it must also partially offset the leader's natural cost advantage due to scale, first mover advantages, or other causes. Unless a challenger maintains cost proximity, the leader will use its cost advantage to neutralize (or leapfrog) the challenger's differentiation. Similarly, if the challenger bases its attack on a cost advantage, it must create an acceptable amount of value for the buyer. Otherwise, the leader will be able to sustain a price premium over the challenger, yielding the leader the gross margin needed to retaliate vigorously.

3. *Some impediment to leader retaliation.* A challenger must also possess some means for blunting the leader's retaliation. The leader must be disinclined or constrained from protracted retaliation against the challenger, either because of the leader's own circumstances or because of the strategy chosen by the challenger. Without some impedi-

ment to retaliation, an attack will trigger a response by the leader that can overwhelm a challenger despite its competitive advantage. A committed leader with resources and an entrenched position can, through aggressive retaliation, force a challenger to bear unacceptable economic and organizational costs.

The three conditions for successfully attacking a leader flow directly from the principles of competitive advantage described in Chapter 1. The odds of success in gaining position increase with the challenger's ability to meet each condition. P&G's Folger's coffee, Coca Cola's Wine Spectrum, and IBM copiers did not decisively meet any of the conditions, and this explains their disappointing experiences.

The difficulty of meeting the three conditions hinges largely on a leader's strategy and its aggressiveness. If a leader is "stuck in the middle" with no competitive advantage, a challenger can often achieve a competitive advantage in either cost or differentiation quite easily. In these instances, a challenger need only recognize the leader's vulnerability and implement a strategy that exploits it. On the other hand, attacking a leader that is aggressively pursuing a cost leadership or differentiation strategy will usually require that a challenger conceive of a major strategic innovation, such as developing a new value chain, if it is to mount a successful challenge.

An example of an industry in which challengers met all three conditions was corn wet milling. Cargill and Archer-Daniels-Midland (ADM) successfully entered against CPC International, A. E. Staley, and Standard Brands, the traditional industry leaders. Cargill and ADM entered the industry with new continuous process plants that embodied recent changes in process technology. They also restricted themselves to a narrow product line, consisting only of higher-volume items, and reduced overhead through streamlined sales forces. These choices allowed Cargill and ADM to gain a significant cost advantage over traditional producers. At the same time, Cargill and ADM achieved parity or proximity in differentiation, despite the efforts at differentiation by the industry leaders. The product itself is a commodity and many buyers did not value extensive service. In addition, several factors impeded retaliation by the traditional industry leaders. They preferred not to retaliate against the challengers for fear of upsetting the industry equilibrium, where rivalry in the industry had traditionally been characterized as a gentlemen's club. At the same time, CPC (the number one firm) and Standard Brands had embarked on diversification programs, diverting attention and resources from corn milling.

While the corn milling example illustrates a situation where challengers met all three conditions, meeting one condition very well can offset a challenger's inability to meet another. The successful entry of "no frills" airlines such as People Express and Southwest provides a case where challengers met two conditions strongly enough to offset barely meeting the third. Chapter 3 has described how the no-frills carriers achieved a significant cost advantage over the trunks by employing a different value chain. At the same time, many passengers perceived the no-frills carriers' product as similar to that offered by trunks, since differentiation in airline transportation is difficult. However, the no-frills carriers faced a major threat of retaliation by the trunks as the trunks sought to defend their market share. Though the trunks hesitated to retaliate because of the high cost of cutting prices and the fear of eroding their quality images, the threat posed by the no-frills carriers was so great that retaliation eventually occurred. Though the no-frills carriers enjoyed only a relatively short period free of retaliation, their significant cost advantage greatly increased the cost of retaliation for the trunks. Many trunks never attempted to match the prices of the no-frills carriers.

Federal Express's successful entry against Emery Air Freight provides another illustration of a challenger using a strong advantage in one area to offset a leader's lingering strengths. Federal Express's unique delivery system, utilizing its own planes and a Memphis hub, quickly gave it differentiation in overnight delivery of small packages. It achieved higher reliability as well as other forms of differentiation, described in Chapter 4. While Federal Express would ultimately achieve cost parity or even a cost advantage, however, the greater scale sensitivity of its value chain meant that its initial cost position was high relative to Emery's. This cost disadvantage and Federal's heavy debt load made it initially very vulnerable to retaliation. Emery, however, did not take Federal Express seriously. It chose not to retaliate until Federal Express had gained enough share to establish cost proximity. As the Federal Express example illustrates, slow retaliation by the leader buys a challenger time (and resources) to overcome disadvantages in cost or differentiation. The principle of responding quickly, described in Chapter 14, proves once again important in determining a leader's ability to defend position.

Avenues for Attacking Leaders

Successfully attacking a leader always requires some kind of strategic insight. A challenger must usually find a *different* strategy in order to neutralize the leader's natural advantages, and recognize or create impediments to leader retaliation. While the strategies that have succeeded against leaders differ widely from industry to industry, three avenues of attack emerge as possible:

- *Reconfiguration.* A challenger innovates in the way it performs activities in the value chain or in the configuration of the entire chain.
- *Redefinition.* A challenger redefines its competitive scope compared to the leader.
- *Pure spending.* A challenger buys market position through superior resources or greater willingness to invest, out of which competitive advantage grows.

Each of the three avenues changes the rules of competition in an industry to offset a leader's advantages and allow the challenger to gain a cost or differentiation advantage of its own. The three avenues are *not* mutually exclusive and have been successfully pursued in tandem. Redefinition of scope usually requires parallel reconfiguration of the value chain, for example. Employing more than one of these avenues of attack generally raises the odds of success in attacking a leader. The three avenues are displayed in Figure 15–1.

The avenues of attacking a leader differ along two important dimensions that are represented in Figure 15–1: the configuration of the challenger's value chain compared to the leader and the competitive

		CONFIGURATION OF THE VALUE CHAIN		
		Same Chain as Leader	New Activities	New Chain
COMPETITIVE SCOPE	Same as Leader	**Pure Spending**	**Reconfiguration**	**Reconfiguration**
	Different from Leader	**Redefinition**	**Reconfiguration and Redefinition**	**Reconfiguration and Redefinition**

Figure 15–1. Avenues for Attacking Leaders

scope of the challenger compared to the leader's. A challenger can employ the same value chain or one in which it has reconfigured individual activities or the entire chain. At the same time, a challenger may compete with the same scope of activities as the leader or for a wider or narrower scope. As described in Chapter 2, scope encompasses segment scope within the industry, degree of integration, geographic scope and industry scope, or the range of industries in which the firm competes with a coordinated strategy.

Pure reconfiguration involves reconfigured activities or ultimately a significantly different value chain, though with the same scope as the leader. Pure redefinition involves a different scope but the same basic value chain for competing. Reconfiguration and redefinition combines both a new chain and a different scope. Pure spending neither reconfigures the value chain nor redefines scope, but relies on greater investment by the challenger to lead to competitive advantage.

Reconfiguration

Reconfiguration allows a challenger to compete differently though it is competing with the same scope of activities as the leader. The challenger performs individual value activities differently or reconfigures the entire chain to either lower cost or enhance differentiation. Reconfiguration of the value chain must be sustainable against imitation if it is to serve as the basis for attacking leaders. Sustainability comes from first-mover advantages and the other sources described in Chapters 3 and 4.[1]

The ways in which reconfiguration leads to competitive advantage have been discussed throughout this book, and can involve any activity in the value chain. Chapters 3 and 4 described in detail how reconfiguring the value chain can lead to cost advantage or differentiation. In wine, for example, Chapter 3 described how Gallo was able to achieve a significant cost advantage through reconfiguring value activities in procurement, blending, bottling, logistics and marketing compared to competitors. In frozen entrees, similarly, Chapter 4 described how Stouffer's reconfigured marketing, technology developments, procurements, and broker relations to achieve and sustain differentiation.

[1]Yip's (1982) discussion of how firms can find "gateways" to entry shows how leaders can be vulnerable. Yip describes how innovations in technology development and marketing can allow entrants to overcome incumbents.

The more value activities that can be reconfigured, the greater the possibility will usually be that the challenger's competitive advantage over the leader is sustainable. Reconfiguring the entire chain, as in the no-frills airline and Iowa Beef examples described earlier in the book, is usually the most potent source of advantage against leaders who are often highly committed to the traditional industry value chain.

Some illustrative examples of reconfigurations that have been the basis of successful attacks on leaders are the following:

Product Changes. A challenger can attack a leader through changing the product.

SUPERIOR PRODUCT PERFORMANCE OR FEATURES. Products with attributes that are valuable to buyers grow out of an understanding of the buyer's value chain (Chapter 4). P&G's Charmin bathroom tissue was softer and more absorbent than Scott Paper's product, which allowed P&G to emerge as a leader. Similarly, CooperVision's and Barnes-Hind/Hydrocurve's (a Revlon division) extended-wear soft contact lenses provided the vehicle for attacking Bausch and Lomb.

LOW-COST PRODUCT DESIGN. Chapter 3 describes how product design can affect relative cost position. Canon's NP200 copier, using toner projection development technology, required many fewer parts than competitors' machines. This low-cost design allowed Canon to improve position significantly in small plain paper copiers.

Outbound Logistics and Service Changes. A challenger can attack a leader through changing such things as product support, after-sale service, order processing, or physical distribution.

MORE EFFICIENT LOGISTICAL SYSTEM. Chapter 3 described how opportunities to improve relative cost position in the logistical system can be analyzed. Relative cost position can sometimes be significantly reduced by reconfiguring its value activities as Federal Express did.

MORE RESPONSIVE AFTER-SALE SUPPORT. Chapter 4 showed how to assess the parameters of service that are most valuable to buyers. A challenger can create differentiation if it reconfigures the value chain to make it more responsive in terms of response to buyer inquiries, documentation, etc. Vetco, for example, a division of Combustion Engineering that sells offshore oil drilling equipment, has gained position significantly through providing excellent training materials and other after-sale support to help its buyers master the complex underwater drilling task.

ENHANCED ORDER PROCESSING. Chapter 4 described how possible enhancements to the delivery system can be identified and evaluated, and create differentiation. Enhancements include such things as performing new functions like controlling buyer inventory—this, in effect, takes over activities in the buyer's value chain. Several wholesaling firms, for example, have created differentiation by allowing on-line ordering to take over inventory management for their retail customers. McKesson, for example, has substantially improved its position through its 3PM order processing system for distributing pharmaceuticals. The system allows pharmacists to order directly and provides them other valuable information.

Marketing Changes. Challengers have employed innovations in marketing value activities to launch successful attacks against leaders in many industries. Some of the most common innovations include:

INCREASED SPENDING IN AN UNDERMARKETED INDUSTRY. Challengers can attack a leader by escalating marketing spending. In mustard, frozen entrees, and frozen potatoes, for example, Grey Poupon, Stouffer's, and Ore-Ida respectively have succeeded or are now undertaking to raise the traditional rates of advertising spending. Higher spending levels allow firms to signal value better, gaining high levels of brand recognition and premium prices.

NEW POSITIONING. A challenger can conceive of a new way to position a product in order to attack a leader. Stouffer's repositioning of frozen entrees as a gourmet item was one of the key elements of its ascendancy, as discussed in Chapter 4.

NEW TYPE OF SALES ORGANIZATION. A new type of sales organization, perhaps with a different type of salesperson, can sometimes be the basis of a successful attack on a leader. Crown Cork and Seal's technically proficient sales force, reorganized to sell the complete line of Crown's cans, bottle caps, and packaging machinery to canners, was one of the reasons for Crown's success against American Can and Continental Can.

Operations Changes. Changes in operation's value activities that lower costs or enhance differentiation have provided the basis for many successful attacks on leaders. As was discussed in Chapter 3, Iowa Beef pioneered an entirely new value chain in meat packing. Cargill and ADM employed new continuous process plants to enter corn wet milling. A modified production process that enhanced quality also contributed to Ore-Ida's success in frozen potatoes. Sometimes entirely new technologies emerge that change the process, or a subtechnology changes that allows an old process technology to be re-invigorated (Chapter 5).

Downstream Reconfiguration. Employing channels neglected by the leader or preemptively concentrating on emerging channels have served as avenues of attack against industry leaders. Some examples of downstream innovations include:

PIONEER A NEW CHANNEL. Timex opened up the drug store and mass merchandisers as channels for watches in the 1950s, allowing it to gain a leadership position in the industry despite the entrenched position of Bulova and the Swiss watchmakers. The traditional leaders had employed the jewelry store channel.

PREEMPT AN EMERGING CHANNEL. Richardson-Vicks pioneered the sale of quality skin care products in supermarkets with its Oil of Olay product line. Supermarkets were an emerging channel for this type of product, and Richardson-Vicks gained substantial first-mover advantages that have allowed Oil of Olay to remain a leader.

GO DIRECT. YKK, the Japanese zipper company, took on Talon successfully by bypassing wholesalers and selling directly to apparel companies.

The most successful attacks on leaders often involve *more than one innovation* in the value chain. Stouffer's combined a product change with several significant marketing innovations. Cargill and ADM combined a process change with product line and marketing changes. Timex combined a new channel with low-cost manufacturing technology and unprecedented TV advertising. Competitive advantage that is sustainable usually stems from multiple sources, as Chapters 3 and 4 have illustrated.

Structural changes often create the opportunity for reconfiguring of the value chain. Timex's attack on the Swiss exploited the emergence of TV and mass distribution channels, in addition to wartime improvements in manufacturing technology. At the same time, growth in buyer income and shifting attitudes made a watch a product purchased for everyday use. In many industries, however, reconfiguration hinges on rethinking what has been done rather than exploiting external changes. Ultimately, however, reconfiguring the value chain is a creative act that is difficult to achieve routinely or predictably. Industry analysis, value chain analysis, technology analysis, industry scenarios, and other concepts in this book can help identify possibilities for reconfiguration.

Redefinition

The second broad avenue for attacking a leader rests on redefining the scope of competition. Broadening scope may allow the achievement of interrelationships or the benefits of integration, while narrowing scope can allow the tailoring of the value chain to a particular target. As I have discussed extensively in earlier chapters, particularly Chapters 2, 7, 9, and 12, the scope of a firm's activities can greatly influence competitive advantage. A challenger can change competitive scope in four ways which reflect the four types of scope. These four modes of redefinition are not mutually exclusive:

- *Focus within the Industry.* Narrowing the basis of competition to a segment rather than across the board.
- *Integration or De-integration.* Widening or narrowing the range of activities performed in-house.
- *Geographic Redefinition.* Broadening the basis of competition from a region or country to worldwide, or vice versa.
- *Horizontal Strategy.* Broadening the basis of competition from a single industry to related industries.

Focus

Successful focus strategies against leaders have taken all the forms described in Chapter 7:

- *Buyer focus.* Motel firms such as La Quinta have focused on middle-level business travellers and created a new low-cost value chain to meet their particular needs.

- *Product focus.* Canon, Ricoh, and Savin focused on small, plain paper copiers to challenge Xerox.
- *Channel focus.* Stihl focused on serving buyers only through servicing dealers to succeed against Homelite and McCulloch in chain saws.

A focus strategy often has the advantage of being difficult for a leader to retaliate against without compromising its own strategy. This delays leader retaliation until the challenger has gained a secure foothold in the industry. In addition, focus strategies to attack leaders can serve as part of *sequencing* strategies.[2] In a sequencing strategy, the challenger initially attacks a leader through focus, and then broadens its scope over time to compete across-the-board with the leader. Japanese producers have employed this strategy in such industries as TV sets and motorcycles. In each instance, they began at the low end of the product range and gradually broadened their lines. NIKE also used this approach against ADIDAS in running shoes, beginning with a focus on the premium segment and then leveraging the reputation gained there to broaden its line downward. Sequencing strategies rest on the presence of segment interrelationships (Chapter 7) that allow a firm in one segment to gain competitive advantages in others. Sequencing has the added advantage of not provoking the leader to retaliate early in the process.

Integration or De-integration

A challenger may employ integration or deintegration as a means of attacking a leader. Backward or forward integration can sometimes lower cost or enhance differentiation.[3] In the wine industry, for example, Gallo's integration in bottles is an important part of its cost advantage. Migros, the leading Swiss food retailer, owes a part of its dramatic ascendancy in its industry to backward integration into products and packaging. Changing circumstances may also make deintegration a means of gaining competitive advantage against a leader who is integrated.

[2]Sequenced entry strategies are described in *Competitive Strategy,* Chapter 16. Sequenced repositioning employs the same principles.
[3]See *Competitive Strategy,* Chapter 14.

Geographic Redefinition

A leader operating in one or a few countries may sometimes be attacked successfully with a regional or global strategy.[4] The challenger widens the geographic boundaries of the market to gain cost or differentiation advantages through geographic interrelationships. A global strategy, that integrates and coordinates value activities in many countries, may allow economies of scale in production or product development, create the ability to serve worldwide buyers better, and other advantages I have described elsewhere. Globalization of an industry has been an important part of successful strategies of challengers in such industries as autos (Toyota and Nissan versus General Motors), motorcycles, lift trucks, TV sets, and various types of medical equipment.

Where an industry is multidomestic, however, local country differences imply that a global strategy is counterproductive. Here a leader with a global strategy is vulnerable to a challenger who tailors its strategy on a country-by-country basis. Castrol has been successful in automotive motor oil with such an approach. Even within global industries there may also be segments where a country-centered strategy can be sustainable though other segments require a global strategy. In both cases, de-globalization can be the route to attacking a leader.

In many industries, firms have concentrated on a particular city or area of a country to succeed against national or even global competitors. Where competitors are local, however, competitive advantage may come from taking a national approach. Gannett's *USA Today* is attempting this in newspapers.

Horizontal Strategy

Challengers may exploit interrelationships among business units as another means of broadening the scope of competition. As Chapters 9 and 10 discussed in detail, interrelationships may lead to a competitive advantage for a firm operating in related industries. A challenger with a horizontal strategy encompassing related industries may successfully attack a leader operating in a narrower or different range of industries. In personal computers, for example, IBM exploited interrelationships with its other business units to overwhelm early leaders

[4]The competitive advantages of a global strategy and the circumstances where global strategies are appropriate are discussed in *Competitive Strategy,* Chapter 13, and in Porter (1985).

such as Apple and Tandy. Interrelationships also serve as a possible substitute for market share in any one industry and neutralize a leader's competitive advantage.

A particular form of interrelationship, complementary products, has been discussed in Chapter 12. Bundling can create competitive advantage in some industries, while unbundling can do so in others. Merrill Lynch's CMA, a bundled product combining previously separate financial services, allowed Merrill to gain significantly vis-à-vis other broad line financial services firms.

Multiple Redefinitions

The four modes of redefinition are not mutually exclusive. A challenger can globalize its strategy and pursue interrelationships at the same time, as Matsushita has done in consumer electronics. Matsushita employs shared manufacturing, distribution channels, and other value activities across its many consumer electronics products. It also integrates and coordinates its strategy worldwide. The strategy has overwhelmed single-product, single-country competitors.

A challenger can also combine narrow scope in one dimension with broad scope in another. A challenger can attack a leader by focusing on a segment (scope within an industry) at the same time as it competes globally (geographic scope). A firm may also focus within an industry but exploit interrelationships with related industries, another example of combining broad and narrow scope. Redefining competitive scope simultaneously in several ways has proven to be a powerful source of competitive advantage, because the competitive advantage from each redefinition cumulates.

The scope diagrams in Figure 15–2 illustrate several dimensions of scope schematically. They suggest how challengers should examine each dimension of scope to see if it might be a means of attacking a leader. A leader's scope is plotted, and then alternative redefinitions (narrower or broader or both) are probed to see if they might create a significant competitive advantage for a challenger. The top diagram, for example, represents the situation in automobiles in the 1970's. General Motors (GM) competed with a broadly targeted strategy involving a full range of models. While GM competed internationally as well as in the U.S., its strategy was essentially country-centered and global coordination was minimal. Toyota and Nissan chose to focus instead on small cars, and employed coordinated global strategies. They gained a substantial competitive advantage over GM in the process.

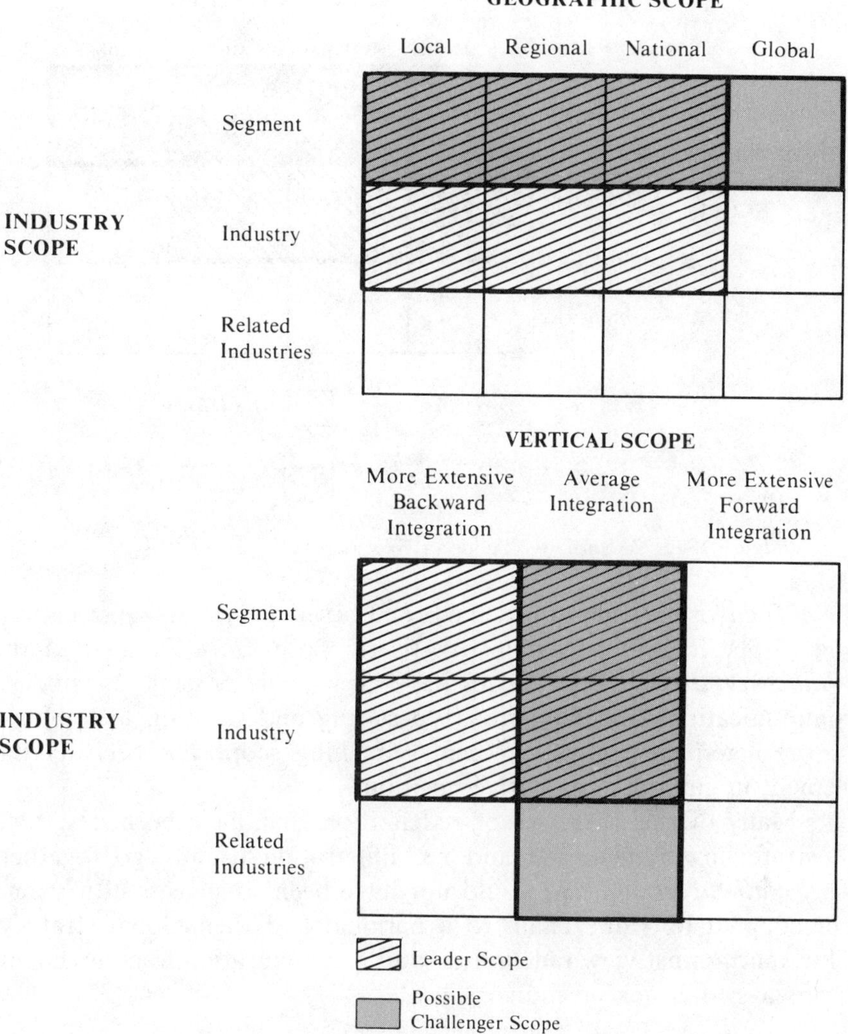

Figure 15–2. Alternate Scope of Leader and Challenger Strategies

Figure 15–3 uses the scope diagram to illustrate the pattern of competition in the U.S. newspaper industry. The traditional strategy in the industry has been to serve a single city with a broad range of news, even though a number of city papers might be part of the same chain. The *Wall Street Journal* and to a lesser extent the *New York Times* have adopted national strategies aimed at segments of the market. The *Wall Street Journal* has recently embarked on a partial global strategy involving European and Asian editions. At the same time,

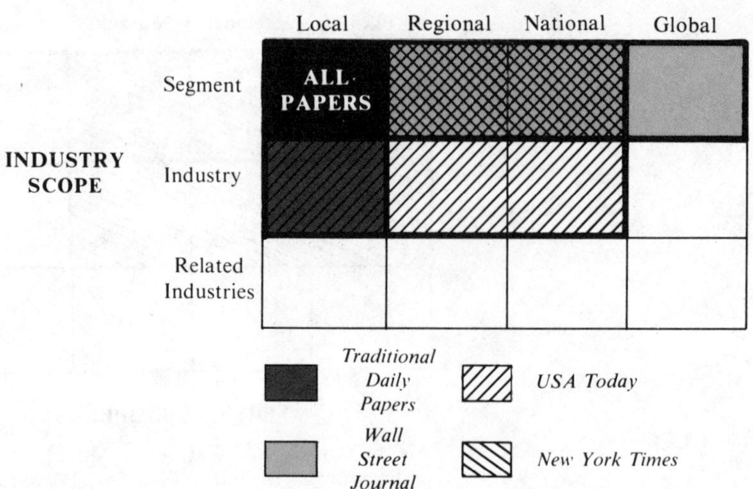

Figure 15–3. Alternative Scope in Newspapers

USA Today is an attempt to sell a broad-based daily newspaper nationwide, appealing to national advertisers. Both *USA Today* and the *Wall Street Journal*'s strategies have been made possible by modern communications and computer typesetting and printing technology. In the newspaper industry, then, redefining scope has been a vital element in gaining competitive position.

Many of the examples of redefinition that have been described illustrate how redefinition and reconfiguration usually go together. The *Wall Street Journal* would not have been so successful if it had not adapted its value chain to a national and then global strategy. Thus a firm must view redefinition and reconfiguration as complementary ways to attack an industry leader.

Pure Spending

The final and riskiest way to attack a leader is through pure spending, without reconfiguration or redefinition. Pure spending involves investment to buy market share, cumulative volume, or brand identification through low pricing, heavy advertising, and so on. By making sufficient investment, a challenger seeks to gain enough market share, volume, or reputation to take the lead in relative cost position or differentiation. The challenger does not do anything differently or better than the leader, but simply overwhelms the leader with resources or with a greater willingness to invest.

This approach to offsetting a leader's advantage is often costly and frequently fails. Leaders typically have sufficient financial resources to counteract such a strategy, when coupled with their advantages in cost or differentiation. Leaders also are usually commited enough to be willing to spend heavily to defend position. A particularly vivid example of the risks of pure spending is the diversification of oil companies into fertilizer and chemicals. Despite enormous financial resources, their lack of a competitive advantage gained through reconfiguration or redefinition has led to a generally dismal track record.

The success of pure spending rests on superior access to financial resources by the challenger, or on unwillingness by the leader to invest in the industry. Even a well-financed leader may be complacent, have a higher hurdle rate, have other priorities, or be under corporate pressure to generate cash. Pure spending has proven most successful in industries where leaders are small and undercapitalized. These leaders may not be able to afford to mount sufficient retaliation to discourage the challenger, despite possessing a competitive advantage.

Pure spending, by itself, remains the least preferred approach for attacking leaders. However, superior willingness to invest is often an important supplement to strategies based on reconfiguration or redefinition. In cans, for example, Crown Cork invested heavily while American and Continental were harvesting, accelerating the process by which Crown gained a cost advantage through having more modern equipment.

Alliances To Attack Leaders

A challenger may need to form an alliance to obtain the necessary resources, technology, market access, or other strengths to attack an industry leader. Alliances can be a *means* of achieving reconfiguration, redefinition or pure spending, though in-and-of-themselves they are no guarantee of success. Alliances of various types have played important roles in many successful attacks against leaders. The two broad forms of alliances are the following:

- *Acquisition.* A firm either acquires another firm (or firms) or is itself acquired.
- *Coalitions.* A firm joins forces with another firm without out-

right merger, through such means as licensing, joint ventures, and supply agreements.[5]

Acquisitions provide a way to broaden a firm's scope through adding positions in new segments, positions in new geographic areas, greater integration, or a beachhead in a new related industry. IVECO, which merged a number of European truck builders, has produced a greatly strengthened competitor. Acquisitions can also play a key role in reconfiguration or pure spending strategies. Acquisitions can allow two organizations to combine resources and skills in such a way that reconfiguration or pure spending is possible.

Coalitions also bring together skills and resources of firms in ways that may allow reconfiguration, redefinition, or pure spending. Japanese TV set producers licensed RCA's color TV technology, providing an important starting point for their own product and process innovations, for example. Similarly, the coalition that led to Airbus Industries has made a world-class competitor out of a group of struggling national firms. Coalitions are also frequently pursued in tandem with a firm's own activities to broaden scope. In the valve industry, for example, WKM sells only in the U.S. and uses licensees elsewhere in the world.

Coalitions can also play a more subtle role in attacking leaders. Challengers sometimes form coalitions with leaders that later provide the basis for attacking the leader, as discussed in Chapter 5. Licensing technology from a leader, or joint ventures in marketing or manufacturing, may allow a challenger to learn a leader's strengths, making it possible to leapfrog. A number of Japanese firms have licensed foreign technology from leaders which they later improved.

Acquisitions and coalitions are not without their problems, however. Acquisitions are difficult to integrate, and coordination among coalition partners can prove troublesome. In copiers, for example, Canon has benefitted from the problems Xerox has had in coordinating with its joint venture partners Rank Xerox and, through Rank Xerox, Fuji Xerox. Canon's greater global coordination leads to some of its competitive advantages.

Impediments to Leader Retaliation

A successful challenger must also discover or create impediments to leader retaliation. This serves to blunt the natural advantages of

[5]See the chapter on coalitions in Porter (1985).

the leader and reduces the cost of mounting an attack. A variety of factors can inhibit a leader's retaliation to a challenger:[6]

Mixed Motives. If a challenger's strategy creates mixed motives for a leader, it will inhibit the leader's ability to retaliate. A leader that must undermine its past strategy to match or respond to the challenger faces mixed motives. A leader that has built its competitive advantage on service, for example, will invalidate its hard-won reputation by responding to a challenger's strategy that makes service unnecessary. The leader may choose instead to maintain its past strategy and suffer a market share loss. Another case is provided by the introduction of the low-priced, throw-away pen by BIC Corporation, which created mixed motives for Gillette's Papermate division. Papermate had patiently developed a brand image of quality. Matching the BIC strategy would undermine this image, and Papermate ultimately had to introduce an entirely new brand (Write Brothers) to counter BIC.

Any interrelationships between the leader and other business units in its parent company may also serve as the basis for mixed motives, because interrelationships can involve a cost of inflexibility (Chapter 9). Interrelationships can constrain the way a leader can respond without hurting its sister business units. Mixed motives can also arise when a leader is employing a bundled strategy, as described in Chapter 12. A leader may allow a challenger to gain a modest share rather than unbundle and thereby cause the entire industry to unbundle.

High Leader Response Costs. A leader may refrain from retaliation if the challenger's strategy inflicts high response costs on the leader. A leader's large market share may inhibit it from costly retaliatory actions such as across-the-board price cuts and warranty increases, for example. Response costs can also be high when a leader has inappropriate or outdated facilities, equipment, or labor contracts. Chapter 14 has discussed how the cost of defensive tactics can be assessed.

Different Financial Priorities. A leader with different financial priorities may not respond to a challenger's attack. A leader emphasizing short-term profits, for example, will give up share to a challenger willing to forgo them. Similarly, a leader desiring high cash flow may not retaliate if retaliation demands heavy reinvestment. Tampax provides an example of a leader whose different financial priorities invited

[6]Diagnosing impediments requires a competitor analysis of the leader. See *Competitive Strategy,* Chapter 3, for a framework plus a discussion of concepts such as mixed motives and blind spots employed here.

attack. Maintaining extraordinary returns in feminine hygiene products seems to have become a preoccupation inside Tampax, and caused it to respond very little to repeated attacks until recently. Differences in financial priorities also underlie the success of many foreign firms against U.S. leaders.

Portfolio Constraints. A leader may not retaliate if its commitment or attention is directed to other industries. Corporate parents can constrain a business unit's resources or dictate its goals. For example, a leader treated as a cash generator by its parent company may not get the resources to fend off a challenger's attack. Similarly, a leader actively pursuing diversification may be diverted from closely monitoring and defending its core industry. Crown Cork and Seal's success against American Can and Continental Can, for example, is partly due to these two leaders' attempts to diversify into other forms of packaging.

Regulatory Pressure. A leader may not retaliate if it believes itself to be constrained from taking actions because of regulatory pressure. Antitrust scrutiny, safety standards, pollution regulations, and many other types of regulation can constrain leader responses. Some observers believe that pressures on the franchise bottler system emanating from Washington distracted Coca-Cola from responding to Pepsi's challenge, and that regulatory fears are inhibiting ATT as it faces new competition today.

Blind Spots. A leader can suffer from faulty assumptions, or blind spots, in interpreting industry conditions. If a leader has false perceptions of the true needs of buyers or the significance of an industry change, for example, a challenger may gain position by moving before the leader does. Moreover, the leader may well perceive the actions of the challenger as inappropriate and nonthreatening, until the challenger has gained enough market position to become established.

Blind spots have been important to the success of many challengers. Harley Davidson misperceived the need for a small motorcycle and watched while Honda became established. Xerox seems to have misunderstood the importance of small copiers, and Zenith clung to handcrafted TV sets despite improvements in design and automated production technology. Careful analysis of competitor assumptions can reveal such blind spots.

Incorrect Pricing. A leader may set prices based on average cost, rather than on the cost of delivering a given product to a given buyer.

If a challenger targets the overpriced products/buyers and offers lower prices, the leader may well be slow to recognize its true costs and be unwilling to reduce its gross margins. Leaders often respond to such strategies by retreating from one segment after another until the challenger emerges as the leader.

Part of a Gentlemen's Game. A leader may respond slowly if rivalry in its industry has been a gentlemen's game. A leader in such industries often feels constrained from retaliating against a challenger for fear of upsetting its relationship with other rivals. Coca-Cola's long history as a statesman in the soft drink industry, where firms followed established rules, seems to have contributed to its less-than-vigorous retaliation against Pepsi until recently.

The impediments to leader retaliation result from a variety of different underlying causes. Some impediments rest on tangible factors such as mixed motives or resource allocation priorities, while others rest on perceptual errors by the leader, as in the case of blind spots and incorrect pricing. A challenger's odds of success are greatest when tangible impediments to leader retaliation exist. Multiple impediments compound the leader's problem. In responding to Timex, for example, Swiss watch firms had a blind spot about the saleability of Timex's disposable, everyday watch. They also had high response costs in matching Timex's automated facilities given the labor intensity of Swiss watch factories, as well as mixed motives in alienating jewelers if they followed Timex into the drug store channel.

Reconfiguration and redefinition strategies frequently exploit impediments to leader retaliation. They often create mixed motives, high response costs, or are incorrectly perceived by leaders. One of the difficulties with the pure spending strategy, however, is that it is less likely to be associated with impediments to leader retaliation than the other two avenues of attack. Pure spending works best where a leader has different financial priorities and is unwilling to match the challenger's investment.

Signals of Leader Vulnerability

The preceding discussion suggests a variety of signals that can indicate that a leader is vulnerable. These fall into two groups—industry signals and signals based on leader traits.

Industry Signals

Structural change provides perhaps the strongest signal that an industry leader might be vulnerable. Structural change emanating from *outside* an industry is a particularly strong indication of leader vulnerability, since entrenched leaders often misinterpret it.

Some important industry signals of leader vulnerability include:

Discontinuous Technological Change. Discontinuous technological change raises the possibility that a leader's competitive advantage can be circumvented, as discussed in Chapter 5. In tires, for example, the radial tire provided the discontinuity that allowed Michelin to challenge Goodyear and Firestone. In typewriters, electronics proved the undoing of Underwood and is threatening SCM. It is more likely that the leader will be favorably positioned to respond to continuous technological change than the challenger, because of its scale economies or cumulative learning.

Buyer Changes. Any changes in the buyer's value chain, for whatever reason, may signal new opportunities for differentiation, new channels, unbundling, or other opportunities. An increasing number of women in the workforce, for example, created opportunities to challenge leaders in many industries producing women's or household products. New buyer segments are also a sign of opportunity because the leader may not be well placed to serve them.

Changing Channels. The emergence of new channels provides a potential opportunity to attack a leader dominant in existing channels. The shift of sales of many consumer goods toward supermarkets, for example, has created the conditions for attacking a number of leaders.

Shifting Input Costs or Quality. Shifts in the quality or cost of significant inputs may signal an opportunity for a challenger to gain a cost advantage through a new production process, locking up new sources of raw materials, or reengineering product designs to reduce or alter material content. The dramatic rise in power costs, for example, is providing opportunities for repositioning in aluminum smelting.

Gentlemen's Game. As discussed earlier, an industry with a long history of stability may signal that a leader has played the role of statesman and may retaliate slowly.

Leader Signals

The following traits of industry leaders are signs of possible vulnerability:

Stuck in the Middle. A leader that has become stuck in the middle (lacking cost leadership or differentiation vis-à-vis other incumbents) provides an inviting target. The challenger may find it easy to meet the three conditions outlined at the beginning of this chapter.

Unhappy Buyers. A leader with unhappy buyers is often vulnerable. Unhappy buyers suggest that the leader has exercised its bargaining power or that leader personnel have developed an attitude of arrogance based on past success. Unhappy buyers may actively encourage and support a challenger.

Pioneer of Current Industry Technology. A leader who pioneered the current generation of industry technology may be reluctant to embrace the next one and may also be inflexible because of its investment in the current technology. Ford seems to have suffered from this problem in the early years of the auto industry.

Very High Profitability. A leader making extraordinary profits may provide an umbrella for a challenger, if high profits more than offset the costs of attack. Very profitable leaders can also be reluctant to diminish their profits to retaliate. Moreover, extraordinary returns may also signal that a leader might yield share in less profitable parts of the product line, providing opportunities for focus by challengers.

History of Regulatory Problems. A leader with a history of regulatory problems, such as antitrust, may be actually constrained from vigorous retaliation or believe itself to be.

Weak Performer in the Parent Company Portfolio. A leader perceived as a weak performer by its parent company may well not get the capital to keep up with the latest technological change, or have sufficient discretion over profitability to retaliate vigorously against challengers.

Attacking Leaders and Industry Structure

A final test for attacking a leader is to weigh the effect on overall industry structure. A challenger's attack on a leader is unwise if it destroys industry structure. Challengers must find a new way of competing compared to the leader's to succeed. However, the new way of competing, in some cases, may undercut possibilities for differentiation, lower entry barriers, or have other adverse structural effects as described in Chapter 1. A closely related risk is where a challenger gains market share but does not gain a clear advantage over the leader, and the leader and the challenger are thus relatively balanced in competitive position. This may guarantee a long period of instability in the industry. The resulting war can be protracted and expensive for both sides, creating a situation where no firm has any competitive advantage.

It is also important to recognize that some leaders are "good" leaders, as was discussed in Chapter 6. Attacking a good leader may worsen, not improve, a challenger's profitability if the umbrella provided by the good leader is lost in the process. In such cases a challenger should refrain from attacking the leader at all. Instead, it should choose another industry as a vehicle for growth.

Bibliography

ABERNATHY, WILLIAM J., AND JAMES M. UTTERBACK. "Patterns of Industrial Innovation," *Technology Review,* Vol. 80, No. 7 (June–July 1978).

ABERNATHY, WILLIAM J., KIM B. CLARK, AND ALAN M. KANTROW. *Industrial Renaissance.* New York: Basic Books, 1983.

ADAMS, WILLIAM J., AND JANET L. YELLEN. "Commodity Bundling and the Burden of Monopoly," *Quarterly Journal of Economics*, Vol. SC (August 1976), pp. 475–498.

AMERICAN EXPRESS COMPANY, 1982 Annual Report.

BASS, FRANK M. "A New Product Growth Model for Consumer Durables," *Management Science*, Vol. 15 (January 1969), pp. 215–227.

BAUMOL, WILLIAM J., JOHN C. PANZAR, AND ROBERT D. WILLIG, with contributions by Elizabeth E. Bailey, Dietrich Fischer, and Herman C. Quirmbach, *Contestable Markets and The Theory of Industry Structure*, New York: Harcourt Brace Jovanovich, 1982.

BLOOM, PAUL N., AND PHILIP KOTLER. "Strategies for High Market Share Companies," *Harvard Business Review* (November-December 1975), pp. 62–72.

BONOMA, THOMAS V., AND BENSON P. SHAPIRO. *Segmenting the Industrial Market.* Lexington, Mass.: Lexington Books, 1983.

BOSTON CONSULTING GROUP. "The Rule of Three and Four," *Perspectives* No. 187 (1976).

BOWER, JOSEPH, L., "Simple Economic Tools For Strategic Analysis," Harvard Business School Case Study, No. 9–373–094.

BUARON, ROBERTO, "New-Game Stategies," The McKinsey Quarterly (Spring, 1981), pp. 24–40.

BUZZELL, ROBERT D. "Are There Natural Market Structures," *Journal of Marketing* (Winter 1981), pp. 42–51.

CAVES, RICHARD E., M. FORTUNATO, AND PANKAJ GHEMAWAT. "The Decline of Monopoly, 1905–1929," Discussion Paper 830, Harvard Institute of Economic Research, Cambridge, Mass., June 1981.

COASE, RONALD H., "The Nature of the Firm," *Economica* (November 1937), pp. 386–405.

COASE, RONALD H., "Industrial Organization: A Proposal for Research," in V. R. Fuchs, ed., *Policy Issues and Research in Industrial Organization*, New York: National Bureau of Economic Research, 1972.

DIXIT, AVINASH K., "The Role of Investment in Entry-Deterrence," *Economic Journal* (March 1980), pp. 95–106.

DIXIT, AVINASH K., AND VICTOR NORMAN. *Theory of International Trade: A Dual, General Equilibrium Approach*, J. Nisbet: Cambridge, England: Cambridge University Press, 1980.

ECCLES, ROBERT G. *The Transfer Pricing Problem: A Theory for Practice*, Lexington, Mass.: Lexington Books, 1985.

FISHER, JOHN C., AND ROBERT H. PRY. "A Simple Substitution Model of Technological Change," *Technological Forecasting and Social Change*, Vol. 2 (May 1971), pp. 75–88.

FORBIS, JOHN L. AND NITIN T. MEHTA, "Economic Value to the Customer," McKinsey and Company Staff Paper (February 1979).

GALBRAITH, JAY. *Designing Complex Organizations*, Reading, Mass.: Addison-Wesley, 1973.

"GENERAL CINEMA CORPORATION," Harvard Business School Case Services 9–377–084, 1976.

GHEMAWAT, PANKAJ. "Building Strategy on the Experience Curve," *Harvard Business Review*, forthcoming.

GLUCK, FREDERICK W., "Strategic Choice and Resource Allocation," The McKinsey Quarterly (Winter 1980), pp. 22–23.

GUPTA, ANIL K., AND VIJAYARAGHAVAN GOVINDARAJAN. "Resource Sharing Among SBU's: Strategic Antecedents and Administrative Implications," Working Paper, Boston University, December 1983.

HAMILTON, RONALD H. "Scenarios in Corporate Planning," *Journal of Business Strategy*, No. 2 (Summer 1981), pp. 82–87.

HASPESLAGH, PHILLIPE. "Portfolio Planning: Uses and Limits," *Harvard Business Review,* No. 1 (January-February 1982), pp. 58–73.

KLEIN, HAROLD E., AND ROBERT E. LINNEMAN. "The Use of Scenarios in Corporate Planning: Eight Case Histories," *Long Range Planning*, No. 14 (October 1981), pp. 69–77.

KOTLER, PHILIP. *Marketing Management: Analysis, Planning and Control,* 4th ed., Englewood Cliffs, N.J.: Prentice-Hall, 1980.

KOTTER, JOHN P. *The General Manager,* New York: The Free Press, 1982.

LAWRENCE, PAUL R., AND JAY W. LORSCH. *Organization and Environment: Managing Differentiation and Integration*, Cambridge, Mass.: Harvard Graduate School of Business Administration, Harvard University, 1967.

LEVITT, THEODORE. "Marketing Intangible Products and Product Intangibles," *Harvard Business Review*, No. 3 (May-June 1981), pp. 94–102.

LEVITT, THEODORE. "Marketing Myopia," *Harvard Business Review* (July-August 1960), pp. 26–37.

LORSCH, JAY W., AND STEPHEN A. ALLEN. *Managing Diversity and Interdependence: An Organizational Study of Multidimensional Firms.* Cambridge, Mass.: Harvard Graduate School of Business Administration, Division of Research, 1973.

MAHAJAN, VIJAY, AND EITAN MULLER. "Innovation Diffusion and New Product Growth Models in Marketing," *Journal of Marketing*, Vol. 43 (October 1979), pp. 55–68.

MALASKA, PENTTI, MARTTI MALMIVIRTA, TARJA MERISTO, AND STEN-OLOF HANSEN. "Multiple Scenarios in Strategic Management: The First European Survey" Working Paper, Turku School of Economics and Business Administration. Turku, Finland, 1983.

MANDELL, THOMAS F. "Scenarios and Corporate Strategy," *Planning in Uncertain Times.* Business Intelligence Program, SRI International, November 1982.

MANSFIELD, EDWIN "Technological Change and the Rate of Imitation," *Econometrica*, Vol. 29, No. 4 (October 1961), pp. 741–766.

MORIARTY, ROWLAND T. *Industrial Buying Behavior: Concepts, Issues and Applications,* Lexington, Mass.: Lexington Books, 1983.

PORTER, MICHAEL E. *Competitive Strategy: Techniques for Analyzing Industries and Competitors*, New York: The Free Press, 1980.

PORTER, MICHAEL E., ed., *Competition in Global Industries*, Cambridge, Mass.: Harvard Graduate School of Business Administration, 1985, forthcoming.

ROBERTSON, THOMAS S. *Innovation Behavior and Communication.* New York: Holt, Rinehart & Winston, 1971.

SALOP, STEVEN C. "Strategic Entry Deterrence," *American Economic Review*, Vol. 69 (May 1979), pp. 335–338.

SCHAMLENSEE, RICHARD. "Entry Deterrence in the Ready-to-Eat Breakfast Cereal Industry," *Bell Journal of Economics,* Vol. 9, No. 2 (Autumn 1980), pp. 305–327.

SCHELLING, THOMAS C., *The Strategy of Conflict*, Cambridge, Mass.: Harvard University Press, 1960.

"SHELL'S MULTIPLE SCENARIO PLANNING," *World Business Weekly*, April 7, 1980.

SCHOCKER, ALLAN D., AND V. SRINIVASAN, "Multiattribute Approaches for Product Concept Evaluation and Generation: A Critical Review, *Journal of Marketing Research*, XVI (May 1979), pp. 159–180.

STENGREVICS, JOHN M. "The Group Executive: A Study in General Management," Doctoral Dissertation, Harvard Graduate School of Business Administration, 1981.

STENGREVICS, JOHN M. "Making Cluster Strategies Work," *Journal of Business Strategy*, forthcoming.

STUART, ALEXANDER. "Meat Packers in Stampede," *Fortune*, June 29, 1981, pp. 67–71.

TEECE, DAVID J., "Economies of Scope and the Scope of the Enterprise," *Journal of Economic Behavior and Organization*, Vol. 1 (1980), pp. 223–247.

WACK, PIERRE A. "Learning to Design Planning Scenarios: The Experience of Royal Dutch Shell," Working Paper, Harvard Graduate School of Business Administration, 1984.

WELLS, JOHN R. "In Search of Synergy: Strategies for Related Diversification," Doctoral Dissertation, Harvard Graduate School of Business Administration, 1984.

WILLIAMSON, OLIVER E. *Markets and Hierarchies: Analysis and Antitrust Implications*, The Free Press: New York, 1975.

World Business Weekly, September 21, 1981, p. 36.

YIP, GEORGE, *Barriers to Entry: A Corporate Strategy Perspective.* Lexington, Mass.: Lexington Books, 1982.

Index